The Libertarian Alternative

El sueno de la rason produce monstruos

GOYA'S TITLE FOR ONE OF HIS CAPRICHOS

... that value is inescapable in human experience and conduct is one of the facts of life. ...

STANLEY CAVELL (1969)

This ceaseless effort to compel each other, in turn for each new object that is clamored for by this or that set of politicians, this ceaseless effort to bind chains round the hands of each other, is preventing progress of the real kind, is preventing peace and friendship and brotherhood, and is turning the men of the same nation, who ought to labor happily together for common ends, in their own groups, in their own free unfettered fashion, into enemies, who live *conspiring* against and dreading, often hating each other. ...

AUBERON HERBERT (1906)

The Libertarian Alternative

Tibor R. Machan, editor

NELSON-HALL nh CHICAGO

ISBN 0-088229-511-X

Library of Congress Catalog Card No. 73–80501

Manufactured in the United States of America

to Leona and Cappy—
with love

Contents

Preface

THE ROOTS OF INDIVIDUALISM and libertarianism may be traced as far back as Aristotle who acknowledged the moral significance, that is, the fundamental value and purpose, each individual's life and happiness constitute for him. Aristotle emphasized the rule of organized society as a *means* by which man could secure the best living conditions in which to develop his highest potentials. But his focus upon human self-sufficiency was in sharp contrast to the political and moral philosophy expressed in Plato's *Republic*, especially when the latter is interpreted as the paradigm of the total state. We need not quarrel with those who hold that Plato never really proposed the *Republic* as an actual goal to be achieved, a view that gains its plausibility in the light of Plato's drastic separation of the real from the ideal. What is important is that as an answer to Plato, Aristotle's ethics and politics were the *first* step in the direction of the overall philosophy of man and society expressed in this collection of articles.

When more than twenty authors are brought together in a book of essays on individualism, it is not likely that a totally integrated position will unfold. And the differences among those who would accept the characterization of "individualist" or "libertarian" are sometimes very significant. To some, these differences make it almost impossible to be classified among others in the first place. When dealing with scholars and authors who do not shy from making responsible claims and who have a commitment to knowledge, such differences can be extremely important.

These authors find their differences even more significant—and so might we—when they accept the possibility of moral knowledge. Someone who maintains that it not only is possible to know what acts and policies are right in human affairs, but that it is one of man's responsibilities to pass moral judgment on such affairs, will find it difficult to abstain from occasional severe criticism of other relatively like-minded thinkers, not to mention those who differ with him more seriously on such counts.

As editor of this volume, I want the reader to realize that one of the important aspects of a book such as this is that the authors—or at least many of them—believe that moral and political judgments *can* be right (and wrong). Also, many of the authors accept openly the responsibility of arguing for the standard by which judgments within these areas of human concern must be assessed. In these pages there will be numerous moral and political judgments and if the very possibility that they are right is denied, the purpose and legitimacy of judgments of this sort, by individualists, collectivists, pragmatists (e.g., Milton Friedman, John Kenneth Galbraith, Richard Nixon, respectively), must be called into question.

Many intellectuals like to dismiss moral and political judgments as mere emotional outbursts, expressions of wishful thinking, myths, etc., that are, however, couched in objective language so as to render them respectable. This (subjectivist) theory of value judgments is stimulated by a widespread fear present in our culture—the fear of dogmatism and authoritarianism. What with Hitler and Stalin just a few decades back, who would ever accept the kind of self-righteousness implicit in the claim that someone can and does know what is right and wrong in (at least some) human affairs (even if only concerning their most general aspects)!

Yet, despite this fear, man's need to make true moral and political judgments is inescapable. To deny this must lead to error or pretence, including widespread injury and harm.

Today, as ever, people, including teachers, scientists, and politicians, make value judgments they believe to be true day in and out—even while they announce the impossibility of doing so. Their judgments are expressed in actions, policies, decisions, programs, and plans, some of which affect the entire world, sometimes for centuries. Also, today in the aftermath of several years of domestic conflict, mostly on America's university and college campuses, the voice of moral agnosticism is no longer as fervent and self-righteous as in previous decades. Philosophers as well as other intellectuals are reinvestigating the doctrine that ethics, politics, and aesthetics fall outside the realm of the meaningful, rational, and the possibly true (or false), and the doctrine that they be viewed as so much well-disguised poetry or emotion venting.

The philosophy of reductionism which gave intellectual support to moral skepticism for more than two centuries is now in great trouble—mostly as a result of the identification of its blatant equivocation between various realms of human interest and what standard of meaningfulness must be employed in discussing each. Reductionism has, for the most part, run aground. Outside the few staunch followers of B. F. Skinner and other social pseudoscientific theorists (who cling to Humean sensationism and/or reductive materialism for fear of losing their meager scientific respectability), the dissatisfaction with the reductionist/empiricist approach is quite serious. Any cursory perusal of various theoretical journals in the social sciences and the philosophy of science will testify to this.

Many in our culture have reverted to mysticism after the failure of the reductionist epoch. If man is not reducible to the subject matter of physics, why, then he *must* be supernatural! Wrong. No such implication holds. Instead, we need to acknowledge that reality comes neither in one form nor in just two irreconcilable forms. The situation is more complex than this. That, of course, needs to be—and has been—argued at length. But nothing points to the fundamental incomprehensibility of it all, mysticism notwithstanding.

I ask the reader not to reject precipitately the claims that are made in this volume of essays. I know that the treatment of topics in essays rarely can be comprehensive. Thus, some authors may give the impression of unwarranted confidence—even faith. And some of them may accept elements of their views as a matter of faith—but more likely as simply not fully investigated assumption. Yet, the positions the essays give voice to, by their very inclusion in this volume, are considered to be within the confines of the *rationally* defensible. In a word, the individualism outlined in this book is not dependent on arbitrary assumptions—although some premises not reasonably questionable may be detected. The unquestionability of certain fundamental principles, for example, some of those of logic, metaphysics, and epistemology, is no proof of arbitrariness—quite the contrary. Whether they are unquestionable may itself be examined by anyone. There is no claim of exclusivity either—to some kind of unique, private access to truths, a type of subjective but still absolute knowledge—in this book. Individualism would indeed be a defective philosophical and political *solution* of some of our problems if it permitted the automatic exclusion of some people from among those who are qualified to discuss its tenets.

As editor, I collected those essays which would contribute to the demonstration and analysis of a reasonably cohesive point of view concerning the areas of politics and social studies. I am aware that in some circles it is academically disrespectable to *commit* oneself to ethical or political positions. Many intellectuals, among them numerous distinguished philosophers, believe that a scholarly approach requires neutrality.

One of the defects of the neutral point of view about ethics and politics is that it is, after all, a commitment to something with ethical and political consequences. Skepticism about what is right in private or public affairs needs support and argumentation just as other positions do—and to be committed to skepticism forever is precisely the sort of commitment that can have severe consequences—as any *blind* commitment must. The neutral stance is plausible mainly because it is confused with being objective. Objectivity is quite rightly considered to be indispensable to accuracy, fairness, justice and all those virtues on which sound scholarship depends. Not to be objective (for instance in one's evaluation of alternative codes of conduct and political theories) implies the serious likelihood of distortion, bias, and wrongheadedness—all of which are demonstrable obstacles to the discovery of truth, certainly a cardinal purpose of scholarship.

But the equivocation between neutrality and objectivity rests on a questionable philosophical view—namely that it is impossible to answer questions about ethics and politics using standards of objectivity, accuracy, precision, and truth. Although no longer as widely accepted as before, this view has been entertained and advocated widely enough to influence the attitudes of most social scientists. (Some distinguished scholars who have contributed to this volume may consider it valid. From my point of view, however, this is irrelevant—I am concerned with their scholarship, not with the views that they may have accepted from what I consider mistaken philosophical theories, for example about the relationship between descriptions and evaluations.) Unfortunately even those philosophers who no longer accept the divorce of values and knowledge are timid about ethics and politics, thereby perpetuating the fact/value dichotomy.

What I hope for in this book is that the reader will approach the subject as freshly as is possible for him. The rest of the work is up to the essays to accomplish. Unfortunately the observations above are needed these days, if only to render more probable an unbiased reading of the works of those who have so generously contributed to the present volume.

Let me close by acknowledging the help of the managements of the *New Individualist Review, Rampart Journal, Left and Right, The Freeman, Reason, The Intercollegiate Review, Persuasion,* and the *Southern California Law Review* in securing permissions to include some of the articles in this collection. I want to express my special thanks to those who have written their papers exclusively for this work.

Next I would like to offer my gratitude to the Institute for Humane Studies, the Koch Foundation, and Reason Enterprises for the help I received from them throughout the years of my preparation of this volume. I want also to mention the invaluable support I have received from Ms. Marilynn H. Walther, without whom it would not have been possible to bring this book to publication. Finally, I would like to point out my indebtedness to novelist/philosopher Ayn Rand and her contributions to the individualist political and moral tradition. I hope that this volume will contribute in some measure to the realization of those values which the works of Miss Rand have first called to my attention.

Tibor R. Machan
Santa Barbara
Summer 1973

The Libertarian Alternative

part one
Justice, Liberty and the Individual

Perhaps the central issue a political thinker must consider is whether there is a need for politics, the systematic organization of society, in man's life. For if it be demonstrable that people would be better off without legal, political, governmental systems, we could advocate the abolishment of them and thereby work for a better life. Anarchism is the viewpoint which argues, pure and simple, that institutions such as governments are bad for people or, at least, serve no real, objective need. (However, some anarchists maintain that legal institutions are all right so long as no centralized seat of authority and power is assigned and the allocations of authority and jurisdiction are left, in some way, to the free choice of those involved. Such individualist anarchists, for example, Lysander Spooner, Benjamin Tucker, Josiah Warren and, today, Murray N. Rothbard and R. A. Childs must be put into a special category of political thinkers. The reader might note that the last two in the above list are contributors to this volume. It is their basic commitment to the concept of societal nonaggression and human rights, including the institution of the free market, that justifies their inclusion. Their anarchism–archism is, to my mind, a matter of dispute, whereas their contribution to an understanding of the nature of the state and liberty is well established.)

1

Assuming, however, that we start from scratch, what is the relationship, if any, between people and politics? To this question the first group of essays is addressed. Most of the contributors to this volume think that the capacity of men to do harm to each other gives rise to the institution of a legal system, or government. In their private affairs people usually require no outside agency to settle disputes or right wrongs. But when the infliction of harm on others occurs, the situation changes. The harmful action will not necessarily also result in damage to the person who inflicted it, at least not in principle. (No doubt, if I hurt another too often, he will make sure I don't get the chance after a while. But the point is that people can respond to the *possibility* of interpersonal injury systematically, and the construction of a legal system based on the definition of each man's limits of authority, sphere of jurisdiction—i.e., human rights—is one way to do it.)

The need for politics, then, arises only within a social context. And when it does, we need to discover how we can meet it without depriving ourselves of other values which we need as well, for example, human liberty—the freedom to judge and act by our judgments. The traditional problem emerges, then: is there a way to secure the protection of our rights without at the same time violating them? Must and will an agency, which is chosen to serve us, violate the code that it was selected to uphold and enforce?

Today the answer commonly given is that a compromise is generally necessary. Although most political philosophers are not sufficiently Hobbesian to be willing to sacrifice liberty in toto in favor of order, many say that a system of just order necessarily abridges some human rights. And this view excludes all of those political thinkers and laymen who believe firmly that (*a*) human rights are mythical, (*b*) human rights are less important than other values which majorities or organized ("legitimate") groups ought to secure (for example, general welfare, space travel, public recreation, consumer protection, and international goodwill), and (*c*) some people exclusively are in possession of powers to know what ought to be pursued by anyone capable, so they ought to govern everyone. People holding any of these views would not even regard the issue of human rights as significant, except historically, as a matter of Western political heritage (or neurosis). But even those who explicitly value the concept of human rights find it unacceptable to advocate the restriction of legal agents to the protection of these rights. Nor can they advocate the enforcement of conduct in conformity with the admittedly complex implications of human rights for our daily lives.

The first group of essays, then, defends the idea and practice of such legal institutions and agents that make no compromise in disfavor of human liberty and rights.

John Hospers

1 What Libertarianism Is

THE POLITICAL PHILOSOPHY that is called libertarianism (from the Latin *libertas*, liberty) is the doctrine that every person is the owner of his own life, and that no one is the owner of anyone else's life; and that consequently every human being has the right to act in accordance with his own choices, unless those actions infringe on the equal liberty of other human beings to act in accordance with *their* choices.

There are several other ways of stating the same libertarian thesis:

1. *No one is anyone else's master, and no one is anyone else's slave.* Since I am the one to decide how my life is to be conducted, just as you decide about yours, I have no right (even if I had the power) to make you my slave and be your master, nor have you the right to become the master by enslaving me. Slavery is *forced* servitude, and since no one owns the life of anyone else, no one has the right to enslave another. Political theories past and present have traditionally been concerned with who should be the master (usually the king, the dictator, or government bureaucracy) and who should be the slaves, and what the extent of the slavery should be. Libertarianism holds that no one has the right to use force to enslave the life of another, or any portion or aspect of that life.

2. *Other men's lives are not yours to dispose of.* I enjoy seeing operas; but operas are expensive to produce. Opera-lovers often say, "The state (or the city, etc.) should subsidize opera, so that we can all see it. Also it would be for people's betterment, cultural benefit, etc." But what they are advocating is nothing more or less than legalized plunder. They can't pay for the productions themselves, and yet they want to see opera, which involves a large number of people and their labor; so what they

are saying in effect is, "Get the money through legalized force. Take a little bit more out of every worker's paycheck every week to pay for the operas we want to see." But I have no right to take by force from the workers' pockets to pay for what I want.

Perhaps it would be better if he *did* go to see opera—then I should try to convince him to go voluntarily. But to take the money from him forcibly, because in my opinion it would be good for *him,* is still seizure of his earnings, which is plunder.

Besides, if I have the right to force him to help pay for my pet projects, hasn't he equally the right to force me to help pay for his? Perhaps he in turn wants the government to subsidize rock-and-roll, or his new car, or a house in the country? If I have the right to milk him, why hasn't he the right to milk me? If I can be a moral cannibal, why can't he too?

We should beware of the inventors of utopias. They would remake the world according to their vision—with the lives and fruits of the labor of *other* human beings. Is it someone's utopian vision that others should build pyramids to beautify the landscape? Very well, then other men should provide the labor; and if he is in a position of political power, and he can't get men to do it voluntarily, then he must *compel* them to "cooperate"—i.e. he must enslave them.

A hundred men might gain great pleasure from beating up or killing just one insignificant human being; but other men's lives are not theirs to dispose of. "In order to achieve the worthy goals of the next five-year-plan, we must forcibly collectivize the peasants . . ."; but other men's lives are not theirs to dispose of. Do you want to occupy, rent-free, the mansion that another man has worked for twenty years to buy? But other men's lives are not yours to dispose of. Do you want operas so badly that everyone is forced to work harder to pay for their subsidization through taxes? But other men's lives are not yours to dispose of. Do you want to have free medical care at the expense of other people, whether they wish to provide it or not? But this would require them to work longer for you whether they want to or not, and other men's lives are not yours to dispose of.

The freedom to engage in any type of enterprise, to produce, to own and control property, to buy and sell on the free market, is derived from the rights to life, liberty, and property . . . which are stated in the Declaration of Independence. . . . [but] when a government guarantees a "right" to an education or parity on farm products or a guaranteed annual income, it is staking a claim on the property of one group of citizens for the sake of another group. In short, it is violating one of the fundamental rights it was instituted to protect.[1]

3. *No human being should be a nonvoluntary mortgage on the life of another.* I cannot claim your life, your work, or the products of your effort as mine. The fruit of one man's labor should not be fair game for every freeloader who comes along and demands it as his own. The orchard that has been carefully grown, nurtured, and harvested by its owner should not be ripe for the plucking for any bypasser who has a yen for the ripe fruit. The wealth that some men have produced should not be fair game for looting by government, to be used for whatever purposes its representatives determine, no matter what their motives in so doing may be. The theft of your money by a robber is not justified by the fact that he used it to help his injured mother.

It will already be evident that libertarian doctrine is embedded in a view of the rights of man. Each human being has the right to live his life as he chooses, compatibly with the equal right of all other human beings to live their lives as they choose.

All man's rights are implicit in the above statement. Each man has the right to life: any attempt by others to take it away from him, or even to injure him, violates this right, through the use of coercion against him. Each man has the right to liberty: to conduct his life in accordance with the alternatives open to him without coercive action by others. And every man has the right to property: to work to sustain his life (and the lives of whichever others he chooses to sustain, such as his family) and to retain the fruits of his labor.

People often defend the rights of life and liberty but denigrate property rights, and yet the right to property is as basic as the other two; indeed, without property rights no other rights are possible. Depriving you of property is depriving you of the means by which you live.

. . . All that which an individual possesses by right (including his life and property) are morally his to use, dispose of and even destroy, as he sees fit. If I own my life, then it follows that I am free to associate with whom I please and not to associate with whom I please. If I own my knowledge and services it follows that I may ask any compensation I wish for providing them for another, or I may abstain from providing them at all, if I so choose. If I own my house, it follows that I may decorate it as I please and live in it with whom I please. If I control my own business, it follows that I may charge what I please for my products or services, hire whom I please and not hire whom I please. All that which I own in fact, I may

dispose of as I choose to in reality. For anyone to attempt to limit my freedom to do
so is to violate my rights.

Where do my rights end? Where yours begin. I may do anything I wish with
my own life, liberty and property without your consent; but I may do nothing with
your life, liberty and property without your consent. If we recognize the principle
of man's rights, it follows that the individual is sovereign of the domain of his own
life and property, and is sovereign of no other domain. To attempt to interfere
forcibly with another's use, disposal or destruction of his own property is to initiate
force against him and to violate his rights.

I have no right to decide how *you* should spend your time or your
money. I can make that decision for myself, but not for you, my
neighbor. I may deplore your choice of life-style, and I may talk with you
about it provided you are willing to listen to me. But I have no right to
use force to change it. Nor have I the right to decide how you should
spend the money you have earned. I may appeal to you to give it to the
Red Cross, and you may prefer to go to prizefights. But that is your
decision, and however much I may chafe about it I do not have the right
to interfere forcibly with it, for example by robbing you in order to use
the money in accordance with *my* choices. (If I have the right to rob you,
have you also the right to rob me?)

When I claim a right, I carve out a niche, as it were, in my life,
saying in effect, "This activity I must be able to perform without
interference from others. For you and everyone else, this is off limits."
And so I put up a "no trespassing" sign, which marks off the area of my
right. Each individual's right is his "no trespassing" sign in relation to me
and others. I may not encroach upon his domain any more than he upon
mine, without my consent. Every right entails a duty, true—but the duty
is only that of *forbearance*—that is, of *refraining* from violating the other
person's right. If you have a right to life, I have no right to take your life;
if you have a right to the products of your labor (property), I have no
right to take it from you without your consent. The non-violation of
these rights will not guarantee you protection against natural cata-
strophes such as floods and earthquakes, but it will protect you against
the aggressive activities *of other men.* And rights, after all, have to do with
one's relations to other human beings, not with one's relations to
physical nature.

Nor were these rights created by government; governments—some
governments, obviously not all—*recognize* and *protect* the rights that
individuals already have. Governments regularly forbid homicide and

theft; and, at a more advanced stage, protect individuals against such things as libel and breach of contract.

It cannot be by chance that they thus agree. They agree because the alleged creating of rights [by government] was nothing else than giving formal sanction and better definition to those assertions of claims and recognitions of claims which naturally originate from the individual desires of men who have to live in presence of one another.

. . .Those who hold that life is valuable, hold, by implication, that men ought not to be prevented from carrying on life-sustaining activities. . . . Clearly the conception of "natural rights" originates in recognition of the truth that if life is justifiable, there must be a justification for the performance of acts essential to its preservation; and, therefore, a justification of those liberties and claims which make such acts possible.

. . . To recognize and enforce the rights of individuals, is at the same time to recognize and enforce the conditions to a normal social life.[2]

The *right to property* is the most misunderstood and unappreciated of human rights, and it is one most constantly violated by governments. "Property" of course does not mean only real estate; it includes anything you can call your own—your clothing, your car, your jewelry, your books and papers.

The right of property is not the right to just *take* it from others, for this would interfere with *their* property rights. It is rather the right to work for it, to obtain non-coercively, the money or services which you can present in voluntary exchange.

The right to property is consistently underplayed by intellectuals today, sometimes even frowned upon, as if we should feel guilty for upholding such a right in view of all the poverty in the world. But the right to property is absolutely basic. It is your hedge against the future. It is your assurance that what you have worked to earn will still be there, and be yours, when you wish or need to use it, especially when you are too old to work any longer.

Government has always been the chief enemy of the right to property. The officials of government, wishing to increase their power, and finding an increase of wealth an effective way to bring this about, seize some or all of what a person has earned—and since government has a monopoly of physical force within the geographical area of the nation, it has the power (but not the right) to do this. When this happens, of course, every citizen of that country is insecure: he knows that no matter how hard he works the government can swoop down on him at any time and confiscate his earnings and possessions. A person sees his life savings wiped out in a moment when the tax-collectors descend to deprive him of the fruits of his work; or, an industry which has been fifty years in the making and cost millions of dollars and millions of hours of time and planning, is nationalized overnight. Or the government, via inflation, cheapens the currency, so that hard-won dollars aren't worth anything any more. The effect of such actions, of course, is that people lose hope and incentive: if no matter how hard they work the government agents can take it all away, why bother to work at all, for more than today's needs? Depriving people of property is *depriving them of the means by which they live*—the freedom of the individual citizen to do what he wishes with his own life and to plan for the future. Indeed, only if property rights are respected is there any point to planning for the future and working to achieve one's goals. *Property rights are what makes long-range planning possible*—the kind of planning which is a distinctively human endeavor, as opposed to the day-by-day activity of the lion who hunts, who depends on the supply of game tomorrow but has no real insurance against starvation in a day or a week. Without the right to property, the right to life itself amounts to little: how can you sustain your life if you cannot plan ahead? and how can you plan ahead if the fruits of your labor can at any moment be confiscated by government?

Without property rights, no other rights are possible. If one is not free to use that which one has produced, one does not possess the right of liberty. If one is not free to make the products of one's work serve one's chosen goals, one does not possess the right to the pursuit of happiness. And—since man is not a ghost who exists in some non-material manner—if one is not free to keep and to consume the products of one's work, one does not possess the right of life. In a society where men are not free privately to own the material means of production, their position is that of slaves whose lives are at the absolute mercy of their rulers. It is relevant here to remember the statement of Trotsky: "Who does not obey shall not eat."[3]

Indeed, the right to property may well be considered second only to the right to life. Even the freedom of speech is limited by considerations of property. If a person visiting in your home behaves in a way undesired by you, you have every right to evict him; he can scream or agitate elsewhere if he wishes, but not in your home without your consent. Does a person have a right to shout obscenities in a cathedral? No, for the owners of the cathedral (presumably the Church) have not allowed others on their property for that purpose; one may go there to worship or to visit, but not just for any purpose one wishes. Their property right is prior to your or my wish to scream or expectorate or write graffiti on their building. Or, to take the stock example, does a person have a right to shout "Fire!" falsely in a crowded theater? No, for the theater owner has permitted others to enter and use his property only for a specific purpose, that of seeing a film or watching a stage show. If a person heckles or otherwise disturbs other members of the audience, he can be thrown out. (In fact, he can be removed for any reason the owner chooses, provided his admission money is returned.) And if he shouts "Fire!" when there is no fire, he may be endangering other lives by causing a panic or a stampede. The right to free speech doesn't give one the right to say anything anywhere; it is circumscribed by property rights.

Again, some people seem to assume that the right to free speech (including written speech) means that they can go to a newspaper publisher and demand that he print in his newspaper some propaganda or policy statement for their political party (or other group). But of course they have no right to the use of his newspaper. Ownership of the newspaper is the product of his labor, and he has a right to put into his newspaper whatever he wants, for whatever reason. If he excludes material which many readers would like to have in, perhaps they can find it in another newspaper or persuade him to print it himself (if there are enough of them, they will usually do just that). Perhaps they can even cause his newspaper to fail. But as long as he owns it, he has the right to put in it what he wishes; what would a property right be if he could not do this? They have no right to place their material in his newspaper without his consent—not for free, nor even for a fee. Perhaps other newspapers will include it, or perhaps they can start their own newspaper (in which case they have a right to put in it what they like). If not, an option open to them would be to mimeograph and distribute some handbills.

In exactly the same way, no one has a right to "free television time" unless the owner of the television station consents to give it; it is his station, he has the property rights over it, and it is for him to decide how to dispose of his time. He may not decide wisely, but it is his right to decide as he wishes. If he makes enough unwise decisions, and courts enough unpopularity with the viewing public or the sponsors, he may have to go out of business; but as he is free to make his own decisions, so is he free to face their consequences. (If the government owns the television station, then government officials will make the decisions, and there is no guarantee of *their* superior wisdom. The difference is that when "the government" owns the station, you are forced to help pay for its upkeep through your taxes, whether the bureaucrat in charge decides to give you television time or not.)

"But why have *individual* property rights? Why not have lands and houses owned by everybody together?" Yes, this involves no violation of individual rights, as long as everybody consents to this arrangement and no one is forced to join it. The parties to it may enjoy the communal living enough (at least for a time) to overcome certain inevitable problems: that some will work and some not, that some will achieve more in an hour than others can do in a day, and still they will all get the same income. The few who do the most will in the end consider themselves "workhorses" who do the work of two or three or twelve, while the others will be "freeloaders" on the efforts of these few. But as long as they can get out of the arrangement if they no longer like it, no violation of rights is involved. They got in voluntarily, and they can get out voluntarily; no one has used force.

"But why not say that everybody owns everything? That we *all* own everything there is?"

To some this may have a pleasant ring—but let us try to analyze what it means. If everybody owns everything, then everyone has an equal right to go everywhere, do what he pleases, take what he likes, destroy if he wishes, grow crops or burn them, trample them under, and so on. Consider what it would be like in practice. Suppose you have saved money to buy a house for yourself and your family. Now suppose that the principle, "everybody owns everything," becomes adopted. Well then, why shouldn't every itinerant hippie just come in and take over, sleeping in your beds and eating in your kitchen and not bothering to replace the food supply or clean up the mess? After all, it belongs to all of us, doesn't it? So we have just as much right to it as you, the buyer, have. What happens if we *all* want to sleep in the bedroom and there's not room for all of us? Is it the strongest who wins?

What would be the result? Since no one would be responsible for anything, the property would soon be destroyed, the food used up, the facilities nonfunctional. Beginning as a house that *one* family could use, it would end up as a house that *no one* could use. And if the principle continued to be adopted, no one would build houses any more—or anything else. What for? They would only be occupied and used by others, without remuneration.

Suppose two men are cast ashore on an island, and they agree that each will cultivate half of it. The first man is industrious and grows crops and builds a shelter, making the most of the situation with which he is confronted. The second man, perhaps thinking that the warm days will last forever, lies in the sun, picks coconuts while they last, and does a minimum of work to sustain himself. At the time of harvest, the second man has nothing to harvest, nor does he assist the first man in his labors. But later when there is a dearth of food on the island, the second man comes to the first man and demands half of the harvest as his right. But of course he has no right to the product of the first man's labors. The first man may freely choose to give part of his harvest to the second out of charity rather than see him starve; but that is just what it is—charity, not the second man's right.

How can any of man's rights be violated? Ultimately, only by the use of force. I can make suggestions to you, I can reason with you, entreat you (if you are willing to listen), but I cannot *force* you without violating your rights; only by forcing you do I cut the cord between your free decisions and your actions. Voluntary relations between individuals involve no deprivation of rights, but murder, assault, and rape do, because in doing these things I make you the unwilling victim of my actions. A man is beating his wife involves no violation of rights if she *wanted* to be beaten. *Force is behavior that requires the unwilling involvement of other persons.*

Thus the use of force need not involve the use of physical violence. If I trespass on your property or dump garbage on it, I am violating your property rights, as indeed I am when I steal your watch; although this is not force in the sense of violence, it *is* a case of your being an unwilling victim of my action. Similarly, if you shout at me so that I cannot be heard when I try to speak, or blow a siren in my ear, or start a factory next door which pollutes my land, you are again violating my rights (to free speech, to property); I am, again, an unwilling victim of your actions. Similarly, if you steal a manuscript of mine and publish it as your own, you are confiscating a piece of my property and thus violating my right to keep what is the product of my labor. Of course, if I give you the manuscript with permission to sign your name to it and keep the proceeds, no violation of rights is involved—any more than if I give you permission to dump garbage on my yard.

According to libertarianism, the role of government should be limited to the retaliatory use of force against those who have initiated its use. It should not enter into any other areas, such as religion, social organization, and economics.

Government

Government is the most dangerous institution known to man. Throughout history it has violated the rights of men more than any individual or group of individuals could do: it has killed people, enslaved them, sent them to forced labor and concentration camps, and regularly robbed and pillaged them of the fruits of their expended labor. Unlike individual criminals, government has the power to arrest and try; unlike individual criminals, it can surround and encompass a person totally, dominating every aspect of one's life, so that one has no recourse from it but to leave the country (and in totalitarian nations even that is prohibited). Government throughout history has a much sorrier record than any individual, even that of a ruthless mass murderer. The signs we see on bumper stickers are chillingly accurate: "Beware: the Government is Armed and Dangerous."

The only proper role of government, according to libertarians, is that of the protector of the citizen against aggression by other individuals. The government, of course, should never initiate aggression; its proper role is as the embodiment of the *retaliatory* use of force against anyone who initiates its use.

If each individual had constantly to defend himself against possible aggressors, he would have to spend a considerable portion of his life in target practice, karate exercises, and other means of self-defenses, and even so he would probably be helpless against groups of individuals who might try to kill, maim, or rob him. He would have little time for cultivating those qualities which are essential to civilized life, nor would improvements in science, medicine, and the arts be likely to occur. The function of government is to take this responsibility off his shoulders: the government undertakes to defend him against aggressors and to punish them if they attack him. When the government is effective in doing this, it enables the citizen to go about his business unmolested and without constant fear for his life. To do this, of course, government must have physical power—the police, to protect the citizen from aggression within its borders, and the armed forces, to protect him from aggressors outside. Beyond that, the government should not intrude upon his life, either to run his business, or adjust his daily activities, or prescribe his personal moral code.

Government, then, undertakes to be the individual's protector; but historically governments have gone far beyond this function. Since they already have the physical power, they have not hesitated to use it for purposes far beyond that which was entrusted to them in the first place. Undertaking initially to protect its citizens against aggression, it has often itself become an aggressor—a far greater aggressor, indeed, than the criminals against whom it was supposed to protect its citizens. Governments have done what no private citizens can do: arrest and imprison individuals without a trial and send them to slave labor camps. Government must have power in order to be effective—and yet the very means by which alone it can be effective make it vulnerable to the abuse of power, leading to managing the lives of individuals and even inflicting terror upon them.

What then should be the function of government? In a word, the *protection of human rights*.

1. *The right to life:* libertarians support all such legislation as will protect human beings against the use of force by others, for example, laws against killing, attempted killing, maiming, beating, and all kinds of physical violence.

2. *The right to liberty:* there should be no laws compromising in any way freedom of speech, of the press, and of peaceable assembly. There should be no censorship of ideas, books, films, or of anything else by government.

3. *The right to property:* libertarians support legislation that protects the property rights of individuals against confiscation, nationalization, eminent domain, robbery, trespass, fraud and misrepresentation, patent and copyright, libel and slander.

Someone has violently assaulted you. Should he be legally liable? Of course. He has violated one of your rights. He has knowingly injured you, and since he has initiated aggression against you he should be made to expiate.

Someone has negligently left his bicycle on the sidewalk where you trip over it in the dark and injure yourself. He didn't do it intentionally; he didn't mean you any harm. Should he be legally liable? Of course; he has, however unwittingly, injured you, and since the injury is caused by him and you are the victim, he should pay.

Someone across the street is unemployed. Should you be taxed extra to pay for his expenses? Not at all. You have not injured him, you are not responsible for the fact that he is unemployed (unless you are a senator or bureaucrat who agitated for further curtailing of business, which legislation passed, with the result that your neighbor was laid off by the curtailed business). You may voluntarily wish to help him out, or better still, try to get him a job to put him on his feet again; but since you have initiated no aggressive act against him, and neither purposely nor accidentally injured him in any way, you should not be legally penalized for the fact of his unemployment. (Actually, it is just such penalties that increase unemployment.)

One man, A, works hard for years and finally earns a high salary as a professional man. A second man, B, prefers not to work at all, and to spend wastefully what money he has (through inheritance), so that after a year or two he has nothing left. At the end of this time he has a long siege of illness and lots of medical bills to pay. He demands that the bills be paid by the government—that is, by the taxpayers of the land, including Mr. A.

But of course B has no such right. He chose to lead his life in a certain way—that was his voluntary decision. One consequence of that choice is that he must depend on charity in case of later need. Mr. A chose not to live that way. (And if everyone lived like Mr. B, on whom would he depend in case of later need?) Each has a right to live in the way he pleases, but each must live with the consequences of his own decision (which, as always, fall primarily on himself). He cannot, in time of need, claim A's beneficence as his right.

If a house-guest of yours starts to carve his initials in your walls and break up your furniture, you have a right to evict him, and call the police if he makes trouble. If someone starts to destroy the machinery in a factory, the factory-owner is also entitled to evict him and call the police. In both cases, persons other than the owner are permitted on the property only under certain conditions, at the pleasure of the owner. If those conditions are violated, the owner is entitled to use force to set things straight. The case is exactly the same on a college or university campus: if a campus demonstrator starts breaking windows, occupying the president's office, and setting fire to a dean, the college authorities are certainly within their rights to evict him forcibly; one is permitted on the college grounds only under specific conditions, set by the administration: study, peaceful student activity, even political activity if those in charge choose to permit it. If they do not choose to permit peaceful political activity on campus, they may be unwise, since a campus is after all a place where all sides of every issue should get discussed, and the college that doesn't permit this may soon lose its reputation and its students. All the same, the college official who does not permit it is quite within his rights; the students do not own the campus, nor do the hired trouble-makers imported from elsewhere. In the case of a privately owned college, the owners, or whoever they have delegated to administer it, have the right to make the decisions as to who shall be permitted on the campus and under what conditions. In the case of a state university or college, the ownership problem is more complex: one could say that the "government" owns the campus or that "the people" do since they are the taxpayers who support it; but in either case, the university administration has the delegated task of keeping order, and until they are removed by the state administration or the taxpayers, it is theirs to decide who shall be permitted on campus, and what non-academic activities will be permitted to their students on the premises.

Property rights can be violated by physical trespass, of course, or by anyone entering on your property for any reason without your consent. (If you *do* consent to having your neighbor dump garbage on your yard, there is no violation of your rights.) But the physical trespass of a person is only a special case of violation of property rights. Property rights can be violated by sound-waves, in the form of a loud noise, or the sounds of your neighbor's hi-fi set while you are trying to sleep. Such violations of property rights are of course the subject of action in the courts.

But there is another violation of property rights that has not thus far been honored by the courts; this has to do with the effects of *pollution* of the atmosphere.

From the beginnings of modern air pollution, the courts made a conscious decision not to protect, for example, the orchards of farmers from the smoke of nearby factories or locomotives. They said, in effect, to the farmers: yes, your private property is being invaded by this smoke, but we hold that "public policy" is more important than private property, and public policy holds factories and locomotives to be good things. These goods were allowed to override the defense of property rights—with our consequent headlong rush into pollution disaster. The remedy is both "radical" and crystal clear, and it has nothing to do with multi-billion dollar palliative programs at the expense of the taxpayers which do not even meet the real issue. The remedy is simply to enjoin anyone from injecting pollutants into the air, and thereby invading the rights of persons and property. Period. The argument that such an injunction prohibition would add to the costs of industrial production is as reprehensible as the pre-Civil War argument that the abolition of slavery would add to the costs of growing cotton, and therefore should not take place. For this means that the polluters are able to impose the high costs of pollution upon those whose property rights they are allowed to invade with impunity.[4]

What about automobiles, the chief polluters of the air? One can hardly sue every automobile owner. But one can sue the manufacturers of automobiles who do not install anti-smog devices on the cars which they distribute—and later (though this is more difficult), owners of individual automobiles if they discard the equipment or do not keep it functional.

The violation of rights does not apply only to air-pollution. If someone with a factory upstream on a river pollutes the river, anyone living downstream from him, finding his water polluted, should be able to sue the owner of the factory. In this way the price of adding the anti-pollutant devices will be the owner's responsibility, and will probably be added to the cost of the products which the factory produces and thus spread around among all consumers, rather than the entire cost being borne by the users of the river in the form of polluted water, with the consequent impossibility of fishing, swimming, and so on. In each case, pollution would be stopped at the source rather than having its ill effects spread around to numerous members of the population.

What about property which you do not work to earn, but which you *inherit* from someone else? Do you have a right to that? You have no right to it until someone decides to give it to you. Consider the man who willed it to you: it was his, he had the right to use and dispose of it as *he* saw fit; and if he decided to give it to you, this is a windfall for you, but it was only the exercise of *his* right. Had the property been seized by the government at the man's death, or distributed among numerous other people designated by the government, it *would* have been a violation of his rights: for he, who worked to earn and sustain it, would not have been able to dispose of it according to his own judgment. If he doesn't have the right to determine who shall have it, who does?

What about the property status of your intellectual activity, such as inventions you may devise and books you write? These, of course, are your property also; they are the products of your mind; you worked at them, you created them. Prior to that, they did not exist. If you worked five years to write a book, and someone stole it and published it as his own, receiving royalties from its sales, he would have stolen your property just as surely as if he had robbed your home. The same is true if someone used and sold without your permission an invention which was the product of your labor and ingenuity.

The role of government with respect to this issue, at least most governments of the Western world, is a proper one: government protects the products of your labor from the moment they materialize. Copyright law protects your writings from piracy. In the United States, one's writings are protected for a period of twenty-seven years, and another twenty-seven if one applies for renewal of the copyright. In most other countries, they are protected for a period of fifty years after the author's death, permitting both himself and his surviving heirs to reap the fruits of his labor. After that they enter the "public domain"— that is, anyone may reprint them without your or your heirs' permission.

Patent law protects your inventions for a limited period, which varies according to the type of invention. In no case are you forced to avail yourself of this protection; you need not apply for patent or copyright coverage if you do not wish to do so. But the protection of your intellectual property is there, in case you wish to use it.

What about the property status of the airwaves? Here the government's position is far more questionable. The government now claims ownership of the airwaves, leasing them to individuals and corporations. The government renews leases or refuses them depending on whether the programs satisfy authorities in the Federal Communications Commission. The official position is that "we all own the airwaves"; but since only one party can broadcast on a certain frequency at a certain time without causing chaos, it is simply a fact of reality that "everyone" cannot use it. In fact the government decides who shall use the airwaves, and one courts its displeasure only at the price of a revoked license. One can write without government approval, but one cannot use the airwaves without the approval of government.

What policy should have been observed with regard to the airwaves? Much the same as the policy that was followed in the case of the Homestead Act, when the lands of the American West were opening up for settlement. There was a policy of "first come, first served," with the government parcelling out a certain acreage for each individual who wanted to claim the land as his own. There was no charge for the land, but if a man had not used it and built a dwelling during the first two-year period, it was assumed that he was not homesteading and the land was given to the next man in line. The airwaves too could have been given out on a "first come, first served" basis. The first man who used a given frequency would be its owner, and the government would protect him in the use of it against trespassers. If others wanted to use the same frequency, they would have to buy it from the first man, if he was willing to sell, or try to buy another, just as one now does with land.

Laws may be classified into three types: (1) laws protecting individuals against themselves, such as laws against fornication and other sexual behavior, alcohol, and drugs; (2) laws protecting individuals against aggressions by other individuals, such as laws against murder, robbery, and fraud; (3) laws requiring people to help one another; for example, all laws which rob Peter to pay Paul, such as welfare.

Libertarians reject the first class of laws totally. Behavior which harms no one else is strictly the individual's own affair. Thus, there should be no laws against becoming intoxicated, since whether or not to become intoxicated is the individual's own decision; but there should be laws against driving while intoxicated, since the drunken driver is a threat to every other motorist on the highway (drunken driving falls into type 2). Similarly, there should be no laws against drugs (except the prohibition of sale of drugs to minors) as long as the taking of these drugs poses no threat to anyone else. Drug addiction is a psychological problem to which no present solution exists. Most of the social harm caused by addicts, other than to themselves, is the result of thefts which they perform in order to continue their habit—and then the *legal* crime is the theft, not the addiction. The actual cost of heroin is about ten cents a shot; if it were legalized, the enormous traffic in illegal sale and purchase of it would stop, as well as the accompanying proselytization to get new addicts (to make more money for the pusher) and the thefts performed by addicts who often require eighty dollars a day just to keep up the habit. Addiction would not stop, but the crimes would: it is estimated that 75 percent of the burglaries in New York City today are performed by addicts, and all these crimes could be wiped out at one stroke through the legalization of drugs. (Only when the taking of drugs could be shown to constitute a threat to *others*, should it be prohibited by law. It is only laws protecting people against *themselves* that libertarians oppose.)

Laws should be limited to the second class only: aggression by individuals against other individuals. These are laws whose function is to protect human beings against encroachment by others; and this, as we have seen, is (according to libertarianism) the sole function of government.

Libertarians also reject the third class of laws totally: no one should be forced by law to help others, not even to tell them the time of day if requested, and certainly not to give them a portion of one's weekly paycheck. Governments, in the guise of humanitarianism, have given to some by taking from others (charging a "handling fee" in the process, which, because of the government's waste and inefficiency, sometimes is several hundred percent). And in so doing they have decreased incentive, violated the rights of individuals, and lowered the standard of living of almost everyone.

All such laws constitute what libertarians call *moral cannibalism*. A cannibal in the physical sense is a person who lives off the flesh of other human beings. A *moral* cannibal is one who believes he has a right to live off the "spirit" of other human beings—who believes that he has a moral claim on the productive capacity, time, and effort expended by others.

It has become fashionable to claim virtually everything that one needs or desires as one's *right*. Thus, many people claim that they have a right to a job, the right to free medical care, to free food and clothing, to a decent home, and so on. Now if one asks, apart from any specific context, whether it would be desirable if everyone had these things, one might well say yes. But there is a gimmick attached to each of them: *At whose expense?* Jobs, medical care, education, and so on, don't grow on trees. These are goods and services *produced only by men*. Who, then, is to provide them, and under what conditions?

If you have a right to a job, who is to supply it? Must an employer supply it even if he doesn't want to hire you? What if you are unemployable, or incurably lazy? (If you say "the government must supply it," does that mean that a job must be created for you which no employer needs done, and that you must be kept in it regardless of how much or little you work?) If the employer is forced to supply it at his expense even if he doesn't need you, then isn't *he* being enslaved to that extent? What ever happened to *his* right to conduct his life and his affairs in accordance with his choices?

If you have a right to free medical care, then, since medical care doesn't exist in nature as wild apples do, some people will have to supply it to you for free: that is, they will have to spend their time and money and energy taking care of you whether they want to or not. What ever happened to *their* right to conduct their lives as they see fit? Or do you have a right to violate theirs? Can there be a right to violate rights?

All those who demand this or that as a "free service" are consciously or unconsciously evading the fact that there is in reality no such thing as free services. All man-made goods and services are the result of human expenditure of time and effort. There is no such thing as "something for nothing" in this world. If you demand something free, you are demanding that other men give their time and effort to you without compensation. If they voluntarily choose to do this, there is no problem; but if you demand that they be *forced* to do it, you are interfering with their right not to do it if they so choose. "Swimming in this pool ought to be free!" says the indignant passerby. What he means is that others should build a pool, others should provide the materials, and still others should run it and keep it in functioning order, so that *he* can use it without fee. But what right has he to the expenditure of *their* time and effort? To expect something "for free" is to expect it *to be paid for by others* whether they choose to or not.

Many questions, particularly about economic matters, will be generated by the libertarian account of human rights and the role of government. Should government have no role in assisting the needy, in providing social security, in legislating minimum wages, in fixing prices and putting a ceiling on rents, in curbing monopolies, in erecting tariffs, in guaranteeing jobs, in managing the money supply? To these and all similar questions the libertarian answers with an unequivocal no.

"But then you'd let people go hungry!" comes the rejoinder. This, the libertarian insists, is precisely what would not happen; with the restrictions removed, the economy would flourish as never before. With the controls taken off business, existing enterprises would expand and new ones would spring into existence satisfying more and more consumer needs; millions more people would be gainfully employed instead of subsisting on welfare, and all kinds of research and production, released from the stranglehold of government, would proliferate, fulfilling man's needs and desires as never before. It has always been so whenever government has permitted men to be free traders on a free market. But *why* this is so, and how the free market is the best solution to all problems relating to the material aspect of man's life, is another and far longer story. It is told in detail in chapters 3 to 9 of my book, *Libertarianism*.

Notes

Professor John Hospers is Director of the School of Philosophy at the University of Southern California. He has written widely on all aspects of philosophy. His books include *Meaning and Truth in the Arts, Introduction to Philosophical Analysis, Human Conduct; An Introduction to Ethics,* and *Libertarianism*. Professor Hospers was the presidential candidate of the Libertarian Party in 1972 and received about 5,000 votes plus an electoral college vote.

1. William W. Bayes, "What Is Property?" *The Freeman,* July 1970, p. 348.

2. Herbert Spencer, *The Man vs. the State* (1884; reprint ed., Caldwell, Id.: Caxton Printers, 1940), p. 191.

3. Nathaniel Branden, *Who Is Ayn Rand?* (New York: Random House, 1962), p. 47.

4. Murray Rothbard, "The Great Ecology Issue," *The Individualist,* 2, no. 2 (Feb. 1970), p. 5.

Eric Mack

2 Individualism, Rights, and the Open Society

IN THIS ESSAY I shall discuss certain of the connections between what I shall term ethical individualism, natural or human rights, and the need for an open and unregulated society. By *ethical individualism* I mean the view that the proper and appropriate goal of each human being's choices and actions is his own wellbeing. I shall refer to the claim that each person should adopt his own wellbeing as the purpose of his actions as the *individualist principle*. By *natural* or *human rights*, I mean rights that each person has by virtue of some characteristic which he possesses as a human being, and not by virtue of considerations of utility or contractual arrangement. When a person has a natural or human right he has a moral claim against interference of a certain type. When such interference occurs, his rights are violated and the person who brings about the interference has acted in an unjustified way. By an *open* and *unregulated society,* I mean a society in which people are at liberty to pursue, in a great variety of ways, their respective happiness and wellbeing. Such a society will exist if rights are respected. And, I shall argue, the existence of such a society insures that the concept of rights and the correlative concept of obligation are applicable in judging human action.[1]

There are a great number of issues that I shall not attempt to cover in this paper. I will not provide a detailed philosophical argument for the view that each individual human being should seek to secure and maximize his own wellbeing. I will, however, say something in favor of the plausibility of this ethical doctrine and of its import. I will not take up the serious and difficult question of the nature of wellbeing, that is, the question of exactly what constitutes a person's achieving his wellbeing. Nor shall I deal, in a very technical way, with the transition from the ethics of the individualist principles to the politics of individual rights. The last section of this paper is devoted to a brief discussion of various exemplifications of the basic right against coercion and to the justification of defense against rights-violating actions.

The Individualist Principle and the Principle of Noncoercion

The individualist principle simply claims that, for *any* given individual person, his own life, wellbeing, and happiness are the things of ultimate value. Ultimately, the only good reason for a particular individual to choose a certain course of action is that this course serves to secure and maximize his wellbeing at least as much as any other course of action.[2] The individualist principle repudiates sacrifice, where *sacrifice* is construed not as the intelligent ordering of priorities, but as a person's surrender of what is of higher value to his life and wellbeing for something which is of lower value. With regard to any choice that faces a person, if it is true that one alternative really is of greater value to his life and wellbeing, then the pursuit of that alternative is nonsacrificial. Of course, the individualist principle does not exclude, but rather recommends, all of those interactions between persons which lead to, and to a great extent constitute, the wellbeing of life.

As classically conceived, the bearer of natural (or human) rights has a moral claim against at least certain types of interference with his person. The obligation to act in accordance with these claims is the only natural (i.e., noncontractual) obligation that men are subject to. Whenever I speak of rights and obligations, unless otherwise specified, I mean natural, noncontractual, rights and obligations. Historically, the advocacy of the individualist principle (or something like it) and natural rights which are, of course, *individual* rights have often been linked together. Consider the two great classical English political philosophers, Hobbes and Locke. In Hobbes we find a law of nature, "by which a man is forbidden to do, that which is destructive of his life or taketh away the means of preserving the same; and to omit, that by which he thinketh it may be best preserved." The law of nature is distinct from but compatible with the right of nature which "is the Liberty each man hath, to use his own power, as he will himself, for the preservation of his own Nature."[3] Locke also links the moral requirement that each person preserve himself with the idea of human rights although the connection is of a different sort. He states the connection as follows:

Everyone as he is bound to preserve himself, and not quit his Station willfully; so by the like reason when his own Preservation comes not in competition, ought he, as much as he can, to preserve the rest of Mankind, and may not unless it do Justice on an Offender, take away, or impair the life or what tends to the Preservation of the Life, Liberty, Health, Limb or Goods of another.[4]

There is a great deal of commonsensical plausibility in the association of the individualist principle with the belief in natural rights. The former maintains that each man's own wellbeing is a special, numerically unique goal toward which that man can and should act while other men can and should move toward the attainment of their own wellbeing. The concept of individual rights seems to protect the autonomy of individual goal-seeking. It serves to sanction the moral pluralism involved in each man's pursuing his own life values and to condemn the destruction of this pluralism which takes place when one man interferes, at least in certain ways, with the activity of another. However, despite this plausibility and despite the historical precedent of linking ethical individualism and individual rights, we must seriously consider the possibility that these two doctrines are not compatible.

Why might one doubt the compatibility of the individualist principle and individual rights? Rights always have obligations as their correlatives. If Jones has a right against action *s* performed by Smith, then Smith is obligated *to Jones* to abstain from action *s*. Now there is a certain feature about the concepts of rights and obligations which may suggest that the application of the individualist principle to a given person is not consistent with that person's having obligations, even negative obligations to abstain from interfering with others. And this further suggests that such obligations are not consistent with the general advocacy of the individualist principle.

To bring out this feature, imagine a case of Smith proposing to slit Jones' throat. Jones objects. He claims a right against having his throat slit. He claims, indeed, that Smith is obligated not to slit his (Jones') throat. Assuming the individualist principle, one way of showing that Smith should not slit Jones' throat is to show that this action would not contribute to Smith's wellbeing. Except for very extreme situations, invoking considerations related to an agent's own wellbeing will provide good reasons for his abstaining from aggressive acts such as slitting people's throats.[5] However, when Jones claims that he has a right against

Smith's slitting his throat, Jones certainly does not *mean* that this action is not in Smith's interest and that Smith should abstain for *this* reason. Jones means that there is something condemnable about the action independently of the disutility of the action for Smith. That is, when Jones invokes his *right* not to have his throat slit and/or Smith's obligation not to slit it, he is claiming that, *aside* from considerations of the usefulness of this action to Smith, the action is unjustified. If the only reason for saying that Smith's slitting Jones' throat is unjustified were the fact that such an action is not in Smith's interest, then while it would be correct to claim that Smith *should* not slit Jones' throat, it would be incorrect to claim that Smith is *obligated* not to slit Jones' throat. In short there is a distinction between "Smith should not do *s*" and "Smith is obligated not to do *s*".

It may be true that Smith should not burn his manuscript (it being a brilliant work which will bring him wealth and happiness), yet it is obviously false that he is obligated to the manuscript not to consign it to the flames.[6] The manuscript has no right against being consumed. If one ascribes a right to Jones, or to any other entity, against a certain action performed by Smith, then there must be some consideration that can be invoked against that action aside from the disutility of the action for Smith. But it may well appear that, given the individualist principle, the only consideration that could be presented to Smith against any action that he might perform is the consideration that the action does not serve his wellbeing. In short, our problem is this: how can a moral theory be both individualist (endorse the view that ultimately the only end of moral value for any particular person is his own wellbeing) and also allow for the existence of rights and obligations?[7]

Philosophers distinguish between ethical principles that are teleological and those that are deontic. Although there are philosophical problems with this distinction, I will apply it here though merely as a means of presenting an answer to the question of the compatibility of ethical individualism and individual rights. According to teleological principles, the moral value or moral disvalue of an action is a function of the consequences of the action. According to deontic principles the rightness or wrongness of an action is based on some feature of the action other than its consequences. Often it is said that a deontic principle focuses on a feature of the action itself (as opposed to its consequences). For instance, punishing a guilty person is often said to be right just because *such* actions *are* just.

The individualist principle implies that the only *consequences* which count in determining the moral value or disvalue of an action are the consequences of the action for the agent's wellbeing. And we have just seen that if, in evaluating Smith's action, one considers only the consequences of the action for Smith, then one can never reach any conclusion as to whether Smith is obligated to abstain from the action. One could never reach any conclusion as to whether Jones has a right against it. Hence, if we are to incorporate judgments about rights and obligations into our moral theory, we must identify an additional and, in the current terminology, a nonteleological, or deontic, ground for considering certain actions to be condemnable. If an action is unjustified on deontic grounds, it is an action from which a person is obligated to abstain. There is a reason aside from its degree of utility for abstaining from it. Given the correlation between obligations and rights, if Smith is obligated to Jones to abstain from action s, then Jones has a right against Smith's performance of s.

But in searching for a deontic principle on the basis of which we could judge actions to be actions that persons are obligated to abstain from, and hence are actions against which persons have rights, we must be careful that the deontic principle does not clash with the individualist principle. We cannot endorse a deontic principle that may require an individual to sacrifice his own wellbeing. In addition, we cannot simply pull out of the air a deontic principle which defines rights and obligations. We must see if one flows from the individualist principle.

The aim, then, is to sketch the outlines of an individualist moral theory which subsumes a doctrine of obligations and rights based upon the teleological individualist principle. Any principle which is to define obligations and rights within this moral theory must meet three conditions. First, its employment must be justified on the basis of the individualist principle. Second, there must be a significant sense in which the employment of the deontic principle cannot require that a person forego those actions that best serve his wellbeing. Third, if the deontic principle does not apply in all cases of human action, there must be a clear rule for determining when it is applicable. Smith will be obligated to abstain from a certain action toward Jones and Jones will have a right against that action, if the deontic principle (*a*) is appropriately invoked with respect to this action, and (*b*) the action is unjustified in terms of the deontic principle.

The following pair of arguments outlines how some actions by Smith may lack justification. In the second argument, the lack of justification does not depend upon the action's failure to be in Smith's interest.

Indeed, the second argument indicates how the individualist principle
can itself be invoked to produce judgments about obligations and rights
and can thereby serve, in the current terminology, as a deontic principle.

1. Why does this action by Smith lack justification? Because Smith is
acting as if it is not the case that Smith ought to act in his own interest.
(He is acting, say, as if Smith ought to act in Jones' interest.)

Why is it wrong for Smith to act as if it is not the case that Smith
ought to act in his own interest? Because all persons ought to act in their
own interest, that is, because of the truth of the individualist principle.

2. Why does this action by Smith lack justification? Because Smith is
acting as if it is not the case that Jones ought to act in his own (Jones')
interest. (He is acting, say, as if Jones ought to act in Smith's interest.)

Why is it wrong for Smith to act as if it is not the case that Jones
ought to act in his own (Jones') interest?

Because all persons ought to act in their own interest, that is,
because of the truth of the individualist principle.

The crucial point to be gleaned from a comparison of these two
arguments is that there are two distinct ways in which a person can act in
a manner which is unjustified in terms of the individualist principle. He
can fail to treat his own wellbeing as his ultimate value. This is an error
on the basis of the individualist principle. And he can fail to treat other
persons as beings who also have their own unique moral goals. This too
is an error on the basis of the individualist principle.

But what, specifically, is meant when we speak of Smith acting as if it
is not the case that Jones ought to act in his own (Jones') interest? We
mean treating Jones as if he were a being who, lacking any moral
purpose of his own, is at the disposal of other persons. Let us suppose
that Smith is acting, pursuing certain goals. In the course of this pursuit,
Jones is used. That is, as a result of the actions performed by Smith some
portion of Jones' life is consumed. Smith acts in a way that would be
justified only if that portion of Jones' life were at his disposal, in the
same sense that an unclaimed natural resource might be at Smith's
disposal.[8] It is actions of this sort, wherein persons used are treated as
natural resources at the disposal of the agents involved that are done as
if it is not the case that the person who suffers the action ought to act in
his own interest. Such actions are ruled out by the individualist principle
in virtue of the principle's implication that a person's life is not a free-
floating resource that can properly be consigned to any (anyone's)
purpose, but that for each person the proper purpose of his life and
actions is his own wellbeing.

When one acts as if it is not the case that a person Jones again, ought to act for his own wellbeing, one directs that person, or a portion of the life of that person, or actions of that person, toward a goal which is not his goal. When one acts in such a manner, one directs a person to a goal that he has not chosen, or toward a goal he has chosen under an influence which was itself not chosen and which involved his being treated as if it were not the case that he ought to act on his own behalf. Such actions are coercive actions. The deontic principle for which we have been searching can be stated, then, as follows: an action is unjustified if it involves coercion of some person. Note that the presence of coercion is not a teleological ground for ruling the action unjustified. Thus, when an action is unjustified on the basis of the presence of coercion, he who would perform that action is *obligated* to abstain from performing it. There is a reason against the action aside from the possible disutility of the action for the agent. And the person who would suffer the action has a right against it. Stated generally, this is the right against coercion or the right not to be coerced. The only obligation correlative to this fundamental right is the negative obligation to abstain from coercive action.

The Applicability of the Principle of Noncoercion

We know what principle it is that can be developed on the basis of the teleological individualist principle, and that defines obligations and rights: the principle of noncoercion. However, it seems that an unlimited application of the rule against coercion would sometimes require an individual to sacrifice his own wellbeing. For sometimes men find themselves in situations where they have to choose between acting coercively and surrendering their overall self-interest. To apply the rule against coercion in such cases is to maintain that in these cases persons are obligated to sacrifice their wellbeing. As we previously noted, we cannot endorse any application of any deontic principle if that particular application would require an individual to sacrifice his wellbeing. The endorsement of such an application would be incompatible with the advocacy of the individualist principle. The advocacy of the individualist principle, therefore, demands a limitation on the application of the derived principle of noncoercion such that the proper application of the principle never requires an individual to surrender his overall self-interest. It is a matter of utmost importance that this limitation be properly identified. For the range of the proper application of the principle of noncoercion determines the scope of human rights. We must investigate, then, the conditions for the proper application of the principle of noncoercion. In the terminology which I will employ in this investigation, we must see what must be true about person A's performance, at time *t*, of a coercive action *c* in order for one to be justified in condemning A's performance of *c* at *t* by invoking the principle of noncoercion.

My claim is that it *is* appropriate to invoke this deontic rule in condemning A's performance of *c* at *t* if and *only if* A's performance of *c* at *t* is not necessary to A's overall wellbeing. If doing *c* at *t* is not necessary to A's overall self-interest, then A is obligated to abstain from the coercive action *c*; and other persons have rights against A's performing *c* at *t*. Clearly, an explication of my claim requires a discussion of the concept of an action being necessary to an agent's wellbeing. In this discussion I will speak of series of actions which are open to a person at a given point in time *t*. Each series is defined by its constituent actions and is to be thought of as commencing at *t*. Except under the most unusual circumstances, a person has an almost infinite number of series of actions open to him. The performance of action *c* is necessary for person A's wellbeing only if *c* is the first constituent of *every* series of actions (of those available to A at *t*) which serves A's interest at least as well as any other series of actions. This is to say that A's performance of *c* at *t* is necessary only if (i) *c* is the first constituent of a series of actions which is *more* in A's interest than any other series open to him or (ii) *c* is the first constituent of *every* one of a number of series of actions each of which is as much in A's interest as any other series of actions. Only if one or another of these conditions is fulfilled is it a sacrifice for A to abstain from performing *c* at *t*. (Notice, then, that only a small percentage of the actions open to a person—indeed, only a small percentage of the actions which are first constituents of series of actions which are in his interest— are necessary to that person's interest.)

A's performance of *c* at *t* is *not* necessary to A's self-interest if there is some other action, say *q*, which is the first constituent of a series of actions open to A at *t* and which is at least as much in A's interest as the series which commences with *c*. Action *q* may be the first constituent of a series of action that is more in A's interest than any other series. Here it is obvious that A can nonsacrificially abstain from doing *c* at *t*. Indeed, the individualist principle requires that A choose *q* over *c* at *t*. Action *q* may be the first constituent of a series of actions that is (along with a series commencing with *c*) as much in A's interest as any series of actions open to A at *t*. In such a case it is still true that A can nonsacrificially abstain from doing *c* at *t*. The individualist principle requires only that at *t* he do *c* or *q* (or some other equally beneficial action). It is perfectly consistent with the individualist principle that A abstain from one of these actions. In fact, he must abstain from either c or q for he can only perform one of them. Hence as long as A's performance of coercive action c at t is not necessary to A's self-interest, there is no inconsistency in advocating the individualist principle and claiming that A is obligated to abstain from c at t. In general, then, when an action s is not necessary to A's wellbeing, A can abstain from performing s and still act as he should according to the individualist principle. Hence, if the performance of s is not necessary, it is *possible* for A to be obligated to abstain from s. Fulfilling this obligation would not require that A abstain from acting as he should act on the basis of the individualist principle. If the performance of s is not necessary for A, then B *can* have a right against A's doing s. Of course, A *will* be obligated to abstain from action s only when (a) s is not necessary to his wellbeing and (b) the performance of s involves the coercion of others. B will have a right against A's performance of s only when this act is not necessary for A *and* it involves the coercion of B. In terms of the applicability of this deontic principle which states that coercive acts are unjustified, we are saying that it is appropriate to invoke this principle whenever the action in question is not necessary to the wellbeing of the agent. And if the action is coercive, the agent is obligated to abstain from performing it, and he who would suffer its performance has a right against it.

As an illustration of these points, consider the case of two men adrift on the open sea with a plank which can only support one man. Let us assume that in this case it serves the wellbeing of each man to survive, even if this survival costs the other's life. In this case, there is only one possible series of actions for each man that is sufficient for achieving his wellbeing. These actions are necessary for each of the men. In such an emergency case, rights are significantly absent. Each man ought, given the individualist principle and the assumptions in the case, to seek his own survival at the expense of the other. But neither can be said to have a right to survival. For to ascribe this right to either party would be to ascribe to the other party the obligation to allow the first party's survival at the expense of his own life. But the second party cannot be obligated to allow this, since we know that, given the individualist principle, he ought not to allow it. Undoubtedly there are actions for each person that are necessary to that person's life and wellbeing. Each person must, for instance, breathe. What is significant, however, is that those actions that *are* necessary to a person, and which, therefore, he *could not* be obligated to abstain from, are, in any case, actions which he *does not seem* obligated to abstain from (for example, breathing).

As the plank example illustrates, in abnormal, crisis situations, actions that are necessary to the wellbeing of the persons involved increase. Concerning the possibility of obligations and rights (the applicability of the principle of noncoercion) in such circumstances, persons are less capable of being the subject of obligations and less capable of being the bearers of rights (that is, the principle of noncoercion does not apply). This also accords with reasonable particular judgments about obligations and rights. Persons are absolved from obligations in crisis situations. The reason that rights appear only when reasonably sane societal conditions prevail, and not in emergency and purely chaotic situations, is that one person, say Jones, can only have rights against another, say Smith, to the extent that coercive actions against Jones by Smith (the actions from which Smith *would* be obligated to abstain, if he *could* be obligated to abstain from them) are not necessary to Smith's wellbeing. The key feature of reasonably sane societal conditions is that they provide each person with multiple and noncondemnable means of seeking his own wellbeing. The reason that it behooves all persons to encourage an open society in the sense of the existence of freedom of broad alternatives for the pursuit of wellbeing is that (with an exception soon to be noted) the man who *must* perform a particular act to preserve his wellbeing cannot be obligated to abstain from this action. And so, although defense against this act may be justified on the basis of the defender's wellbeing, the intended victim of the act cannot claim that his right against coercion is threatened. The more open society is, the less likely the occurrence of such necessary acts.

I have been claiming that if action *s* is necessary to A's wellbeing, then the deontic rule that coercive acts are unjustified cannot properly be invoked, that if *s* is necessary, A cannot be obligated to abstain from *s* and persons cannot have a right against the performance of *s*. There is an exception to this rule which I shall discuss only briefly. The exception is that the rule against coercive action *does* apply to an action *s* which is necessary for A's wellbeing *if A himself brings it about that s is necessary*. This exception is to be explained on the basis of the principle that, whereas the course of events (other than one's own actions) can result in one's being absolved from obligation, one cannot absolve oneself from obligation.

Consider Jones and Smith in a modified plank case. In this case, Jones is on the oneman plank and Smith is on an oceanliner that is passing by. We can say that Smith could be obligated (and what is more, *is* obligated) to abstain from causing Jones' death since, presumably, causing Jones' death is not necessary to Smith's overall wellbeing.

However, in this case, Smith, who is the only person to hear Jones' pleas for help, throws himself overboard. He swims toward the plank feeling a deep relief. For he reasons that since causing Jones' death is now necessary to his own overall wellbeing, he is finally free of the obligations to abstain from causing Jones' death, and he has always wanted to justifiably kill Jones. Yet Smith reasons incorrectly. To suppose that a person's performance of any actions which would make a particular coercive action c necessary to that person's wellbeing is sufficient for relieving that person of the obligation not to do c is to suppose that the existence of his obligation not to do c is utterly dependent upon whether he exercises his liberty to perform actions which would make action c necessary. The supposition vitiates the meaning of the word "obligation." There are no obligations if one can absolve oneself from the alleged obligations.

Indeed, it is clear that the modified plank case that I have just described is radically different from the first case in which two men, each unexpectedly, find themselves on or near the plank after the oceanliner explodes and sinks. If an action s is necessary to a person's self-interest because *he himself created the necessity for s*, and if alternatives to creating the necessity for s were available and these alternatives did not involve surrender of his wellbeing, then the person is obligated to abstain from s.[9]

Let us consider one additional example. Suppose that an act of theft becomes necessary to Jones' wellbeing. Either Jones does not bring this necessity upon himself, or he does bring it upon himself. Suppose that he did not, that, for example, he is an innocent victim in a war devastated country. On the surface, there is no problem. Due to the course of events, Jones must "steal" food. He cannot be obligated to ?bstain from this action. In the war devastated area, persons do not have rights to the food they possess; not against victims such as Jones. However, the following objection can be raised. Undoubtedly some series of actions other than the series that Jones engaged in would have been at least as much in his interest as the series of actions that he has engaged in.

For example, Jones might have fled the country at an earlier stage in the war. We might wonder whether his failure to do so, his mistake, does not imply that Jones *did* bring it upon himself that the acts of theft were necessary. After all, alternatives to bringing the necessity to steal upon himself, which did not involve the surrender of his wellbeing, were available to him.[10] But, in Jones' defense, we must note that Jones did not bring it upon himself that the path that he chose required this coercive action. Jones may very well have made a mistake in not fleeing the country. The path he embarked upon while staying in the country, the path which turns out to involve coercive actions as Jones' only means of protecting his wellbeing, may very well serve his interests less than some alternative path would have. But his making this mistake, and his having brought it about that the theft is necessary are two different things. Other persons are responsible for the theft being necessary. This is implied in Jones' innocence. And this is why the course of events absolves Jones of certain of his natural obligations. If Jones himself had brought this necessity about, for instance, by carefully destroying all his own resources, he would be obligated to abstain from the theft. For there would have been, in this case, another course of action, fully available to Jones which did not require an act of theft and which would have been at least as much in his interest as the course of action which brought about the necessity for and included the act of theft. Of course, in actual cases of human action we must worry about to what extent the agent brings about the necessity for him to act in a condemnable way. This is just one of the complications which tends to block precision in ethical judgments.

The Application of the Principle of Noncoercion

The difficulty of explaining the relationship between an ethics of individualism and a doctrine of noncontractual rights and obligations has been resolved. This was accomplished by deriving the principle of noncoercion in conjunction with recognizing when that principle is properly applied to a particular action. The application of the principle of noncoercion defines the (negative) obligations and the rights to which all persons are subject. The proper application of this principle is such that persons can never be brought to the point that their obligations to others, or the correlative rights of these other persons, require that they sacrifice their wellbeing. In the final section of this paper I want to display how other human rights can be accounted for in terms of the fundamental right against coercion.

To begin with, let us consider such commonly ascribed rights as the right to assembly or the right to free speech. The phrases *the right to assembly* and *the right to free speech* are misleading. For Jones can be prevented from assembling or from speaking without having his rights violated. For instance, the owner of the place of assembly may choose not to rent his hall to Jones and his cohorts. This may well prevent Jones from assembling, but it does not violate Jones' rights. The hall owner is under no obligation, assuming the absence of a contract, to rent to Jones. It is clear that persons are at liberty to assemble, speak, etc., (always construing such actions as noncoercive) in the sense that they are under no obligation to abstain from assembling, speaking, and so on. But one's right to R, where R represents any activity or sequence of activities, consists in something more than not being obligated to abstain from R. What? Simply the right not to be coerced in attempting to do R, or preparing for, or doing R. It is only from coercive intervention that other persons are obligated to abstain. By letting R stand for *life*, we arrive at the phrase *the right to life* which can be clarified as the right against coercion. Possession of the right to life does not mean that one has a right to be provided with the means for living, or that one has a right against being deprived (say, through competition) of the possession of some specific object or opportunity which would be a means to living. For no one is *obligated* (again assuming the absence of prior contracts) to insure that one has the means to live. Certainly, each man is at liberty to live in the sense of not being obligated to abstain from living. The additional element present in the right to life is simply the right against coercion in attempting, preparing for, and performing life sustaining actions. The right to life consists in the fact that under normal societal conditions any coercive action, and, *a fortiori*, any coercive action against one's life sustaining actions, is unjustified.

Persons have rights against being lied to and to the keeping of promises that are made to them. In the case of fraud and a lying promise (that is, a promise that is made with the intention of not keeping it and is not kept), it is clear that he who perpetrates them uses or manipulates the object of the fraud or lying promise in much the same way as trained animals are used in circus acts. The failure to fulfill any promise (under normal conditions, and ignoring any possible "escape clauses" built into the promise) will violate the rights of the person to whom the promise was made if, on the basis of the expectation produced by the promise and its subsequent frustration, the person to whom the promise was made is rendered less capable of attaining his own goals. What I have in mind is this. Promises produce expectations; and, given these expectations induced by the promiser, persons may reorder their plans, goals, and actions. The fact that the expected (promised) event does not occur renders the person who received the promise and reordered his plans less efficacious as a direct result of the promise that was made to him. Thus, his power to act, to achieve his own goals, is reduced without his consent and not merely through the withdrawal of any privilege which he enjoyed. Such a reduction of goalseeking efficacy is another instance of coercion. I shall postpone a discussion of the right against threats of coercion until after my remarks on property rights.

Persons have specific rights to property. I shall be concerned only with discussing the original right to any piece of property, assuming that nonfraudulent contractual transfer of property already rightfully possessed is not problematic. The classical account of the right to property in the tradition in which this essay falls is the doctrine enunciated by John Locke:

Every man has a property in his own person. . . . The labour of his body and the work of his hands, we may say are properly his. Whatsoever, then, he removes out of the state that nature hath provided and left it in, he hath mixed his labour with it, and joined to it. Something that is his own, and thereby makes it his property.[11]

I think that in basic spirit Locke's position is correct (despite the apparent definition of property in terms of property). But this Lockean doctrine can be better expressed in terms of the investment of (some of) the time of one's life and the right against being deprived of this investment. We have seen previously that all persons have a right against the consumption by other persons of portions of their lives. The creation of a right to property merely provides another instance of this right. For persons invest and thereby save up portions of their lives by intentionally directing their actions toward the production of specific and nonfleeting objects and states of objects. A man has a right to the tool he fashions out of an unclaimed stone by virtue of the fact that he cannot be deprived of the tool without depriving him of the invested time involved in fashioning it. A man has a right to a field by virtue of the fact, and to the extent, that it cannot be used by others without depriving him of the time invested in clearing and otherwise preparing it.

The case of the right against threats of coercion is more difficult.[12] Suppose A threatens B as follows: "Your money or your dissertation manuscript"; and B succumbs to this threat by handing over his money. Now, there is a clear sense in which what B has done, he has done voluntarily. Consider the fact that he clearly *decides* to hand over the money. But since this action is voluntary, must one not conclude that A's acquisition of B's money involves no violation of B's rights? Certainly A is free to accept voluntary contributions from B. So what if A *did* make a certain factual prediction, namely, that if B did not hand over the money, his manuscript would be incinerated. The key to seeing what *is* wrong with successful threats begins with the observation that the threats that appear to be rights violating are those threats wherein the threatened party has a right to the object which is threatened (or a right to perform the action whose prevention is threatened). The phrase "your *x*, or your *y*" is revealing here. For it shows that what the threatener offers is an exchange, an exchange that will be found to be advantageous to the threatened party. And the sense in which he who succumbs to the threat acts voluntarily is directly linked to this exchange; he is willing to give up his money in return for not having his manuscript burnt.

But there is a great problem in assimilating this "exchange" to other cases of voluntary exchange. The problem is that what A offers B in exchange for B's money is not something that A has a right to—indeed, it is something to which B has a right, namely, B's manuscript. Hence, although B's manuscript is in A's power, it is not A's to exchange in the sense that is required if A's receipt of B's money is to be part of a paradigmatic voluntary exchange between A and B. B does voluntarily offer to A his (B's) money as the price for his (B's) manuscript, but what B receives in exchange from A (the manuscript) is not A's to offer. We have an invalid exchange, just as the exchange would be invalid if A offered C's automobile in exchange for B's money. A cannot *rightfully* deliver the profferred goods. Hence, B's voluntary surrender of the money may be rescinded because of A's default. B, or his appointed agents, may properly take such steps as are necessary to reclaim his money.

The justification for self-defense cannot follow the same pattern as, say, the establishment of the right to property or the right against frauds. For the latter are fundamentally rights against coercion and are correlative to obligations on the part of other persons to abstain from coercive and manipulative actions. In the case of self-defense, we want to justify *actions* directly. The right against certain aggressive actions is *not* identical with the right to perform defensive acts, acts which in the absence of prior aggression would themselves be rights violating. Unfortunately, from the fact that action *s* violates A's rights it does not follow that A has a right to forcibly defend himself against *s*. This point is the central feature of any well-developed pacifistic position. Nor can it be overturned. It can, however, be circumvented by invoking the limitation on the applicability of the noncoercion principle which we have previously noted. That is, A cannot be obligated to abstain from action *d* if the performance of action *d* is necessary to A's life and/or wellbeing. The performance of defensive acts (including, say, the commissioning of a defensive agent) in the face of rights-violating aggression is necessary to the wellbeing of the intended victim, A. Thus, A cannot be obligated to abstain from such actions. He is at liberty to perform them, that is, he is not obligated not to perform them and the aggressor has no rights against them.

Notes

Eric Mack is Assistant Professor of Philosophy at Eisenhower College. He has published several papers in the area of ethics and political philosophy.

1. For an excellent historical overview of the parallel growth of ethical individualism, the recognition of individual rights, and the breakdown of feudal social structure see: Michael Oakeshott, "The Masses in Representative Democracy," in *American Conservative Thought in the Twentieth Century*, ed. W. F. Buckley, Jr. (Indianapolis: Bobbs-Merrill, 1970), pp. 103–123.

2. For a detailed argument in favor of the individualist principle see: Eric Mack, "How to Derive Ethical Egoism," *The Personalist*, Autumn 1971, pp. 735–743, and the references cited therein. For a detailed discussion of the transition from the individualist principle to the principle of noncoercion and the applicability of the latter principle see: Eric Mack, "Egoism and Rights," *The Personalist*, Winter 1973, pp. 5–33.

3. Thomas Hobbes, *Leviathan*, ed. Michael Oakeshott (Oxford: Basil Blackwell, 1966) p. 84.

4. John Locke, *Two Treatises on Government*, ed. Peter Laslett (Cambridge: Cambridge University Press, 1967) p. 289.

5. See especially Nathaniel Branden, "Rational Egoism Continued," *The Personalist*, Summer 1970, pp. 305–313.

6. Of course, Smith may have a *contractual* obligation to other persons to abstain from burning the manuscript. More on contractual obligations later.

7. Note that one *cannot* argue as follows: since each person's acting for his own wellbeing has moral value, each person should act in such a way that each other person may act for *his* (the latter's) wellbeing—as long as such actions themselves do not prevent some third party from acting in his respective self-interest. For this argument assumes that the individualist principle implies that Jones' acting for Jones' wellbeing is a valuable end for Smith—hence, Smith ought to pursue this end. But the individualist principle involves no such implication.

8. Hence the obscenity of Commissioners of Human Resources.

9. To be strictly correct, "nor a greater number/degree of coercive actions" should be added to the antecedent.

10. To be strictly correct, "nor a greater number/degree of coercive actions" should be added at this point.

11. Locke, *Two Treatises*, p. 306.

12. On this issue I am indebted to Mary Sirridge for her insightful suggestions.

John O. Nelson

3 The Two Opposed Theories of Freedom of Our Philosophical Inheritance

WHATEVER SHADOW OF doubt the existence of ultimate or metaphysical freedom may stand under, there can be no doubt that in practice we sometimes use the term *freedom* to make assertions that are confirmed as true. I shall call what we affirm in such cases *practical freedom*. Since there can be no doubt that we sometimes make true references to practical freedom, there can be no doubt that practical freedom sometimes exists. If it were necessary to do so, I should argue that the existence of practical freedom rests upon the existence of metaphysical freedom. For the purposes of our present discussion it is not necessary to enter into the last, more profound subject. We shall be able to say what we have to say without granting, or asking that there be granted, anything more than practical freedom; that is to say, a practical meaning and application of the term *freedom*. The two theories that I shall examine make no further demand. We shall not therefore need to consider in our assessment of them the question, "Does freedom exist?"

I have indicated in the title of this lecture that two opposed theories of freedom comprise our philosophical inheritance. This may seem either like a gross oversimplification or a gross exaggeration. Philosophical theories of freedom are almost as numerous, on the one hand, as philosophers themselves. A contemporary author, for instance, lists eighty-four philosophical theories of freedom, falling under five main categories.[1] On the other hand, if by the word *our* is meant persons other than philosophers it may be wondered whether there is even one theory of freedom within our inheritance. If the ordinary man in the street is asked, he will probably offer or be able to offer no explicit theory of freedom at all. The title of this lecture obviously needs some further explanation.

To begin with, let me explain that in speaking of theories of freedom I am referring to theories which (1) present an analysis of individual freedom—by *individual freedom* I mean such practical freedom as one would be referring to in saying that a particular person had gained or lost his freedom or was now not free where he had been before; (2) relate individual freedom to the political condition of man; and (3) exercise a direct influence upon the political condition of man today.

Having so narrowed my reference, I do not hesitate to assert, though I shall not try to prove, that two opposed theories of freedom constitute our philosophical inheritance. Philosophers may vary slightly in their interpretations of these theories, but not significantly. Ordinary men may not be explicitly aware that these theories exist; but it is certain that they are made implicitly aware of their existence. The lives they lead are significantly shaped by them, even though it is through the hands of others and not, unfortunately, through their own minds and evaluations.

The two theories I have been referring to might be called, for obvious historical reasons, "the English theory of freedom" and "the Continental theory." As I have already mentioned, both are in contention for the minds of contemporary men, and where not their minds, their lives. It is, I should agree, important that these lines of influence be traced. But before that is done we should certainly want to know whether the influence of each theory was good or bad; and in order to know that, we should need to examine and assess the theories themselves. It is these two latter tasks to which this lecture will be devoted.

Specifically, my strategy will be this. Having defined and distinguished between the Continental and English theories of freedom I shall first show that the Continental theory amounts to a fallacy of division; in short, to the illicit imposition of a collective concept upon distributed or individual terms. Next, in support of the thesis that errors in logic or philosophy are not merely ridiculous but pernicious, I shall argue that the adoption of the Continental theory not only has had the effect but can only have the effect of fostering and even legitimatizing the sort of political oppression and barbarity that has disfigured this century. I shall argue, third, that the English theory, which is conceptually sound, provides a bulwark, though not perhaps an impregnable one, against the same political oppression and barbarity. Finally, I shall deal with a major objection that has been advanced, and that seems advanceable, against the English theory. I shall suggest, but no more than suggest, a possible way out of the difficulty in question.

The Two Theories

A classic statement of the English conception of freedom would be contained in Hobbes's definition of natural right. The essence of natural right, argues Hobbes, is liberty. And "liberty," says Hobbes, "is the absence of external impediments; which impediments may oft take away part of a man's power to do what he would, but cannot hinder him from using the power left him according to how his judgment and reason shall dictate to him."[2] Because, in Hobbes, reason and judgment are the instruments of passion or desire, we may read Hobbes as decomposing freedom into these two parts: an absence of external hindrances, but also, a power to desire and to exercise that power. This power, in turn, must be construed as being itself uncompelled externally. If, for instance, a person desired to leave a room, and there existed no external impediment, but he desired to do so because a gun was placed at his back and he was ordered to leave, or if he desired to leave the room because he had been given some sort of drug which it was known would produce such a desire, he would not be exercising freedom, according to Hobbes's and the English conception. For an impediment by definition is what "takes away from a man's power to do what he would . . . according to how his judgment and reason dictate to him." The presence of the gun or the ingestion of the drug is not something which the person desires; hence, his decision to leave the room cannot be accounted as the dictate of his reason based upon his own desires; and hence, it cannot be accounted freedom.

Freedom or liberty, as defined by Hobbes, is *prima facie* the sort of freedom that an individual possesses or fails to possess. A child may truly complain that he has no freedom when his parents do not let him do what he wants to do, and when they do, he may truly claim that he has been given freedom. It might be added that this is the sort of freedom that not only children but almost all human beings seem to prize. It is the sort of freedom, for example, that we withdraw when we punish a man by putting him in prison. It can exist or fail to exist, in various degrees, within the circle of a family or some other non-political group. But it also exists or fails to exist in various degrees within a state. Where it is considered within the context of a state and it meets certain other qualifications, Hobbes calls it "the liberty of the subject."[3]

In Hobbes, as is well known, freedom and law are treated as "contraries." The increase of the one entails the diminution of the other. In extending law we give up freedom, and vice-versa, in extending freedom we restrict law.[4] For the time being I shall say no more of this opposition of law and freedom in Hobbes, except to point it out.

The Continental theory of freedom is first expounded by Rousseau; from Rousseau it passes into the moral philosophy of Kant; and from there into the "mainstream" of Continental thought.[5] In a nutshell, the theory maintains that "the mere impulse of appetite is slavery, while obedience to the law which we prescribe to ourselves is liberty."[6] As can be seen at once, in this conception freedom is opposed to appetite or desire and is assimilated to law. Thus it represents an almost opposite conception of freedom from the English which bases freedom in desire and, at the very least, separates it from law.

The practical difference between the two theories is brought out in Rousseau's contention that "whoever refuses to obey the general will shall be compelled to do so by the whole body. This means nothing less than that he will be forced to be free . . ."[7] In the English conception it is impossible to be free and to be compelled at the same time in respect to the same thing. The Continental definition makes freedom and compulsion compatible by assimilating freedom to law. If freedom equals obeying a law that I myself have prescribed, then obviously in obeying that law I am free, whether I am forced to obey or whether I do so on my own volition.

Now, both the English and Continental theories purport to describe the essence of what we have called individual freedom. In carrying out what he wishes to do, an individual is free, according to the English theory; in obeying a law that he himself prescribed, an individual is free, according to the Continental theory. But either one of these theories is in error or else two entirely different sorts of individual freedom exist and each theory refers to a different existence. Otherwise, we shall have to suppose that it is possible for an individual to be free and not to be free with respect to the very same thing at the very same time in the very same sense of *free*, and that is not possible. It does not appear, however, that two different sorts of individual freedom are being referred to by the two theories. If that were the case, the proponents of the two theories could not conceivably consider themselves in disagreement on the description of freedom, any more than one person who describes a raven as black would or could consider himself in disagreement on that account with another person who describes a swan as white. But the proponents of these two theories do consider themselves in disagreement. What Hobbes and the English refer to as freedom, Rousseau and his followers say is really slavery, and that freedom is instead obedience to law. Thus, Rousseau and his followers show that they mean to be defining the very same concept as Hobbes and the English, only they disagree on its description.

Our first reflections on the subject showed that doing what we wish to do, and not being compelled, constitutes individual freedom. Further reflection simply confirms this conclusion. It is, for instance, a palpable contradiction in practical terms either to assert that one is able to do whatever he wishes but that he possesses no freedom, or that he is compelled in all things to do what he does not wish to do but that he possesses freedom. It follows, therefore, that the sort of practical freedom, if any, which is described as obedience to the law does not constitute individual freedom. But if the Continental definition of freedom does not represent the concept of individual freedom, what concept of freedom, if any, does it represent?

A Collective Concept

Some reflection will show that the Continental definition is not purely empty; it does represent an intelligible and familiar sense of the term *freedom* but a sense of the term that has to do essentially with collections of individuals and not individuals *per se*. We say that a people are free when they can make and obey their own laws. People under the political hegemony of another people, we say, "lack freedom." In the same sense, we speak of the American Revolution of 1776 as being a war in which the American people gained their freedom. In this sense of the term *freedom* it is possible for a people to attain freedom while finding themselves individually less free than they were before. Rightly or wrongly it could be argued, for instance, that the American colonists were individually less free after they gained their freedom as a people than they were before. In short, the equation *freedom is obedience to the law we ourselves prescribe* describes a collective, as opposed to a distributive or individual, sense of the term *freedom*.

But may this not be an accident of ordinary language usage? Is it not possible that the Continental theory of freedom could be extended to individuals, even though in fact it has not been in ordinary thought? It will be important for our purposes to show that this is not possible; that the Continental concept of freedom is intrinsically and unalterably collective. This, in turn, can be demonstrated by showing that the concept of law is intrinsically and unalterably collective.

I have already remarked that Continental philosophers—at least since the time of Rousseau—have generally wanted to maintain that individuals, and hence not merely collections of individuals, are free in the sense of "obeying the law that they themselves prescribe." In order to arrive at this conclusion these philosophers have had to assume that it is possible for an individual, given simply himself, to make laws for himself. This assumption is, for instance, the very foundation of Kant's system of morality. But is this assumption really thinkable? We can conceive, it is true, a person laying down laws for another particular person—for example, a monarch might have a single subject and lay down laws for him, as Prospero did for Caliban. But even in this case we must think of the law as covering a potential many: it is simply an accident that the subject of the law happens to be one person. If we can really think of such a thing as a law that is the law for an individual rather than a collective many, we shall have to be able to conceive, for example, Robinson Crusoe, completely alone on his island, legislating law. Can we, then?

We may be tempted to think: Well, could he not legislate law for himself as he might for some other person, say, Friday? And if we do not try to think the matter out in explicit detail, we may indeed have the illusion that we can conceive such a case, just as when we do not think the matter out in explicit detail we may think that we can conceive time machines that return men to the past. When we think the matter out in detail, however, we shall see that except for the name *law* that we employ, nothing of the concept, *law*, remains.

Let me, for instance, put myself in Crusoe's shoes. Suppose I now try seriously to prescribe laws for myself. I say and do what? At the most I might say aloud, "Hear ye, Crusoe. This is now the law: you will wear a hat whenever the sun is up." But surely there is no point to Crusoe's talking to himself aloud or even under his breath. If Crusoe is making laws for Crusoe, promulgation of the law becomes absurd. But how, next, is it to be decided whether the law that has not been promulgated is being observed? Who does this, and how? Let us say that I go into the sun without my hat on: what now? I might say to myself, "Crusoe, you are not following the law about hats." But could I not say in the same breath, "But that was never a valid law." Or could I not say, "The law this instant is changed: one may go without his hat in the sun." What is to prevent me from making a new and different law every time it suits me? Is there a law that says that I cannot? But did I prescribe this last law? If I did not, then we have violated the conditions of our test-case. If I did, then I can discard or amend it. In short, what difference does observance or non-observance of law make here? None at all. And what can enforcement or application of the law amount to? Again, nothing at all. Or interpretation or adjudication? Still again, nothing at all; for when I go out without my hat in the sun, I can as easily say as not, if it concerns me to say anything, "The law did not mean on Sunday—only on week-days."

The upshot is: if I am both the law-giver and the law-given, the judge, jury, prosecutor, and the accused, the court and the indicted, does it make any real difference whether I go through the verbal motions of passing laws for myself or simply do what I wish to do in silence? It makes absolutely no difference. By the same token, though, we can as meaningfully call this species of talking to oneself "wishing and doing" as "making laws for oneself." But laws and legislation are not in fact anything like the same thing as simply wishing and doing. Hence, what we have been calling "making laws for oneself" cannot *be* making laws.

What an individual can do in a non-collective context that has in some measure the appearance of legislating law is to make resolutions. Robinson Crusoe can, for instance, make the resolution on his lonely island not to go out in the sun without a hat. He can adhere to this resolution or fail to. I shall have occasion later to refer to the possibility of individuals non-collectively making resolutions. But as we have seen, there exists no such thing as non-collective legislation. Making and obeying laws is a collective enterprise. As it takes at least two to make a quarrel, it takes at least two to make a law or, rather, at least two for a law to be made. Thus, the term *freedom* when defined in terms of law can have only a collective sense. One might say: *freedom* so defined is intrinsically and unalterable collective in its sense.

Now, since the term *freedom* as it occurs in the equation, *freedom is obedience to the laws we ourselves prescribe*, has only a collective sense, the attempt to describe individual freedom as such freedom must involve us at once in a fallacy of division. Our philosophical fallacy may not wear its equivocation quite so plainly on its sleeve as the laughable textbook illustration of division: "The American Indian is vanishing; Tom is an

American Indian; therefore, Tom is vanishing." We may therefore be tempted to swallow the one conclusion where we are not tempted to swallow the other. But it should be clear that this is only a matter of our carelessness and even penchant for swallowing glittering generalities. The two conclusions—the Continental theory's conclusion on the nature of individual freedom and the conclusion that Tom is vanishing—are no different in the absurdity that they contain and the bad reasoning that generates them.

Spelled out, the two syllogisms proceed side by side as follows: Major premise—The American Indian is vanishing (collective sense of *vanishing*); major premise—Freedom is obedience to the laws that we (collective sense) prescribe to ourselves (collective sense). Minor premise —Tom is an American Indian; minor premise—We have prescribed laws x, y, z. Conclusion: Tom is vanishing (illicit passage from collective to distributed sense of *vanishing*); conclusion: I am free in obeying laws x, y, z (illicit passage from collective to distributed sense of *free* and the pronoun *us*). Patently, when put into the scales of logic, both arguments and both conclusions weigh out as pure chicanery.

An Inevitable Effect

This brings me to the second of my contentions. I said that in support of the thesis that errors in logic or philosophy are not merely ridiculous but pernicious, I should argue that the adoption of the Continental theory of individual freedom not only has had the effect but can only have the effect of fostering and even legitimatizing the sort of political oppression and barbarity that has disfigured this century. I shall now show why this is so.

We have noted that when the collective sense of the term *freedom*, embodied in the Continental theory, is used in the definition of individual freedom, individual freedom becomes in effect assimilated to law. This, it might be added, is a result that Continental theorists, far from trying to evade, have welcomed. Thus, as one of his Continental commentators points out with manifest approval, in Kant "law and freedom are, to a certain extent, one and the same."[8] But if freedom is assimiliated to law, then no separate existence can be predicated to either; nor can one be put in opposition to the other. To repeat and expand Rousseau's staggering equation: Freedom is obedience to the laws we ourselves prescribe; and, conversely, obedience to the laws we ourselves prescribe is freedom.

Now, one can see that if freedom and obedience to law are in effect one and the same thing, freedom can have a value or be prized only to the extent that the laws prescribed are good or non-oppressive. But individual freedom is in fact prized everywhere. Hence, in order to maintain at least a facade of plausibility, Continental theorists have been forced to define law in such a way that only good laws are really laws. Rousseau, for example, finally defines a law to be that which is legislated by all for the good of all; anything falling short of these criteria is not law.[9] It follows necessarily that there cannot in Rousseau be an evil law; or not, in any event, unless we want to maintain that a law that everyone subscribes to and that is for everyone's good is evil; and how can we do that, especially when freedom itself has been assimilated by hypothesis to law? Attempts, however, to conceive law in such a way that only good laws are really laws break down, as everyone knows, when we pass from mere definition to practice. In practice we are reduced to the ordinary state and understanding of men; and in that state and understanding, laws can be either good or bad, oppressive or non-oppressive.

Suppose, then, that oppressive political forces become ascendant and evil laws are legislated. Suppose, further, that we have adopted the Continental theory of freedom. I ask: from what position, conceptually and emotionally, can we now oppose ourselves to those laws? Appeals to the general welfare are much too indeterminate to be effective. Our oppressors can claim with as much appearance of evidence as we are likely to be able to muster that they are in fact legislating for the general welfare. Hitler, Mussolini, Stalin, Roosevelt, Truman, Eisenhower, Kennedy, and Johnson have all made this claim and no doubt seriously, and great masses of persons have believed them.

Do we not, though, possess in the distributed sense of the term *freedom*, a solid and determinate standpoint from which to oppose the laws in question? Such freedom, as we have noted, is prized by almost all men; moreover, its boundaries are definite. There can be no mistaking when I am free and to what extent I am free in this sense, and when I am not. When I cannot do what I wish to do, I am not free; when I can, I am free. And certainly I have no trouble determining when I am doing what I wish to do and when I am prevented from doing what I wish to do. Possession of English freedom provides us, consequently, with a definite foot-place, separate from law, from which, emotionally and conceptually, we can resist and even attack oppressive laws.

It must, however, be remembered that we have hypothetically adopted the Continental definition of individual freedom. In doing so, we have forfeited any appeal to the distributive sense of the term *freedom*. Freedom, including individual freedom, is merely—we are saying—law and obedience to law. From this standpoint, how can we oppose oppressive laws?

Certainly we cannot oppose them on the ground that they infringe or take away from our freedom. For we have agreed that just obeying the law is freedom, and disobeying the law must, conversely, constitute an attack upon freedom. We might try to claim, perhaps, that we had not ourselves prescribed the laws in question. We might exclaim that before a law is a law for us, we must assent to it personally. But if we try to carry through this line of argument, we shall be overwhelmed by absurdities. Must a thief, for example, personally assent to a law against robbery before it is a law binding on him? It is hard to see how, from our present collective standpoint, we could suppose so.

Moreover, on what grounds are we to withhold our assent to a law? We cannot say: because it takes away from our freedom. For that objection can be met by our simply assenting to the law in question. The minute we do, we possess total freedom: we need only obey the law to be free. Shall we say that we refuse to assent to the law in question because it does not correspond to our desires? But even if we do not go to the lengths of Rousseau and Kant and treat the attempt to satisfy desire as a form of slavery, surely we cannot want to propose that desire, divorced from freedom, serves as a good reason for either assenting or refusing to assent to a law. Desire that is not an expression of freedom—and desire cannot be that according to the Continental theory—justifies nothing. I can merely cite my desires against yours, and vice-versa. Once we adopt the Continental theory of freedom, therefore, it looks as if our refusal to assent to a law can only be interpreted as an arbitrary whim on our part. And how can we meaningfully oppose our oppressors on the ground of arbitrary whim? Would they not be justified in retorting: "You could be free just by assenting to and obeying our laws. For no good reason you refuse to be free. How can you complain if we make you free—which we now do by forcing you to assent to our laws"? Does this last argument seem far-fetched and contrived, a mere academic straw-man? But consider: where in the world today is not the equation, freedom= democracy, either greedily embraced or at least given lipservice? And does not this equation mean simply, freedom=obedience to the general will? And does not the last equation, every day in our lives, come to the following proposition: in the name of freedom the individual must submit or be made to submit to the general will? If you do not believe me, ask what our draftees are fighting for in Vietnam. They are fighting, we are told, for their freedoms and our freedoms. And now see what happens and what is said if you refuse to report for induction.

Not only abstract reasoning but daily experience shows, then, that the practical upshot of replacing the English theory of freedom by the Continental theory is to remove from our use, if not all our conceptual and emotional weapons against the imposition and legislation of oppressive or evil law, in any event the most considerable and effective one. We have in effect agreed not to argue against the legislation or imposition of any law that it opposes freedom. And this means that we have in many instances deprived ourselves of all argument and of all justification for being in opposition.

At the same time we have removed, if not the only, at least one fundamental end of rational legislation; namely, the preservation of freedom. For if freedom is obedience to the law, it makes neither sense nor can it particularly appeal to anyone as a benefit to pass a law favoring freedom, since the law we pass can say merely, "Obey all laws." Thus, we are left with the general welfare or the general security as the only possible ends of rational legislation. But intrinsically the general welfare and the general security are ends that foster the legislation and imposition of laws that restrict individual freedom, and extrinsically they are ends that encourage the use of repressive measures and institutions, such as concentration camps, slave labor, censorship, and the police state. On the first score, the general welfare and the general security by their very definition oppose individual freedom. On the second, never in human affairs is the general welfare or the general security in such a prosperous condition that it will not seem to governments that human hands are threatening or undermining both.

Thus, adoption of the Continental theory of freedom, both by depriving us of the most solid arguments we have against the legislation and imposition of oppressive laws, and by restricting the ends of legislation to those that lend themselves intrinsically and extrinsically to the oppression of individuals and groups of individuals, turns out to have practical consequences matching in their perniciousness the conceptual fallaciousness of the theory itself. Nor is this, let me repeat, a purely academic deduction. The fruits of the Continental theory have for a century and a half been eaten in Europe. The distress, both physical and intellectual, that has been occasioned, is a secret to no one. In this country, where the Continental theory is in the process of replacing the English theory of our older traditions, we begin, as already noted, to find everywhere symptoms of the same distress.

We shall therefore think ourselves justified in refusing to elect the Continental theory of freedom to the congress of our beliefs. Indeed, if we accompany our rejection with scorn and derision, we shall be serving a calamitous falsehood exactly as it deserves to be served. We have seen, on the other hand, that the English theory accurately depicts the concept of individual practical freedom. We have remarked, in passing, that it provides us with the sort of foot-place we need in order to oppose oppressive or evil legislation. But these observations cannot terminate our discussion. Objections that demand a hearing must be heard out.

Relation Between Freedom and Law

The first and most obvious of these objections might be stated as follows. Since freedom, according to the English theory, is doing what one wishes, and since law appears to be a restriction upon one's doing what he wishes, one can be free only at the expense of being without law, or one can live under law only at the expense of being without freedom. And this, we have seen, is in fact something like Hobbes's conception of the relation between freedom and law. The two, we have noted him saying, are "contraries." The increase of the one entails the diminution of the other. Supposing, then, that both freedom and law are things to be prized, it would appear that the English theory of freedom forces upon our lives a kind of irrational system: two goods, freedom and law, claim our embrace; but rational bigamy is prohibited. We are doomed to deny ourselves one good or the other.

This pessimistic view of the relationship between freedom and law, which finds expression in Hobbes's mournful assertion that "the state of man can never be without some incommodity or other,"[10] is not, however, the only possible view according to the English theory. Locke, for instance, conceives freedom in the same terms as Hobbes but treats freedom and law, not as opposing each other, but supporting and supplementing each other. Freedom is secured within a framework of law, according to Locke; and although he does not use quite these words, he clearly implies that, though both are separate things, law is the necessary condition of freedom. Thus he says, ". . . the end of law is not to abolish or restrain but to preserve and enlarge freedom; for in all the states of created beings capable of laws, where there is no law, there is no freedom."[11]

The difference between Locke and Hobbes on the relationship between freedom and law stems from their differing definitions of man's nature. Both would agree with Aristotle that man is a rational animal. But Hobbes assumes that men are primarily passionate; reason is but the scout of our passions; and hence, our passions, preceding reason as they do, are essentially animal. Locke takes men to be primarily rational, and hence, he takes our desires to follow after our reasons, and hence to be essentially rational. Irrational or merely animal desires must on the face of it oppose and be opposed by law; but rational desires would naturally cohere with proper law. Since men must reason in order to survive, and since mankind has notably survived, we may safely assume that men's desires are generally rational desires and that, therefore, Locke's conception of the relationship of freedom and law is more just than Hobbes's conception.

It remains a difficult question to answer, though, how, specifically, we are to conceive law and freedom in a complementary as against a mutually destructive relationship. Now, one way in which we might distinguish between animal and rational desires is in terms of foresight and what might be called wide-sight. Through reason we are able to project conditions, make inferences from present conditions to possible future conditions, and also extend cases from the particular to the general. Without reason, we should be limited to the immediate and particular. Rational desires might be expected, consequently, to conform to generalized conditions of desire. But here we are very likely to fall into a deadly trap. We are confronted, as it were, with two avenues: one all primrose and descent, and the other all rock and steepness upward. I need not point out which we are tempted to take and which we ought to take, or where each eventually leads.

The primrose path in our figure of speech is the common good or the general welfare. This is one approach to the generalized condition of desire. But we have already seen that the general welfare, like the general security, is intrinsically opposed to individual freedom. And nowhere is this theoretical conclusion more plainly confirmed than in the current history of man. Throughout the world today men are in a condition of enforced servitude that can rarely be matched if at all in the past; and never were their actions and motives so constantly referred to the general welfare.

A second way in which we can project and generalize desire—and in our figure of speech this way is, of course, the straight and narrow path that ends in happiness and freedom—a second way is in terms of the private ownership of property. Let me merely sketch out in this connection what various profound thinkers are working out in detail. I shall be very summary, not because the subject does not deserve the most circumspect analysis, which it does, but because, short of a summary statement, the subject can only properly be treated in terms of hours, not minutes; pages, not paragraphs.

If we generalize our desires, we project the condition where what I am allowed to desire, you must be allowed to desire also; where I am allowed to exercise desire, you may also. In short: where I may be free, so may you. If we think to fulfill this condition in terms of the common good or general welfare, we must end by minimizing the exercise of desire or freedom.

But let us reconceive the matter in this way. A person is, among other things, a physical being, occupying space. His very existence, as well as his exercise of desire, requires, then, the use of some space. Alone on his desert island, Robinson Crusoe needs no title to the use of space. But where the bodies and actions of persons can spatially collide, some sort of arrangement of titles to space must be agreed upon and instituted. Now, in fact, each individual person recognizes and constantly harkens to this demand. Where men fail is in properly generalizing their use of space, and that is to say, in setting up a proper arrangement of titles to space. By "proper," I mean "maximizing freedom."

What I have said regarding space may also be said regarding objects of all kinds and their use. Without meaning to exclude other considerations I shall, however, restrict my discussion to the generalized use of space. For certainly the titles we may claim to anything else are subject to the titles we may claim to the use of space. We cannot, for example, speak but speak from nowhere. The title to say what we please rests upon the conjoint title to the use of some space or other.

Properly generalized, the use of space would take the form of absolute private ownership, established within a system of mutual consent or trade, and, it seems also, within some sort of framework of un-owned commons or public passageways. For if we wished to order some person out of the private space or land we owned, we should have to be able to, and if all spaces were privately owned, we would not be able to. We should have to order him to trespass upon some other person's private property in ordering him to quit our property, and we should have no right, clearly, to do that. On the other hand, if all space were in the state of un-owned commons, all title to the use of space would belong to the general will alone; and this would mean that the general will would have the right to do as it pleased, but never any individual. Thus, individual practical freedom would be minimized. If we are to successfully generalize individual practical freedom, therefore, almost all but not quite all space must be available, it seems, to private ownership, taking the form: *within a privately owned space one can do anything he pleases*.

I am assuming here, of course, that our actions and their consequences are contained in the space we privately own or that they do not infringe upon the titles of other persons.

When the condition of desire is generalized in the above way, individual freedom is not only maximized but it is maximized at the expense of no one's individual freedom. Suppose, for example, that you in fact own no private space or land. You want to shoot a gun at a target. Assuming, as we have, that the system of private ownership of spaces exists within a system of private ownership of objects and trade, you may attempt to make this sort of arrangement with someone who does own an appropriate amount of land—say, ten acres: for an ounce of gold he will grant you the right of shooting a gun at a target on his property during weekends. Suppose that no one is willing to rent you such space for such a purpose. You work hard and save enough money to buy ten acres of your own. Now you may shoot your gun at a target as you please. Was there any real limitation on your freedom? There was upon the *how* of your freedom, I agree. You could not, just because you wanted to shoot a gun at a target, commence shooting. But there was no limitation on the *what* of your freedom, short of that which by your nature or the natures and titles of others it was impossible to possess or acquire. For example, even though you might desire to jump one hundred feet straight up into the air, you were not and could not be made free to do so—either in the system of privately owned spaces or any other system. Nor can one actualize two conflicting desires, such as, for example, the desire to overeat and the desire to be healthy. Preferences will always have to be set up and the realization of one desire be forfeited for the realization of another.

To the extent that it establishes, defines, and ensures a system of privately owned spaces or land, law is visibly compatible with, and not, as in Hobbes, the contrary of, individual freedom. Is such law also, as Locke would argue, a necessary condition of individual freedom? I am inclined to think not. But we can say, I think, that it is a sufficient condition.

Yet, even in this sufficient condition of individual freedom there lurks its possible subversion. Law, we have observed, is a collective concept; individual freedom is a distributed concept. One involves a collective many; the other, the individual as such. In theory we can conceive an equilibrium's being established between the two. This is just in case law has for its only end the definition and protection of the private ownership of property and most notably the private ownership of space. But how is this equilibrium to be preserved in practice? What is to ensure that its collective side, law, being the more powerful in fact though not in right, in numbers though not in virtue, does not become converted to the instrument of the common good or some other specious good and undermine freedom? Here is the problem that finally confronts us. It seems that if we try to ensure the existence of individual freedom through law and legislation, we may have brought into our fortress a Trojan Horse filled with implacable enemies. And if we are to believe the teachings of history, it would seem that we have. Law that is first adopted as the paladin of private property, in the end becomes its destroyer. Witness once again what has happened in our own country.

I shall not present a solution to this last problem. Indeed, to be honest, I do not know what its solution is. I can make out, however, one interesting route that may just possibly take us where we want to go. It is clear, for instance, that law can remain proper law only as long as persons are individually of the persuasion or resolution to be free. Apparently, therefore, right resolution is both prior to and independent of proper law—that is, law that maximizes freedom. But if this is so, might we not establish, define, and protect the private ownership of property and space through resolution and not through law? The making of resolution is a distributed concept. We saw that Robinson Crusoe, for example, could make resolutions, though he could not make laws, alone on his deserted island. By basing, then, our system for private spaces upon resolution instead of law, we should skirt the conflict between the collective and the individual that law and freedom, when brought together, seem finally to evoke. Nor would it appear that we are indulging here in a purely academic fancy. We can cite empirical evidence that supports at least the claim that law and legislation are not the necessary condition of ordered practical freedom. For example, Benjamin Franklin in his *Autobiography*, in the section titled, "Remarks Concerning the Savages of North America," recounts from his own observation that "the Indian men, when young, are hunters and warriors; when old, counselors; for all their government is by the counsel or advice of the sages. There is no force, there are no prisons, no officers to compel obedience or inflict punishment. Hence they generally study oratory, the best speaker having the most influence."[12] But because a primitive and constricted system of freedom can be founded upon tradition and individual resolution rather than law and legislatures, can we safely say that a system of freedom, involving not only an industrialized society but immense, urbanized populations, can be? I do not know. Nor do I know whether we might not find more workable some combination of principles that neither I or anyone else has yet thought of.

The further exploration of these last questions is a matter of great and engaging enterprise. To achieve anything like final answers will require the keenest effort of the keenest minds.

Although the time could not be darker and the way ahead is little traveled and menaced on all sides by baleful Pied Pipers and the quagmires of false theories and false goods, there was never a time, either, for higher hope. For surely as the monstrous systems of collectivism which now dominate men's minds and actions grind to their inexorable halt in poverty, misery, and undisguisable slavery, man must awaken from his present trance of infatuations and ask for new and correct answers to the problems of his existence and freedom. And when he does, he will find at hand the answers he needs already largely hammered out, thanks to those stubborn armorers of thought like Bastiat, Von Mises, Rand, LeFevre, and the others, who worked at their forges through the night.

Notes

John O. Nelson is Professor of Philosophy at the University of Colorado. He is a distinguished philosopher who has written articles for many scholarly journals including, *The Review of Metaphysics, Ratio, Philosophy and Phenomenological Research, Analysis,* etc.

"The Two Opposed Theories of Freedom of Our Philosophical Inheritance" is reprinted with permission from *Rampart Journal* (Summer 1967).

1. Mortimer J. Adler, *The Idea of Freedom* (New York: Doubleday & Co., 1958), I, pp. 592—594.

2. Thomas Hobbes, *Leviathan* (Cleveland, Ohio: The World Publishing Co., 1963), Part I, chap. 14.

3. *Ibid.,* Part II, chap. 21.

4. Hobbes, *Philosophical Rudiments concerning Government and Society,* in *The English Works of Thomas Hobbes,* ed. Molesworth (London, 1939), II, p. 186. "There is great difference therefore between law and right. For law is a fetter, right is freedom; and they differ like contraries."

5. Paradoxically, one should have to except here France, whose intellectual roots are embedded in Cartesianism and the Enlightenment.

6. Jean Jacques Rousseau, *The Social Contract* (trans., G.D.H. Cole,

The Social Contract and Discourses [New York: Everyman's Library, 1947]), chap. 8.

7. *Ibid.*, chap. 7.

8. Harold Hoffding, *History of Modern Philosophy* (New York: Dover Publications, Inc., 1966), II, p. 87.

9. See Rousseau, *The Social Contract*, II, chap. 6.

10. *Leviathan*, chap. 18.

11. John Locke, *The Second Treatise of Civil Government* (London: J. M. Dent & Sons, Ltd., 1955), chap. 6, para. 57.

12. Benjamin Franklin, *Autobiography* (New York: The Macmillan Co., 1924), p. 195.

J. Roger Lee

4 Reflections on Punishment

PUNISHMENT IS A REACTION to a wrong. It is an action taken by one or more persons against another who has performed an action which is thought to be wrong.

Not all reactions to wrongdoings are punishment. Acts in compliance with the injunction to turn the other cheek fail to be acts of punishment. Punishment involves acts against a wrongdoer which result in (real or fancied) negative value for the wrongdoer. All acts of revenge may be acts of punishment, but revenge differs from punishment by, of necessity, containing some element (fancied or real) of advantage to the person to whom the initial act of wrong was done—advantage acquired through the return of an act of wrongdoing. Thus, if A stole money from B, B might take revenge on A by stealing money from him or simply by reinforcing his feelings of mastery over the situation by beating A to a bloody pulp or by destroying some of A's property. In both cases, B's action results in something which he takes to be of positive value to himself and of negative value to A.

Not all acts of punishment, however, are acts of revenge. If A, rather than falling prey to B, was incarcerated by the state for his misdeed, then A would have been punished but there would have been no act of revenge involved. Reparation is distinct from revenge in that it is not fundamentally concerned with the return of wrong, but is concerned with reestablishing the situation which obtained prior to the initial wrongdoing. This essay will concern itself solely with punishment.

Punishment is of interest to philosophers primarily because of the elements of wrongdoing and the return of harm. On the surface we seem to be able to treat the subject as a legal issue and thus say: punishment is the response of the state to the violation of its rules. In extreme cases, however, such legalism breaks down. If acts of the state directed against certain of its citizens are not responses to what are, in fact, ethically wrong actions by those citizens, then we call such acts of the state acts of persecution, not acts of punishment. The incarceration of liberal thinkers by the Nazi state was the persecution of those individuals.

It is a rather prevalent view[1] that individuals may not punish other individuals—that punishment can be performed only by legally constituted authority. This view cannot be correct, however, since all legitimate powers of a government are delegated to it by their prior possessors—the people. If the view at issue here were true, then either government would not have the power to punish or, having it, all such exercises as it put it to would be illegitimate.

Many, if not most, of the people who have come to the libertarian position in the last decades have, as a matter of fact, come to it through the writings of Ayn Rand. Since Rand claims to give a moral justification of capitalism as a social system based on egoism as an ethical view, if Rand and those who have accepted her arguments are correct, then it is of interest to libertarians to consider what a theory of punishment would be which was consistent with ethical egoism. I propose, in this essay, to formulate such a theory of punishment.

The standard way of classifying ethical theories of punishment is to say that there are two theories, the utilitarian and the retributive. According to the utilitarian view, we punish someone solely to achieve a greater good than would be the case were he not punished. If the infliction of harm on another brings about more intrinsic good, then it is right to inflict that harm.

The libertarian must reject the utilitarian approach to the issue of punishment since the person who holds that theory cannot distinguish between the justification of an act of punishment and of an act of social engineering. *If it maximizes good* for A to be incarcerated or killed, *then* it is *right* for the responsible officers of the government to incarcerate or kill A, regardless of whether or not A has done anything wrong. Libertarian egoists must reject the utilitarian account of punishment since they must reject utilitarianism as an ethical account of right and wrong actions. If, as utilitarianism maintains, that act is right which maximizes good, then, as Bertrand Russell so ably puts it:

It is indeed so evident that it is better to secure a greater good for A than a lesser good for B, that it is hard to find any still more evident principle by which to prove this. And if A happens to be some one else, and B to be myself, that cannot affect the question, since it is irrelevant to the general maxim who A and B may be.[2]

The position that has been characterized as retributivist cannot be the entire answer for the egoist, either. The retributivist reportedly maintains that someone's doing wrong is both a necessary and a sufficient condition for his deserving punishment. Hence the retributivist claims that the inference from

$$(1)\ (\exists x)\ (x\ \text{did wrong})$$

to

$$(2)\ (\exists x)\ (x\ \text{ought to be punished})$$

is valid. The consistent egoist, however, cannot accept this inference because it leads to a denial of the fundamental tenet of egoism, which is

$$(3)\ (y)\ (z)\ (y\ \text{ought to do}\ z \equiv y\ \text{doing}\ z\ \text{is in}\ y\text{'s self-interest}).$$

The inference in question is simple. It is a conceptual truth that (2) entails

$$(4)\ (\exists y)\ (\exists x)\ (y\ \text{ought to punish}\ x).$$

Thus since (1) entails (2) and (2) entails (4), (1) entails (4). But while (1) entails (4) on this reasoning, (1) does not entail

$$(5)\ (\exists y)\ (\exists x)\ (y\text{'s punishing}\ x\ \text{is in}\ y\text{'s self-interest})$$

thus leaving open the possibility of

$$(6)\ (\exists y)\ (\exists x)\ (y\ \text{ought to punish}\ x.\sim (y\text{'s punishing}\ x\ \text{is in}\ y\text{'s self-interest}))$$

which would be a denial of (3), the fundamental principle of ethical egoism.

One need not look far for a state of affairs which would realize the possibility expressed in (6). Let x be some harmless heroin user, in which case (1) is satisfied. Further, let y be some fellow citizen of x. Then y's punishing x for his "victimless crime," would not be in y's self-interest because of its implications of a loss of human freedom. Since that (1) entails (2) and (2) entails (4) entails that (1) entails (4) and (4) leaves open the possibility of (6), the egoist must either reject the claim that (1) entails (2) or that (2) entails (4). Since the latter is a conceptual truth, it is the former that the egoist is compelled to reject. Thus, the egoist must say, contra retributivism, that someone's doing wrong is not a sufficient condition for his deserving punishment.

It is often said of a wrongdoer who has received punishment that he "got what he deserved"; in saying that, what people seem to mean is that the wrongdoer behaved so badly that the punishment was appropriate to the wrong act.

In the light of the preceding, it would seem that such an appraisal would be unwarranted since if everyone should get what he deserves then someone *ought* to have punished the individual who deserved to be punished. Were that the case, then the inference from (1) to (2) would have been reintroduced.

Before such a widely received reaction is consigned to the realm of the unreasonable, however, it would be well to make some further examination of the issue.

Quite apart from the difficulties presented by the wrongdoer's putative ability to impose obligations upon others merely by his doing wrong, there are other problems with the notion that the wrongdoer *deserves* punishment. It is far from clear what is meant by the word 'deserve' in the phrase "he got what he deserved." I think that the phrase 'he got what he deserved' is used with some precision in those cases in which people use it to describe someone's achievement of something which is taken to be a positive value. In these cases, most frequently, what the person who "got what he deserved" got was the causal consequences of his actions. Thus, the man who builds a fortune by diligent work and by keeping his funds in capital at the early stages of his life gets what he deserves for so doing—his wealth. Consequently, in these cases in which we say of a success that it was what the person deserved, we mean by 'deserved' that he, by his planning and actions, caused that which was a consequence of those actions.

It may be objected that we also think that people sometimes don't get what they deserve to get; but such cases, I suggest, fall into two types and the claims of desert involved in both of them have their meaning rooted in the causal analysis. The first type of case is the result of human intervention and has the structure: A acted in such a way as to cause the thing in question and B came along and seized it before A could take possession of it. The second type is further removed and has the form: A acted in such a way as would have caused the thing in question had not some chance event α occurred which no reasonable man at the time could have foreseen even as a possibility. In this last case, A, who deserved the thing in question, could not be said to have caused it. But we recognize with our use of the word 'deserved' that a reasonable man projecting the future could not have described at the time of A's planning and acting, what would be the case other than: A will cause the thing in question to come into being and thus possess it, barring personal intervention. I suspect that the legal phrase 'acts of God' to describe such events as α has been an attempt to avoid the complexities involved with the epistemological concept of context of knowledge while at the same time not abandoning the causal notion at the base of 'deserve'.

If these reflections on the causal meaning of 'deserve' are correct, then it is difficult to make sense out of the claim that someone who did wrong and then was punished, by being punished, got what he deserved. If a man, A, has done something wrong, then that wrong action has causal consequences each of which A has received (barring personal intervention) prior to any independently initiated actions of others to punish him. A person gets all the causal consequences of his action without being punished. Punishment is something which is added to his life by the actions of others, not as a causal consequence of his own acts. Consequently, in the usual sense of desert, punishment is not deserved.

The analysis of desert into causal consequences is not complete, however. We often claim that a man who is in the good graces of the other men in his community, who has earned the good will of his fellow men as manifested in such concretes as testimonial dinners and friendships, has got what he deserved or that it was no more than he deserved. But this voluntary good will of his fellow men may not be a *causal* consequence of his actions. In this sort of case we must, to explain it, appeal to the distinction between causes of actions and reasons for action. We may say of this man that he has acted so as to make for himself a character such that if a reasonable man were to recognize the nature of his character that recognition would be a sufficient reason for thinking well of and extending good will toward him. But the appeal to this sort of case would not support the claims of those who maintain that wrongdoers deserve punishment because it was shown above that '($\exists x$) (x did wrong)' does not entail that '($\exists x$) (x ought to be punished)' and, hence, recognition of the fact that someone did wrong is not a sufficient reason for someone else to punish him. So even in this rather remote sense of 'desert' it seems to be unwarranted to say that the wrongdoer deserves punishment.

I suggest, however, that these reflections are inconclusive because a possibility has been left open. It may yet be the case that a reasonable man, B, by coming to believe that A did wrong, or more properly, performed a wrong action of a certain sort, introduces a new proposition into the context of his knowledge which, when conjoined with other true propositions that he also believes, entails that A ought to be punished. If this were the case, then A may be said to deserve punishment in the sense that the introduction of the recognition of the fact of A's wrongdoing into the context of knowledge of a reasonable man gives that man a sufficient reason to punish A. In fact, I think that these conditions are often met and that people often deserve punishment. But this, we may note by way of closing what has been a long and tortured analysis, does nothing to give support to the retributivist position. The retributivist maintains that it is the fact of a person's doing wrong *simplicitor* that makes him worthy of punishment, but that is precisely what we have had to deny to make sense of the claim that some people deserve punishment.

The foregoing paragraphs serve to show that, in some cases at least, the fact of someone's having done wrong does not give rise to anyone's obligation to punish that wrongdoer. It may well be the case both that some individual A did wrong and that A ought not be punished.

One consideration which people often seem to take as that which, when combined with the claim that an individual did wrong, entails that the individual ought to be punished is that *men deserve the consequences of their actions*, and that *if someone has done wrong, then he deserves bad consequences from his wrong act*. This point, which I take to be true, seems to enter into people's reflections on punishment in the following way. Not all of the actions which people take to be wrong have obviously bad consequences. Thus, if some person, A, spends a Sabbath morning in bed indulging in pleasures of the flesh rather than observing the Sabbath in some church or other, certain of his fellow citizens may well think that he has done wrong. That he seems to suffer no bad consequences for his actions is a situation which many people would themselves find unpleasant and perhaps take to be wrong in itself. Some people have seemed to reason that since the act is wrong and it has had no bad consequences as yet, it is up to them to make the account balance, as it were, and provide the bad consequences themselves in the form of punishment. However, if every wrong act has bad consequences and we know that a certain act has had no bad consequences, then the proper thing to say about it is that it could not have been a wrong act—not that its existence brings about a state of affairs in which we are required to get the moral order right (or some such thing) through acts of our own, such as punishment. And, if the act in question is not wrong, then any action taken against the person who performed the act in question would fail, of necessity, to be punishment and would, in fact, be persecution. Thus, the appeal to the principle that the person who acts wrong deserves bad consequences is not helpful to one searching for a good reason to punish someone. If the action is in fact wrong, then it already has its bad consequences (even if only a relative lack of good consequences) without our acts of punishment; if it does not have the bad consequences (even if only a relative lack of good consequences), the act in question was not wrong, thus leaving us nothing to punish. Consequently, punishment is not required to insure bad consequences for a large number of (if not all) wrong actions. Punishment, in fact, would seem superfluous in these cases. If a man has carelessly squandered away his fortune, leaving himself in a destitute state with nothing but years of penury ahead of him, we do not, I suspect, feel that we should add to his miseries through punishing him. Rather, if we just leave him to his miseries, then that is recompense terrible enough for his wrongdoing. And thus we can come to a seductively simple proposition —that there is no need for punishment, that if we who do right actions merely leave the perpetrators of wrong actions alone, then reality will insure that the wrongdoers fail while we who do the right thing prosper.

While the above position is seductive, I think that it is mistaken on three counts: (1) men are of value to one another solely in relations of production and trade; (2) it is of value for an individual to associate with others in society only on the basis of freely chosen exchanges of goods and services; (3) it is of interest to each man in a society to insure that such freely chosen value exchanges are the only such exchanges that occur within the society, that men deal with each other on the basis of rational interchange, not in terms of force and fraud. The seductive picture above is false because while what can be called the harmony principle (that every wrong act directed at another has bad consequences for the actor, that the interests of men are harmonious) is true, its being true does not suffice to insure that the society of men will contain only those relations that are worthwhile to the individuals involved. Indeed, while there is probably nothing which would insure that all interactions will be of the sort desired, the presence of some sort of punishment will act against the three weaknesses of the false view given above and will thus maximize the good for *each* individual that can be found in the society in which he lives.

And thus, to pick up a lately neglected strand of our analysis, the egoist ought to endorse the punishment of perpetrators of these wrong acts which have victims other than the actor, for *his own* good.

The first mistake seems to be that while it may be true that wrongdoers come out worse off than rightdoers, the average wrongdoer may not know this. In fact, the bad consequences in question often are fairly abstract, and while that in no way diminishes their reality, the average criminal type is not known for his acumen at abstract specula- tion of the sort usually required. Consider the following which has been offered as just part of an answer to the question of why one ought not to rob banks even if he is certain not to be found out:

since presumably he intends to go on living in society, he evidently intends to live among and deal with other men as a permanent fraud—in that he hopes to be regarded as a respectable citizen, who earns his living, but he knows that he is not, he knows that any esteem he gains is possible only because of other people's ignorance of his actual nature, he knows that he is a liar and a cheat and must go on lying and cheating to protect himself, so he consigns himself to being a permanent outcast, psychologically, from all rational (or semi-rational) human beings.[3]

These considerations, I believe, afford good reason to avoid robbing banks, but I am sceptical as to the effect they would have on the average bank robber even if he could understand them.

Second, while Ayn Rand and Nathaniel Branden have done enough to show that any attempt on the part of a person A to exploit, to attempt to acquire the unearned from, B has bad consequences for A, it is by no means clear whether in all cases the bad consequences would outweigh the values dishonestly acquired from B.

Last, whatever neatness the picture of social relations without punishment seemed to have, this appearance is at least diminished when we consider that although in all cases in which A acts wrongly toward B, A suffers bad consequences (or the lack of good consequences), it can be and often is the case that B, through no fault of his own, also suffers bad consequences of A's act, and in some cases the consequences to B are worse than the consequences to A.

There are a set of wrong actions such that, if an individual performs any one of them, as a direct consequence of his so doing, someone else, B, undergoes a loss of his values. No man, B, who has a reasonable concern for his own interest can tolerate A's so acting, and consequently each man has the obligation to *defend* against others who would act in the way specified. In civilized societies these defense activities are made subject to both the division of labor and the rule of objective law via the institution of government and its police.

Defense, however, is anticipatory. After the wrong action has been performed, something other than defense is required—retribution, first, and then punishment. What form punishment is to take, however, is a function of the context in which a person finds himself. If a person were to find himself in a frontier society in which the power of the law had not yet really manifested itself as sovereign over the area, then he probably would find it advantageous to take the most extreme measures against those who harmed him or his family. It would perhaps be best in that context to hang horse thieves, for it is the reputation of being a "bad person to mess with," rather than the nonexistent patrol cars, which would keep the thief, the barn burner, the murderer away from the door on subsequent long isolated nights. The reputation of being an understanding and decent fellow of liberal sentiment to those who wronged him would be an invitation to those who would leave behind only financial ruin or death.

The conditions of the frontier, fortunately, are not the conditions in which most, if any, of us find ourselves. Thus, we are not forced to the extreme measures outlined above. Unfortunately, neither do we find ourselves in a fully free society of the sort envisioned by libertarians. What we ought to do in the way of punishment would vary from one of these situations to another. In general, however, punishment is a practice which is designed to help keep society a place for peaceful exchange among reasonable men by: (1) making the cost of deviating from this pattern of interaction by the introduction of force and fraud so high as to make such deviance perspicuously unattractive thus reducing people's motives to so act, and (2) expressing people's repulsion by and implementing their dissociation from someone who by his actions has shown himself not to be in agreement with and to be likely again to act against the fundamental principle of proper human interaction—to seek a value exchange with another only through voluntary agreement based on a reasonable appreciation of each party's advantage. Whether it has been by ostracism or by imprisonment, the essential feature of punishment, historically, has been the loss of the capacity to freely associate with one's fellow men. This estrangement from one's fellow men is painful to the one estranged and insures the tranquility of the society, not so much by removal of one likely to act against it (there are probably better indicators of likelihood of criminal action than past criminal behavior, but only the most jaded utilitarian would use them), but by the reaffirmation by the members of the society which punishes of the basic principle of proper social interaction and of their abhorrence of those who would act otherwise.

I believe that the following proposals, if put into practice in a libertarian society would allow for the legitimate aims of punishment to be met. Certain geographical areas ought to be set off from the rest of the community by the government to which those who are to be punished would be removed, in which they would be subject to intense surveillance by police to insure the absence of violence, and from which they would be denied exit. While in these areas they would be free to engage in whatever work they desire and amass whatever wealth they are capable of producing and acquiring through trade (including trade with communities outside the area from which they may not leave, should outsiders and inmates wish such trade).

Any monies made inside the area in question shall be taxed by the government authorities at a fixed percentage such that the cost of the intense police supervision and other administrative costs of the area are borne solely by the "inmates" (it is the wrongdoers who must bear the costs of their wrongdoing, not the other members of the society), and such that retribution is made in a prompt fashion to the victims of their crime.

It is not my purpose in this essay to develop an ideal penal system, but to sketch a theory of punishment and show it to be practicable in a libertarian society. What is broadly sketched is sufficiently unpleasant to make the obscurity of bad consequences overcome by its mere presence as punishment—as an additional bad consequence. The provisions for reparation insure as far as possible (nothing can be done for the murder victim) that wrongdoers shall bear the cost of their wrongdoing. But neither this informative aspect nor the requirement of reparation is, strictly speaking, punishment. Reparation is an act done to the victim. The publicity attaching to this new bad consequence of wrong action is just that—publicity—and insofar as it deters others from acting wrongly, it is defense. Punishment is an action done to a wrongdoer: our refusal to recognize his liberty, our removing him from free association with a large segment of society. And, in part, because of what goes on inside these punative institutions, the society outside of them remains a place of voluntary association and trade which quickly removes any deviations from that pattern by removing the cause and undoing the effect of such deviations.

We are finally in a position to say in what sense people may be said to deserve punishment. A reasonable man, B, coming to believe that A did a wrong act that resulted in an individual other than A suffering a loss of value which he in no way chose, in conjunction with what B knows about the only type of social interaction that is conducive to anyone's long-range well being, concludes that A acted in such a way as to undermine those relations in B's society. B also is in a position to conclude that A's actions show that he is not willing to search out reasonable agreement with his fellow men and thus not to be trusted in the free association with his fellow men which the libertarian society embodies. Thus B has acquired good reason to think that A ought to be made to undo the harm he has done so that the net effect to others, if possible, is as if he had not done the wrong act, and that A ought to be excluded from free association with those members of the free advanced society who have not so acted. Such a loss of freedom is severe punishment indeed.

Notes

J. Roger Lee is doing his graduate work in philosophy at the University of Southern California. He is concerned with the philosophy of logic, Existentialism, and political theory.

1. See Antony Flew, "The Justification of Punishment," *Philosophy* (1954); 291–307. Reprinted in Wilfrid Sellars and John Hospers (eds.), *Readings in Ethical Theory*, 2nd ed. (New York: Appleton–Century–Crofts, 1970), pp. 620–632, especially p. 632. Also, Kurt Baier, "Is Punishment Retributive?" *Analysis* (1955); among others.

2. Bertrand Russell, "The Elements of Ethics" in Sellars and Hospers, *op. cit.*, p. 23.

3. Nathaniel Branden, "Rational Egoism—Continued," *Personalist* (1970); 307–308.

part two
State and Societies

A complete discussion of society is neither possible nor advisable to aim at in this or any other work. This is especially true for those intent on defending and explaining the free society simply because the problems of individuals, ranging anywhere from alcoholism to the style of their clothes, should not be confused with politics. So, although most discussions of contemporary society tend to project a sense of total concern and/or wisdom, I have selected only a few of the more pervasive and truly politically related issues for general discussion. From the point of view of the libertarian, the high divorce rate, hippies, TV violence, and the like are not proper concerns of political or social philosophy as such.

Instead, my aim has been to offer the reader a few key topics discussed from the libertarian perspective. I do not mean, however, to give anyone the impression that the thinking of libertarians does not reach beyond political concerns, only that there is, in most cases, a deliberate division of labor and distinction of fields of inquiry. Political theory is one of the few fields with necessarily broad relevance—whereas techniques of psychotherapy, child rearing methods, building construction, the states of contemporary music and literature, while very possibly on many people's minds, cannot be regarded as the proper subject of political studies. It is the characteristic of collectivists and statists to obliterate the distinction between the political and private, thus rendering everything accessible to the influence of those responsible for administering political matters only. For the libertarian, a person's political concerns must be definable, within limits, so that when he turns to his political interests, he can hope to become reasonably well-informed about them. In turn, those aspiring to become political representatives need, lest they fail at the outset, a clear idea as to what their job might be.

Today, congressmen must be omniscient in order to be good at their jobs because a government which is gradually becoming more and more involved with the particular and diverse affairs of each and every person in a society needs, in principle, to know about each and every possible problem people may have. As people, however, administrators, governors, and bureaucrats have their own lives to lead, just as do others. This makes it impossible for them to be good at either running their own lives or doing their jobs.

The members of the public, in turn, cannot possibly be well-informed about the qualifications of those aspiring to serve them in political capacities. Senators and representatives throughout the American political system are called upon to pass judgments on anything from the quality of baby foods to the desirability of airbags in automobiles. And the inevitable incompetence of government is not surprising; nor can we wonder about the thousands of cases of corruption that come to the fore concerning virtually all segments of government. When incompetence is coupled with the duty to be omniscient, one can hardly be shocked by total confusion on the political scene, whether it stems from ill will or negligence or some other category of human failure. The system renders the entire scene incomprehensible even though the Ralph Naders of the nation seem to be ready to fix it all in a jiffy if we just hand the job to them.

By restricting his concerns to some basic issues of the relationship between politics and society, the libertarian is, to my mind, engaging in the wise policy of not extending himself until he inevitably becomes a bungler.

Murray N. Rothbard

5 The Anatomy of the State

I. What the State Is Not

THE STATE IS almost universally considered an institution of social service. Some theorists venerate the State as the apotheosis of society; others regard it as an amiable though often inefficient organization for achieving social ends; but almost all regard it as a necessary means for achieving the goals of mankind, a means to be ranged against the "private sector" and often winning in this competition of resources. With the rise of democracy, the identification of the State with society has been redoubled, until it is common to hear sentiments expressed which violate virtually every tenet of reason and common sense: such as "we *are* the government." The useful collective term "we" has enabled an ideological camouflage to be thrown over the reality of political life. If "we are the government," then anything a government does to an individual is *not only* just and untyrannical; it is also "voluntary" on the part of the individual concerned. If the government has incurred a huge public debt which must be paid by taxing one group for the benefit of another, this reality of burden is obscured by saying that "we owe it to ourselves"; if the government conscripts a man, or throws him into jail for dissident opinion, then he is "doing it to himself" and therefore nothing untoward has occurred. Under this reasoning, any Jews murdered by the Nazi government were *not* murdered; instead, they must have "committed suicide," since they *were* the government (which was democratically chosen), and therefore anything the government did to them was voluntary on their part. One would not think it necessary to belabor this point, and yet the overwhelming bulk of the people hold this fallacy to a greater or less degree.

We must therefore emphasize that "we" are *not* the government; the government is *not* "us." The government does not in any accurate sense "represent" the majority of the people,[1] but even if it did, even if 70 per cent of the people decided to murder the remaining 30 per cent, this would still be murder, and would not be voluntary suicide on the part of the slaughtered minority.[2] No organicist metaphor, no irrelevant bromide that "we are all part of one another," must be permitted to obscure this basic fact.

If, then, the State is not "us," if it is not "the human family" getting together to decide mutual problems, if it is not a lodge meeting or country club, what is it? Briefly, the State is that organization in society which attempts to maintain a monopoly of the use of force and violence in a given territorial area; in particular, it is the only organization in society that obtains its revenue not by voluntary contribution or payment for services rendered, but by coercion. While other individuals or institutions obtain their income by production of goods and services, and by the peaceful and voluntary sale of these goods and services to others, the State obtains its revenue by the use of compulsion, i.e., by the use and the threat of the jailhouse and the bayonet.[3] Having used force and violence to obtain its revenue, the State generally goes on to regulate and dictate the other actions of its individual subjects. One would think that simple observation of all States through history and over the globe would be proof enough of this assertion; but the miasma of myth has lain so long over State activity that elaboration is necessary.

II.   What the State Is

Man is born naked into the world, and needing to use his mind to learn how to take the resources given him by nature, and to transform them (i.e., by investment in "capital") into shapes and forms and places where the resources can be used for the satisfaction of his wants and the advancement of his standard of living. The only way by which man can do this is by the use of his mind and energy to transform resources ("production") and to exchange these products for products created by others. Man has found that, through the process of voluntary, mutual exchange, the productivity, and hence the living standards, of all participants in exchange may increase enormously. The only "natural" course for man to survive and to attain wealth, therefore, is by using his mind and energy to engage in the production-and-exchange process. He does this, first, by *finding* natural resources, and then by transforming them (by "mixing his labor" with them, as Locke puts it), to make them his individual *property,* and then by exchanging this property for the similarly obtained property of others. The social path dictated by the requirements of man's nature, therefore, is the path of "property rights" and the "free market" of gift or exchange of such rights. Through this path, men have learned how to avoid the "jungle" methods of fighting over scarce resources so that A can only acquire them at the expense of B, and, instead, to multiply those resources enormously in peaceful and harmonious production and exchange.

The great German sociologist Franz Oppenheimer pointed out that there are two mutually exclusive ways of acquiring wealth; one, the above way of production and exchange, he called the "economic means." The other way is simpler in that it does not require productivity; it is the way of seizure of another's goods or services by the use of force and violence. This is the method of one-sided confiscation, of theft of the property of others. This is the method which Oppenheimer termed "the political means" to wealth. It should be clear that the peaceful use of one's reason and energy in production is the "natural" path for man: the means for his survival and prosperity on this earth. It should be equally clear that the coercive, exploitative means is contrary to natural law; it is *parasitic,* for instead of adding to production, it subtracts from it. The "political means" siphons production off to a parasitic and destructive individual or group; and this siphoning not only subtracts from the number producing, it also lowers the producer's incentive to produce beyond his *own* subsistence. In the long run, the robber destroys his own subsistence by dwindling or eliminating the source of his own supply. But not only that; even in the short run, the predator is acting contrary to his own true nature as a man.

We are now in a position to answer more fully the question: what *is* the State? The State, in the words of Oppenheimer, is the "organization of the political means"; it is the systematization of the predatory process over a given territory.[4] For crime, at best, is sporadic and uncertain; the parasitism is ephemeral, and the coercive, parasitic lifeline may be cut off at any time by the resistance of the victims. The State provides a legal, orderly, systematic channel for the predation of private property; it renders certain, secure, and relatively "peaceful" the lifeline of the parasitic caste in society.[5] Since production must always precede preda-tion, the free market is anterior to the State. The State has never been created by a "social contract"; it has always been born in conquest and exploitation. The classic paradigm was a conquering tribe pausing in its

time-honored method of looting and murdering a conquered tribe, to
realize that the time-span of plunder would be longer and more secure,
and the situation more pleasant, if the conquered tribe were allowed to
live and produce, with the conquerors settling among them as rulers
exacting a steady annual tribute.[6] One method of the birth of a State
may be illustrated as follows: in the hills of southern "Ruritania," a
bandit group manages to obtain physical control over the territory, and
finally the bandit chieftain proclaims himself "King of the sovereign and
independent government of South Ruritania," and, if he and his men
have the force to maintain this rule for a while, lo and behold! a new
State has joined the "family of nations," and the former bandit leaders
have been transformed into the lawful nobility of the realm.

III.   How the State Preserves Itself

Once a State has been established, the problem of the
ruling group or "caste" is how to maintain their rule.[7] While force is
their *modus operandi*, their basic and long-run problem is ideological. For
in order to continue in office, *any* government (not simply a "democratic" government) must have the support of the majority of its subjects.
This support, it must be noted, need not be active enthusiasm; it may
well be passive resignation as if to an inevitable law of nature. But
support in the sense of acceptance of some sort it must be; else the
minority of State rulers would eventually be outweighed by the active
resistance of the majority of the public. Since predation must be
supported out of the surplus of production, it is necessarily true that the
class constituting the State—the full-time bureaucracy (and nobility)—
must be a rather small minority in the land, although it may of course
purchase allies among important groups in the population. Therefore,
the chief task of the rulers is always to secure the active or resigned
acceptance of the majority of the citizens.[8,9]

Of course, one method of securing support is through the creation
of vested economic interests. Therefore, the King alone cannot rule; he
must have a sizable group of followers who enjoy the perquisites of rule,
i.e., the members of the State apparatus, such as the full-time bureaucracy or the established nobility.[10] But this still secures only a minority of
eager supporters, and even the essential purchasing of support by
subsidies and other grants of privilege still does not obtain the consent of
the majority. For this essential acceptance, the majority must be persuaded by *ideology* that their government is good, wise, and, at least,
inevitable, and certainly better than other conceivable alternatives.

Promoting this ideology among the people is the vital social task of the "intellectuals." For the masses of men do not create their own ideas, or indeed think through these ideas independently; they follow passively the ideas adopted and disseminated by the body of intellectuals. The intellectuals are therefore the "opinion-moulders" in society. And since it is precisely a moulding of opinion that the State almost desperately needs, the basis for age-old alliance between the State and the intellectuals becomes clear.

It is evident that the State needs the intellectuals; it is not so evident why intellectuals need the State. Put simply, we may state that the intellectual's livelihood in the free market is never too secure; for the intellectual must depend on the values and choices of the masses of his fellow-men, and it is precisely characteristic of the masses that they are generally uninterested in intellectual matters. The State, on the other hand, is willing to offer the intellectuals a secure and permanent berth in the State apparatus; and thus a secure income, and the panoply of prestige. For the intellectuals will be handsomely rewarded for the important function they perform for the State rulers, of which group they now become a part.[11]

The alliance between the State and the intellectuals was symbolized in the eager desire of professors at the University of Berlin, in the nineteenth century, to form the "intellectual bodyguard of the House of Hohenzollern." In the present day, let us note the revealing comment of an eminent Marxist scholar concerning Professor Wittfogel's critical study of ancient Oriental despotism: "The civilization which Professor Wittfogel is so bitterly attacking was one which could make poets and scholars into officials."[12] Of innumerable examples, we may cite the recent development of the "science" of strategy, in the service of the government's main violence-wielding arm, the military.[13] A venerable institution, furthermore, is the official or "court" historian, dedicated to purveying the rulers' views of their own and their predecessors' actions.[14]

Many and varied have been the arguments by which the State and its intellectuals have induced their subjects to support their rule. Basically, the strands of argument may be summed up as follows: (a) the State rulers are great and wise men (they "rule by divine right," they are the "aristocracy" of men, they are the "scientific experts"), much greater and wiser than the good but rather simple subjects, and (b) rule by the extant government is inevitable, absolutely necessary, and far better than the indescribable evils that would ensue upon its downfall. The union of Church and State was one of the oldest and most successful of these ideological devices. The ruler was either anointed by God or, in the case of the absolute rule of many Oriental despotisms, was himself God; hence, any resistance to his rule would be blasphemy. The States' priestcraft performed the basic intellectual function of obtaining popular support and even worship for the rulers.[15]

Another successful device was to instill fear of any alternative systems of rule or nonrule. The present rulers, it was maintained, supply to the citizens an essential service for which they should be most grateful: protection against sporadic criminals and marauders. For the State, to preserve its own monopoly of predation, did indeed see to it that private and unsystematic crime was kept to a minimum; the State has always been jealous of its own preserve. Especially has the State been successful in recent centuries in instilling fear of *other* State rulers. Since the land area of the globe has been parcelled out among particular States, one of the basic doctrines of the State was to identify *itself* with the territory it governed. Since most men tend to love their homeland, the identification of that land, and its people, with the State, was a means of making natural patriotism work to the State's advantage. If "Ruritania" was being attacked by "Walldavia," the first task of the State and its intellectuals was to convince the people of Ruritania that the attack was really upon *them,* and not simply upon the ruling caste. In this way, a war between *rulers* was converted into a war between *peoples,* with each people coming to the defense of its rulers in the erroneous belief that the rulers were defending *them.* This device of "nationalism" has only been successful, in Western civilization, in recent centuries; it was not too long ago that the mass of subjects regarded wars as irrelevant battles between various sets of nobles.

Many and subtle are the ideological weapons that the State has wielded through the centuries. One excellent weapon has been *tradition.* The longer that the rule of a State has been able to preserve itself, the more powerful this weapon; for then, the X-Dynasty or the Y-State has the seeming weight of centuries of tradition behind it.[16] Worship of one's ancestors then becomes a none-too-subtle means of worship of one's ancient rulers. The greatest danger to the State is independent intellectual criticism; there is no better way to stifle that criticism than to attack any isolated voice, any raiser of new doubts, as a profane violator of the wisdom of his ancestors. Another potent ideological force is to deprecate the *individual* and exalt the collectivity of society. For since any given rule implies majority acceptance, any ideological danger to that rule can only start from one or a few independently thinking individuals. The new idea, much less the new *critical* idea, must needs *begin* as a small minority opinion; therefore, the State must nip the view in the bud by ridiculing any view that defies the opinions of the mass. "Listen only to your brothers" or "adjust to society" thus become ideological weapons for crushing individual dissent.[17] By such measures, the masses will never learn of the non-existence of their Emperor's clothes.[18]

It is also important for the State to make its rule seem *inevitable*; even if its reign is disliked, it will then be met with passive resignation, as witness the familiar coupling of "death and taxes." One method is to induce historiographical determinism, as opposed to individual freedom of will. If the X-Dynasty rules us, this is because the Inexorable Laws of History (or the Divine Will, or the Absolute, or the Material Productive Forces) have so decreed, and nothing any puny individuals may do can change this inevitable decree. It is also important for the State to inculcate in its subjects an aversion to any "conspiracy theory of history"; for a search for "conspiracies" means a search for motives, and an attribution of responsibility for historical misdeeds. If, however, any tyranny imposed by the State, or venality, or aggressive war, was caused *not* by the State rulers but by mysterious and arcane "social forces," or by the imperfect state of the world, or, if in some way, *everyone* was responsible ("We Are All Murderers," proclaims one slogan), then there is no point to the people's becoming indignant, or rising up against such misdeeds. Furthermore, an attack on "conspiracy theories" means that the subjects will become more gullible in believing the "general welfare" reasons that are always put forth by the State for engaging in any of its despotic actions. A "conspiracy theory" can unsettle the system by causing the public to doubt the State's ideological propaganda.

Another tried and true method for bending subjects to one's will is inducing guilt. Any increase in private well-being can be attacked as "unconscionable greed," "materialism," or "excessive affluence," profit-making can be attacked as "exploitation" and "usury," mutually beneficial exchanges denounced as "selfishness," and somehow with the conclusion always being drawn that more resources should be siphoned from the private to the "public sector." The induced guilt makes the public more ready to do just that. For while individual persons tend to indulge in "selfish greed," the failure of the State's rulers to engage in exchanges is supposed to signify *their* devotion to higher and nobler causes—parasitic predation being apparently morally and esthetically lofty as compared to peaceful and productive work.

In the present more secular age, the Divine Right of the State has been supplemented by the invocation of a new god, Science. State rule is now proclaimed as being ultra-scientific, as constituting planning by experts. But while "reason" is invoked more than in previous centuries, this is not the true reason of the individual and his exercise of free will; it is still collectivist and determinist, still implying holistic aggregates and coercive manipulation of passive subjects by their rulers.

The increasing use of scientific jargon has permitted the State's intellectuals to weave obscurantist apologia for State rule that would have only met with derision by the populace of a simpler age. A robber who justified his theft by saying that he really helped his victims by his spending giving a boost to retail trade would find few converts; but when this theory is clothed in Keynesian equations and impressive references to the "multiplier effect," it unfortunately carries more conviction. And so the assault on common sense proceeds, each age performing the task in its own ways.

Thus, ideological support being vital to the State, it must unceasingly try to impress the public with its "legitimacy," to distinguish its activities from those of mere brigands. The unremitting determination of its assaults on common sense is no accident, for as Mencken vividly maintained:

> *The average man, whatever his errors otherwise, at least sees clearly that government is something lying outside him and outside the generality of his fellow men—that it is a separate, independent, and hostile power, only partly under his control, and capable of doing him great harm. Is it a fact of no significance that robbing the government is everywhere regarded as a crime of less magnitude than robbing an individual, or even a corporation? . . . What lies behind all this, I believe, is a deep sense of the fundamental antagonism between the government and the people it governs. It is apprehended, not as a committee of citizens chosen to carry on the communal business of the whole population, but as a separate and autonomous corporation, mainly devoted to exploiting the population for the benefit of its own members. . . . When a private citizen is robbed, a worthy man is deprived of the fruits of his industry and thrift; when the government is robbed, the worst that happens is that certain rogues and loafers have less money to play with than they had before. The notion that they have earned that money is never entertained; to most sensible men it would seem ludicrous. . . .* [19]

IV.   How the State Transcends Its Limits

As Bertrand De Jouvenel has sagely pointed out, through the centuries men have formed concepts designed to check and limit the exercise of State rule; and, one after another, the State, using its intellectual allies, has been able to transform these concepts into intellectual rubber stamps of legitimacy and virtue to attach to its decrees and actions. Originally, in Western Europe, the concept of divine sovereignty held that the kings may rule only according to divine law; the kings turned the concept into a rubber stamp of divine approval for any of the kings' actions. The concept of parliamentary democracy began as a popular check upon absolute monarchial rule; it ended with parliament being the essential part of the State and its every act totally sovereign. As De Jouvenel concludes:

> *Many writers on theories of sovereignty have worked out one . . . of these restrictive devices. But in the end every single such theory has, sooner or later, lost its original purpose, and come to act merely as a springboard to Power, by providing it with the powerful aid of an invisible sovereign with whom it could in time successfully identify itself.*[20]

Similarly with more specific doctrines: the "natural rights" of the individual enshrined in John Locke and the Bill of Rights became a statist "right to a job"; utilitarianism turned from arguments for liberty to arguments against resisting the State's invasions of liberty, etc.

Certainly the most ambitious attempt to impose limits on the State has been the Bill of Rights and other restrictive parts of the American Constitution, in which written limits on government became the Fundamental Law to be interpreted by a judiciary supposedly independent of the other branches of government. All Americans are familiar with the process by which the construction of limits in the Constitution has been inexorably broadened over the last century. But few have been as keen as Professor Charles Black to see that the State has, in the process, largely transformed judicial review itself from a *limiting* device to yet another instrument for furnishing ideological legitimacy to the government's actions. For if a judicial decree of "unconstitutional" is a mighty check to government power, an implicit or explicit verdict of "constitutional" is a mighty weapon for fostering public acceptance of ever-greater government power.

Professor Black begins his analysis by pointing out the crucial necessity of "legitimacy" for any government to endure, this legitimation signifying basic majority acceptance of the government and its actions.[21] Acceptance of legitimacy becomes a particular problem in a country such as the United States, where "substantive limitations are built into the theory on which the government rests." What is needed, adds Black, is a means by which the government can assure the public that its increasing powers are, indeed, "constitutional." And this, he concludes, has been the major historic function of judicial review.

Let Black illustrate the problem:

The supreme risk [to the government] is that of disaffection and a feeling of outrage widely disseminated throughout the population, and loss of moral authority by the government as such, however long it may be propped up by force or inertia or the lack of an appealing and immediately available alternative. Almost everybody living under a government of limited powers, must sooner or later be subjected to some governmental action which as a matter of private opinion he regards as outside the power of government or positively forbidden to government. A man is drafted, though he finds nothing in the Constitution about being drafted. . . . A farmer is told how much wheat he can raise; he believes, and he discovers that some respectable lawyers believe with him, that the government has no more right to tell him how much wheat he can grow than it has to tell his daughter whom she can marry. A man goes to the federal penitentiary for saying what he wants to, and he paces his cell reciting . . . "Congress shall make no laws abridging the freedom of speech" . . . . A businessman is told what he can ask, and must ask, for buttermilk.

The danger is real enough that each of these people (and who is not of their number?) will confront the concept of governmental limitation with the reality (as he sees it) of the flagrant overstepping of actual limits, and draw the obvious conclusion as to the status of his government with respect to legitimacy.[22]

This danger is averted by the State's propounding the doctrine that *some one* agency must have the ultimate decision on constitutionality, and that this agency, in the last analysis, must be *part of* the federal government.[23] For while the seeming independence of the federal judiciary has played a vital part in making its action virtual Holy Writ for the bulk of the people, it is also and ever true that the judiciary is part and parcel of the government apparatus and appointed by the executive and legislative branches. Black admits that this means that the State has set itself up as a judge in its own cause, thus violating a basic juridical principle for aiming at just decisions. He brusquely denies the possibility of an alternative.[24]

Black adds:

The problem, then, is to devise such governmental means of deciding as will (hopefully) reduce to a tolerable minimum the intensity of the objection that government is judge in its own cause. Having done this, you can only hope that this objection, though theoretically still tenable, will practically lose enough of its force that the legitimating work of the deciding institution can win acceptance.[25]

In the last analysis, Black finds the achievement of justice and legitimacy from the State's perpetual judging of its own cause as "something of a miracle."[26]

Applying his thesis to the famous conflict between the Supreme Court and the New Deal, Professor Black keenly chides his fellow pro-New Deal colleagues for their shortsightedness in denouncing judicial obstruction:

> . . . *the standard version of the story of the New Deal and the Court, though accurate in its way, displaces the emphasis. . . . It concentrates on the difficulties; it almost forgets how the whole thing turned out. The upshot of the matter was (and this is what I like to emphasize) that after some twenty-four months of balking . . . the Supreme Court, without a single change in the law of its composition, or, indeed, in its actual manning, placed the affirmative stamp of legitimacy on the New Deal, and on the whole new conception of government in America.*[27]

In this way, the Supreme Court was able to put the quietus on the large body of Americans who had had strong constitutional objections to the New Deal:

> *Of course, not everyone was satisfied. The Bonnie Prince Charlie of constitutionally commanded laissez faire still stirs the hearts of a few zealots in the Highlands of choleric unreality. But there is no longer any significant or dangerous public doubt as to the constitutional power of Congress to deal as it does with the national economy. . . .*
> *We had no means, other than the Supreme Court, for imparting legitimacy to the New Deal.*[28]

As Black recognizes, one major political theorist who recognized—and largely in advance—the glaring loophole in a constitutional limit on government of placing the ultimate interpreting power in the Supreme Court was John C. Calhoun. Calhoun was not content with the "miracle," but instead proceeded to a profound analysis of the constitutional problem. In his *Disquisition,* Calhoun demonstrated the inherent tendency of the State to break through the limits of such a constitution:

> *A written constitution certainly has many and considerable advantages, but it is a great mistake to suppose that the mere insertion of provisions to restrict and limit the power of the government, without investing those for whose protection they are inserted with the means of enforcing their observance will be sufficient to prevent the major and dominant party from abusing its powers. Being the party in possession of the government, they will, from the same constitution of man which makes government necessary to protect society, be in favor of the powers granted by the constitution and opposed to the restrictions intended to limit them. . . . The minor or weaker party, on the contrary, would take the opposite direction and regard them [the restrictions] as essential to their protection against the dominant party. . . . But where there are no means by which they could compel the major*

party to observe the restrictions, the only resort left them would be a strict construction of the constitution. . . . To this the major party would oppose a liberal construction. . . . It would be construction against construction—the one to contract and the other to enlarge the powers of the government to the utmost. But of what possible avail could the strict construction of the minor party be, against the liberal construction of the major, when the one would have all the power of the government to carry its construction into effect and the other be deprived of all means of enforcing its construction? In a contest so unequal, the result would not be doubtful. The party in favor of the restrictions would be overpowered. . . . The end of the contest would be the subversion of the constitution . . . the restrictions would ultimately be annulled and the government be converted into one of unlimited powers.[29]

One of the few political scientists who appreciated Calhoun's analysis of the Constitution was Professor J. Allen Smith. Smith noted that the Constitution was designed with checks and balances to limit any one governmental power, and yet had then developed a Supreme Court with the monopoly of ultimate interpreting power. If the federal government was created to check invasions of individual liberty by the separate states, who was to check the federal power? Smith maintained that implicit in the check-and-balance idea of the Constitution was the concomitant view that no one branch of government may be conceded the ultimate power of interpretation: "It was assumed by the people that the new government could not be permitted to determine the limits of its own authority, since this would make it, and not the Constitution, supreme."[30]

The solution advanced by Calhoun (and seconded, in this century, by such writers as Smith) was, of course, the famous doctrine of the "concurrent majority." If any substantial minority interest in the country, specifically a state government, believed that the federal government was exceeding its powers and encroaching on that minority, the minority would have the right to veto this exercise of power as unconstitutional. Applied to state governments, this theory implied the right of "nullification" of a federal law or ruling within a state's jurisdiction.

In theory, the ensuing constitutional system would assure that the federal government check any state invasion of individual rights, while the states would check excessive federal power over the individual. And yet, while limitations would undoubtedly be more effective than at present, there are many difficulties and problems in the Calhoun solution. If, indeed, a subordinate interest should rightfully have a veto

over matters concerning it, then why stop with the *states*? Why not place
veto power in counties, cities, wards? Furthermore, interests are not only
sectional, they are also occupational, social, etc. What of bakers, or taxi
drivers, or any other occupation? Should *they* not be permitted a veto
power over their own lives? This brings us to the important point that
the nullification theory confines its checks to *agencies of government itself*.
Let us not forget that federal and state governments, and their respective branches, are still States, are still guided by their own State interests
rather than by the interests of the private citizens. What is to prevent the
Calhoun system from working in reverse: with states tyrannizing over
their citizens, and only vetoing the federal government when it tries to
intervene to *stop* that state tyranny? Or for states to acquiesce in federal
tyranny? What is to prevent federal and state governments from
forming mutually profitable alliances for the joint exploitation of the
citizenry? And even if the private occupational groupings were to be
given some form of "functional" representation in government, what is
to prevent them from using the State to gain subsidies and other special
privileges for themselves, or from imposing compulsory cartels on their
own members?

In short, Calhoun does not push his path-seeking theory on
concurrence far enough: he does not push it down *to the individual*
himself. If the individual, after all, is the one whose rights are to be
protected, then a consistent theory of concurrence would imply veto
power by every individual, i.e., some form of "unanimity principle."
When Calhoun wrote that it should be "impossible to put or to keep it
[the government] in action without the concurrent consent of all," he
was, perhaps unwittingly, implying just such a conclusion.[31] But such
speculation begins to take us away from our subject, for down this path
lie political systems which could hardly be called "States" at all.[32] For one
thing, just as the right of nullification for a state logically implies its right
of *secession*, so a right of individual nullification would imply the right of
any individual to "secede" from the State under which he lives.[33]

Thus, the State has invariably shown a striking talent for the
expansion of its powers beyond any limits that might be imposed upon
it. Since the State necessarily lives by the compulsory confiscation of
private capital, and since its expansion necessarily involves ever-greater
incursions on private individuals and private enterprises, we must assert
that the State is profoundly and inherently anti-capitalist. In a sense, our
position is the reverse of the Marxist *dictum* that the State is the
"executive committee" of the ruling class—in the present day, supposedly the capitalists. Instead, the State—the organization of the political

means—constitutes, and is the source of, the "ruling class" (rather, ruling *caste*), and is in permanent opposition to *genuinely* private capital. We may therefore say, with De Jouvenel:

> Only those who know nothing of any time but their own, who are completely in the dark as to the manner of Power's behaving through thousands of years, would regard these proceedings [nationalization, the income tax, etc.] as the fruit of a particular set of doctrines. They are in fact the normal manifestations of Power, and differ not at all in their nature from Henry VIII's confiscation of the monasteries. The same principle is at work; the hunger for authority, the thirst for resources; and in all of these operations the same characteristics are present, including the rapid elevation of the dividers of the spoils. Whether it is socialist or whether it is not, Power must always be at war with the capitalist authorities and despoil the capitalists of their accumulated wealth; in doing so it obeys the law of its nature.[34]

V.   What the State Fears

What the State fears above all, of course, is any fundamental threat to its own power and its own existence. The death of a State can come about in two major ways: (a) through conquest by another State, or (b) through revolutionary overthrow by its own subjects—in short, by war or revolution. War and revolution, as the two basic threats, invariably arouse in the State rulers their maximum efforts and maximum propaganda among the people. As stated above, any way must always be used to mobilize the people to come to the State's defense in the belief that they are defending themselves. The fallacy of that idea becomes evident when conscription is wielded against those who refuse to "defend" themselves and are therefore forced into joining the State's military band: needless to add, no "defense" is permitted them against this act of "their own" State.

In war, State power is pushed to its ultimate, and, under the slogans of "defense" and "emergency," it can impose a tyranny upon the public such as might be openly resisted in time of peace. War thus provides many benefits to a State, and indeed every modern war has brought to the warring peoples a permanent legacy of increased State burdens upon society. War, moreover, provides to a State tempting opportunities for conquest of land areas over which it may exercise its monopoly of force. Randolph Bourne was certainly correct when he wrote that "war is the health of the State," but to any particular State a war may spell either health or grave injury.[35]

We may test the hypothesis that the State is largely interested in protecting *itself* rather than its subjects by asking: which category of crimes does the State pursue and punish most intensely—those against private citizens or those against *itself*? The gravest crimes in the State's lexicon are almost invariably not invasions of private person or property, but dangers to its *own* contentment, e.g., treason, desertion of a soldier to the enemy, failure to register for the draft, subversion and subversive conspiracy, assassination of rulers, and such economic crimes against the State as counterfeiting its money, or evasion of its income tax. Or compare the degree of zeal devoted to pursuing the man who assaults a policeman with the attention that the State pays to the assault of an ordinary citizen. Yet, curiously, the State's openly assigned priority to its *own* defense against the public strikes few people as inconsistent with its presumed *raison d'être*.[36]

VI. How States Relate to One Another

Since the territorial area of the earth is divided among different States, inter-State relations must occupy much of a State's time and energy. The natural tendency of a State is to expand its power, and, externally, such expansion takes place by conquest of a territorial area. Unless a territory is stateless or uninhabited, any such expansion involves an inherent conflict of interest between one set of State rulers and another. Only one set of rulers can obtain a monopoly of coercion over any given territorial area at any one time: complete power over a territory by State X can only be obtained by the expulsion of State Y. War, while risky, will be an ever-present tendency of States, punctuated by periods of peace, and by shifting alliances and coalitions between States.

We have seen that the "internal" or "domestic" attempt to limit the State, in the seventeenth through nineteenth centuries, reached its most notable form in constitutionalism. Its "external," or "foreign affairs," counterpart was the development of "international law," especially such forms as the "laws of war" and "neutrals' rights."[37] Parts of international law were originally purely private, growing out of the need of merchants and traders everywhere to protect their property and adjudicate disputes. Examples are admiralty law and the law merchant. But even the governmental rules emerged voluntarily, and were not imposed by any international super-State. The object of the "laws of war" was to limit inter-State destruction *to the State apparatus itself*, thereby preserving the innocent "civilian" public from the slaughter and devastation of war.

The object of the development of neutrals' rights was to preserve private civilian international commerce, even with "enemy" countries, from seizure by one of the warring parties. The overriding aim, then, was to limit the extent of any war, and particularly to limit its destructive impact on the private citizens of the neutral, and even the warring, countries.

The jurist F. J. P. Veale charmingly describes such "civilized warfare" as it briefly flourished in fifteenth-century Italy:

> . . . the rich burghers and merchants of medieval Italy were too busy making money and enjoying life to undertake the hardships and dangers of soldiering themselves. So they adopted the practice of hiring mercenaries to do their fighting for them, and, being thrifty, business-like folk, they dismissed these mercenaries immediately after their services could be dispensed with. Wars were, therefore, fought by armies hired for each campaign. . . . For the first time, soldiering became a reasonable and comparatively harmless profession. The generals of that period maneuvered against each other, often with consummate skill, but when one had won the advantage, his opponent generally either retreated or surrendered. It was a recognized rule that a town could only be sacked if it offered resistance: immunity could always be purchased by paying a ransom. . . . As one natural consequence, no town ever resisted, it being obvious that a government too weak to defend its citizens had forfeited their allegiance. Civilians had little to fear from the dangers of war which were the concern only of professional soldiers.[38]

The well-nigh absolute separation of the private civilian from the State's wars in eighteenth-century Europe is highlighted by Nef:

> Even postal communications were not successfully restricted for long in wartime. Letters circulated without censorship, with a freedom that astonishes the twentieth-century mind. . . . The subjects of two warring nations talked to each other if they met, and when they could not meet, corresponded, not as enemies but as friends. The modern notion hardly existed that . . . subjects of any enemy country are partly accountable for the belligerent acts of their rulers. Nor had the warring rulers any firm disposition to stop communications with subjects of the enemy. The old inquisitorial practices of espionage in connection with religious worship and belief were disappearing, and no comparable inquisition in connection with political or economic communications was even contemplated. Passports were originally created to provide safe-conduct in time of war. During most of the eighteenth century it seldom occurred to Europeans to abandon their travels in a foreign country which their own was fighting.[39]
> And trade being increasingly recognized as beneficial to both parties, eighteenth-century warfare also countenanced a considerable amount of "trading with the enemy."[40]

How far States have transcended rules of civilized warfare in this century needs no elaboration here. In the modern era of total war combined with the technology of total destruction, the very idea of keeping war limited to the State apparati seems even more quaint and obsolete than the original Constitution of the United States.

When States are not at war, agreements are often necessary to keep frictions at a minimum. One doctrine that has gained curiously wide acceptance is the alleged "sanctity of treaties." This concept is treated as the counterpart of the "sanctity of contract." But a treaty and a genuine contract have nothing in common. A contract transfers, in a precise manner, titles to private property. Since a government does not, in any proper sense, "own" its territorial area, any agreements that it concludes do not confer titles to property. If, for example, Mr. Jones sells or gives his land to Mr. Smith, Jones' heir cannot legitimately descend upon Smith's heir and claim the land as rightfully his. The property title has already been transferred. Old Jones' contract is automatically binding upon Young Jones, because the former had already transferred the property; Young Jones, therefore, has no property claim. Young Jones can only claim that which he has inherited from Old Jones, and Old Jones can only bequeath property which he still owns. But if, at a certain date, the government of, say, Ruritania, is coerced or even bribed by the government of Walldavia, it is absurd to claim that the governments or inhabitants of the two countries are forever barred from a claim to reunification of Ruritania on the grounds of the sanctity of a treaty. Neither the people nor the land of North-west Ruritania are *owned* by either of the two governments. As a corollary, one government can certainly not bind, by the dead hand of the past, a later government through treaty. A revolutionary government which overthrew the king of Ruritania could, similarly, hardly be called to account for the king's actions or debts, for a government is not, as is a child, a true "heir" to its predecessor's property.

VII.   History As a Race Between State Power and Social Power

Just as the two basic and mutually exclusive inter-relations between men are peaceful cooperation or coercive exploitation, production or predation, so the history of mankind, particularly its economic history, may be considered as a contest between these two principles. On the one hand, there is creative productivity, peaceful exchange and cooperation; on the other, coercive dictation and predation over those social relations. Albert Jay Nock happily termed these contesting forces: "social power" and "State power."[41] Social power is man's *power over nature*, his cooperative transformation of nature's resources and insight into nature's laws, for the benefit of all participating individuals. Social power is the power over nature, the living standards, achieved by men in mutual exchange. State power, as we have seen, is the coercive and parasitic seizure of this production—a draining of the fruits of society for the benefit of non-productive (actually *anti*-productive) rulers. While social power is over nature, State power is *power over man*. Through history, man's productive and creative forces have, time and again, carved out new ways of transforming nature for man's benefit. These have been the times when social power has spurted ahead of State power, and when the degree of State encroachment over society has considerably lessened. But always, after a greater or smaller time lag, the State has moved into these new areas, to cripple and confiscate social power once more.[42] If the seventeenth through the nineteenth centuries were, in many countries of the West, times of accelerating social power, and a corollary increase in freedom, peace, and material welfare, the twentieth century has been primarily an age in which State power has been catching up—with a consequent reversion to slavery, war and destruction.[43]

In this century, the human race faces once again the virulent reign of the State—of the State now armed with the fruits of man's creative powers, confiscated and perverted to its own aims. The last few centuries were times when men tried to place constitutional and other limits on the State, only to find that such limits as with all other attempts, have failed. Of all the numerous forms that governments have taken over the centuries, of all the concepts and institutions that have been tried, none has succeeded in keeping the State in check. The problem of the State is evidently as far from solution as ever. Perhaps new paths of inquiry must be explored, if the successful, final solution of the State question is ever to be attained.[44]

Notes

Professor Murray N. Rothbard is the most prolific and eloquent representative of the Austrian school of economics actively working in his field as well as making numerous contributions to political theory and general social studies (history, political science, etc.). He teaches economics at the Polytechnic Institute of Brooklyn. His monumental *Man, Economy and State* is now a classic. His other books include

America's Great Depression, The Panic of 1819 and *Power and Market*. He is editor of *Libertarian Forum*.

"The Anatomy of the State" is reprinted with permission from *Rampart Journal*, vol. I, no. 2 (Summer 1965).

1. We cannot, in this paper, develop the many problems and fallacies of "democracy." Suffice it to say here that an individual's true agent or "representative" is always subject to that individual's orders, can be dismissed at any time, and cannot act contrary to the interests or wishes of his principal. Clearly, the "representative" in a democracy can never fulfill such agency functions, the only ones consonant with a libertarian society.

2. Social democrats often retort that democracy—majority choice of rulers—logically implies that the majority must leave certain freedoms to the minority, for the minority might one day become the majority. Apart from other flaws, this argument obviously does not hold where the minority *cannot* become the majority, e.g., when the minority is of a different racial or ethnic group from the majority.

3. "The friction or antagonism between the private and the public sphere was intensified from the first by the fact that . . . the State has been living on a revenue which was being produced in the private sphere for private purposes and had to be deflected from these purposes by political force. The theory which construes taxes on the analogy of club dues or of the purchase of the services of, say, a doctor only proves how far removed this part of the social sciences is from scientific habits of mind." Joseph A. Schumpeter, *Capitalism, Socialism, and Democracy* (New York: Harper and Bros., 1942), p. 198.

Also see Murray N. Rothbard, "The Fallacy of the 'Public Sector,'" *New Individualist Review* (Summer, 1961), pp. 3 ff.

4. "There are two fundamentally opposed means whereby man, requiring sustenance, is impelled to obtain the necessary means for satisfying his desires. These are work and robbery, one's own labor and the forcible appropriation of the labor of others. . . . I propose in the following discussion to call one's own labor and the equivalent exchange of one's own labor for the labor of others, the 'economic means' for the satisfaction of needs, while the unrequited appropriation of the labor of others will be called the 'political means'. . . . The State is an organization of the political means. No State, therefore, can come into being until the economic means has created a definite number of objects for the satisfaction of needs, which objects may be taken away or appropriated by warlike robbery." Franz Oppenheimer, *The State* (New York: Vanguard Press, 1926), pp. 24–27.

5. Albert Jay Nock wrote vividly that "the State claims and exercises the monopoly of crime. . . . It forbids private murder, but itself organizes murder on a colossal scale. It punishes private theft, but itself lays unscrupulous hands on anything it wants, whether the property of citizen or of alien." Nock, *On Doing the Right Thing, and Other Essays* (New York: Harper and Bros., 1928), p. 143; quoted in Jack Schwartzman, "Albert Jay Nock—A Superfluous Man," *Faith and Freedom* (December, 1953), p. 11.

6. "What, then, is the State as a sociological concept? The State, completely in its genesis . . . is a social institution, forced by a victorious group of men on a defeated group, with the sole purpose of regulating the dominion of the victorious group of men on a defeated group, and securing itself against revolt from within and attacks from abroad. Teleologically, this dominion had no other purpose than the economic exploitation of the vanquished by the victors." Oppenheimer, *op. cit.*, p. 15.

And De Jouvenel has written: "the State is in essence the result of the successes achieved by a band of brigands who superimpose themselves on small, distinct societies. . . ." Bertrand De Jouvenel, *On Power* (New York: Viking Press, 1949), pp. 100–101.

7. On the crucial distinction between "caste," a group with privileges or burdens coercively granted or imposed by the State, and the Marxian concept of "class" in society, see Ludwig von Mises, *Theory and History* (New Haven: Yale University Press, 1957), pp. 112 ff.

8. Such acceptance does not, of course, imply that the State rule has become "voluntary"; for even if the majority support be active and eager, this support is not unanimous by every individual.

9. That every government, no matter how "dictatorial" over individuals, must secure such support has been demonstrated by such acute political theorists as Étienne de la Boétie, David Hume, and Ludwig von Mises. Thus, cf. David Hume, "Of the First Principles of Government," in *Essays, Literary, Moral and Political* (London: Ward, Locke, and Taylor, n.d.), p. 23; Étienne de la Boétie, *Anti-Dictator* (New York: Columbia University Press, 1942), pp. 8–9; Ludwig von Mises, *Human Action* (New Haven: Yale University Press, 1949), pp. 188 ff. For more on the contribution to the analysis of the State by La Boétie, see Oscar Jaszi and John D. Lewis, *Against the Tyrant* (Glencoe, Ill.: The Free Press, 1957), pp. 55–57.

10. ". . . whenever a ruler makes himself dictator . . . all those who are corrupted by burning ambition or extraordinary avarice, these gather around him and support him in order to have a share in the

booty and to constitute themselves petty chiefs under the big tyrant." La Boétie, *op. cit.*, pp. 43–44.

11. This by no means implies that all intellectuals ally themselves with the State. On aspects of the alliance of intellectuals and the State, cf. Bertrand De Jouvenel, "The Attitude of the Intellectuals to the Market Society," *The Owl* (January, 1951), pp. 19–27; De Jouvenel, "The Treatment of Capitalism by Continental Intellectuals," in F.A. Hayek, ed., *Capitalism and the Historians* (Chicago: University of Chicago Press, 1954), pp. 93–123, reprinted in George B. De Huszar, *The Intellectuals* (Glencoe, Ill.: The Free Press, 1960), pp. 385–99; and Schumpeter, *op. cit.*, pp. 143–55.

12. Joseph Needham, "Review of Karl A. Wittfogel, *Oriental Despotism*," *Science and Society* (1958), p. 65. Needham also writes that "the successive [Chinese] emperors were served in all ages by a great company of profoundly humane and disinterested scholars." *Ibid.*, p. 61. Wittfogel notes the Confucian doctrine that the glory of the ruling class rested on its gentleman-scholar-bureaucrat officials, destined to be professional rulers dictating to the mass of the populace. Karl A. Wittfogel, *Oriental Despotism* (New Haven: Yale University Press, 1957), pp. 320–21 and *passim*. For an attitude contrasting to Needham's, cf. John Lukacs, "Intellectual Class or Intellectual Profession?" in de Huszar, *op. cit.*, pp. 521–22.

13. ". . . strategists insist that their occupation deserves the dignity of 'the academic counterpart of the military profession.'" Jeanne Riha, "The War Plotters," *Liberation* (August, 1961), p. 13. Also see Marcus Raskin, "The Megadeath Intellectuals," *New York Review of Books* (November 14, 1963), pp. 6–7.

14. Thus, the historian Conyers Read, in his presidential address, advocated the suppression of historical fact in the service of "democratic" and national values. Read proclaimed that "total war, whether it is hot or cold, enlists everyone and calls upon everyone to play his part. The historian is not freer from this obligation than the physicist. . . ." Read, "The Social Responsibilities of the Historian," *American Historical Review* (1951), pp. 283 ff. For a critique of Read and other aspects of court history, see Howard K. Beale, "The Professional Historian: His Theory and Practice," *The Pacific Historical Review* (August, 1953), pp. 227–55. Also cf. Herbert Butterfield, "Official History: Its Pitfalls and Criteria," in *History and Human Relations* (New York: Macmillan, 1952), pp. 182–224; and Harry Elmer Barnes, *The Court Historians Versus Revisionism* (n.d.), pp. 2 ff.

15. Cf. Wittfogel, *op cit.*, pp. 87–100. On the contrasting roles of

religion *vis a vis* the State in ancient China and Japan, see Norman Jacobs, *The Origin of Modern Capitalism and Eastern Asia* (Hong Kong: Hong Kong University Press, 1958), pp. 161–94.

16. "The essential reason for obedience is that it has become a habit of the species . . . Power is for us a fact of nature. From the earliest days of recorded history it has always presided over human destinies . . . the authorities which ruled [societies] in former times did not disappear without bequeathing to their successors their privilege nor without leaving in men's minds imprints which are cumulative in their effect. The succession of governments which, in the course of centuries, rule the same society may be looked on as one underlying government which takes on continuous accretions." De Jouvenel, *On Power, op. cit.*, p. 22.

17. On such uses of the religion of China, see Jacobs, *passim*.

18. "All [government] can see in an original idea is potential change, and hence an invasion of its prerogatives. The most dangerous man, to any government, is the man who is able to think things out for himself, without regard to the prevailing superstitions and taboos. Almost inevitably he comes to the conclusion that the government he lives under is dishonest, insane and intolerable, and so, if he is romantic, he tries to change it. And even if he is not romantic personally he is very apt to spread discontent among those who are." H. L. Mencken, *A Mencken Crestomathy* (New York: Knopf, 1949), p. 145.

19. *Ibid.*, pp. 146–47.

20. De Jouvenel, *On Power, op. cit.*, pp. 27 ff.

21. Charles L. Black, Jr., *The People and the Court* (New York: Macmillan, 1960), pp. 35 ff.

22. *Ibid.*, pp. 42–43.

23. ". . . the prime and most necessary function of the [Supreme] Court has been that of *validation*, not that of invalidation. What a government of limited powers needs, at the beginning and forever, is some means of satisfying the people that it has taken all steps humanly possible to stay within its powers. This is the condition of its legitimacy, and its legitimacy, in the long run, is the condition of its life. And the Court, through its history, has acted as the legitimation of the government." *Ibid.*, p. 52.

24. To Black, this "solution," while paradoxical, is blithely self-evident: ". . . the final power of the State . . . must stop where the law stops it. And who shall set the limit, and who shall enforce the stopping, against the mightiest power? Why, the State itself, of course, through its judges and its laws. Who controls the temperate? Who teaches the wise? . . ." *Ibid.*, pp. 32–33. And: "Where the questions concern governmental

power in a sovereign nation, it is not possible to select an umpire who is outside government. Every national government, so long as it is a government, must have the final say on its own power." *Ibid.,* pp. 48–49.

25. *Ibid.,* p. 49.

26. This ascription of the miraculous to government is reminiscent of James Burnham's justification of government by mysticism and irrationality:

"In ancient times, before the illusions of science had corrupted traditional wisdom, the founders of cities were known to be gods or demigods. . . . Neither the source nor the justification of government can be put in wholly rational terms . . . why should I accept the hereditary or democratic or any other principle of legitimacy? Why should a principle justify the rule of that man over me? . . . I accept the principle, well, . . . because I do, because that is the way it is and has been." James Burnham, *Congress and the American Tradition* (Chicago: Regnery, 1959), pp. 3–8. But what if one does *not* accept the principle? What will "the way" be then?

27. Black, *op. cit.,* p. 64.

28. *Ibid.,* p. 65.

29. John C. Calhoun, *A Disquisition on Government* (New York: Liberal Arts Press, 1953), pp. 25–27. Also cf. Rothbard, "Conservatism and Freedom: A Libertarian Comment," *Modern Age* (Spring, 1961), p. 219.

30. J. Allen Smith, *The Growth and Decadence of Constitutional Government* (New York: Henry Holt and Co., 1930), p. 88. Smith added: "It was obvious that where a provision of the Constitution was designed to limit the powers of a governmental organ, it could be effectively nullified if its interpretation and enforcement were left to the authorities it was designed to restrain. Clearly, common sense required that no organ of the government should be able to determine its own powers." *Ibid.,* p. 87. Clearly, common sense and "miracles" dictate very different views of government.

31. Calhoun, *op. cit.,* pp. 20–21.

32. In recent years, the unanimity principle has experienced a highly diluted revival, particularly in the writings of Professor James Buchanan. Injecting unanimity into the present situation, however, and applying it only to *changes* in the *status quo* and not to existing laws, can only result in another transformation of a limiting concept into a rubber stamp for the State. If the unanimity principle is to be applied only to *changes* in laws and edicts, the nature of the initial "point of origin" then makes all the difference. Cf. James Buchanan and Gordon Tullock, *The*

Calculus of Consent (Ann Arbor: University of Michigan Press, 1962), *passim*.

33. Cf. Herbert Spencer, "The Right to Ignore the State," in *Social Statics* (New York: D. Appleton and Co., 1890), pp. 229–39.

34. De Jouvenel, *On Power, op. cit.*, p. 171.

35. We have seen that essential to the State is support by the intellectuals, and this includes support against their two acute threats. Thus, on the role of American intellectuals in America's entry into World War I, see Randolph Bourne, "The War and the Intellectuals," in *The History of a Literary Radical and Other Papers* (New York: S. A. Russell, 1956), pp. 205–22. As Bourne states, a common device of intellectuals in winning support for State actions is to channel any discussion *within* the limits of basic State policy, and to discourage any fundamental or total critique of this basic framework.

36. As Mencken puts it in his inimitable fashion: "This gang ('the exploiters constituting the government') is well-nigh immune to punishment. Its worst extortions, even when they are baldly for private profit, carry no certain penalties under our laws. Since the first days of the Republic, less than a few dozen of its members have been impeached, and only a few obscure understrappers have ever been put into prison. The number of men sitting at Atlanta and Leavenworth for revolting against the extortions of the government is always ten times as great as the number of government officials condemned for oppressing the taxpayers to their own gain." Mencken, *op. cit.*, pp. 147–48. For a vivid and entertaining description of the lack of protection for the individual against incursion of his liberty by his "protectors," see H. L. Mencken, "The Nature of Liberty," in *Prejudices: A Selection* (New York: Vintage Books, 1958), pp. 138–43.

37. This is to be distinguished from modern international law, with its stress on maximizing the extent of war through such concepts as "collective security."

38. F.J.P. Veale, *Advance to Barbarism* (Appleton, Wisc.: C. C. Nelson Publ. Co., 1953), p. 63. Similarly, Professor Nef writes, of the War of Don Carlos, waged in Italy between France, Spain, and Sardinia against Austria, in the eighteenth century: "at the seige of Milan by the allies and several weeks later at Parma . . . the rival armies met in a fierce battle outside the town. In neither place were the sympathies of the inhabitants seriously moved by one side or the other. Their only fear was that the troops of either army should get within the gates and pillage. The fear proved groundless. At Parma the citizens ran to the town walls to watch the battle in the open country beyond . . ." John U. Nef, *War*

and Human Progress (Cambridge: Harvard University Press, 1950), p. 158. Also cf. Hoffman Nickerson, *Can We Limit War?* (New York: Frederick A. Stoke, Co., 1934).

39. Nef, *op. cit.*, p. 162.

40. *Ibid.*, p. 161. On advocacy of trading with the enemy by leaders of the American Revolution, see Joseph Dorfman, *The Economic Mind in American Civilization* (New York: Viking Press, 1946), I, 210–11.

41. On the concepts of State power and social power, see Nock, *Our Enemy the State* (Caldwell, Ida.: Caxton Printers, Ltd., 1946). Also see Nock, *Memoirs of a Superfluous Man* (New York: Harpers, 1943), and Frank Chodorov, *The Rise and Fall of Society* (New York: Devin-Adair, 1959).

42. Amidst the flux of expansion or contraction, the State always makes sure that it seizes and retains certain crucial "command posts" of the economy and society. Among these command posts are a monopoly of violence, monopoly of the ultimate judicial power, the channels of communication and transportation (post office, roads, rivers, air routes), irrigated water in Oriental despotisms, and education—to mould the opinions of its future citizens. In the modern economy, *money* is the critical command post.

43. This parasitic process of "catching up" has been almost openly proclaimed by Karl Marx, who conceded that socialism must be established through seizure of capital *previously accumulated* under capitalism.

44. Certainly, one indispensable ingredient of such a solution must be the sundering of the alliance of intellectual and State, through the creation of centers of intellectual inquiry and education, which will be independent of State power. Christopher Dawson notes that the great intellectual movements of the Renaissance and the Enlightenment were achieved by working outside of, and sometimes against, the entrenched universities. These academies of the new ideas were established by independent patrons. See Christopher Dawson, *The Crisis of Western Education* (New York: Sheed and Ward, 1961).

Bruce Goldberg

6

Skinner's Behaviorist Utopia

THAT A STATEMENT or a theory is true or false is a matter which is, presumably, to be decided by the employment of the various canons of scientific (in the widest sense of that term) observation and inference. A theory, for example, is tested by its ability to explain the facts on the basis of which it was introduced, and also by its ability to explain new facts which were not explicitly taken into account in its construction. And there are considerations irrelevant in determining the acceptability of putative truths. One obviously irrelevant factor is the aesthetic satisfaction anyone might get from contemplating a given theory. Whatever the poet may have thought, beauty is not the same as truth. Less obvious, and perhaps worth mentioning for that reason, is that the moral consequences of a statement are not relevant determinants of its truth or falsity. It may be that the general acceptance of some statement would lead to universal misery. Conceivably this could be a reason for keeping the statement secret. It could *not* be a reason for concluding that it was false. All men *are* mortal, whatever *Angst* might be occasioned by recognition of the fact.

That these considerations are not truth determinants would seem to be hardly susceptible of dispute. And yet, without explicit avowal, antagonists of scientific theories have all too often allowed aesthetic or moral upset to count against those theories. The Einsteinian conception of time as a relativistic magnitude did indeed shatter a well-established *Weltanschauung*. The relatively simple picture of Newtonian mechanistic interactions embedded in an absolute temporal framework died hard. That death, however, should have been an easy one. The major test of a scientific theory is its ability to explain the phenomena, and the new theory was better at this than the old. And for most (although not absolutely all) physicists, this was enough. But for others—theologians, philosophers, aestheticians, even laymen (though certainly not for all the members of any of these groups)—this was not enough. The aprioristic defenses of the old order began. "It's perfectly self-evident," ran one defense, "that time is absolute throughout the universe. One simply can't conceive of it being any other way." "It's in the nature of time," ran another, "to be the same everywhere." And in the background was the—unexpressed—objection that the adjustment was too difficult to make, that the new picture was not anything so much as repulsive.

Nowhere does this anti-scientific resistance to new theorizing assume more vigor than with respect to explanations in psychology. While physicists may displease, they are in possession of a mathematical apparatus which frightens. The critics, for all their resistance, remain more or less quiet and, at times, even a little ashamed. However, the language of, say, Freudian theory is ordinary English (or German). The technical terms are no more awe-inspiring than those of a competent aesthetician: "drive cathexis" is no more intimidating than "aesthetic distance." This releases inhibitions, and the defenders of received opinion feel that they have a free hand.

But there is a feature of psychological theory more important in this connection than that its propositions are unmathematized.[1] Psychological theory concerns people. It attempts, among other things, to explain why they act the way they do. And often the answers are such that the actor would not unreflectively acknowledge their correctness. Further, the critic may have a stake in the answers' being incorrect. How often has Freudian theory been attacked because of its "repulsive" doctrines of infantile sexuality? Or on the ground that our traditional views of human responsibility would have to be discarded? But such objections are absolutely worthless. The repulsiveness of Freudian theory is no more relevant to its truth or falsity than its country of origin. But it is one thing to point up the utter irrationality of an objection, and quite another to dispel the fears which prompt it.

As objectionable as Freudian theory was, however, it was sufficiently anthropomorphic to pose less of a threat to "man's dignity" than the mechanistic view associated with a certain other psychological theory. While Freud, the standard version goes, moved the springs of action from the conscious mind to the unconscious, later twentieth century psychology removed it from the psyche altogether. This new dehumanization of man is called behaviorism. Behaviorism not only eliminated the mental as a factor—it combined this with a thoroughgoing determinism which left no room for free action at all. The moral conscience revolted. Behaviorism was castigated as evil, and therefore, presumably, false. But the argument is no more legitimate here than it was in the preceding cases. Behaviorism simply cannot be shown to be incorrect by showing that its alleged consequences are undesirable, morally repugnant, or even evil. Those who adopt this approach deserve our ears no more than the critics of another theory, who insisted that man's dignity required that his planet be at the center of the universe.

These observations on what is relevant and what is irrelevant in the evaluation of a scientific theory such as behaviorism are necessary, for in this essay I shall be concerned with the behaviorist-based recommendations for social organizations of Professor B. F. Skinner, the eminent Harvard University psychologist, as set forth in his utopian novel, *Walden Two*.[2] If his proposal for a society rigidly controlled by behaviorist psychologists is to be rejected (as I think, in reason, it must be), it will have to be on the basis of logical analysis, and not of foolish sloganizing.

The blurb on the book informs us that *Walden Two* "provocatively pictures a society in which human problems are solved by a scientific technology of human conduct—and in which many of our contemporary values are obsolete." That anyone has presented us with a solution for human problems should make us listen, especially when the donor is a psychologist of unquestionable achievement. If in the end we will be skeptical, no part of the cause should be lack of gratitude for the attempt.

Walden Two is an attempt, in fictional form, to outline a system of social organization based on behaviorist psychological theory. "The methods of science have been enormously successful wherever they have been tried," Skinner says in another place;[3] "let us then apply them to human affairs." The scene of most of the book is a utopian community (Walden Two). Frazier, the creator of the experiment, defends his theories of social organization against Professor Burris, a slightly skeptical but generally sympathetic antagonist, and Professor Castle, a tender-minded philosopher and a bumptious, nasty, and unreasonable caviller, who interrupts the discussion from time to time with generally strawmannish objections.

A good deal is said in this novel, and I shall not try to examine every point that is made. What I shall do is consider certain of the central ideas of *Walden Two*, on the falsity of which the claims of the book would founder. Occasionally I shall bring to bear illustrative evidence from one of Skinner's nonfiction works, *Science and Human Behavior*.

The initial picture of the inhabitants of Walden Two with which we are presented is an attractive one. "These were delightful people," Professor Burris muses; "their conversation had a measure and a cadence more often found in well-wrought fiction than in fact. They were pleasant and well-mannered, yet perfectly candid; they were lively, but not boisterous; affectionate, but not effusive" (page 28). And in the course of the book, we come to learn that the inhabitants of Walden Two possess most of the desirable character traits one can think of and almost none of the bad ones. Indeed, with the exception of Frazier himself (who did not have the benefit of a Walden Two upbringing) everyone seems to be supremely happy and well-adjusted. This is not to be scoffed at. Only those with no social concern at all (and they don't count) could be indifferent to the possibility of establishing a form of social organization which has such results.

How does one go about producing such desirable characters? Well, babies at Walden Two are reared in community nurseries. At the age of one year, they graduate to community playgrounds, being subjected during these formative years to an intensive and highly scientific program of conditioning. All this provokes much resistance from the antagonistic Castle. But the questions of the techniques of Walden Two seem to me less interesting than the question of whether Skinner has even provided a coherent account of what can be accomplished by those techniques. If that account is itself internally inconsistent, the details are unimportant.

What I mean is this. Skinner's general program is the behavioral conditioning of certain kinds of emotions and behavioral responses. This conditioning is to have the result that only certain kinds of emotions appear in the members of Walden Two, while others, the undesirable ones, disappear through lack of positive reinforcement. The result is lots of people with good emotions, and very few or none with bad ones. It might immediately be objected that this could never come about, that human nature cannot be changed, or something of the sort. But this Castle-type move is a bad one. Talk about human nature is far too vague to permit a reasonable decision to be made as to whether or not it could be changed.

"As to emotions—we aren't free of them all, nor should we like to be. But the meaner and more annoying—the emotions which breed unhappiness—are almost unknown here, like unhappiness itself. We don't need them any longer in our struggle for existence, and it's easier

on our circulatory system, and certainly pleasanter, to dispense with
them" (page 101). To the objection that emotions are fun, Frazier
replies, "Some of them, yes. The productive and strengthening emotions
—joy and love. But sorrow and hate—and the high-voltage excitements
of anger, fear and rage—are out of proportion with the needs of
modern life, and they're wasteful and dangerous. Mr. Castle has
mentioned jealousy—a minor form of anger, I think we may call it.
Naturally we avoid it" (page 102). And so it is conditioned out, along
with the other unpleasant emotions, presumably simply by never receiving any positive reinforcement on any occasion of its occurrence.
This is the account one must examine, not, I should add, to determine
whether or not it would be *advisable* to condition out the emotions
referred to but to determine whether such a conditioning out would be
even a theoretical *possibility*.

The behaviorist picture (at least as Skinner presents it) is in some
ways an excessively simplistic one. There seems to be the idea that, with
respect to any given person and the various emotions he is capable of
experiencing, one could, given a proper technology, pluck out some
while leaving the others intact. Occurrences of emotions are, on this
account, something like pains. Just as one can eliminate a given pain (by
administering a drug, say), so one can eliminate a given emotion (by a
proper administration of behavioral engineering). In this sense, the
account of the emotions is an atomistic one. Each emotion can be
considered separately, and the relevant conditioning techniques can be
applied to it. The good ones stay and the bad ones go.

This picture is a radically misconceived one, and it requires no
experimentation at all to show this. Is it even possible to become clear
about what the picture suggests? Skinner wants to retain joy (because it is
productive) and eliminate sorrow (because it isn't). Under what circumstances might one experience joy? Well, suppose one has not seen one's
mother for twenty years. One goes to meet the plane on which she is
expected to arrive. The door opens, she descends the stairs and comes
running to meet one, arms outstretched, tears in her eyes. Presumably,
on this occasion one is happy, joyful, and the inspiration provided
enables one that very evening to make some important new contribution
to knowledge.[4] But suppose that just as one is about to embrace one's
mother, an unknown assailant shoots her in the back. Doesn't one then
feel at least sorrow, or even grief? Is one neutral? Indifferent? Isn't it
obvious that joy and sorrow are not atomistic states with no stronger
connection than that they are both emotions? If the death of one's

mother (in the situation described above) did leave one indifferent, how *could* the embrace produce joy? In order for one to experience joy in the situation described, it must (logically must) be true that whether or not one's mother lives or dies makes *some* difference to one. But if that's true, then one could not remain indifferent if she does die.

Perhaps another example will make the point clearer. Skinner is pro-happiness. The people in Walden Two are a happy group. They are often engaged in creative enterprises, and they are happy in their work. But unhappiness is unproductive. Presumably it's also to be conditioned out. Again, the question arises about the theoretical possibility of such a state of affairs, i.e., a state of affairs in which people are only happy. Suppose I have been working on a project for ten years, have constructed an elaborate theory which has only to receive its final experimental confirmation. The laboratory technicians bring in the results of a series of experiments which they have been running for the past two weeks. Now what is Skinner's claim? Am I indifferent to the results of my experiments? Suppose I am. In that case, it's odd to say that I'm very happy, even overjoyed, when I learn that my theory has been confirmed. Suppose that I'm not. Then it's equally odd to say that I'm not even a little bit unhappy when I learn that the experiments have falsified the theory. Given that people sometimes fail to achieve what they want very much (and not even *Walden Two* promises to fulfill all desires), it follows that they are sometimes unhappy. Isn't it patently obvious that happiness and unhappiness are not independent atomic states? But if that's true, then it doesn't even make sense to suppose that one could condition people never to experience the one and always (or almost always) to experience the other.

The principle illustrated by these examples is that many emotions have what might be called quasi-logical counter-parts. Pairs such as love-hate, joy-sorrow, happiness-unhappiness are familiar. To suppose that (whatever technique one might employ) one could condition out one member and leave the other intact is to believe a fiction. And this has nothing to do with the nature of man or the limitations of scientific technique. It is, rather, a matter of the logic of emotional predication. "Whenever a particular emotion is no longer a useful part of a behavioral repertoire, we proceed to eliminate it," Frazier tells us (page 103). Presumably, on this account we could, if we wanted, "engineer" a person to feel only grief or only love or only nostalgia. We decide which emotions we want, and then instill them. But this is something we shall never be able to do (at least not in the way implied in *Walden Two*). And the reason is that to say that we can do it doesn't even make sense.

The above is not mere philosophic pedantry. One of the attractions of *Walden Two* is that it seems to offer us an escape from the unpleasant, and this through the application of an allegedly scientific theory. But that theory, whatever its other merits, cannot at least succeed in this. If the inhabitants of Walden Two can experience joy, then they can experience sorrow. And it is a logical mistake to suppose that things could be otherwise.

We have, then, eliminated one major piece of the theoretical groundwork of *Walden Two*, at least as Skinner views his system. There is another view advanced by Skinner, of even greater importance than the view that one can selectively condition emotions. This is the idea that free will is an illusion. Skinner regards a behavioral technology as being incompatible with free will. Since he regards the former as possible, he denies the latter. Now, the problem of free will is an enormously complicated one. What I shall try to do here is merely to show that Skinner's view of what it would mean to have free will is a confused one, and that nothing he says even tends to show that free will is an illusion.

Skinner regards adherence to the idea that man has free will as essentially a relic of pre-scientific ways of thinking. And this is a fairly widespread notion. Without discussing the merits of this claim—my own opinion is that it is much too vague for argumentation on either side—it might be worthwhile to see just how Skinner proposes to demonstrate the falsity of the free will doctrine. In a way, this is a difficult thing to do, for Skinner seems not altogether clear about what view he is attacking. Sometimes it is the view that human actions are spontaneous, at other times it is that their actions are the actions of responsible agents, at still other times it is the view that human actions are uncaused. This last is probably the most substantial, so let us deal with that one. Skinner argues that it is a mistake to regard actions as uncaused. The most we are justified in saying is that for various actions we do not know what the causes are. However, the advancing march of science gives us every reason to believe that in time the causes of human behavior will present no greater problem than the causes of heat transfer in gases. The issue of free will is often discussed in these terms. That is, those who assert that we have free will generally regard this as committing them to the view that human action is uncaused. Those who opt for a general determinism regard this as implying that human action is unfree.[5] One of the unfortunate aspects of this controversy is that both sides seem to have thought that they had pretty clear ideas about the meaning of the key expression, i.e., determinism. The allegedly unproblematic explication of this notion has most often been: "the theory that every event has a cause." But a number of contemporary philosophers have seen that this explication is by no means as clear as has been thought. Some have gone so far as to assert that they do not know what the thesis of determinism is.[6] And there is good reason for this. For example, if one sees how Skinner fills out his account of what determinism with respect to behavior is, one cannot but find it surprising that he does regard the truth of determinism as incompatible with human freedom.

In Chapter Three, "Why Organisms Behave," of *Science and Human Behavior*, Skinner says that "we are concerned . . . with the causes of human behavior. We want to know why men behave as they do. Any condition or event which can be shown to have an effect upon behavior must be taken into account. By discovering and analyzing these causes we can predict behavior; to the extent that we can manipulate them, we can control behavior" (page 23).

Initially such a picture of a general determinism of behavior seems to many people to be a frightening one. The suggestion is that we are mere ciphers in a causal stream over which we have no control. And this is a picture to which Skinner frequently alludes in a favorable way in the course of his writings. We can manipulate causes and control people. A Brave New World (if one is frightened) or a Walden Two (if one is pleased) looms up before us.

But is there reason, given Skinner's view (which is a widely held one), for either fear or pleasure? Is there, indeed, anything excitingly new being said?

What are the causes of behavior on Skinner's showing? "Any condition or event which can be shown to have an effect upon behavior. . . ." Suppose I am a devotee of Shakespeare and a friend tells me that a new production of *King Lear* has just come to the Lido. Excited, I rush down to reserve tickets for the next performance. Now it is unquestionably true that my friend's informing me that the play was being performed is an event which had an effect on my behavior. If he hadn't told me I wouldn't have done what in fact I did do, *viz.*, go to the theater to reserve the tickets. Of course I might later have learned on my own that the play was being performed and would have then bought the tickets, but I wouldn't have done that when, as a matter of fact, I did. Suppose that I go to the play, and, after having thoroughly enjoyed it, applaud wildly when the performers take their curtain calls. Again, the appearance of the performers on the stage is an event which had an influence on my behavior. If they hadn't come out I would have returned home without applauding, wondering what went wrong, and perhaps feeling a bit sad because I didn't have the opportunity to show my appreciation. We have here, then, two examples of events which had an influence on my behavior. Were they causes of it?

It is not altogether easy to answer this question. For Skinner, of course, the answer is clear. They *are* causes. According to the quoted passage *any* condition or event which has an influence on behavior is a cause. But there are difficulties. Consider another kind of case. I tell someone, "I was just in the psychology laboratory with John and I caused his leg to rise." When asked how, I reply that I hit his knee in the familiar spot with a small hammer. But suppose that, when asked how I caused John's leg to rise I reply, not that I hit his knee with a small hammer, but that I asked him if he would raise his leg. Ordinarily, we would say that if *this* is how I got John's leg to rise (by asking him to raise his leg), then I didn't *cause* his leg to rise, although what I said was certainly relevant to bringing it about that John's leg did rise. It would at least be misleading, under these circumstances, to say that I did cause his leg to rise. In a context like this one, it would in general be assumed that if I *caused* John's leg to rise, I did something which in some way put it out of John's control that his leg did rise. When this assumption turns out to be wrong, i.e., when it turns out that I simply asked John to raise his leg and he did so, then it sounds very odd indeed to say that I caused his leg to rise. This is not always true. If John were hypnotized and raised his leg at my command, then it would be perfectly in order for me to say that I caused what occurred. One can easily think of other cases in which it wouldn't sound odd to say that I caused John's leg to rise. But in the case where I simply ask John to raise his leg (and he's fully conscious— not hypnotized, etc.), it does. But why should this be true if, as Skinner says, a cause is *any* condition or event which can be shown to have an effect upon behavior? Why does it sound at all odd to say that the performers' appearing on the stage *caused* me to applaud?

Above I hinted at what seems to me to be at least a partial explanation. It seems to be a legitimate inference that if someone is caused to do something, then that thing is in some way out of his control, that he is in some way not at liberty not to do it. And Skinner appears to be aware of the legitimacy of this inference. Notice that he says that to the extent to which we can manipulate behavior we can *control* it. If I am controlling someone's behavior, then he certainly isn't. This is surely the source of the doctrine that if someone's behavior is determined, then he isn't free. If the behavior is determined, then it's caused; if it's caused, then it is out of his control; and if it is out of his control, then he's not free. Assuming this argument to be legitimate, then one cannot at the same time grant that a bit of behavior was determined and that it was free. From the fact that the behavior was determined, it would follow that it was not free. But does it follow from the fact that there were events which *influenced* the behavior that the behavior was unfree? Put in another way, from the fact that the agent was influenced by certain circumstances to act in a certain way, does it follow that the action was out of his control? As we ordinarily speak about behavior, this certainly does not follow. Let us take still another example.

One of the factors influencing a general's decision to attack may be the intelligence information that the enemy is shortly going to concentrate its forces against his weak flank. Is his subsequent behavior (giving instructions to his subordinates to attack, preparing certain false reports which he is going to allow to fall into enemy hands, etc.) something which is out of his control? Surely not. Such a situation is just the sort of situation in which we say someone's behavior *is* under his control. Under what circumstances would we say that his behavior was out of his control? Well, suppose that he received the intelligence information and instead of calmly preparing plans for the coming attack, went berserk. Suppose he ran out of the Command Headquarters raving about the imminent destruction of his forces, and ordered each individual soldier (with or without a weapon) to attack the enemy at once. Suppose, too, that he himself starts running in the direction of the enemy camp, knife in hand, screaming that he is going to kill the mad beasts. Here, most probably, we would say that his behavior was not under his control. Surely our estimate of the situation must be different when he calmly sits down to prepare the attack, and gives his subordinates intelligent instructions, involving what, in the opinion of all, is a master military move. And yet there are events which influenced this behavior, just as there are events which influenced the berserk behavior. But if we allow that, in the case of the intelligent action, simply from the fact that there were indeed events which influenced his behavior it does not follow that the behavior was out of his control, then we must either reject the argument that causality implies non-freedom or reject Skinner's assumption that any event which influences behavior is a cause of that behavior.

And indeed how would one go about trying to show that any event which influences behavior *is* a cause of that behavior? Skinner, in the passage I quoted, seems to want to do this by definition. But this can show absolutely nothing. Presumably Skinner must regard the assertion that all behavior is, because determined, unfree, as an interesting assertion about behavior, i.e., about actions which people perform. That is, presumably he doesn't regard the contention that behavior is unfree as a simple definition. For if it were a mere definition, then while we might agree (accepting his definition for a moment) that "behavior" will imply unfreedom, we could not say about any of the events which we normally call cases of human action that they were in fact cases of "behavior."

Let us assume, then, that the statement at issue is not a simple definition. Now, to say that behavior is determined, is to say that it is caused. Therefore, by the original argument, caused behavior is unfree. And if any event or condition which influences behavior is a cause, then behavior which is to any extent influenced by events or conditions is unfree. What is it to say that a bit of behavior was influenced by an event or condition? Presumably, that the event or condition would be relevant in explaining why the behavior occurred, why the man acted as he did. From all of the above, it follows logically that the only behavior which *could* be free is that behavior for which there is no explanation at all. The only behavior which could be free is that behavior which is completely irrelevant to the circumstances in which it occurred, in the sense that nothing could be brought to bear to explain why the agent acted as he did. And from this it follows that every case of goal-directed behavior (that is, behavior in which the agent acts to achieve some end) is, to the extent to which the end was relevant to his behavior, *unfree*. And finally, it follows that all behavior, in so far as it is rational, is unfree. This, I submit, is absurd, for if behavior is unfree, then it is impossible that it be rational. Any argument which has as its conclusion the assertion that all rational behavior is unfree (in the last analysis, *because* it is rational) must be rejected. Skinner's argument about free will thus results in a palpable contradiction. His reasons for thinking that free will is an illusion are no reasons at all.

I have spent a good deal of time on what might be called the philosophical underpinning of *Walden Two*, the two theses, namely, that it is possible selectively to condition emotions and behavior, and that all behavior is unfree. If the truth of these theses were granted, much (though not all) of what Skinner recommends would be extremely difficult to deny. Mere charges that it is all diabolical would, in this case (and actually, in any case), be pointless. Now that we have seen that they are false, we can go on to see how they lead to the advocacy of Walden Two.

In Walden Two, things are controlled from the top. There are various managers (of play, of social activity, of work, etc.) who decide what sorts of enterprises are conducive to the psychological welfare of the members of the community, and are therefore to be permitted. The society is thus a rigidly controlled one, and the reason is that "when a science of behavior has once been achieved, there's no alternative to a planned society. We can't leave mankind to an accidental or biased control" (page 264). Why, one might ask, is the only alternative to planning (controlling) the lives of people by Skinnerian managers that of leaving them to the (accidental and/or biased) control of others? The historical tradition of liberalism would seem clearly to have shown us another alternative, that of letting people shape their own lives as they see fit. But, it should by now be clear, this is not an alternative which Skinner, in terms of the framework he has constructed, could even suggest. Since all behavior, whether we like it or not, is, in fact, controlled, we might as well let it be controlled by the good guys. Why is all behavior controlled? In the last analysis, because there are events and conditions which influence that behavior. Because of his mistaken idea that no behavior can be free, Skinner is rendered incapable of seeing the distinction between planning someone's life and letting him plan it himself.

This is a most important point. *Prima facie* there would seem to be two alternatives (with lots of gradations in between)—either people are controlled, or they are not. But for Skinner, this last is not even a possibility. The argument about free will makes it impossible that anyone is uncontrolled. The only real alternatives are good control and bad control (page 263). But this is simply the product of a bit of sham reasoning. What, one wants to ask, do you say about the possibility of establishing a society in which people are not subject to a rigid condi-tioning process in the hands of "behavioral engineers," but in which they are able to encounter many and diverse influences and make up their own minds about which they regard as the more important and which the less? Skinner's answer is clear. This, he would presumably say, is just the situation I am trying to avoid; it is the one I was talking about when I described a situation in which there was accidental and biased control.

It seems to me that therein lies, for the superficial reader, the main attraction of *Walden Two*. Only the unreasonable would prefer a system of biased and accidental control to one of intelligent control. Walden Two is, after all, better than Russia. It is to expose the view that these are our only choices that I spent as much time as I did examining Skinner's argument about free will.

In actuality, there are a number of alternatives open to us who would recommend a form of social order. There are at least the three just alluded to: a Russian system controlled from the top by foolish and arbitrary men, a Walden Two in which this control is exercised by intelligent men of good will, and an uncontrolled society.[7] These are, of course, not the only alternatives, but if we recognize the fallaciousness of Skinner's free will argument, we see that there are at least these three.

And, granting that Walden Two is preferable to Soviet society, we must raise the question concerning whether it is better than an uncontrolled one. Frazier, in effect, raises this very question, ". . . what do you say to the design of personalities? Would that interest you? The control of temperament? Give me the specifications, and I'll give you the man! . . . Let us control the lives of our children and see what we can make of them" (page 292). Notice that Skinner relies, in characterizing his own alternative, on the view which we discovered earlier was not even coherent. It is not true, irrespective of the techniques one employs, that one can generate people according to any arbitrary list of specifications: one could not (logically) make people who were only happy. But leaving this aside, the question is whether we should allow a central committee in control of society consciously to design personalities. *Prima facie* the answer to the question would seem to depend on which values the central committee is concerned to instill. It might seem that if these values are good ones, then we can accept Skinner's recommendation, and that if they are bad ones, we should reject it. What are the character traits and social values which Skinner accepts? In general, they are the very best. Happiness, productivity, lovingness, etc. This is another reason, I suspect, for the attraction which *Walden Two* exerts. If the answer to the question *did* depend on whether or not Skinner's choices were good ones, then there would be little more to say.[8] But it does not. What must be decided is the question of the desirability of a controlled society.

An initial question, preparatory to deciding the matter, might be the following: given that we can produce artists, scientists, musicians, at will, how could anybody reasonably decide about the desirable proportions? This seems to be the sort of value question which the behavioral scientist is in no better position to answer than any of the rest of us. Suppose that the behaviorist were to reply that this isn't a value question at all. It's purely an economic matter, i.e., the question is one of the allocation of resources: we want to provide the people in our behaviorist utopia with the maximum possible satisfaction of their various desires, and our decision about what sort of people to produce (artists, musicians, scientists, etc.) will depend not on our values, but on the values of the community.

Now there would be difficulties in proceeding in this way. I mean that the behaviorist in his controlled socialist society would have the same problems in the effective allocation of resources as any other socialist planner. But this sort of objection is, at this point, not the relevant one. Can we really allow that, as far as we have presented it, the behaviorist's problem is one of resource-allocation? I think not. Remember that the important idea about Walden Two is that we are conditioning values, i.e., likes and dislikes. We are not simply taking an arbitrary society and discussing the question about how best to satisfy the needs of that society given its (and not our) set of values. What this means in the present case is that the problem about how many musicians to produce is not an economic question. We are deciding not merely how to satisfy desires—we are deciding what those desires shall be, i.e., we must decide how many people are going to want to hear music, how many people enjoy art, etc.

Thus the behavioral scientist is faced with a question of value, a question of the order in which various goods are to be placed on a preference scale, and the behavioral scientist is in no better position to resolve this problem than we are. Indeed what criteria *could* be employed to decide such a question? This is surely not a scientific question, in the sense that there are generally accepted ways of finding out the answer, *finding out* the answer. The very best one could do is suggest an answer, and that answer will be an expression of the particular value scheme embraced by the suggester. There is no reason at all to suppose that the behaviorist is possessed of any expertise in this matter which is denied to the rest of us.[9]

It begins to look as though distinctly unscientific elements of arbitrariness (which arbitrariness, remember, Skinner was concerned to avoid) are being introduced into the design of the behaviorist utopia. But there are further difficulties. Skinner argues that a free society (in the ordinary sense) is an extremely undesirable thing. The reason is that all sorts of elements of arbitrariness and haphazardness are introduced by people pursuing incompatible (and often unpraiseworthy) goals. The various efforts which these people make in the attempt to persuade their fellows that the goals are desirable ones are causal factors which can change, in the last analysis, the value orientation of that society. This arbitrariness, the possibility of bad values being substituted for good ones as a result of the free (again in the ordinary sense) interplay of competing goals, is perhaps the chief evil against which *Walden Two* is directed. This is *the* reason Skinner advocates a controlled society.

We must then investigate whether or not it is *possible*, even on Skinner's terms, to eliminate arbitrariness in this sense. Let us suppose that we have a scientific procedure for determining not only how to condition various abilities, character traits, and values, but also for determining which ones we *should* condition. Now, it is not so easy to know what we are supposing here. With respect to musical ability, for example, are we supposing ourselves to be conditioning general ability in this area, ability at baroque music, ability at Bach, Vivaldi, or what? The same question arises for musical tastes. Do we condition people to like baroque music or do we condition a fondness for music in general? This is by no means an academic question for the behavioral engineer. We shall see that his failure to solve this problem will result in the emergence of new values in society, which the behaviorist psychologist cannot have taken into consideration in his scheme of conditioning, and for the control of which he will have to resort to methods which have nothing of the respectable air of science about them.

We can distinguish various levels of what we might call value generality, and the behavioral engineer must decide, assuming him to have the suitable techniques, on which level to operate. For purposes of the discussion, we might call music in general the first, or highest, level of generality; the various periods—baroque, classical, romantic, etc.— the second level of generality; particular composers, the third level; and so on. Let us call an ability or a liking on the first level an Ability$_1$ or a Value$_1$, and so on.

Now the question is: at what value or ability level are our conditioning procedures supposed to operate? Presumably the behaviorist is not going to condition each miniscule preference or ability in each member of society. I mean he is not going to decide that so and so many people should be devotees of the late Beethoven quartets, and that so and so many people are going to be admirers of Bach piano sonatas played without the pedal. Let us assume, then, that conditioning procedures are going to be applied at the first level: we are going to produce so and so many musicians, and so many artists, etc. We are not going to produce as a matter of deliberate policy a given number of baroque pianists, a given number of impressionists, and so on. Thus, Value$_2$ choices are not, as the Value$_1$ choices are, the direct result of policies and practices instituted by the planners.

This is the situation we are envisaging. What could we reasonably expect from such a situation; what would be the natural result of this absence of Value$_2$ conditioning? Well, one thing we could reasonably expect would be that, in an important sense, $Value_2$ would not be anything like as stable as $Value_1$. While the number of people who have musical interests and abilities is something that we can expect to be constant (because we are fixing it) the number of people who like any *kind* of music and the number who are skilled in the production of any *kind* of music is something that is likely to vary.

So, to restrict ourselves to this specific case, we can expect there to be periods in which one sort of music is in the ascendancy and periods when this sort of music is replaced by another in the favor of the inhabitants of the society. More interesting is the fact that we can expect *new* values to be created on this level. Since, to the extent to which values on this level are unconditioned there is an area for what we might call a free interplay of competing values, there is reason to expect that there will be some sort of building on what is already in existence. Gifted musicians will see the possibility of innovating, of building upon the stock of values and knowledge which they already possess, in the same way that this was done in the old society, in the way, for example, in which Mahler is said to have built on Wagner, and Schoenberg on Mahler. And we can also expect that some of these innovations will receive acceptance on the part of some of the music lovers of the society. Remember that we are supposing their $Values_2$ choices to be unconditioned.

Thus new and unplanned values have come into existence in the society. What interest, if any, should the planners take in this fact? Presumably they are going to be very interested indeed. After all, this new sort of music, when it is performed, is going to be one of the causal factors influencing the behavior of the inhabitants of the society. And there will be all sorts of factors, on this level, which will be determinants of the behavior of the inhabitants of the society—new art forms, new ways of painting, new ways of writing and performing plays; innovations in technology; new ways of building homes, new alloys for use in such building. The possibility of a literally endless number of changes in the established order opens up. These new elements are going to be competing with each other for the attention and approval of society at large. Were the planners to step back disinterestedly from this development the very element of arbitrariness and randomness which Skinner was concerned to eliminate would reappear.

So the planners must act. If it could be shown that some new $Value_2$ —some new style of painting, for instance—was likely to have what in the judgment of the planners would be an adverse influence on the populace, it must be stopped. The whole point of the society is that such adverse influences are to be eliminated. Thus, control is introduced at this lower level of value generality.

Or is it? When we speak of "control" at this level are we speaking about the same sort of thing with which we began? The answer is no. In our initial attempt at describing the behaviorist utopia, how did we suppose control to be introduced? What counted as control? Clearly, it was the conditioning of certain likes and dislikes, certain abilities and character traits. This is what Skinner seems to mean throughout *Walden Two*. This, for Skinner, is an innocuous sort of control. The planners of the society are not acting against the wishes of the members—they are shaping those wishes. People do what they want to do, although what they want to do is determined by what some others want them to want. It is in this sense, for Skinner, that Walden Two is a controlled society in which all the inhabitants are free. But the control of which we are now speaking is nothing like this at all. It consists simply in the proscription, by the authorities, of certain kinds of activities. If the planners decide that a certain type of music is likely to have an injurious effect, they will forbid it. This is political control pure and simple.

Interestingly enough, Skinner admits that control of the kind takes place in Walden Two (page 164). If someone in the society comes up with something new, he does *not* try to bring it about that the society at large accept his innovation. He goes to the relevant planning board. It is there that the decision about the acceptability of what he has done is made. If the planners decide against his idea they will prohibit its circulation. Thus is met the threat of "arbitrariness."

It is of absolute importance to recognize the difference between control in this latter sense and behavioral conditioning. *Walden Two* seems to present us with a picture of a society in which the ordinary, "nasty" elements of political control are absent. I suppose that many readers of the book have found this to be one of its most attractive features. But, as we have shown above, this is an illusion. As long as the planners of the behaviorist utopia do not condition values and abilities down to the last thinkable atom, it will be absolutely necessary to control the society (in the ordinary sense) in order to insure that the chosen values maintain their supremacy. Whatever merits Walden Two may have, the absence of rigid political control is not one of them.

This last point obviously raises the question of freedom, now in the political sense, and not in the sense of freedom of the will. Skinner argues that the former question is one that finds an easy solution in

Walden Two. If people do what they want to do (whether or not their wants have been selected by someone else) then they are free. Suppose we accepted this account. Would it then follow that the inhabitants of the behaviorist utopia are free? Surely not. Consider a citizen of the society going to the planning board convinced that his new idea will result in enormous progress in sundry fields. He wants (if the word is not too weak) to have the idea introduced. But after many hours of pleading with the planners (whom he comes to look on, at least in part, as thick-headed), he is turned down. He asks, as a last desperate move, to be permitted to give a public address on the merits of his new scheme. This too is turned down. The planners, we may suppose, feel that any propagation of the ideas they have just heard will have a markedly deleterious effect on the rest of society. This sort of situation is clearly possible in the behaviorist utopia. Skinner admits as much when he says that new ideas will have to be cleared through the relevant planning boards. But the situation we have described *is* a situation in which someone is not allowed to do what he wants to do. Thus we can grant Skinner all he asks for (in the way of a definition of freedom) and still the society he envisages is an unfree one. Not only are wants and desires (on some level) conditioned by the behavioral engineers, but any deviation from the established pattern is suppressed by those behavioral engineers when it does not accord with their own views. Walden Two may now begin to look, not like an excitingly new departure in the theory of social organization, but like an old-fashioned totalitarian society of a kind with which we are already familiar.

Thus we have seen that at every important stage in the argument for the behaviorist utopia, the position adopted by Skinner is one that cannot be maintained. But let us suppose now that none of this was shown. Let us suppose, that is, that Skinner's argument, up to this point, has been a good one. Would even that show that his recommendations are worthy of acceptance? Is a controlled society (assuming that it can do most of what Skinner says) a desirable thing? Again, I submit, the answer is no. But, given our assumption, it is not possible to show this by pointing up internal contradictions in the theory behind Walden Two. We are assuming, in some vague sense, that Walden Two can "work."

Is a working Walden Two a more desirable social organization than a free society? The answer to this question obviously depends, in part, on the sort of criteria one employs in assessing the merits of a particular form of social organization. Given certain ends, Walden Two *is* more desirable. Frazier indicates, in the course of his advocacy of Walden Two, that an important feature of the society is that it provides the opportunity to make controlled social experiments. Obviously, Walden Two would provide a more effective medium in which to conduct controlled social experiments (of a certain kind) than would a free society. But this is, after all, a rather restricted goal. And the fact that it is so restricted renders it untenable as a justifying goal for a form of social organization. One doesn't construct a society for the purpose of experimenting with its members. Skinner recognizes this, and what he regards as justifying the society is something else. Walden Two is supposed to represent an extremely progressive society, and one remarkably well adapted to achieve the goals set for it. It is in these terms that the issue between Walden Two and a free society must be discussed.[10]

One of the most important criteria by which we judge societies, of course, is a great degree of satisfaction of material wants—that is, the society must be an economically successful one. And the economic question is especially important in regard to Walden Two: much of the glamor of the life there proceeds from the fact that the inhabitants, having to work no more than four hours a day, have a great deal of leisure for the pursuit of culture and general self-improvement. Unfortunately, I am afraid that there is not much use in discussing this aspect of Skinner's ideas. He states, in his book, that the economics of a society are "child's play," and, indeed, he proceeds to deal with economic problems much as a child would. His ideas here are simply naive socialism, of the silliest sort. One example: once in a while, the children in Walden Two are sent out into the world and given a

sort of detective assignment. The game is to establish a connection in the shortest possible time between any given bit of luxury and some piece of poverty or depravity. The children may start with a fine residence, for example. By going in the service drive they may be able to speak to a colored laundress hanging out clothes. They induce her to let them drive her home. That's enough [page 206].

Enough for what? To prove that all wealth in a free enterprise system is gotten unfairly? To prove that wealth in a society is like a pie, and that if some have more others must necessarily have less? Does Skinner know what an economic cost is, and that there are fortunes to be made by entrepreneurs who can discover ways of cutting costs which their competitors have not yet realized? Does Skinner know that there exists a question of the practicability of rational allocation of resources in the absence of a market for capital goods—in such a situation as obtains in Walden Two, for instance? Offhand, one would have considered an economics primer required reading for a society-builder. But in any case, the economic problems of a utopian socialist community are much beyond the scope of our discussion here. Let us, therefore, pass on to the more general question of social control vs. the decentralization characteristic of a free society.

I have mentioned that Skinner admits the necessity for political control over new ideas. This concession occurs in his discussion of the "Walden Code," a system of maxims regulating the conduct of the members of the community in an incredibly detailed way: the Code even governs how introductions between people are to be made, establishes what is to count as rudeness in a conversation and prohibits (for the sake of psychological health) the deliberate expression of gratitude between members of the society. Now, in regard to this Code, Skinner states:

As to disagreement, anyone may examine the evidence upon which a rule was introduced into the Code. He may argue against its inclusion and may present his own evidence. If the Managers refuse to change the rule, he may appeal to the Planners. But in no case must he argue about the Code with the members at large. There's a rule against that.[11]

What this involves, then, is that every innovation in social life will have to gain the approval of the behavioral engineers. Thus, the distinction between Walden Two and the open society becomes as clear-cut as possible, and we are in a position to introduce what is probably the chief argument for freedom.

Let us attempt to state this argument in the form of an analogy—the analogy between society as a whole considered as an organization for the acquisition and communication of knowledge, and any given semi-organized field within society serving the same function. If advances in social knowledge (in the best ways of meeting the problems that arise in human life) are best promoted by a system of rigid controls such as Skinner's why not apply this system to science and the arts? If we established a commission of the best physicists, say, who would decide what lines of thought subordinate physicists would be allowed to follow up, is it likely that breakthroughs in this science would be as frequent as in these past centuries of "anarchy," when each physicist has done as he wished? In other fields, to cite illustrations is virtually to close the case as far as these disciplines are concerned: who would wish that Bradley and Bosanquet—the outstanding British philosophers of their day—had been commissars of philosophy, empowered to decide whether Russell and Moore would be allowed to present their ideas to the public? Who would wish to have set Haydn in a similar way as arbiter over the young Beethoven?

These examples illustrate the principle that the progress of ideas is not served by casting over any given field—and *a fortiori*, over society as a whole—the mental limitations of one mind or one group of minds, no matter how superior a position they occupy in regard to other individual minds.

Now, it may be objected that the analogy is a false one; that the behaviorist psychologists would occupy, in relation to their wards, an extremely superior position, not at all comparable to that of Haydn to Beethoven. That is, the behaviorist might argue: "Of course, we would not wish a young innovating genius to have his hands tied by the established and conservative leaders in his field. But this would not be the case with human behavior. It is not the ideas of a young Beethoven that will be 'suppressed' by our behavioral engineers; it is simply the 'ideas' of the masses of uninspired, generally mediocre men and women, and they will assuredly gain in our system."

But such a rebuttal fails to see the full implications of the problem of innovation. Very often, innovation depends not only on qualities internal to the innovator (which conceivably could be predicted by a system of testing), but on a unique combination of circumstances in which the innovator finds himself. As Hayek describes the situation:

. . . we have no way of predicting who will at each step first make the appropriate move or what particular combinations of knowledge and skills will suggest to some man the suitable answer, or by what channels his example will be transmitted to others who will follow the lead. It is difficult to conceive all the combinations of knowledge and skills which thus come into action and from which arises the discovery of appropriate practices or devices that, once found, can be accepted generally. But from the countless number of humble steps taken by anonymous persons in the course of doing familiar things in changed circumstances spring the examples that prevail. They are as important as the major intellectual innovations which are explicitly recognized and communicated as such.[12]

To put anyone in charge of a field of human activity—or of human activity in general—is necessarily to place him in a position of arbiter over every potential innovator. The original question remains: "Why doesn't Skinner propose establishing commissions in each science and art, to pass judgment on the efforts of all its practitioners?"

It seems clear, then, that innovation will not be promoted by a controlled society. But perhaps a controlled society is in the best position to make use of the knowledge already available (we are speaking now of "social knowledge"—the sort of thing with which the "Walden Code" deals). Actually, it is difficult to know what to say here, because Skinner appears to be maintaining a position little short of incredible. When he says, for instance, that the expression of gratitude is not to be allowed between members of society—does he mean this literally? Will it, under all possible circumstances, represent an infraction of the Code to express gratitude? What if a man saves my life at the risk of his own? Or, to put it more strongly, what if he submits to torture, in order to conceal my place of hiding from my would-be murderers? Does Skinner mean to say that I will have to clear it with a board of behavioral engineers before I express my gratitude? Perhaps the rule concerning gratitude, when it emerges from the laboratories, will contain a clause permitting its expression in certain cases. But then, how many clauses will it contain? In general, how will it be possible for a group of men—endowed, as we may assume them to be, with a great deal of scientific psychological knowledge—to foresee all the possible combinations of circumstances which occur in social life, circumstances which often include the pitting of one generally accepted rule against another?

Since it is clearly impossible, perhaps Skinner could allow a certain leeway in the interpretation of his gratitude rule. But it requires little insight to see that this would be a fatal breach in his system. Once people are permitted a degree of personal discretion in the application of a behaviorist "truth," it becomes possible for them to modify the rule itself, in the way that judges have made deadletters of various laws by their interpretations of them. Control over behavior would once more pass from the hands of the psychologist to those of society at large, the very situation Walden Two was created to eliminate. Thus, we must assume that no leeway will be allowed in the interpretation of the various behaviorist maxims. Now, what does this imply? It implies that the only place where society's accumulated knowledge can be refined and fitted for application to an infinitely great variety of circumstances is in the laboratories of the behavioral psychologists. If someone thinks that a received rule ought to be modified in its application to the particular situation in which he finds himself, he is not allowed to do so. He must obey the rule as it has been handed down to him, and await the judgment of the behavioral engineers as to the permissibility of his suggested modification. Isn't it obvious that this would bring about virtually the *least* flexible and *least* adaptable society imaginable? To arbitrarily exclude by far the larger segment of society from the work of adapting received rules and maxims to various situations is to eliminate all these minds as centers for acquiring, refining and passing on knowledge. Such a procedure would make sense if there were good reason to believe that the minds put in control were omniscient—but our previous discussion of free will and selective conditioning does not support that claim, at least as far as one important behaviorist is concerned, and it is unlikely that the case would be different with his fellows.

The argument for freedom is—quite unfortunately, from the viewpoint of the prospects for a free society—an enormously complicated and abstract one, and we have only touched the surface here.[13] But, I hope that enough has been said to suggest that Walden Two is hardly a rival to a free society with respect to its ability both to adapt to changing conditions and to promote progress.

A word is perhaps in order for those who have read *Walden Two* and are made enthusiastic by its promise of a better existence for all, with less frustration and fewer misdirected lives than we see around us today. The important thing to realize is that the choice before us is not between whatever improvements behavioral psychology offers us in the problems of arranging our lives, and the benefits a free society offers us in the way of innovation and progress. Skinner's utopia indeed precludes the advantages accruing from the free play of ideas and the clash of values of the open society, but the reverse is not the case. In an uncontrolled social setting, people are free to adapt their lives in the light of behavioral psychology, and, if a substantial part of what Skinner claims for his ideas is true, then the same society which gave birth to them will be free to apply them to advantage.

The real value of the book, I think, is that it performs one of the functions credited by John Stuart Mill to even the most erroneous doctrines: by energetically presenting the case for a centrally directed social order, it leads us to reconsider fundamentals, and forces us to re-examine and refine the arguments for the open society. Thus, while we may thank Skinner for promoting this end—which was indeed no part of his intention—those of us who are reasonable must decline the offering.

Notes

Professor Bruce Goldberg teaches philosophy at Cornell University and has written numerous articles for scholarly journals, including *Philosophical Review, Analysis, The American Philosophical Quarterly*.

"Skinner's Behaviorist Utopia" is reprinted with permission from the *New Individualist Review*, vol. 3, no. 2.

1. I am, of course, ignoring those areas of psychology where mathematics is becoming increasingly important, e.g., learning theory.

2. Originally published in 1948. I have used the paperback edition published by Macmillan in 1962.

3. *Science and Human Behavior* (New York: Macmillan, 1953), p. 5.

4. For joy, Skinner tells us, is a productive emotion (page 102). This seems hardly to be a "scientific" remark. What is it for an emotion to be "productive"? Is the view something like that joyful people do more productive work than sad ones? Is there any empirical evidence for this? Skinner provides no experimental evidence; and even if one were to make a historical survey which showed that joyful people are, in fact, more productive than sad people, that wouldn't establish the claim. Their greater productivity might be attributable to all sorts of other factors. But Skinner probably doesn't mean anything as precise as this. More likely, all he means by calling joy a productive emotion is that he has a favorable attitude towards joy and not towards sorrow. In any case, nowhere are any criteria presented for what is to count as a productive emotion.

5. There have been exceptions in the history of philosophy. Hume and John Stuart Mill accepted both determinism and free will. But this is no place for a historical account of the question.

6. Cf. P. F. Strawson, *Freedom and Resentment* (London: Oxford University Press, 1962), p. 187.

7. It should be clear that by uncontrolled society I don't mean one in which there is no control over behavior. Obviously, a society which prohibits certain acts (e.g., murder) is to that extent controlling behavior. By an uncontrolled society, I don't mean an anarchic one. This is not the place to enter upon an extended discussion of the semantics of "control." For my purposes it is enough to say that by an uncontrolled society I mean one in which the sorts of control that are characteristic of both Walden Two and Soviet society are absent—thought control, thoroughly propagandized education, etc.

8. Of course, in this discussion I am accepting something which I spent much time earlier in denying, *viz.*, the possibility of creating people to order.

9. While Skinner seems to be vague enough on how questions of value are decided in Walden Two, he is at least candid in admitting that science plays no part in the decisions. "The philosopher in search of a rational basis for deciding what is good has always reminded me of the centipede trying to decide how to walk. Simply go ahead and walk! We all know what's good, until we stop to think about it" (page 159). If

Skinner means by this that universal agreement can be obtained on what is and what is not good, his statement is obviously false—suffering, promiscuous sexual behavior, etc., are things concerning the goodness of which a Christian and a hedonist might well disagree. But even assuming that we could cleanly separate good from bad things, this would in no way solve the problem of the behavioral engineer. Since he is charged with arranging the value systems of the members of society, and since very often a choice must be made among good things (at the very least because they can't all be realized at the same time), he must have a good idea of the order in which goods are to be ranked among themselves—which are the more important ones, and which the less. This problem scarcely permits of a ready answer.

10. Of course, a free society does not have goals set for it in the same sense that Skinner's controlled society would, for there is no one in a position to set goals for everyone else. All we mean here by the goals of a free society are the ends which, in considering it, we would like it to achieve.

11. It ought to be pointed out, incidentally, that the "scientific" nature of Walden Two is always stated rather than shown. That is, Frazier's defense of a particular practice in his community takes the form not of the presentation of any pointer readings, but simply of suggestive inferences about human beings, much as might occur in a conversation between two educated persons with an interest in "what makes people tick." (Sometimes, indeed, it descends somewhat beneath this level—see for instance his argumentation concerning the irrelevancy of history, with his vague but impassioned championship of "the *Now*" [page 239].) But, presumably, Skinner is not calling for the acceptance of any of the particular practices he describes (for which he gives no "laboratory evidence" at all); it is rather the method which he wants us to accept.

12. F. A. Hayek, *The Constitution of Liberty* (Chicago: University of Chicago Press, 1960), p. 28.

13. Much the most profound discussion of these problems which I have come across is contained in Hayek's *Constitution of Liberty*. An interesting discussion of Skinner's social ideas from a psychological point of view is provided by Carl R. Rogers, "The Place of the Individual in the New World of the Behavioral Sciences," in *On Becoming a Person* (Boston: Houghton Mifflin, 1961), pp. 384-402.

James Sadowsky, S.J.

7

Private Property and Collective Ownership

PHILOSOPHY HAS FATHERED a number of other sciences. It is, as we all know, the father of physics which used to be known as *natural philosophy*. And no one is ignorant of the fact that economics was launched by a moralist whose name was Adam Smith. Nor should this be really surprising when we reflect on the fact that the most general notions in all these sciences are basically philosophical and that the methods of unfolding their implications are basically philosophical. There is, of course, the problem of determining whether there is anything in reality which corresponds to the notions whose depths we attempt to plumb. In general the answer to this problem is not given to us by philosophical methods; it is given to us by observation.

How then does philosophy differ from the other sciences? No hard and fast line can be drawn between them. Both the scientist and the philosopher analyze concepts. Both of them engage in observations. But the people called philosophers have usually begun the analysis of the concepts and have made the most general observations. Others continue where they leave off. These we may call the scientists. They prolong the work which was begun by the philosopher, leaving him to open up new areas which are in their turn to be handed over to future scientists for further refinement.

Consider the idea of free exchange. We can analyze this notion and work out all of its logical implications. We can also concern ourselves with finding out whether there is such a thing as free exchange in reality and to what extent. Now let us ask ourselves whether this notion is proper to philosophy or to economics. *In vacuo* there really is no way of answering the question. In the abstract it is no more the one than the other. We may note, however, that the full working out of the idea and its application has been achieved by a group of people known as *economists*. And we could therefore define an economist as one who has developed this and other more or less closely related ideas.

There is an enormous quantity of metaphysics in Newton's *Principia* just as there is an enormous quantity of science in Aristotle's *Physics*. It is, therefore, simplistic to speak of the one as being a philosopher and the other as being a scientist. It is rather a question of more or less. We can say that Newton belonged to the class of those who pushed a certain line of inquiry to an extraordinary degree and that there are enough of such people to enable us to speak of a class of physicists.

So, perhaps, we should not ask whether so and so is talking philosophy or economics. About all we can say is that he has gone further into a certain type of question than most people called philosophers care to go. If he does a bad job we tend to say he is out of his field; it would probably be better simply to say that he is out of his depth. But we should not say: "He is out of his depth. Therefore, he did a bad job." Rather we should say: "He did a bad job; therefore, he is out of his depth."

If all this begins to look like an apology for what I am going to discuss this will be because it is. Had I not written this preface the reader would be tempted to wonder whether I, a philosopher, was doing philosophy or economics. I trust that this question will now seem a less interesting one. I propose to attempt a justification of private ownership and then to analyze the term "collective ownership." I hope to show that this latter term is without any meaning. Unfortunately, it is often assumed to have meaning and the existence of such a thing in reality is frequently taken for granted even by would-be defenders of individual ownership. I shall conclude by pointing up a number of cases where this occurs—to the great detriment of economic debate.

Self-Ownership and Property Right

We shall begin by stating our fundamental thesis concerning private property. *Any man has the right to acquire previously unowned goods, keep or give them away at his pleasure, use or not use them at his pleasure.* We shall now attempt to justify this proposition.

Lest there be any confusion, it would be well to define exactly the manner in which we are employing the term "right." When we say that one has the right to do certain things we mean this and only this, that it would be immoral for another, alone or in combination, to stop him from doing this by the use of physical force or the threat thereof. We do *not* mean that any use a man makes of his property within the limits set forth is necessarily a *moral* use. We do not deny, therefore, that one may in many instances have an obligation to share his property with various of his fellows. It does not follow that one may with propriety produce and sell addictive drugs to whomsoever desires them. What is wrong, however, is the use of physical force to stop these things from happening.

We mention this to point up the fact that we do not give automatic approval to whatever occurs on the free market. Not only this, but the market itself provides suitable punishments to what we may regard as undesirable forms of conduct. As an example, let us mention the "Legion of Decency." In the early thirties there was widespread disapproval of many of the films being turned out in Hollywood. The Legion was extremely active in organizing a boycott of such films. Now whether we approve of the particular effort or not, we should note that it did not rely on physical force and that it was effective to a considerable degree. It relied on voluntary activity and relied entirely on the right of free speech. There is also the old remedy of the raised eyebrow. Most of us do not like to be known as skinflints; on the contrary, we like to be known as great benefactors of mankind and some of us even want to *be* that way. Doubtless factors such as these had considerable influence on much of the philanthropy during this and the last century. We may say that a man's right to property tells us not so much what *he* may properly do but rather what *others* may not properly do to him. It is fundamentally a right not to be interfered with.

We may now ask ourselves on what this right rests. It derives, we would say, from the prior right of self-ownership. Each of us owns himself and his activities. This means that we may not *initiate* violence against others. We say "initiate" because we may certainly employ violence against those who have initiated it against us. In other words, we may repel violence. Now let us suppose that in various manners I deploy my activity upon material non-human goods that are previously unowned. By what right does anyone stop me? There are but two possible justifications: either he has the right to direct my activities by using violence (in other words he owns me) or else he owns the material goods in question. But this contradicts the assumptions we have already made: that each human being is self-owned and that the material goods in question are not *previously* owned. This man is claiming either to own me or the property I think I have acquired. The only factor open to question is whether the other man had peacefully acquired the land before me. But to raise this question is to concede the right of private property which is the thing we are trying to establish. Now, if no one man has the right to do this, it follows that no greater number may do so, for the same question that was asked of A may be asked concerning C, and so of all the others. Surely, if this is true of any of them taken singly, there is no reason to suppose that they could properly do this if they banded together.

There is, then, an unlimited right of acquisition. This applies, however only to what others have not already acquired. This sounds obvious, but apparently it is not for many. One frequently hears the claim that there should be a redistribution of property on the grounds that its present division does not enable everyone to be a landowner and each one has the right to be a property owner. The equivocation should be clear: each one has the right to appropriate what no one else has appropriated. The right to appropriate is without content unless he who does so may keep what he has taken. And if one may keep what has been taken, it follows that nobody has the authority to wrest it from him.

The right of self-ownership implies the right to give away property either *gratis* or in exchange for something else. By what right could one force an individual to retain ownership of his property? Likewise, if an individual may give away his property then by the same token a person may receive it. One is the corollary of the other. All the objection to inherited wealth is an attack on the right of a man to give away his property. Where do we derive the authority to force a man to give his property to the individuals whom *we* designate? Surely *their* income is just as much unearned as the one to whom the original owner desires to bequeath his goods.

There appears to be an extremely powerful prejudice against unearned wealth. But it is as selective as it is powerful. The "liberals" object to it when the recipients are wealthy and favor it when they are poor. Some "conservatives" select in the opposite direction. These latter will object to the guaranteed annual income on the grounds that it is unearned by the recipient and it removes from him the stimulus to produce. Neither of these reasons is valid. The mere fact that an income is unearned is totally irrelevant and although the fact that a person is not productive is bad for the rest of us, we do not have the authority to force him to be productive. The true answer to the advocates of such subsidies is that they involve stealing from legitimate owners. This has nothing to do with whether we favor the "Protestant Ethic." By using this type of argument "conservatives" fall into the hands of their opponents, who have a field day in raising all manner of difficulties against that ethic. The unearned income of the rich is justified because it belongs to them; whereas that of the man on government relief is not because it is stolen from its rightful owner. It is certainly proper to point out to those who favor such measures that most of the people whom this kind of income would motivate not to produce would eventually become poorer than they already are—this because they are unaware of long-range economic efforts. But the primary issue still remains ethical. Suppose that even without welfare payments the leisure preferences of most people increased enormously. All of us would then be poorer because of their failure to produce. But this fact would not justify our forcing them to produce. The only legitimate alternative would be for us to move elsewhere.

Man also has the right to use or not to use his property as he sees fit. By use we mean any alteration in the physical constitution of the thing owned. Once the property has been appropriated the owner may either leave it alone or alter it in any manner whatsoever. Many object to the continued ownership of "unimproved" land on the grounds that the owner has done nothing to increase its value. Were he later to sell it he would be obtaining something without any effort on his part. Here again is implicit the fallacy that gain is justified only to the extent that it is the result of previous misery—a doctrine that Marx and others inherited from the Schoolmen. But more basically, it relies on a totally false supposition: that by transforming an object we can increase its value. There is no such thing as value *in* the object. Objects are valued by people: what is valued by people is the physical reality. People do not value values! The only way to increase another's valuation of what I have is by hypnotism.

True, we may so change the physical constitution of objects that they correspond to the future values of people. But note that there is no absolute certainty as to what their values will be. It may very well be the case that what people will value will be the object in its *original* form. If this happens then all my efforts will have been in vain. I then would have benefitted him and myself far more by doing nothing. In other words, the owner of property performs an entrepreneurial function. He must predict the future valuations that he and others will make and act or not act accordingly. He is "rewarded" primarily, not for his work, but for his good judgment.

This is a simple lesson the learning of which would have spared the world a tremendous amount of misery. Unfortunately the world seems as far from accepting it as always. The view that one should be rewarded for one's efforts is part of the Conventional Wisdom and one finds it on the tongue of both the liberal and the conservative. One of the reasons why Marxism always finds such a ready ear is the fact that before hearing about it people already hold its basic theory of value. And it is an easy matter for the Marxist to show such a person that the way in which wages are paid accords very poorly with commonly accepted ideas of justice. Far from retarding the acceptance of Socialistic ideas his religious convictions will tend to accelerate the process. Witness the numbers of clergymen who have been caught in this trap.

Justice and Property in Land

So much, then, for the basic principles connected with the notion of private property. The sad reality of England at the end of the eighteenth and the beginning of the nineteenth century was rather different from the ideal situation. Undoubtedly the extent of the misery that prevailed after the introduction of more or less free economies has been grossly exaggerated. Indeed there would have been even greater misery had this system not been introduced. This leads us to believe that there was something radically wrong before the change that has never been given the proper attention. While most of the frightful restrictions on economic action were removed, the enormous feudal land-holdings were left untouched in the name of respect for private property.

As we know these holdings were mostly the result either of conquest or state land-grants. It is highly dubious that these holdings could ever have attained their size on the free market. Justice would have dictated the division of these lands among the agricultural workers. Unfortunately this was not done. The result was that a few individuals had votes in the market far beyond their due and were thereby enabled to determine the course of events. These were responsible for the spectacular amount of investment and consequent economic growth of the area. There is no doubt that we have more goods at our disposal now because of what happened then.

Suppose the land had been divided up. Probably agriculture would have been a much more important industry in England. It is also likely that the rate of consumption would have been higher. This would have meant less investment, less "growth." We would not be where we are today. Supposing all this to be true, what of it? The primary question is the one of justice. Where does a man get the authority to require that someone else use his property in the manner that the outsider judges to be the most economic? It is his property and he has the right to use it in the way which satisfies him. If he does not want to "grow" that is his business.

The fact that a future generation may be better off because of a forced rate of growth during the previous generations excuses nothing. This would be tantamount to allowing future generations to impose taxes on their ancestors. The forced abstinence from consumption is constantly being justified on the grounds that "we will be better off in a hundred years." Just who is "we?" In a hundred years we will all be dead. Even if we were not, suppose we want to be better off *now*. Should not individuals be allowed to function in accordance with their own time-preferences?

The unwillingness of some to remedy an unjust distribution of holdings on the ground that to do so would be uneconomic is positively scandalous. After all, if not to remedy such an iniquitous distribution is justifiable in the name of economics, then would it not also be legitimate to *create* an unjust system for the same reason? Why not seize small holdings and give them to those men who would choose to save rather than to consume? But this would be unjust. True, but so it is if people are allowed to retain holdings that really do not belong to them.

We can go further, however, and challenge the thesis that the system of holdings that obtained at the time the free market was instituted was the most economic one. How can anyone tell? On the supposition that a free market had obtained from the beginning we can say that the distribution of wealth is the most economic one. The size of anyone's holdings will tend to reflect the extent to which he satisfied the desires of those with whom he engaged in business. Since, *ex hypothesi*, there never was coercion everybody benefitted by the exchanges. Certainly no such claims can be made in behalf of a system that preexisted the unhampered market. All we can say is that if the holdings are left untouched and if free exchange is introduced, then *eventually* a satisfactory system will develop. Here, however, the long run may be long indeed, and what about the *rights* of the people in the meanwhile? They will prefer to consume the smaller pie that is theirs by rights. That people who possess what is rightfully yours are busy making a larger pie which can be consumed only by your descendants is cold comfort indeed.

These considerations surely raise numerous questions about the situations in the undeveloped areas of the world. Obviously one of the big problems is what to do with the vast holdings of land. There is little doubt that these were not acquired by legitimate means. Because these exist large numbers of individuals are doomed to a life of misery even by their own standards. One can sympathize with the misguided concern of the Marxist reformer. On the other hand, we must deplore his forked-tongued approach to the propaganda problem. Interestingly he will appeal to the peasant by his proposals to divide the land—an effective appeal because by instinct the peasant firmly believes in private property and feels he has been defrauded of it. To the factory workers, however, he has an entirely different story to tell. He gives them to understand that the capitalistic mentality of the peasant is his real enemy and promises that the land will be taken over by the state, so that the *kulaks* will not be able to charge the workers in the city exorbitant prices.

Anybody who understands the workings of the free market can see that the policies advocated by collectivists are doomed to failure. For the most part, however, those who pay lip-service to the market show little desire to question the property arrangements in these areas. This is why they have little to say that would interest the poor and downtrodden in these countries. These people have therefore come to associate the free market system with approval of the *status quo*. They would not be greatly helped by the fact that from now on their oppressors would be able to exchange with each other on an unhampered basis. All this means is that for the foreseeable future a few more crumbs might fall from the tables of those who profit by facilitated exchange.

Here again the spirit of growthmanship is operative. "These countries will never become industrialized unless the vast holdings are allowed to continue and the land will not be well used if divided up." Could a Marxist be more critical of the free market than these people? Is it not the right of the real owners to decide to what extent their area shall be industrialized?

Also operative are certain special interests who want justice here but not abroad. Some of them have bought land from people who had no right to it in the first place; others have been given land by governments who had previously expropriated it. This makes them a party to the injustice. Obviously much of the justifiable complaining in these areas is misdirected. Just as these foreign companies will object to any expropriation by appealing to the sanctity of property, so the natives will blame their troubles on the system of private property itself, or they will attack foreign investment as something which is evil in itself. As in so many instances people are unable to locate their real enemy. Surely if these people do blame their troubles on free enterprise, the defenders of this system are partly responsible for their error.

We have given a general analysis of what is involved in the notion of private, individual property. We have attempted to show that this system is justified by the more basic right of self-ownership. We then pointed out that the only ground on which others could prevent a person from acquiring ownership is an implicit claim to previous ownership by somebody else. But to concede that somebody else owned the property is to admit that there is such a thing as the right to property. Then we established that no one has the authority to interfere with the non-aggressive use of that property. It is finally important to realize that goods that have been illegitimately acquired do not become lawful property by virtue of the mere passing of time.

"Society" and Collective Ownership

We have put off until now reckoning with one final notion: that the goods of the earth belong to no individuals, but rather are vested in an entity called "society." Somehow this entity is a whole of which each one is a part. It is conceived as having rights and also duties. The actions of the parts may be permitted only to the extent to which they aid the whole. The organ through which society expresses itself can be either a king, a parliament, or simply the majority of its members. Supposedly, whatever these organs want "we" want. Pervasive as it is, this theory is quite difficult to formulate, and for good reason. It is often enough used as the ultimate justification of government.

The question we should ask is not so much whether society has the rights attributed to it as whether such an entity can be meaningfully said to exist at all. When, however, you ask what kind of entity this could possibly be you are referred to various analogies. Just as we are made up of cells so society is made up of individuals. "If you claim that the notion of 'society' is unintelligible, you must also claim that the notion of a whole is meaningless." It is, indeed, difficult to admit that the one could exist and not the other. If, therefore, the notion of "society" derives its plausibility from these analogies it might pay us to inquire a bit into them. Are there really, anywhere, entities that are made up of entities, or are we the victims of a linguistic trick? If nowhere are such entities to be found, then automatically this notion of "society" will fall to the ground.

Perhaps the best approach to the matter would be through an examination of what is meant by a collective noun. As an example, let us take "baseball team." We use this term to designate many things that are united in some particular respect. In the case at hand each man acts in conjunction with others in order to bring about a certain pattern of activities. Do we literally have a new being which did not exist before these people joined forces? Certainly not. We do as a matter of fact speak *as if* there were now a single entity, we use the word "team" as the subject of a sentence, we replace the word "team" by "it." But we are conscious that in so doing we are simply using a convenient manner of speaking which is designed to save time. The proof of this is that we could simply eliminate the word "team" from our language and substitute a more prolix language that referred to "those men who are united for the purpose of playing baseball." This is quite a complicated formula and it is well we have discovered more convenient fashions of expressing ourselves. Nor does this cause any problem as long as we realize exactly what we are doing.

Note that in the example given there is no "Ego" over and above that of the individuals who have pooled their activities. Nor, strictly speaking, is there a collective activity; there are only individual activities directed by individual persons towards a mutually agreed upon end. The "whole" is nothing but the individual players insofar as they cooperate. The only real entities are the individuals or the "parts." This suggests that we could in principle eliminate "whole" sentences from our language and replace them by more complicated sentences whose subject is "parts" or "individuals."

In what sense can we speak of these organizations or societies as owning property? These groups vary considerably from one another but there are a few general remarks that should apply to all. The first thing to realize is that no matter what else may be true of the arrangements, these groups own what they do because of the free choice of the individuals who have entered into this type of cooperation. Indeed, the very existence of the organization presupposes the willingness of individuals to join together and its continuance requires new decisions on the part of those willing to collaborate with the already existing members. It is certain that the organization cannot have preceded its first members. The financial arrangements will be those decided upon by the original members, for even if changes are later to be made, the procedure for introducing them will have been set up by the founders. So, from first to last the societal ownership is ultimately that of its individual members.

Let us now return to the contention that the original owner of the property is not the individual but "Society." We have seen that the only real entities are individuals, so that nothing can be true of a society which is not true of the individuals that make it up. Consider first the ownership of the individuals. In so doing we shall suppose a society made up of two individuals, A and B. There are but two possibilities: A owns A, B owns B; or A owns B or B owns A. There is no third entity that can own them both. But there must be a third if both of them are to be owned; that is, for them to belong in the literal sense to Society. If we suppose that A owns B or the opposite, we still do not have societal ownership but individual ownership. Now since the appropriation of non-human goods can only take place via the activities of people, it follows that what is appropriated by the individuals will belong to the owners of the individuals. Since it is impossible that Society own the individuals, it cannot own what they appropriate.

It is true that the two members of our little society can agree jointly to appropriate land of which they will be co-owners. But in this case the initial decision is entirely voluntary, and each one is an individual part-owner of that property and may abandon his share of ownership at his own pleasure.

Thus we see that the thesis that Society is the original owner of land cannot stand up under analysis. This is not simply a question of historical fact. In the very nature of the case, the individual precedes society and this includes the ownership of the individual. All the rest must be the result of contractual relationships, itself dependent on the free decisions of individuals.

Though the concept that there are goods that belong to Society is unacceptable, there are many occasions where it is taken for granted that Society is an entity in its own right and that it automatically does own things. This constitutes the unspoken major premise of many political proposals. We would like briefly to examine a number of cases where this assumption is made.

"It is necessary to conserve Society's valuable resources." This is the famous problem of waste. As we have already seen, these resources are either unowned or else their ownership is distributed among various individuals. There is no third possibility. The first alternative presents little difficulty. How come nobody owns these resources? Surely if it were in the interest of the economy various individuals would be appropriating such resources. Why do they fail to do so? Why is it not to their interest to acquire them? The fundamental reason appears to be the fact that such goods are not sufficiently scarce to justify the cost (and there is such) of appropriating them. In other words the very fact that there are goods which no one sees fit to acquire for his exclusive use is of itself a sign that no problem exists concerning their conservation. Surely, if there were, some entrepreneurs would notice the fact and do something about it. It is surely suspicious when the only one who can see that it is worthwhile to acquire resources is the government.

The other possibility is that the resources are already distributed among individual owners. In which case the only ones who have the right to speak about wasting "our" resources are the owners themselves. Each owner will make use of his resources in the way he sees fit. He can be said to have wasted his resources only when he makes mistaken predictions, and the more resources he has the ability to acquire the less likely he is to be the kind of person who makes the wrong predictions. The same may be said concerning those who make eccentric use of their resources, e.g., setting their oil fields afire in order to produce spectacles. Here we cannot say that the man is wasting something. He may be so constituted that he gets more satisfaction out of doing this than from other uses to which he might put his property. All we can say is that in a free society people of this type are unable to acquire any considerable amount of property unless someone makes a gift of it to them. In an unhampered market the entire tendency is that one may grow wealthy only by serving in large measure the interest of his fellows. If the wealth were given to someone of this nature, again, he would not be able for any length of time to preserve his position. So we can say that full freedom to perform non-aggressive actions tends to prevent any large scale use of resources that is not *mutually* beneficial. Not only is it meaningless to speak of Society's resources; it is not even helpful.

"Our country is importing too much." Here is another statement which, given a free society, is without content. Countries do not import. Only people do. How can an individual import too much except by failing properly to predict his future wants? If he is that poor a guesser he will not be around for long, and the less wealthy he is the more quickly he will cease importing. In any area some people will import a great deal, others much less, but no one can go on importing too much for his good for any length of time. But perhaps some people are importing too much for the good of others in the sense that they are failing to help the others. We must note, first of all, that a person's importing is not the reason why those around him are not helped. Suppose he were to cease importing and not buy the goods from those near him. Are they any better off because he stopped importing? We may also add that to the extent that the importer has wide relationships with those near him, his imports from elsewhere will positively benefit them because these extensive relationships can continue only because what he imports is of greater benefit to them. Obviously, the fewer economic ties he has with his neighbors, the less they will be helped by his imports. But then to complain about this is to stake a claim to the effect that simply because X lives within a certain radius of Y, he should be forced to help Y.

One of the common complaints against an unmanaged currency is that the people are unable to control their money. The ambiguity lies in the expression "the people's money." Does it mean that there is collective ownership of the medium of exchange? If so, the phrase is unintelligible. Given the free economy each individual owns whatever money he is able to acquire. He values it as he sees fit, controls it as he sees fit, and manages it as he sees fit. The people control their money in the same way they control their television sets. Of course, the last thing that advocates of government planning want is for people to have control of their money. What they want is for the government to control it. What they mean by "uncontrolled" is precisely that it is controlled but not by those whom they would like to see control it. One of the great problems of the world is the fact that money is not controlled by its rightful owners.

Then there is the old chestnut that has it that our country is losing gold. Supposing that each individual owns whatever gold he has, it is obviously impossible for a country to lose gold. *It* doesn't have it in the first place. Only the individuals who have the gold can lose it—not a very likely contingency. Normally people do not lose gold. They exchange it for things that they would rather have. We would be somewhat astonished to hear someone maintain in all seriousness that he "lost" two dollars because he went to the movies. The real truth behind such claims is that the government which has expropriated the people's gold is being called upon by other governments to redeem its currency. But this would never have happened had not the government engaged in an inflationary policy.

I will end with a particularly weird example from Robert Heilbroner's *The Making of Economic Society,* pp. 96–97:

Yet England experienced difficulties enough in launching the Great Transformation. As we can now see, many of these difficulties were the direct consequences of the problems which our model highlighted for us. The industrialization process of the eighteenth and nineteenth centuries did, indeed, necessitate a great amount of saving—that is, of the releasing of consumption—and much of the social hardship of the time can be traced to this source.

For who did the saving? Who abstained from consumption? The manufacturers themselves (for all their ostentatious ways) were among those who plowed back a substantial portion of their profits into more investment. Yet the real savers

were not the manufacturers so much as another class–the industrial workers.
Here, in the low level of industrial wages, the great sacrifice was made–not
voluntarily, by any matter of means, but made just the same. From the resources
they could have consumed was built the industrial foundation for the future.

We have already referred to what we believe were the great injustices of
the period of the "Great Transformation." Had there been a more equal
distribution of property individuals would have been consuming more
of what they produced, simply because each of them would have been
producing a smaller quantity and, therefore, a lesser tendency to save.
Since Heilbroner's reasoning does not depend on any prior unjust
distribution of property, let us take for granted the justice of the
arrangement and see if his analysis makes any sense.

It is true that non-consumption is a necessary condition for saving.
But the non-consumption in question concerns *one's own* resources, not
those of other people. I can hardly be said to be saving for you when I
fail to consume your resources. This is not the place to discuss the
problem of wages. Suffice it to say that had less been produced real
wages would not have been as high as they were at any given time. The
increased production was mutually beneficial to the owners and the
workers. The fact that the owners saved rather than consumed made the
workers' condition far better than otherwise. They were perhaps victimized by the fact that the producers had the money that rightly belonged
to them. But not by the fact that the money was *saved*. It is absolutely
ridiculous to assert that the workers actually did the saving for they did
not have the resources to save. Even if someone takes my money away
from me and saves it, it is hardly enlightening for me to claim that I am
doing the saving. It is only because he indulges in this type of collective
thinking that Heilbroner was able to write such nonsense. Its plausibility
can only rest on the analogy of a family where some members, anxious to
increase the total wealth, deliberately abstain from consuming their
earnings in order to contribute them to the investments of the more
productive individuals of the group.

In the next paragraph we are told that "England had to hold down
the level of its working class consumption in order to free its productive
effort for the accumulation of capital goods." What on earth is the *entity*
that ever made such a decision? Practically the only entities making
decisions in nineteenth century England were those who owned resources. There were many decisions on the part of many people, but
none by England. And I am quite sure that no one thought himself

capable of "holding down the consumption of the working class" or desired to do so "in order to free its productive effort for the accumulation of capital goods." Decisions of this kind *are* made today, however. But they are made, not by property owners, but by dictators.

If there is a lesson to be learned from this paper it is that the only enlightening way of analyzing economic and property problems is by always returning to the individual who, alone, is real. People are ill served by the manufacture of spurious entities.

Note

Professor James Sadowsky, S.J., teaches philosophy at Fordham University. His papers have appeared in *Left and Right* and *The Personalist.*

"Private Property and Collective Ownership" is reprinted with permission from *Left and Right* (Fall 1966).

Tibor Machan

8

Justice and the Welfare State

IMAGINE SOMEONE WHO stole a composition from its creator and claimed it as his own. Surely, the fame and fortune which may result from this theft could not be considered *justly* acquired. Imagine, again, someone who has been bound and gagged in a chair in his home and misses an important appointment as a result, the consequences of which are disastrous. The blame, punishment, or related adverse result our victim suffers if people do not believe his story cannot justly be considered his due. A mere case of intentionally tripping another where the result can be a broken watch or a broken head suffered by the victim further shows that where agency cannot be established—where harm or advantage befalls someone other than the person who caused the injury or benefit—we cannot justly assign responsibility for consequences. Nor do we praise a student who passes an examination by copying the answers from another's paper.

The examples could continue. But what is their point? They serve, in this case, the purpose of an introduction to a discussion of political philosophy.

Take any political system in which it is impossible to determine who is responsible for the various events, situations, etc. that result from human action, one in which responsibility is misassigned or indeterminate because the laws and regulations which comprise the *legal* system of the *political* system render correct determination impossible—such a political system is in its most important respects *unjust*. While some elements of justice may be a *de facto* part of that society, as an organized institution the society is unjust. In this paper I will show that ours is this kind of a society; i.e., I will show that the legal system we have, comprised of various laws (and regulations, backed by laws), make it impossible correctly to determine the responsibility for the consequences of the actions of citizens.

By examining any one of the examples listed earlier, it can be seen that the reason for the distortions in determining the responsibility for the events which ensued was that those who partook of the situation were either coerced or coercing others in some way—freedom of action was hampered. It is only if the coercion becomes evident, and the agent of the coercion is identified, that determination of responsibility can be made and the various situations can be treated justly. The thief gained fame and fortune by depriving the composer of his freedom to act (such as to sell or keep his composition). The bound and gagged victim was suffering consequences unduly when his failure to attend the meeting in question had adverse consequences for him (and others). The man who was tripped was deprived of his freedom to act as well, while the chap who copied the answers from his schoolmate reaped unearned grades, both cases being paradigms of injustice. In all these examples the central feature is—with varying degrees of complexity—that one man deprived another of his freedom to act as he could have chosen.

On a socio-political scale the situation is markedly similar. Slavery, to take a rather drastic example, makes it impossible to determine who is responsible for consequences of the slave and slave-owner's actions as a matter of law. In other words, while retrospectively we can assign the proper responsibility in many cases, within the context of a political system where slavery is legally sanctioned, the determination of justice will be impossible, in fact. If a slave is *made* to do the various chores his master wants him to do, the resulting consequences, whether beneficial or harmful, are clearly not the slave's responsibility; the slave *might have* acted very differently had he been free to choose his own goals, though, of course, he *might have* done just what the slave-owner made him do. The slave-owner himself cannot be held solely responsible for the results, for it is indeterminable whether he would have pursued his goal had slavery not been permitted by law. Whatever we might say about degrees of responsibility, what is clear is that, within a slavery sanc-tioning political system, the linking up of causes and effects regarding human action is rendered virtually impossible—impossible, that is, correctly. To be sure, a slave will most often be blamed when what he was told to do involved harmful consequences. If a slave is told to drive to town and in doing this he runs over a person, the slave will surely be held responsible; yet no one can say whether he would have undertaken the drive had he had the freedom to choose his course of action.

Furthermore, within the slave's private life the linking of

causes with effects cannot be achieved. For we cannot tell just what personal tragedies were brought about by the slaveowner's whim, as distinguished from consequences which followed decisions of the slave that he would have made whether living as freeman or slave. Illnesses, eccentric traits, over- or undernourishment and the variety of possible states men find themselves in may all be the results of this person's status as a slave; yet they may have nothing to do with it.

With serfdom the situation is not fundamentally different. Here again the society's legal system sanctions the conditions which serfs suffer and the responsibility for events and situations in which serfs are involved cannot be assigned justly within the system.

What is common to these is that the persons involved are not free to choose their own goals, the means of attaining them, etc., but are consistently interfered with by others. Furthermore, this condition is sanctioned by law and is officially considered the most appropriate. When persons are allowed by law—or caused by law—to suffer the consequences of actions actually performed by others, when citizens must forever live as cripples because the state used them in scientific experiments against their will, or when persons are legally punished for performing badly on a job which they were forced to take—then what we have is clearly a condition of injustice within the respective political systems. And what is characteristic about injustice *in law* is that it obtains from the *legal* sanction of the coercion of some people by others, that is, the *legal* unavailability of freedom. If anything is properly designated unjust, it is a situation where someone is either enjoying or suffering consequences not *caused* by him. (This, incidentally, may be applied to the enjoyment of gifts and inheritance; however, to prevent the resulting injustice would involve a more serious form of injustice, in most cases—the usurpation of the rights of individuals to distribute what is theirs to willing takers.)

To suffer unjustly is to suffer for something caused by another. To benefit unjustly is to benefit from something achieved by another at the other's expense. (Clearly, I may benefit from another's achievements, say his tasteful dressing habits or his use of the right kind of deodorant —nowhere do I delimit his own opportunity to enjoy the consequences of his acts, however.) With some risk we may put it thusly: injustice denies, justice links cause and effect.

If a political or legal system fosters the denial of cause and effect, then it is, to that extent, unjust. In order to see whether our political system can be so characterized, and why, I will consider some of the results of the laws our political system incorporates. Clearly, the impact of these laws, if there is any, may not be so severe as to cause the degree of injustice—or the scope of it within the society—that we are familiar with in connection with the kind of societies depicted above where slavery and serfdom were legally sanctioned and supported practices of the society as a whole. Surely, in contemporary oppressive societies the discussion of justice, in a manner as directly critical as this essay may turn out to be, would not be permitted. Yet, the simple fact that injustice has not (in America) reached a degree of pervasiveness we know it can reach and has reached elsewhere needn't soften our aversion to it, nor need it prompt us to dismiss the issue as insignificant in comparison to other harmful or evil situations which are also present.

Some of the laws which I will proceed to show to contribute to injustice are not all pervasive. There are ways in which one can avoid being submitted to the legal measures of a society. Yet, in the end, it is very hard to tell whether any member of society can escape the results of unjust laws, especially if some of these results may be welcome.

The broadest of the laws which are in this category—productive of injustice, that is—is the federal taxation law; it is broad because it covers all citizens who are engaged in any kind of productive enterprise. Yet, tax laws, while the broadest, are not the most consequential in impact. The law of our political system which fits the characterization of "most unjust" is the military conscription law, better known to all as the draft. Related but less widely known noted laws which can be seen as unjust are: laws and bills permitting the subsidization of businesses; laws imposing tariff restrictions and quotas against foreign businesses (indi-rect subsidization); the law prohibiting the ownership of gold; laws and bills which permit the dispensation of tax-payers' funds for selected scientific endeavors, cultural ventures, educational projects, etc.; zoning laws (which operate in many of the smallest communities of the country); *eminent domain* laws; property and sales tax laws; price fixing laws; anti-trust laws; "right-to-work" laws (which forbid business firms and labor groups to enter into free contractual agreements); censorship laws; conservation laws; laws against gambling, prostitution, or the use of drugs or narcotics; "public accommodation," "fair employment," "fair housing," and related laws aimed at integration; and thousands of others . . . one could go on forever.

What is evident in the above list is that all of the laws included deviate from the purpose of government most widely accepted, namely the protection of the rights of individuals against the usurpation or abridgment of these rights by other men; in other words, the list includes laws which are "progressive" and render government an agent toward bringing about certain preferred human aims as against others, even when some members of the citizenry would prefer to neglect these aims. Laws, on the other hand, which protect the right of persons to act in line with their judgment, provided others' right to this is unimpinged, are not in the above list. The distinction, though a controversial one among philosophers interested in the concept of "human rights," is evident between progressive and protective laws. In this discussion, however, I cannot defend the distinction in detail. What I want to say about it is simply that the laws which I call protective are equally related to all citizens since they deal with the rights all human beings possess, with something which is common among the members of a society; the laws, however, which are in the list deal with the particular aims, goals, interests, difficulties, preferences and tastes of segments of the citizenry. For this reason I call them "progressive" laws: they contribute to the progress of these aims and goals; they do so, however, at the expense of other people's ability to make progress in the aims they have chosen or might have chosen for themselves.

The laws I have included in my list can be seen to comprise a substantial portion of what is called welfare legislation in our country (or elsewhere). It is the thesis of my paper that elements of the welfare state render the realization and attainment of justice in our society impossible. It is of no importance how the laws come into being—in principle they are no different from laws established by dictators, monarchs, the communist or fascist ruling groups, or a tribal lord, as regards their content; they serve to deprive individuals of their freedom to run their lives in line with their own judgments and capacities. It is unimportant here whether the people who are thus affected like or dislike their condition—the story of the happy southern slave is widely known and repeated by those who argue for the security and other "advantages" of slavery as against the benefits of justice. It is another issue entirely whether justice is to be preferred to other factors which could be secured in a political society.

Some have said that a just law has to satisfy no other requirement than that it is applicable to all citizens equally. This may indeed be an important rule (measure) for justice in the *application* of laws but it is not central to the productivity of justice by laws. A law, universally applied, which would hold guilty of murder not the person who did the killing but one who was in closest spacial proximity to him would be open to "just" application but be productive of injustice, nevertheless.

At this point let me return to the central purpose of my paper and give some illustration of the way in which some of the laws I listed are productive of injustice. Let us take taxation and see in what manner it produces injustice, i.e., in what way taxation renders the assignment of responsibility for various events, situations, circumstances, be they harmful or helpful to taxpayers, impossible. In what way, that is, do tax laws break the link between cause and effect in human action as this relates to the operation of the *assignment* of responsibilities?

When a person is taxed, he must, under threat of legal punishment (fines, jail, etc.), give up a certain amount of his earned income for purposes planned by past or present lawmakers. Here it is not important and relevant that *some* of these purposes may be shared by the taxpayer himself; he *must* support them—he does not enjoy the option of supporting them or not supporting them. What is central is that the taxpayer is *not free to withhold his support* from the purposes in point. In being deprived of his freedom to use his earned income for purposes designated wholly by him, the taxpayer's resources for advancing his own goals and purposes have been limited considerably.

The above is often rejected as a correct characterization of the nature of taxation on the following grounds: the citizen has gained immensely from many of the goals which have been achieved without his consent, in the past; for this reason it is only right and just that he should share the cost of these accomplishments. This is highly spurious. It is clearly unjust that a person, having been "given" something, for which he never had even the opportunity to ask, is made to share the cost of the "gift" at a later date, when he does not enjoy the option of rejecting the gift. The injustice arises out of the imposition of a responsibility upon the person when he does not share in the assumption of that responsibility. The reply that "He can leave the country any time he does not prefer the conditions" is equally spurious: after all it is merely an admission of injustice to tell a person that if he does not like the injustice he has still the option to escape the premises where it is the existing political or legal condition. Furthermore, if injustice is accepted within the legal system in principle, there is no ground for limiting it to those who wish to remain within the territory covered by that legal system; the next step may include the injustice of disallowing people to depart. (Such a measure is being contemplated in Great Britain as a result of the "brain drain" on the very grounds that the people who are leaving received their "free" education in England; it is, of course, the status quo within the communist block.)

Considering that the issue at hand is the determination of whether justice is possible *within* a political system correctly characterizable as a welfare state, we can proceed to investigate the manner in which taxation relates to this question. It should, however, be kept in mind that when one speaks of a society and its political system, it is a mistake to compare the situation to that of a social club or a fraternal organization. These latter are voluntarily formed groups which exist *within* a society and do, in fact, qualify very frequently as a "legal person" in their treatment by the law. The groups do *not* resemble society in many ways; most importantly, however, one is free to join or not to join them, free to take one's leave from them once his selfassumed debts to the organization have been paid, and the organization has no police force of itself but operates within the legal system of the society of which it is a part. Society, in general, does not have this character: its members are born such, in the main; one does not have the choice to assume one's "obligations" to the general society; society's governing body is not legally responsible to yet some greater or higher organization (with *its* own legal system). The fact that there are in existence different nationstates and that there is some toying with the idea of a super-world-legal-system (world law, United Nations, etc.) does not invalidate my point; the governmental system preferred by someone is usually the same that he would like for the whole world to adopt. This is true of those who find the welfare state as the best kind of organization for human beings. This clearly is not the case with social and fraternal organizations such as the Lions or Kiwanis Clubs, the Red Cross, Optimists, and the thousands of other groups, each of which has its own special (group of) goals, aims, purposes, methods, interests, emphases, and so forth, representing the goals, etc., of its members, all of whom joined the groups presumably knowing of these and free to stay out. The contract theory of society, promulgated by political philosophers such as Jean-Jacques Rousseau, is a totally invalid conception of the state, both historically and theoretically.

Now, to return to the investigation, let me note that the taxpayer's own choices are not the determinants of what he will do. He will be forced to support programs—with his presumably honestly earned taxed income—he *might* never support were he free to refrain, and again, he *might* never undertake goals that he *would* have chose to pursue had he been free to do so. What he will do, in areas where he is free to act, will be the complicated outcome of choices with possibly crucial alternatives removed. With these alternatives lacking, it is now—when we attempt to attain justice in appraising him, both legally and otherwise —simply impossible to determine whether this lack did in fact contribute to the various events, circumstances, and states of affairs of his life.

Let us just imagine that the individual in question would have been free to invest his earnings in some business venture; he might have spent it on further education for himself or his children; he might have gambled it away—the possibilities are innumerable. *However* he *might* have spent his income had he been free to do so is indeterminable. What is more important is that equally indeterminable is *who* precisely is responsible for this condition in which we find the taxpayer.

If the abstract account given above has no impact, perhaps a more concrete one will. We can easily imagine a citizen who needs a new car because the motor of his old one is defective. He cannot, however, both pay his taxes and purchase a new vehicle. One morning he gets into an "accident" and suffers serious injuries, all as a consequence of the failure of his automobile. It is obvious that we cannot determine who is to be held responsible for the "accident" and the resulting injuries, etc. The individual could not buy a better car after he paid his taxes; furthermore, we cannot tell whether he *would* have bought one, had he been free to do so. So, the case is closed—with his earnings taken as taxes he certainly could not buy a car, and of his own free choice, with all his earnings, he could have, but might not have, bought one. The responsibility for the ensuing situation: indeterminable; a just appraisal of the situation: impossible.

It may be replied that "After all, the sheer fact that our social, economic and other interactions are complicated—not to mention the issue of psychological and sociological theories which make the matter even more complex—can contribute to numerous situations wherein the assignment of responsibility and, therefore, *just* appraisal, are rendered impossible." Granted the objection, there is a fundamental distinction between injustice which is the result of default, complications, and the like, and injustice which is brought about through the consciously planned actions of members of society, human beings, who might have refrained from making the laws which now contribute to the widespread injustice. From complications injustices arise which, however, are not planned to occur and are not desired, at any rate. From laws, which are not the result of the complexities of life itself but the ideas men have about dealing with some of these complexities, injustice can only be seen as avoidable.

The impact of taxation on a man's life is immense—yet, very few respected and prominent philosophers would argue that taxation is a contributing factor to injustice, taxation as an institution; they may argue that certain features of it produce injustice, of course. And this is not surprising. The interventions into the life of individuals in our society are so widespread and common, so well embedded, that they are virtually impossible to sort out. We may benefit from modeling the situation on what happens to the balls in a pinball machine: by the time they reach the end of their run they will have gone through various interferences, obstacles, shoves and pushes, all of which contribute to the end result. With a person the situation is a thousand times more complex due, in part, to the fact of human agency itself. The interferences are both caused and suffered by people, yet the intermediary, the law, serves to break the link between the interferer and the interfered unlike the pinball case and unlike, even, the case where a person suffers the interference not from the law but from a private individual or group, as in the case of theft, murder, extortion, and fraud. In these latter, interference has occurred but the law instead of perpetrating it, works to prevent injustice by linking the parties with their responsibility as best as can be done by human beings.

I have, thus far, been talking about just one of the hundreds of thousands of laws which can be characterized as depriving people of their freedom to pursue their own chosen ends, that is, laws which are productive of injustice. I will mention only one other law of this kind. This is conscription. The draft deprives a man of at least two years of his life if he is subject to it. Yet, there is absolutely no cogent justification for this law within a society the legal system of which has long rejected slavery as one of its features.

Conscription is defended most frequently on two grounds: (1) A person owes his country certain services in return for the benefits he has accrued by being born in the given country; (2) a country has a right to defend itself against possible aggression and such defense is unattainable without conscription. Both of these arguments uphold the welfare of the society (the state) as prior to the welfare of the individual citizens involved in providing that welfare. This is why I consider them classic arguments in behalf of the welfare state.

I have already dealt with argument (1) in connection with the alleged duty of a citizen to pay for services from which he gained benefits but which he never asked for. We saw that we were dealing with a variant of the social contract theory of society the model for which was provided by fraternal clubs and other private organizations which are indeed formed by contract.

Argument (2) is somewhat complicated because it presupposes a theory of nationhood still in question. Does any *kind* of country have the right to defend itself? What kind of right would it be that would grant legitimacy to a dictator's attempts, for instance, to defend the country which he rules? Presumably it would not be a moral right but a right of fiat, i.e., a right claimed by reason of rulership. If we are to talk of the right of a country or society to defend itself against aggressors, we must be open to the possibility that some countries cannot claim that right. This leads to problems of legitimate authority.

When does a government have legitimate authority to govern? Presumably when it is representative, when the governed have freely chosen to delegate to the government certain responsibilities to be carried out by that government. The crucial feature then is the freedom of the governed, the citizens. If conscription involves the usurpation of the rights of individuals to act in accordance with their own wishes, judgments, goals, etc.—the usurpation of freedom—then a government could not possibly conscript its citizens without losing its legitimacy in the process.

If, then, a country has the right to defend itself, it cannot do so by conscription without losing that right (by losing its legitimacy and, thereby, its right of exercising authority).

It is clear that conscription limits freedom of action; thus, the consequences of military conscription—or any other kind—are such that it is impossible to speak of the draftee as one who is responsible for his actions—his life is largely not in his own hands, the actions which he undertakes are not strictly his own, and the responsibility which ordinarily goes with the performance of actions by persons cannot, therefore, be his own either. Of course, some decisions and acts, once the limits of decision-making have been set by law, are the draftee's own. It would, therefore, be false to hold that he was responsible for *nothing*. Even this fact becomes obscured by the constant factor of interference, however.

It is obvious from the above that conscription is productive of grave injustices in society and renders the determination of responsibility—the linking of cause and effect in human action—impossible. In various more or less complicated and direct ways laws such as price-fixing, minimum-wage regulations, racial quotas, censorship, anti-gambling ordinances, and others are productive of similar injustices. Minimum-wage laws, for instance, *force* an employer to pay more for work than the market can bear; this can result in cutting down the workload; as a result people will be dismissed; others gain higher wages not as a result of better work but because of direction from the government; the higher wages can lead to higher prices, thereby eliminating the general effect of higher wages altogether. When companies collapse, employees are dismissed, children go hungry, illnesses cannot be cured for lack of funds, etc., etc.—thousands of consequences follow as a result of the initial governmental action which deprived men of their right to act in line with their own judgment; once again the link between the cause of the results and the results is broken and responsibility cannot be assigned.

Governmental subsidies to businesses are productive of similar results. And so are tariffs and quota systems, both of which deprive buyers in this country of alternative courses of action by force. When a manufacturer simply withholds his products from the market the situation is different, since it is he who makes the product and he, therefore, is not depriving anyone of something to which there exists a right. If Frank Sinatra refuses to sing to me when I offer to pay him for it, he is not depriving me of something to which I have a right. If another person stops him from singing by cutting his throat both Sinatra and I have been interfered with. The government's tariff and quota policies can be modeled on the above example without any change in the essentials.

I believe that I have listed enough examples. Clearly, every law mentioned earlier and thousands of others can be put to similar scrutiny. What would be discovered is that at some point laws of this type interfere with the freedom of individuals in such a way that their activities will be impervious to being appraised concerning matters of responsibility, blame, desert, or accomplishment. And such a state of affairs renders justice within society an impossibility.

I have not ventured in this paper to suggest a governmental system within which the attainment of justice would be possible. That would certainly require not only another paper but several books. The fact that the society which I think would come closest to one within which justice is possible has been approximated within this country, with drastic contradictions evident within that approximation, would render the task of arguing for that sort of a system even more difficult than would ordinarily be the case. I am speaking, of course, about the system of government known as constitutional democracy, with government being limited to the duties of administering laws, protecting the innocent, and prosecuting the guilty. Within the society itself the police and the courts would represent the government, and for purposes of contact with other nations the military—pertaining to aggressors—and the diplomatic corps—relating to international legal matters—would represent the body and functions of such a government. The economy, morality, culture, sports, entertainment, education, etc., of the people would be their own individual business (or collective, whenever the collective body can be organized voluntarily). The financing of the government would be through the charging of fees for contracts which might be in need of legal backing and protection. Unlike a utopia, that kind of a system would secure justice for people, while it would be the people who would have to secure all else for themselves.

To argue for such a system would take us into ethics, metaphysics and, finally, epistemology. So I must refrain from doing this now. My present aim has been to discern whether justice is possible within the framework of a governmental system commonly known as the welfare state. The conclusion of my inquiry was that it is impossible to have both justice within a society and the governmental system of the welfare state.

As I mentioned, this conclusion does not establish the undesirability or impropriety of the welfare state. There might be other considerations which must be brought to bear upon those questions, considerations which might lead us to abandon justice as a desirable state of affairs within a legal system in favor of some other commodity, say security or happiness or racial purity.

Needless to say, *I* cannot think of any commodity which is more important than justice. Thus I will confess my preference for a social system within which it is attainable. But a preference is not enough in philosophy; arguments are needed. To argue in favor of justice, as against other possible and competing benefits a governmental or legal system may provide, is necessary. Hopefully, despite the anti-political philosophy trend of contemporary philosophy, discussions related to such matters will attend to that question also.

Note

"Justice and the Welfare State" is reprinted with permission from *The Personalist* (Summer 1969).

part three

Contemporary Statism: Libertarian Critiques

Although criticism is always a bit more convenient than advocacy of constructive alternatives, it is not due simply to laziness. Criticism is always directed toward what already exists either in practice or in theory; the object one addresses himself to need not be discovered or invented—it is there waiting to be abused.

Still, responsible criticism requires the demonstration, either explicitly or implicitly, of some standard of judgment. Thus, such criticism lays itself open for examination, as well. (One of the central faults of Marx's *Das Kapital* is the absence of any clear point of critical reference—only the barest hints about the standards of a good social order are offered. Marx's constant reference to social utility—what today goes by the term "public interest"—is backed with no clear presentation of a standard which could itself be checked for its reasonableness and availability.)

While some of the following critical essays focus on issues which may not be the fad of the day (fads change so quickly—concern for the environment has given way to concern about TV violence, prison reform, and child care centers) most of them attack the common theme that human problems in general, involving medicine, technology, education, art, travel, communication, science, and so on interminably, can be dealt with successfully by a political system, by politicians, through political means. The idea of the essays is that the means of solving a problem must be appropriate to the nature of that problem—so, when not related to politics, a problem can be only mishandled through political means. This is, above all, what the philosophy of science—the general field in which the nature of the scientific method is considered— can tell the social scientist.

Yale Brozen

9   Is the Government the Source of Monopoly?

When Adam Smith wrote *The Wealth Of Nations*, there was no doubt in the mind of anyone that monopolies were the result of governmental power. Few felt they could flourish without government support. The only prominent monopolies were the result of governmental grants. Even they were difficult to maintain despite the use of government power. Competition kept breaking out in spite of governmental attempts to suppress it. The following account is illustrative.

In 1631 the King granted to a group of projectors the exclusive right to make soap of vegetable oil for fourteen years. They agreed to pay the King £4 a ton and to make five thousand tons a year at 3d. a pound; they were permitted, in view of the supposed superiority of their soap to examine all other manufactured soap and impound or destroy any that they thought below standard. At a test held in private in London, their soap was certified better than that of the London soap-makers. It did not fare so well at Bristol where a tavern maid and a laundress lathered away in public at some soiled linen napkins with the projectors' soap and with soap made by the Bristol soap-makers; they demonstrated that the Bristol soap washed whiter and more economically than the projectors' soap. In spite of this the King ordered the closing down of seven out of Bristol's eleven soap-boiling workshops.

In London the struggle went on with unabated venom. The King's projectors prevailed on the King to prohibit the use of fish oil in soap altogether; on the strength of this they seized the stock of the London soap-makers and prosecuted them in the Star Chamber, following this up by an offer to buy them out of business. The London soap-makers refused the bait and some of them were imprisoned. Murmurs were now rising on all sides. While fishing companies were affected by the prohibition on whale oil, the people in general declared that the projectors' soap was bad. The projectors mobilized the Queen's ladies to write testimonials to the excellence of their soap but laundresses and—more important— cloth-workers throughout the country continued to condemn it. In response the King prohibited the private making of soap altogether and gave the projectors the right to enter and search any private house. All in vain. By the summer of 1634 illicit soap was being sold at a shilling the pound or six times its original price, so low was the general opinion of the projectors' soap. At this point the projectors gave up their plan of using only vegetable oil and took to using the fish oil, which they had made illegal for everyone else. In a final effort to drive their rivals out of business the King put a tax of £4 a ton on Bristol soap. The Bristol soap-boilers refused to pay, and fourteen of them followed the London soap-makers to prison. The farce could not continue much longer and in 1637 the King wound up the project and bought in the projectors' rights for £40,000, of which he made the London soap-makers contribute half. He then allowed the London men to go back to their interrupted manufacture on payment of a tax of £8 a ton to the Crown. [1]

The very word monopoly was, in its usage in the eighteenth century, a label for a special privilege granted by the monarch—the privilege of being the sole supplier of some commodity or service. The royal grant of a monopoly was usually made to a subject of the monarch who, for some reason, the monarch felt deserved enrichment, and it was cheaper to the monarch to award such a privilege than to make a direct grant from the royal purse.

In some cases the excuse for the grant was the encouragement of a trade—as in the case of the grant to the East India Company (famous in American history for the fate of one of its tea cargoes in Boston Harbor in the early 1770's).

As is clear from American history, one of the causes of the American Revolution was the attempt to enforce the Trade & Navigation Acts. These laws were intended to monopolize certain activities for the benefit of Englishmen living in the British Isles. One might say that the American Revolution and the Declaration of Independence were a reaction to the attempt by the British government to create a monopoly by its trade regulation.

Adam Smith wrote his book in part to demonstrate that a nation will fail to enrich itself if it fosters monopoly. The wealth of a nation grows more rapidly by avoiding monopoly. This was heresy in Adam Smith's day but is now a part of accepted doctrine and embodied in our statutes in the form of the Sherman Act, the Clayton Act, and dozens of state anti-trust statutes.

With such statutes on the law books and with a government born out of reaction to regulations which fostered monopolies, why is a discussion of monopoly necessary? Certainly government support of monopoly privileges must be an archaic practice of interest only to antiquarians. We certainly can not have revived the very practices which led us to overthrow a previous government and to establish a new one. The sad truth, notwithstanding our history, is that we have not only re-instituted the very practices against which we once revolted, we have instituted new ones with a much wider reach than those of the British government in the eighteenth century.

Monopolies Directly Created by Government

In 1965, Congress passed a Sugar Act. The act is designed to monopolize the trade in sugar for favored growers of cane in Florida and Louisiana, favored growers of sugar beets mostly located in the western states, and certain favored foreign suppliers who are allotted a share of the American market. American consumers are to be granted the dubious privilege of being protected from the politically impure supply of sugar which some are willing to sell to them at two cents per pound in order that they may be sure of obtaining politically pure sugar at seven cents a pound. When the constituents of the sugar senators ask, "What have you done for me lately?", the senators will be able to tell them.

The Sugar Act is only one of many such acts. The regulations of government which foster monopoly in both domestic production and foreign production are legion. We have a coffee agreement with several foreign governments which allots to them a monopoly of the American coffee market. The Department of Agriculture regulates the production of tobacco, and many other commodities, on a basis which monopolizes the privilege of growing tobacco for those who have land which has a history of growing tobacco—a history which has been officially acknowledged by the issuance of an appropriate certificate.

This confinement of the right to be in a given economic activity to a designated few is, of course, the essence of monopoly—that is, the prevention of free entry into a line of business or an occupation. If you or I want to get into the business of growing tobacco or supplying electricity, it is not enough to rent land capable of growing tobacco or to buy a generator and let potential customers know that we are ready to supply them. We have to have governmental permission—and I assure you that you cannot get such permission. The only way you can get into these businesses is by buying out one of the monopolists who is already in the business. The privilege of supplying such commodities and services is reserved for them (or their heirs or assigns).

These few examples of governmental actions which foster monopoly are illustrative of numerous regulatory activities which are quite consciously aimed at reserving the privilege of supplying goods and services to favored persons—quite consciously aimed at fostering monopoly and restricting the right to engage in certain businesses to the favored few. I will return to an analysis of the economic consequences of this type of regulation later when I will deal in detail with transportation regulation, the monopoly it fosters, and the losses in national welfare which are caused.

Monopolies Indirectly Created by Government

For the moment, let us turn away from regulations deliberately aimed at creating monopolies where none would otherwise exist to another kind of regulation. This is regulation aimed at other purposes whose net effect is the creation of more monopoly—more restrictions on entry into various businesses with the result that labor and capital are forced into inferior, alternative uses where they cannot contribute as much to our national and individual welfare as they could and would if allowed the freedom to enter areas of economic activity now barred to them. These restrictions on the freedom of laborers and capitalists to enter some types of activity hurt them as well as hurting the national economy, causing many to fall into the group labeled as poverty stricken and creating a greater poverty problem.

An example of governmental regulation which indirectly fosters monopoly is minimum wage legislation—the federal statutes known as the Fair Labor Standards Act, the Davis-Bacon Act, and the Walsh-Healy Act, and the many state statutes setting minimum wage rates for various occupations not covered by the Federal statutes. Presumably, the aim of these statutes is the prevention of exploitation of employees by employers. However, the result of these statutes has been to provide a monopoly of some businesses for those firms located nearer to major markets or with a more highly skilled set of employees available to them. Crab meat packing plants located closer to Washington, Baltimore, Philadelphia, and New York, for example, no longer need be concerned with the competition of North Carolina crab meat packers. When the minimum wage went to $1.25 on September 3, 1965, North Carolina crab packing plants shut down causing 1,800 women to lose their jobs and eliminating an outlet for the hundreds of crab fishermen who supplied these plants. These North Carolina plants could not pay $1.25

an hour and the transportation costs required to ship their product to their major markets. The crab meat packing plants which have lower transportation costs because they are located closer to major markets now have a monopoly of those markets. They need not concern themselves with their former competitors located on remote portions of the North Carolina shore.

The fact that minimum wage legislation results in a monopoly of some kinds of business for those in favorable locations is well recognized by some groups. The New England textile manufacturers have always supported increases in the minimum wage rate. They know that any increase knocks out some of the competition from Southern textile producers and gives New England fabricators a more monopolistic position.

The increase in the minimum wage by Federal statute from 40 cents to 75 cents an hour in 1950 played an important role in knocking out 10 percent of the individually owned textile plants (between 1947 and 1954) and 25 percent of those owned by partnerships. Textile plants owned by corporations increased by five percent in this period, in large part because of the large number of non-corporate plants driven out of business by the higher minimum wage rate.[2]

The increase in the minimum wage rate from 75 cents to $1 an hour in 1956 also served to reduce the number of textile plants in operation, leaving the remaining firms with fewer competitors and a more monopolistic position.

The cigar and cigarette industry and the leather industry had even more competition knocked out by the federal minimum wage law amendments of 1950 and 1956 than the textile industry. Fifty percent of individually owned tobacco manufacturing establishments and 60 percent of partnership owned plants went out of business because of the 1950 minimum wage increase. Another 35 percent disappeared in each category after the enactment of the 1956 minimum wage increase. In the leather goods industry, 10 percent of individually owned factories and one-third of partnership-owned factories disappeared after the enactment of the 1950 increase. The 1956 increase knocked out three percent of the remaining individually owned leather product factories and 25 percent of the partnership-owned factories.

We do not have any data available as yet to measure the consequence of the minimum wage increases of 1961, 1963, 1965, and 1967, although we do know there has been a strong impact. I have already described one instance of the impact of the 1965 increase in the case of the crab meat packing industry.

Incidentally, these decreases in the number of individually owned establishments which I have described are not the result of a general trend in manufacturing. In all other manufacturing, the number of individually owned factories increased by 17 percent in the period in which the 1950 minimum wage increase was applied and by eight percent in the period in which the 1956 increase was applied. These other industries use more highly skilled labor whose pay rate was not affected by the minimum wage law, and most of their plants have market oriented locations.

Here, then, is an instance of monopoly fostered by a governmental regulation which was not intended for that specific purpose, but which had that effect.

Other governmental regulations have a similar, largely unintended effect in promoting monopoly. The recent amendments to the food and drug act have reduced competition in the drug industry. Clearance procedures for new drugs have been made so costly that no company will embark on the research program to develop a new drug unless the drug can be expected to have a sales volume of at least $500,000 per year. Under the old law, investors were willing to put capital into a research program if a drug could be developed which might be expected to have a sales volume of $100,000 per year. The number of new drugs becoming available to compete with old drugs has been greatly reduced by the new law. Incidentally, one of the consequences of the new law was an increase in the profitability of the drug industry.

The Transportation Monopolies
Created by Government

Perhaps the most thoroughly regulated activity in our economy is transportation. It is, I would argue, more completely regulated than agriculture or even the narcotics industry. First, let me describe some of the regulatory activities in transportation in terms of the monopoly aspect of the regulations and then discuss some of the consequences.

The Interstate Commerce Commission (ICC) limits the number of firms allowed to engage in common carrier transportation. In addition, it actually sets minimum rates below which transportation companies are not allowed to sell. It maintains a price umbrella for truckers, barge lines, coastal steamship operators, and railroads.[3]

The Civil Aeronautics Board (CAB) sets minimum air cargo rates and passenger rates. It even attempts to regulate the service provided at these rates to prevent one airline from offering a more comfortable seat or more leg room at a given price than another.[4]

The Federal Maritime Board forces steamship lines into the ocean conferences—the privately operated cartels which regulate ocean freight rates and attempt to prevent rate cutting.[5] Forty states regulate intrastate trucking and prevent rate cutting just as the ICC prevents rate cutting in the inter-state movement of freight.[6] Most cities regulate the taxi business with the same result.[7]

The regulatory agencies not only prevent those in the transportation industry from competing with each other—they also protect those in the industry from the entry of additional competitors. You cannot get into the trucking business, the airline business, the bus business, the taxi business, or the pipeline business as you would enter retailing or manufacturing. You must be certified by the CAB if you wish to enter the airline business. The CAB has not certified an additional scheduled airline in continental United States since it began operating in 1938. The ICC will certify an additional common carrier truck company to operate on a given route only if it can be demonstrated that adequate truck service is not available on the route in question. The only major city in which you can start a taxi business simply by applying for a taxi license and demonstrating that you carry the necessary public liability insurance and have safe equipment and drivers is Washington, D.C. All other major cities stop any additional taxi operators from entering the business. They even prevent present taxi operators from increasing the size of their fleets. Transportation regulation very effectively protects transportation companies from new competition and produces the exact opposite of the situation which our anti-monopoly laws were designed to produce in other industries.

Regulation Causes High Rates

The original *raison d'etre* for transportation regulation was the prevention of extortionate rate setting by railroad monopolies and discriminatory treatment of shippers. Yet, from its very inception, the ICC has caused rates to be higher than they otherwise would be and forced some users of freight services to pay very much higher rates than other shippers had to pay.

Before the ICC began operation, agreements between railroads were made in order to maintain certain rate levels for the shipment of corn, for example, from Chicago to New York. However, the railroads seldom observed their agreements. They constantly undercut the agreed rates with very beneficial results for mid-West farmers. With the enactment of the Interstate Commerce Act, undercutting of the published corn rates from Chicago to New York ceased.

The Act provided that short haul rates were not to be higher than long haul rates. Since this meant that any reduction in long haul between points joined by competing railroads would have to be accompanied by reductions in short haul rates, railroads ceased trying to compete by setting low long haul rates. Rates between Chicago and New York went up and stayed up after 1887, the year when the Interstate Commerce Commission began operation.[8]

Since this may sound like such ancient history that it has little application to present circumstances—although I assure you it does—let me discuss a more recent illustration of the impact of regulation in causing rate increases. Although truck transportation of agricultural commodities is exempted from regulation, the ICC regulated truck rates for semi-processed agriculture goods before 1952. The Courts held, in 1952, that the agricultural exemption applied to semi-processed items as well as raw commodities. Following the deregulation of these goods, motor carrier rates for fresh dressed poultry fell by 33 percent and for frozen poultry by 36 percent over the next five years.[9]

With the passage of the Transportation Act of 1958, motor carriage of semiprocessed items was placed under regulation again. Rates for transporting these goods promptly rose by 20 percent.

Incidentally, I should point out that in the 17 years before the ICC came into operation, average railroad rates dropped from $19 per 1,000

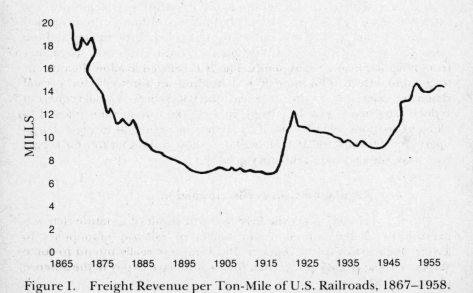

Figure I.   Freight Revenue per Ton-Mile of U.S. Railroads, 1867–1958.

ton-miles to $8.50. It seems that competition was working very well indeed in the rail industry from 1870 to 1887. In the 17 years after the ICC began operating, rail rates dropped from $8.50 per 1,000 ton-miles to $7.80 (see figure I). If there was a large monopoly profit in railroad prices at the time the ICC began operating, the Commission does not seem to have done much about it. Certainly, the record of decreasing rates after the Commission began regulating the industry is nowhere near as impressive as the record in the period when there was no regulation.

The fall in railroad rates from 1870 to 1898 may be attributed to the generally deflationary circumstances of the times. The general level of prices in the United States fell until the time of the Klondike gold strike in 1898. The important point to recognize is that the ICC did nothing to accelerate the decline in rates which had been taking place before the ICC began operating, that it actually caused an increase in rates which had been competitively determined between points joined by more than one railroad, and that in recent years railroads which wanted to offer lower prices to their customers have been refused permission to reduce rates.

A few examples of this refusal are illustrative of a much larger number of instances. In 1951, the Commission denied railroads permission to institute proposed reductions of rates on scrap iron. In this instance, the Commission was holding an umbrella for the barge lines. The Commission also denied a rail request to reduce petroleum product rates that same year to protect trucker business, although the proposed rates were compensatory and railroads would have made money at these rates. In 1954 railroads filed a proposal to reduce rates on magazines from Philadelphia to Texas points. The ICC refused to allow the rate cut to go into effect. This time it was holding an umbrella for coastal steamship operators. In the same year, the ICC rebuffed a rail request to reduce rates on aluminum articles. In 1955 the Commission refused to allow reductions of rail rates on sugar in order to protect barge operators. In 1961 the ICC denied a request to lower rates on piggy-back movements. And so the story goes.

Regulation Causes Discrimination

This is, to say the least, a weird result of a statute that was presumably designed to limit the ability of railroad monopolies to extract high prices from shippers. Did Congress really intend to force shippers to pay higher prices than they would have to pay in the absence of regulation?

Perhaps Congress did not intend to reduce competition among railroads when it passed the Interstate Commerce Act in 1887, although this was the immediate result. There appears to be no ambiguity on this score since 1920, however. The Transportation Act of 1920 instituted minimum rate regulation of railroads. If it was monopoly about which Congress was concerned, it would hardly have been necessary to place floors under rates. Presumably, the purpose of regulating monopolies is to prevent prices from being high. The usual method and aim in monopoly regulation is to put ceilings on prices at the levels which restrict the monopolist's return on investment to the rate earned in competitive industries of comparable risk and progressiveness. In this conception of the regulatory process, there is no place for minimum rate regulation. The Transportation Act of 1920 frankly converted the ICC into an operator of a cartel, not a regulator of monopolies.[10]

However, the ICC had behaved as a cartel authority long before this time. Presumably, another purpose of the regulation of monopolies is the prevention of monopolistic practices. It is not regarded as equitable for anyone to possess and exercise the power to extract higher prices from some people for the same service which is sold at lower prices to others. Such a practice is regarded by the courts as evidence of the use and exercise of monopoly power and would lead to punitive findings by the courts under the Sherman and Clayton Acts.

Yet, under ICC regulation, different rates are set for the transportation of different commodities even when there is no difference in the service or in the cost of providing the service. Before the Interstate Commerce Act was passed, railroads classified freight into four categories on which they attempted to maintain different rates. However, competition among roads in Trunk-Line territory caused rate differentiation to almost disappear.[11] After the ICC began operating, rate differentiation proliferated to the point where rates have become a morass of discriminatory charges based on more than 200 classifications. Despite the prohibition of railroad discrimination in the Act to Regulate Commerce of 1887, discrimination increased with the blessing of the ICC. The rates charged on the movement of some commodities range up to ten times as much on some as on others between the same pair of points for essentially the same service.

The following chart, which simply breaks up rail movement into ten equal classes in terms of the amount of car miles in each class, shows that the ten percent of car miles charged for at the highest rates pay six times as much per car mile as the ten percent of car miles charged at the lowest rates.

You will notice that this chart greatly simplifies the rail rate structure to show the gross effects of the discriminatory treatment of shippers. These ten groupings are an amalgam of 261 different commodity groups each charged a different rate with the highest rates being 35 times as high as the lowest rates. Some differences in commodity rates are justifiable on the basis of differences in costs. These differences in costs wash out to a large extent when we look at revenue results in dollars per carload mile terms, however. And we still see a carload mile of some commodities yielding more than ten times as much revenue as a carload mile of other commodities.

Congress has certainly put us on notice by giving the ICC power to set minimum rates that it is not interested in preventing monopoly or the exercise of monopoly power. If it were, it would give the ICC only the power to set maximum rates. I would also argue that Congress not only wishes to support monopoly and create monopolies where none exist, but it also is in favor of discrimination among shippers. It is not interested in eliminating discrimination despite the proclamation to that effect in the preamble of the Act to Regulate Interstate Commerce.

What Congress is interested in doing is taxing some shippers by seeing that they are charged above-cost rates in order to subsidize other shippers and make freight service available to them at below-cost rates. This has been the intent of Congress and of the regulatory agencies.[12] The net result, however, has been that the shippers that Congress is attempting to favor are paying higher rates than they would be paying if Congress had not attempted to legislate such favors. The situation is reminiscent of the old wisecrack, "With friends like these, who needs enemies?"

Economic legislation in the transportation field produces the opposite of its intended result just as so much other economic legislation does. The imposition of regulation on the pricing of natural gas in the field, which was intended to produce lower prices for consumers, has caused an increase in the field price of gas.[13] Our tariff legislation, which presumably protects high wage American workers from the competition of low-paid foreigners actually monopolizes low paying jobs and prevents Americans from moving into higher paying jobs.[14] Our minimum wage legislation, which is supposed to eliminate poverty by raising the pay of low-paid workers, is creating more poverty by causing unemployment and by forcing people out of higher paying jobs into poorly paid jobs.[15] Our legislation favoring low income regions such as the Tennessee Valley and Appalachia which is supposed to benefit the poor, is maintaining pockets of poverty and benefiting the highly paid workers in high income areas.[16] Our agricultural program, presumably designed to help poor farmers, has hurt poor farmers and enriched rich farmers.[17] Our urban renewal programs, which are supposed to benefit the slum dweller, have hurt slum dwellers and small business men and enriched building contractors, landlords, and the most highly paid workers in the country, the members of the building trades unions.[18]

The Result of Congressional Intent in Transportation

Despite the Congressional intent to tax some shippers through imposition of high rates in order to subsidize other shippers by making below cost rates available, the net result has been that the shippers who are supposed to be favored are paying higher rates than they would be paying if Congress had not tried to do them a favor. Congress has tried to keep common carriers profitable while extending below cost rates to small shippers and to shippers of agricultural commodities by giving the ICC the power to set high rates—above-cost rates—for less worthy shippers. In this way, it was hoped, common carriers could earn enough to attract the necessary capital to the transportation business and yet provide below cost service to the worthy shippers—those with political preference (or, should I say, political clout).

How has it happened, then, that the shippers who are subsidized are worse off than if there had been no attempt to subsidize them? Perhaps the way to explain this is to begin with a paradox. In 1956, after rising labor rates had greatly eroded the return on railroad capital, the ICC raised rail rates by six percent. The St. Louis-San Francisco R.R., after putting the new rates into effect, found that its volume of freight movement increased by two percent in the following year, but that its total revenues dropped by one percent. Now how can you charge higher prices, do more business, and end up with less revenue?

To explain the paradox, let us look at the following set of figures. Suppose a railroad is doing 150 billion ton-miles of business and realizing $4 billion of revenue with an average revenue of 2.67 cents per ton-mile. This average is the result of doing 100 billion ton-miles at one cent per ton-mile, let us say, and 50 billion ton-miles at six cents per ton-mile. Some shippers are being charged a high price, but this does not result in a handsome return to the railroad. The profit from the high-price business subsidizes the loss suffered on the business done at a low price.

Now let us assume that the loss becomes so great that prices must be

Figure II

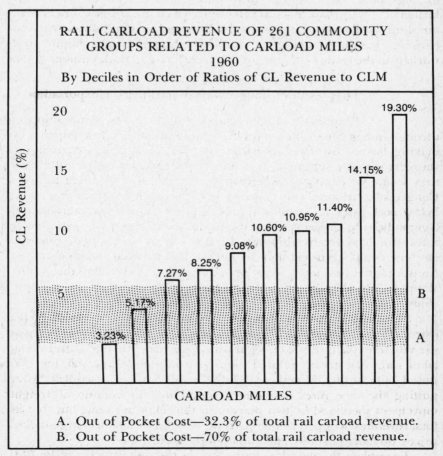

**RAIL CARLOAD REVENUE OF 261 COMMODITY
GROUPS RELATED TO CARLOAD MILES
1960
By Deciles in Order of Ratios of CL Revenue to CLM**

CL Revenue (%)

20 — 19.30%

15 — 14.15%

11.40%

10.95%

10.60%

10 — 9.08%

8.25%

7.27%

5 — 5.17% — B

3.23% — A

CARLOAD MILES

A. Out of Pocket Cost—32.3% of total rail carload revenue.
B. Out of Pocket Cost—70% of total rail carload revenue.

raised if the railroad is to stay in business. For this example, let us
assume they are raised 10 percent. This amounts to a 0.1 cent increase
on the subsidized business and a 0.6 cent increase on the high-rated
business. As a consequence of the increases, the high-rated business falls
off. The railroad has a substantial increase in low-rated business and its
volume increases by two percent, but revenues fall, despite the higher
prices charged. The reason lies in the decline in high-rated business
which more than offsets the price increase and the rise in volume of low-
rated traffic.

High-rated shippers have been leaving the railroads and common carrier truckers in large numbers because the price of service is high and has been increased. They are finding it cheaper to buy their own trucks and barges and to build their own pipelines rather than allow themselves to be grossly overcharged.

We can see the net result of this in terms of the rapid growth of private carriage from 23 percent of total intercity ton-miles in 1948 to 32 percent in 1960. This growth in private carriage came at the expense of the high-rated traffic of the railroads and common carrier trucks. Although the common carrier share of intercity traffic dropped only from 77 to 68 percent of the total between 1948 and 1960, their share of the intercity freight bill which they collected dropped from 74 to 57 percent. Their share of freight revenues dropped by 23 percent while their share of ton-miles dropped by only 12 percent.

Because high-rated traffic is fleeing the railroads, the high-rated business done by railroads declined by one-third during the last 15 years while total intercity traffic was rising by 50 percent. This reduction in volume means that the rates to preferred shippers have had to be

Figure III

Examples of Increased Freight Rates With Increased Volume and Reduced Revenues			
	Freight Rate	Volume	Revenue
Class I	1¢/ton-mile	100 bil. ton-miles	$1.000 bil.
Class II	6¢/ton-mile	50 bil. ton-miles	3.000
		150 bil. ton-miles	4.000
10% increase across-the-board			
Class I	1.1¢/ton-mile	112 bil. ton-miles	$1.232 bil.
Class II	6.6¢/ton-mile	41 bil. ton-miles	2.706 bil.
		153 bil. ton-miles	3.938 bil.
Average	2.57¢	+2%	−1.5%

increased because of the decline in the share of the overhead burden carried by the vanishing high-rated traffic. Rates paid by the preferred traffic have now been increased to a level higher than they would have been if there had been no attempt to tax some shippers for the benefit of the preferred traffic.

The ICC, in its attempt to favor low volume shippers, suppressed the railroads' initial attempts to institute multi-car and trainload discounts for volume shipments.[19] The result has been that much of this large volume traffic has now moved to pipelines and barges. Low volume shippers, as a consequence, are now paying higher rates than they would have if the ICC had allowed some so-called discrimination in favor of large volume shippers. The supposedly scandalous behavior of the railroads in the nineteenth century in giving rebates to large shippers was simply an attempt to hold traffic which would have been lost without the rebates.

The ICC has now allowed train load volume discounts on coal since the electric utilities would have built slurry pipe lines and high voltage transmission lines from mine mouth generating plants if this had not been done. If volume rates had been allowed when railroads first requested them, there would be far more traffic on railroads today, less overhead or burden per unit of traffic, and lower current prices to the shippers Congress and the ICC were trying to subsidize.

Who Has Benefited from Regulation

The value-of-service rate-making principle which has been enforced by the ICC is one designed to extort monopoly returns from the carriage of high-value commodities. Since the evidence indicates that low volume shippers and low-value commodities have not benefited from the monopoly returns extracted from some shippers, who has received these returns? Certainly investors in railroads have not received them! The return on railroad investment has averaged less than five percent for at least the past 45 years. The monopoly profits made on some transportation business appear to have gone almost entirely to members of labor unions, to labor union officers, and to subsidizing the employment of unneeded employees.

In this period in which trucking regulation was instituted and in which strong support was given to the unionization of employees (1929–1947), average earnings of employees in the highway freight and warehousing industry rose by 135 percent. This may be compared with the 86 percent rise in the annual earnings of the average employee in all private industry. I would estimate that by 1947, employees in the regulated trucking industry were being overpaid by at least 10 percent. By 1966, the extent of overpayment had grown to at least 15 percent.

In an industry whose wage bill exceeds $6 billion, this means that overpayment of employees consumes $800 million of the industry's revenues. Since profits in common carrier trucking were on the order of $300 million in 1966, employees of the industry received about three times as much in *overpayment* as investors received as a return on their capital. Certainly not as much as half of the return to trucking companies could conceivably be considered as monopoly profits conferred by the ICC. Using a maximum estimate of the monopoly profits of investors and a minimum estimate of the monopoly profits of unionized employees, employees received five times the amount of monopoly profits as investors in regulated trucking companies. The example of this one mode indicates that if any monopoly returns are being earned in the transportation industry, practically all of it goes to the employees.

In the railroad industry, investors as a whole obtain no monopoly profits. Their capital is earning less than it could have earned in alternative uses. Employees probably receive about $600 million in overpayment for their services, although a major part of this may be regarded as coming at the expense of railroad investors rather than at the expense of shippers. Monopoly profits extracted from some rail shippers by the railroad industry are practically all consumed in providing unneeded services (services worth less than their cost) and in employing unneeded employees. The railroad industry has estimated that it has been paying $500 million per year for unneeded employees (for firemen who do not tend fires, brakemen who do no braking, yard crews who do no yard work, and so on). If the experience of the Florida East Coast Railroad in operating its road since it was struck is any guide, $500 million is a great underestimate of what the railroad industry has been paying for unneeded employees. The figure should be at least double this amount for employees used in freight service alone.

Since federally regulated truckers and railroads do over 90 percent of the business (by dollar volume) done by federally regulated freight carriers, the extraction of monopoly returns to overcompensate trucking employees and to employ unneeded workers in the railroad industry means that most of our common carrier freight services have been overpriced by at least 10 percent. Given value-of-service rate-making, part of the services offered by common carriers has been very greatly overpriced (with the result that some rates came to be called "phantom" rates —rates for traffic which ceased to exist because the rate was so high).

These very high rates for some kinds of business drove this kind of business off the common carriers. The growth of private carriage and the decline of common carriage in the past 35 years has been a result of this regulatory policy—a policy which operated as if the ICC regulated portion of the industry were a total monopoly when, at best, it was only a partial monopoly.

The Costs of Regulation

To conclude this analysis, let us sum up the costs imposed on our nation by the cartelization and monopolization of the transportation industry under the aegis of government.

First, we are using approximately one billion dollars worth of labor services in the railroad industry which are totally wasted. These services could be producing products for us worth one billion dollars. Instead, they are producing nothing. These unneeded laborers would not be employed in the rail industry if they could not have been paid for—and they could not have been in the absence of monopolistic prices set on some traffic by the ICC.

Second, we are overpaying employees in trucking, railroading, and airlining at least another billion dollars. If this overpayment were simply a transfer of income from one group to another, we might regard it as inequitable, but not as wasteful or uneconomic. Inasmuch as these overpaid employees are in the upper half of the population in terms of status measured by income, and a major part of their overpayment is at the expense of the poorer half of the population, we may be particularly resentful of such inequity. However, as a professional economist, I have nothing to say on this point.

As an economist, I should point out that the overpayment of employees in transportation causes other results besides a simple transfer of income from the poor to the rich. The $40,000 a year airline pilot and the $20,000 a year milk truck driver can receive these rates of pay only because many transportation services are over-priced. The over-pricing restricts the rate of purchase of these services, prevents resources (manpower and capital) from being used in the most productive way, and causes a loss in net national income because much goes unproduced which would otherwise be turned out. Of the 15 billion dollars worth of common carriage trucking services purchased each year, about $10 billion would not be purchased if railroads were allowed to reduce their rates on high-rated traffic and innovate special services at premium rates. If this traffic moved by rail, the job could be done with the expenditure of about $3 billion per year of manpower, fuel, and material instead of $10 billion. This would mean a saving of $7 billion a year. It would be possible to add that amount of housing, schooling, medical services, research, recreation, and so on, to our total output of goods and services if we did not waste these resources.

These are the major wastes caused by transportation regulation. We could add various amounts resulting from uneconomic locations chosen to economize on over-priced transportation, uneconomic airline scheduling which results from minimum fare regulation, etc. To the eight billion dollars of waste described above, these would add approximately two billion dollars more.

This is the cost of only one set of monopolies fostered by the government. If we were to add the costs resulting from the cartels in agriculture operated by the Department of Agriculture, the costs of monopolies by license and franchise such as taxi, utility, barber, electrician, plumber, medical, and others, the total cost would come to over $50 billion per year.

I would estimate, then, that our governmentally fostered and supported monopolies cost the country $50 billion per year. In return, we have our freedom to choose our occupation restricted, the value of corrupting civil servants and Congressmen increased, and a larger poverty problem on which to work. I, for one, am willing to give up these doubtful values produced by regulation in order to increase our national income by $50 billion or to increase the leisure time available for the pursuit of truth, beauty, and goodness by 15 billion hours.

Notes

Professor Yale Brozen is one of the most distinguished members of the Chicago school of economics. His articles have appeared in *The Journal of Law and Economics, The American Economic Review, Econometrica, Land Economics, Ethics, Social Research, Il Politico, Political Science Quarterly, Revista Brasileira de Economia, Saturday Review, Barron's, New Individualist Review, The Intercollegiate Review, The Freeman, Reason,* etc. He is professor of business economics at the Graduate School of Business, University of Chicago.

"Is Government the Source of Monopoly?" is reprinted with permission from the *Intercollegiate Review* (Winter 1968–69).

1. The quotation is from pp. 160–161 of *The King's Peace* (Collins, 1960). Permission to reproduce the passage has been given by Miss Wedgwood.

2. D. E. Kaun, "Minimum Wages, Factor Substitution and the Marginal Producer," *Quarterly Journal of Economics*, August 1965.

3. G. W. Hilton, "Barriers to Competitive Ratemaking," *I.C.C. Practitioners Journal*, June 1962; C. D. Stone, "ICC: Some Reminiscences on the Future of American Transportation," *New Individualist Review*, Spring 1963.

4. S. Peltzman, "CAB: Freedom from Competition," *New Individualist Review*, Spring 1963.

5. John S. McGee, "Ocean Freight Rate Conferences and the American Merchant Marine," *The University of Chicago Law Review*, Winter 1960 (Vol. 27, No. 2).

6. Donald Harper, *Economic Regulation of the Motor Trucking Industry by States* (Urbana, 1959).

7. Stephen Sobotka, *The Operation and Regulation of Taxicabs in the City of Chicago* (Evanston: Transportation Center, 1958).

8. Paul MacAvoy, *Truck Line Railroad Cartels and the Interstate Commerce Commission 1870–1900: A Case Study of the Effects of Regulation on Price* (multilith, 1963).

9. Department of Agriculture estimates reported in "Problems of the Railroads," Hearings before the Subcommittee on Surface Transportation of the Committee on Interstate and Foreign Commerce (U.S. Senate, 88th Congress, Second Session, 1958) p. 2103.

10. "The Great U.S. Freight Cartel," *Fortune*, January 1957. S. P. Huntington, "The Marasmus of the Interstate Commerce Commission," *Yale Law Journal*, 1952.

11. P. Locklin, *Economics of Transportation* (Richard D. Irwin, Homewood, Illinois, Sixth edition, 1966).

12. Robert A. Nelson, "Interest Conflicts in Transportation," *Journal of Business*, April 1964. Robert A. Nelson, "Rate-Making in Transportation—Congressional Intent," *Duke Law Journal*, 1960.

13. R. W. Gerwig, "Natural Gas Production: A Study of the Cost of Regulation," *Journal of Law and Economics*, October 1962.

14. Y. Brozen, "The New Competition—International Markets: How Should We Adapt?" *Journal of Business*, October 1960.

15. Y. Brozen, "Minimum Wage Rates and Household Workers," *Journal of Law and Economics*, October 1962.

16. Y. Brozen, "The Role of Open Markets in Coordinating and Directing Economic Activity," in *Futures Trading Seminar* (Mimir Publishers, Inc. Madison, Wis., 1966).

17. D. G. Johnson, "Output and Income Effects of Reducing the Farm Labor Force," *Journal of Farm Economics*, November 1960.

18. Joel Segall, "The Propagation of Bulldozers," *Journal of Business*, October 1965, an article reviewing Martin Anderson, *The Federal Bulldozer* (Cambridge, MIT Press, 1964).

19. Paul W. MacAvoy and James Sloss, *Interstate Commerce Commission Regulation of Technical Change: The Case of Unit Trains of Coal to the Eastern Seaboard* (multilith, 1965).

D. T. Armentano

10

Capitalism and the Antitrust Laws

LIBERTARIANS DO NOT need to be told at length that laissez-faire capitalism and antitrust are philosophically incompatible. Capitalism is a social system founded on the principle of private ownership and voluntary exchange. Antitrust is a set of laws either restricting or prohibiting unpopular but, nonetheless, *voluntary* uses of private property[1]. Since antitrust explicitly interferes with private willing exchange, it is completely antithetical to the concept of capitalism.

Non-libertarians (which means just about everyone we deal with as workers, teachers, or businessmen) are not so easily convinced of the antithesis outlined above. Almost all economists, for example, have held that a capitalist economic system cannot exist without antitrust to protect it. They have accepted the notion that free-market capitalism has a fatal "flaw," an inherent tendency to eat itself up, to destroy the very essence of its own economic mechanism: business competition. And they point to the latter part of the nineteenth century in America as empirical proof of their theory[2].

Capitalism and Competition

Since Adam Smith, economists have sought to justify their belief in capitalistic economic systems by falling back on "competition." It was competition that would keep business costs and prices down and lead greedy businessmen, as if by some "invisible hand," to maximize the public's economic interest. Government intervention, not opposed in principle, was unnecessary in such situations since competition was "regulating the allocation of scarce resources."

If competition could not exist, however, or if competition tended toward monopoly, the economist's classic utilitarian defense for the free market collapsed. A truly free, unhampered market implied a market *free of all governmental regulation.* Yet, if the declining competition thesis was correct, a competitive capitalism was impossible unless the state itself, through antitrust legislation perhaps, sought to maintain competition. Thus those who would support capitalism were pushed into the ironical position of having to support active governmental intervention in the economy to keep it competitive—a blatant contradiction in terms. Yet almost all economists have (somehow) coexisted with such a contradiction and have held such a position on monopoly, competition, and antitrust. The intellectual support for a competitive capitalism without antitrust is nonexistent in the academic community.

Can the "conventional wisdom" and political economy of more than a half-century be wrong on this crucial issue? Of course it can. The "declining competition" thesis as outlined above has no basis in logical theory or empirical fact. The entire argument is premised on mighty assumptions that are not true. It is not true that there is an inherent tendency for competition to break down in a truly free market[3] or, accordingly, that actual business competition was declining in the latter part of the nineteenth century. And it is also not true, emphatically not true, that an examination of the leading antitrust cases in business history demonstrates that active governmental intervention is necessary to "preserve competition."

Those who hold that competition was declining in the nineteenth century have a confused notion of business competition (as will be demonstrated below) and have never studied the empirical data of that period with respect to costs, prices, outputs, or any other relevant benchmark of economic performance. And those who hold that antitrust theory is sound or that antitrust cases demonstrate the need for and justify the existence of the antitrust laws have never taken the time actually to read the leading cases in antitrust history. To "believe" in antitrust is never to have read a leading antitrust case.

While there are some excellent revisionist histories of the nineteenth century (see, for example, Gabriel Kolko's *The Triumph of Conservatism*, originally published by Macmillan in 1963), the theory and practice of antitrust has yet to be formally challenged. This author will soon provide that challenge when Arlington House of New Rochelle,

New York, publishes his volume titled, *The Myths of Antitrust: Economic Theory and Legal Cases*[4]. As a brief introduction to the more formal work, it might be interesting to explore some basic antitrust dogmas.

Antitrust Theory

Antitrust theory is founded rock-bottom on an admittedly impossible concept: *pure competition*. If you are unfamiliar with the term, you must first forget everything that you know about real-world business rivalry, since *pure competition* has nothing at all to do with that. Instead, pure competition is that friction-less, profit-less, never-never land, where strange robot-like firms produce "homogeneous" products at prices that just equal the marginal costs of production and the minimum average cost of production[5].

Economists by and large rejoice at such an occurence and agree that it is a wonderful state of affairs. For in this purely competitive situation, the firms involved would not have any "price control" or "monopoly power" by which they might "exploit" the unsuspecting consumer. Hence, consumer welfare is being "optimized" and the economy is functioning "efficiently."

Departures from this blissful state of affairs are unanimously regarded as movements away from "consumer optimality" and, accordingly, movements toward the opposite of pure competition: *monopoly*. As business firms get larger, as they merge perhaps, and as they begin to innovate, and advertise, and differentiate their products, and acquire locational and promotional advantages, and engage in interdependent rivalry for the consumers' dollars, *they wreck pure competition and any chance at it*. The market place, economists have concluded, is becoming less competitive. And that, as you may realize by now, is the sort of "competition" that was "declining" in the latter part of the nineteenth century!

The concept of pure competition is the most destructive "straw man" in all economics and one of the most destructive in all political economy. The intellectual charade goes something like this (and every student of economics has heard it at one time or another): the free market system would be ideal if pure competition existed; pure competition does not or cannot exist; a free market system is impossible, i.e., government regulation is an absolute necessity[6]. Enter antitrust on a white charger. A convenient and cute bit of "logic" but absolute nonsense, and don't let your economics professor forget it or get away with it.

Pure competition is impossible in reality, and we wouldn't want it even if it could exist. The concept was conceived by the mathematically oriented classical economists because it lent itself to precise mathematical analysis. Any resemblance between the concept and reality or reality-oriented competition between flesh-and-blood firms was purely coincidental. And something that cannot exist in reality, and would not be desirable even if it could, cannot rationally be used as a "standard" to measure "resource misallocation" or "monopoly power." Yet antitrust is founded entirely on this sort of approach, and it is the only *economic* rationalization ever offered for antitrust activity.

Antitrust History

The so-called empirical case for antitrust is worse—if that is possible—than the theoretical approach outlined above. A long accepted dogma in the area of governmental regulation of business is that the "classic" monopoly cases of antitrust history clearly demonstrate the need for and justify the existence of the antitrust laws. The impression certainly created by all the leading textbooks on this subject is that the "trusts" indicted in the past were (as the textbook theory suggests) actually raising prices, lowering outputs, exploiting suppliers, driving competitors from the market through predatory practices and generally lowering consumer welfare[7]. Ironically, few if any of these leading texts provide the student of antitrust with the necessary empirical information that might allow an independent judgment as to the relative conduct and performance of these "monopolies." The empirical evidence is not provided, this author has discovered, because it would completely destroy the antitrust myth and expose antitrust as a complete hoax. *The Myths of Antitrust* will reveal this information in systematic detail for *all* the leading cases in antitrust under *all* the important sections of the antitrust laws. The following is the briefest possible peek under the window shade of antitrust.

There are six leading "monopoly" cases in antitrust history. These cases involve *Standard Oil* in 1911, *American Tobacco* in 1911, *United States Steel* in 1920, *Alcoa* in 1945, *United Shoe Machinery* in 1953 and *DuPont* in 1957[8]. If these trusts were abusing consumers or competitors in the marketplace, surely the information presented at Court in these long cases would reveal such behavior.

Without exception, however, the Court record in each of these classic antitrust cases reveals no such thing[9]. All the firms involved were actually lowering prices, expanding outputs, engaging in research and innovation at a rapid rate, and not, as a general rule, employing predatory practices toward their competition. In a word, the firms' actions in the market were entirely consistent with competitive and not monopolistic behavior, and the Court's own records confirm this. Yet the student of antitrust, let alone the general student of business history, cannot become aware of these facts by reading the standard textbook approach to antitrust. As mentioned before, the standard texts conveniently do not provide such information.

Price Fixing

Antitrust cases dealing with so-called "price fixing" are treated even worse. Economists so dislike price collusion that their hatred has blurred their objective treatment of such cases. Students are led to assume that antitrust history contains ample empirical proof that businessmen can successfully collude and raise prices above competitive levels. Actually antitrust history reveals no such thing.

The author has written elsewhere of the inherent difficulties associated with price collusion in a free market[10]. It should only be noted here that price fixing antitrust cases illustrate the theoretical argument of that article, namely, that *successful "conspiracy" is impossible without government intervention*. Although it may be difficult to believe, the leading price fixing antitrust cases *do not involve successful price fixing*.

As an illustration, take the most famous price fixing case in all business history, the electrical equipment conspiracy of the late 1950s. The case, as you may remember, involved some of America's leading corporations such as General Electric, Westinghouse, Allis-Chalmers, Federal Pacific, and many others. The charge was that they had "raised, fixed, and maintained" unreasonable prices and that they had "restrained, suppressed, and eliminated" price competition on many important electrical products.

Was there an elaborate "conspiracy" to restrain trade with respect to price competition in the industry? Of course there was. But, different question, did the conspiracy raise, fix, and maintain unreasonable prices and suppress price competition between the "conspirators"? The answer is an emphatic *NO*, not at all. No one can read the Hearings on Administered Prices, *Price-Fixing and Bid-Rigging in the Electrical Manufacturing Industry*, held by the United States Senate Committee on the Judiciary in the spring of 1961, without being overwhelmed by two facts: 1) there was clear evidence of meetings among various firms to "do something" about prices; 2) the meetings were, on balance, "a complete waste of time." The firms were eventually convicted (like many firms before them) for *having* what the Court refers to as a "conspiracy" and *not* for successfully fixing prices. Firms cannot defend themselves in a "price fixing case," therefore, by arguing that the prices were not fixed; that sort of information is "immaterial" at Court in such cases.

Merger

The most exciting (and, therefore, saddest) area of antitrust today is mergers. Most economists dislike mergers, particularly large ones, since they hold the market structure approach to "measuring" competition. They mistakenly assume that the number of firms in a "market," or the relative size of the firms, is the crucial determinant of competitive behavior. Since mergers reduce numbers and increase relative size (concentration), some economists argue that they automatically reduce competition. The Courts, unfortunately, have simply adopted this cute, kneejerk approach to merger and competition. In doing so, they have rendered some of the most blatantly absurd decisions in all antitrust.

The *Brown Shoe* case of 1962 is a good illustration of this argument. The Supreme Court finally ordered Brown Shoe to divest themselves of Kinney Shoes since the merger of the two companies would have, in fact, made competition *more vigorous* in the shoe industry. By the Court's own admission, the merger would have allowed specific economies in the sale of shoes that were likely to be passed along to Brown's customers[11]. But since Brown's competitors might then have been at a competitive disadvantage, and since the Court's myopic view of mergers and competition would not have permitted similar mergers between competitors to realize similar economies, the Brown merger had to be dissolved. Thus consumers were explicitly deprived of shoe purchasing economies because the Court, with much academic advice, thought it important to preserve the existing market structure in the shoe industry for its own sake. Absurd; yet similar decisions in similar cases are rendered almost daily.

Present merger policy is even more irrational, if that is possible to imagine. The Justice Department has argued in some very recent cases that it is "concentration in the American economy" (not concentration in any given industry or market) and reductions in "potential competition" (not actual competition!) that should determine the legality of particular mergers[12]. Although the Lower Court cases decided so far have rejected such nonsense, that such wonderland notions can be offered as serious theory is enough to indicate the present intellectual state of antitrust. Antitrust today is more of a religion, a mystical experience, than anything else; yet the juggernaut rolls on through the business system.

Conclusion

Is there a "monopoly problem" in the American business system? Of course there is, but it has nothing to do with antitrust. In fact the monopolistic situations in the American economy have been, for the most part, immune from antitrust anyway. I am, of course, referring to the monopoly or cartel-type arrangements maintained by the Interstate Commerce Commission, the Federal Communications Commission, the Federal Power Commission, the all too numerous state regulatory commissions, and other regulatory authorities. The cartels that these governmental agencies protect and shield from competition could not last a week without such protection; the forces of the free market would take them apart immediately. Indeed, these industries prove the very point of this article, that is, that "monopoly" is not a free market problem at all, and that antitrust does not and has not restored "competition" to the American marketplace. To end the "monopoly problem" in America, end *all* governmental involvement in economic affairs, including antitrust.

Notes and References

D. T. Armentano teaches economics at the University of Hartford. He wrote *The Myths of Antitrust*. He has written for *Reason*, *The Freeman* and various scholarly journals.

"Capitalism and the Antitrust Laws" is reprinted with permission from *Reason* (January 1972).

1. The most important antitrust statutes are: The Sherman Antitrust Act of 1890; the Clayton Act of 1914; the Federal Trade Commission Act of 1914; the Robinson—Patman Act of 1936; and the Celler—Kefauver Antimerger Act of 1950. Under certain circumstances that may, supposedly, reduce "competition," these laws restrict attempts to "restrain trade," "monopolize," "price discriminate," engage in "tying agreements" and "merge."

2. For a typical (and much respected) view of this position see Joseph W. McGuire's *Business and Society*, McGraw-Hill, 1963.

3. See, of course, the works of von Mises and Rothbard or, for a brief argument along these lines, see Rod Manis' "Free Enterprise and the Monopoly Myth," *Reason*, Vol. 3, No. 6, September 1971.

4. Scheduled for publication in May 1972.

5. For an elaboration of this position, see any micro-economics text or, specifically, Richard H. Leftwich, *The Price System and Resource Allocation*, Fourth Edition, The Dryden Press, 1970.

6. For a recent account of exactly this sort of "argument," see Milton H. Seencer's *Contemporary Economics*, Worth Publishing, Inc., 1971, p. 327.

7. Probably the best selling college text in "Government and Business" courses is Clair Wilcox's *Public Policies toward Business*, Irwin, 1971. See this particular text for *all* the distortions and misrepresentations suggested in this article.

8. For a brief review of these cases see my article, "The Antitrust Hoax," *The Individualist*, January 1971.

9. For a detailed history of the American Tobacco Company and the tobacco industry prior to the antitrust case in 1911, see my article "Antitrust History: The American Tobacco Case of 1911," *The Freeman*, March 1971.

10. "The Inherent Weakness of Price Collusion," *The Freeman*, January 1970.

11. *Brown Shoe Company v. United States*, 370 U.S. 294. See, specifically, p. 344.

12. See the Justice Department's argument in their recent suits against International Telephone and Telegraph's purchase of the Grinnell and Canteen Corporations. Or see *The Wall Street Journal*, 6 July 1971.

Lynn Kinsky

11

The FDA and Drug Research

Introduction

How do you know that the drugs you take are safe? Most people, in response to this question would reply—"Well—the *government* takes care of it. I don't have to worry . . . do I?" Few people really have any idea *how* the government goes about this task, and still less idea whether the job it does is a good one. The agency charged with the responsibility for controlling the drug industry is the Food and Drug Administration (FDA). The Nader report on the FDA covered only regulation of foods; the 292-page report gives strong evidence to support its charges that the FDA, having become a political rather than a scientific entity, is failing miserably at this task:

> *The FDA is not a happy place for scientists to work in . . . Several researchers showed the students "atrocity logs" in which they kept detailed accounts of "assaults on their scientific integrity" . . . The most common complaint was that the FDA "constantly interferes" with medium and long range research projects, at least partly from fear that the results will embarrass the agency. The students also criticized the FDA for retaliating against scientists who disagree with its positions.* [1]

In an attempt to learn whether the FDA does any better at assuring safe drugs than it does at assuring safe food, the editor of this magazine requested persons connected with the drug industry to relate their experiences in dealing with the FDA. The president of a small drug firm, among other comments, wrote the following:

177

Our company, as are the others, is continually harassed on all sorts of nonsensical inspections by FDA. They take up large amounts of executive and employee time, and generally amount to nothing. The ordinary FDA inspector has become a snooper, assiduously trying to find something he can pin on a drug company at any time, with no apparent thought of the avowed purpose of FDA to cause better drugs to be sold. Thus it is necessary to stay with these boys the whole time they are in the drug plant, for once alone they will rummage through the most personal desk drawers and correspondence. Then if they get thrown out after being caught rifling someone's desk, they go to no end in attempting to pin false criminal charges on the man who threw them out, as was the case of a friend of mine in St. Louis; they well knew that he wouldn't be convicted in court, but also knew that it would cost him many thousands of dollars which he could ill afford to spend.

This man is obviously very bitter about the way a *political* agency is controlling his business. Yet is there any alternative way of ensuring that people are not poisoned or cheated by dangerous or worthless drugs? To answer this question requires an examination of what drugs are, how they are developed, how they are marketed and prescribed, and how the FDA regulates them. Unlike many other industries, where regulations were frequently *asked* for by the established firms, the modern drug industry came into being after the federal drug regulations had already been established, primarily to deal with foods. Thus, since there has never really been an unregulated drug market in the United States, it is not surprising that few people have ever considered alternatives to the present system.

A drug can be defined as any non-[food] substance designated to produce some change of body chemistry on a molecular level in a living entity. So far as government regulatory agencies are concerned, drugs fall into two main categories: proprietary drugs, which are sold over the counter without a prescription, and ethical drugs, which are sold only by prescription. Our main concern here will be with ethical drugs.

The definition of a drug says nothing about the specific *kind* of change in body chemistry that it may produce. A drug may cure disease —or cause it, alleviate pain—or create it. Drugs may heighten or decrease or alter consciousness, abate or accentuate psychological reactions, rearrange genetic makeup, or cause death. Whatever can be done to a human body, eventually drugs could probably be created to do it.

To this date, there is no such thing as a "perfect drug." Differences in human physiology make even the most innocuous drug a potential killer for some people, while certain drugs that mean certain death for "normal" people are an absolute necessity for the survival of others. So far as physiology—and concomitant reaction to drugs—is concerned, all [people] are created unequal.

Thus aspirin, which by any standards is man's safest pain-killer, can be dangerous to a minority with a certain genetic background. And while large doses of water can cause death in a "normal" person, they mean life for the [person] with diabetes insipidus.

Nor are the effects of many drugs independent of dosage. Some drugs reach a plateau of dosage, beyond which further administration is useless and generally harmful. A standard dose of aspirin (.65 grams or two tablets), for example, is sufficient to reduce fever, but a larger dose won't help, and may cause gastrointestinal bleeding. Other drugs have no such plateau. The barbiturates, for example, tranquilize at low levels, sedate at moderate levels, and, at high levels, produce coma and death.

Sometimes, drugs taken in conjunction with other drugs can produce results quite different from those of either drug alone. A well known example is that of alcohol and barbiturates, a mixture that is an American suicide favorite.

When evaluating drugs, physicians use a therapeutic index: toxic dosage/pharmacological dosage.[2] If the ratio is large the drug is fairly safe to use; if small, the dosage must be carefully controlled. (On the other hand, some drugs take advantage of a low ratio to produce special effects. Anti-cancer drugs, with a ratio of [almost] unity, capitalize on the fact that cancerous cells absorb chemicals quicker than normal cells. The tricky and delicate work involves poisoning the malignant cells without killing the organism with the malignant cells.)

The therapeutic index is not sufficient in itself for drug prescription because, as we have pointed out, drug reaction differs from individual to individual, not only quantitatively, but qualitatively as well. One [person's] medicine may be another's poison. To illustrate: oral contraceptive users have a death rate of 22.3 per million woman years from thromboembolism (fatal blood clot)[3]—Diabinase (anti-diabetic drug) causes jaundice at a rate of 4 cases per 1,000[4]—Chloromycetin causes fatal anemia in 1 per 225,000.[5]

Some of the factors that account for varied or unanticipated reaction to a drug include genetic differences, aging, sex, multiple or undetected disease, acquired reactions and tolerances developed from previous drugs, other drugs a patient may be taking, psychosomatic disturbances, reactions and tolerances developed from environmental conditions, such as heavy doses of various industrial pollutants, and physical states, such as pregnancy.

There are two types of adverse reactions to drugs: side effects and idiosyncrasies. If most people respond to a drug with an unwanted reaction, this is called a side effect. If only a few do, this is termed an idiosyncrasy. What a drug firm tries to do (in theory), through research, is produce drugs that produce no side effects, while developing tests that alert doctors to the presence of genetic or other differences in patients that could produce adverse reactions. "Have you ever had penicillin before?" your doctor asks you, during a recent [visit] for the flu. He's checking to see that you don't have a sensitivity to the drug before he prescribes it.

Much current controversy and alarm centers around bad drug effects that are not [as] immediately evident as penicillin sensitivity or blood clots from oral contraceptives. Thalidomide, one of a class of drugs known as teratogens that act directly on embryos, is a sedative, which if taken between days 20 and 40 of pregnancy, results in an infant with deformities,while the mother remains totally unaffected except for the sedation effects.

More subtle still are the mutagens[6] which attack a cell's genetic material, possibly causing cancer if somatic (body) cells are affected, or birth defects if germinal (sex) cells are affected. Among some suspected mutagens are LSD, caffein, cyclamate, sodium nitrite, and tobacco smoke components.

The problem of adverse drug reaction is a central one, not only to pharmaceutical research and retailing and the medical profession, but is the core of the rationale for the existence and activities of the FDA. People—and thus the bureaucrats of the FDA—are concerned about drug effectiveness and safety.

Drug Research

Every company doing research has a program detailing what type of drugs it wants developed. The programs are based on estimates of probable results, which are in turn based on accumulated research data, available personnel and their specialties, and facilities. Their decisions are also based on estimates of profitability, and likelihood of government regulation, restriction, or delay on domestic or foreign markets.

Because of economic and technological advantages, companies often develop specialties in addition to their standard lines of research. Syntex, for example, concentrates on hormones—Smith, Line, and French, mind drugs—Sandoz, headache remedies.

Seeing the combination of a large market and the relative likelihood of producing a drug to capture that market, a company may attempt to cure some specific disease. Drugs for heart disease, birth control, mental illness, and arthritis are examples of such attempts. A cure for cancer, on the other hand, although there is a market, because so little is known of cancer's cause, would today more likely come by accident than by systematic research.

Generally, companies do not seek out cures for rare disease. Instead, most progress in this area comes either by accident or through the efforts of university research labs, which are often supported by grants from pharmaceutical firms.[7] These specialized drugs are marketed at a fraction of actual cost, the loss written off to good will, scientific reputation, and concern for human suffering. If the company can obtain a broad enough patent, other more profitable drugs produced during the same project can sometimes recap such losses.

Once an area of research emphasis is chosen, the work of the organic chemist begins. He examines what is known of successful drugs in the area of concern; he then either devises syntheses of slightly different compounds (a process known as molecular modification), or produces radically different compounds until he finds one that looks promising, which he determines via animal testing, proceeding then to further molecular modifications. Twenty-five years ago, devising a new drug was mostly a random affair often involving animal tests ("screening") on any handy chemical, often plant extracts. Today, chemistry and pharmacology have progressed to a point where rational, ordered inquiries are possible. The chemist has large quantities of data which indicate what general chemical structure a drug must have to produce a particular effect. Even so, research and development of a new drug averages about seven million dollars and requires five or six years from conception to market.[8] Please keep these figures, five years and seven million dollars, firmly in mind, for they are extremely significant in judging the actual and probable effects of government regulation on pharmaceutical research and retail.

Once a chemist has produced a reasonable drug prospect (perhaps 30–50 a year) he sends it to the biologists and pharmacologists for animal screening. The first tests establish dose and toxicity levels in the particular experimental animal used, and provide a general idea what biological effects the drug might have. The drug is then screened for specific effect both on the basis of the results of the first series of screens and what the chemist is seeking. These specific tests can be expensive; often specially bred or modified animals and time consuming, involved procedures are required.

If the drug passes the screens, (a rare occurence), it is then subjected to long term toxicity and teratrongenic tests in several species of animal (including primates). Here is where less reputable firms have been known to cut costs and compromise safety. Only after a drug has come through this process does a reputable drug firm release it for human testing.

Under current Investigational New Drugs (IND) regulations, before humans can use the new drug, or more precisely, before a drug company is allowed to give it to them, an application must be filed with the FDA that sets forth all knowledge of the drug and includes an outline of planned investigation, a summary of investigators' qualifications, and so forth. The investigator must also promise to keep the required records, permit inspections, comply with patient-consent rules. If the proper reports are not made, or if there is any indication that the drug is unsafe or ineffective, the FDA may halt the investigation.[9] If a company halts a project of its own initiative, it must give account to the FDA.

The investigation's first step is usually to establish dose and toxicity level, with prisoners and medical students often the volunteers. Later the drug is tested on a small group of patients, primarily with their knowledge and consent (although consent is not required by either law or medical ethics if the physician doesn't think it is in the patient's best interest to know he is receiving an experimental drug), and in the final stages before full marketing the study is broadened to include a large number of physicians and patients.

Once a manufacturer has established a drug's safety and effectiveness to his own satisfaction, he can file a New Drug Application with the FDA and see if it meets their acceptance. The material of an application can fill several volumes. In the past, processing time for a NDA was several months, but, as paperwork piles up, it is increasing. The quantity of new drugs receiving approval each year, therefore, whether original formulations or combinations of old drugs, or molecular modifications of patented drugs, is dwindling.[10]

History of the FDA

The FDA was created in response to the greed or dishonesty of many nineteenth century food producers and the ability of modern science to both aid them and expose them. As the transportation network grew in the U.S. after the Civil War and canned and packaged foods became more common, the manufacturer became more remote from his customers both in physical distance and in the complexity of production. Science provided chemicals to change flavors, prevent spoilage, enhance colors, etc., and while these made possible the enjoyment of all foods in all places, regardless of season, they also made fraud much easier. Strawberry jam could be made without strawberries, rotten eggs could be deodorized and rancid butter could be revived.[11] Not surprisingly the first pressure for anti-adulteration laws came from farmers who saw their market for real eggs, butter, etc. cut by the cheaper fraudulent stuff—state and federal departments of agriculture soon hired chemists to detect product fraud. One of these chemists— Harvey Washington Wiley—proved to be a real crusader, making even Ralph Nader pale by comparison. Through speeches, books, and sheer force of personality he managed to unite the consumers (who were fearful of fraud and poison) and the manufacturers (who feared the competition of the adulterers and sensed the public's growing mistrust of all producers) behind several omnibus food and drug bills culminating—largely as a result of Upton Sinclair's novel *The Jungle*[12]—in the Pure Food and Drugs Act of 1906 (also known as the Wiley Act). This Act established the FDA, with Wiley as its director, to protect the consumer from injury, deception, and fraud: it had wide police powers to induce compliance with the law (which was amended frequently, always in the direction of greater control). Dr. Wiley didn't stay with the FDA for very long—in 1908 he conducted some research which proved to him that benzoate of soda and saccharin were harmful and he requested President Roosevelt to ban their use in food and drugs. President Roosevelt had used saccharin himself—"President Roosevelt characterized Dr. Wiley's position in these words: 'Anybody who says saccharin is injurious to health is an idiot,'"[12] and he designated a board to run the FDA. (Dr. Wiley joined the staff of *Good Housekeeping* magazine.)

The next major revision of the Food and Drug Act came in 1938, again after a period of crusading, led mainly by Consumers' Research organization and the FDA itself. But the S. E. Massengill Company of Tennessee is generally conceded most of the credit—in 1937 their "Elixir of Sulfanilamide" came on the market, and while their chief chemist had tested the mixture of diethylene glycol (a relative of permanent antifreeze) and sulfanilamide for appearance, flavor and fragrance, he had neglected to test it for safety: 107 people, mainly children, died from the 11-3/4 gallons dispensed (the chemist made it 108 with his suicide). The FDA seized the rest of the manufactured supply because it was falsely labeled—elixir implies an ethyl alcohol solution. The 1938 revision, therefore, "required a manufacturer to test any new drug for safety and report the result to the Food and Drug Administration. The agency also was authorized to remove from the market a drug it could prove to be unsafe."[14] In addition the FTC and FDA were empowered to regulate patent medicine advertising to prevent false or misleading claims.

The most recent major amendments were those introduced by Kefauver and Harris in 1962. Among other things they required that a drug be shown by the manufacturer to be "substantially efficacious" as well as safe; the FDA, however, was denied the power to sit in judgement of efficacy—the law dealt only with the quantity of evidence a manufacturer must supply before marketing a new drug. A far-sighted observer commented at the time: "Once more we find the Congress refusing to abridge the basic philosophy of our drug law by recognizing again that in the long run the physicians of this country must be the judges of a drug's efficacy and of its safety. The Congress, however, has not stopped [the FDA's usurpation of power] and we can certainly look forward to further expansion by the FDA of its jurisdiction in opinion areas, through the promulgation of regulations and various other administrative techniques including the use of the vast punitive sanctions that are at its disposal."[15] In 1966 the FDA had the National Academy of Sciences and the National Research Council (a group of scientists but *not* M.D.s or pharmacists) review nearly 7000 *previously licensed* drugs for effectiveness. By 1969 the NAS-NRC evaluation was completed and at least 90 drugs were ordered to be withdrawn from the market, with many others being severely restricted in their advertising, despite the fact that physicians had been prescribing them for years. In essence the FDA *is* practicing medicine, Congress not withstanding.

In taking these drugs from the market the FDA is using some of the strongest enforcement powers of any government agency. "For any given violation of the Food, Drug and Cosmetic Act, the FDA has a variety of enforcement weapons, from a mere suit for an injunction to an outright seizure of the offending drug before trial and even to criminal prosecution. These remedies can be invoked whether or not the drug itself is safe and effective in fact, for the manufacture of a safe and effective drug by unapproved methods or its marketing with unapproved labeling or advertising is sufficient to violate the Act, whether or not the violation is intentional."[16] The FDA can't lose—a drug manufacturer can't make a cent and he'd better think twice before fighting the FDA, no matter how arbitrary the sanction they have brought against him. In addition those few with the temerity to take the case to court really haven't much chance to win—between 1938 and 1964 only one manufacturer requested a hearing to protest the withdrawal order of a previously approved prescription drug—he lost.[17] (The FDA has very persuasive lawyers—what judge wants to be responsible for thousands of deaths if he OK's the drug against the FDA's judgement?)

The Costs of FDA Protection

The FDA, like many government bureaus, represents a basically sound idea—protection against fraud—perverted by means of political power into a fiefdom which literally *rules* the drug industry, arbitrarily deciding what products to approve and disapprove. Certainly there is a consumer demand for information on the relative safety and effectiveness of drugs; but are the FDA's coercive methods the proper way to provide this information? Emphatically not.

The most important defect lies in the very nature of the FDA as a *political* entity. As such, entrusted with the absolute power of the state, the FDA is subjected to a vast assortment of competing pressures—from Congress, consumer organizations, and drug firms—in the hope that it will come up with a set of rules and regulations which precisely define which drugs are "good" and which are "bad." Yet, as has been shown previously, there exists no preordained dividing line of this sort; the nature of drugs and the nature of human physiology are such that the effectiveness of *any* drug must be described as a continuum or frequency distribution, from "very harmful" through "no effect" through "very beneficial," depending upon the individuals' unique biochemistry, state of age and health, the size of the dosage, etc. Experimentation can and does establish the nature of this distribution of effects; given this knowledge and data on the particular patient in question, the physician can weigh the benefits and risks, and decide on an *individual* basis whether or not it is wise to administer the drug.

But the FDA does not operate in terms of individuals—its concern is with the "public interest," i.e., the supposed welfare of the "population as a whole." For this reason, despite the fact that it is impossible, the FDA seeks to define and enforce a black-and-white judgement that a drug is either "effective" or "ineffective." Attempting to put this impossible aim into practice results in several characteristic modes of FDA behavior:

1. The uppermost concern of the bureaucratic mind is rules and procedures, expressed in countless official forms and paperwork. The inference, in the FDA's case, is that if the bureaucrat does not know how to ensure that a drug is "effective," the next best thing is to require such

a mountain of paperwork that the bureaucrat is "covered" at every possible turn. As a result, since the FDA began requiring "effectiveness" documentation, the length of time it takes to get a New Drug Application processed has *tripled*.[18] Preparing the monumental paperwork adds millions of dollars to a drug firm's research budget—which has the effect of discouraging smaller (perhaps more innovative) firms from even attempting to get new drugs approved. In 1968 only 14 new drugs were approved, compared with 63, 45 and 41 in 1959, 1960 and 1961,[19] the last three years before the "effectiveness" requirement went into effect.

2. A second characteristic of this mentality is the FDA's strongly conservative position with respect to radically new drugs. Since the FDA's black or white verdict on effectiveness is taken by most people as the last word, the bureaucrats are naturally very cautious about which drugs they will "endorse." Thus, promising new drugs which come from sources other than the most prestigious companies or which are based on fundamentally new principles are extremely suspect in the FDA's view. The cases discussed here further on provide some indication of the serious effects of this policy in keeping new drugs from people who would willingly assume the risks associated with their use.

3. The third aspect of the FDA's mentality is merely the ultimate consequence of its simplistic good/bad view of drugs—the forcible intervention in the marketplace to prevent the sale or use of "bad" drugs. The FDA has absolute, unchallengeable power to declare illegal the manufacture, sale, or use of any drug which it deems ineffective by its arbitrary general welfare standards. This means that the essential scientific and medical judgement of the doctor and patient as to the value of a particular drug in a particular case is thrown aside in favor of a government decree, backed up by force. The following cases illustrate the effects of this policy ... DMSO was not discovered by a large prestigious drug firm; it is a common commercial solvent, a byproduct of pulp manufacture, whose medicinal properties were first discovered in 1963 by Robert Herschler of Crown Zellerbach Corp. and Dr. Stanley Jacob of the University of Oregon Medical School. DMSO is applied directly to the skin, rather than orally or by injection; its effectiveness is well-documented for treating bursitis, arthritis, scleroderma (a fatal skin-hardening disease), and useful as a local anesthetic. Most important, there is strong evidence that DMSO is effective against leukemia, cervical cancer, and possibly other types of cancer.[20]

Without warning, however, on Nov. 25, 1965, the FDA banned all clinical testing of DMSO, due to the fact that laboratory dogs, rabbits, and pigs developed changes in the lenses of their eyes when fed huge doses of DMSO. No such changes were found in the eyes of rhesus monkeys, nor in any of the many human patients who had received the drug. No animals developed lens changes when the DMSO was applied to their skins, as it had been with humans, rather than being given orally; moreover, the humans received only 1 percent of the proportional dose which caused the animals' lens damage.

But to the bureaucratic mind in its impossible quest for certainty DMSO was a *dangerous* chemical (i.e. one which the bureaucrats might conceivably be blamed for someday). It was not until a year later, after DMSO was regularly used in Germany and Austria, that the FDA backed off slightly and allowed limited testing to be resumed—under stringent FDA controls requiring each study to be specifically approved in advance. DMSO's developer, Dr. Stanley Jacob, commented, "Under the current law and its interpretation, were the cure for cancer discovered tomorrow, it would not be available as a prescription drug in the United States for at least seven years. How many people would needlessly die of cancer while the drug was going through FDA red tape?"[21]—if in fact it made it through at all.

Thalidomide

Everyone is aware of the FDA's heroic actions in saving America from the deformed babies produced when the tranquilizer is given to pregnant women. Very few people, however, realize the full impact of the FDA's action in this case. The FDA did not merely warn pregnant women; it enacted and enforces a total ban on the sale of thalidomide within the United States—to anyone, male or female, married or single, young or old, for many of whom thalidomide might be the optimum tranquilizer.

But [an] Associated Press story reveals an even more important use of thalidomide which is being kept from the public by the FDA; it appears that thalidomide is useful in treating leprosy. Under a special FDA exemption, with thalidomide donated by the Merrell Co., doctors at the U.S. Public Service Hospital in Louisiana have reported "very successful results" in halting or arresting extreme leprosy reactions which lead to the crippling, deformity, and paralysis associated with the disease. So far the drug has been used on only 22 patients. "If we had sufficient quantities, we probably would use it in more cases," reports Dr. John R. Trautman, the hospital director.[22] The article goes on to say that "the doctors decided to use thalidomide on the basis of other evidence *from other countries* that the drug, despite its bad reputation, is beneficial in halting leprosy reactions." (Italics added) "We shouldn't let something like [the fetus deformities] throw out a medicine completely," states Dr. Carl D. Enna, chief of the hospital's clinical branch.[23] Yet for the duration of the *five year* Louisiana study, thalidomide will continue to be totally banned, everywhere else in the U.S. And people with leprosy will continue to suffer unnecessarily.

Oral Contraceptives

Despite the emotionalism of the ... Senate hearings on the Pill, the fact remains that pregnancy is over *ten times* more dangerous than treatment with oral contraceptives (based on all available figures of comparative death rates per million people).[24] Despite this, in recent years the FDA has imposed more stringent requirements on oral contraceptives than on virtually any other drug. For example, toxicity studies with very high daily doses must be made for seven years in dogs and ten years in monkeys before any female contraceptive agent can be tested on humans. This, despite the opinion of many researchers, including the World Health Organization Scientific Group,[25] that extrapolation of experimental animal data to human females is of questionable value when dealing with contraceptives—due to the animals' different sex cycles and the difficulties in defining comparative dosages. Dr. Carl Djerassi, one of the pioneers of oral contraception, reported that these FDA requirements "have resulted in the recent discontinuance of at least two clinical trials of promising compounds. Even more serious is the fact that, as a consequence, this experience with FDA's practical power to determine scientific protocol has led one of the largest of American drug companies (which does not market any contraceptive agent) to discontinue virtually all research on contraceptive agents chemically related to female steroids."[26] Dr. Djerassi adds, "There is little doubt that if the present climate concerning clinical testing of contraceptive agents had existed 15 years ago, none of the steroid oral contraceptives now being used would ever have been developed."[27]

We may never know how many other promising, life-saving drugs have been held up or cancelled because of the FDA. Suffice it to say that the overall effect of all of the FDA regulations and legal weaponry is to make a manufacturer think several times before even taking a drug out of his lab. Why should he go through the bother of filling out the huge IND forms, the even larger NDA forms, pay for testing, manufacturing, and advertising?—His drug stands a slim enough chance in the very competitive drug field anyway without having to face constantly expanding regulations and police powers. Many companies handle the problem by canceling a drug rather than developing it;[28] others seek out less regulated foreign markets[29]—either way patients and doctors in the U.S. lose a chance to try a new and possibly better drug.

Some Thoughts on an Alternative

The most subtle—and perhaps most damaging—aspect of FDA regulations is not their effects on the drug industry, but their effects on the general public and physicians. Everyone, including the doctors, feels that "someone" is seeing to it that drugs are safe and production standards high. The result is an uncommon amount of ignorance and misplaced trust. As Morton Mintz points out in *Therapeutic Nightmare* (a very pro-regulation book), the FDA simply isn't doing the protecting that everyone assumes it is. Thalidomide was their big and nearly only coup.

As has been pointed out, fraud is a proper concern of the law; whether the specialized knowledge required to deal with drug fraud implies the need for a special, full-time agency (rather than merely allowing suits against the drug companies), is an interesting question which this article will not attempt to cover. What is of concern, however, is to investigate how an unregulated market could deal with the issue of relative safety and effectiveness.

In his article, "The Assault on Integrity,"[30] Alan Greenspan points out that reputation is a major tool in an unregulated economy and that manufacturers would vie to have a reputation for honest dealing and quality products. Unfortunately he chose the drug industry as his example: even in a free economy this industry is one of the least amenable to rating by the consumers. Specialized knowledge is needed in order to judge the quality and purity of the product; the consumer is generally using the product under orders from someone else (i.e., the doctor), and in many cases, he may not be in a condition to make a carefully reasoned judgement—he may be sick or frantic with worry about someone else who is. This does not excuse the consumer, particularly one with chronic medicinal needs, from being as well informed as possible (most people today can't even identify by name what they are taking let alone know what side effects to be alert for or what to do in case of accidental overdose); this suggests, however, that for the purposes of judging drugs the doctors are the ones who count as consumers. This is certainly true today when drugs can only be gotten via a doctor's prescription (and the doctors are the objects of all prescription drug advertising), but even in an unregulated market most people still would go to a doctor simply because he has the specialized knowledge and they do not (just as people currently consult lawyers even though a lawyer is not officially required in most cases). Certainly then it would be in the doctor's interest, as a man of professional integrity and also as a businessman who wants to keep customers, to prescribe the best drugs he could.

At the present time the doctor gets most of his information through drug company salesmen, the *Physician's Desk Reference* (the PDR)—in which drug companies do their own product write-ups, the AMA's *New and Non-Official Drugs* (produced once a year by the Council on Drugs), or, if he has the time in his busy practice, from journal articles and letters. It should be obvious that over half of his information is coming from a biased source—the companies themselves. It is common (in some groups) to think of all industrialists as virtuous capitalists, and many are; but it must also be remembered that the FDA was originally set up with the legitimate function of detecting fraud and mislabeling, and even in recent years some drug companies (e.g. Merrill in the case of MER/29) have been convicted of falsifying data and suppressing knowledge of severe drug reactions.

What is needed, and what would almost certainly exist in the absence of the FDA, is an independent agency similar to Consumer's Union that would evaluate company claims and tests, run tests of its own where necessary, keep abreast of the medical literature, collect physician reports of drug reactions (the AMA is currently working on a computerized system), and then dispense the information to its subscribers (or members, if the AMA were to expand its Council on Drugs). Certainly it would be in the interest of physicians and some laymen to use such a service. In today's regulated environment, in which the government is presumed to be taking care of everything, only *one-eighth* of all U.S. physicians subscribe to the one modest newsletter which reports systematically on drug side-effects.[31] The fortnightly, nonprofit "Medical Letter" costs only $12.50 per year and has established an excellent reputation—but most doctors continue to rely on company sales brochures and the FDA as their primary sources of information.

Such is the pervasiveness of government regulations and the mentality that trusts them—it is no wonder that people scream that if the FDA were to be abolished we'd all be poisoned: if people were to continue to use so little caution and intelligence in selecting drugs and physicians to advise them, that could very well happen. Any industry needs an incentive for excellence if the [crooks] are not to take over. The

FDA provides an incentive based on fear, via a government-backed gun. If the FDA were abolished, physicians and consumers, by means of testing labs and computerized information systems, could provide an incentive based on reputation. Doctors and patients would at last be free to make their own decisions about what risks to take in using a particular drug, free of government coercion. And one's full ownership of his own body would advance another step towards being a legal reality.

Footnotes

Lynn Kinsky is a chemist and anthropologist who consults for a number of research firms on the West Coast. She is one of the editors of *Reason* magazine and among her articles is "Freedom and Long Time Coming ..." a discussion of John Stuart Mills' theories pertaining to the legal treatment of women. Ms. Kinsky obtained her degree from the University of Wisconsin (B.S.) and has done graduate work at Dartmouth College.

"The FDA and Drug Research" is reprinted with permission from *Reason*, vol. 2, no. 9.

1. "Nader's Raiders on the FDA: Science and Scientists 'Misused'," *Science*, 17 April, 1970, pp. 349–352.

2. Green and Goldberger, *Molecular Insights into the Living Process*, p. 363.

3. Morton Mintz, *The Therapeutic Nightmare*, p. 277.

4. Ibid., p. 18.

5. Ibid., p.9.

6. See "Chemical and Engineering News," May 19 and June 2, 1969.

7. This industrial support is likely to be lost if the government persists in its policy of not allowing patents for anything resulting from government funded work, no matter how minor the government support. The drug industry is vitally dependent upon patents, but few university projects are without NIH, NSF, NIMH, or PHS grants of some sort. The impact will most likely be felt in the development of rare disease drugs, and in the clinical testing of industrially developed drugs (the largest clinics are generally part of a medical school).

8. "Key Facts About the U.S. Prescription Drug Industry"—Pharmaceutical Manufacturers' Association publication.

9. *Proceedings, Commission on Drug Safety*, James H. Luther, speaker, 1963.

10. "Drug Industry," May 9, 1969, p. 509.

11. Young, "Social History of American Drug Legislation," *Drugs in Our Society*, p. 218.

12. [Dr. Wiley was just ahead of his time—the FDA is once again considering banning saccharin.]

13. Klumpp, *Proceedings; Committee on Drug Safety*, p. 157.

14. *Therapeutic Nightmare*, p. 49.

15. Klumpp, *op. cit.*, p. 165.

16. Cutler, Lloyd, "Practical Aspects of Drug Legislation," *Drugs in Our Society*, p. 153.

17. Ibid., p. 154.

18. *The Value Line Investment Survey–Drug Industry*, May 9, 1969, p. 510.

19. Ibid.

20. Jacob, Dr. Stanley W. and Donald C. Wood, Ph.D., "Dimethyl Sulfoxide (DMSO)—Toxicology, Pharmacology, and Clinical Experience," *American Journal of Surgery*, September 1967.

21. Mosely, Hazel, "A Case of Overprotection," *Analog*, April 1970, pp. 61–71.

22. "Thalidomide Combats Leprosy," Associated Press dispatch, as reported in the *Boston Globe*, June 29, 1969.

23. Ibid.

24. Djerassi, Carl, Ph.D., "Prognosis for the Development of New Chemical Birth Control Agents," *Science*, 24 October, 1969, p. 470.

25. "Hormonal Steroids in Contraception," World Health Organization Technical Report Ser. No. 386, 1968.

26. Djerassi, *op. cit.*

27. Ibid.

28. The author's company . . . pulled a promising cardiovascular drug out of clinical testing after a FDA staff scientist reported at a conference that a structurally similar drug caused mutations in bacteria.

29. "Drug Industry," May 9, 1969, p. 510.

30. Alan Greenspan, "Assault on Integrity" in Ayn Rand's *Capitalism, The Unknown Ideal*, 1966.

31. Joseph Garland, "Dissemination of Information on Drugs," *Drugs in Our Society*, p. 209.

Robert W. Poole, Jr.

12

Fly the
Frenzied Skies...

A PRIVATE BUSINESS whose sales volume had increased 15-20 percent annually for seven years (and showed many signs of continuing to do so) would probably view its future with eager anticipation. In the government controlled, privately-owned cartel known as commercial aviation, however, the expected growth in air travel is viewed, in part, with horror. For as the volume of air traffic rises, a monumental crisis appears imminent, a crisis that threatens the complete paralysis of air transportation. What is the source of this seeming paradox? How can it be that the same industry that is flying, fueling, and servicing the huge 747 is unable to solve seemingly simple problems of supply and demand? The answer is not at all difficult to arrive at, provided one views the problem in its full scope, without recourse to the self-imposed blind spots that have plagued mass media analysis of the subject.

Commercial aviation consists of three distinct parts: the airports, the airways linking airports, and the airlines.

Although there are 10,000 airports in the United States, many of them privately owned, all 525 of those large enough to handle scheduled airline service are owned by city governments (except Dulles and Washington National which belong to the federal government). Municipal airport financing comes primarily from three sources: municipal bonds (for basic equipment and taxiways), airline investment (for terminal buildings), and federal tax money (for control towers, instrument landing aids, and runways). Since limited federal aid tax money is available for building runways at these airports, many citizens quite remote from airports are thus forced to pay for them. During the last ten years, the pace of airport expansion has lagged far behind the growth in air traffic, because: (1) local governments have little political incentive (or expertise) to accurately forecast passenger demand, (2) Congress has let the annual appropriation for airport aid gradually decrease, despite constantly increasing requests for such aid, and (3) local taxpayers are increasingly reluctant to commit themselves to large-scale bond issues, especially for things not of direct benefit to themselves. Hourly capacity restrictions have already been imposed by the federal government at major East Coast airports, because of the increasing congestion at terminals and on runways. When the 365-passenger 747 and the 300-passenger airbuses went into service, only a handful of airports had terminal facilities or access roads adequate for such large concentrations of people.

The airways consist of a number of paths in the sky, defined by ground-based radio navigation stations (navaids). The Federal Aviation Administration (FAA) owns and operates the navaids and polices the airways. Anywhere above 3,500 feet and in the vicinity of airports, all aircraft must fly under FAA control. Although modern electronics and computer technology make nearly-automatic air traffic control technologically feasible, the FAA still relies on the early 1950's method of using navaids only as references, with all control and decision making in the hands of a (human) FAA air traffic controller. Because of limited funding by Congress, there aren't enough controllers, their salaries are low, and their training is poor. Combined with the high volume of air traffic, these conditions make today's controller extremely overworked, in many cases literally a nervous wreck. Another consequence of the controller shortage is the fact that these men are "daily forced to compromise with safety procedures"[1] in order to handle their work load. The controllers' slowdowns of 1968 and 1969 with their disastrous effects on flight schedules, illustrate how close to collapse the existing system is.

The FAA's operations are financed out of general federal tax receipts (the tax on airline tickets goes into general revenue, while the tax on aviation gasoline goes into the highway trust fund!). Thus, as long as there aren't many crashes, Congress is content to appropriate meager sums for the FAA.[2] The taxpayers, 60 percent of whom have never flown at all, justifiably feel little desire to be taxed even further to provide airways for the mere 15 percent who fly commerical airlines regularly.

Finally, the airlines themselves present an interesting picture.

Though nominally private companies, the airlines in fact are controlled by the Civil Aeronautics Board (CAB) in every essential aspect of their business. The routes between cities are divided up among the airlines as a huge cartel, originated and enforced by the CAB, thus making free entry into the market illegal. Likewise, it is nearly impossible for an airline to leave a particular market (by dropping a city from its schedule) —the "public convenience and necessity" must be served, apparently regardless of losses. The prices charged customers for a particular route are fixed by the CAB, in order to prevent "destructive" price competition. Price increases are permitted to the airlines only as a group, and price decreases, while allowed on an individual basis, must still be run through the mill of CAB. If companies in the steel industry tried to set up such an arrangement, they would be prosecuted by the Antitrust Division of the Justice Department. Indeed, the contradiction between the CAB's philosophy and the antitrust laws was illustrated in the summer of 1969 when the CAB had to grant the airlines temporary immunity from antitrust action so that they could meet together to discuss coordinating their schedules, so as to relieve rush hour airport congestion.

As if this were not enough, thirteen local service airlines, which were formed after World War II with surplus aircraft and "temporary" subsidies, continue to receive about $60 million per year in subsidy payments, out of general tax revenues. Thus, taxpayers are forced to pay huge direct subsidies, in addition to the countless indirect subsidies they provide in the form of "free" airways, weather reports, landing aids, and mail contracts.

The net result of these government activities is that at least three distinct groups of people are being victimized. First, the vast majority of taxpayers who do not use the airlines are being unjustly taxed so that those who do fly can have air travel at less than its true cost. Second, the most competent, aggressive airline owners (and potential airline owners) are being prevented from engaging in competition with the less competent companies, with the result that neither the more competent companies nor their stockholders can benefit as fully as they could and should. Third, the people who do fly are getting less efficient and less safe air service than, in the absence of government interference, they might; less efficient because of the lack of competition, and less safe because of the antiquated, underfunded, congested airport and airways system.

The question which should be obvious by now is: How, in "capitalist" America did such a horrendous tangle of vested interests and government control ever come to pass? The standard "conservative" mythology holds that all of America's economic troubles began with FDR's New Deal. The sad fact of the matter is that government interference with, and subsidy to, American aviation has a long nonpartisan history.

History of a Crisis

Throughout the history of American aviation, the general rule has been that each expansion of government control was preceded by requests for such regulation from one or another group of people involved in aviation. At each step of the way, of course, the proponents did not foresee or advocate any further government involvement—they merely wished blindly to promote their own short-range special interest.

Federal involvement began in 1915 when President Wilson selected a number of aviation enthusiasts to form the National Advisory Committee on Aeronautics (NACA) to "study . . . the problems of flight, with a view of their practical solution." The impetus for setting up NACA was World War I, but as with many government agencies, NACA emerged in 1919 as a permanent entity and became a vigorous advocate of government control of aviation.

Former wartime aircraft producer Howard Coffin strongly supported NACA's position. During the war, Coffin had been picked to head the government's Aircraft Production Board, which passed out over $1 billion in aircraft contracts to his own company and those of his fellow auto producers.[3]Coffin and his friends ignored the advice of many aircraft designers and mass-produced the Liberty aircraft engine along automotive lines, which made it a poor aircraft power plant. They also produced 10,500 DH–4 aircraft, only a few of which ever reached Europe. The remaining planes were subsequently sold as war surplus for 2 percent of their cost and the resulting postwar glut of cheap aircraft greatly depressed the market for new designs. The DH–4 with Liberty engines won the nickname of "flaming coffin" in the postwar years.

In 1918, at the urging of NACA, the Post Office inaugurated airmail service, using Army planes. Using the "coffins," Post Office service was risky at best. By 1925, thirty-one of the first forty airmail pilots had been killed in crashes. Somehow, during the same six-year period, the safety record of many of the fledgling private operators was much better. In 1925, a government investigating board recommended that the Post Office let airmail contracts to private companies, rather

than having the Army fly the mail. Congress agreed, and passed the
Kelly Airmail Act. One of the results was the formation of three
"conglomerate" aviation companies—United Aircraft and Transport,
North American (under GM control), and AVCO—which proceeded to
win most of the longer airmail routes.

During these years NACA continued to propose bills calling for
federal regulations. These bills received support from such diverse
sources as state and local bar associations, the American Legion, presidents Wilson and Harding, and Secretary of Commerce Herbert
Hoover. In addition, a number of airline owners (and would-be owners)
asked Congress for regulations and subsidy—regulation to win public
confidence, and subsidy to keep them in business regardless of the
market or their ability. One of the most common appeals was that the
United States must not fall behind Europe, where governments were
setting up airlines and subsidizing their operations.

The outgrowth of this lobbying was the Air Commerce Act of 1926,
which firmly asserted the government's authority over aviation, giving it
authority to "foster air commerce," provide airways and navaids, conduct research and design, issue licenses and aircraft certificates, and
investigate accidents. Both President Coolidge and Secretary Hoover
had worked for the passage of this act, considering it only as a means of
"strengthening private enterprise." As Professor Donald Whitnah points
out, "in 1926 rate fixing and the awarding of exclusive operating
franchises to airlines were hardly conceivable to the majority of the
framers of the legislation."[4]

By 1930, however, the government had already begun to flex its
newly authorized muscle. Hoover's Postmaster General, Walter F.
Brown, decided that there was too much "chaos" and competition in
aviation and decided to "foster air commerce" by forcing mergers and
consolidation, using airmail contracts as his "persuader." Previously, of
course, these contracts had been let to the lowest bidder. Brown
proposed a new law allowing him to select contractors "by negotiation"
(on the basis of cooperation with his master plan), and to pay them on
the basis of the size of their aircraft, rather than the amount of mail they
carried. Congress approved the latter idea but refused to allow Brown
full discretion in selecting contractors. Nonetheless, Brown proceeded
on his own, attempting at first, to persuade various airlines to merge.
When that failed, he "arbitrarily selected those companies he believed
most suitable,"[5] and awarded them the routes. Lines that didn't cooperate had their contracts (and thereby their route authority) cancelled.

When the Democrats came to power in 1932, Senator Hugo Black conducted a sweeping investigation of airmail contracting and exposed the entire shameful situation to public view. In the uproar which followed, Roosevelt ordered all mail contracts cancelled and called upon the Army to resume carrying the mail. The Army responded, but it was unprepared and poorly equipped; in the first week, twelve pilots died and six more were seriously injured. The Army's mail service this time lasted only a few months (at an average cost per mile of $2.21 versus 54c for the airlines!). In the Airmail Act of 1934, competitive bidding was restored, but as a result of the previous scandals, aircraft manufacturers were forced to sell their airline operations. Thus, with one blow the government destroyed the three largest aviation companies in the country.

A further consequence of the airmail scandals was the Civil Aeronautics Act of 1938, sponsored by Senator Pat McCarran (another hero of the conservatives). Beginning in 1934, Senator McCarran began a legislative campaign for economic regulation of scheduled air carriers. In 1935 a federal study group recommended treating air transport as a public utility, with subsidies and fare regulation. Meanwhile, with the resumption of competitive bidding for airmail contracts, and with the depression rolling along, many airlines lost money, and began looking to Washington for help. The newly formed Air Transport Association began lobbying for federal regulation and subsidy, in effect threatening that if the airlines didn't have more money available, they couldn't guarantee safe operation (!). This argument apparently worried FDR, who didn't want the New Deal blamed for a wave of air crashes.

The resulting Civil Aeronautics Act "gave the airlines almost all they desired."[6] It provided blank-check subsidy, eliminated competitive bidding on airmail contracts (substituting "need" as the criterion), and protected against competition the routes of existing airlines. The major airlines welcomed passage of the new law; even staunch free enterpriser Eddie Rickenbacker supported it. In addition to these provisions, the Act set up an independent agency known as the Civil Aeronautics Authority to carry out the regulation of the industry. Two years later the agency was split in two, with the Civil Aeronautics Board (CAB) performing economic regulation and the Civil Aeronautics Administration (CAA) responsible for safety and air traffic control. Except for the CAA being renamed the FAA in 1958, and becoming a part of the Transportation Department in 1966, the government's regulatory structures have remained essentially as they were in 1940.

There is one further incident in the history of aviation that deserves mention, because it illustrates the nature of the effects of the CAB on competition. At the close of World War II a number of entrepreneurs purchased surplus transport planes in order to start new airlines. Since the established airlines had monopolies on the most profitable routes, the newcomers were legally forbidden to compete with them—as scheduled carriers. But the CAB exempted nonscheduled cargo and coach service from the "certification" (monopoly-granting) procedures, as well as from subsidy. Thus, the newcomers, with their own money, began nonscheduled cargo and coach flights, the latter service an unheard-of innovation in the industry.

The scheduled lines, free enterprisers all, attacked the concept of coach flights as "economically unsound" and implored the CAB to put the nonskeds out of business. But coach service proved to be so popular with customers that the scheduled lines soon began to offer it themselves, undercutting their own arguments. Even so, the CAB began putting pressure on the nonskeds, who then asked Congress for an investigation to determine the full extent of federal subsidies received by the "ins." The scheduled airlines, through their lobbying group, the Air Transport Association, conducted a massive campaign against the nonskeds, charging that they "were making no public contribution and constituted a drain and diversion of needed revenue from the scheduled carriers."[7]Eventually, this type of propaganda was successful; the CAB adopted regulations which put the nonskeds out of business.

Suggested Solutions, Their Flaws, and the Proper Solution

That a crisis in aviation is impending is widely acknowledged; aviation and aerospace publications have been rife with analyses and recommendations for several years. Now newspapers and news magazines are beginning to pick up the story, alerted by growing flight delays, air controller slowdowns, and hopelessly congested airports. And so, there is no dearth of proposed solutions. In evaluating these proposals, however, it is vital to keep one point clearly in mind: the essential nature of the problem is not technological nor political, but economic. As with any other case of government intervention, the normal relationships between supply and demand have been grossly distorted with the result that, on the one hand, massive needs (electronic "area navigation," larger and more modern airports) are being ignored, while on the other hand, the present consumers of airline service are not paying anything like the full costs of the service they are getting. For this reason, any solution that deals only with politics or technological improvements is actually dealing with effects, rather than causes.

The government's short-term approach will be some variation of the "user tax" plan developed by the Administration. Under this plan, additional taxes will be levied on tickets, a new tax levied on airfreight, and fuel for private planes will be taxed. About half of the money raised by these taxes (i.e., $5 billion over ten years) will be earmarked exclusively for airports and airways improvements, with the remainder going into "general revenue." According to Transportation Department projections, some $14 billion is needed for airport and airways modernization over the next ten years—thus, the remaining $9 billion would have to come from Congress and/or local communities.

The only real merit of the user-tax proposal is that it gives token recognition to the fact that the users are not currently paying the full costs of the service they are receiving. But this recognition is given in so minimal a way as to be almost worthless. The proposal still leaves all essential funding decisions to be made politically, with the result that millions of taxpayers will still be forced to pay most of the costs, for the benefit of a few. Since the plan doesn't identify the principle of full-cost pricing versus indirect subsidies, it is easy for vested interests to attack it as costing them more than they are accustomed to paying (the Air Transport Association and the Airline Owners and Pilots Association have already done just that.) In addition, the proposal makes the error of assuming that simply providing more money is the answer to all the problem without ever questioning whether the government's bureaucracies might themselves be part of the problem.

A proposal that does raise this question was made in December 1968 by Glen A. Gilbert, aviation consultant and one of the originators of the existing Air Traffic Control (ATC) system.[8] After many years of experience in aviation, both in government and industry, Mr. Gilbert has concluded that the FAA's structure and policies are not conducive to continuing progress in developing and implementing advanced technology systems. He proposes that the FAA get out of the airways business altogether, in favor of a COMSAT-type corporation financed directly by the users, based on the actual costs of the services provided. This idea, predictably, has received little publicity outside of aviation circles. It is certain to be opposed by the same organizations and interests that oppose the user-charge taxes.

Probably, the most popularized approach of recent years is to call for a "total systems approach" to the entire airport–airways–airline–ground transportation problem. It is difficult to argue with this approach, per se, since all it really says is that a complex problem is not likely to be solved by piecemeal solutions considered in isolation from the total system. Yet, what most proponents of this approach end up calling for is merely more of the same: more federal spending and more government regulations. A genuine systems approach must look beyond conventionally perceived boundaries of the problem and determine to what extent the established order (the FAA, the CAB, and the special interest groups) may be the cause of the problem.

Political control of airports, airways, and airlines prevents the normal market mechanism from operating. It is impossible to determine the true demand for air navigation service, since the users, the airlines and "general aviation," (private pilots) do not pay for it. Airport construction lags traffic growth by a decade—because taxpayers and those using airlines are very different groups of people. Hundreds of short-haul transport aircraft crowd airports and airways, aircraft whose average passenger load is too small to be profitable and whose owners would be long since bankrupt, but for decades of subsidy at public expense.

If the present system is collapsing, and increased government intervention does not attack the core of the problem, what then is the answer? The basic economic problem cannot be solved by legislative fiat —if supply and demand are distorted by arbitrary regulations, they cannot be forced back to normal, since "normal" means what supply and demand would be, free of force. What the government must do is get out of the way and let the market mechanism take over. Since people are volitional beings, it is impossible to spell out in advance exactly how, once free, they would solve these (or any other) problems. Nonetheless, it is possible to set forth the principles that apply in this case and draw some logical conclusions from them.

The first principle is that everything that is of value to someone has a market value, which the objective forces of the free market can (and should) determine. Any violation of this principle (by subsidy, "free" services, coercive barriers to entry and exit, or enforced price fixing) distorts the market process and unjustly benefits some at the expense of others. The second principle is that the proper role of government in a capitalist society is to protect rights, in this case, property rights. It is impossible to peaceably conduct business unless there are objective ground rules that define what constitutes particular types of property, how such property rights are originally acquired, and how the right is to be legally protected. By misunderstanding this crucial principle, modern legal theory has applied the ancient concept of "public ownership" to such uniquely twentieth century property as radio and TV frequencies and air routes.

Under free market capitalism, airports would be **private businesses,** operated for profit, deriving revenues directly from customers (airlines, individual airplane owners, passengers, concessionaires, etc.). Such an airport would be free to float bonds and to sell stock (as does Madison Square Garden) in order to raise capital. In order to remain profitable, the airport's management would have a strong incentive to plan for the future, developing the same type of forecasting expertise possessed by aircraft manufacturers and airlines. Such planning would probably include the acquisition of large amounts of surrounding land, both for expansion and as a noise buffer zone. In some cases, it might prove economical to build the airport offshore, either as a floating platform or as an artificial island.

The airport management would be free to make whatever contracts it could with the various airlines which would compete for terminal space and landing privileges. In the interest of attracting the largest number of passengers, the airport company would seek the most competent airlines in terms of quality and quantity of service. At the same time, by means of those individual contracts, the airport company could control arrival and departure times (probably by variable landing fees) to prevent rush hour congestion of runways. To assure customers of convenient access to the airport, it would be in the company's interest to cooperate with local high speed transit companies in planning and building airport access links.

It is quite possible that airline customers using such airports would pay more for their trip than they do now. Without the power of eminent domain, the airport company would have to acquire land at full value, rather than by condemnation; in addition, it would have to bear full legal liability for accidents and noise, like any other business. And, of course, without access to tax money, it would be unable to force the local citizenry to make up any operating losses. On the other hand, the customers, while paying their way, would enjoy the benefits of well-planned, low-congestion terminals, rational scheduling, on-time operation, a wider choice of services, and probably greater safety due to the airport's full liability status.

As far as air traffic control (ATC) is concerned, the basic concept of an ATC "utility" has already been presented. The only flaw in Glen Gilbert's proposal is the automatic assumption of a nonprofit or quasi-governmental status for such a company. If AT&T can provide high-quality telephone service at low rates, while making a healthy profit, why couldn't the same be true of an ATC company? Interestingly, the existing ATC system was begun by a private company formed by the airlines back in the thirties. When the federal government took over control of the skies, it inherited a functioning system, including system, en route navaids and control towers.

The largest single benefit of a privately-owned ATC system is that sufficient funding and motivation would be available to implement up-to-date electronic navigation techniques. Much of today's air traffic congestion results from the FAA's requirement that airlines fly exclusively over the limited number of paths linking VOR ground stations (navaids). For over a decade, on-board computers and pictorial displays have been available, which, when installed in an aircraft, permit the pilot to define a new path instead of being restricted to the old station-to-station ones. This technique, known as area navigation, has the potential of increasing the amount of navigable airspace by orders of magnitude, as well as substantially reducing air traffic controller work load (since the pilot does most of his own controlling). After years of lethargy and indifference, the FAA in the summer of 1969 finally began allowing limited experimental usage of area navigation, but did so only under the threat of total saturation of the existing airways.

This bureaucratic stagnation is typical of the FAA. As airline pilot Vernon Lowell relates, "the inflexibility of these [FAA] regulations . . . is the bane of every pilot's existence."[9] Furthermore, once it has chosen a wrong policy (such as opposing area navigation) the FAA is loath to admit its error. Since protecting its political existence, rather than providing profitable service, is its standard, "the FAA has degenerated into a bureaucracy which often engages in face-saving of its public image rather than the pursuit of air safety."[10] In attempting to obtain ATC services "for free" the airlines have paid the price in the form of a bureaucratic nightmare of flight rules that compromise safety. The FAA's "endless flow of rules forces pilots into a conflict: fly legally but less safe, or violate the rules and fly safer."[11]

Once again, breaking the link between supply and demand has produced a situation in which nobody wins. A profit-making ATC company is today completely feasible, technically and economically. The airlines and other users would have to pay for the services they received, but because of this they could demand—and receive—the latest innovations that advanced electronics and computer technology could provide. As a result they could expect an unprecedented increase in capacity and safety of the airways.

With airports privately run, and airways privately defined, what would be the position of airline companies with regard to free access to specific airspace? The crucial question here is the proper definition of the property rights to an air route. Because two aircraft cannot fly over the same airway in the same place, at the same time, and because the number of airways, though large, is ultimately limited, it is clear that individual airways constitute a class of property and ought to be protected as such. As Ayn Rand points out in "The Property Status of Airwaves,"[12] the right of ownership (to any kind of property, be it a radio frequency, an airway, or a gold mine) belongs to whomever first applies his knowledge and effort to make use of it. As technology develops an ever-increasing variety of property, it is the government's task to "formulate the laws by which . . . rights[to this property] are to be implemented and adjudicated."[13] Thus, in the case of airways, the first person or company to make the effort of flying a particular air route has the first claim on it; that is, his right to use it has priority over anyone else's. The specific details of this right—the dimensions of an airway, the time or distance between successive users, etc.—are a function of the level of technology at a particular point in time. These are matters that would be worked out when formulating—and periodically revising—the laws dealing with airway property rights. The air traffic control companies would offer their services as a means of enabling all users, through the expedient of knowing exactly where they are flying, to comply with airway laws.

The other important issue concerns which airlines would serve which cities. The advocates of government control claim that under laissez-faire every airline would attempt to serve every city, with the result that all (or most) would go bankrupt. When challenged on the absurdity of this assumption, they usually give as an alternative their fear that the airlines would form a huge cartel, dividing up the markets among them, and fixing the prices. (This is, of course, precisely what the CAB presently forces them to do.)

As pointed out earlier, it is impossible to predict exactly what would happen to air service in a free market. But because of competition for the limited airport space, the number of airlines, or more precisely, the number of planes, serving a particular city-port would probably be limited (though in many cases, there would be more planes than at present). The important point to remember is that the market, rather than politicians, would be allocating the routes and that difference could mean significant improvements in service. In the early fifties Eastern Airlines asked the CAB for permission to link Florida and California— a market not then served. For a number of years the CAB held hearings, acquiring mountains of inconclusive testimony from various city governments and airlines; eventually the route was awarded to National Airlines on the basis of its "need" for it. Thus, Eastern, with three times as many planes, was completely frozen out. Examples such as this dot the history of the CAB. The CAB's policies prevent greater service on many profitable routes, and force excess service on many marginally-profitable or loss-producing routes. In the free market, the quantity and quality of service to or from any city would bear a direct relationship to the demand for service, as reflected in the prices people were willing to pay.

Thus, unrestricted competition, far from causing chaos, would promote orderly, harmonious growth in air services, with everyone paying his own way. It is certainly possible that some cartel-type agreements would be attempted—this is a possibility in any free market. But as in any other market, neither technology nor competition stands still; no price can be fixed at a highly profitable level for very long (except by the government) without attracting competition. The unrestricted operation of supply and demand provides real-time feedback of information to both consumers (via prices) and producers (via profits) about the state of the market. When liberated from the distortion of government intervention, the market mechanism will provide whatever air services people—as individuals, rather than as special-interest groups —are willing to pay for.

Steps Toward Freedom and Order

If the Administration became convinced that government was the cause of the aviation crisis, it could take three specific steps towards decontrol. The highest priority should be given to selling the FAA's air traffic control system to the highest bidder (the proceeds to be added to income tax refunds). The new owners, after a transition period in which to raise capital, could put all their efforts into implementing electronic area navigation. As soon as the change over were complete, they would begin charging all users for their services.

Once area navigation were operational, and the air congestion crisis over, the government's next step would be to cancel the Federal Aid to Airports (FAAP) program. This would leave municipalities with the alternatives of greatly increasing local taxes (very unlikely) or selling the airports to private companies. Those cities which did neither would probably soon find their obsolescing airport competing with newly built or newly acquired privately owned and operated airports.

The government's third step would be to abolish the CAB. Not a single one of the CAB's functions is justifiable in a free society; none is without harmful economic consequences. Abolishing the CAB would immediately end millions of dollars of subsidies to smaller airlines, probably causing a number of mergers and failures. At the same time, with the elimination of route certificates, all air routes would be opened to competition. The airlines would be free to negotiate with all airport owners (private and government) and much new service would be made available in short order (and easily could be accommodated via area navigation). At the same time, the government would be obliged to promulgate an air route property law, precisely defining the means of establishing and enforcing usage priority for individual airways.

These steps, to be sure, would be vociferously opposed by the multitude of vested interests and their lobbyists that have proliferated in response to the government's policies. Such individuals and organizations, the embodiment of status quo and special privilege, are the natural result of the attempt to substitute politics for economics, fascism for freedom, "pull" for trade. It will take people of integrity, in business and in government, to stand up to these people and answer their pleadings of "need" and "public interest" with reason and economics. Such people of integrity are essential if aviation (along with our nation) is to escape the stagnation which is the end result of government control.

Notes

Robert Poole, Jr. is a systems engineer for a West Coast firm. He earned a B.S. and M.S. from MIT. He is managing editor of *Reason* magazine and has written articles dealing with social change, ecology, and federal regulation of technological aspects of society. He contributed to Dorothy James' (ed.) *Outside Looking In* (Harper & Row, 1972).

"Fly the Frenzied Skies ..." is reprinted with permission from *Reason* (September 1969).

1. F. Lee Bailey, attorney for the Professional Air Traffic Controllers Organization, in *Aviation Week*, June 30, 1969, p.28.

2. A graph on p. 53 of the May, 1969 issue of *Space/Aeronautics* illustrates the direct relationship between air crashes and Congressional appropriations for FAA facilities and equipment.

3. Charles J. Kelly, Jr., *The Sky's the Limit—The History of the Airlines*, (New York: Coward McCann, 1963), pp. 25–29.

4. Donald R. Whitnah, *Safer Skyways—Federal Control of Aviation, 1925–1966*, (Ames, Ia.: Iowa State Univ. Press, 1966), p. 27.

5. Kelly, op. cit., p. 75.

6. Ibid., p. 102.

7. Ibid., p. 180.

8. Glen A. Gilbert, "Gilbert Offers ATC 'Master Plan,'" *American Aviation*, December 23, 1968, pp. 28–37.

9. Capt. Vernon W. Lowell, *Airline Safety is a Myth*, (New York: Bartholomew House, 1967), p. 180.

10. Ibid., p. 178.

11. Ibid., p. 174.

12. Ayn Rand, *Capitalism, the Unknown Ideal*, (New York: New American Library, 1966), pp. 117–124.

13. Ibid., p. 118.

R. A. Childs, Jr.

13

Big Business and the Rise of American Statism

Preface

THIS ESSAY CONSTITUTES a part of "revisionism" in history, largely domestic history. The term *revisionism* originally came into use referring to historiography after World War I. A group of young historians, eager to uncover the realities behind the blanket of myths surrounding the origins of this crucial conflict, discovered as a result of their investigations that Germany and Austria were *not*, contrary to popular mythology, solely responsible for the outbreak of that crisis. Thus, reevaluating the history of the immediate past, these historians came to see the Treaty of Versailles, forced upon the losers of that war, as monstrously unjust, and maintained that the rigid enforcement of its terms would lead to further world conflict. They came to advocate a radical overhauling and revision of the Versailles treaty—whence the term "revisionism."

Since then, revisionism has been applied to virtually *any* renegade school of thought in historiography that took issue with the "official government line" on important events in history. As it is used today, revisionism is a general concept subsuming a wide diversity of schools, or integrated conceptions of man's past. For at the time when any set of events occurs, in any context, there is almost always a specific set of interpretations of events, a given historical paradigm, which spreads throughout a given culture to the relative exclusion of other interpretations.

Those schools of historiography that are responsible for refuting the popular myths, for *revising* the historical record in accordance with new evidence, are thus called revisionist in nature. In this preface, it is my intention to sketch briefly what I consider to be the nature and status of history as a field of investigation. I want especially to focus on the crucially important, yet neglected, relationship of philosophy to history. In the nineteenth century, practically every great philosopher made extensive use of history, particularly in fields such as social philosophy; and, every great historian was usually well acquainted with philosophy. Yet today historians and philosophers often seem to be completely cut off from one another. This is unfortunate, for history is vitally important to the philosopher, at the very least in illustrating his theories, in filling in the outlines of an abstract theory with concrete units and events. Similarly, philosophy is critically important to history in at least two interrelated ways: philosophy necessarily serves as a critic, and a guide, on two important levels—methodology, and evaluation. No one who deals with questions of responsibility, causality, or even the problem of "knowing" concrete events to which the human mind no longer has direct access through immediate awareness (as opposed to inference), can escape the importance of philosophy.

But the problem is more complicated than that. Today, certain philosophers tend to dismiss specific social theories, such as libertarianism and laissez-faire almost out-of-hand, usually because of alleged historical facts regarding centralization of economic power, depressions, unemployment, imperialism, war, and so forth. And certain historians (usually those operating from an *implicit* philosophic base such as Marxism), in an attempt to pump "relevance" into history, insist on drawing explicitly *nonhistorical* conclusions from purely historical data. Thus, such key revisionist authors as Gabriel Kolko and William Appleman Williams often mention in the course of their historical studies that such-and-such was "a necessary consequence of American capitalism." Aside from the enormous problems involved in the question of "necessity" *as such* in all fields, surely we face here more than a strictly historical judgment! At the barest minimum, such a statement would put the responsibility of proof on the shoulders of the proponent, who must marshall not only historical data, but economic theory and social philosophy as well—not to mention epistemology, which alone can provide him with a systematic methodology. Notice this intricate statement in Joyce and Gabriel Kolko's masterly *The Limits of Power:* "A society's goals, in the last analysis, reflect its objective needs—economic, strategic, and political—in the light of the requirements of its very specific structure of power." This is certainly *not* a strictly historical judgment. These questions immediately arise: what does it mean to talk of "society's goals"? what are a "society's" objective needs, and how does one determine them? what are the "requirements" of a specific structure of power, and what is meant here by the term "specific structure of power"? The point is not to fall back on agnosticism and skepticism, but to raise the question of whether or not such questions can be answered— or even *raised*—from within the context of history *alone*. If they cannot be, then we obviously fall into such fields as economics and philosophy. But philosophy *first*: it is only philosophy that, properly speaking, will give us the means of *answering* the very question of whether or not such-and-such a problem can be answered by historical inquiry alone.

Although I have stressed the dependence of history on philosophy, I do not mean to imply that history is merely tangental to philosophy. The philosopher, in my view, should, if nothing else, regard history as a testing ground, an experimental laboratory in which he conceptually can apply his theories (particularly social and political theories, and ethics) in an attempt to see if they make sense. A philosopher who preaches total state control of individual human actions and decisions, for instance, might profitably look at history for instances of what has happened as his ideal has been approached, approached as a limit case. If he finds destruction, chaos, and the like, then the burden of explaining this within the confines of his assertions of the supposedly beneficial nature of State control comes into play. Similarly, if an advocate of laissez-faire holds that depressions are impossible or unlikely in a free market economy, then he must be prepared to explain the nature and genesis of historical depressions by another theory than the prevalent ones, and to call into play historical data which other schools either neglect or misinterpret. Finally, the philosopher can profitably regard historical evaluations and interpretations as *practice* for actually applying his theories in interpreting contemporary events.

Since space does not permit me to detail every major issue in the philosophy of history, I shall restrict myself to presenting some of the more interesting points which a developed philosophy of history should focus on. And within these limits, I shall summarize my own approaches to some key problem areas.

What is history? History is a selective recreation of the events of the past, according to a historian's premises regarding what is important and his judgment concerning the nature of causality in human action. This selectivity is a most important aspect of history, and it is this alone which prevents history from becoming a random chronicling of events. And since this selectivity is necessary to history, the only remaining question is whether or not such judgments will be made explicitly or implicitly, with full knowledge of what one considers to be important and why, or without such awareness. Selection presupposes a *means, method*, or *principle* of selection. The historian's view of the nature of causality in human action also is determined by a principle of selection. He can have a conscious theory, such as economic determinism, or attempt to function without one. But without one, the result of historical investigation is likely to appear disintegrated and patched together. In this case, the historian depends necessarily on philosophy, on economics, and on psychology. If he is not aware of his selections and presuppositions, then the result is a bad historian, or at best a confused one. Charles A. Beard was more self-conscious than most about the problems of historical method, yet he still could write, at the apex of his career, an essay entitled "Written History as an Act of Faith." Of philosophical evasion and bankruptcy are bad historians born, as are professionals in so many other fields. A professional in any field has the unshakeable responsibility to be aware of and name his primaries, those presuppositions which function as axiomatic in his field. If he intends to be taken seriously, then he should be prepared to defend them. Evasion on any level produces disastrous consequences for man; on the highest political and intellectual levels, evasion can result in such things as physical destruction, or in entire generations of scholars being misled in their scholarly pursuits.

A popular philosophical doctrine holds that the methodology of history is entirely different from the methodology of other sciences. Yet *fundamentally* the methodology of *all* sciences is the same—*logic*. The nature of the evidence relevant to one field may differ from that relevant to another, and this indeed accounts for the *apparent* differences of method. Yet truths in any field are in fact verified by a process of applying man's reason to objective evidence. By 'reason' I mean simply the faculty of integrated awareness which is responsible for all of man's *knowledge* above the perceptual level; by 'objective evidence' I mean reality as presented to the intellect—'objective' meaning that which is determined by the nature of the entities existing in reality, and 'evidence' referring to that context or "segment" of reality which a consciousness has become aware of.

The nature of the objective evidence which is largely considered in history is simply *human testimony*, direct or indirect. History as a field deals with past human thought and actions. Since we have no direct awareness of the contents of anyone's consciousness but our own, we must rely on inference from what a person says, and what he does.

Considered from a different perspective, history deals with the ends that men have held in the past, and the means that they have adopted to attain these ends. Since no two individuals are specifically alike in every particular characteristic, it is impossible to recreate the past in the form of a laboratory experiment and to observe the effects of single causal factors on human action. Thus, all that one can do is to collect evidence concerning the context of individual men, their ideas, and their actions. Using a theory or model of the nature of causality in human action, one then interprets or selectively reconstructs events of the past, omitting what one judges to be unimportant, and offers an explanation for what one does consider to be important, in light of the evidence available. Utopian "completeness" is neither possible nor necessary in knowledge —in history or anywhere else. All knowledge is contextual, but this does not in any way hinder knowledge from being *valid*.

Turning from this sketch of historical *method*, I shall indicate, briefly, the *value* of history. Traditionalists often seek to use history as a guide to action, spurning abstract guides to conduct provided by the science of ethics, and adopting conventions and traditions instead. Yet it should be noted at the outset that to use history in any reasonable way to find rules of conduct *presupposes* a rational ethic. One must use a rational ethic to differentiate "good" traditions from "bad," and in fact to supersede history altogether in projecting what is *possible* to man. If something has happened in history, then one rationally can conclude that it *is* possible for man; if something has *not* happened in history, the reverse is not true—one *cannot* conclude that it is *not* possible for man. History can *illustrate* principles, but cannot verify or refute them. It is important to point out the submission of history to a rational ethic in this regard.

People distraught with the present often seek stability and refuge in the past, idealizing it beyond recognition. Such an attitude, however, will only lead to a life built on illusions, to despair that tomorrow things will only be worse, and a general feeling of impotence and inefficacy, with the result that those who accept such a view will *not* act to attain a better future.

But to act to change things for the better presupposes not only that one understands a rational ethic and its principles, but that one has some idea of "where one is," historically speaking. One has to answer the question: what is the present context of man? To answer this takes a knowledge of what ends men have sought up to now, in a broad cultural and political sense, and what means they have adopted to attain them. One then applies the principles of a rational philosophy to his actions;

understanding his context, he acts to change things in a certain direction.

If either history or philosophy, specifically, ethics, is left out of this, an ideology is necessarily incomplete. On the one hand, there is the error of those who, like William Appleman Williams, "are committed to the proposition that History is the most consequential way of learning who we are and what we should do." On the other hand, there is the fallacy of those who develop a social philosophy and attempt to apply it without any knowledge of what is going on in the world.

In response to Williams, it can be said that history *cannot* tell us "what we should do." At best, it can pinpoint problems which people historically have faced and solutions which they have attempted to apply.

In response to the others, it should be stated that the application of the most consistent philosophy to real events requires a journalistic knowledge of the state of the world. This differentiates ideology from philosophy. Whereas philosophy abstracts from time, and hence from history, the fundamental truths about man and his relationship to reality, ideology is a consistent world view. It integrates philosophy with one's context, applies the principles of philosophy to the concrete realities of the world. Philosophy is concerned with the nature and validity of human knowledge, with validating and detailing the precepts of a rational ethic, with *truth*. Ideology is concerned with applying philosophy to any given historical context—with *making truth relevant*, which comes from an integrated focus on man as he is in any historical context.

The transition from philosophy to ideology is largely accomplished by history. To use an analogy, philosophy discovers a rational ethic, but every given individual must apply its precepts to his own life by identifying the context he faces and making concrete choices by means of logic. The "major premise" in this version of the Aristotelian "practical syllogism" is the ethical premise itself. The "minor premise" is the concrete in anyone's life which the principles subsume. The "conclusion" is the action to be taken.

Similarly in the transition from philosophy to ideology, the major premise is the ethical–philosophic principle; the minor premises are the concrete details, or "existential premises" which summarize some aspect of the context of man in some historical period. The conclusion is the ideological stand to be taken.

It is important to emphasize the overwhelming necessity of having a valid existential premise in either the individual or general case. In ideology, invalid historical or existential premises can make the stand taken totally inconsistent with the basic thrust of the philosophy which generated it initially. The result of errors may be that the ideological stand ends up on the wrong side of the fence.

Now a word on some of my own positions on basic issues. Believing that the universe consists of a number of distinct entities which are related to each other by both real and mental relations (having an objective foundation in fact), I hold that things necessarily act in accordance with their individual natures, producing results in accordance with such natures. Concepts and theories are therefore formed by integrating particulars according to common characteristics into new mental entities.

In history, I hold that events consist of the actions of *individuals* motivated toward certain ends using certain means to attain them. But since individuals often have the same values and conceptions of appropriate means to attain their ends, they often work together. In fact, the whole function of institutions is to enable individual human actions to be systematically and consciously integrated in producing common ends. It is this fact which gives rise to all classifications, and hence all "class analysis." "Classes" in social theory, or political theory, or historical investigation, must of necessity be groups of individuals having common characteristics. It is my view that man has free will, and that the concept and existence of such free will is a necessary postulate if an obvious fact of man's nature is to be explained: his capacity for conceptual thought and propositional speech, and his ability to identify facts of reality. Determinism, in the strict sense, is self-contradictory. For if man's mental processes—specifically, his attempts at reasoning—are not free, if they are determined by environment and heredity, then there is no means of claiming that theory x is true and y is false—since man can have no way of knowing that his mental processes might not be conditioned to force him to believe that x is logical, when in fact it is not.

This means that "classes" in history are not primarily economic, in the usual sense of the term, but rather, are *ethical*. Man is not born with values, or preferences except on a sensory level (pleasure and pain), and he does not merely absorb values from a culture like a sponge absorbs water. Rather, men must *choose* their values, by intention or default. And the realm of chosen values is the realm of ethics. This belief in ethical classes is the *root* of my disagreement with Marxism.

A related fallacy of Marxism, especially in relation to its effect in guiding historical investigation, is its simplistic conception of what constitutes a class "interest."

"Interests" are not primary, nor automatic. Apart from that category of things which actually benefit men (whether or not men are aware of them), "interests" can only be arrived at through a process of consciousness; *evaluation*. This means that, given an objective standard of the organism's life and well-being, a given man's values and conceptions of his own, or his "class's" interests, can be right or wrong. More importantly, *classes are derived from and validated by reference to concrete individuals, actions, and values, not vice versa*. Classifications are derived from things, not vice versa.

This is important to focus on for a moment. For Marx, despite all his anti-Idealistic and anti-Hegelian rhetoric, is really an Idealist and Hegelian on the issue of classification. Whatever attempts he makes to get around this point, Marx is still asserting, at root, that a classification (a social class) precedes and determines the characteristics of those who are members or units of the classification. Marx is, in fact, very unclear on the nature of the exact process of causation which occurs in the interaction between those people who own the "means of production," their ideas ("interests") and actions, and those people relating to them. Since any such theory of causality in human action is vitally important in historical investigation, it is to be expected that Marxism corrupts historical investigation.

Interestingly enough, this is very relevant to the subject of this essay: the role of big business in promoting American statism. For if nothing else, this essay shows that the "class lines" in American history are different from what they were thought to be. Some of the men in larger businesses supported and even initiated acts of government regulation, while others, particularly relatively smaller and more competent competitors, opposed such regulation. Thus we have a clear-cut case in American history that contradicts Marxian theory: the lines of battle and conflict were *not* drawn merely over the issue and criterion of individuals' relation to the means of production, but on much more complicated grounds. A better classification might be along the lines set down by Franz Oppenheimer: the state-benefitted and the state-oppressed, those who gained their wealth by means of confiscation, robbery, and restriction of other people's noncoercive activities, and those who gained their wealth by means of free trade in a free market, by the method of voluntary exchange. But even here the lines are not clear-cut, and we find cases of those who were honest producers sanctioning theft and parasitism, as well as cases of those who were parasites and benefitors from statism opposing controls—twin sides of hypocrisy and altruism.

Needless to add, many contemporary Marxists have responded to the challenge with ever new wings being added onto classical Marxist theory to "explain," in an ad hoc fashion, the events which do not fit into classical Marxist paradigms. Historically, *whenever* defenders of some classic paradigm, in any field, begin to confront problems which conflict with the basic theory, they begin increasingly to modify the particulars of the theory to conform to fact, without ever questioning the basic paradigm itself. But sooner or later any such imitation of the path taken by the followers of Ptolemy must end in the same way: the paradigm will collapse and be replaced by a new paradigm which explains all the known facts in a much simpler manner, thus conforming to a fundamental rule of scientific methodology: Occam's razor.

The new paradigm, I think, will be the paradigm of libertarianism.

The purpose of this particular essay is simply to apply some of the principles of libertarianism to an interpretation of events in a very special and important period of American history. I have attempted to give a straightforward summary of New Left revisionist findings in one area of domestic history: the antitrust movement and Progressive Era. But I have done so not as a New Leftist, nor as a historian proper, but as a *libertarian*, that is, a social philosopher of a specific school.

In doing this summary, I have two interrelated purposes: first, to show Objectivists and libertarians that certain of their beliefs in history are wrong and need to be revised under the impact of new evidence, and simultaneously to illustrate to them a specific means of approaching historical problems, to identify one cause of the growth of American statism, and to indicate a new way of looking at history. Secondly, my purpose is to show New Left radicals that far from undermining the position of laissez-faire capitalism (as opposed to what they call state capitalism, a system of government controls which is not yet socialism in the classic sense), their historical discoveries actually *support* the case for a totally free market. Then, too, I wish to illustrate how a libertarian would respond to the problems raised by New Left historians. Finally, I wish implicitly to apply Occam's razor by showing that there is a simpler explanation of events than that so often colored with Marxist theory. Without exception, Marxist postulates are not necessary to explain the facts of reality.

Conflicting Schools of Thought

In historiography different schools of thought exist in much the same way and for the same reason as in many other fields. And in history, as in those other fields, different interpretations, no matter how far removed from reality, tend to go on forever, oblivious to new evidence and theories. In his book, *The Structure of Scientific Revolutions*, Thomas Kuhn shows in the physical sciences how an existing paradigm of scientific explanation tends to ignore new evidence and theories, being overthrown only when: (a) the puzzles and problems generated by a false paradigm pile up to an increasingly obvious extent, so that an ever-wider range of material cannot be integrated into the paradigm, and an ever-growing number of problems cannot be solved, and (b) there arises on the scene a new paradigm to replace the old.

In history, perhaps more than in most other fields, the criteria of truth have not been sufficiently developed, resulting in a great number of schools of thought that tend to rise and fall in influence more because of political and cultural factors than because of epistemological factors. The result also has been that in history there are a number of competing paradigms to explain different sets of events, all connected to specific political views. In this essay, I shall consider three of them; the Marxist view, the conservative view, and the liberal view. I shall examine how these paradigms function with reference to one major area of American history—the Progressive Era—and with respect to one major issue: the roots of government regulation of the economy, particularly through the antitrust laws and the Federal Reserve System. Other incidents will also be mentioned, but this issue will be the focus.

Among these various schools, nearly everyone agrees on the putative facts of American history; disagreements arise over frameworks of interpretation and over evaluation.

The Marxists, liberals, and conservatives all agree that in the economic history of America in the nineteenth century, the facts were roughly as follows. After midcentury, industrialization proceeded apace in America, as a consequence of the laissez-faire policies pursued by the United States government, resulting in increasing centralization and concentration of economic power.

According to the liberal, in the nineteenth century there was an individualistic social system in the United States, which, when left unchecked, led inevitably to the "strong" using the forces of a free market to smash and subdue the "weak," by building gigantic, monopolistic industrial enterprises which dominated and controlled the life of the nation. Then, as this centralization proceeded to snowball, the "public" awoke to its impending subjugation at the hands of these monopolistic businessmen. The public was stirred by the injustice of it all and demanded reform, whereupon altruistic and far-seeing politicians moved quickly to smash the monopolists with antitrust laws and other regulations of the economy, on behalf of the ever-suffering "little man" who was saved thereby from certain doom. Thus did the American government squash the greedy monopolists and restore competition, equality of opportunity and the like, which was perishing in the unregulated laissez-faire free market economy. Thus did the American state act to save both freedom *and* capitalism.

The Marxists also hold that there was in fact a trend toward centralization of the economy at the end of the last century, and that this was inherent in the nature of capitalism as an economic system. (Some modern, more sophisticated Marxists maintain, on the contrary, that historically the state was *always* involved in the so-called capitalistic economy.) Different Marxists see the movement towards state regulation of the economy in different ways. One group basically sees state regulation as a means of prolonging the collapse of the capitalistic system, a means which they see as inherently unstable. They see regulation as an attempt by the ruling class to deal with the "inner contradictions" of capitalism. Another group, more sophisticated, sees the movement towards state regulation as a means of *hastening* the cartelization and monopolization of the economy under the hands of the ruling class.

The conservative holds, like the liberal, that there was *indeed* such a golden age of individualism, when the economy was almost completely free of government controls. But far from being evil, such a society was near-utopian in their eyes. But the government interfered and threw things out of kilter. The consequence was that the public began to clamor for regulation in order to rectify things that were either not injustices at all, or were injustices imposed by initial state actions. The antitrust laws and other acts of state interference, by this view, were the result. But far from seeing the key large industrialists and bankers as monopolistic monsters, the conservatives defend them as heroic innovators who were the victims of misguided or power-lusting progressives who used big businessmen as scapegoats and sacrifices on the altar of the "public good."

All three of the major schools of interpretation of this crucial era in American history hold two premises in common: (a) that the trend in economic organization at the end of the nineteenth century was *in fact* towards growing centralization of economic power, and (b) that this trend was an outcome of the processes of the free market. Only the Marxists, and then only a portion of them, take issues with the additional premise that the actions of state regulation were anti-big business in motivation, purpose, and results. And both the conservatives and the liberals see a sharp break between the ideas and men involved in the Progressive Movement and those of key big business and financial leaders. Marxists disagree with many of these views, but hold the premise that the regulatory movement itself was an outgrowth of the capitalistic economy.

The Marxists, of course, smuggle in specifically nonhistorical conclusions and premises, based on their wider ideological frame of reference, the most prominent being the idea of *necessity* applied to historical events.

Although there are many arguments and disputes between adherents of the various schools, none of the schools has disputed the fundamental *historical* premise that the dominant trend at the end of the last century was toward increasing centralization of the economy, or the fundamental *economic* premise that this alleged increase was the result of the operations of a laissez-faire free market system.

Yet there are certain flaws in all three interpretations, flaws that are both historical and theoretical, flaws that make any of the interpretations inadequate, necessitating a new explanation. Although it is not possible here to argue in depth against the three interpretations, brief reasons for their inadequacy can be given.

Aside from the enormous disputes in economics over questions such as whether or not the "capitalistic system" inherently leads towards concentration and centralization of economic power in the hands of a few, we can respond to the Marxists, as well as to the others, by directing our attention to the premise that there was in fact economic centralization at the turn of the century. In confronting the liberals, once more we can begin by pointing to the fact that there has been much more centralization since the Progressive Era than before, and that the function, if not the alleged purpose, of the antitrust and other regulatory laws, has been to increase, rather than decrease, such centralization. Since the conservatives already question, on grounds of economic theory, the premise that concentration of economic power results inevitably from a free market system, we must question them as to why they believe that (a) a free market actually existed during the period in question, and (b) how, then, such centralization of economic power resulted from this supposed free market.

Aside from all the economic arguments, let us look at the period in question to see if any of the schools presented hold up, in any measure or degree.

The Roots of Regulation

In fact and in history, the entire thesis of all three schools is botched, from beginning to end. The interpretations of the Marxists, the liberals, and the conservatives are a tissue of fallacies.

As Gabriel Kolko demonstrates in his masterly, *The Triumph of Conservatism* and in *Railroads and Regulation*, the dominant trend in the last three decades of the nineteenth century and the first two of the twentieth was not towards increasing centralization, but rather, despite the growing number of mergers and the growth in the overall size of many corporations,

toward growing competition. Competition was unacceptable to many key business and financial leaders, and the merger movement was to a large extent a reflection of voluntary, unsuccessful business efforts to bring irresistible trends under control. . . . As new competitors sprang up, and as economic power was diffused throughout an expanding nation, it became apparent to many important businessmen that only the national government could [control and stabilize] the economy . . . Ironically, contrary to the consensus of historians, it was not the existence of monopoly which caused the federal government to intervene in the economy, but the lack of it.[1]

While Kolko does not consider the causes and context of the economic crises which faced businessmen from the 1870's on, we can at least summarize some of the more relevant aspects here. The enormous role played by the state in American history has not yet been fully investigated by anyone. Those focusing on the role of the federal government in regulating the economy often neglect to mention the fact that America's ostensive federalist system means that the historian concerned with the issue of regulation must look to the various state governments as well. What he will find already has been suggested by a growing number of historians: that nearly every federal program was pioneered by a number of state governments, including subsidies, land grants, and regulations of the antitrust variety. Furthermore, often neglected in these accounts is the fact that the real process of centralization of the economy came not during the Progressive Era, but rather (initially) during the Civil War, with its immense alliance between the state and business (at least in the more industrialized North). Indeed, such key figures in the Progressive Era as J. P. Morgan got their starts in alliances with the government of the North in the Civil War. The Civil War also saw the greatest inflationary expansion of the monetary supply and greatest land grants to the railroads in American history. These and other related facts means that an enormous amount of economic *malinvestment* occurred during and immediately after the Civil War, and the result was that a process of liquidation of malinvestments took place: a depression in the 1870's.

It was this process of inflationary boom caused by the banking and credit system spurred by the government and followed by depressions, that led the businessmen and financial leaders to seek stabilizing elements from the 1870's on. One of the basic results of this process of liquidation, of course, was a growth in competition. The thesis of the Kolko books is that the trend was towards growing competition in the United States before the federal government intervened, and that various big businessmen in different fields found themselves unable to cope with this trend by private, economic means. Facing falling profits and diffusion of economic power, these businessmen then turned to the state to regulate the economy on their behalf. What Kolko and his fellow revisionist James Weinstein [*The Corporate Ideal in the Liberal State*, 1900–1918] maintain is that business and financial leaders did not merely react to these situations with concrete proposals for regulations, but with the ever more sophisticated development of a comprehensive *ideology* which embraced both foreign and domestic policy. Weinstein in particular links up the process of businessmen turning to the state for favors in response to problems which they faced and the modern "corporate liberal" system. He maintains that the ideology *now dominant* in the U.S. had been worked out for the most part by the end of the First World War, not during the New Deal, as is commonly held, and that the "ideal of a liberal corporate social order" was developed *consciously and purposefully* by those who then, as now, enjoyed supremacy in the United States: "the more sophisticated leaders of America's largest corporations and financial institutions."[2] In examining this thesis, I shall focus predominantly on the activities of the National Civics Federation (NCF), a group of big businessmen that was the primary ideological force behind many "reforms."

Since the basic pattern of regulation of the economy was first established in the case of the railroads, a glance at this industry will set the basis for an examination of the others.

American industry as a whole was intensely competitive in the period from 1875 on. Many industries, including the railroads, had overexpanded and were facing a squeeze on profits. American history contains the myth that the railroads faced practically no competition at

all during this period, that freight rates constantly rose, pinching every
last penny out of the shippers, especially the farmers, and bleeding them
to death. Historian Kolko shows that:

*Contrary to the common view, railroad freight rates, taken as a whole, declined
almost continuously over the period [from 1877 to 1916] and although
consolidation of railroads proceeded apace, this phenomenon never affected the
long-term decline of rates or the ultimately competitive nature of much of the
industry. In their desire to establish stability and control over rates and
competition, the railroads often resorted to voluntary, cooperative efforts. ...
When these efforts failed, as they inevitably did, the railroad men turned to
political solutions to [stabilize] their increasingly chaotic industry. They advocated
measures designed to bring under control those railroads within their own ranks
that refused to conform to voluntary compacts ... from the beginning of the 20th
century until at least the initiation of World War I, the railroad industry resorted
primarily to political alternatives and gave up the abortive efforts to put its own
house in order by relying on voluntary cooperation ... Insofar as the railroad men
did think about the larger theoretical implications of centralized federal regulation, they rejected ... the entire notion of laissez-faire [and] most railroad leaders
increasingly relied on a Hamiltonian conception of the national government.*[3]

The two major means used by competitors to cut into each other's
markets were rate wars (price cutting) and rebates; the aim of business
leaders was to stop these. Their major, unsuccessful, tool was the "pool"
which was continuously broken up by competitive factors.[4] The first
serious pooling effort in the East, sponsored by the New York Central,
had been tried as early as 1874 by Vanderbilt; the pool lasted for six
months. In September 1876, a Southwestern Railroad Association was
formed by seven major companies in an attempt to voluntarily enforce a
pool; it didn't work and collapsed in early 1878. Soon it became obvious
to most industrial leaders that the pooling system was ineffective.

In 1876 the first significant federal regulatory bill was introduced
into the House by J. R. Hopkins of Pittsburgh. Drawn up by the attorney
for the Philadelphia and Reading Railroad, it died in committee.

By 1879, there was "a general unanimity among pool executives ...
that without government sanctions, the railroads would never maintain
or stabilize rates."[5] By 1880, the railroads were in serious trouble; the
main threat was identified as "cutthroat competition."

Far from pushing the economy toward greater centralization,
economic forces indicated that centralization was inefficient and unsta-

ble. The push was towards decentralization, and smaller railroads often found themselves much less threatened by economic turns of events than the older, more established, and larger business concerns.

Thus the Marxist model finds itself seriously in jeopardy in this instance, for the smaller firms and railroads, throughout the crises of the 1870's and 1880's often were found to be making larger profits on capital invested than the giant businesses. Furthermore, much of the concentration of economic power which was apparent during the 1870's and on, was the result of massive state aid immediately before, during, and after the Civil War, *not* the result of free market forces. Much of the capital accumulation—particularly in the cases of the railroads and banks—was accomplished by means of government regulation and aid, not by free trade on a free market.

Also, the liberal and conservative models which stress the supposed fact that there was growing centralization in the economy and that competition either lessened or became less intense, are both shaken by the historical facts. And we already have seen that it was the railroad leaders, faced with seemingly insurmountable problems, who initiated the drive for federal government regulation of their industry.

Rate wars during 1881 pushed freight rates down 50 percent between July and October alone; between 1882 and 1886, freight rates declined for the nation as a whole by 20 percent. Railroads were increasingly talking about regulation with a certain spark of interest. Chauncey Depew, attorney for the New York Central, had become convinced "of the [regulatory commission's] necessity . . . for the protection of both the public and the railroads."[6] He soon converted William H. Vanderbilt to his position.[7]

Agitation for regulation to ease competitive pains increased, and in 1887, the Interstate Commerce Act was passed. According to the Railway Review, an organ of the railroad, it was only a first step.

The Act was not enough, and it did not stop either the rate wars or rebates. So, early in 1889 during a prolonged rate war, J. P. Morgan summoned presidents of major railroads to New York to find ways to maintain rates and enforce the act, but this, too, was a failure. The larger railroads were harmed most by this competition; the smaller railroads were in many cases more prosperous than in the early 1880's. "Morgan weakened rather than strengthened many of his roads . . . [and on them] services and safety often declined. Many of Morgan's lines were overexpanded into areas where competition was already too great."[8] Competition again increased. The larger roads then led the fight for further regulation, seeking more power for the Interstate Commerce Commission (ICC).

In 1891, the president of a midwestern railroad advocated that the *entire* matter of setting rates be turned over to the ICC. An ICC poll taken in 1892 of fifteen railroads showed that fourteen of them favored legalized pooling under Commission control.

Another important businessman, A. A. Walker, who zipped back and forth between business and government agencies, said that "railroad men had had enough of competition. The phrase 'free competition' sounds well enough as a universal regulator," he said, "but it regulates by the knife."[9]

In 1906, the Hepburn Act was passed, also with business backing. The railroad magnate Cassatt spoke out as a major proponent of the act and said that he had long endorsed federal rate regulation. Andrew Carnegie, too, popped up to endorse the act. George W. Perkins, an important Morgan associate, wrote his boss that the act "is going to work out for the ultimate and great good of the railroad." But such controls were not enough for some big businessmen. Thus E. P. Ripley, the president of the Sante Fe, suggested what amounted to a Federal Reserve System for the railroads, cheerfully declaring that such a system "would do away with the enormous wastes of the competitive system, and permit business to follow the line of least resistance"—a chant later taken up by Mussolini.

In any case, we have seen that: (a) the trend was not towards centralization at the close of the nineteenth century—rather, the liquidation of previous malinvestments fostered by state action and bank-led inflation worked against the bigger businesses in favor of smaller, less overextended businesses; (b) there was, in the case of the railroads anyway, no sharp dichotomy or antagonism between big businessmen and the Progressive Movement's thrust for regulation; and (c) the purpose of the regulations, as seen by key business leaders, was not to fight the growth of "monopoly," and centralization, but to foster it.

The culmination of this big business-sponsored "reform" of the economic system is actually today's system. The new system took effect immediately during World War I when railroads gleefully handed over control to the government in exchange for guaranteed rate increases and guaranteed profits, something continued under the Transportation Act of 1920. The consequences, of course, are still making themselves felt, as in 1971, when the Pennsylvania Railroad, having cut itself off from the market and from market calculation nearly entirely, was found to be in a state of economic chaos. It declared bankruptcy and later was rescued, in part, by the state.

Regulation Comes to the Rest of the Economy

Having illustrated my basic thesis through a case study of the origins of regulation in the railroad industry, I shall now look at the rest of the American economy in this period, and examine, however briefly, the role that big business had in pushing through acts of state regulation.

I should also mention, at least in passing, big businessmen not only had a particularly important effect in pushing through domestic regulation, but they fostered interventionism in foreign policy as well. What was common to both spheres was the fact that the acts of state intervention and monetary expansion by the state-manipulated banking system had precipitated depressions and recessions from the 1870's through the 1890's. The common response of businessmen, particularly big businessmen—the leaders in various fields—was to promote further state regulation and aid as a solution to the problems caused by the depressions. In particular vogue at the time—in vogue today, as a matter of fact—was the notion that continued American prosperity required (as a necessary condition) expanded markets for American goods and manufactured items. This led businessmen to seek markets in foreign lands through various routes, having fulfilled their "manifest destiny" at home.

Domestically, however, the immediate result was much more obvious. From about 1875 on, many corporations, wishing to be large and dominant in their field, overexpanded and overcapitalized. Mediocre entrepreneurship, administrative difficulties, and increasing competition cut deeply into the markets and profits of many giants. Mergers often were tried, as in the railroad industry, but the larger mergers brought neither greater profits nor less competition. As Kolko states: "Quite the opposite occurred." There was *more* competition, and profits, if anything, declined." A survey of ten mergers showed, for instance, that the companies earned an average of 65 percent of their *preconsolidation* profits after consolidation. Overcentralization inhibited their flexibility of action, and hence their ability to respond to changing market conditions. In short, things were not as bad for other industries as for the railroads—they were often worse.

In the steel industry, the price of most steel goods declined more or less regularly until 1895, and even though prices rose somewhat thereafter, there was considerable insecurity about what other competitors might choose to do next. A merger of many corporations in 1901, based on collaboration between Morgan and Carnegie, resulted in the formation of U.S. Steel. Yet U.S. Steel's profit margin declined *over 50 percent* between 1902 and 1904. In its first two decades of existence, U.S. Steel held a continually shrinking share of the market. Due to technological conservatism and inflexible leadership, the company became increasingly costly and inefficient. Voluntary efforts at control failed. U.S. Steel turned to politics.

In the oil industry, where Standard Oil was dominant, the same situation existed. In 1899 there were 67 petroleum refiners in the U.S.; within ten years, the number had grown to 147 refiners.

In the telephone industry, things were in a similar shape. From its foundation in 1877 until 1894, Bell Telephone (AT&T) had a virtual monopoly in the industry based on its control of almost all patents.[10] In 1894 many of the patents expired. "Bell immediately adopted a policy of harassing the host of aspiring competitors by suing them (27 suits were instituted in 1894–95 alone) for allegedly infringing Bell patents."[11] But such efforts to stifle competition failed; by 1902, there were 9,100 independent telephone systems; by 1907, there were 22,000. Most had rates lower than AT&T.

In the meat packing industry too, the large packers felt threatened by increasing competition. Their efforts at control failed. Similar diffusion of economic power was the case in other fields, such as banking, where the power of the eastern financiers was being seriously eroded by midwestern competitors.

This, then, was the basic context of big business; these were the problems that it faced. How did it react? Almost unanimously, it turned to the power of the state to get what it could not get by voluntary means. Big business acted not only through concrete political pressure, but by engaging in large-scale, long-run ideological propaganda or "education" aimed at getting different sections of the American society united behind statism, in principle and practice.

Let us look at some of the activities of the major organizational tool of big business, the National Civics Federation. The NCF was actually a reincarnation of Hamiltonian views on the relationship of the state to business. Primarily an organization of big businessmen, it pushed for the tactical and theoretical alliance of business and government, a primitive version of the modern business–government partnership. Contrary to the consensus of many conservatives, it was not ideological innocence that led them to create a statist economic order—they knew what they were doing and constantly said so.

The working partnership of business and government was the result of the conscious activities of organizations such as the NCF created in 1900, (coinciding with the birth of what is called the "Progressive

Movement"), to fight with increasing and sustained vigor against what it considered to be its twin enemies: "the socialists and radicals among workers and middle class reformers, and the 'anarchists' among the businessmen" (as the NCF characterized the National Association of Manufacturers). The smaller businessmen, who constituted the NAM, formed an opposition to the new liberalism that developed through cooperation between political leaders such as Theodore Roosevelt, William H. Taft, and Woodrow Wilson, and the financial and corporate leaders in the NCF and other similar organizations. The NCF before World War I was "the most important single organization of the socially conscious big businessmen and their academic and political theorists." The NCF "took the lead in educating the businessmen to the changing needs in political economy which accompanied the changing nature of America's business system."[12]

The early leaders of the NCF were such big business leaders as Marcus A. Hanna, utilities magnate Samuel B. Insull, Chicago banker Franklin MacVeagh (later Secretary of the Treasury), Charles Francis Adams, and several partners in the J. P. Morgan & Co. The largest contributor to the group was Andrew Carnegie; other important members of the executive committee included George W. Perkins, Eldrige Gary (a Morgan associate and a head of U.S. Steel after Carnegie), Cyrus McCormick, Theodore N. Vail (president of AT&T), and George Cortelyou (head of Consolidated Gas).

The NCF sponsored legislation to promote the formation of "public utilities," a special privilege monopoly granted by the state, reserving an area of production to one company. Issuing a report on "Public Ownership of Public Utilities," the NCF established a general framework for regulatory laws, stating that utilities should be conducted by legalized independent commissions. Of such regulation one businessman wrote another: "Twenty-five years ago we would have regarded it as a species of socialism"; but seeing that the railroads were both submitting to and apparently profiting from regulation, the NCF's self-appointed job of "educating" municipal utilities corporations became much easier.

Regulation in general, far from coming against the wishes of the regulated interests, was openly welcomed by them in nearly every case. As Upton Sinclair said of the meat industry, which he is given credit for having tamed, "the federal inspection of meat was historically established at the packers' request. . . . It is maintained and paid for by the people of the United States for the benefit of the packers. . . ."[13]

However, one interesting fact comes in here to refute the Marxist theory further. For the Marxists hold that there are fundamentally two opposing "interests" which clash in history: the capitalists and the workers. But what we have seen, essentially, is that the interests (using the word in a journalistic sense) of neither the capitalists nor the workers, so-called, were uniform or clear-cut. The interests of the larger capitalists seemed to coincide, as they saw it and were clearly opposed to the interests of the smaller capitalists. (However, there were conflicts among the big capitalists, such as between the Morgan and Rockefeller interests during the 1900's, as illustrated in the regimes of Roosevelt and Taft.) The larger capitalists saw regulation as being in their interest, and competition as opposed to it; with the smaller businessmen, the situation was reversed. The workers for the larger businesses also may have temporarily gained at the expense of others through slight wage increases caused by restrictions on production. (The situation is made even more complicated when we remember that the Marxist belief is that one's relationship to the means of production determines one's interests and hence, apparently, one's ideas. Yet people with basically the same relationship often had different "interests" and ideas. If this in turn is explained by a Marxist in terms of "mystification," an illuminating concept in a libertarian context, then mystification *itself* is left to be explained. For if one's ideas and interests are an automatic function of the economic system and one's relationship to the means of production, how can "mystification" arise *at all*?)

In any case, congressional hearings during the administration of Theodore Roosevelt revealed that "the big Chicago packers wanted more meat inspection both to bring the small packers under control and to aid them in their position in the export trade. Formally representing the large Chicago packers, Thomas E. Wilson publically announced: "We are now and have always been in favor of the extension of the inspection."[14]

In both word and deed American businessmen sought to replace the last remnants of laissez-faire in the United States with government regulation—for their own benefit. Speaking at Columbia University in February 1908, George W. Perkins, Morgan associate, said that the corporation "must welcome federal supervision administered by practical businessmen."[15]

As early as 1908, Andrew Carnegie and Ingalls had suggested to the NCF that it push for an American version of the British Board of Trade, which would have the power to judge mergers and other industrial actions. As Carnegie put it, this had "been found sufficient in other countries and will be so with us. We must have our industrial as we have a Judicial Supreme Court."[16] Carnegie also endorsed government actions to end ruinous competition:

It always comes back to me that government control, and that alone, will properly solve the problem. . . . There is nothing alarming in this; capital is perfectly safe in the gas company, although it is under court control. So will all capital be, although under government control.[17]

AT&T, controlled by J. P. Morgan as of 1907, also sought regulation. The company got what it wanted in 1910, when telephones were placed under the jurisdiction of the ICC, and rate wars became a thing of the past. President T. N. Vail of AT&T said, "we believe in and were the first to advocate . . . governmental control and regulation of public utilities."

By June of 1911, Elbert H. Gary of U.S. Steel appeared before a congressional committee and announced to astonished members, "I believe we must come to enforced publicity and governmental control even as to prices. . . ." He virtually offered to turn price control over to the government. Kolko states that

the reason Gary and Carnegie were offering the powers of price control to the federal government was not known to the congressmen, who were quite unaware of the existing price anarchy in steel. The proposals of Gary and Carnegie, the Democratic majority on the committee reported, were really 'semisocialistic' and hardly worth endorsing.[18]

Gary also proposed that a commission similar to the ICC be set up to grant, suspend, and revoke licenses for trade, and to regulate prices.

In the fall of 1911, the NCF moved on two fronts: it sent a questionnaire to 30,000 businessmen to seek out their positions on a number of issues. Businessmen favored regulation of trade by three to one.

In November of 1911, Theodore Roosevelt proposed a national commission to control organization and capitalization of all interstate businesses. The proposal won an immediate and enthusiastic response from Wall Street.

In 1912, Arthur Eddy, an eminent corporation lawyer, working much of the time with Standard Oil, and one of the architects of the FTC, stated boldly in his magnum opus, *The New Competition*, what had been implicit in the doctrines of businessmen all along. Eddy trumpeted that "competition was inhuman and war, and that war was hell."

Thus did big businessmen believe and act.

Meanwhile, back at the bank, J. P. Morgan was not to be left out. For Morgan, because of his ownership or control of many major corporations, was in the fight for regulation from the earliest days onward. Morgan's financial power and reputation were largely the result of his operations with the American and European governments; his many dealings in currency manipulations and loans to oppressive European states earned him the reputation of a "rescuer of governments." One crucial aspect of the banking system at the beginning of the 1900's was the relative decrease in New York's financial dominance and the rise of competitors. Morgan was fully aware of the diffusion of banking power that was taking place, and it disturbed him.

Hence, bankers too turned to regulation. From very early days, Morgan had championed the cause of a central bank, of gaining control over the nation's credit through a board of leading bankers under government supervision. By 1907 the NCF had taken up the call for a more elastic currency and for greater centralization of banking.

Nelson Aldrich proposed a reform bank act and called a conference of twenty-two bankers from twelve cities to discuss it. The purpose of the conference was to "discuss winning the banking community over to government control directed by the bankers for their own ends." A leading banker, Paul Warburg, stated that "it would be a blessing to get these small banks out of the way."[19]

Most of his associates agreed. In 1913, two years after the conference, and after many squabbles over specifics, the Federal Reserve Act was passed. The big bankers were pleased.

These were not the only areas in which businessmen and their political henchmen were active. Indeed, ideologically speaking, they were behind innumerable "progressive" actions, and even financed such magazines as the *New Republic*. Teddy Roosevelt made a passing reference to the desirability of an income tax in his 1906 message to Congress, and the principle received support from such businessmen as George W. Perkins and Carnegie, who often referred to the unequal distribution of wealth as "one of the crying evils of our day." Many businessmen opposed it, but the *Wall Street Journal* said that it was certainly in favor of it.

The passage of the Clayton Antitrust Act and the creation of the Federal Trade Commission occurred in 1914. Once established, the FTC began its attempt to secure the "confidence" of "well-intentioned" businessmen. In a speech before the NCF, one of the proregulation powerhouses, J. W. Jenks, "affirmed the general feeling of relief among the leaders of large corporations and their understanding that the FTC was helpful to the corporations in every way."[20]

In this crucially important era, I have focused on one point: big business was a major source of American statism. Further researches would show, I am convinced, that big business and financial leaders were also the dominant force behind America's increasingly interventionistic foreign policy, and behind the ideology of modern liberalism. In fact, by this analysis sustained research might show American liberal intellectuals to be the "running dogs" of big businessmen, to twist a Marxist phrase a bit.

Consider the fact that the *New Republic* has virtually always taken the role of defender of the corporate state which big businessmen carefully constructed over decades. Consider the fact that such businessmen as Carnegie not only supported all the groups mentioned and the programs referred to, but also supported such things as the big Navy movement at the turn of the century. He sold steel to the United States government that went into the building of the ships and he saw in the Venezuela boundary dispute the possibility of a large order for armor from the United States Navy.[21] Carnegie, along with Rockefeller and, later, Ford, was responsible for sustained support of American liberalism through the foundations set up in his name.

J. P. Morgan, the key financial leader, was also a prime mover of American statism. His foreign financial dealings led him to become deeply involved with Britain during World War I, and this involvement in turn led him to help persuade Wilson to enter the war on Britain's behalf, to help save billions of dollars of loans which would be lost in the event of a German victory.

In a more interesting light, consider the statements made in 1914 by S. Thruston Ballard, owner of the largest wheat refinery in the world. Ballard not only supported vocational schools as a part of the public schools (which would transfer training costs to taxpayers), restrictions on immigration, and a national minimum wage, he saw and proposed a way to "cure" unemployment. He advocated a federal employment service, public works, and if these were insufficient, *"government concentration camps where work with a small wage would be provided, supplemented by agricultural and industrial training."*[22]

Consider the role of big businessmen in pushing through public education in many states after World War I. Senator Wadsworth spoke before a NCF group in 1916, pointing out that compulsory government education was needed to "protect the nation against destruction from within. It is to train the boy and girl to be good citizens, to protect against ignorance and dissipation." This meant that the reason to force children to go to school, at gunpoint if necessary, was so that they could be brainwashed into accepting the status quo, almost explicitly so that their capacity for dissent (i.e., their capacity for independent thinking) could be destroyed. Thus did Wadsworth also advocate compulsory and universal military training: "Our people shall be prepared mentally as well as in a purely military sense. *We must let our young men know that they owe some responsibility to this country.*"

Indeed, we find V. E. Macy, president of the NCF at the close of the war, stating that it was not "beside the mark to call attention to the nearly thirty million minors marching steadily toward full citizenship," and ask "at what stage of their journey we should lend assistance to the work of quickening . . . the sense of responsibility and partnership in the business of maintaining and perfecting the splendid social, industrial, and commercial structure which has been reared under the American flag." The need, Macy noted, was most urgent. Among American youths there was a widespread "indifference toward, and aloofness from, individual responsibility for the successful maintenance and upbuilding of the industrial and commercial structure which is the indispensable shelter of us all."[23]

Big business, then, was behind the existence and curriculum of the public educational system, *explicitly to teach young minds to submit and obey, to pay homage to the "corporate–liberal" system which the politicians, a multitude of intellectuals, and many big businessmen, created.*

My intention here simply has been to present an alternative model of historical interpretation of key events in this one crucial era of American history, an interpretation which is neither Marxist, liberal, nor conservative, but which may have some elements in common with each.

From a more ideological perspective, my purpose has been to present an accurate portrait of one aspect of "how we got here," and indicate a new way of looking at the present system in America.

To a large degree it has been and remains big businessmen who are the fountainheads of American statism. If libertarians are seeking allies in their struggle for liberty, then I suggest that they look elsewhere. Conservatives, too, should benefit from this presentation, and begin to see big business as a destroyer, not as a unit, of the free market. Liberals should also benefit, and reexamine their own premises about the market and regulation. Specifically, they might reconsider the nature of a *free* market, and ponder on the question of why big business has been opposed to precisely that. Isn't it odd that the interests of liberals and key big businessmen have always coincided? The Marxists, too, might rethink their economics, and reconsider whether or not capitalism leads to monopoly. Since it can be shown scientifically that economic calculation is impossible in a purely socialistic economy, and that pure statism is not good for man, perhaps the Marxists might also look at the real nature of a complete free market, undiluted by state control.

Libertarians themselves should take heart. Our hope lies, as strange as it may seem, not with any remnants from an illusory "golden age" of individualism, which never existed, but with tomorrow. Our day has not come and gone. It has never existed at all. It is our task to see that it will exist in the future. The choice and the battle are ours.

Notes

R. A. Childs, Jr., is one of the most active intellectual theoreticians in this country. His articles have appeared in the *Individualist, Libertarian Forum, Outlook, Reason, Rampart Journal* and elsewhere. He taught at Rampart College, managed Books for Libertarians, and has participated in numerous workshops dealing with political philosophy, ethics, and economics.

"Big Business and the Rise of American Statism" is reprinted with permission from *Reason*, vol. 2, nos. 11 and 12.

1. Gabriel Kolko, *The Triumph of Conservatism* (Chicago: Quadrangle Publishing Co., 1967), pp. 4–5.

2. James Weinstein, *The Corporate Ideal in the Liberal State* (Boston: Beacon Press, 1968), p. ix.

3. Gabriel Kolko, *Railroads and Regulation* (Princeton: Princeton University Press, 1965), p. 3–5.

4. See both Kolko books for factual proof of this. Weinstein does not take this fact into account in his book, and thus underestimates this as a motivating force in the actions and beliefs of businessmen. For a theoretical explanation, see Murray N. Rothbard, *Man, Economy and State* (Los Angeles: Nash Publishing Co., 1971), 2:566–585.

5. Kolko, *Railroads*, p. 26.

6. Ibid, p. 17.

7. The twin facts here that Vanderbilt needed "converting" and that he had other options open to him should by themselves put to rest the more *simplistic* Marxist theories of "class consciousness," awareness of interests and relationships to the means of production.

8. Kolko, *Railroads,* pp. 65–66.

9. Ibid., p. 74.

10. It is instructive to note that most of these patents were illegitimate according to libertarian ownership theories, since many other men had *independently* discovered the telephone and subsequent items besides Bell and the AT&T group, yet they were coercively restrained from enjoying the product of such creativity. On the illegitimacy of such patent restrictions, see Rothbard, *Man, Economy and State,* pp. 652–660.

11. Kolko, *Triumph,* p. 30–39.

12. Weinstein, *op cit.,* pp. 5–7.

13. Kolko, *Triumph,* p. 103.

14. Ibid., p. 103.

15. Ibid., p. 129.

16. Weinstein, *op cit.,* p. 82.

17. Kolko, *Triumph,* p. 180.

18. Ibid., p. 173–74.

19. Ibid., p. 183.

20. Weinstein, *op cit.,* p. 91.

21. Walter LeFeber, *The New Empire: An Interpretation of American Expansion, 1860–1890* (Ithaca: Cornell U. Press, 1963), pp. 239, 273n. The note on Carnegie's linking of the Venezuela boundary dispute with obtaining large orders of steel from the Navy was taken from Carnegie's correspondence.

22. Weinstein, *op cit.,* pp. 209–210.

23. Ibid., p. 133–35.

Joan Kennedy Taylor

14

Slavery: America's Fatal Compromise

JOHN LOCKE, THE PHILOSOPHER who most influenced the founders of America, stated that a man's life, liberty and estate were all his property, and that governments were founded for the preservation of property. "The State of Nature has a Law of Nature to govern it," he said, "which obliges everyone, and Reason, which is that Law, teaches all Mankind who will but consult it, that being all equal and independent, no one ought to harm another in his Life, Health, Liberty, or Possessions."

On June 12, 1776, the Virginia Declaration of Rights, written by George Mason, was adopted by the Colony of Virginia. Its Article I held "That all Men are by Nature equally free and independent, and have certain inherent Rights, of which, when they enter into a State of Society, they cannot, by any Compact, deprive or divest their Posterity; namely, the Enjoyment of Life and Liberty, with the Means of acquiring and possessing Property, and pursuing and obtaining Happiness and Safety."

And yet we now live in an age in which a popular political play has as its supposedly idealistic hero a presidential candidate who says that he is not sure whether or not property rights exist; an age in which a real-life President, Lyndon Baines Johnson, invoked in his inaugural address "Justice, Liberty and union" as this nation's founding principles, and characterized justice as "the promise that all who made the journey would share equally in the fruits of the land."

What has happened to the right of property? It seems to be very clear that life, liberty and property were once considered to be interconnected aspects of a new view of the proper relationship of man to the state. Has the concept of rights been repudiated in the intervening years? No, it has not. Everyone in American political life is for rights. It is merely hard for people to agree on exactly what they are.

The answer to the question, What has happened to the right of property in American political thought? is the explosion of the truism that politics is the art of compromise. It is because politicians and theoreticians were willing to compromise on an issue of rights in the early years of our history that we face today a split concept of rights— property rights are considered in opposition to "human" rights, the rights to life and liberty.

Politics should be considered the art of implementing rights. Because it has not been so considered, the concept of rights itself has been clouded, and therefore so has the concept of the proper limitations of government. And of all the issues which have been improperly the subject of compromise in American political history, by far the most important is the issue of slavery.

The sad fact is that for many years those who were most brilliant in their analysis of rights, those who were most incisive in their understanding of free trade and a free market, were willing to use the concept of rights to violate the rights of others.

The Declaration of Independence was originally drafted by Thomas Jefferson, who was one of a committee appointed by the Second Continental Congress for that purpose. Changes were made in the document before it was adopted by Congress—and one of the most startling changes was the omission of the following passage about George III of England:

He has waged cruel war against human nature itself, violating its most sacred rights of life and liberty in the persons of a distant people who never offended him, captivating & carrying them into slavery in another hemisphere, or to incur miserable death in their transportation thither. This piratical warfare, the opprobrium of infidel powers, is the warfare of the Christian king of Great Britain. Determined to keep open a market where MEN should be bought & sold, he has prostituted his negative for suppressing every legislative attempt to prohibit or to restrain this execrable commerce: and that this assemblage of horrors might want no fact of distinguished die, he is now exciting those very people to rise in arms among us, and to purchase that liberty of which he has deprived them, by murdering the people upon whom he also obtruded them: thus paying off former crimes committed against the liberties of one people, with crimes which he urges them to commit against the lives of another.

Why was this omitted? Jefferson speculated about it in his notes on the subject: "The clause too, reprobating the enslaving the inhabitants of Africa, was struck out in complaisance to South Carolina and Georgia, who had never attempted to restrain the importation of slaves, and who in the contrary still wished to continue it. Our Northern brethren also I believe felt a little tender under those censures; for tho' their people have very few slaves themselves yet they had been pretty considerable carriers of them to others."

Whoever they were, very apparently there were others besides the King of England who were "determined to keep open a market where men should be bought & sold," and they were able to prevail upon the majority. This was the first opening chink in the fabric of rights in the United States, and it occurred even before there was a United States. It must have seemed like such a small thing—not a real compromise with principle, merely a decision not to discuss a certain area.

But once it had been admitted that for purposes of political unity the subject of slavery was one that could rightfully be made the object of political compromise, such compromise inevitably went further.

And so the next step in the weakening of the theory of rights was taken in the Constitutional Convention. Thomas Jefferson wasn't there. George Mason of Virginia and others fought for an anti-slavery clause—and lost the fight. Worse than that, the Constitution as finally adopted sanctioned slavery in three places by recognizing its existence. Article I, Section 2, Paragraph 2, which provided for the apportionment of representation and direct taxes by population, "which shall be determined by adding to the whole Number of free Persons, including those bound to Service for a Term of Years, and excluding Indians not taxed, three fifths of all other Persons." Article I, Section 9, Paragraph 1, was the compromise result of disagreement over the slave trade. "The Migration or Importation of such Persons as any of the States now existing shall think proper to admit, shall not be prohibited by the Congress prior to the Year one thousand eight hundred and eight, but a tax or duty may be imposed on such Importation, not exceeding ten dollars for each person." (The African slave trade was prohibited in 1808.) And lastly, the Fugitive Slave provision, which was to be the basis on which the Abolitionists exhorted people to obey a "higher moral law" than the law of the land: Article IV, Section 2, Paragraph 3: "No Person held to Service or Labour in one State, under the Laws thereof, escaping into another, shall, in Consequence of any Law or Regulation therein, be discharged from such Service or Labour, but shall be delivered up on Claim of the Party to whom such Service or Labour may be due."

Now, there were other sections in the Constitution which today might be seen as institutionalizing the violation of rights. The powers of eminent domain and of taxation, to name but two, have served as precedents to enlarge government power far beyond the scope originally planned by the framers of the Constitution. But these areas had not yet been identified as explicit contradictions to the principles on which the Constitution was supposedly based. It is not so with the clauses dealing with slavery. George Mason said in 1787, "Slavery brings the judgment of heaven upon a country. As nations cannot be rewarded or punished in the next world, they must be in this." The very language which was finally adopted shows a reluctance to put into plain words what was being discussed: the word "slave" is never mentioned. The result was a document which guaranteed that all men are created equal and shall not be deprived of life, liberty and property without due process of law—except Other Persons.

To many Europeans the contradiction of principle was obvious and inexcusable. A young Irish poet, Tom Moore, who was nine years old when the American Constitution was ratified, later wrote:

> The patriot fresh from Freedom's councils come,
> Now pleased retires to lash his slaves at home;
> Or woo, perhaps, some black Aspasia's charms,
> And dream of freedom in his bondsmaid's arms.

As the years passed, few indeed were the voices raised publicly against slavery in the name of rights. Instead, many of those who were not economically dependent on slavery, and so disdained it, allowed the slaveholders to assert that they were the true defenders of property rights. The anti-slavery people grew to dislike the strict assertion of property rights; the defenders of slavery righteously invoked the right of property as their explicit defense.

In a historical description of slavery in the antebellum South in the book *The Peculiar Institution*, Professor Kenneth M. Stampp quotes an editorial in the Austin, Texas *State Gazette*, December 18, 1858: "The same reason which would induce us to oppose a high protective tariff . . . leads us to protest against the fanatical laws passed to prohibit the African slave trade. We can distinguish no great difference between the trade in African negroes, and the trade in any other article of property. Nothing but sectional malice and narrow bigotry prevents the trade in slaves from being left to the great laws of commerce, which can best adjust the relation between supply and demand." (p. 272)

The institution of slavery had existed in this country prior to the

Revolution, and the fact that it was already established admittedly posed some economic problems. Were those who had not chosen to live in a slave economy, but had inherited slaves, to be economically ruined? And what of the slaves themselves? Where were they to go; how were they to live? But the fact that slavery could not be dissolved casually without consideration of the consequences was confused with the "rights" of the slaveholders. The desire to enslave someone cannot be asserted as a right. If, when I am declaring my rights, what I mean is my right to enslave you—how can I defend this as a moral basis for a government? The fact that an innocent inheritor of slaves may be harmed by universal liberty should be no more of a consideration than the fact that an innocent inheritor of stolen property may be harmed by the property's return.

Avoiding the economic and moral problems posed by slavery did not solve them. Northern states dissolved the institution in time; Southern states did not. According to Kenneth Stampp, "Not because slave labor was unprofitable, but because they were given no choice, northern slaveholders accepted a domestic application of the principles which had justified resistance to British authority. During the 1780's, these states put slavery 'in the course of ultimate extinction,' usually through a system of gradual emancipation which took a generation to complete." (pp. 19–20)

Servitude of one sort or another was common in colonial days. Indentured servants whose contracts were sold on arrival to the highest bidder, transported felons serving out their time, and slaves from Africa —what was the difference? The crucial difference was that the felons had sentences, and the indentured servants had contracts, which limited their terms of service. In the seventeenth century, the status of the Negro slave was undefined, and it was often assumed that he was to be freed after a number of years, or upon his conversion to Christianity. But he had no contract.

And so, gradually, his status was defined by law, and his status became that of a chattel. In the 1660's, Maryland and Virginia passed statutes providing that Negroes were to be slaves for life and that this status was not changed by baptism. It was defined by statute that the child of a slave mother was a slave. In 1669, the Lords Proprietors of Carolina issued a constitution which established slavery in that colony. By 1750, Georgia had rescinded her original prohibition of slavery. The slave population in Southern colonies increased. Virginia's landholders relied chiefly on white labor until the end of the seventeenth century— but by the time of the Revolution, half her population was slave.

By the eve of the Civil War, the problem had grown. There were six million white inhabitants of the South, owning three million slaves, which was a vested interest of hundreds of millions of dollars. The legal defining of the slave's lack of rights had continued. There were laws against the education of slaves, against social fraternization between whites and Negroes, against such an exercise of property rights as freeing one's own slaves. There were cruelties in the selling of slaves, in the training of slaves, in the daily lives of slaves which were widespread and which no one could totally ignore. But they *were* ignored, by brilliant political writers who supported slavery on the so-called moral basis of property rights. And finally, to protect these rights, the Southern states seceded from the Union. Jefferson Davis, the President of the Southern Confederacy, was a serious student of Adam Smith, John Locke, and Thomas Jefferson; in his inaugural address he invoked "honor and right and liberty and equality," and stated: "Our present political position has been achieved in a manner unprecedented in the history of nations. It illustrates the American idea that government rests on the consent of the governed, and that it is the right of all those to whom we would sell, and from whom we would buy, that there should be the fewest practicable restrictions upon the interchange of these commodities."

Meanwhile, Northern reformers were willing to cede the defense of property rights to the slaveholders. The main voices against slavery were the abolitionists, who preached civil disobedience, in the name of a higher moral law, to people called on to obey the Fugitive Slave Act. Books like Harriet Beecher Stowe's *Uncle Tom's Cabin* and Theodore Weld's *American Slavery as It Is* inflamed their audiences by depicting the cruelties of slavery. It was clear that a gross injustice had been institutionalized. But the South's position, so totally untenable in principle, was correct in law.

The laws were based on the Constitution, which in turn was supposedly based on the natural rights of man. Slavery had been recognized by the Constitution. It was ultimately the principle of rights that had to suffer for that fact.

The North could not take the position that the Confederacy was a tyranny—officially, slavery was totally legal. The North took the position that the Union was more important than States' Rights, which is a collectivist position. Historians may disagree on the journalistic causes of the Civil War, but it seems obvious that millions of Northerners were willing to fight for this position because of the issue of slavery.

The South, aided by the fatal Constitutional compromise, had an unimpeachable legal defense. The Dred Scott decision in 1857 held that a Negro "whose ancestors were ... sold as slaves" had no rights as a Federal citizen, and that Congress had no power to prohibit slavery in the territories, as that would be a violation of the Fifth Amendment in that it would deprive slaveholders of their property without due process. Many a Northerner found it obvious that if the institution of slavery was defensible in the name of property rights, then property rights would have to be abrogated, and the slaves freed by force.

Thus the original contradiction had blossomed. Those who were actually tyrants were the avowed defenders of rights and constitutionality and free trade; while the advocates of expanded federal power had been enabled to pass the first draft laws, the first income tax laws, and to assert federal regulation of the iron, steel, textile and munitions industries in the name of defending "human" rights which were higher than the right to property.

There were those who held that the right to property was in fact exalted out of proportion by John Locke and by the Founding Fathers; that a rigid observance of property rights must inevitably lead to violations of the rights to life and liberty. One of the observers of the Civil War was a political exile living in London who had been the London correspondent of Horace Greeley's *Tribune* prior to 1862. His name was Karl Marx. He was to promote the pre-Lockean concept that property was not an individual right, but that nations and groups ideally should own land and possessions in common. He was by no means the only person to hold such a point of view; it had a long historical tradition, bolstered by certain passages in the Bible. This collectivist, statist view was now granted the status of an appeal to rights. Northerners in America, having been incensed by the cruelty of slavery, were ready to see little difference between the plight of a slave and the plight of a "wage-slave." Property rights had supposedly been abrogated in the name of humanity to save the slave—what answer was to be given to the collectivists who wished to question the rich factory owner's property right? It was not too long to the passage of the first anti-trust act.

But the right to property cannot be separated from the rights to life and liberty—they are in fact interconnected aspects of a view of the proper limitations of state power. The attempt to do so resulted in the erosion of all rights. The direct result of the South's defense of "property" was not only the permanent denial of life and liberty to one-third of its inhabitants, but the forcing of a garrison state upon the holders of such property. The law not only defended a *right* to property in other people, it insisted upon property in other people. By the time of the Civil War, all the states of the Deep South had not only provisions in their state constitutions prohibiting the legislatures from freeing slaves, but laws against private manumission as well. Compulsory segregation, the prohibition of education for slaves, and like measures to ensure the safety of the society, served further to chain the slaveholder to his property.

Similarly, the failure of the North to identify the importance of the property right that had been so travestied in the South resulted in the gradual entrenchment of federal power and statism; and the War which gained its moral fervor from a supposed defense of the rights of life and liberty attacked those very rights by the wartime suspension of *habeas corpus* and by the draft.

So we return to our first question, what happened to John Locke's brilliantly identified philosophy of the rights of man?

And here we find a surprising answer; an answer which illustrates anew the enormous importance of theoretical consistency in politics. Because, on closer examination, we find that what happened in American history to the ideas of John Locke was no more than John Locke deserved. The contradiction goes all the way back to him and his *Two Treatises of Government*.

In 1703, John Locke wrote to a young relative, "Property I have nowhere found more clearly explained, than in a book entitled, *Two Treatises of Government*." The editor of the most recent critical edition of the treatises, Peter Laslett, says of Locke's doctrine of property, "It remains an original document, particularly important in its bearing on the way men analysed social and political origins, and his own judgment on it must stand—no man has ever done quite this before or since." (John Locke, *Two Treatises of Government*, A critical edition with Introduction and Notes by Peter Laslett, p. 120) In 1932, which was the tercentenary of Locke's birth, Sir Ernest Barker wrote in an article in *The Times* Literary Supplement: "The Declaration of Independence with its initial appeal to 'The Laws of Nature and of Nature's God,' shows one side of Locke, who lived in American thought in 1776 even more than he lived in England. The deep sense of property evident in American thought, including even property in the person of others, showed another. The two sides had already been conjoined in Locke's draft of a constitution for Carolina."

John Locke held, among other minor political offices, the secretary-ship of the associated proprietors of the Colony of Carolina. He is the author (perhaps with the help of his friend and patron, Lord Shaftes-bury) of the Carolina constitution mentioned previously as establishing slavery in that colony in 1669. In his *Second Treatise, Of Civil Government*, the document which most influenced the founders of the United States,

John Locke later defended slavery as an institution: "But there is another sort of servants, which by a peculiar name we call *Slaves*, who being captives taken in a just War, are by the Right of Nature subjected to the Absolute Dominion and Arbitrary Power of their Masters. These Men having, as I say, forfeited their Lives, and with it their Liberties, and lost their Estates; and being in the *State of Slavery*, not capable of any Property, cannot in that state be considered as any part of *Civil Society*; the chief end whereof is the preservation of property." (*Of Civil Government*, paragraph *85*)

Says Peter Laslett of this and two other paragraphs in the *Second Treatise* which also justify slavery: "It may seem unnecessary, and inconsistent with his principles, but it must be remembered that he writes as the administrator of slave-owning colonies in America. As Leslie Stephen pointed out ... the *Fundamental Constitutions of Carolina* provide that every freeman 'shall have absolute power and authority over his negro slaves.' ... The Instructions to Governor Nicholson of Virginia, which Locke did so much to draft in 1698 ... regard negro slaves as justifiably enslaved because they were captives taken in a just war, who had forfeited their lives 'by some Act that deserves Death.' ... Locke seems satisfied that the forays of the Royal Africa Company were just wars of this sort, and that the negroes captured had committed such acts."

Even granting some persuasiveness to the argument that if one has forfeited his right to life one has forfeited other rights as well, nothing in this argument even attempts to justify such a contradiction as the concept of being born a slave, on which the economy of the South, including the Carolinas, was being led to base itself.

When one reads John Locke in a historical context of other influential political philosphers, he stands out like an island of defense of individual rights in a sea of centuries of collectivist thinking. Why didn't this concept transform the world and abolish tyranny forever? Why did collectivist attacks on individualism and private property flourish after John Locke, as well as before? Because he did not consider it vital to be totally consistent. And no one who put Locke's philosophy into practice corrected his fault.

Bibliography

Becker, Carl L., *The Declaration of Independence: A Study in the History of Political Ideas*, Vintage Books, New York, 1958. (Originally published, 1922)

Furnas, J. C., *Goodbye To Uncle Tom*, Sloane, New York, 1956.

Introduction to Contemporary Civilization in the West, Vol. I, 3rd ed., Columbia University Press, New York, 1960.

Locke, John. *Two Treatises of Government*, with Introduction and Notes by Peter Laslett, Mentor, New York, 1965.

Sideman, Belle Becker, and Lillian Friedman, eds., *Europe Looks at the Civil War*, Orion Press, New York, 1960.

Social Contract, Essays by Locke, Hume, and Rousseau, with an Introduction by Sir Ernest Barker, Oxford University Press, New York, 1962.

Stampp, Kenneth M., *The Peculiar Institution*, Knopf, New York, 1956.

Strode, Hudson, *Jefferson Davis, American Patriot: 1808–1861*, Harcourt, Brace & Co., New York, 1955.

Note

Joan Kennedy Taylor was the founder and editor-in-chief of *Persuasion*, a libertarian magazine that started as the newsletter of the Metropolitan Young Republican Club of New York during the Goldwater presidential campaign and became an independent corporation early in 1965. It appeared monthly until May 1968. Ms. Taylor is co-author, with Lee M. Shulman, of *When to See a Psychologist*, and has made a musical out of Oscar Wilde's story "The Canterville Ghost," with the composer George Broderick. She and her husband, David J. Dawson, now live in Stockbridge, Mass.

"Slavery: America's Fatal Compromise" is reprinted with permission from *Persuasion* (February 1967).

Tibor Machan

15 "The Schools Ain't What They Used to Be and Never Was"

To say that American education is at a point of extreme self-consciousness does not seem to require extensive justification. Just being awake and reading the newspapers will suffice to avail us of this fact.

There are probably more things the matter with education in America today than anyone could discuss in a short essay. An understanding of our educational problems, even if we grant that it is in principle possible, would take extensive and very careful hard work. I shall confine myself to some more or less basic points.

To start off I will have to propose a definition of education that can be defended without extensive philosophical argumentation about definitions, knowledge, and the nature of truth. That itself is difficult. It may seem like wanting to escape the burden of dealing with the really difficult issues. But things are not always what they seem, so I will proceed.

Education will be taken to be, in the present context, an endeavor of human cooperation for purposes of assisting individuals to develop their intellectual capacities to cope with their world *so that they may lead their lives well*. This, I think, is broad enough to be noncontroversial. The acceptance of this definition will, however, commit one to certain propositions which may not be obvious at first.

Although education in America is something that occurs at many different levels of complexity, appropriate to age and circumstance, in an investigation which aims to treat *fundamentals* it is not advisable to ponder over the *variations* of education.

There are a few points which must be developed before we can discuss the place of education within a culture. These have to do with some of the basic principles which all levels of education must observe in order for them to be education. For example, if we take the concept "cooperation" as central to education, it will be clear that those involved in the endeavor of education must be *active* parties. Those who assist and those who seek assistance need to play *active* parts. Once one party to the cooperative enterprise defaults of his active role, the element of *cooperation* has been lost and education itself may falter to a corresponding extent.

On the level of everyday educational activities, John Holt illustrates well, in his work *How Children Fail*, just what happens when either pupil or teacher fails to play an active role. We may summarize his conclusion to the effect that instead of becoming facilitated in the particular field of learning and teaching, both pupil and teacher will resort to evasiveness in order to hide disinterest and lack of participation. Children from their earliest years tend to respond to educational ventures which they do not want, or, therefore, enjoy, with distaste and with clever methods whereby their unwillingness to cooperate is hidden from teachers and other observers.

The practice of lying and "psyching out" the teacher starts way before a student's undergraduate or even high school years. In colleges this practice emerges through the answering of questions on tests with reams of nonsense so as to present the impression that learning has taken place. Here, as in earlier schooling experiences, the aim is not to perform well but to avoid pain, punishment, or a bad image. (Personally I have always tried to induce in myself and others the habit of admitting ignorance both in test and classroom situations. I would recommend showing appreciation for such admissions, even when accompanied by advice for improvement.)

What, beside the fact that those partaking in educational endeavors must play an active role, is *basic* to all educational ventures? The *possibility* of actually learning something, of attaining knowledge, and of attaining knowledge that relates to some area of a pupil's values has to obtain in all educational ventures. Education is the development of capacities, the "bringing out" of ignorance into knowledge for someone—presumably the pupil. If either teacher or student is basically convinced that we *cannot* have knowledge of things, that all we may achieve is subjective beliefs, and that other than perhaps direct experience (so called) there simply is no road toward learning something—if these convictions or feelings prevail, education cannot take place.

We may have indoctrination: we might *pump* some beliefs into our pupils' minds, or we may have certain beliefs pumped into our own; but that is not education. It is something that we do with horses, dogs, and perhaps computers; but if we presume that *that* is what we are doing in engaging in the educational endeavor, we violate the first principle, namely the recognition that education requires *active participation*. Pumping is a one-sided venture, and so are programming, indoctrinating, and training. A total skeptic, one who believes that knowledge is impossible for human beings, cannot have a viable approach to education. His conviction contradicts one of education's basic requirements— in effect, if there is no knowledge, there *is* no way to assist the pupil out of his ignorance.

In addition to the above, education must presume some form of *free will* on the part of all those engaging in educational activities. If a pupil is not free to attend to the subject being taught, if his activity in the learning process is simply reactive, prodded out of him by clever stimulation of his brain cells or expected of him by virtue of some inherent instincts, then we are not talking, again, of an *active* pupil (nor, of course, of an active teacher). If we are determined to do what we do, either through prodding or through our inherited or early acquired drives, then it is not really we who engage in the activity of learning. We are, like complex biochemical organisms without the power of self-generated action, simply moving through behavior patterns. One may have this view of human nature and believe in indoctrination, training, programming; one cannot, however, think that a man could be party to an *educational* endeavor.

Arguments against free will abound, of course, and one would do them injustice to treat them as briefly as this discussion permits. My grounds for believing that they all fail is that without the element of human freedom in at least one area of human activity, namely in the assessment of the truth or falsity of judgment, there would be no way in which to assess *the truth or falsity of the view that "free will does not exist."* If *we* are entirely determined, then, of course, so are our judgments of whether something is or is not the case. Since all judgments would have to be products of determined behavior, including judgments about whether this or that view of free will is right or wrong, then one's view of human nature would be neither correct nor incorrect but simply *there*. Which would make nonsense of the contention that "free will does not exist" *in the face of any denial* of that judgment. Both judgments, though contradictory, have equal merit—which is to give way to blatant contradictions and cannot govern thinking. No doubt more could be said, but I simply want to make clear where I stand on this matter, should it arise in later discussion.

Finally, in order to have a viable conception of education, one which is distinguishable from indoctrination, training, etc., we must admit of the distinction between the knower and the known. The pupil must be viewed as a being *capable of gaining knowledge* but not identical to that which is to be learned. In other words, we cannot accept solipsism (or idealism) as our model for the human mind. If our *mind creates* what is known, then we cannot learn about something; nor could we learn about something from someone else. Information would be part of the pupil's mind to begin with, and it would make little sense to speculate on what meanings we could attach to our terms—e.g., learning, ignorance, discovery, inattention, research, etc.—within educational theory and practice if we denied the distinction between the knower and the known. (Of course, the nature of that distinction is not at issue here. Once again, that issue is a complex one which would take us far into other matters than education.)

It seems then that we are left with some basic components of education: it must be achievable; those engaged in learning must enjoy some kind of freedom to learn, to achieve or not to achieve what they are after; and those taking part in education as knowers must be distinguishable from what they are to learn or to come to know. These basic elements support our initial definition in the following manner: cooperative endeavors require free and active participants or it is not cooperation that we have at all; the development of capacities to cope with the world requires that such capacities *can be* developed, which *in this context* means that knowledge *can be* achieved, in principle.

(You may notice that I have assumed that coping with the world for human beings requires knowledge. And this is true; but to call it an assumption is to speak loosely. It is such a fundamental point that debate about it would be irrational, in most cases. Surely even minimal success by a child, say in building a sand castle, requires that this child know something about building such a castle. "Human vegetables" would not be said to be incapacitated if knowledge were not so essential a part of being able to cope with the world. Of course, knowledge alone may not do the job; still, it is a necessary element of it.)

Education also presumes that those being educated, the knowers, are different from what they are to be educated about, what they are to learn or to come to know; they cannot be the creators of what they know in the drastic sense, at least, in which solipsism would have it. Education without something to be educated about that is distinct from the one being educated would simply be something other than education (though I could not tell you what it would be, inasmuch as such a view is simply beyond comprehension, even if seriously proposed by some thinkers).

The question arises now whether the American educational system is consonant with some or all of these features of education; if it is, at least in most cases, then our troubles may have to do with matters other than education itself. If it is not, then improvements must be made within education itself in order to improve matters.

Most likely, however, troubles abound on many sides and contribute heavily to the overall picture we get of education in general. There is one area where education American style is certainly not consistent with the features which I have claimed were essential for any educational endeavor. From the earliest stages, American students attend school independently of their choice. Elementary school students *must attend* schools and as things go, they must attend schools which have been built with the support of people who must build schools. Which is to say, elementary education is compulsory and schools are financed by taxes. Even so-called private education in America has become a tax burden. ... It is, I think, fair to say that education in America has become a public enterprise, like the police, the military, the building of highways, and the delivery of mail. Except that if one does not want to write letters or receive them, one needn't, and if one wants to refrain from becoming a cop, one may. It is a bit different with the military, but even in this there are avenues of escape. With going to school there is no escape—you *must*.

You probably know what I am going to say next. It has been said by others and it is being said by more people every day. To presume that one can conduct educational endeavors when parties to the action are forced to join the action flies in the face of what education must be. It makes little difference whether we conduct educational endeavors in pink houses, in fields of grass, or in barn yards. It makes no difference if we use books or take notes or write on blackboards; all these and similar matters are incidental and depend much on the particular context of a given educational undertaking. But it makes all the difference to whether someone is really receiving an education and participating in the educational enterprise whether he is *forced* or comes because he *wants* to.

Now it may be replied that children really have nothing to do with when they start their educational processes; it is the parents who would be forcing kids to enter school if the law refrained from doing so. This may be right, in some cases; but it is at least safe to say that without compulsory education some parents would be able to determine more accurately just when it is more appropriate to send their children to school than they are now able—since there is no question about the issue for parental decision. The issue may be put at least as follows: should the State or should the parents determine when a child should go to school? In terms of what I said earlier, the answer would depend on which method would ensure the least amount of compulsion within the various educational institutions available to children today.

Before we can consider the question raised above, it will be necessary to look at the other feature of American education which appears, at least, to violate the requirements of education proper previously established. This feature is the public or State supported character of U.S. education. I have already acknowledged that not all educational institutions are actually run and directly funded by governments. I have also noted that even private, elementary, secondary and higher education, e.g., church and secular schools, receive special considerations from the State in the way of exemptions, deductions, etc. Thus when I include all American education in my characterization of them as public, I do so with good reason.

How do these two elements of our educational system pertain to the basic features I have argued education proper must involve? First, is there a connection between the need for free choice on the students' part and the fact of compulsion in public education? Second, is there a connection between the possibility of exercising free choice and the publicly financed character of American education?

Compulsion in education amounts to the following: if a parent does not send his child to a State accredited educational facility (or obtain credentials to provide State approved educational procedures in his home to his children) at a prescribed age limit, the parent is liable to the punitive measures of the laws of the state. Fines, jail terms, suits of child neglect, and similar measures will be administered upon parents who refuse to comply with the compulsory provisions of education.

The fact that education is financed through taxation amounts to the following: all wage earners and property holders must finance American education on all levels such that the refusal to do so results in punitive measures against non-payers.

The question now arises, what if anything, does this result in for the education of children and the ability of parents to secure the education their children require? The compulsory feature of education has the consequence that a child must be *sent to* school at an age prescribed by law; the law in a democratic political system, assuming at least some approximation to the principle of majority rule (via "taxation with representation" which entails avenues of taxpayer control on all features of that area of education which is financed by taxpayers), decides for each parent (and child) the correct age for school entry and attendance. The State decides, at least semi-democratically, what is good for children and parents—for, of course, the latter must also be considered when the family as a unit is being dealt with; the students are children, and children of some parents in most cases, one may surmise. At least one thing is clear: parents are forced to comply with the State's conception of what is right for their children, not regardful primarily of the individual characteristics, talents, needs, aspirations, interests, qualifications, etc. of any given child. Beyond this we will have to consider whether there need be any relationship between our educational crisis and the coercion of parents to live by the educational theories of the State (not to mention the factors of politics, bureaucracy, and majority decisions). For the time being, however, all that need be shown is that compulsory education limits the judgment and choice of individual parents in the matter of selecting the education or non-education of their children. (I am not, of course, arguing that outside the legal provisions no other harmful factors may influence a child's education).

When we combine the compulsory character of education with its public character, that is to say, with the fact that education is funded through the mechanism of taxation, with its corresponding features of politicalized administration as described above, additional matters arise. First of all, a parent has no choice but to finance public education. This entails that he may have to support a system of which he disapproves; and he will have less of an opportunity to finance his children's education through avenues which escape the State system. The chances for supplying alternative means of education by educators who wish to offer such means will also decrease. When the public is forced to support one system, the possibility for supporting another will be seriously limited. Thus non-State supported education is not only made less available to the customer but, correspondingly, the producers of such education will have their entry into the market place of education restricted through the provisions of the legal system for tax financed education.

More important, perhaps, than the above is the State-funded education as accompanied by State-established standards for qualification as an educational institution proper. The case of the Amish people being physically forced into public schools bears this out most vividly, but, of course, there are less obvious examples than the Amish case we must take into consideration. Here we must remember that the evidence is not easily obtained, simply because much of what *might be* the case, were it possible and economical to provide private education, simply *is* not the case. Yet we can speculate intelligently about what might be and might have been the case without state education, with its compulsory and public character as it presently exists. An example of how things might be can be produced if we permit an analogy that is quite real.

Nursery schools, unlike all others, are still not under State supervision—though that is not entirely true either. Licensing provisions have been established even in this area. Yet nursery schools have the opportunity to experiment, to work on providing the best service, and to work on suiting special needs of special types of children without having to account for their actions to political bodies. In other words, the "taxpayers at large"—i.e., the State—need not be consulted.

One more factor to be considered is that with taxation as the source of finances for education, many pay for something from which they do not benefit in the way those benefit who have children in school. Thus also, many have a *say* in education without the kind of stake those who have school aged children have in it. This itself indicates that the connection between education and those who are funding it is different from the connection between those who buy the services of non-tax supported producers and the product itself. The barber I pay to cut my hair works for me alone in our relationship; he is not committed to listen to and follow the rules others set for his job when he cuts my hair, even if my haircut is a concern to others. My psychiatrist or doctor (unless I am involved in some State financed medical care program) also treats me without having to answer to people who do not receive his services (though my health may indeed benefit others, just as education may have consequences for others than those who receive it).

Now the important question arises. Do all these features of American education aid or hinder the furtherance of those conditions which must accompany education proper?

We have already admitted that both parents and the State can use force to send children to schools. The former can do so, if he is allowed to, wisely or unwisely; he may consult the child, examine his needs, base his decision on this examination, and change his mind in the light of improved knowledge; he may also default on this. If education were merely public but not compulsory, parents could keep their children out of schools as long as they choose, take them out when they choose, and so forth. Clearly if no compulsion existed and yet school would be provided for everyone at everyone's expense there would still exist financial pressures to utilize the public school system; the burden of supporting a private school would still be an addition to what has already been paid into the public system. Still, variations and experimentation to improve would increase. Also, it is unlikely that such a system could survive long: it would probably be considered unjust to tax everyone when many could legally keep children at home or send them to private schools. Under the compulsory system there is at least the double edged sword: kids *must attend* schools and schools *must be provided* for them to attend. This has the air of "justice" about it. If, on the other hand, education would be totally private and yet compulsory, a different problem would exist: in order to force everyone into schools it would be necessary to provide the schools; and there is no guarantee that the kind of education prescribed for everyone would be what private schools would choose to provide.

But what does this have to do with the relationship between State compulsion and education proper? If parents and State both coerce kids, why choose one over the other? This question can only be dealt with within the context of the total picture, namely compulsory, public financed educational practices. If we accept compulsion without public education, we are still left with coercion and the distinction between State education and total private education cannot be discerned. If we abolish compulsion but retain public education, we are still allowing a great deal of legal pressure favoring public education, namely the economic security provided by a guaranteed supply of funding.

First I want to establish the manner in which compulsion—either directly or via the existence of economic pressures established by law in favor of public education (though without necessarily involving outright compulsion)—affects education. The choice of schools must necessarily be limited when public education prevails; the choice of timing and circumstances must be limited when compulsion itself exists. Without either, a parent has the option to send the child to a school or instructor or tutor of his choice, not to send the child to school at all, or to send him for a time period the parent himself chooses. This would be the case even though different income groups would find themselves limited by different economic and other circumstances. Obviously, no one can argue that a free, privately provided educational system would guarantee the satisfaction of everyone's wishes. As an example, probably no one could provide the equivalent of an aristocratic tutorial education to those who cannot pay for it and even, sometimes, for those who could: such a service would cost a great deal and may not even exist. But this is no argument against a free, private system—clearly there is far less of a chance for such quality education within the context of the present system. With the State, most of the parents have essentially one option open to them: to send the child to a public school within the context of the laws governing such matters as age, neighborhood, curriculum, physical facilities, space, etc. And within the American political system these conditions generally reflect the more-or-less-well-considered unhappy medium of judgments of voters, their representatives, and their appointees. There are, of course, variations from school to school, district to district, and state to state. But in all cases the resulting conditions are reflective of the collective decision of the politically active majority of voters (no doubt, with variations which can only be identified in retrospect in most cases).

Is there any important difference between the result of such State directed and supervised compulsion and the non-legal compulsion or direction parents carry out (or would have to carry out) in a free, private system? This difference would have to be more than simply the earlier established mere greater diversity of possibilities. For, one might ask, is there any special value of increasing opportunities for parents with respect to the education of their children? For instance, one may wonder if the option of not sending a child to school may not itself pose enough of a disadvantage for children in general to warrant opposition to a free, private educational system. Clearly in a free, private educational system this option would exist. (Not all educators are frightened of this. At the White House Conference on Children ninety experts suggested that being kept out of school may be better for some children educationally.)

If it were a matter of what adults could do with their own lives perhaps no great problem would exist—though, of course, even with respect to adults the idea of freedom is often rejected in favor of "protecting people from themselves" (as, e.g., in drug laws, social security and unemployment compensation measures, and restrictions on the sale of pornographic entertainment). With this issue, however, we are talking about whether parents or the State should dictate the means by which a child is provided for in his need to become intellectually equipped to live his life well. So the question really amounts to whether in general the State or individual parents (or guardians) can best supply what children need.

We have already seen that a child, as pupil, needs to have his interests, talents, and circumstances consulted in order that the educational endeavor in which he may be involved should have the greatest chance for success. The freedom to attend to what is being taught him cannot be divorced from the conditions under which the child enters the educational endeavor. If he is forced into something that he would rather not be part of, the attitude with which he will approach this will differ from what it would have been had his interests and values been paid attention to in the first place. Granted that it is not always possible to discover what children want—they may not know it; they may even want something that is bad for them. So there will, undoubtedly, be some degree of compulsion in most children's education. The questions are: what kind is *better* for them; how can we determine this; and will parents not forced to send their children to public schools (a more or less universal type of educational program) pay more attention to these matters than the State does and can?

Here, I think, we have reached an important question: will people in freedom bring up their children better or worse than people whose lives are controlled by the educational system of the democratic process? The former will, to a great extent, be left to their own resources, individually, through voluntary cooperation. The latter will be freed from having to think too much about this matter except in so far as the relationship between their children and the political process makes possible. (There is absolutely no guarantee that taxpayers will demand what they want from their representatives, whether in education or something else. In fact, because of the relatively small significance of their own individual desires and decisions, alienation from the political process which leads to adverse results in publicly financed education or anything else is more likely. In that case the politically astute have the most to say about everything, whether they are qualified to say what is right or not—just so long as politics has something to do with the matter.)

Remembering, then, that in a free, private system, there is no guarantee that each child will receive what is good for him, and also that under the present system every child receives a uniform education whether or not it is *good for him*, the probability of better overall results for children under the free educational system seems to be clear. It is, after all, the *parents* of this or that child who will make the decision for the welfare of the child. These may not be excellent or even responsible at all times; but the relationship between parent and child, characterized at least by affection and some sense or a feeling of responsibility on the parents' part, has a good chance of resulting in maximum personal concern over education. Since no public education would be available and, therefore, no guarantee of at least some, however misconceived, education would exist, the decision about having children would also be checked. If a couple knows that it must take care of its offspring through its own efforts, the habit of bringing children into the world without caring what will happen to them would decrease considerably. Schools would improve, also, since they would need to gear their practice to the judgment of an ever critical clientele; the parent could take his child out of a school simply on the grounds that the child is not improving his life by attending it or because he judges the school to be bad. The child's needs, in terms of various conceptions of life-styles, morality, intellectual capacity, degree of knowledge and skills required for the many areas of the prevailing social, cultural, and economic circumstances, would play an important part in the minds of many parents—there would, after all, be no one to dictate by law *how* children must be educated. The conception of education advanced at the outset of this essay would have a chance to gain prevalence; those who, accordingly, would prefer an educational experience in which the interests, talents, and values of children are considered as priorities would have the chance to look for and build schools which shared this concern. Such schools would arise (as a matter of mere need) to supply what concerned parents demand. Not unlike the nursery school system we have, an appeal would be made to the public on the basis of the various conceptions of education which educators and administrators have. Communication between parent, child, and teacher would improve. And while all this would presume some degree of rationality on the parts of all concerned, including parents, children, and educators, the element of free choice on all sides would enable rational thought to become more and more pervasive.

Last, though certainly not least, there would be greater diversity of scholarship *and* ideology. Education, contrary to what some think, cannot be divorced from values. When the State runs education, values have to be suppressed in view of certain obvious fears all democracies have about using State run institutions for purposes of indoctrination. Since, however, one cannot separate fact from value, especially in such fields as history, literature, civics, law, economics, etc., such attempts at suppression must fail and result in deception. Explicit indoctrination is eschewed, though the implicit favoring of certain views of life, morality, religion, politics, law, sexual behavior, etc. is evidenced throughout public education. The hypocrisy which overshadows the system adds to its other flaws and provokes resentment.

Free, (not financially, but politically) private education would make such hypocrisy unnecessary and, therefore, less prevalent. Schools, colleges, and universities could freely admit their commitment to certain views, be they controversial or not. Unlike governmentally run projects, which must refrain from violating the First Amendment, private institutions cannot be prevented by law from voicing their moral, religious, political, or other preferences. And while other sorts of pressures may exist, no doubt, they will be quite different from pressures which are backed by threats of legal punishment. (In a private system no problem about "prayer in school" could exist. Since uniformity is not enforced, changing from one school to another may solve the problem of clashes of values between family and school.) Here again the present nursery school system comes to mind. Such schools openly proclaim their adherence to certain moral, political, and educational values and advise parents of different persuasions to take their children elsewhere.

Ultimately the matter becomes, of course, an issue of one's view of human nature, morality, and the relationship between a citizen and his government. In America it would seem that the suggestion that freedom is better for people than coercion would be well received. Unfortunately, again, things don't always seem as they are.

In order to do full justice to the effects of government financing, running, and assisting of American education, we have to conduct some economic analysis. I am not an economist and will, therefore, like most of us, pick my favorite economists to testify in my behalf. One such economist/political scientist/philosopher is E.G. West of Kent University, England. His book *Education and the State* and his article "The Political Economy of American Public School Legislation" (in *The Journal of Law and Economics*, October 1967) give evidence for the contention that neither was private education economically unfeasible, given the goal of providing the educational needs of Americans, when public education first became an established institution in the early 1800s, nor is it the case that private education could not accomplish the task of satisfying education needs today if public education were phased out. Needless to say, authority is not argument, so I would simply wish to claim that there is solid support for the above contention throughout the intellectual community. (Those interested in examining this issue with a view to making fundamental changes in the educational practices found in this country may find the best source The Center for Independent Education, 9115 East 13th, Wichita, Kansas 67206.) Incidentally, the idea that education should be severed from the state entirely was endorsed not only by such radical political philosophers as Ayn Rand, F.A. Harper,

E.G. West, Henry M. Levin, Murray N. Rothbard, Herbert Spencer, Albert J. Nock, *et al*, all of them proponents of laissez-faire capitalism; but Oliver LaFarge (who openly challenged ex-Harvard President Conant's denunciation of private schooling in *The Atlantic Monthly*), Ivan Illich (who argued in the *New York Review of Books* for an amendment to the U.S. Constitution which would prohibit governmental interference with education), Professors Arman Alchian and James Buchanan (who argue again on economic grounds, that private education is better for us) and others, from various sides of the political spectrum, have held that governmental schooling is harmful. Though these individuals may not all be concerned with the overall violation of the principle of individual rights and object to public education incidentally, only, they are concerned, as are libertarians, about the consequences of public education. And these consequences must be measured against the definition of education offered at the outset of this article. What is important, then, ultimately, is whether pupils are being educated; whether schools, colleges, universities, and other educational institutions can provide what people need when they seek education. Ultimately it is the *pupil* who must be the concern of those interested in education. And by all counts (e.g., at the White House Conference on Children) it is the pupils who are complaining the most. They complain explicitly, though admittedly inarticulately; they complain implicitly, by acting so that one can observe that they have no love for education as it exists today.

I will not attempt to list all the symptoms of the disease. We hardly associate all things with matters I have been discussing; but in the classroom one cannot escape the fact that students are not excited about learning; they consider it a chore; they are in school mostly out of habit or duty or whatever, but rarely because they have developed a love for learning, a desire to cope with various subjects, an anticipation for the challenge of tackling assignments which require intellectual effort. I think the experiences of most educators will bear this out. By the time students reach colleges and universities, the matter becomes *almost* irreversible. It is often embarrassing for a teacher to do his job because so much time must be spent on "turning people on." The atmosphere of give and take is virtually absent. This is not confined to such schools as junior and teachers' colleges, those, that is, which are traditionally *thought* to absorb students who are less facilitated in intellectual respects. The major universities are finding this problem to be all pervasive, too. Those who have analyzed the recent upheavals on our campuses do not, I think, do justice to the problems when they blame them on agitators, communists, extremists, administrators, or any single group. They will do justice to the problems only when they examine the total context of the American student's educational experience.

From the point of view of philosophy, there are a few additional remarks which should be made. First, we must examine our methodology of education. Here advances will depend on our conception of the relationship between pupil and the school. Here the conception of knowledge as a static picture, pieces of information or data, can only work against the task of bringing pupils out of ignorance, though for indoctrination such a conception is appropriate. Knowledge is possible; but it is not something stale and fixed. To acquire knowledge it is necessary that the student's mind be active; it is, perhaps, more important to cultivate the intellectually active feature of the educational process than what it results in, namely the knowledge of facts. Here again removal of politics would work for the good.

Those who argue about whether pure intellectual *effort* or *experience* fosters learning are only obscuring the very important fact that neither of these *alone* can produce anything educationally worthwhile: experience without intellectual participation may produce a mind which works like a camera—it records uninterpreted pictures, at the same time, thinking without paying attention to material about which thinking is to be done produces theoretical machines which cannot be employed in practice. Man needs both his mind and the world in order to know.

It is impossible to end this story, of course. Much work has to be done in order to produce something that will lead to progress in the field of education. At the base of it all, however, must lie concern for the most prominent parts of education, namely pupils capable of learning and teachers bent on teaching. It is these which lie at the center of any fruitful investigation of educational theory. Questions about techniques to be used to promote knowledge of mathematics or about the methods to be pursued to *provide* any kind of educational services must not lose sight of the purpose of education, namely assisting a young person to become able to lead a fruitful human life.

My views on this matter have been called naïve. I appreciate the fears of pragmatists and realists in dealing with hypotheses which are not likely to gain immediate popular support. And no one will argue that the suggestion of freeing education from the State is going to get wide reception among our politicians, academicians, or humanists. The first like to have some control over the population by way of education, though I am sure many believe they are doing noble things forcing kids into schools indiscriminately and forcing people to pay for any or all kinds of schooling equally indiscriminately. The second have really never considered the plausibility of free education—just as some people never even thought of abolishing slavery: were not at least some of the slaves very happy? Humanists—and there are many among politicians and educators—feel that they will hurt the poor by abolishing public education. It is only the latter who, I think, deserve an answer.

Will the poor suffer most from making education private? From what we know about what education does for poor children, taking into account the kind of teachers who teach at poor neighborhood schools, the monies available to such schools, the political football-playing done with such schools, and the time consuming attention the parents at such schools would have to pay to the political maneuverings necessary to be informed about their childrens' education—in all this and more there is no ground for the contention that privatizing education will hurt the education of poor students. Quite the contrary; it has been argued convincingly that poor children are badly hurt by what compulsory education does for (to) them, on the whole. They are the ones who get most "turned off" to intellectual matters. They become anti-intellectual and hostile toward matters of the mind. One need only consult the books Holt, Silberman, Dennison, and others have written recently to become convinced of this. Actually one need only look at the students of his local elementary and high schools; the poor gain very little, if anything at all. Just *ask them.*

Furthermore, when we come to colleges, it has been shown that the poor are in fact financing the education of the rich. *TransAction* magazine—not a right or left wing radical journal—investigated who is funding whose college education, and in California the "superrich" have to pay least, proportionately, while the "superpoor" pay the most when their tax rates and educational costs are tabulated. . . . So the humanists may rest assured that no one here is forgetting the poor child; it is, in fact, because of what is happening to him and to all other children and young people that the proposals and suggestions of this article are made.

Perhaps eventually they will be considered seriously and something may even happen that will foster real education in America. As of now, it seems, that many have only learned about the disease—hardly anyone in educational theory expresses satisfaction with the present system. But the political and economic sophistication of educational theorists and administrators is minimal, unfortunately. Instead of urging the freeing of education, many are simply demanding more money and more State intervention. The question is, will they ever seriously examine a truly radical proposal, such as that offered by free market economists and libertarian educational theorists? Or will they simply talk up their dissatisfactions, thereby affecting serious concern without paying serious attention to the problem?

Note

"'The Schools Ain't What They Used to Be and Never Was'" is reprinted with permission from *Reason*, vol. 3, nos. 1 and 2.

Cheri Kent and T. R. Machan

16

The Misuses of the University

FOR CENTURIES SCHOLARS have proposed, analyzed, and debated their conceptions of the ideal university—its nature, purposes, functions, responsibilities, and goals. In the mid-twentieth century, the "Berkeley Rebellion," the first explosion of the New Left's "student revolt," brought the debate into the streets. Professorial arguments about the relationship between the university and society began appearing in the newspaper; students protesting university involvement with the military-industrial complex received front-page and prime-time coverage; taxpayers' and citizens' committees organized to influence university policy; the general public argued the issues raised by demonstrators. In the last ten years, the universities have become the center of social turmoil, a major topic of social conversation, and a hot subject for volumes of print supporting the publishing industry.

Many Americans' unbounded faith in the glory of higher education has come face to face with their despair about its major institutions' future. They have watched the university suffer continual dissection in the realm of ideas and continual assault in the realm of practice. They have seen it torn apart by protestors and demonstrators who halt its operations and burn its buildings; by politicians, alumni, and taxpayers who retaliate by refusing it funds; by faculty, administrators, and trustees who cannot agree on what is to be done next.

Certainly the vast majority of colleges and universities continue to function predominantly with business as usual. But the extent and spread of damage since 1965 at Berkeley make it impossible to assume any longer that any institution of higher education is immune to serious trouble.

An apt symbol of the issue that confronts all concerned with the university today appeared in that first Berkeley "revolt," in the form of a lone student carrying a picket sign that read: "I am a student. Please don't fold, bend, staple or mutilate me." His protest against the vast academic bureaucracy in which individual students are often treated as just one more number on an IBM card expressed the disappointment felt by many students who are quickly disillusioned by the kind of university they find when they arrive. Clark Kerr, then president of the University of California, had enunciated the liberal academic establishment's acceptance of what the modern university has become:

The ends are already given–the preservation of the eternal truths, the creation of new knowledge, the improvement of service wherever truth and knowledge of high order may serve the needs of man. The ends are there; the means must be ever improved in a competitive, dynamic environment. There is no single "end" to be discovered; there are several ends and many groups to be served.[1]

In other words, Kerr—with a host of his fellows—accepts the modern "multiversity" as what his opponents identify as a "social service station." The service station pumps knowledge into students' heads that will make them "useful national resources" for a burgeoning technological society. And it provides men and facilities for huge corporate and governmental research projects that in many cases have little immediate relevance to the education of its students. The extent to which the modern university is supported by corporate and governmental grants and research contracts, the extent to which its senior professors are hired and promoted for their research rather than for their teaching, has made undergraduate education a secondary priority in the daily function of the institution.

The radical leaders of the so-called Free Speech Movement at Berkeley viewed it this way:

The multiversity is not an educational center, but a highly efficient industry: it produces bombs, other war machines, a few token "peaceful" machines and enormous numbers of safe, highly skilled, and respectable automatons to meet the immediate needs of business and government.[2]

In the October 9, 1969 issue of the *New York Review of Books*, Christopher Lasch and Eugene Genovese repeated the charge:

The university both provides facilities and training for a managerial elite allied to the military and to the big corporations and also trains, on a much larger scale, intellectual workers who . . . are necessary precisely in the way the working class is necessary . . . . The universities, moreover, serve, like the secondary schools, as places of detention and custody for young people in general.[3]

But perhaps the most succinct explanation of the university's role has been offered by Mario Savio:

[T]he schools have become training camps—and proving grounds—rather than places where people acquire education. They become factories to produce technicians rather than places to live student lives . . . .

He [Clark Kerr] looks at a university this way . . . these are his metaphors, not mine. It's a factory and it has a manager . . . that's Kerr . . . and a Board of Directors . . . that's the Board of Regents . . . and employees, the faculty and teaching assistants, and raw materials . . . that's us . . .

His view . . . is that we serve the rational purpose by being "a component part of the military-industrial complex." Well, I haven't felt much like a component part . . . .[4]

What this amounts to is that the ivory tower conception of the university still idealized by many Americans is functionally a myth. Some in the academic community still enunciate the ideal of the university removed from immediate practical concerns and dedicated to the "liberal education" of its students—the university as a haven for intellectual theorists who transmit the knowledge accumulated by men through centuries of effort so that "the best that has been thought and said in the world," as Matthew Arnold put it, may become part of the minds of increasing numbers of students—the university that, in so doing, raises the intellectual level of the culture—the university that encourages the advancement of theoretical knowledge and humane letters.

In the mid-nineteenth century this conception of the university was already under heavy attack. Its most famous defender, John Henry Cardinal Newman, then delivered a series of lectures (published as *The Idea of a University*) in which he declaimed:

A University . . . is a place of teaching universal knowledge. This implies that its object is, on the one hand, intellectual, not moral; and, on the other, that it is the diffusion and extension of knowledge rather than the advancement. If its object were scientific and philosophical discovery, I do not see why a University should have students . . . .[5]

Newman thus considered the cultivation of the intellect to be the primary purpose of higher education.

Many protesting students in the mid-twentieth century have advanced a similar conception with similar arguments as an alternative to the contemporary multiversity. The initial cries for "student power" were sometimes backed by the argument that educational institutions exist to meet the intellectual needs of their students rather than the practical needs of the social order. They advocated a return to student-centered institutions. Paul Goodman, a social critic and theorist widely admired among young people, advocated in his *Community of Scholars* a decentralized, "free" university modeled on medieval institutions that were created by secession from existing ones, and some young people founded and joined attempts at establishing such centers of learning. Others, of course, demanded that the multiversities themselves reform by increasing the power of students to direct policy and hire faculty, by eliminating requirements and grades, and by discarding university regulations of students' activities. Still others suggested a compromise:

> *One would like to see some attempt to establish, within the multiversities, true centres of learning, creativity and scholarship, with no obligation to train useful citizens. Because they will have no connection with the labour market, there will be no need to issue licenses, certificates or degrees, and what necessarily goes with them, exams and grades . . . .*
>
> *I would propose that a guaranteed annual income be provided for all citizens who wish to participate in this community of life, and for as long as they may wish to remain there.*[6]

The impulse to such reforms, which would supposedly reorient the university toward its true educational, as opposed to its "training," function is understandable. What is interesting to notice is that "society," the public, is still considered to be the beneficiary of the reformed university and is still expected to furnish its funding. This conception of the university is often justified not by its value for individual students (in which case they would presumably be expected to pay for it); it is justified by its value to society as a whole. What changes is the nature of that value: instead of being an institution that supports the existing structures of society, the university is to be an institution that criticizes and foments change in society:

> *The major purpose of a university in a free society is a criticism of society for its own improvement . . . the university should be the conscience of the community, the seedbed of dissent where the worst departures between the ideals and the realities of the community can be pointed out and criticized.*[7]

Both the New-Left protestors and the liberal academic establishment share the view, then, that the university exists primarily to serve
"social needs." They disagree only upon which social needs the university should serve. The issues in New-Left protests after Berkeley focused
more and more not upon the educational needs of students, but upon
which social functions the university should fill. The second major
eruption of protest, at Columbia University in the spring of 1968,
ostensibly was in reaction to the university's policies in regard to military
research and to its surrounding "ghetto" community. The majority of
New-Left dissidents have demanded that universities end those activities
that they consider harmful to society (military research, ROTC programs, recruiting for big business and military-governmental agencies)
and that universities instead undertake activities that they consider
beneficial to society (minority racial group and poverty programs;
antiwar activities; conservation programs, and so on). Not one demand
was for the reorientation of the university toward the education of
students in whatever fields and methods are conducive to their *individual*
well-being.

In other words, the New Left, while calling upon the university to
radically restructure itself, is in fact only one more political movement
attempting to use the university for *its* social purposes. Some more
militant New Leftists have even demanded that the university turn itself
into a training ground for revolution by offering courses in everything
from revolutionary theory to guerrilla warfare tactics. Few, of course,
take this view. The majority—joined by increasing numbers of the
"establishment"—see the university as a solver of "social problems."
(What these people do not see is that if the university should not engage
in projects in business and government to the detriment of the educational process, then neither should it engage in solving social problems
to its detriment.)[8]

Today, the university finds itself attacked and besieged from all
sides, including from within, by all manner of groups demanding that it
take up and carry forth their cause. Its impossible position has been
excellently delineated by Jacques Barzun in *The American University*:

> [*The universities*] *spend huge sums and are desperately poor; their students
> attack them; their neighbors hate them; their faculties are restless; and the public,
> critical of their rising fees and restricted enrollments, keeps making more and more
> peremptory demands upon them. The universities are expected, among other
> things, to turn out scientists and engineers, foster international understanding,
> provide a home for the arts, satisfy divergent tastes in architecture and sexual*

*morals, cure cancer, recast the penal code, and train equally for the professions
and for a life of cultured contentment in the Coming Era of Leisure.*[9]

*. . . Whatever the individual and the society cannot do for themselves is entrusted
to the likeliest existing agency. Faith in education and faith in the integrity and
good will of those called educators have accordingly wished upon the midcentury
university a variety of tasks formerly done by others or not done at all. Just as the
lower schools must organize transportation, free lunches, dental care, and "driver
education," so the university now undertakes to give its students, faculties, and
neighbors not solely education but the makings of a full life, from sociability to
business advice and from psychiatric care to the artistic experience. Again, every
new skill or item of knowledge developed within the academy creates a new claim
by the community. Knowledge is power and its possessor owes the public a prompt
application, or at least diffusion through the training of others. It thus comes
about that the School of Social Work aids the poor, the School of Architecture
redesigns the slum, the School of Business advises the small tradesman, the School
of Dentistry runs a free clinic, the School of Law gives legal aid, and the
undergraduate college supplies volunteers to hospitals, recreation centers, and
remedial schools.*
*. . . the main tendency . . . is to think: we will get the school to do it; we will find the
money and urge the university to take it on.*[10]

And working away at the university from within are the students,
whose

*extracurricular ventures must be subsidized: earning or raising the money would
take time away from the work; their encounter with the police must be condoned, as
in the past, on the ground of studentship*–in status pupillari *being the
counterpart of* in loco parentis; *their sociable desires must be served through a
diversity of expensive arrangements; any initiative–an art show, a welfare scheme
–must at once be received hospitably and made possible; and, passing over the
insurance, employment, and health services that everyone now takes for granted,
students assume that the university owes them the rest of the full life, expressed in a
growing list of necessities, such as: free contraceptives, free legal aid in disputes
with their landlord for those who live off campus, free theater tickets, free
secretarial staff and* research funds *for self-appointed groups that want to
investigate the mismanagement of the place.*[11]

This is the state, these are the problems of major universities (and,
following their precedent, of other educational entities). Considering
the facts, perhaps talk of *the* philosophy of the university is functionally
pointless at present. The campuses are hosts to such a variety of people,

groups, and, subsequently, problems, that ideal conceptions (though necessary for planning the future) are a matter of luxury. However, we do need to understand what facts and attitudes and assumptions have resulted in the university's present plight and to discover ways of attending to its existing problems.

The Need for Educational Autonomy

One must first note that the connections between government and education are so widespread in scope and diversity that, in order to launch an examination of the university, one must establish whether any connection between state and education is to be tolerated, supported, or encouraged.

On the simplest level, the idea that the state—a political and therefore coercive agency, the activities of which are necessarily backed by physical threats—should conduct the delicate activity of human education is clearly repulsive. Education and its related enterprises, such as research, creativity, and so on, must be conducted with a degree of individual freedom that only the nonpolitical conditions of man will make possible. Although it is clear that even without political constraints other factors—such as social pressures and the goal of prestige—will distort aspects of the educational enterprise, these factors do not have the wide-ranging effects of the presence of a political agent as the final authority in decision-making procedures related to education (nor are they so easily removed). What educational undertakings require is total autonomy from coercive agencies.

The idea of total private education in the United States, involving even the high-school and elementary levels, is not ridiculous, it is merely absent. Several suggestions have been made toward the establishment of such private education. Benjamin Rogge's "Financing Higher Education,"[12] Dilman M. K. Smith's "Why Not Full Tuition?"[13] and Robert L. Cunningham's "Education: Free and Public"[14] point up not only the viability of moving education into the private sector but the definite advantages of such a move to students.[15]

It is no less revealing to consider the findings of E. G. West in his essay "The Political Economy of American Public School Legislation." Professor West, of the University of Kent, England, describes the rationale for public education:

Economists have often "justified" parts of our inherited educational legislation by arguing that originally they must have been built upon the basis of "scientific" propositions in welfare economics. Compulsory laws, to take one instance, are sometimes considered to have arisen as the logical outcome of the recognition of external benefits in education. Such a view betrays excessive rationalization . . . .[16]

The first honor [of adopting compulsory laws] is usually given to the state of Massachusetts whose laws of 1642 and 1647, in the words of one historian, "constitute the precedents upon which the subsequent universal free education program of the country has been established . . . ."[17]

[N]othing could have been more alien to the spirit of the American Constitution than the early legislation in Massachusetts. For it was passed at a time when the policy of the state being that of the church, a puritan theocracy was in full power. Certainly nothing can be further from the spirit of the Fourteenth Amendment than the idea of compulsory religious instruction which was contained in the 1642 measure.[18]

Our account of the nineteenth century evolution of school legislation therefore draws to its conclusion with the observation that whether or not it was appropriate to apply compulsory laws unconditionally to all classes of individuals, the laws which were actually established did not in fact secure the nineteenth century an education which was universal in the sense of 100 percent school attendance by all children of school age. If, on the other hand, the term "universal" is intended more loosely to mean something like "most," "nearly everybody," "over 90 percent" then we lack firm evidence to show that education was not already universal prior to the establishment of laws to provide a schooling which was both compulsory and free.[19]

Public education has thus come under close scrutiny of late. The Center for Independent Education in Wichita, Kansas is involved with an extensive examination of the effects of compulsory mass education upon those who are part of the educational system. In addition, the works of John Holt (*How Children Fail, How Children Learn, The Underachieving School*) and Charles Silberman ("Murder in the Schoolroom," *The Atlantic*, June-July-August 1970) indicate that not only is public mass education economically unnecessary, as argued by Professor West, but it actually does more damage than benefit to those who partake of it.

Granted that the removal of the state from education is not likely, in considering solutions to university problems one must keep in the forefront of his awareness that such separation is desirable and that one should strive for the lessening of the dependence on the state of all phases of education. The solutions to distinctively university-oriented problems, then, will have to come from thinking of the university as an autonomous, free institution in society. (Otherwise, one is likely to look to the state to "solve" the university's problems—with money, for example—which would only obscure the real issues.)

Dismantling the University "Service Station"

One way to work toward the ideal of the university—an institution in which scholarship that is conducive to the teaching of the universal concerns of man takes place *and* where the teaching of these concerns occurs—is to remove from its realm those concerns that have been thrust upon it by virtue of its being one of man's most persistent and stable institutions. The status of the university, like that of governments, at first makes it appear to be the last resort; yet it is in fact the first resort today in attempts to get problems solved in society. Our present obsession with the need and potential of institutions, our reliance upon them on an abnormally wide scale (which is backfiring all around us at present), leads us to beset man's most sustained institutions—universities——with many problems that are not by nature university related. In doing so we have made the university both the villain and the savior of mankind and rid ourselves of the responsibility of solving problems and of answering our failure to solve them. In the final analysis, by this transference of duty and responsibility, we will very likely have overloaded the university to such an extent as to destroy it *qua* university altogether.

What appears to be required at the outset is the infrequent acknowledgment that persons are capable of solving problems outside of and/or apart from institutions. Thus, even though one is closely attached to a university and perceives problems *at* a university, it need not follow that one's response to such problems must be *qua* member of the university as an institution. In other words, solutions to problems recognized at universities do not necessarily require solutions by universities. Nevertheless, almost all problems at and around major educational institutions, as has been noted, are posed to them. At present this view of the university's purpose manifests itself in the wide-scale concern about the social responsibility of the university—a responsibility, according to some, derived from the fact that it receives financial support from society, and, according to others, derived from the nature of the university as an institution. How mistaken the latter assumption is can be discerned simply by noting that virtually all the services included under the label *social responsibilities* are accomplished in places where universities do not exist by institutions that cannot be characterized as universities. Such services clearly are not central to the nature of the university.

Both as a cause and a consequence of America's obsession with group projects and group efforts, the view of persons as agents capable of attending to *and* solving problems has almost vanished. Although we grant as a basic truth that all collective action is, in the final analysis, individually initiated, most people today think of individuals as fundamentally incompetent to solve "social" problems. In most people's minds, all problems require the responses of committees, organizations, institutions, governments . . . groups. This orientation is manifest particularly in the immense trust invested in political action—followed by total disappointment once it proves ineffective (which, according to the New Left, supposedly warrants revolutionary action). Nowhere is the assumption of individual incompetence more vociferously proclaimed than in today's university; it is not surprising that so many of its students have accepted these ideas.

The New Left does not reject the notion that the university can solve all social problems and meet all social needs while effectively educating students—the New Left simply wants the universities out of some extraeducational businesses and into others. (The same is true of political institutions: many in the New Left agree with the dominant "establishment" view that the state should control individuals' activities for the "social good"—they simply want the state to control individuals in different ways, e.g., instead of forbidding the use of marijuana the state should forbid the ownership of property; or instead of financing a space program, the state should finance a poverty program.) No wonder that the impetus for individual action in response to social ills (which are in reality the personal tragedies of individual human beings) is lacking.

Yet, of course, the individual *can* correct or cure ills and *can* solve or help to solve problems; we need not turn to institutions of one kind or another. (Perhaps the time has come to realize not only that individuals *can* correct and cure ills but that *only* individuals can do so; if there really is a serious problem, the most effective approach to it is to leave the solution to the individuals who are most closely connected with it. The whole idea of politicalization of virtually all levels of human life—today with state-run animal protection agencies even nonhuman animals have fallen within the range of politics—is a very destructive aspect of current culture.) Despite the current *actual* inertness of individuals faced with social ills, the *potential* for a successful response exists. However, men must consider a course of action sound or fruitful in order to undertake it, and if the culture constantly fails to reaffirm that they are efficacious agents, their confidence will be undermined and action will not ensue. (It is one of the few well-established tenets of the science of psychology that men will not be motivated to take action they believe will fail to achieve their goals.)

In order to solve problems that exist around a university, problems that the university itself can solve only at the expense of its intellectual and moral autonomy, the idea of human efficaciousness must gain wide acceptance. And such acceptance will require that those who are aware of this must do everything they can, both in talk and action, to insure the desired result. Although it may not receive the national TV coverage provided mass demonstrations, the helping of just one black student to pay his fees, the bringing about of a new course at a university, the hiring of just one handicapped person to do library research, or the tutoring of one freshman—all these, individually, are possible small-range yet effective courses of action contributing to the solution of major problems that surround universities (Berkeley and Columbia, in particular). One will do more to solve the problem of unemployment, for example, if he starts an enterprise that provides jobs rather than if he sits in a campus plaza protesting "the establishment."

Frequently, suggestions such as those offered above are shunned and belittled by people who respond that they are asking for *constructive* programs of reform or remedy. The fact that such solutions are immediately assumed to be inadequate (as evidenced if not by verbal disparagment then by drifting attention in the eyes of those who ask for solutions) is just another indicator of how deep-seated the prejudice against individual, personal human efficacy is. It is not the case that such suggestions are rejected *after* they have been considered and found unworkable—these kinds of suggestions are rarely, if ever, given a hearing. Suggestions are considered to be solutions only if they manifest themselves in immediate social changes, which means reform evidenced by widespread social turnovers. The individuals who constitute the concrete substance of social problems and changes are virtually forgotten.

This neglect has been the fate of many people, especially the students who want to learn in our constantly overextended universities. The mass programs undertaken to solve problems have created new bureaucracies, added several miles of red tape, provided several more plush administrative posts, and punched millions of more holes into millions of more IBM cards. They have provided more issues for dissection and have more firmly compromised the university's autonomy. And it does not appear that anyone is more satisfied with the university as a result.

There is, however, no inevitability to this trend. We can start in small ways to change our course and put ourselves and other institutions in charge of those activities not central to a university, improving the university thereby—particularly in those realms that no other institutions in society can reasonably be expected to manage. The fact that the depoliticalization of the university may require drastic changes in the long run need not deter anyone. The troubles that face us did not spring into existence overnight, and there is no reason to expect that their remedies should do so; nor should we fear that these remedies might require major changes. The attempts of today's radicals to reform institutions have proved only to push universities farther in the direction they were already going. Fundamental improvement will necessarily require a more truly revolutionary approach; that individuals assume responsibility for problems and that institutions assume accountability to individuals.

Footnotes

Cheri Kent was for several years active in writing and lecturing on student politics and the university. Currently she is completing her doctoral for a Ph.D. in English and American Literature at the University of California, San Diego. She plans a career in teaching and writing.

"The Misuses of the University" was originally a chapter in a larger work. Copyright © 1971 by Jacquelyn Estrada. From *The University Under Siege*, edited by Jacquelyn Estrada and published by Nash Publishing Corp., Los Angeles. It is reprinted with permission.

1. Clark Kerr, *The Uses of the University* (Cambridge, Mass.: Harvard University Press, 1963).

2. Brad Cleaveland, "A Letter to Undergraduates," distributed to Berkeley students in 1964, quoted in *The New Radicals*, eds. Paul Jacobs and Sal Landau (New York: copyright 1966, Random House, Inc.), p. 224. Quoted by permission.

3. Christopher Lasch and Eugene Genovese, "The Education and the University We Need Now," *New York Review of Books*, October 9, 1969, p. 25.

4. Mario Savio, "Berkeley Fall: The Berkeley Student Rebellion of 1964," in *The Free Speech Movement and the Negro Revolution* (Detroit: *News and Letters*, July, 1965).

5. John Henry Cardinal Newman, *The Idea of a University* (New York: Holt, Rinehart and Winston, 1960), p. xxxvii (preface).

6. C. W. Gonick, "Self-Government in the Multiversity," in *The*

University Game, eds. Adelman and Lee (Toronto, Anansi, 1968), pp. 45, 46.

7. Sanford H. Kadish, "Essay IV," in *Freedom and Order in the University*, ed. Samuel Gorovitz (Cleveland, 1967), p. 134.

8. Some professional intellectuals who have in the past favored the New Left's demands for reform are beginning to identify the unrevolutionary nature of many demands. Barrington Moore, Jr., writing in the April 23, 1970 *New York Review of Books*, lamented that the demand for "relevance" in educational curricula has become "a cover for all sorts of historical and cultural provincialism and the demands of special interest groups" and thus "a mirror image of the demand that universities become service stations for the status quo" (p. 35).

9. Jacques Barzun, *The American University* (New York: Harper & Row, 1968), p. 2.

10. *Ibid.*, pp. 10, 11.

11. *Ibid.*, p. 73.

12. *New Individualist Review 4* (Summer 1965): 3–14.

13. *Princeton Alumni Weekly*, November 26, 1968, pp. 11–13.

14. *New Individualist Review 3* (Summer 1963): 3–15.

15. The suggestion that the state should be severed from education is today being heard from all points on the political compass. The left-liberal *New York Review of Books*' July 2, 1970 issue featured an article titled "Why We Must Abolish Schooling." Its author, Ivan Illich, writes, "Two centuries ago the United States led the world in a movement to disestablish the monopoly of a single church. Now we need the constitutional disestablishment of the monopoly of the school, and thereby of a system which legally combines prejudice with discrimination. The first article of a bill of rights for a modern humanist society would correspond to the first amendment to the U.S. Constitution: 'The State shall make no law with respect to the establishment of education'" (p. 11. Copyright 1970 The New York Review). Quoted by permission.

16. E. G. West, "The Political Economy of American Public School Legislation," *The Journal of Law and Economics* 10 (October 1967): 101.

17. *Ibid.*, p. 126.

18. *Ibid.*, p. 126.

19. *Ibid.*, p. 127.

Aubrey T. Robinson

17 Government and Public Health

(PARIS: 1832). ON MARCH 29TH, the night of Mi-careme, a masked ball was in progress, the chahut in full swing. Suddenly, the gayest of the harlequins collapsed, cold in the limbs, and, underneath his mask, "violet-blue" in the face. Laughter died out, dancing ceased, and in a short while carriage-loads of people were hurried from the *redoute* to the Hotel Dieu to die and, to prevent a panic among the patients, were thrust into rude graves in their dominoes. Soon the public halls were filled with dead bodies, sewed in sacks for want of coffins. Long lines of hearses stood *en queue* outside Pere Lachaise. Everybody wore flannel bandages. The rich gathered up their belongings and fled the town. Over 120,000 passports were issued at the Hotel de Ville. A *guillotine ambulante* was stalking abroad, and its effect upon the excitable Parisians reduplicated the scenes of the Revolution or of the plague at Milan.[1]

If you had been present at such a scene, wouldn't you want to help? Mightn't your concern even amount to feelings that you should help? People traditionally have confused such feelings of moral obligation with the idea that a *legal* obligation must be involved—that people should be *forced* to help. Out of such reactions to similar episodes have grown the large government operations and controls in the field of public health. Such spectres from the past, and knowledge of the evils overcome by governmental activity in the area of health, retain their psychological pull today. They help secure public support for future public health projects and for the professional public health officer, they justify not simply his occupational existence, but any program in which he is engaged.

Although there is a legitimate basis for someone to engage in many health projects of a "public" nature, such as health research, contagious disease control and environmental sanitation, the lack of any precise definition of what the government's role should be in this area makes the present-day public health scene a mixture of legitimate, dubious, and wrong activities.

No one has ever differentiated between public health activity as a potentially useful service and government activities of a public health nature. Most of the activities labeled "public health" form a distinct social service which can be performed by private businessmen, and is not ipso facto a political or governmental area of responsibility. From the beginnings of civilization, activities such as garbage disposal (which includes sewage systems), supplying water in quantity for towns and cities, rodent control, and the cleaning and maintenance of city streets have been considered proper, almost fundamental areas of government operation and control. The rationale for this opinion was that no individual would undertake a project in which his own benefit was so small a part of the benefit to all—a rationale that is not even necessary in this day of mass markets and mass services.

To these social services has been added a mixture of strictly medical services (hospitals, clinics, and district nurses), some research and experimental work (testing new drugs and pesticides), and many welfare activities (free milk for babies, marriage counseling, and nutritional advice). Today, the public health field in America is becoming one gigantic, confused, loosely constituted institution, composed largely of government activities (with private organizations playing adjunctive and supporting roles), presided over by the Department of Health, Education and Welfare. And these public health activities all come indirectly under the influence of the World Health Organization (WHO) of the United Nations, whose medical research is 100 percent financed by United States tax dollars.

Basically, the question that must be answered is: what is the proper relationship of the government to the public health field? That is the primary concern of this article.

What is public health? There are many "definitions" put forward, almost all of which give an idea of public health rather than an actual *definition*.

Almost all definitions in use today agree on two points: (a) the group or community is the basic unit (or patient) to be treated, and (b) this care or treatment is brought about through "organized community effort." In this respect, *Webster's Third New International Dictionary* is fairly concise: public health is the "Art and Science dealing with the protection and improvement of community health by organized community effort." Further, in *Introduction to Public Health*, it is called "that body of knowledge and those practices that contribute to health in the aggregate."[2]

However, the definition still considered by public health professionals to be one of the most authoritative is by C. E. A. Winslow in an article entitled "The Untilled Field of Public Health," which appeared in *Modern Medicine* in March, 1920:

Public Health is the Science and Art of preventing disease, prolonging life, and promoting health and efficiency; through organized community effort; for the sanitation of the environment, control of communicable infections, education of the individual in personal hygiene, organization of medical and nursing services for the early diagnosis and preventive treatment of disease, and development of the social machinery to insure everyone a standard of living adequate for the maintenance of health, so organizing these benefits as to enable every citizen to realize his birthright of health and longevity.

It must be noted that the focus of all three definitions is on the group treating a group, which does not in fact happen. It is the individual nurse or public health officer who deals with an individual citizen, to educate him, to treat him, to quarantine him, or to send him to the hospital. If, in fact, it was the health of the group rather than of the individual that was important, then of course, individual rights would not matter. You cut off a leg to save the person's life without reference to the leg's "rights"—it has no rights where the health of the whole is concerned. It is this attitude that the devotee of public health legislation would have us take toward the individual citizen when "group health" is at stake.

Also, notice that all three definitions have a lack of definite or precise meaning, which makes it possible to include any sphere of human activity. Hence, the so-called comprehensive approach (euphemism for *include everything*) in which one treats *every* aspect of the patient (social, economic, psychological). The result is Big Brother's dreams come true.

If public health professionals can't or won't specify the boundaries of their field, then perhaps an investigation of historical developments may provide a context in which to formulate a more proper definition and area of responsibility.

Most ancient civilizations had no governmental medical services of any kind. Health research was practically nonexistent; contagious diseases were controlled by social ostracism and, in the case of epidemics, by governmentally enforced banishment or isolation. But sanitary services were instituted very early.

The Minoans and Cretan rulers from 5000 to 1800 B.C. had constructed public water systems, and their houses had water closets with flushing systems. The Egyptian Pharaohs (about 1000 B.C.) constructed public drainage systems with slave labor and also developed earth closets, in addition to numerous pharmaceutical preparations. The Jews are considered to be the first to have developed a formal hygienic code. Their Mosaic law set rules for such activities as disinfection, disposal of refuse, and maternity care.

The Greeks had few government social services of the sort we have been discussing. Their culture emphasized matters of personal cleanliness, exercise, and dietetics rather than environmental sanitation and public water systems. They did have some public baths and aqueducts, which were constructed by wealthy citizens for their own use and on their own lands.

The Roman Empire developed extraordinary water and sewage systems and paved streets, many of which still exist today. It was the Romans who first formulated the concept of governmentally collected vital statistics, later to become an important adjunct to public health activities. At the height of the Roman Empire, laws existed for the registration of citizens and slaves and for periodic census-taking. The Romans also started government activities in related areas—supervision of weights and measures and of public bars and houses of prostitution, the .destruction of unsound goods, and the regulation of building construction.

By the time of the fall of the Roman Empire, public drainage and flushing systems, public water supplies, methods of disinfection and refuse disposal, maternity care, environmental sanitation, regulation of merchant and industrial practices, census-taking, control of rodents, housing laws, and regulation of health hazards and care in industrial establishments had all been thought of in at least some civilization as practices instituted by the government on behalf of "the health of the public." The Middle Ages added control of epidemics through primitive government-enforced quarantine and isolation measures.

The Middle Ages in general were marked by mysticism and a

"mortification of the flesh" that considered the world and the body evil. This resulted in a pronounced unconcern on the part of the people with personal hygiene and sanitation. It was a time of plague and epidemic. Two of the most feared diseases of these times were leprosy and bubonic plague (black death) which often reached pandemic proportions, wiping out one-half or two-thirds the population in each settlement or area. It has been said that "nothing before or since so nearly accomplished the extermination of the human race. . . . When Pope Clement VI asked for the number of the dead, some said that half of the population of the known world had died. . . . The total mortality from the Black Death is thought to have been over sixty millions. In Avignon where sixty thousand people died, the Pope found it necessary to consecrate the Rhone river in order that bodies might be thrown into it without delay, the churchyard no longer being able to hold them. Europe, particularly during 1348, was devastated.

"Leprosy apparently was a far more acute and disfiguring disease than presently observed in the Western world and, because of the terror to which it gave rise, laws were passed all over the continent regulating the conduct and movement of those afflicted. In many places lepers were declared civilly dead and banished from human communities. They were compelled to wear identifying clothes, and to warn of their presence by means of a horn or bell. . . . As a result, these victims died either from starvation, exposure or lack of treatment and care." By the sixteenth century, leprosy in Europe was practically nonexistent.[3]

As a result of these plagues, the first formal quarantine measure was instituted in this period. The government of Rogusa in 1377 forced infected or suspected ships or travelers to remain outside of port, free of disease for two months before being allowed to enter the city.[4]

Although the Renaissance was not dramatic for its innovations in public health work as such, the medical discoveries during this period founded modern medicine. All of the discoveries that constitute the basic medical knowledge on which public health practitioners build their professions were the result of the thinking and brilliant innovations of individual men like Leonardo da Vinci (1452–1519), whose sketches and drawings added to his other accomplishments a well-founded reputation as a physiologist; Ambroise Paré (1510–1590), still considered one of the greatest surgeons of any age; and Andreas Vesalius (1514–1564), probably the greatest anatomist of all time. These basic advances were all made possible because of the general spirit of inquiry and free thought that characterized this period.

The modern public health movement, and the modern concern

with social legislation in general, developed in England and America—mainly in England. The Poor Laws in Elizabethan England set a precedent that was extended to include health care services and facilities to mothers, children, and the aged and infirm. It was the English who were to give the real impetus and sophistication to the public health movement, not only in this country but in much of the world.

In colonial America, the British government was generally concerned with gross insanitation and with preventing the entrance of exotic diseases. However, vital statistics were early considered essential to sound public health practice. In 1639, an act was passed by the Massachusetts colony ordering the registration of each birth and death and outlining the required administrative responsibilities and procedures.

In England, the first sanitary legislation was passed in 1837. Also, during the nineteenth century, because of the increasing concentration of people in cities, the previously existing poor health habits and insanitary conditions were emphasized. The legislation of this time included bills concerning factory management, child welfare, care of the aged and infirm, mental illness, and education, along with other social reforms. Under the guise of protecting children, the power of the government was systematically increased in such areas as factory regulation and inspection and the prohibition of health hazards.

It is important to note that much of the government monopolization of public health reforms could not have been accomplished without the demands, urgings, and active support from professionals in every occupational field, from medicine to law to social work. There is a long line of men in the eighteenth and nineteenth centuries who championed various public health laws, projects, and programs.

In this country, Lemuel Shattuck (1793–1859) published his now-famous *Report of the Massachusetts Sanitary Commission,* which included a census of health, housing, and sanitation in Boston in 1845. Although this and other such documents were concerned mainly with those health problems that were most obviously the result of human beings living in close proximity, they served to focus public interest and attention on problems of sanitation and preventive medicine.

In England, three men were particularly influential. Jeremy Bentham (1748–1832), student of law and utilitarian philosopher, enlisted the doctrine "the greatest happiness of the greatest number" in support of his contention that public health legislation was needed and that the government must do much more in this area. He has been called the father of modern preventive medicine.[5]

Thomas Southwood Smith (1788–1861), London physician, wrote a treatise on *The Use of the Dead to the Living*, which led to the passing of the Anatomy Act (permitting the dissection of cadavers in medical schools) in England in 1832.

Sir Edwin Chadwick (1800–1890), lawyer, furthering Bentham's philosophy through what he called "the sanitary idea," persuaded the British government to appoint a Sanitary Commission in 1839. This led to the establishment of the General Board of Health in 1848.

All these men contributed significantly to a philosophical climate in which intellectuals demanded that the government provide health and welfare services for all. There can be no true understanding of the public health movement without understanding the philosophy of "social betterment" which has determined the extent and manner of the development of this field. Although extensive, the following quote eloquently summarizes this point of view:

—*As health is an essential factor in human welfare, its maintenance and protection are necessarily of social importance.*

—*Under a system where individualism obtains, society tends to take only those public health measures which are beyond the scope of individual action: organization for the prevention and control of epidemics, the provision of public water supplies, sewer systems, milk sanitation, research, hospital facilities, etc.*

—*Since, for generations, the social philosophy in the United States was largely one of individualism, quite naturally health problems have been left to the individual, public health work assuming responsibility only for those measures which the citizen, alone, could not institute.*

—*Within recent years, society has shown a tendency to assume an increasing responsibility for the individual* as an individual, *for his education, his employment, his general welfare.* [Italics mine.]

—*Out of this evolution there has come a tendency to broaden and intensify public health work; and in this expansion government, representing society, appears more and more inclined to regard provision of adequate public health and medical care as society's responsibility to each individual if he cannot himself procure such service.*[6]

It is the view of man (and therefore society) that is the basis for social philosophy. The view of man implied by the above statement is one of a basically helpless, irrational creature requiring the enforcement of an altruistic moral dogma guaranteeing his existence through the resources (i.e., life and property) of other men.

It is imperative to remember that public health activities traditionally have been regarded primarily as government responsibility and only secondarily as a voluntary community function. It was not, in the beginning, government that encroached upon private agencies taking public health responsibility; it was assumed to be a field for government prerogative. The government has mixed various unrelated health control measures with voluntary community health activities into the field we now recognize as public health.

In late nineteenth- and early twentieth-century America, many private agencies did develop. Most hospitals and clinics have been built with private funds. The American Red Cross, although chartered by Congress and working in cooperation with government agencies, is supported by voluntary contributions and staffed by volunteer workers. Margaret Sanger's birth control movement and the National Tuberculosis Association are good examples of private agencies that have provided medical and health–educational services to millions.

But in the 1930s, the American government's public health measures began to expand under the New Deal administration. And then, by a sort of natural impetus peculiar to governments, the administration extended its control and influence through administrative fiat and legislation, under pressure from special interest groups, both governmental and private. The recent trend has been toward the continued incorporation of various social welfare schemes into one giant federal organization: the Department of Health, Education and Welfare (1953). This department (now of cabinet status) is so large and so complex that a library of books would be needed for a complete study of its bureaus and divisions potentially involved in *one* health area, such as maternal and child care. Once this consolidation of agencies was well started, the government then proceeded to utilize social security funds (as it is now doing) for such programs as mental health, heart disease, and dental health.

In his paper, *The Impact of the Great Society on Public Health Practice,*[7] Edward S. Rogers, M.D., professor of Public Health and Medical Administration at the University of California School of Public Health at Berkeley, quotes Secretary John Gardner, of the Department of Health, Education and Welfare:

The whole movement of events in recent years has been not *toward the separation but toward the interweaving of the Department's various objectives. With the enactment of Medicare legislation, health and social security are inextricably linked. It is impossible to conceive of a modern welfare program without a strong educational component. Programs concerned with juvenile delinquency, mental retardation, and aging cut across the old categories. An adequate attack on poverty defies bureaucratic boundary lines.*

For a graphic illustration of the relationships that exist between private medicine and the forces for social medicine, the following quote from the same article is unequaled. Professor Rogers states:

Between the time of the passage of the heart disease, cancer and stroke legislation (DeBakey Program) in the same year, a total change in the relations between the Federal government and the AMA occurred. . . . The AMA suddenly changed its course in favor of working constructively in support of the bill. . . . The government welcomed this cooperative approach—and the lion and the lamb lay down together. *This was a significant event because these two great forces for better health services had too long been at odds with each other. In the philosophy of creative federalism, the government needed the AMA. In the philosophy of pragmatism, the AMA recognized the growing pressure of a public consensus.* [Italics mine.]

There are two questions left to ask: which one is the lion and which is the lamb? and, what happens to the lamb?

We now have a general idea of how the gradual development of the field presently called public health led to the government's present predominance.

Intellectually, this predominance was accomplished through: lack of any context for defining proper governmental public health concerns; the failure to differentiate between public health as a field of private endeavor and government activities of a public health nature; and the philosophy of pragmatism which evades principles and focuses only on methods and concretes.

Morally and *politically,* the government's predominance was accomplished through the doctrine of "social betterment" and the concept of the "right to housing, jobs, health and other necessities of life," and the large, tacit, assumed government responsibility for the general welfare, all of which bastardize and mock the legitimate concepts of rights and individualism.

Psychologically, it resulted, in part, from a distortion of the valid respect many people hold for medicine in general. Through handling and treating health problems, the health practitioner acquires familiarity and efficacy in dealing with situations of fundamental necessity to health and life: in a very special way he "knows what makes life tick." This knowledge inspires respect and a sense of awe in many people which indiscriminately may be extended to envelop anything that is *said* to be of a medical nature. The result is a kind of charisma attached to the field of medicine and health. This charisma sometimes prevents people from critically evaluating any public health project: if it will improve health, it must be good. Today the government is cashing in on this charisma.

What is wrong with government public health work? Apart from being an expense of millions of dollars to the unwitting taxpayers, apart from the inefficiencies of sprawling agencies rife with red tape and duplicate services, government agencies are forcing private competing agencies out of business, and public health laws are used to extend the tyranny of the bureaucrat over the citizen.

The question is: *How does one apply the standard of protection of individual rights to delimit government operations, responsibilities, and authority in the field of public health?*

Some areas of responsibility now included in public health work are validly governmental in nature. These must be explicitly defined and recategorized under a heading such as *Health Law*. The only justification for government involvement in any area of the citizen's life is the protection of rights (by which I mean life, liberty, and property). Health law would be concerned exclusively with infringements of rights of a health nature. It would be applied through civil law suits and standard courts, never through administrative agencies, and would employ the legal weapons of search warrants, injunctions, contempt of court proceedings, arrest and trial—*never* regulation and regulatory inspection. The foregoing description obviously excludes the operation or control of any public health facility or organization by the government.

Valid areas of government assumption of public health responsibility would therefore be areas in which the use of retaliatory force or the threat of force is required in order to protect the legitimate rights of other citizens. Such areas would be, for example, the arrest and prosecution of persons specifically accused of polluting the air or water supply; the enforcement of laws against maintaining known health hazards to neighbors on one's property; the enforcement of laws against selling polluted or disease-carrying products; provision for institutions for the criminally insane; and some quarantine laws. Those areas (such as air pollution) that have been handled mainly in a regulatory manner to date would present special problems because of the scarcity of legal precedents. Although we don't know all the answers to these problems, the standards for drafting legislation would always be that government actions (no matter how "good" for the "public welfare") cannot violate rights of property and that the rights of property do not permit the maintenance of uncontrollable health hazards on one's land affecting the health of one's neighbors. Such areas as emergency provisions for lifesaving measures on the part of the police would not be affected, as these are not properly considered public health measures, but protection against possible death from crime or criminal neglect. This area of police work does not basically change the nature of government activities as here stated.

Most of the present public health activities of the government would be considered illegal. The medical services now provided by public agencies would be provided by private agencies which would have no power to force treatment on the individual (however, criminal or civil law suits could apply). Sewage disposal, the provision of water systems, and similar social services would be performed by privately owned companies. The control of health research, hospitals, and clinics would, of course, be in private control.

If the government feels that an infringement of rights of a public health nature is involved, it institutes a lawsuit or provides the means for other citizens to institute one. Therefore, major government costs may be judicial operating expenses (along with military and police forces). Financing can be obtained for these costs in much the same way that it is obtained by insurance companies—through government premiums to users and potential users.

As an intermediary step in returning the field of public health, and health in general, to private control (this is the literal meaning of "power to the people"), the government could establish a system contracting for public health, utility, and medical services, using private companies. For a complete exposition of this idea read the article, "Contracts—Key to Urban Rebirth" by Robert Poole, Jr.[8]

In this country, medicine traditionally has been a free enterprise operation, not a state service. Why did the medical profession acquiesce to the incorporation into the government colossus of so many areas that were theirs? In large part, because present public health services are not thought of as being based on the use of force. Taxation rarely is recognized as a use of force, neither is ruinous government competition through near monopoly. In public health, more than in most areas of government activity, methods of operation are through persuasion, research studies, dissemination of health literature, consultations and evaluation services, and grants-in-aid. For an interesting illustration of the effect of government grants on the field of ideas, read: Ayn Rand's "The Establishing of an Establishment."[9]

As in every other area of human endeavor, destruction of institutions and systems requires the destruction of the concepts on which they rest. When the concept of human rights is destroyed, then the destruction of a particular concept—public health—is possible. However, in this case, the destruction goes beyond these two phases because the goal is the change in the modus vivendi of a society in all spheres of activity. But the destruction of rights only applies to its literal or objective meaning; the emotional connotation (i.e., moral force) of human rights is retained. Next, pseudorights are created such as jobs, housing, and medical care, which are, in reality, actual needs or necessities of life. This application of terminology insures a sympathy for those without these necessities (i.e., "rights"). Since society has already been "intellectually disarmed," it does not distinguish between the legitimate meaning of rights and human needs. The moral force of the idea of rights is retained but attached to the necessities or concretes of life. In effect, rights become physical things or conditions.

The result of the foregoing is that the philosophy of altruism in the field of public health has expanded its scope and context to include the general welfare of the citizen in terms of education, jobs, housing, and so forth. The idea of the general welfare (in this sense) of the individual affecting his psychological and physical health is not illogical as stated. The political and moral danger is the use of political force (i.e., government agencies, laws, taxes) to implement a concept involved with the total care, responsibility and—by fiat—control of a person's existence.

The three relevant points here are that: (1) the concept of public health has broadened to mean any health condition affecting a group of people or individuals, regardless of whether the condition is publicly contagious or not (e.g., venereal disease); (2) concepts of health are focused on the *total* person—that is, his education, economic stability, and living conditions contribute to his resulting state of health and should accordingly be treated; (3) through government actions in the fields of health, education, and economics, a particular philosophy (altruism) is forced upon the citizen who is forced to support it with his own money.

Quite naturally, then, an agency that operates directly or indirectly by force and coercion and has the responsibility for the health, education, and welfare of citizens, logically acquires over the citizen's life the authority and control that follows that responsibility. The control, in this country, is exercised primarily through regulating the amount of money the citizen is allowed to retain from his salary. The result is totalitarian control of the individual's life through assumed government responsibility for his health.

The most reprehensible fact of modern life is this cynical willingness of men (conservatives in the area of personal, sexual, and moral values; liberals in the realm of economics and social policy) to force their beliefs on other men. From this point of view, it is totally irrelevant how great the need, how well-intentioned the motivations, or whether the philosophy or belief forced on the society is socialized medicine, capitalism, or communism. The important consideration is that members of no group (intellectuals, lobbyists, government agencies) have the moral authority and/or legal power to facilitate their beliefs on a society through its political system. Political and social philosophies are not decided and imposed by "the rule of the majority." A political system, as such, should exist only for the protection of legitimate human rights—period. Therefore, in terms of an organized system of social and political ideas, a government must be philosophically neutral.

It is quite appropriate to have various political and philosophical orientations competing for the minds of the citizen—but always through intellectual, rational persuasion, not through force (i.e., laws, taxes). This idea of persuasion would be just as applicable to changing an altruistic society to a capitalistic society. The absence of any government enforced philosophy leaves society—as individuals—free to actualize and choose (through monetary contributions, volunteer organizations, etc.) their own beliefs.

America is a curiosity in respect to the exercise of force; she specializes in the indirect, rather than the direct, use of force. Because she still has some respect for individual rights, her infringement of these rights necessarily takes a different form from that in countries in which there is little respect for this moral principle—which is most of the world. America is kinder, more considerate, more well-intentioned, less brutal, and, as a consequence, less obvious. How does the average nonpolitical, nonideological professional refuse money for research projects, medical school construction, and various other endeavors. Given his situation, he doesn't.

We are "economic man." Control a man's money and you control his health, education, and welfare. You control his life.

Notes

Aubrey T. Robinson is in the Department of Nursing of the Manhattan Community College of the City University of New York.

"Government and Public Health" is reprinted with permission from *Persuasion* (October 1967).

1. F.H. Garrison, *History of Medicine,* 4th ed. (Philadelphia: W.B. Saunders Co., 1966), p. 775.

2. H.S. Mustard and E.L. Stebbins, *Introduction to Public Health,* 4th ed. (New York: Macmillan Co., 1962), p. 16.

3. John J. Hanlon, *Principles of Public Health Administration,* 2nd ed. (St. Louis: C.V. Mosby Co., 1955), pp. 29–32.

4. Ibid., p. 31.

5. Douglas Guthrie, *A History of Medicine,* (Philadelphia: J.B. Lippincott Co., 1946), p. 387.

6. Mustard, *op. cit.,* pp. 3–4.

7. Paper given at the 1966 American Nurses Association Convention.

8. Robert Poole, Jr., "Contracts—Key to Urban Rebirth," *Reason,* April 1972.

9. Ayn Rand, "The Establishing of an Establishment," *The Ayn Rand Letter, vol. 1, nos. 16–17, May 8 and May 22, 1972.*

Alan Reynolds

18 The Case against Wage and Price Controls

MR. NIXON'S ECONOMIC proposals since his presidency essentially repudiate his earlier faith in free trade and free markets. Concern over a general upward trend of wages and prices is one thing, a strait-jacket on *relative* price and wage changes is quite another. There is no reason to believe that the existing relationships among myriad prices and wages are the most efficient or most equitable possible—even right now, much less after three months of change. Exemption of taxes and interest rates from the "freeze" leaves our frozen incomes vulnerable to the two fastest rising elements in the typical family budget.

So-called "direct" price controls are no such thing: They are a deceptive attack on the *results* of monetary mismanagement, rather than on the cause. The current suppression of price increases should cause few *short-run* problems, since the price index has been rising insignificantly (0.2 per cent last month). The impact of the enormous May increase in the money supply, however, may well hit about the same time the freeze is due to be lifted. Add this monetary snowball to three months of postponed labor demands, and we can be sure of a November explosion of wages, prices and strikes (as occurred in Britain after controls were lifted in late 1969). This situation will create a myopic clamor for still more controls, though controls were largely the cause of the wage explosion. Frozen wages and prices prevent the smooth, continual adjustments which free markets would otherwise make in response to government's inept management of debt and money.

The President's 10 per cent surcharge on non-quota imports is a blatantly inflationary move, designed to "protect" consumers from low, foreign prices. Foreigners trade their goods for dollars so that they can spend those dollars on U.S. products. They don't collect dollars as a hobby. A tariff between the U.S. and Japan no more benefits the U.S. than a tariff between California and New York would benefit California.

By giving new names to old ideas, ancient arguments can be continually reborn with fresh, new trademarks and slogans. In this way, the tyranny of government wage and price control has been transformed into the thoroughly respectable notion of an "incomes policy."

The idea is simple enough; it goes something like this: "The inflation of the Seventies is something altogether new. Unions bargain for wages in excess of productivity gains, and these wage-costs are simply passed on, by monopolistic firms, in the form of higher administered prices. Orthodox prescriptions of tight money are simply irrelevant to this fundamentally new situation, in which inflation continues despite massive unemployment. The only solution, which will combine reasonable price stability with a tolerable level of unemployment, is government control of wages and/or prices—at least in highly concentrated industries."

There is, of course, nothing "new" about all this, except the slogans. Shifting the blame for inflation has been attempted by most governments throughout history. The Democratic Party has consistently embraced this scapegoat theory of inflation since before 1960, when Chester Bowles explained his party's platform by describing "a relatively new type of inflation in which prices in a few tightly controlled semimonopolistic industries are raised regardless of market consideration." More recently, AFL-CIO President George Meany has been especially vocal in demanding wage and price controls.

In *The New Industrial State*, even John Kenneth Galbraith has lost the indecision on this subject which plagued his earlier books. "The seemingly obvious remedy for the wage-price spiral is to regulate prices and wages by public authority." Unemployment, says Galbraith, "occurs when there is insufficient demand; the spiral operates when there is too much and also, unfortunately, when there is just enough . . . since the system is unstable at full employment, there is no alternative to control. However regretted, it is inescapable."

But why should wage and price controls be regretted? Aside from the inherent risk in granting anyone such potentially awesome power over incomes, there are several regrets that Galbraith forgot to mention. First of all, controls may block price or wage increases related to genuine shortages. Prices and wages act as signals for businessmen and laborers to move to areas and occupations where they're most urgently needed. Controls stop this movement of scarce productive equipment and skills, and thereby limit the economy's ability to produce what is wanted.

Second, because of the enormous complexity of our economy, even fairly comprehensive (i.e., fascistic) efforts at control are necessarily selective and discriminatory. Very conspicuous industries are singled out for "restraint," while sectors where inflation may be greatest—professional incomes, food and services—gain even more from the resulting diversion of demand. Controlling a few wages and prices doesn't eliminate inflationary pressure, it simply shifts the pressure elsewhere.

These objections to controls are not just theoretical, but express actual effects of the wage-price guideposts of the Sixties. Indeed, the disillusioning experience with unenforced guidelines is the reason why stronger measures are now often being proposed. But the problems of price control arise from *following* the rules, not from evading them. The *less* room left for hidden price and service adjustments, the more inefficient and inequitable the distortions of repressed inflation will become.

The Chicken and the Egg

These ill effects are often admitted, but wage and price controls are nonetheless considered The Only Answer to our dilemma. After all, it is said, monopolistic corporations raise prices to pass on the cost of rising union wages; these prices then justify further wage demands, and so on. February articles in *Look* and *Fortune* blamed unions for starting this cost-push "spiral"; George Meany blames corporations. Galbraith, the diplomat, claims neither the chicken nor the egg came first: "Wages force up prices and prices force up wages."

In a famous essay, MIT Professor Paul Samuelson offers a brief explanation of cost-push inflation: "Just as wages and prices may be sticky in the face of unemployment and overcapacity, so may they be pushing upward beyond what can be explained in terms of levels and shifts in demand."

Now, suppose a businessman is somewhat reluctant to take markdowns and cut his employees' wages. How does this reluctance relate in any way to the same businessman's ability to *raise* prices without losing sales to his competitors, or to *raise* wages without worrying about the effect on profits? Samuelson's conclusion simply doesn't follow. Downward price and wage rigidity proves nothing at all about upward "pricing power." Moreover, as Professor George Stigler of the University of Chicago demonstrated, the alleged "rigidity" of those prices which Gardiner Means whimsically classified as "administered" decreases as more firms are examined, and disappears altogether when we consider actual prices rather than prices from price lists and catalogs. No association has been found between concentration of production (the portion of business done by a few firms) and the size and frequency of price increases.

Most firms are continually searching for the combination of price and sales which will best maximize their wealth. Sure, *any* firm, regardless how competitive its market, *could* keep raising its price (even until only one unit could be sold), but such arbitrary pricing power would obviously be suicidal.

By implying no significant connection between wages or prices asked, and the amount of labor and goods actually sold, common remarks about the "new" inflation completely reject elementary economic theory. An imposed increase in the price of, say, steel, causes some steel buyers to use less steel or to substitute aluminum or plastic. The resulting lower output of steel releases productive resources (machines, workers, raw materials) to other goods, whose prices fall as their supply is thereby increased. Similarly, to the extent that relative wage gains of unions have not been an illusion, they have occurred through restrictions on entering a trade (usually by licensing laws), which increased the supply of workers in nonunion sectors and depressed nonunion wages by 3 to 4 per cent. *Specific* price or wage increases do not create general inflation.

Probably the most compelling feature of the cost-push argument for wage and price controls is that it provides an opportunity to criticize big unions or big business. Actually, though, it isn't enough to show that unions and concentrated industries have substantial power to influence wage rates and prices. This would explain why certain prices and wages were *relatively* high at any moment, but such market power alone would not explain why these prices, or why prices generally, were rising. In order to explain generally rising prices, monopolistic influences would, first of all, have to be substantial enough already greatly to affect the general level of all prices. Secondly, such pricing power would also have to be *increasing* at a rate much faster than that of the average price level, since the average also contains many competitive prices. In brief, unions and large corporations would have to command a *predominant and rapidly growing* share of economic activity in order to cause any general increase in prices.

Because it's so newsworthy, the market power of unions and large corporations is often exaggerated. Dr. Albert Rees, a prominent labor economist, estimates that the direct union wage effect on all costs in the economy is about 4 per cent. Moreover, union membership has stabilized at less than one-fourth of the labor force, and some of the strongest unions have experienced substantial membership losses (apparently due to the effect of high wages in reducing employment). Manufacturing unions are an especially poor scapegoat for recent problems, since average wage increases for *non*union manufacturing workers exceeded those for unionized workers in four out of the five years ending with 1969.*

Incidentally, the fact that wages are rising faster than productivity in no way "proves" that wages *cause* inflation. Suppose that wages and productivity both rose at 3 per cent, while prices rose at 6 per cent. Obviously, this would be a 3 per cent decline in real wages, and a terrific boon to employers, because of reduced salary cost. This is, in fact, the main reason why unexpected inflation increases short-run employment, though an explicit wage cut with stable prices would have the same effect. To ask wage-earners to lag behind the general trend of other prices is to ask them to suffer a serious relative decline. As we shall see, the supposition that price increases would then slow down proportionately is more than unlikely.

On the business side, Anthony Harberger has estimated that the annual cost of enterprise monopoly to consumers is less than $1.50 per person, and most of this is government-created monopoly. All major research shows no increase whatsoever in industrial concentration since 1909 (firms are bigger, but do not get a bigger share of the growing market). Big business is a particularly unlikely villain in last year's drama, since after-tax corporate profits were only about 6.5 per cent of Gross National Product, compared with a more typical 9.5 per cent in 1966. The Tax Reform Act of 1969 was, as the President's Council of Economic Advisers admits, "excessively burdensome on business investment." The result was a $4-billion reduction in investment, and a lower real output than in 1969.

So, it appears there is little factual support for the crucial notion that union and industrial power is sufficient to upset greatly the whole economy, and even less justification for the idea that such power is increasing relative to the more competitive sphere. Since manufacturing unions and corporations have not fared too well during recent years, either their power is a bit overstated, or they intentionally "administered" their prices and wages in order to lose wealth.

The Phillips Fallacy

A second flaw, in the idea that inflation can be caused by negotiated wages and administered prices, is that it assumes a passive monetary policy. Without an increase in either the amount of dollars, or the rapidity with which they're spent (velocity), general price and wage increases will result in unsold goods and unemployed laborers. It simply isn't possible for most people to be receiving incomes from continually rising wages and prices unless the Federal Reserve authorities create more and more money units (roughly, by making it easier for banks to create new checking accounts in the form of loans).

In principle, money velocity could increase for a while, to pay the rising prices. But people and businesses have been remarkably stubborn about the amount of cash (in terms of real buying power) that they hold relative to their wealth. More precisely, the demand for currency and checking deposits to hold (the converse of velocity of spending) is *predictably* related to variations in wealth, prices and interest rates. Thus, changes in velocity can be offset by the appropriate Federal Reserve actions to change the money supply.

If we are having inflation, then, it logically *must* be due to excessive increases in the amount of money relative to the amount of goods. In technical terms, if the supply of cash balances is increased beyond the amount which people wish to hold, relative to their wealth, they will spend the difference, thereby bidding up prices (which reduces the real value of their cash holdings). This is the monetarist explanation of inflation, which the archaic "new" theories claim is now suddenly irrelevant to recent experience. What, exactly, is so unique about this recent experience?

From December 1969 to December 1970, the stock of currency and checking deposits rose 5.4 per cent. A more inclusive measure of liquid assets, including various savings deposits, increased in this period by 7.7 per cent. Output per man-hour actually declined somewhat last year, as did Gross National Product. Thus, we had too much money chasing too few goods, and this situation created a 5.6 per cent price inflation last year.

In the first half of 1971, the monetary growth became explosive: an

18.3 per cent annual rate of growth of all monetary assets. Since it takes six to nine months for the full effects of monetary changes to be felt, the Nixon Administration is certainly not being complacent when it says enough has already been done to "stimulate" the sluggish economy. Actually, that's a huge understatement. Whether the impact of the new money will be felt primarily in increasing prices, or in production and employment, cannot be conclusively determined from the fact that unemployment is fairly high. The answer will largely depend on how much of the new money can be channelled into profits and investments, rather than into incomes from unmarketable government activities.

The idea that increased wage inflation will reduce unemployment, and that increased unemployment will reduce inflation, is often called the "Phillips Curve" after the British economist who more or less discovered it. Phillips' figures, for Britain from 1861-1913, show a fairly close relationship between the rate of change in money wages and the portion of the labor force unemployed.

Samuelson and Solow's influential 1960 paper presented their "best guesses ... phrased in short-run terms" about the relevance of the Phillips Curve to the United States. Most editorial "facts" about how much inflation will cure how much unemployment, and vice versa, are derived from these short-run guesses. *Time* Magazine (August 16), for example, somehow deduced that "well over 10 per cent" unemployment would be needed to stop inflation.

Actually, this alleged trade-off between unemployment and inflation occurs while the inflation is unexpected. Once employees realize that they can no longer buy as many things despite their apparent wage increases, their resulting demands for higher *real* wages will restore the previous rate of unemployment. The only way of continually fooling people into thinking a pay cut is really a raise, is to keep increasing the *rate* of inflation, which soon becomes obvious too, and results in a spiraling situation as people rush to unload money for goods.

This is likewise the verdict of most recent factual research on the "Phillips Curve"—that it is a short-run approximation at best, being based on a failure to distinguish between nominal and real wages. It is not true, then, as Samuelson claims, that the combination of high unemployment and price inflation confirms the folklore of cost-push inflation. It would do so only if we were willing to accept the Phillips Curve fallacy as well.

Yet, even if we swallowed a crude trade-off between high unemployment and low inflation, there are at least two reasons why we might expect unemployment and inflation to coexist right now. First of all, at least 45 per cent of the increase in *civilian* unemployment last year (700,000 to 1,570,000) was due to defense cutbacks. This government-planned unemployment clearly has nothing to do with aggregate demand, nor with some inherent instability of the private economy. By subtracting the defense unemployment, we find that 1970 unemployment in this sense was 3.4 million (about 4.3 per cent), which is considerably less, even in absolute numbers, than in any of the years between 1958 and 1965.

Secondly, the 1970 labor force increase of 1.9 million was more than double the increase in nondefense unemployment, largely because of more teen-agers and married women filing for unemployment benefits. These benefits rose from $1,890,900,000 in 1966 to a mere $3,-960,000,000 in 1970. Average weekly checks increased more in the last two years than in all the years from 1961–67 and the average check is now equal to about thirty hours of work at the minimum wage.

Perhaps it would not be too cynical to suggest that we should *expect* more housewives and students to list themselves as "unemployed," when their leisure time is so limited, child care so costly, and unemployment benefits so lucrative relative to part-time employment.

The President's Council of Economic Advisers (CEA) is usually noted for its ability to whitewash existing governmental policy. The latest *Economic Report of the President*, however, is remarkably candid about government's role in raising the cost of living, and in discouraging efficient investment.

First, there is government suppression of competition through import restrictions, maximum interest payments on bank deposits, restrictive residential building codes, laws fostering closed entry into unionized trades, and minimum rate regulation in the transportation industry. Journalists make much of the strikes and "administered" prices in the auto industry. But how many of us are affected by (fictitious) new car list prices, which have only risen a total of 7 per cent in the last three years anyway? How often do we hear mentioned the government's deliberate increases of regulated transportation rates—which affect nearly everything everyone buys? Professor Yale Brozen estimates the wastes and overcharges resulting from transport regulation amount to $10 billion a year. If that's a sample of government price control, it surely isn't too encouraging.

A related source of inflated prices and restricted output is government tinkering with wages and prices (*more* of which is now, paradoxically, suggested as a cure for inflation!). As the CEA put it: ". . . where government has intervened to set prices for certain goods and services and otherwise to control their availability, the results have often prevented the efficient use of resources." Examples of such distortions could be found in farm and dairy price supports, state "fair trade" laws, subsidized recreational areas, minimum-wage laws and restrictive professional licensing laws.

Government Fraud

If governments are to decree the "proper" level of private incomes, it seems worthwhile to ask who will regulate the regulators' incomes. The Federal Government is the largest employer in the country, with more than 2.5 million civilians on its payroll. Employment of all levels of government is 16 per cent of total employment. The number of state and local government employees has more than doubled since 1955.

In the first quarter of 1970, the Federal Government pay raise added 1.2 percentage points to the whole economy's measured annual rate of inflation. This price index increase has now become part of the "proof" that we need more government regulation of incomes—of *private* incomes, of course.

Quoting the *Economic Report* again (page 34): "State and local government purchases, which have been rising steadily for many years, continued to increase at a rapid rate . . . . Employment by state and local governments rose almost 5 per cent over the average level in 1969 . . . . The rise in wage and salary rates was especially large last year." So much for Galbraith's remark that "those who depend for their pay on the public treasury are . . . especially likely to suffer during inflation."

The relevance of all this is that government is the only sector which is immune to monetary policy, as was emphasized by Arthur Burns many years ago. Here we have a legitimate need for wage control, as well as an example of how effective governments might be in resisting wage demands.

The Federal Government can finance any salary expense by increased taxes or by selling bonds to the banking system—which become reserves for inflationary loan expansion. State and local governments can and do finance unusually generous salaries by unusually large tax-rate increases, or by issuing tax-exempt bonds at artificially low interest rates.

Thus, government officials, since they have little incentive to worry about the pinch of salary costs on revenues, are in a unique position to create a fourfold inflationary pressure: 1) highly productive employees are induced out of less remunerative private employment, thus reducing the supply of marketable goods and services; 2) regulated rates are increased in government enterprises, such as the postal service monopoly; 3) some of the added salary expense is usually financed with inflationary management of government debt; and 4) the rest of the expense is passed on in enlarged tax requisitions, which have an obvious direct effect on the cost of living.

Table C-30 of the *Economic Report of the President* shows average gross weekly earnings by type of employment—except that government is conspicuously absent. We can arrive at an estimate of mean weekly earnings in government employment by dividing government annual wage and salary disbursements ($114 billion; Table C-17) by the number of government employees (12,599,000; Table C-27). The result is $174 a week, which is 45 per cent higher than the nonagricultural private economy's average of $120, and 14 per cent higher than the supposedly monopolistic manufacturing sector. Moreover, the corresponding gap between public and private averages was only 27 per cent in 1960 and 39 per cent in 1965, indicating a growing source of inflationary expenditure. As we have seen, wage-push inflation can originate only in the government sector, because only governments are immune to the incentives of monetary restriction.

The plight of the *private* employee is neatly summarized in Table C-32 of the *Economic Report*. Average gross weekly earnings rose from $95.06 in 1965 to $119.78 in 1970, for an illusory increase of $24.72. Adjusting for inflation by converting to 1967 prices, however, shows only a $2.58 real improvement, or .5 per cent per year. Subtracting only Social Security and income taxes, we find average real spendable earnings, for a family of four, actually *declined* $1 from 1965 to 1970. Neither inflation nor federal taxes have risen so rapidly as regressive state and local taxes, however, so average real private income, net of all taxes, has doubtless declined even more than this figure shows.

There is a subtle dishonesty in editorializing about the "cost of living," while not even mentioning taxes. Ralph Nader should investigate consumer fraud originating in government. According to tax authority Joseph Pechman, families with annual incomes between $2,000 and $4,000 received 11 per cent of their 1965 incomes from government welfare payments—but they *paid* 27 per cent of their incomes in taxes. The most quickly increasing taxes are the highly regressive Social Security, property and sales taxes. Social Security payroll deductions already take over $1.5 billion from families officially classified as poor, and rates have risen from 6 per cent of incomes up to $4,800 in 1960 to 9.6 per cent of incomes up to $7,800 in 1969. State and local tax receipts have risen from 7.1 per cent of GNP in 1951 to 11.9 per cent in 1968. Federal, state and local taxes claimed at least 44 per cent of the incomes of families earning less than $2,000 in 1965, thereby creating most of the poverty problem these agencies claimed to be solving.

Pull, Not Push

The CEA's *Economic Report* (page 100) illustrates the deceptive way in which this tax burden is typically glossed over: "The sectors where strong growth *in demand* has occurred are education, health and general government .... Those sectors where expenditures are increasing are also the sectors where prices have risen very rapidly." Much of the fantastic inflation in the price of medical services is indeed due to the fact that government greatly increased the "demand" for such services by paying 40 per cent of the bills, while allowing the AMA to legally restrict the supply by controlling the licensing of medical schools (the number of medical students was the same in 1955 as it was in 1904).

But how can we believe there has been an increase in *demand* for education and general government? The growth has been in *supply*, despite well-publicized, overwhelming taxpayer disapproval. On the CEA's definition, the "demand" for the Vietnam war must still be enormous.

Of the private sector's price increases, we could well argue that much of the apparent inflation represents significant *quality* improvement: polyester knit apparel instead of cotton, more low-cost restaurant meals appearing in the food budget, self-cleaning ovens, aerosol cans, disc brakes on cars, etc. It would certainly be difficult to create a comparable argument about bloated statism: Hard to say, for example, that the doubling since 1963 of state and local expenditures on education and welfare is due to a tremendous improvement in quality.

What we are experiencing is more of a tax-pull than a wage-push situation. Inflated government has raised the cost of living through high regulated rates and excess money creation, while it reduced real incomes and economic growth with oppressive taxation. Now, some people are seriously suggesting that what we need is even more government intervention, with price controls and an onerous state-freeze on private wage "increases." The logic involved is reminiscent of the rock concert where some genius hired several members of the Hell's Angels to promote peace and order.

Notes

Alan Reynolds is the associate editor of the *National Review*.
"The Case against Wage and Price Controls" is reprinted with permission from the *National Review* (September 24, 1971).
Economic Report of the President (U.S. Gov't., 1971) p. 59. All subsequent statistics are also from this source, unless otherwise noted.

part four
Free Societies and Foreign Affairs

The philosophy of libertarianism is not predicated on the possibility of a total, final unchangeable answer to all of man's political problems. Knowledge and reality aren't static systems, so it is only within a given context of the evolution of human knowledge that solutions can be provided. Perhaps the least well-developed area of political solution concerns the realm we may call "foreign affairs." The term is ambiguous; in a free society it is not clear in terms of what criteria one would distinguish the domestic from the foreign over any length of time. And this alone indicates the problem.

Assuming, however, that a free society would have borders, separating it from other, more or less free (as well as statist) societies, how ought it to relate to these neighbors, if at all?

The problems connected with foreign relations are complicated if only because they are the least well explored. And understandably so: the data on how various approaches of such a society to its neighbors might work are nonexistent. My own evaluation is projective. Following the motto "if it is a human problem, it is humanly manageable," and reflecting on the dismal conduct of foreign affairs by states throughout history, I conclude that it is reasonable to expect better performance on the part of free societies than on the part of statist ones.

The articles in this chapter will offer an insight into some of the libertarian thinking about foreign affairs and the affairs of foreign societies. Hopefully, the thinking thus reflected will give a good indication of the sort of approach a society grounded on libertarian political principles would use within the realm of international affairs.

John O. Nelson

19 The Economic Failure and War Ethos of Socialist States: No Accident

HISTORY ABOUNDS WITH evidence that highly socialized economies are able to produce war goods in abundance but are unable to produce consumer goods in anything like adequate supply. We read, for instance, that when the Inca rulers began their socialization of the Peruvian economy in the late twelfth century, an increase in number and scope and success of military operations occurred, but also the oppression of the ordinary peasant and worker increased, along with a gradual decline in his living standard. Thus, by the fifteenth century, the Inca King, Pachacutec, having "completed his work of unification by laws which regulated work with great precision, established compulsory military training and reduced the standard of living of the people to the lowest point. No more feather ornaments or clothes of vicuna wool, no more simmering drinks, one drink only—*maize chicha*. This hopeless austerity," adds the author, "is today called basic leveling," and he notes wryly, "One could wish that the ruler had applied to himself and his family the same high principles which he imposed on his people."[1] We might, in our own times, apply the same descriptions to Communist Russia, Red China, or any of the other highly socialized economies that have been spawned in this century.

One would think that this abundant historical evidence on the nature and effects of socialism would give the American intellectual community—and especially the members of its universities—some pause in their advocacy of that doctrine. But not so. Generally, they either blithely ignore the plain evidence of past and present history or they twist it to the account of socialism. Thus, turning light into darkness, they will often argue in this fashion: "Socialist economies are demonstrably productive—consider their ability to produce war goods in abundance. That they do not produce consumer goods in abundance must, therefore, be due to mere accidents of one sort or another. When these accidents are eliminated, socialist economies will produce consumer goods in as much abundance as they now produce war goods."

A more militant form of the same argument is worth our particular attention. It goes: "Communist Russia and her socialist allies are forced to produce great amounts of war goods in order to counter capitalist (laissez-faire) aggressions and threats. It is this production of an abundance of war goods that prevents Communist Russia and her friends from producing an abundance of consumer goods. Once the capitalist (laissez-faire) world is destroyed and the socialist world thus permitted to live in peace, the latter will fulfill the productive dreams of its founders. So our first task must be to destroy capitalism (laissez-faire)."

In this essay I shall show that it is *no* accident at all that socialist economies, though capable of producing war goods, are incapable of producing consumer goods. I shall then show as a corollary that *if* the capitalist or laissez-faire world is destroyed,[2] what will replace it is not a socialist world at peace but a socialist world at total war.

The success of socialized economies in producing war goods and their seemingly discrepant failure in producing consumer goods can be traced to two sources: inherent differences in the distribution of war goods and consumer goods, and inherent differences in the motivations affecting the production of each. I shall deal with the inherent differences of distribution first.

Distribution of War Goods and Consumer Goods

Since the distribution of war goods rests ultimately upon the demands and calculations of a supreme military commander, we shall want to ask at the outset what criteria for requisition motivate this personage or body of personages. Does the supreme military commander, for instance, concern himself with the competition of men's appetites for satisfaction? With respect to war goods themselves, he clearly does not. Men have no appetite for tanks *per se* or bombs *per se*. What competition there is for war goods comes down to a few contending generals arguing matters of tactics, strategy, and logistics. This general argues, for instance, that he needs a thousand tanks placed in such-and-such a location in order to carry out such-and-such a plan; another general argues that the plan in question calls for five hundred tanks placed in such-another location, and so on.

In contrast, the distribution of consumer goods has as its end the contending appetites of everyone. Men do desire food *per se*, clothes *per se*, and cigarettes *per se*. They vie in their consumption of these things; and they are immediately satisfied or dissatisfied in the distributions that eventuate.

We already see, then, the inherent differences characterizing the distribution of war goods and consumer goods. The demand for war goods reduces, finally, to the demands of a single person or a singular group of persons, i.e., high ranking military officers. The demand for consumer goods involves the demands of everyone. The requisition of war goods rests not on the direct gratification of men's appetites, but on such removed and abstract ends as victory and strategic advantage. The ordering and parceling of consumer goods have as their immediate end the gratification of men's appetites.

Flowing from these differences in distribution and purposes are these further ones. The military commander does not have to concern himself with questions of an equilibrium between supply and demand. Thus, he does not have to concern himself with the question whether all the war goods he requisitions will be used up. Rather, the considerations that motivate his requisitions are of these sorts: Will there exist enough war goods to meet any hypothetical battle emergency? How many tanks are necessary to break through such-and-such a defensive line? Now, such questions and their answers are highly speculative and imprecise. Hypothetical emergencies on the battlefield, for instance, can take almost an indefinite number of shapes. One can hardly know what the enemy is going to do in any exact detail, and so on. Typically, therefore, war goods remain crated in warehouses or standing in fields, simply waiting to be used up. And if not used up, they are disposed of by being dumped into the oceans or converted into scrap. No one can be blamed for this wasteful and chaotic distribution. It is dictated by the inherent nature of war and by the fact that the goods produced for war are not *per se* objects of men's appetites.

Those concerned, on the other hand, with the ordering and distribution of consumer goods must concern themselves with questions of equilibrium between supply and demand. For not only do they cater directly to the appetites of everyone, but men's appetites are peculiar in these regards: in some respects, they are practically "bottomless"; in some others, narrowly constricted; in some respects, flexible and changeable, and in some others, rigid and permanent. There is, for instance, almost no limit to most men's appetite for display and luxury. Given the opportunity, one individual can consume the production of a thousand. Yet, men's appetites are narrowly circumscribed also. Men cannot eat hay; they cannot wear shoes of the wrong size; and some men cannot eat beef and others can or will eat very little else. Appetites change in all kinds of ways. The man who likes beef today may detest beef tomorrow. Other appetites and desires of men are as inflexible as rock. Because of the "bottomlessness" of men's appetites, the situation can never exist where men's appetites are exhaustively satisfied; but because of the narrowness of men's appetites, it is perfectly possible to produce an unusable plethora of some consumer goods, say, size two shoes.

Since productive forces are always limited, the manufacture of an unusable entity must be accompanied by the absence of a usable entity. Thus, an unusable plethora of size two shoes may be reflected in a lack of size six shoes and the latter in people going barefooted. Can the person responsible for such erroneous requisitioning excuse himself like the military commander who says, "But who can tell what battlefield emergencies will come to?" Clearly not. What might or might not happen on a battlefield is sheer speculation; a vague cluster of subjunctives. But there is nothing speculative about whether persons are going barefoot or not, and that they are because of just this requisition or that one. Again, the person looking at a thousand unused tanks standing in a field does not see in them shoes that he might have worn, or other consumer goods that might have been produced but were not. He sees in them victory or defeat or security against an enemy. But what can he, barefooted, see in a warehouse filled with unusable size two shoes? He must see the shoes that he might be wearing but is not. And seeing this, he will be unhappy, angered, ready to sulk or riot.

I have sketched some of the crucial differences (but surely not all) that characterize the distribution of war goods and consumer goods. What even this partial sketch shows is that the requisition and distribution of war goods not only can, but must, proceed in a largely arbitrary manner; hence, a largely arbitrary and capricious method of ordering and prorating goods will suffice. But the distribution of consumer goods cannot be arbitrary or capricious. If it is, disequilibriums between supply and demand will be occasioned, and these in turn will make themselves felt in the dissatisfaction and outrage, if not the actual demise, of persons.

One can perceive at once why socialist economies fail in the distribution of consumer goods and why laissez-faire or free economies not only can but historically have succeeded in this enterprise. Socialist methods of requisitioning and distributing consumer goods are essentially the methods of the military's requisitioning and distributing war goods. Socialist requisitions and distribution are based on speculations covering hypothetical emergencies, economic strategy, etc., projected by a supreme economic planner or body of such personages. They are fated, accordingly, to incorporate all the insensitivity, imprecision, and arbitrariness of the military commander's requisitioning and distribution, without possessing, however, his transcendent prerogatives to be wasteful, imprecise, and economically absurd.

In contrast, laissez-faire economies have built into them what one might compare to an organism's homeostasis: a wondrously immediate sensitivity to all shades and variations of supply and demand, men's appetites both fixed and changeable, and the demands of justice. The possibility and basis for this sensitivity consists in the myriad minds and preceptions of knowledgeable entrepreneurs and the principles of trade and profit. This organic, as opposed to mechanical, interaction of individual minds and free wills, combined with the principles of trade and profit, adjusts the requisitioning and distribution of consumer goods with mathematical precision and computer speed to supplies and demands and just proportions.

But why, we must ask, should faulty systems of distribution result in inadequate production of consumer goods? What is the connection?

We have already touched on one factor. Chaotic and arbitrary requisitioning and distribution of consumer goods will necessarily result —men being what they are—in unhappy and frustrated persons. Unhappy and frustrated persons are poor producers. One can expect, therefore, in socialist systems, producers of consumer goods who are indifferent to and even alienated from their work. But abundant production rests on conscientious and prideful labor.

Ignoring, however, the temperament of the producer, we might restate Kant's dictum, "Concepts without percepts are empty; percepts without concepts are blind," to read, economically: "Distribution without production is empty; production without distribution is blind." What I mean in the last connection is this. No matter how productive producers might wish to be—say, even that men worked as industriously as ants, producing (as Lenin thought they would and should) for the sheer love of work—faulty and imprecise requisitioning and distribution must cut off and choke production. For production is not spun simply out of the good wills of men. Production involves the presence of right amounts of productive factors—raw materials, machines, transportation units, workers, etc. One cannot, for instance, manufacture ten thousand pairs of shoes (no matter how willing one's work force) if the proper number of hides has not arrived, if the machinery is not in working order, if the work force consists of unskilled persons, and so on. But the right amount of productive factors requires right requisitioning and distribution. Thus, an economic system that fails inherently to provide precise and sensitive distribution of consumer goods must, *a fortiori*, fail to produce adequate consumer goods. This failure in production must, in turn, cause to open up still further the already existing gap between adequate requisitioning and distribution and the requisitioning and distribution that in fact obtain; the latter, in a still further falling off in production; the latter, in still further disequilibriums in distribution, and so on. Each revolution in this maelstrom of failures carries the economy with ever-increasing speed downward: first, through slow stages of feverish activity and thus seeming, but illusory, prosperity; next, through accelerating stages of grim austerity and exhortations of sacrifice; and then finally into that fragmentizing chaos of cynicism, despair, depravity, and universal misery which is the lot of men who have known but lost freedom. We trace here both the necessary and historical course of socialism as it infects an advanced economy of laissez-faire capitalism.

Motivations Affecting Production

There may still, however, seem to exist a serious lacuna in our argument. If the socialist system of distribution must choke off production of consumer goods, how is it that it does not choke off production of war goods? For have we not already admitted that socialist economies can produce war goods in abundance?

Now again two answers to this question suggest themselves. For one thing, when we speak of an abundance of war goods, we refer to a species of things which, as we have already noted, plays no part in the direct satisfaction of men's appetites. War goods are not subject to being devoured, therefore, in the way that consumer goods are. No "bottomless appetites," for example, yawn under them. The comparatively small maw of the battlefield is all that has to be satisfied. A thousand tanks, for example, may seem a very large number and amount of war goods. But say that these thousand tanks were translatable into automobiles at the ratio of ten automobiles to a tank. Ten thousand automobiles are hardly very many automobiles in terms of consumer appetites. What constitutes, then, an "abundance" of war goods does not translate into an abundance, but rather a meagre outlay, of consumer goods. It does not follow, therefore, that the same productive forces that might be capable of producing an abundance of war goods would be capable of producing an even barely sufficient, much less an abundant, supply of consumer goods.

Motivation also, and no less importantly, enters into the discrepancy we are dealing with. Men are not in fact ants. They do not produce out of the sheer love of work (supposing that ants do). By and large, if able to, men prefer to remain inert or to play. What spurs most men, then, to engage in onerous work?

For one thing, they can be spurred by some ideal or purpose which they consider superior to their own personal likes and interests. Spurred by love of God, for instance, medieval artisans and workers sometimes raised up cathedrals. Spurred by love of country, men not only risk their lives on a battlefield but toil in mines, in factories, in shipyards. But anyone who would depend on such motivations in consumer production should remind himself of Machiavelli's shrewd advice to the Prince: "'Tis better to be feared than loved." In moments of transport, these "transcendent" reservoirs of men's energies may be called upon in consumer production. But they are reservoirs of energy invoking self-sacrifice, and impulses to self-sacrifice are generally either sustained by transcendence of ends or quickly dissipated by self-interest. But transcendent ends must be just that; they must not be visibly akin to oneself. If they are, their transcendence is almost at once eroded. The users of consumer goods, however, are, as such, simply other persons like oneself. Appeals to a person to produce consumer goods for the love of God, or the love of man, or love of country must therefore soon lose their aura of transcendence and, thus, their force.

We might take the concrete case of a workman producing shoes. We may imagine that with some effort he manages for a week to look at the shoes he is producing as shoes serving humanity. Sooner or later, though, he must look at the shoes he is producing as shoes other individuals like himself will wear. And then he must look with a self-interested eye.

In contrast, the producer of war goods cannot look at the tank he is producing as possibly satisfying the appetites of persons like himself, or, indeed, of any persons. Thus, he can look at it transcendently without the erosion of transcendence taking place that one's self-interest brings about in the production of consumer goods.

If, then, we realistically are to conceive the motivations that spur producers, we can call upon transcendent motivations in the production of war goods but we shall not want to in the production of consumer goods. For the production of these, we must appeal to nontranscendent motivations. But which ones in particular?

We can motivate men to produce consumer goods through the threat or actual use of brute force, by subjecting them to the whip, to fetters, prison, and so on. And this, indeed, is the motivation that socialism finally appeals to in consumer production. But here we simply have slavery, and even if no more than history is canvassed, we know that slaves are both noninventive and only minimally productive.

The only other motivation that can be conceived as spurring workers to produce is that which one finds in a free society, the worker's appetites, his self-interest. But now his self-interest is coupled not to fear and coercion as in slavery, but to the right to exercise his own initiative and decision. Since the free worker can choose when and where to work, or not to work at all, and since such options are not tolerated or tolerable in a socialist economy, the free worker cannot exist in a socialist state. Yet, it is only the worker motivated and energized by this sort of freedom who can produce consumer goods, not just for a week or so in rapture, but day in and day out in patient labor, with the conscientious care and pride that are the necessary conditions of an abundant production of consumer goods.

The Inevitability of Total War under Socialism

Both from the side of distribution and the side of the motivations affecting production we can perceive why socialized economies historically have failed and must always fail in the production of adequate consumer goods, though they may succeed in the production of adequate war goods. We can perceive, moreover, that the reason for this failure has nothing to do with accidents; it has to do, instead, with certain hard realities of human nature and the objective conditions of distribution and production in advanced economies. The claim, therefore, that once the laissez-faire world is destroyed and the Socialist–Communist world is left to its own devices, men will enjoy a superabundance of consumer goods shows itself to be a deadly lie. If that time comes (God forbid), the only abundance in production will be in the production of war goods. Here alone will our new rulers be able to point to successful accomplishment. Here they may glorify themselves with May Day parades of tanks and Labor Day flights of rockets. But the production of war goods demands for its *raison d'être* the threat or actual presence of war. It is thus absolutely predictable, politicians and their motives being what they are, that in the Socialist–Communist world which is so devoutly prayed for by so many present dwellers in the grove of Academe, there will reign, not the peace prophesied for it, but war of unprecedented virulence and duration. Our new Socialist rulers may not be so candid as Mussolini as to exclaim, "[We] above all do not believe either in the possibility or utility of universal peace. War alone brings all human energies to their highest tension and sets a seal of nobility on the people who have the virtue to face it."[3] But when the Socialist rulers are confronted with monumental and unrelieved failure in all other endeavours, armament and aggression must be their inmost thought and constant policy.

Notes

John O. Nelson is Professor of Philosophy at the University of Colorado. He is a distinguished philosopher who has written articles for many scholarly journals including, *The Review of Metaphysics, Ratio, Philosophy and Phenomenological Research, Analysis*, etc.

1. Bertram Flornoy, *The World of the Inca* (New York: Vanguard Press, 1965) p. 178; see also pp. 113–116.

2. Or more accurately, the few fragments of a laissez-faire condition that exist or remain.

3. Benito Mussolini, "The Doctrine of Fascism," *Readings in Fascism* (Denver: Swallow Press) p. 15.

Henry Hazlitt

20

The Fallacy of Foreign Aid

THE ADVOCATES OF foreign aid believe that it helps not only the country that gets it but the country that gives it. They believe, therefore, that it promotes worldwide "economic growth." They are mistaken in all these assumptions.

I should make clear at the beginning that when I refer here to foreign aid I mean government-to-government aid. Still more specifically, I mean government-to-government "economic" aid. I am not considering here intergovernmental military aid extended either in wartime or peacetime. The justification of the latter will depend, in each case, only partly on economic considerations, and mainly on a complex set of political and military factors.

It ought to be clear, to begin with, that foreign aid retards the economic growth and the capital development of the country that grants it. If it is fully paid for out of taxes at the time it is granted, it puts an additional tax burden on industry and reduces incentives at the same time as it takes funds that would otherwise have gone into new domestic investment. If it is not fully paid for, but financed out of budget deficits, it brings all the evils of inflation. It leads to rising prices and costs. It leads to deficits in the balance of payments, to a loss of gold, and to loss of confidence in the soundness of the currency unit. In either case foreign aid must put back the donor country's capital development.

All the consequences just described have occurred in the United States. In the last twenty years American foreign aid has reached the stupendous total of $115 billion. As the public debt has increased from $259 billion at the end of 1945 to $321 billion now, this means that $62

billion of this foreign aid was in effect paid for by borrowing and by
inflating the currency, and $53 billion by added taxation. Without the
foreign-aid handouts we could have avoided both the inflation and the
added taxation. We could have avoided both the cumulative deficit of
$27 billion in the balance of payments and the loss of $9 billion gold in
the last eight years. Today, American "liberals" are talking about all the
billions we ought or will need to spend to extend and improve our roads
and highways, to improve and increase our housing and to rehabilitate
our blighted cities, to combat air pollution and water pollution, to bring
more water to the cities and to turn salt water into fresh. The $115
billion that went into foreign aid would have covered practically all the
improvements in this direction that most of these "liberals" are demanding.

The Pump-Priming Argument

We sometimes hear it said by American advocates of
foreign aid (and we very frequently hear it said by many of the foreign
recipients of our aid, and *always* by the communists) that the U.S. has got
great economic advantages out of its foreign aid program. We desperately need "outlets" and "new markets" for our "surplus." We must give
part of our goods away, or give foreigners the dollars with which to buy
them, to keep our factories going and to maintain full employment. This
program was even necessary, according to the communists, to "postpone" the "inevitable collapse" of capitalism.

It should not be necessary to point out that this whole argument is
unmitigated nonsense. If it were true that we could create prosperity
and full employment by making goods to give away, then we would not
have to give them to foreign countries. We could accomplish the same
result by making the goods to dump into the sea. Or our government
could give the money or the goods to our own poor.

It ought to be clear even to the feeblest intelligence that nobody can
get rich by giving his goods away or making more goods to give away.
What seems to confuse some otherwise clearheaded people when this
proposition is applied to a nation rather than an individual is that it is
possible for particular firms and persons within the nation to profit by
such a transaction at the expense of the rest. The firms, for example,
that are engaged in making the exported foreign-aid commodities are
paid for them by the aid-receiving country or by the U.S. government.
But the latter gets the money, in turn, from the American taxpayers.
The taxpayers are poorer by the amount taken. If they had been allowed

to keep it, they would have used it themselves to buy the goods they wanted. True, these would not have been precisely the *same* goods as those that were made and exported through the foreign-aid program. But they would have supplied just as much employment. And Americans, rather than foreigners, would have got what was made by this employment.

Buying Friends

"Yes," it may be conceded, "all of this may be true; but let us not look at the matter so selfishly, or at least not so nearsightedly. Think of the great blessings that we have brought to the aid-receiving countries, and think of the long-run political and other intangible gains to the United States. We have prevented the aid-receiving countries from going communist, and the continuance of our aid is necessary to continue to keep them from going communist. We have made the recipient countries our grateful allies and friends, and the continuance of our foreign aid is necessary to continue to keep them our grateful allies and friends."

First, let us look at these alleged intangible gains to the United States. We are here admittedly in the realm of opinion, in the realm of might-have-beens and might be's, where proof either way is hardly possible. But there is no convincing evidence that any of our aid-recipients that have *not* gone communist *would* have done so if they had not got our economic aid. Communist Party membership in aid-receiving France and Italy did not fall off; in fact it has shown a tendency to increase in both countries with increasing prosperity. And Cuba, the one country in the Western Hemisphere that *has* gone communist, did so in 1959 in spite of having shared freely in our foreign aid in the preceding twelve years. Cuba had been favored by us, in fact, beyond all other countries in sugar import quotas and other indirect forms of economic help.

As for gaining grateful allies or even friends, there is no evidence that our $11 billion of lendlease to Russia in World War II endeared us to the Russian leaders; that our aid to Poland, Yugoslavia, Indonesia, and Egypt turned Gomulka, Tito, Sukarno, or Nasser into dependable allies; that it has made Gaullist France, or India, Mexico, Chile, Laos, Cambodia, Bolivia, Ghana, Panama, Algeria, and scores of other nations that have got our aid, into our grateful friends.

On the other hand, there *is* good reason to suspect that our aid has often had the opposite effect. Countries have found that whenever they look as if they are in danger of going communist they get *more* American aid. This veiled threat becomes a recognized way of extorting more aid. And the leaders of governments getting our aid find it necessary to insult and denounce the United States to prove to their own followers that they are "independent" and not the "puppets" of "American imperialism." It is nearly always the U.S. embassies and information offices that periodically get rocks thrown through their windows, not the embassies of countries that have never offered any aid.

Humanitarian Motives

"Still," it may be (and is) objected, "to mention any of these things is to take a shortsighted and selfish point of view. We should give foreign aid for purely humanitarian reasons. This will enable the poor nations to conquer their poverty, which they cannot do without our help. And when they have done so, we will have the reward of the charitable deed itself. Whether the recipients are grateful to us or not, our generosity will redound in the long run to our own self-interest. A world half rich and half poor is an unsafe world; it breeds envy, hatred, and war. A fully prosperous world is a world of peace and good will. Rich nations are obviously better customers than poor nations. As the underdeveloped nations develop, American foreign trade and prosperity must also increase."

The final part of this argument is beyond dispute. It is to America's long-run interest that all other countries should be rich and productive, good customers, and good sources of supply. What is wrong with the argument is the assumption that government-to-government aid is the way to bring about this desired consummation.

The quickest and surest way to production, prosperity, and economic growth is through private enterprise. The best way for governments to encourage private enterprise is to establish justice, to enforce contracts, to insure domestic peace and tranquillity, to protect private property, and to secure the blessings of liberty, including economic liberty—which means to stop putting obstacles in the way of private enterprise. If every man is free to earn and to keep the fruits of his labor, his incentives to work and to save, to invent and invest, to launch new ventures, to try to build a better mousetrap than his neighbor, will be maximized. The effort of each will bring the prosperity of all.

Under such a system more and more citizens will acquire the capital to lend and invest, and will have the maximum inducement to lend and invest at home. Very quickly more and more foreigners will also notice the investment opportunities in (let us call it) Libertania, and their money will come in to speed its development. They will place their funds where they promise to earn the highest returns consonant with safety. This means that the funds will go, if the investments are wisely chosen, where they are most productive. They will go where they will produce the goods and services most wanted by productive Libertanians or by foreigners. In the latter case they will produce the maximum exports, or "foreign exchange," either to pay off the investment or to pay for the import of the foreign goods most needed.

The surest way for a poor nation to *stay* poor, on the other hand, is to harass, hobble, and straitjacket private enterprise or to discourage or destroy it by subsidized government competition, oppressive taxation, or outright expropriation.

Socialism versus Capitalism

Now government-to-government aid rests on socialistic assumptions and promotes socialism and stagnation, whereas private foreign investment rests on capitalistic assumptions and promotes private enterprise and maximum economic growth.

The egalitarian and socialistic assumptions underlying government-to-government aid are clear. Its main assumption is that the quickest way to "social" justice and progress is to take from the rich and give to the poor, to seize from Peter and give to Paul. The donor government seizes the aid money from its supposedly overrich taxpayers; it gives it to the receiving nation on the assumption that the latter "needs" the money— not on the assumption that it will make the most productive use of the money.

From the very beginning government-to-government aid has been on the horns of this dilemma. If on the one hand it is made without conditions, the funds are squandered and dissipated and fail to accomplish their purpose. But if the donor government attempts to impose conditions, its attempt is immediately resented. It is called "interfering in the internal affairs" of the recipient nation, which demands "aid without strings."

In the twenty expensive years that the foreign aid program has been in effect, American officials have swung uncertainly from one horn of this dilemma to the other—imposing conditions, dropping them when criticized, silently watching the aid funds being grossly misused, then trying to impose conditions again. But now American officials seem on the verge of following the worst possible policy—that of imposing conditions, but exactly the wrong conditions.

President Johnson has announced that our future foreign aid will go to those countries "willing not only to talk about basic social change but who will act immediately on these reforms." But what our aid officials appear to have in mind by "basic social change" is to ask of the countries that receive our grants, not that they give guarantees of the security of property, the integrity of their currencies, abstention from crippling government controls, and encouragement to free markets and free enterprise, but that they move in the direction of government planning, the paternalistic state, the redistribution of land, and other share-the-wealth schemes.

Land Reform Measures

The so-called "land reform" that our government officials are demanding has meant and still means destroying existing large-scale agricultural enterprises, dividing land into plots too small for efficient or economic cultivation, turning them over to untried managers, undermining the principle of private property, and opening a Pandora's box of still more radical demands.

Socialism and welfare programs lead to huge chronic government deficits and runaway inflation. This is what has happened in Latin America. In the last ten years the currency of the Argentine has lost 92 per cent of its purchasing power; the currency of Chile has lost 94 per cent; of Bolivia 95 per cent; of Brazil 96 per cent. The practical consequence of this is the expropriation of wealth on a tremendous scale.

Yet, a United States Senator, recently demanding "land reform" and ignoring this history, made it a charge against the rich in these aid-receiving nations that they do not "invest in their own economies" but place their funds abroad. What he failed to ask himself is *why* the nationals of some of these countries have been sending their funds abroad or putting them in numbered accounts in Switzerland. In most cases, he would have found that it was not only because no attractive private investment opportunities were open to them at home (because of burdensome controls, oppressive taxes, or government competition), but because they feared the wiping out of their savings by rapid depreciation of their home currencies, or even the outright confiscation of their visible wealth.

The Benefits?

In the last twenty years foreign aid has made American taxpayers $115 billion poorer, but it has not made the recipients anything like that much richer. How much good has it actually done them? The question is difficult to answer in quantitative terms, because foreign aid has often been a relatively minor factor out of the scores of factors affecting their economies.

But the advocates of foreign aid have had no trouble in giving glib and confident answers to the question. Where, as in Western Europe and Japan, our aid has been followed by dramatic recovery, the recovery has been attributed wholly to the aid (though just as dramatic recoveries occurred in war-torn nations after World War I when there was no aid program). But where our aid has not been followed by recovery, or where recipient nations find themselves in even deeper economic crises than they were before our aid began, the aid advocates have simply said that obviously our aid was not "adequate." This argument is being used very widely today to urge us to plunge into an even more colossal aid program.

A careful country-by-country study, however, shows pretty clearly that wherever a country in recent years (such as West Germany) has reformed its currency, kept it sound, and adhered in the main to the principles of free enterprise, it has enjoyed a miraculous recovery and growth. But where a country (such as India) has chosen government planning, has adopted grandiose socialistic "five-year plans" arbitrarily directing production into the wrong lines, has expanded its currency but kept it overvalued through exchange controls, and has put all sorts of restrictions and harassments in the way of private enterprise and private initiative, it has sunk into chronic crises or famine in spite of billions of dollars in generous foreign aid.

As Charles B. Shuman, president of the American Farm Bureau Federation, recently put it, the one common denominator in virtually all the hungry nations has been "their devotion to a socialist political-economic system—a government-managed economy. The world does not need to starve if the underdeveloped areas can be induced to accept a market price system, the incentive method of capital formation—competitive capitalism."

Our conclusion is that government-to-government foreign aid, as it exists at present, is a deterrent, not a spur, to world economic prosperity, and even to the economic progress of the underdeveloped recipients themselves.

Wasteful Projects

This is true partly because of the very nature of foreign aid. By providing easy outside help without cost, it often fails to encourage self-help and responsibility. Moreover, government-to-government economic help almost inevitably goes to *government* projects, which frequently mean socialized projects, such as grandiose government steel mills or power dams.

It is true that there are many economic services, such as streets and roads, water supply, harbors, and sanitary measures, that are usually undertaken by governments even in the most "capitalistic" countries, yet which form an essential basis and part of the process and structure of all production. Foreign as well as domestic funds may legitimately go to governments for such purposes. Yet intergovernmental aid is likely to channel a disproportionate amount of funds even into such projects. If governments had to depend more on domestic or foreign *private investors* for these funds, less extravagant projects of this nature would be embarked upon. Private investors, for example, might lend more freely for toll roads and bridges, and similar projects that promised to be self-liquidating, than for those that yielded no monetary return. As a result, the recipient government's planners would make more effort to put their roads and bridges where the prospective use and traffic would prove heavy enough to justify the outlay.

In addition to the conditions in the very nature of government-to-government aid that make it on net balance a deterrent rather than a spur to private enterprise and higher production, there is the recent disturbing trend in the attitude of American aid officials, who have begun to insist that underdeveloped nations cannot get more aid unless they adopt "land reform," planning, and other socialistic measures—the very measures that tend to retard economic recovery.

Conditions for Private Investment

If our aid program were now tapered off, and the underdeveloped nations had to seek foreign private capital for their more rapid development, the case would be far different. Foreign private investors would want to see quite different reforms. They would want assurance (perhaps in some cases even guarantees) against nationalization or expropriation, against government-owned competition, against discriminatory laws, against price controls, against burdensome social security legislation, against import license difficulties on essential materials, against currency exchange restrictions, against oppressive taxes, and against a constantly depreciating currency. They would probably also want guarantees that they could always repatriate their capital and profits.

Foreign private investors would not *demand* the active cooperation or an enthusiastic welcome by the government of the host country, but this would certainly influence their decision considerably. In fact, foreign private investors, unless the would-be borrowers came to them, would not *demand* any conditions at all. They would place their funds where the deterrents and discouragements were fewest and the opportunities most inviting.

What the anticapitalistic mentality seems incapable of understanding is that the very steps necessary to create the most attractive climate for *foreign* investment would also create the most attractive climate for *domestic* investment. The nationals of an underdeveloped country, instead of sending their money abroad for better returns or sheer safekeeping, would start investing it in enterprises at home. And this domestic investment and reinvestment would begin to make foreign investment less and less urgent.

It is unlikely that reforms in the direction of free enterprise will be made by most socialistic and control-minded countries as long as they can get intergovernmental aid without making these reforms. So a tapering off or phasing out of the American aid program will probably be necessary before a private foreign investment program is launched in sufficient volume.

A More Hopeful Alternative

I should like to renew here a suggestion for an interim program that I put forward a few years ago.[1] This is that, from now on out, economic foreign aid would be continued solely in the form of loans rather than grants. These would be hard loans, repayable in dollars. They would bear interest at the same rate that our own government was obliged to pay for loans of equal maturity—as of today, say about 4½ per cent. They would be repayable over not more than twenty-five to thirty years, like a mortgage. Like a mortgage, they would preferably be repayable, principal and interest, in equal monthly or quarterly installments, beginning immediately after the loan was made.

Such loans would not be urged on any country. The would-be borrowers would have to apply for them. They would be entitled to borrow annually, say, any amount up to the amount they had previously been receiving from us in grants or combined loans and grants.

All these requirements would be written into law by Congress. Congress would also write into law the conditions for eligibility for such loans. Among such conditions might be the following: The borrowing government would have to refrain from any additional socialization or nationalization of industry, or any further expropriation or seizure of capital, domestic or foreign. It would undertake to balance its budget, beginning, say, in the first full fiscal year after receiving the loan. It would undertake to halt inflation. The borrowing government, for example, might agree not to increase the quantity of money by more than 5 per cent in any one year, and not to force its central bank to buy or discount any increased amount of the government's own securities. The borrowing government might be required to dismantle any exchange controls. In brief, the borrowing country and government would be obliged to move toward the conditions that would be necessary to attract private domestic or foreign capital.

Anticipated Consequences

My guess is that the mere requirement for repayment of principal and interest, to begin immediately, would in itself probably reduce applications for aid to about a third of the amounts we now pay out. The other conditions of eligibility would probably cut the applications to a sixth or a tenth of these amounts. For the borrowing governments would have to think twice about the advisability of projects for which they would have to start paying themselves. Projects would tend to be reduced to those that were self-liquidating, *i.e.*, demonstrably economic.

The borrowing nations could not complain that we were trying to interfere in or to dictate their domestic economic policies. These would merely be the conditions of eligibility for loans. The borrowing nations would be neither forced nor urged to borrow from us. The American administrators of the foreign loan program would not be authorized either to dictate or remove any conditions or to discriminate among borrowers. In any case, their discretion should be very narrowly circumscribed.

The benefits of such a program would be many and obvious. It would immediately cut down drastically the outflow of American funds in foreign aid. Most of the aid that we granted through such loans would be repaid with interest. We would not be courting foreign favor. The would-be borrowers would have to come to us, openly. We would cease, as now, to subsidize and expand foreign socialism.

I should make it clear that I am not proposing such a program for its own sake, but as a purely transitional measure to phase out our existing foreign-aid program with the least possible disturbance, disruption, or recrimination. This scaled-down lending program might run for, say, a maximum of three years. At the end of that time it could easily be terminated. For meanwhile the borrowing governments, and particularly private enterprises in their respective countries, would have created an attractive climate, and would have become attractive media, for both domestic and foreign private investment.

In such a revitalized capitalistic climate the improvement in world economic conditions might even become spectacular.

Notes

Henry Hazlitt is one of the nation's foremost journalists in economics. He has been a journalist for *The Wall Street Journal*, literary editor for the *New York Sun* and *The Nation*, successor to H. L. Mencken as editor of *The American Mercury*, financial writer for *The New York Times*, and from 1946 to 1966 he wrote the "Business Tides" column for *Newsweek*. His books include *The Failure of the 'New Economics,' Economics in One Lesson*, and the novel *Time Will Run Back*. He has also contributed to *Modern Age, Ethics, The Freeman, Human Events*, etc.

"The Fallacy of Foreign Aid" is reprinted with permission from *The Freeman* (February, 1966).

1. *National Review*, May 6, 1961.

F. A. Harper

21 In Search of Peace

CHARGES OF PACIFISM are likely to be hurled at anyone who in these troubled times raises any question about the race into war. If pacifism means embracing the objective of peace, I am willing to accept the charge. If it means opposing all agression against others, I am willing to accept that charge also. It is now urgent in the interest of liberty that many persons become "peacemongers."

Patrick Henry, that great advocate of liberty, in a speech before the Virginia Convention in 1775, said: "I know of no way of judging of the future but by the past." Were he with us today, he might well repeat that advice to a nation confused and woefully mired in the problems of war and peace—a nation acting in a blind panic.

Probably more wealth and effort have been squandered in a fruitless search for peace by the present generation than by any other in the history of man. For nearly half a century the increasing tempo of war and preparation for war has found the world further and further from peace. Time after time it has been asserted that if only we could crush some particular dictator by the use of military might, the safety of man's freedom would be assured. "One more supreme sacrifice," again and again. And each time dictators "more ruthless than anything the world has seen since Genghis Khan" arose out of the refuse of war, leaving liberty and peace the loser after each bloody conflict.

Not only that, but in nations like the United States and Britain most of the trappings of dictatorship, under different names, have been accepted until the plight of citizens in a "free" country is much the same as that of citizens in a "dictatorship" country. To test this, merely make a detailed comparison, ignoring reasons given in one's own country for this or that abridgment of liberty.

We speak of the impending threat of World War III, even while we are still officially engaged in World War II. The guns have hardly cooled from a war in which we joined Russia to help defeat Germany, Japan, and Italy. Now the veterans of that war are again commanded to pick up arms to defeat Russia, which is operating under the same management and with the same policies and methods as when we were her ally—if, in fact, we are not still officially her ally.

All the while our diplomats have been hastening to arrange something that will pass for a peace agreement with Germany, Japan, and Italy. Unless that is done, it is especially awkward for our legislators to appropriate our money to replenish a military might that we have just finished destroying in these former enemy nations.

A Tito or a Franco or a Peron is one day an "enemy" of liberty and the next day its "friend." Ships frantically rush here and there, first giving and then threatening not to give our wealth as bribes to "friends" and "enemies" alike. And there is no telling which will be which tomorrow.

While all these banners and alignments of nations have been shifting back and forth as with the changing winds, the liberty of the people in "our haven of liberty" has been constantly eroding, until it has now reached the lowest point in the history of this nation. It makes one feel as if he were being whirled through space until he has lost all sense of direction.

Against this confusing picture, it would be well to heed the words of Patrick Henry and pause long enough on a road strewn with the wreckage of liberty and peace to see if we may not have been treading it in the wrong direction. Perhaps the problem of peace should be approached from a new and unconventional direction. On the record, at least, the solution would seem to lie elsewhere than in the methods that have been tried again and again without even a semblance of success.[1]

We must not let pleas for unity paralyze our minds and prevent any review of our past acts. There is no virtue in a unity attained by blinding people and inducing them to join in a mass stampede. Uncommon courage, not cowardice, is demanded of anyone who will remove himself from the stampede long enough to see where he is going.

The Problem of Conflict

Let us start on the problem this way. Many persons consider war to be an evil, but they support it on occasion as necessary "for the long time good." But how can good be attained by means of an evil? That defies simple logic.

A review of the historical consequences of war, so far as its effect on liberty is concerned, supports the belief that war is an evil and that no long time good results from it. Why, then, do we keep getting into war? One study reports that war has engaged the major countries of Europe for about half the time since the year 1500.[2] What mistakes are made in preserving the peace and the liberty of man?

War is conflict on its largest scale. Conflict in all its forms—murder, rebellion, riot, insurrection, mutiny, banditry, war—has caused the death of 59 million persons in the world during the last century and a quarter. Of this number, four-fifths died as a direct result of the larger wars, which are by all odds the major cause of death from conflict. Murders and all the other lesser forms of conflict, though highly numerous, have accounted for only one-sixth of all the deaths from conflict in the world during this period.[3] Conflict probably never can be wholly eliminated, because man is imperfect. But these figures suggest the importance of preventing it from growing into wars.

Only if we identify the cause of conflict can we keep it at a minimum and prevent its growth into war. The cause of conflict is the moral delinquency that allows infringement on liberty and on the rights of men; it is that alone. If liberty were complete, and if each person were to restrict himself to what is his proper scope and concern, there could be no conflict. What would there be to fight about if liberty were thus universal?

Conflict arises when freedom of choice is restricted. If one is free to choose his work and his leisure, to use what he produces and to spend what he earns, to select his own associates, and to choose in all other aspects of his life, he does not have to fight his way out of anything or to maneuver around restrictions and repressions beyond those of his own conscience. This concept may be tested on the everyday conflicts we know best—with one's child, with one's neighbors, in community affairs, between employer and employee. In every instance it is some prohibition, or control, or monopoly that gives rise to conflict. These are the things which prohibit free choice and which therefore generate conflict.

It is true that to whatever extent we violate the rules necessary to a peaceful society, there cannot be unrestricted freedom. That is why the general acceptance of certain rules, governing the use of things that are in limited supply, is necessary to a peaceful society. The concept of private property is one of these, and freedom of exchange is another such rule.[4]

Stated bluntly, conflict results from slavery in some form or degree or from the violation of rules of a peaceful society. Problems of war—all conflict—are exclusively problems of abolished liberty. Thus the prevention of war, or of the threat of war, must take the form of cutting the bonds on liberty wherever they exist.

Peace will exist only as liberty is increased in all its forms among individuals throughout the world. There is no other road to peace. This means that any building up of power anywhere in the world in any of its forms, and under any excuse, leads toward conflict in its worst form—war.

Conflict between humans may be compared with the physical fact of friction. We know that friction exists, but it is one of the most difficult phenomena of the physical world to explain thoroughly. It occurs as the result of contact. Since complete separation of objects is difficult if not impossible, lubrication is necessary to reduce friction to a minimum.

All human relationships are also potential friction. Voluntary arrangement in these relationships acts like a lubricant. It will not eliminate all friction but reduces friction to a minimum. The use of force removes this lubricant and generates heated conflict, because persons then cannot withdraw from contacts not of their liking.

Every conflict, at its origin, is a matter between only two persons. One person may be using force against the other or trespassing on his property. If this conflict cannot be resolved in any other manner, a murder may occur. The outcome could be no more serious than the loss of one life, unless somebody intercedes who is not directly concerned.

Conflict grows, then, as a result of anything which causes opposing sides of any controversy to amass into growing numbers. The larger the number, the greater and bloodier the conflict becomes.

We can see how this works by observing a football game. Someone violates the rules, and two players start to battle it out. If all 22 players joined in, the conflict would become serious. What if 100,000 spectators joined in?

I was deeply impressed by a scene in a recent movie. Two contenders for the kingship of a tribe of uncivilized "savages" in the deepest recesses of Africa were in conflict for possession of the throne. Finally, the two contenders battled it out to the death. The other members of the tribe laid their preferences and their weapons aside, and all stood on the sideline as observers. They had learned that if persons other than the two concerned were to join in the battle, there would be unnecessary bloodshed. Uncivilized? Perhaps we would be more humane and civilized if we were to resolve the present world conflict in some such manner—at least a "victor" by combat could be selected without so much bloodshed and destruction of property.

There would always be some conflict even among free people, but it would be small and localized. There would be a murder now and then, but death would not be nearly so prevalent as from the mass conflict of major wars.

A neighborhood squabble between two persons in China, for instance, might lead to one of them murdering the other. But if we are left to use our individual judgment, not many of us would volunteer in behalf of one or the other and cause it to grow into a war. Numbers do not become amassed that way into a major conflict unless persons are forced to join in.

True, there are always some volunteers in foreign wars. In fact, fighting in foreign wars used to be an accepted hired occupation. But this sort of thing never became prevalent enough to be featured in the history books.

It is a fact that small conflict develops into major war only as a result of involuntary servitude. We can see this much better if we look afar at the "dictatorship" nations.

There is no escaping the fact that some men have a lust for power. And war or the presumed threat of war seems to surpass all other devices by which a ruler can induce the people to thoroughly enslave themselves under his "leadership," to lose their liberty and all rights of choice, to answer to his beck and call. Power becomes concentrated at one end of a long line of authority, which at the other end terminates in complete subservience on the field of battle.

Edmund Burke said that loss of liberty always occurs "under some delusion." By some strange twist of reasoning, fear of losing liberty drives persons to enslave themselves and surrender their liberty in the hope of keeping it. It is argued that this is necessary "to protect the people." How can slavery make them any more brave? This presumes the people to be too ignorant or cowardly to act voluntarily in their own behalf, that they must be forced to protect themselves.

It is indeed a strange notion that I should be compelled by others to protect myself. This "self protection" then becomes labelled "sacrifice," and tribute is paid me, my dependents, and my descendants by those who forced me to "defend myself." Something is wrong there, somewhere.

Power is grasped by the dictator because of the urge to be "great." Lord Acton, the British historian, said: "All power tends to corrupt, and absolute power corrupts absolutely. Great men are almost always bad men."[5] He was speaking here of "great" in the sense of a Caesar or of a Napoleon—whose moral degradation was reflected in one of his remarks. After hurrying back to France from a campaign in Russia that cost the lives of over 500,000 of his countrymen, he rubbed his hands before the fire and said: "Decidedly it is more comfortable here than in Moscow."

Perhaps dictators are evil because power corrupts them, as Lord Acton said. Or perhaps evil men gravitate to the administrations of power, as Hayek said in one notable chapter in his book, *The Road to Serfdom*.[6] I do not know which, but it seems certain that a part of the strategy of maintaining "leadership" in this sense is to keep up a series of crises and emergencies and a confusion that seems to demand the action of a strong and ruthless autocrat. "Greatness" may even be acquired by chasing a series of one's own mistakes, as "leader," into eventual war—backing into "greatness," so to speak.

It is no coincidence that large-scale wars are the product of dictatorships or of the acts of aspiring dictators. Power is first grasped in internal confusion and conflict; then later it bursts into an external conflict, and the dictator calls for national unity.

The Balance of Power

At this point we should take a look at the "balance of power" theory. It calls for bolstering up a lesser power as a protection against a greater power, until it equals or exceeds the power that is "threatening." This theory has been widely followed in international affairs, in labor-management affairs, in politics—everywhere.

It is strictly a power concept. Rulers are given more and more power to guide and control the actions of others, to sound the bugle call of battle at whatever time and place they choose. The persons over whom they rule are first presumed to be incapable of acting voluntarily in their own defense and are then bound in controls and servitude until they actually are unable to defend themselves, even against their own "leader."

Let me illustrate how the balance of power theory works, by a hypothetical case. A threat to peace arises between two persons at a church social. Deacon Jones suspects Deacon Smith of planning to do him some harm—". . . so it is said, by sources usually considered to be reliable but which cannot be revealed for reasons of religious security." Smith is powerful enough to do so, if he chooses. So Jones propositions Deacon Brown to come to his defense. Brown, who sincerely wants peace to prevail, agrees to a treaty whereby he is to be subject to Jones' call to **arms** in case of aggression by Smith. Notice of the treaty is released to **the** "public" through Jones' Department of Public Defense—or perhaps privately to Smith through the "proper" process of a "diplomatic note." Smith, finding himself threatened with a superior force, then proposes the same balance of power theory, in turn, to Deacons Solcefoskiski and Chin, and they sign a treaty with Smith. A counter "diplomatic note" is sent back to Jones. This goes on and on, with personal liberties declining more and more as power accumulates on both sides under the rule of Smith and Jones. Tensions increase more and more on both sides, until a wholesale brawl can be started by someone sneezing or shouting "Boo!" Or perhaps the brawl is intentionally started by one side or the other, as it becomes clear that the burden of "defense" under conditions of an armed truce is too costly and threatens them with starvation, if continued. Going to war then becomes "a matter of self-defense against encirclement and starvation."

War or the threat of war becomes self-generating under the balance of power theory and builds up and up, until abandoned out of sheer exhaustion from battle or from the costs of "defense." But this brings no settlement of the underlying causes of the conflict. The certain outcome is total loss of liberty by individuals on both sides of the conflict. Losers become serfs of the winning side; and on the winning side, all other individuals remain subjects of the ruler, who finds no reason to abdicate at the victorious height of his ruling glory. This "route to liberty" thus becomes a route to servitude.

In carrying out the balance of power idea, it is of course necessary to shift alignments of "allies" and "enemies" on frequent occasion. Treaties and money are both used as the medium of exchange. We should have learned by now that an "ally" bought with dollars will demand a steady stream of dollars in a one way deal and even then does not stay bought. One who can be bribed by us can also be bribed away from us. He is not a friend.

Defense and Self-Defense

What is to be the guide of proper defense, then, that is consistent with the ideals of liberty? Has the libertarian no rights of self-defense? Must he stand idly by while murderers, thieves, and vandals ravage his person and property, his family, or his friends?

My reply is: No. So far as my rights are concerned, the right to life carries with it the right to defend my life. And since my property is the economic extension of my person, it is likewise within my rights to protect my property from theft or destruction. I may, within my rights, protect these in whatever manner seems to me to be the soundest from the standpoint of strategy. I may or may not use force to resist an aggressor or evict a trespasser. When one is forced to decide between preserving his life and protecting his property, he may without cowardice decide that protecting his life is his initial duty. He would, if forced to make that choice, let his property go and keep his life rather than say: "Take my life, but leave me my property."

Now we come to a more perplexing question. Is it my duty to throw my weight against the oppressors of liberty in any instance where it is others rather than myself whose personal rights are being violated? Should I protect my infant child in this respect? My wife? My neighbor? Your neighbor? An Englishman? A Chinese? A Russian peasant who feels oppressed by the iron hand? An officer of the Russian army who is happy in his status? A conscripted soldier of our own army? Where, if at all, is one justified in employing the tools of force to remove trespass on the rights of others?

Since I am responsible for the care and protection of my family, I am also within my rights to defend each of them against an aggressor, a thief, or a vandal by whatever means seems best—assuming, of course, that they agree and want me to help protect them. As for neighbors and others, it is proper to help defend them against acts of crime against their person and property, if I desire and they want me to do so. There should, however, be mutual agreement on the need as well as the means. So far as I can see, this applies to one's next-door neighbor or to a person anywhere else in the world.

One is not necessarily obligated to assist everyone whose liberty is being transgressed. I am certainly not obligated to give my life to protect the property of someone who differs with me as to the nature of liberty. Nor am I morally obligated to assist those who agree with me about the design of liberty and the nature of its violation, if they themselves have not first exposed their lives in its defense. Indeed, I have no right to intervene by the use of force to defend something they have chosen not to defend.

It is also proper for me to induce another to resist trespassers on his own or my liberty. But in doing so I must use only voluntary educational means. His rebellion must be sincere and stem from a personal conviction on his part. It is illiberal for me to use authority over him "to force him to protect his own liberty" or mine.

It is frequently said in defense of wartime controls and centralization of power that liberty is a luxury to be enjoyed in peacetime when things are normal, that we cannot afford the luxuries of liberty during emergencies like the present. One who makes such a statement, if he makes it seriously, does not really understand and believe in liberty. He is one who cannot be depended upon to act in its behalf. He is one who will willingly enslave his fellowmen "in order to defend their liberties." His devotion to liberty is a sham, and he can be expected to conclude later that, if controls and centralized power are desirable in wartime, they are also desirable in peacetime.

One who believes in liberty and who understands it enough to act in its defense does so because he considers liberty to be superior to its alternative—slavery in its various forms. Why does he believe it to be superior? Because it is more just, more in harmony with the design of a good society, more productive. This makes it stronger because it embodies justice and those incentives which bring out the best in man. If, on the other hand, he believes liberty to be less just, less strong, and less productive than slavery, he is on the other side of this great issue even though he salutes the same flag and is one's friendly neighbor.

Relinquish liberty for purposes of defense in an emergency? Why? It would seem that in an emergency, of all times, one needs his greatest strength. So if liberty is strength and slavery is weakness, liberty is a necessity rather than a luxury, and we can ill afford to be without it—least of all during an emergency.

Suppose that a clergyman were to admonish the members of his flock to abandon the practice of Christianity during every emergency because it is a luxury, good only for normal times. If he were to say that, we would certainly believe him to be a religious quack and of negative worth. We would conclude that he did not really believe justice, goodness, and strength to be embodied in religious faith. It is the same with all self-styled lovers of liberty who call for its abandonment during every emergency. They must be counted out of the forces for liberty. Indeed, should they not be counted among the enemies of liberty?

The only person who can effectively defend liberty is one who believes in it and considers it to be the embodiment of strength rather than of weakness. All others will do the wrong thing and support the wrong cause when the chips are down. If by this test the defenders of liberty turn out to be few, then the cause of liberty is that much more desperate than we had assumed.

Finding the Enemy

The first necessity in any defense is to identify the enemy with precision and accuracy. Lacking that, defense measures make no sense. It is like shooting at an unknown target. Could it be that our past efforts for the defense of liberty have failed for the reason that we have failed to identify the real enemy?

What is the basic issue in this conflict? What do we wish to fight against? It is slavery, the enemy of liberty. It is simply that and nothing else.

Slavery takes on many forms and goes by many names. But no matter what its form and name, the enemy is anything that prevents man from being free.

The enemy of liberty is, at its base, an idea—the idea that the enslavement of man is a superior and stronger form of social arrangement than is an arrangement of free men acting together voluntarily. It is the idea that men of a community or a nation can better themselves and strengthen themselves if some of them will enslave others. That idea is the real enemy.

In attacking the enemy of liberty by the use of force, as is commonly assumed to be necessary, how might one proceed? The enemy is basically an idea, which is an abstraction. It has no nose to be punched and no heart to be pierced. The nearest you can get to an idea by the use of force is to attack its host—the person who believes it. This explains the great temptation to personify the enemy of liberty, to recast it in the form of certain persons who can be attacked by the use of force.

Which persons shall be attacked? Every person violates at least some of the tenets of liberty and to that degree is an enemy of liberty in practice. Every person is, then, partly the friend and partly the enemy of liberty. Realizing this, one should abandon the attempt to personify the enemy of liberty and to attack it by force. If he persists in the attempt, he will at this point have already gone astray in its defense. The project will be doomed to failure in the enactments of "necessary wartime controls," no matter what words are emblazoned on the banners of the marching columns.

In the attempt to personify the enemy, who will be tagged? Will they be selected after a careful examination of the beliefs of each of the world's 3 billion inhabitants? To attempt to do so would preclude war, because the political leaders are incapable of doing the testing and because the job is so large that it would never be completed by any central examining committee of this type.

What, then, is to be done? The leaders ignore the fact that they are incapable of examining even one person and hide their incapacity behind a grandiose façade of decoys. They label entire nations, or continents or races, as the enemies of liberty when, in fact, they are unable to judge even one person in this respect and do not even know the questions to be asked.

So the nation goes to war and, while war is going on, the real enemy —long ago forgotten and camouflaged by the processes of war—rides on to victory in both camps. The real enemy is, in fact, immune to the weapons of physical combat used in war.

Further evidence that in war the attack is not leveled at the real enemy is the fact that we seem never to know what to do with "victory." When guns are silenced by the white flag of surrender, what is to be done with the victory? Are the "liberated" peoples to be shot, or all put in prison camps, or what? Is the national boundary to be moved? Is there to be further destruction of the property of the defeated? Or what? The fact that those responsible for the settlements of "liberation" have themselves acquired the disease while administering the processes of war, makes any logical solution even less likely.

False ideas can be attacked only with counter-ideas, facts, and logic. There is no other way. It is necessary to realize that an idea cannot be forced into submission by kicking it in the shins or by beating it over the head. Nor can you shoot an idea.

It is worth remembering that the Roman legions were never able to defeat the Christian idea by this method two thousand years ago. The British military might never was able to defeat Gandhi, the little man without weapons. Christ and Gandhi were both killed, but their murder seemed to give impetus to the spread of their ideas rather than the destruction of them.

Karl Marx perhaps more than any other person developed the body of thought that is today the leading enemy of liberty. It would have made no difference if Marx had died a year earlier or a year later, because the ideas had been put into circulation and were not mortally a part of him. Nor can these ideas of his be destroyed today by murder or suicide of their leading exponent or of any thousands or millions of the devotees. On the contrary, persecution seems to unite those of one faith and spreads their ideas as nothing else will do. Least of all can the ideas of Karl Marx be destroyed by murdering innocent victims of the form of slavery he advocated, whether they be conscripts in armies or victims caught in the path of battle.

Ideas must be met by ideas, on the battlefield of belief.

The Fruits of Aggression

Government in this country was designed as an agent to protect persons and property, to maintain peace and order by resolving conflict through a judicial system. And it was supposed to administer resistance to threats from outside the country, but without ever becoming an aggressor in the outside world.

Our government during the last half century, however, has become the captain of military excursions all over the world. In these wars, the citizens are compelled to give up essentially all their liberty and to respond to the call to arms at the command of one person—one who is presumed to be their servant and not their master. Our war excursions are coming more and more to be without the consent of the people or of their elected representatives. So long as this procedure is tolerated, liberty is at an end in this nation.

The government was originally supposed to serve as policeman and to punish those within the borders who use force or violence against the person or the property of their neighbors. When a government, however, uses force or violence against the person or the property of national neighbors, the process is honored by terms such as "national defense," "victory," and the like.

For performing acts that are the same in the eyes of God, a person may be either executed or decorated, imprisoned or promoted—depending on whether the act is in peacetime against a near neighbor or in wartime against a more distant neighbor. How can either of these properly go by the name of justice and the maintenance of peace?

As previously stated, self-defense is the right of any person. But it seems that many of us are unable to distinguish between a defense properly within this limit of rights and the use of the same tools to generate a "war of self-defense." Perhaps a reason is to be found in the failure to understand how proper defensive measures may become diseased and develop into a cancerous growth of illiberal power. This can best be seen by reviewing the usual nature of war from the standpoint of liberalism.

When at war or in preparation for war, the pattern of affairs in any nation includes all the devices of the socialist-communist state. A centralized power gains control of the economic affairs of the nation and of the acts of the citizens. The armed forces, and perhaps others, are conscripted. Priorities and subsidies, and all such authoritarian devices, become "tools of defense." Capital and its uses "must be controlled, else the selfish interests of the capitalists will sap the defense of the nation." Intellectuals and high executives are drawn into the program of administering socialism in the form of these powers and controls, as a "patriotic duty" and amid great fanfare of flag waving. Power, which first was granted reluctantly in the belief of its necessity during an emergency, soon becomes thought of as a virtue in itself and at any time. All this is financed either by taxes drawn from the smaller and smaller remainder of private enterprise of the nation or by money counterfeited by means of inflation by those in control. The entire process of war is always the direct antithesis of liberalism.

The Honorable R. Hopkin Morris, Member of the House of Commons from Wales, who has great understanding of the subject of liberty, has aptly expressed the present world situation thusly: "War is pre-eminently the breeding ground of the Planned State. . . . Liberalism, silenced as it always is in war, has now in peace time been paralyzed by the prevailing atmosphere of the time."[7]

Yet "liberals" are found embracing, approving, and supporting the process of war. Why? I suspect that it is because, in an atmosphere of panic, they are drawn to an objective which they can comprehend—the defeat of a personalized "enemy" on the field of battle. In the heat of a generated hatred, that objective seems to them to be commendable.

There must be considerable satisfaction to the promoters of the collectivized state in the fact that, heads or tails, they win: that while still being officially at war and preparing at terrific cost to defeat our recent partner in the continuing conflict, we have more and more contributed to the strength of the enemy—compulsory collectivism. Suicide it is, however unwitting. If one were to attempt to design a scheme whereby an easy victory would be handed to the foreign managers of the collectivized state, the pattern of events now being followed could hardly be improved upon. Why should one lend his support to the process or even tolerate it?

If power be an evil, how can the employment of this evil possibly beget a good? Power can, to be sure, be used to displace one power with another that is greater. Displacing one power with another in this manner does not destroy power; it increases the scope of illiberal power. And if power be evil, this process merely increases the magnitude of the evil.

The records of history show how great dictatorships have been built on pleas for defense against some vague, external threat or "enemy." I see no reason to assume that the eventual outcome of now pursuing similar ends can be expected to be any different here. Democratic processes as such are no protection, as Ballinger so well proves in his book.[8] That we possess no miracle of protection against the evil conduct or misuse of power should by now be clear to any person capable of observation. That fact is revealed in a growing and entrenched bureaucracy. It is also revealed by our increasing participation in distant wars—wars sanctioned under the cloak of national defense, but nonetheless the handmaiden of dictatorial power and a factory for the collectivized state.

It is frequently argued these days that force must be used to stop aggression before it starts. That is an untenable position. It is impossible for anyone to tell a future aggressor from one who is not going to be one. Such use of force is never justified, and in engaging in it there will have been opened a floodgate of mayhem which, in its release, can be followed logically to the ultimate obliteration of the human race.

The reason for this rule of restraint can be seen by reducing it to the simple form of its elements. If aggression were to be allowed against an anticipated aggressor, you would not only fight off the murderer-in-progress, and perhaps kill him, you would kill him as he comes over the hill for that presumed purpose; you would not only kill him as he comes over the hill for that purpose, you would kill the one assumed by you to be planning to do so; you would not only kill the one presumably planning to do so, you would kill all who might plan to do so—and that includes everybody.

There must be something wrong in that theory of defense, at its start. Once a person practices aggression, he finds no logical stopping point. It must end in his own defeat. The time to stop it is before starting, no matter what seeming justification may be at hand for initiating aggression.

We are told that to get at an "enemy" and "prevent his attack on us," we must set up "defense" at some distant point. So a foreign battle-ground is selected. Suppose A and B are neighbors, each of whom violently disapproves of the way the other operates his household. The difference is great; the enmity is bitter. Each considers the other to be a serious threat to another neighbor, C, who is not concerned beyond letting A and B each run his own household as each desires. Both A and B know that if there should be battle in one of their own houses, windows would be broken and furniture wrecked and blood would be splattered on the wallpaper and the rugs. Yet each is watching for an opportunity and excuse to attack the other so as to rid the neighborhood of a "dangerous enemy." Finally an occasion arises when both happen to be on C's property. So they go at it, wrecking his house and killing his wife and baby in the process—on the basis that in so doing they are liberating C from the threat of aggression and trespass. It may be seriously questioned, I believe, whether this is the way to generate good will among one's neighbors, even though the action was started for the avowed purpose of neighborhood defense. It is a violation, I believe, of the proper and right conduct.

Perhaps it is for a similar reason, in connection with present world tensions, that most foreign countries seem reluctant to have us mess up their living room by using it as the battlefield for another war. They may not see why, if we want to fight someone, we should not be willing to wait until we have been attacked and then defend ourselves as we see fit in our own house. After all, the people of Europe have had considerable experience in this sort of thing in recent decades, seemingly to no avail.

And what is more, most of these peoples now live under governments that allow very little liberty anyway—governments which we appear to favor, as evidenced by our giving them continuous support to protect them against the effects of their suicidal economic policies. So, obviously, we do not seem to be interested in liberating these people from their own governments. The people themselves probably do not see enough difference between their present governments and the communism that "threatens from without" to warrant fighting a war. So why should they either join the fight or again allow their homelands to be used as battlegrounds in what probably seems to them to be a contest for world power?

That must be the way our neighbors look at it. Deeds, not words, will be necessary to convince these people otherwise. We ourselves must first consistently and for a considerable time live by the principles we espouse and which we claim to be trying to preserve by such wars. What, for instance, must the average Korean citizen think has been the issue of the war in his homeland? Lofty principles and the freedom of man? The one thing that he can see clearly is that his cities and towns have been destroyed and his innocent countrymen killed. The view of these people is likely to be: "Isn't the United States merely fighting for its own power in the world and, in doing so, preferring to have the bloodshed and destruction take place in my dooryard rather than on its own soil?"

One popular proposal these days is to send a "limited" number of warriors to various other countries. Supposedly this is to protect these countries from aggression, perhaps by frightening away the would-be aggressor. If there were to be no aggression, this would be a trespass without a purpose. And if there were to be aggression, a token resistance would be futile.

The sending of a token force probably induces the aggression it is intended to prevent. The "enemy," if he is not so weak as to be no threat anyhow, is thereby invited to become an aggressor on the basis of exactly the same argument used for sending the force there in the first place, except that his aggression then becomes more clearly justified as a counter measure. And others may join him in a consolidation of enmity against us.

Sending "only a few" rather than many is a compromise proposal having as a doubtful virtue the fact that it is certain to be wrong because of being either too much or too little. The crucial question is resolved when the *first* soldier is sent officially. I am not speaking of soldiers who wish to volunteer for service with the army of their choice; they are on their own, and I would allow them their full rights of participation as private individuals on that basis. What I am speaking of is the matter of our government forcing some of our citizens to participate in armed trespass. Once the first one has been sent, the second becomes all the more "necessary" to defend the first, the third to defend the second—on without end and without any place to call a halt with any logic whatsoever.

The difference between sending a few and sending many is a distinction without a difference. The lack of difference becomes clear later when the sending of just a few has become ridiculous and when it has become too late to reconsider the basic issues. We would by then have become involved in a foreign war to an advanced degree.

Many persons can be induced to fight some distant "enemy" they do not know, over some issue they do not understand, while in the abundant company of kinsmen who likewise do not know what the grandiose affair is all about. People are much less inclined to engage in conflict with an "enemy" who is their next-door neighbor, where the issue is clear to both parties; this form of dispute is much more likely to be settled out of conflict, because they can see the issue and resolve it peacefully.

A strange thing happens when people are in a panic of fear over something they neither see nor understand. For instance, they can be induced to give up their liberty by delegation of power over their affairs to others—who also cannot see or understand. They fall for a plan of "collectivized liberty," which is a contradiction in terms. They trade their liberty for the false claim of saving it. This is the same as a person who hands his wealth over to someone who convinces him that it is unsafe in his own hands and promises to take care of it for the victim, but who is a robber using this device for thievery. We know how liberty has thus been lost in Germany and in many other countries. It can happen under any form of government, if the people allow power to grow and rob them of their liberty. It can happen here. In fact, it is happening here.

The Proper Defense of Liberty

Russia is supposed to be the enemy. Why? We are told that it is because Russia is communistic, and our enemy is communism. But if it is necessary for us to embrace all these socialist-communist measures in order to fight a nation that has adopted them—"because *they* have adopted these measures"—why fight them? Why not join them in the first place and save all the bloodshed?

Is it any wonder that a person who is charged with a governmental responsibility for defense, and who does not know the real nature of the enemy, is surprised to discover that many of his close ideological friends are card-carrying members of the Communist party? Why not? They have merely formalized the basic beliefs which both of them share, in the form of allegiance to and membership in the Communist party—which is in no sense an illogical act for anyone who holds those basic beliefs. The only question at issue between them would seem to be that of who is to be the captain of the totalitarian ship—a distinction of no great importance.

If it were possible for more curbs on liberty to become the tools of liberation, why not conclude that slavery is the best route to emancipation, that positives can be created by the accumulation of negatives?

But I insist that ideas rather than persons are the real enemy. If one is not already familiar with this enemy, it can be seen in brief outline in the "ten points" of the *Communist Manifesto*, together with a few paragraphs of comments immediately preceding the listing of the ten points.[9]

These ideas are to be found in operative forms everywhere in our midst, as well as in proposals for further extension. They are to be found in the form of numerous laws and regulations in the United States. A person who does not know the forms in which this enemy is already in our midst is in no position to urge our support in a further surrendering of our liberty at home to protect us against this same enemy in some "communist" nation afar. There is no sense in conjuring up in our minds a violent hatred against people who are the victims of communism in some foreign nation, when the same governmental shackles are making us servile to illiberal forces at home.

One who would serve the freedom of man is bound by his honor to do everything within his power to re-establish liberty and justice at home before concerning himself with its demise elsewhere. On a purely military basis, I believe, it is supposed to be good strategy always to attack the enemy at the closest and most vulnerable point of contact.

For any person who would use force at all, within the limits of his rights of defense, it would seem that the logical place to start defending his liberty is in any area where he, personally, has been reduced to the status of slavery. He need not look afar for an enemy that is still merely a threat to his liberty on his own soil. There are, here and now, specific things to be attacked, things within the proper scope of his action in self-defense. In doing so, he will not be violating the principle that he should never aggressively use force or the threat of force against what is merely a possible future trespasser on his liberty.

And as to preparation for defense against future trespass on his liberty, the best form of preparation is to cut those shackles on his liberty that now exist. If he is to defend remaining liberties, hadn't he better throw off those shackles which now enslave him, rather than to further enslave himself? As more and more individuals do so and engage in opposing the shackles that bind us here and now, there will most certainly emerge a high degree of cooperative defense of liberty without any compulsory planning and without the need of binding us in obedience to any domestic master.

If I am to be servile, one way or another, I find little reward in battling for a better master—if, in fact, there can be such a thing as a better master. I care not about the color of his hair, or his name, or his ancestry, or the language he speaks, or where he may happen to reside. I would not shed blood over such differences, and I would not ask others to do so. Why quibble over who is to administer an evil? There may be something harmonious and proper in having an evil administered by an evil person, if in fact it could be otherwise.

Those who want action because they are in a panic, and who point to "the lateness of the hour," are free to start throwing off the yoke they now endure at any moment they wish. They may use all the fearlessness and boldness they demand of others. Let them throw caution to the winds, if they wish, and wade in! Why don't they? Why do they hesitate to take action against the elements of illiberalism here at home, while demanding haste in squandering money and blood for "defense" against its foreign forms? The reason is, I fear, that they do not know the nature of the enemy.

In view of all the misunderstanding and confusion about liberty and its defense, the thing most to be feared at this time is enslavement from within the nation rather than from without. Slavery from within is no vague threat; it is rapidly approaching a full victory. But the "enemy" from without is still only a threat, and I doubt if a nation of free people could be conquered by him, even if it were to be attacked.

The theme of this analysis has been that liberty and peace are to each other as cause and effect; that war is an evil; that good cannot be attained by evil means; that war is the cancerous growth of minor conflicts, which would remain small if dealt with as issues between the individual persons concerned but which grow into the larger conflict of war as a consequence of amassing forces by means of involuntary servitude; that a person has the right to protect his person and his property from aggression and trespass and to help others if asked and he wishes to do so; that liberty is lost under guise of its defense in "emergencies"; that in emergencies, of all times, the strength and vitality of liberty is needed; that concentrating power in wartime is as dangerous as at any other time; and that power corrupts those who acquire it.

Perhaps these are the reasons why war always seems to demoralize those who adopt its use; why human reason seems to go on furlough for the duration of serious conflict, and in many instances thereafter; why liberty seems always to come out the loser on both sides of war. Bentham's definition of war as "mischief on the largest scale" then comes to have a deeper meaning.

While being fully sympathetic with the unwilling victims of conflict, we must not lose sight of the greatest heroes—the heroes of wars unfought because of what they did to prevent them. Largely unsung and unrecorded are the truly great persons whose wise and timely acts have stopped the makings of aggression at its source and who in this way have prevented major wars. Their greatness, we may trust, is safely recorded in more important places and in a manner more substantial than mere popularity and common renown, more permanent than statue and shrine, in forms where human errors of judgment cannot tarnish or pollute their greatness. Those most deserving of glory are the persons who prevented the battles from being fought. It is such as these whose council we should follow.

Human frailties being what they are, there are always those among us who will use force and trespass against others. The problem of peace is that of how to deal with them and those who blindly serve them. The solution does not lie in doing the same thing under guise of "self-defense," which is usually the use of force and violence offensively against others.

Whether one should use force and violence even in self-defense, where it seems to be within one's right to do so, may be open to question. The decision of whether or not to use it is a matter of strategy and moral right. When Christ's method met the force of great military and political power two thousand years ago, its defensive strength was impressive. It would seem that the Prince of Peace has demonstrated the secret of both peace and defense, for which we search, even though the reason why it works so well may defy some of our instincts and surpass our full understanding.

References

1. Chang Hsin-hai, "The Moral Basis of World Peace," *The Annals*, Vol. 258 (July, 1948), 79–89.

2. Quincy Wright, *A Study of War* (Chicago: University of Chicago Press, 1942).

3. Lewis F. Richardson, "Variation of the Frequency of Fatal Quarrels with Magnitude," *Journal of the American Statistical Association*, December, 1948.

4. F. A. Harper, *Liberty: A Path To Its Recovery* (Irvington-on-Hudson, N.Y.: Foundation for Economic Education, 1949), chap. 3.

5. John Emerich Edward Dalberg-Acton, *Historical Essays and Studies* (London: Macmillan and Co., 1907), p. 504.

6. Friedrick A. Hayek, *The Road to Serfdom* (Chicago: University of Chicago Press, 1944), chap. 10.

7. R. Hopkin Morris, *Dare or Despair* (London: Liberal League of Youth Trust, n.d.), pp. 3–5.

8. Willis J. Ballinger, *By Vote of the People* (New York: Charles Scribner's Sons, 1946).

9. Karl Marx, *Communist Manifesto* (Chicago: Regnery, 1954), pp. 36–7.

Note

F. A. Harper was President of the Institute for Humane Studies until his death in April 1973. Dr. Harper taught marketing at Cornell University, was an economist for the Foundation for Economic Education and researcher for the William Volker Fund. He has written widely on economics.

In Search of Peace (Menlo Park, Calif.: Institute for Humane Studies, 1951, 1971) is reprinted here with permission.

Ludwig von Mises

22

Observations on the Russian Reform Movement

THE BOSSES OF the Russian Communist Administration are disturbed by the fact that economic conditions in the countries which have not adopted the methods of the Communist International are by far more satisfactory than those in their own country. If they could succeed in keeping their "comrades" in complete ignorance of the achievements of Western capitalism, they would not mind the low efficiency of their own plants and farms. But as some scanty information about the "affluence" in the West penetrates to Russia, its masters are upset by the fear of a procapitalist reaction in their own house. This fear impels them on the one hand to foment sedition all over the "capitalist sector" of the earth, and on the other hand to ventilate projects aiming at some minor reforms in their own methods of management.

Nobody is today more firmly convinced of the incomparable superiority of the capitalistic methods of production than the "production tsars" of the countries behind the Iron Curtain. The present-day strength of communism is entirely due to the mentality of the pseudo-intellectuals in the Western nations who still enjoy the products of free enterprise.

Capitalism a Social System of Consumers' Supremacy

The market economy—capitalism—is a social system of consumers' supremacy. There is in its frame only one method of earning a living and of acquiring property, namely, one must try to serve one's fellow men, the consumers, in the best possible way. A daily and hourly repeated plebiscite determines again and again every individual's earnings and place in society. By their buying and abstention from buying the consumers allocate ownership of all the material factors of production to those who have succeeded in satisfying the most urgent of their not yet satisfied wants in the best possible and cheapest way. Ownership of the material factors of production can be acquired and can be preserved only by serving the consumers better than other people do. It is a revocable public mandate as it were.

The supremacy of the consumers is no less complete with regard to labor, the human factor of production. Wage rates are determined by the price the consumer, in buying the product, is prepared to refund to the employer for the worker's contribution to the process of its production. Thus the consumers' valuation fixes the height of every worker's remuneration.[1] And let us not forget: the immense majority of the consumers are themselves earners of salaries and wages and, in this capacity, instrumental in the determination of their own compensation.

The unique efficiency of the capitalistic system is due to the incentive it gives to everybody to exert his forces to the utmost in serving his fellow citizens. Not a vague altruism, but rightly understood selfishness impels a man to put forth all his strength in the service of his fellow men. The system of economic calculation in terms of money, the commonly used medium of exchange, makes it possible to compute precisely all projects in advance and the result of every action performed in retrospect; and, what is no less important, to ascribe to every factor the size of its contribution to the outcome.

Planning for People Control

The characteristic feature of socialism is precisely the fact that it substitutes for this market system of consumers' supremacy a dictatorial system, the "plan." In the planned economy the individuals are not driven by the desire to improve their own conditions but either by dutifulness or by the fear of punishment. It is impossible for the individual workers to improve their own material situation by working better and harder. If they intensify their own exertion, they alone are burdened by the implied sacrifices, but only an infinitesimal fraction of the product of their additional exertion will benefit themselves. On the other hand, they can enjoy in full the pleasures of carelessness and laziness in the performance of the tasks assigned to them while the resulting impairment of the total national product curtails their own share only infinitesimally.

The economists always have pointed to this inherent deficiency of socialism. Today all people in the socialist countries know that this criticism was fully justified. All their projects for an improvement of the quality and an increase in the quantity of economic goods and services turn around this problem. They all aim—unfortunately, in vain—at discovering a scheme that could make the individual members of a socialist system self-interested in the effect of their own contribution to the collective's effort.

That the socialists acknowledge this fact and are anxious to find a solution amounts in itself to a spectacular refutation of two of the most zealously advanced arguments in favor of socialism. On the one hand, the socialists asserted that in the market economy the wage earners are not interested in improving the output of their own work. They expected that socialism would bring about an unprecedented improvement of the individual worker's contributions because everybody will be incited by the knowledge that he does not labor for an exploiter but works for his own best interest. On the other hand, the socialists vilified profit-seeking as the most pernicious and "socially" injurious institution and indulged in reveries about the blessings of what they called a substitution of "production for use" for "production for profit."

No less significant an admission of the viciousness of the socialist ideology is provided by the system of allowing small plots of land to be exploited for the account of the individual rural workers—falsely labeled for "private profit." This capitalistic loophole alone prevented famines in the country that includes a good deal of the world's most fertile arable soil. The urgency of the Soviet productivity problem is due to the fact that in the processing industries no analogous expedient is at hand.

No Fundamental Change

The much discussed reform projects of Professor Liberman and other Russian authors do not refer to the essential characteristics of the Soviet system of central planning of all activities commonly called economic. Neither do they deal in any way with the problem of economic calculation. (For present-day Russian planners this problem does not yet have primary importance; as long as they are operating within a world of the price system, they are in a position to rely upon the prices determined on the markets of the West.)

What the reformers want to attain is improvement in the conduct of factories and workshops turning out consumers' goods by the adoption of new methods for the remuneration of directors, supervisors, or foremen. The salaries of such people should henceforth be meted out in such a way that they should have a pecuniary interest in producing articles that are considered as satisfactory by the consumers.

It is a serious blunder to employ, in dealing with this issue, any reference to the concept of "profit" or to declare that the suggested method of payment would mean something like "profit-sharing." There is within a socialist system no room for the establishment and computation of a magnitude that could be called profit or loss.

The task of production is to utilize the available human and material factors of production for the best possible satisfaction of future wants, concerning which there cannot be any *certain* knowledge today.

The Entrepreneurial Function

Technology indicates for what purposes the various factors of production could be employed; it thus shows goals that could be attained provided this is considered as desirable. To choose from this bewildering multitude of possible ways of production those which most likely are fit to satisfy the most urgent of the future wants of the consumers is in the market economy the specific task of the entrepreneur. If all entrepreneurs were right in their appreciation of the future state of the market, the prices of the various complementary factors of production would already have attained the height corresponding to this future state. As, under these conditions, no entrepreneurs would have acquired some or all of the complementary factors of production at prices lower or higher than those which later events proved to be the correct ones, no profits or losses could emerge.

One profits by having expended less than one—later—receives from the buyers of the product, and one loses if one can sell only at prices that do not cover the costs expended in production. What determines profit or loss is choosing the goal to be set for the entrepreneurial activities and choosing the methods for its attainment.

Thus, it is investment that results either in profit or in loss. In a socialist system, since only "society" invests, only society can profit or suffer losses. But in a socialist system the material factors of production are *res extra commercium*. That means: they can neither be bought nor sold and thus no prices for them are determined. Therefore, it is impossible to find out whether a definite production activity resulted in profit or loss.

The Process of Selection

The eminence of capitalism consists precisely in the fact that it tends to put the direction of production into the hands of those entrepreneurs who have best succeeded in providing for the demands of the consumers. In the planned economy such a built-in process of selection is lacking. There, it does not matter whether the planning authorities have erred or not. The consumers have to take what the authorities offer them. Errors committed by the planning authority do not become known because there is no method to discover them.

In the market economy the emergence of profit demonstrates that in the eyes of the consumers one entrepreneur served them better than others did. Profit and loss are thus the effect of comparing and gauging different suppliers' performance. In the socialist system there is nothing available to make possible a comparison of the commodities fabricated and the services rendered by the "plan" and its executors with something originating from another side. The behavior of the people for whom the plan and its executors are supposed to provide does not indicate whether a better method of providing for their needs would have been feasible. If, in dealing with socialism, one speaks of profits, one merely creates confusion. There are no profits outside the "profit and loss system."

If the authorities promise to the director of a shoe factory a bonus to be determined as a percentage of sales, they do not give him a share in "profits." Still less can this be called a return to the profit system. Profits can only be calculated if one deducts total costs from total receipts. Any such operation is unfeasible under the conditions of the case. The whole factory, fully equipped, was handed over by the authorities to the care of the director and with it all the material needed plus the order to produce, with the help of workers assigned to the outfit, a definite quantity of footwear for delivery to definite shops. There is no method available to find out the costs incurred by all the operations preceding the first interference of the director. The bonus granted to him cannot have any relation to the numerical difference between such total costs and the proceeds from the sale of the final product.

A Significant Difference

In fact, the problem of reform as passionately discussed in the communist countries today does not deal with the profitability of the various plants and productive processes. It turns virtually around a different problem: Is it possible within a socialist system to remunerate a worker, and especially the supreme foreman of a plant, according to the value the consumers, the people, attach to his contribution to the accomplishment of the product or the service?

In the capitalistic or market economy the employer is bound to pay a hired worker the price the consumers are prepared to refund to him in buying the product. If he were to pay more, he would suffer losses, would forfeit his funds, and would be eliminated from the ranks of the entrepreneurs. If he tried to pay less, the competition of other employers would make it impossible for him to find helpers. Under socialism no such connection between the amounts expended in the production of a commodity and its appreciation by the consumers prevails. There cannot therefore, *in general*, be any question of remunerating workers according to their "productivity" as appreciated by the consumers. Only in exceptional cases is it possible to separate the contribution of one worker in such a way from those of all other contributors that its separate valuation by the consumers and therefore its remuneration according to this valuation become feasible. For instance: all seats in the opera house can be sold at the regular price of m. But if a tenor of world fame sings the main part, the house is sold out even if the price of admission is raised to $m + n$. It is obvious that such cases are extremely rare and must not be referred to in dealing with the problem of wage rate determination under socialism.

Of course, a socialist management can determine for many kinds of work "normal" tasks to be performed by the laborer and, on the one hand, reward those who accomplish more and, on the other hand, penalize those who fail to produce their quotas. But such a norm in no way depends on any market phenomena. It is the outcome of a more or less arbitrary decision of the authorities.

In the market economy the salaries paid to people who turn out commodities or render services that cannot be sold on the market, and for which therefore no prices are available, are indirectly determined by the structure of the market. The employer—in such cases, as a rule, the government—must pay to such people enough to prevent them from preferring a job in the orbit of the market. Such indirect determination of the height of wage rates also is unfeasible in a socialist system.

Of course, the government is always free to grant to any of the officials it employs a salary equal to the value the supreme chief or planner attaches to this man's services. But this does not have any reference to the social problem around which the discussion turns.

Notes

Ludwig von Mises is the dean of contemporary free market economics and the most outstanding and respected member of the Austrian School of economics. Professor von Mises, now retired, has taught at the University of Vienna, the Graduate School of International Studies in Geneva, New York University, and elsewhere. His most important works are *Human Action, Socialism, Theory of Money and Credit, Theory and History, Epistemological Problems of Economics, Bureaucracy, Omnipotent Government,* and *The Anti-Capitalist Mentality.*

"Observations on the Russian Reform Movement" is reprinted with permission from *The Freeman* (May, 1966).

1. This is to what the jargon of the Hollywood industry refers in using the term "box office account." But it is no less valid for all other fields of business.

David Osterfeld

23 The Nature of Modern Warfare

IN REFLECTING UPON the intensity of the sentiment and the methods utilized in contemporary antiwar protests, it seems manifest that the preference is always for peace; that nobody wants war. So, one must ask why, if no one wants war, do wars continue to occur?

Perhaps wars result, not from the direct intentions of "war mongering capitalists" or any other group for that matter, but as Edmund Opitz observed, they are the "unexpected by-product," the inevitable culmination, of particular political or economic policies not intended to be aggressive and, in fact, even humanitarianly motivated. What one must, therefore, attempt to discern is the generic nature of these particular policies whose underlying elements propel us toward war. Only if we are cognizant of the processes that cause wars can we ever hope to obviate these warlike tendencies.

The crux of this thesis, however, is nearly diametrically opposed to today's prevailing ethos which attempts to explain war, more often than not, as the result of the insidious machinations of the industrial magnates or the "warmongering capitalists," or insists that by its nature the capitalist system must culminate in violent conflicts and, ultimately, its own catastrophic demise. The position here is to equate classical liberalism and capitalism with peace rather than war. Conversely, it considers the factors begetting war as endemic, not in socialism per se, but in any type of government economic intervention of which socialism is merely one form.

Aggressive Nationalism follows Intervention

While everyone is agreed that the cause of war is aggressive nationalism, the position here is that aggressive nationalism is the necessary outcome of government intervention. In other words, statism fosters nationalism. An in-depth study of nearly 1000 wars fought in the West from 500 B. C. to A. D. 1925 was conducted by the sociologist, Pitirim Sorokin. In contrasting the size of the casualty list to the corresponding population, he determined that the war magnitude of the first quarter of the twentieth century stood at 52 per 1,000,000 (compared with 17 for the nineteenth century) leading Sorokin to conclude that "the twentieth century will unquestionably prove to be the bloodiest and most belligerent of all the twenty-five centuries under consideration."[1]

These figures are in accord with the two salient contentions of this article. If a general date can be given for the beginning of the abandonment of the principles of laissez-faire for those of government intervention and control, it would be the 1870's, highlighted by events such as Germany's appointment of Bismarck as Chancellor and the emergence of the first effects of Britain's Reform Bill of 1867. Since that time, the trend has been conspicuously away from limited democracy and laissez-faire and toward government economic interference. We can say, generally, that the age of classical liberalism was the nineteenth century and that the age of statism extends from the latter part of that century to the present.

In applying Dr. Sorokin's findings to that of our historical sketch, two things we have noted become manifest. On the one hand is the relative peace and tranquility enjoyed by a world embracing largely laissez-faire principles. On the other we see, with the substitution of the deification of the state and rise of the controlled economy for the principles of classical liberalism, the concomitant rise of war and international conflict.

The question to be considered now is why government intervention —whether it be socialism or a "mixed" or welfare economy, and whether for humanitarian or insidious purposes—engenders international conflicts and war.

Domestic Ramifications of Statism

The free market is perpetually heading toward equilibrium. Wages and prices are always heading toward a point at which the supply of laborers and of commodities equals the demand for them. Any attempt to interfere with the natural operation of market pricing is destined to engender economic imbalance, begetting in turn, international conflict.

To illustrate how this occurs, we will follow the linkage of events in any government interference. We will assume, moreover, that the intervention occurs under the most propitious circumstances; that it is, in other words, humanitarianly motivated. We will say, for example, that the government has intervened in an endeavor to raise the wages of the hard-pressed or to set a minimum standard for the lowest strata of the working force. Surely, most would exclaim, this is a generous act; surely there could be nothing sinister or pernicious about such a policy; surely this would ease, not aggravate, tension. However, let's examine it more closely.

If wages are forced up, prices also may rise. Either they will rise nearly simultaneously, or the increased wages will reduce the income of the entrepreneurs, thus driving the marginal producers out of business and discouraging additional investment in those fields. This diminution in the amount of capital investment will entail a reduction in the quantity of commodities produced, thus causing prices to rise. And the same thing is true of endeavors to hold prices down. At the lower prices, more is bought. But the reduced price discourages investment and once again forces the marginal producers out of business, thereby engendering shortages that can only be corrected by either (1) removing the controls and permitting prices to rise or (2) carrying on production through means of subsidies, which requires higher prices in other fields. Any government intervention, therefore, must inevitably create imbalances in the economy; these, in turn, tend to bring a rise in production costs and therefore in prices.

This rise in prices, moreover, must have catastrophic international ramifications. Since domestic wages and prices are artificially held above the level set by the free market, the lower prices offered by imported goods will encourage the buying of the imported commodities in preference to domestically produced goods. As long as prices domestically are maintained at bloated levels, this foreign underselling ultimately will force the domestic firms out of business. Moreover, maintaining wages domestically above their respective equilibrium levels will attract immigrants from abroad. The influx of new laborers will either force the bloated wage level down or engender institutional mass unemployment.

The apparent solution for such problems is a policy of autarchy, viz., economic isolation, as best manifested by recourse to tariff and migration barriers, exchange controls, and the like.

International Ramifications: War

It should now be evident that a country intent upon controlling wages and prices cannot permit either imports or immigration. Such penetration would easily and obviously frustrate the planners. Statism, therefore, becomes synonymous with autarchy. With the possible exceptions of the U.S. and U.S.S.R., hardly any nation is adequately blessed with the means of self-sufficiency; statism and autarchy, therefore, must manifest themselves as a policy of aggressive nationalism. As Lionel Robbins observed: "It is really ridiculous to suppose that such a policy is possible for the majority .... To recommend autarchy as a general policy is to recommend war as an instrument for making autarchy possible."

It may be well to consider this passage further. In the long run, exports must always equal imports. The only reason one gives up an object in trade is to acquire that which he does not possess but values more than what he is giving up; similarly, the only need for exports is to pay for the required imports. Thus, the greater the imports demanded for subsistence, the greater the exports required to pay for them.

A nation, in endeavoring to preserve domestic wage and price increases through recourse to tariff and migration barriers, thereby eliminates the possibility of exporting its surplus commodities and thus acquiring the foreign exchange necessary to purchase imports. There are only three ways to procure the necessities of life: (1) to produce them at home, (2) to trade for them, or (3) to go to war and take them. If a nation does not possess the kind or the necessary quantities of natural resources, and if it does not possess enough fertile agricultural land to provide for its population, then it must trade for these necessities. If it erects tariff barriers and prohibits imports—or if other nations erect tariffs that prohibit exports—a nation is then unable to trade for its necessities. Unless one subscribes to the unlikely proposition that the people of one nation will passively acquiesce in permitting either starvation or a substantial reduction in their standard of living, there is only one recourse left: war.

World Wars I and II are replete with support for this hypothesis.[2] It is important to note that between the wars, for example, all European nations resorted to very strict anti-immigration laws, in most cases prohibiting immigration altogether. Every nation was eager to protect its wage level against encroachment from nations with still lower wage levels. Such policies were bound to engender serious international friction.

Moreover, like the "Sozialpolitik" of pre-1914 Germany, Hitler's Germany endeavored to raise the wage rates of its workers. In doing so, prices were forced up. Since this would have encouraged imports and thus thwarted the statist schemes, tariff barriers were established. However, the German ban on imports meant that no nation could acquire the necessary German exchange to purchase German exports. Germany, an industrial nation, was largely dependent upon foreign foodstuffs. It had to export its industrial commodities in order to obtain much of the needed food. By eliminating imports, it eliminated, in a like degree, the only means by which it could peaceably attain these necessary agricultural and other products. So, Germany had but one alternative; it had to go to war and take them.

Rise of Aggressive Nationalism

The nineteenth century was governed largely by classical liberal principles. It was, for the most part, a peaceful century. The onslaught of war accompanied the abandonment of these principles. The question to be considered, therefore, is precisely why these policies were discarded. The answer can be perceived if one realizes that an integral element of this liberalism was democratic rule. It is imperative, however, to appreciate that this was the democracy of Tocqueville; that is, a limited democracy. Under the classical liberal ideal, the power of the state—the apparatus of compulsion and control—was severely circumscribed. The crux of this concept was the recognition of individual rights; the sole function of the state was simply the suppression of attempts by individuals to suppress other individuals, that is, to provide a secure and peaceful framework to facilitate social cooperation. While the means for determining who held the reins of government was to be decided democratically, the power and functions of government were significantly curtailed; the democracy of the classical liberal tradition was a strictly limited concept.

Before this ideal could be fully implemented, it began, like most ideals, to be abused. As suffrage was extended—which was not necessarily inimical in itself—this democracy became ever less limited. In exchange for votes, the politicians began to promise more and more. The function of the state, accordingly, could no longer be restricted to the protection of the life, liberty, and property of its citizens. The interventionist state thus began to supplant the laissez-faire state, even before the latter had been fully established. These statist measures were, in many cases, humanitarianly motivated, that is, aiding the poor, assistance for the jobless, and so on. Nevertheless, the inevitable corollary of this proliferation of government intervention was the precipitation of aggressive nationalism. It was the inevitable result of an ethos that sanctioned the extension of government into all phases of life. It was, in short, the emergence of the total state. Whether it came as autocracy or as the "despotism of the majority" was irrelevant.

Significance of National Boundaries

In a planned, autarchic economy, territorial boundaries are of supreme importance. An isolated nation must possess all of its required natural resources. The larger the area under control, the better it can provide for its wants and needs. Yet, no country is blessed with a position of complete economic self-sufficiency. Autarchy, accordingly, must manifest itself in aggressive nationalism, in the desire of every country for the control of ever larger areas. What is required to make peace viable, therefore, is a lessening of the significance of boundaries.

This could only be attained, however, if the governments of the world were confined in their activities to protecting the life, liberty, and property of their citizens. Only then would international boundaries lose their significance. It would then make no difference whether a nation were large or small; its citizens could derive no benefit or sustain any damage from the extension or loss of territory. Under a laissez-faire system, where all transactions would take place between individuals unimpeded by government, the size of a nation would not matter. No one would be aided or hurt by a transfer or territorial jurisdiction, since all property would be held by individuals and all transactions would take place between individuals.

If the primacy of private property and free trade were the rule, at least one of the major causes of war would be all but eliminated. No one would be artificially or forcibly excluded, by tariff or immigration barriers, from acquiring any needed goods or natural resources. No one would be penalized for having been born a foreigner or of a different race or in a country of limited natural resources. Under these terms, then, at least one of the causes of war would be effectively ameliorated, if not eliminated entirely.

Conclusion

Statism, in so far as it begets autarchy, engenders international antagonisms for which no peaceful solution can be found within the context of our contemporary politico-economic ethos. These antagonisms can be relieved only by a change in ideologies. What is needed to make peace viable is the acceptance of the principles of limited democracy and its economic corollary, the free market. Only by such an advance can we ever hope to surmount at least one of the underlying factors precipitating international conflicts and war.

If this analysis possesses any cogency at all, then at least one thing is surely manifest: all the antiwar marches, protests, demonstrations, and peace songs from here to China cannot improve the situation one iota. While they may be fun, they are nevertheless futile. They are futile because they are premised upon a misunderstanding of war. Yet, wars continue to occur. Accordingly, war will not be ameliorated, much less abolished, by the mere utterance of platitudes or by shock tactics designed to scare us into peace. Only the elimination of its root cause can greatly diminish the threat of war. Such a policy, to repeat, entails a change in attitude, a policy impossible until the leaders and the people of the world are prepared to accept it.

Notes

David Osterfeld is a political science major, working toward a Master's degree in International Relations at the University of Cincinnati.

"The Nature of Modern Warfare," is reprinted with permission from *The Freeman* (April, 1972).

1. As quoted by Edmund Opitz, *Religion and Capitalism* (New Rochelle: Arlington House, 1970), p. 268.

2. Easily the most lucid and cogent delineation of this position is to be found in Ludwig von Mises' *Omnipotent Government* (New Rochelle: Arlington House, 1969).

part five
Economics and the Free Market

Economics divides people concerned with politics more than any other issue, at least in the beginning stages of their philosophical encounter. The political collectivist or leftist will find many of the conclusions of libertarians appealing, but when it comes to economics, and the capitalistic nature of the libertarian society emerges, the leftist will become totally intransigent. (Libertarians have their problems with conservatives, as well. Consider that Mr. William F. Buckley, Jr.'s anthology of essays on the conservative tradition includes only a very few authors that libertarians would consider consistent advocates of human liberty. That is because conservatives, on the whole, are more interested in establishing morality via order, i.e., force, than in offering the proper conditions, namely liberty, within which moral excellence can and is most likely to emerge.) But it is in the economic realm that much of the confusion about the free society prevails.

One of the central goals and values of societal living is the creation and maintenance of *a market* for trading material goods and services, as well as ideas and ideals (art). Hermits cannot enjoy the fruits of trade nor, of course, the emotions which accompany human companionship. Most people (except those under Hitler, Stalin, Castro, and the Skinner of *Walden II*) find the regimentation of personal relations unacceptable. Therefore, the regulation of their trading activities (through setting conditions and standards which the materials being traded and produced must meet) affords a convenient avenue toward human control. The claim can always be made that *property* is being controlled—not *people*, its owners, traders, and producers. Evidence of this artificial divorce of a person from the goods that he makes and trades is overwhelming in anticapitalist literature.

Also, capitalism has had a very bad press. Identified early in its history with anything that spelled wealth and power and, thus, resented by many, capitalism is still not understood by people. Yet, it is hated vehemently. Capitalism, only rarely viewed as the system which must accompany the marked reduction of governmental power and influence, is generally known to be associated with the institution of private property. And private property is the one moral and legal concept that all collectivists find abhorrent. Generally unable to convince people that everything should be owned collectively, from socks to factories, the left asks that we distinguish between "personal property" and "private property." These days, private property is widely viewed as a concept which implies the tolerance of brutal greed and total lack of compassion and kindness, while public property is regarded in the opposite light.

Of course, there is no such thing as public property, if we remember that property entails the use and control of material or other goods and services *by someone*. Just consider that Air Force One, the president's jet, is public property! And so is every museum, park, beach, military base, post office, staff car, university building, and courtroom paid for by the taxpayer and controlled by people in various branches and levels of government. That hardly a fraction of the public can or does use any of the above properties should be evident to any observer. Yet, we all *must* pay for what is regarded as public property. (The situation in so-called socialist countries is the same, with only minor variations, mostly in the direction of even greater absurdity and inequality. One only need think of how few Chinese people have ever eaten the dinner Chou En-Lai enjoyed with Nixon during the latter's visit to China.)

The essays below are designed to *prove* a point! This is that the economics of the free market is *better* for people in general, and each of us in particular, than any known alternative. It is hoped that any honest examination and comparison will bear out this conclusion. I myself have investigated the contentions against the free market and found that in no case has it been shown that centralized, governmentally run systems are better than free ones. And by "better"* I mean more productive of the just, deserved interests of people in society without the violation of people's rights (something which must, necessarily, hurt all if it occurs). The essays below are designed to show the workings of a free market and how its principles would apply to some of the problems that are commonly considered to be closely related to economics.

*This was written just as *Apollo XVI* was launched, which brought to my mind the fact that very often people criticize free markets for not being able to generate the production of goods and services required to achieve feats of the magnitude of space shots. That space travel might not have come about at the time it did without governmental support is quite true. That space travel must necessarily be the best *possible* thing that could have emerged in a society seriously begs the question of what *might have been* the consequences of letting people invest their monies as they saw fit individually, in *voluntary cooperations*. Surely we cannot assume that Werner von Braun is inherently wise about what is good for people any more than we can assume the inherent stupidity of everyone else whose funds support space explorations.

Frederic B. Jennings, Jr.

24 Values, Exchange, and Profits: The Bedrock of Economic Science

THE MOST BASIC questions in economic theory are those concerning *value*. What determines value? What are those factors that make a mere item have a value? A common error is that of speaking about values out of context. For example, if someone were to ask: "Does that rock have a value?," one's immediate reaction should be, "A value to *whom* for what *purpose*?" If that rock cannot be used (a) by someone (b) to achieve some goal, it has no worth.

Thus, the very employment of the term value presupposes the question, "Of value to whom?"; the concept "value" must be used in context. A given individual has a certain hierarchy of values, whether explicitly or implicitly held in his own mind. However, these values are ultimately referable to the purposes set by that person for himself. A fisherman may consider fishhooks and fishing-line as quite valuable, since they have a high degree of importance relevant to his *purpose* of fishing. A writer will not find fishhooks of much use at all; he will want writing instruments; their worth to *him* is derived directly from the goals *he* has chosen. Thus, an individual's hierarchy of values is based on two things: (a) his hierarchy of purposes and (b) the degree of relevance to those purposes of the objects to be valued.

But then what is the relation of *prices* to value? It must be kept in mind that the existence of prices presupposes the existence of exchange. Without the latter the former would be unnecessary. Thus, in order to understand exactly how prices relate to exchange, the nature of an exchange relationship must be closely examined. Once again we must ultimately refer to individual values, always remembering that these only reflect that person's goals which he has chosen for himself.

Each Trader Gains

A voluntary exchange, by its own nature, always results in the mutual advantage of both parties, at least in their eyes. In terms of an individual's hierarchy of values, he will not tend to be willing to accept a lower value in exchange for a higher one. He will only be willing to act if he will be better off as a result of that action, i.e., if he will *profit* by it. In a barter economy, exchange will only take place if each party considers himself better off in terms of his value-preferences as a result of the trade. If I have a potato and a friend has a pear, it would only be to our mutual advantage to trade if he wanted the potato more than the pear and I the pear more than the potato. Both of us would consider ourselves to be better off after the trade. When a medium of exchange is introduced, longer-range and more complex exchanges are made possible (thus enabling men to plan long-range and hence to expand their potentialities), but the principle remains the same. Voluntary exchange still works to mutual profit, by its very nature.

A common error is that which views exchange as involving two commodities of equal value, thus dropping the context of what a value is. This notion forms the basis for the conclusion that one man's profit must be at another's expense. However, one man cannot gain at another's expense by free exchange. Only when exchange is coerced may one party to the trade incur a loss.

Note that coercion is only necessary if the exchange wouldn't have taken place otherwise, i.e., if the exchange was *not* to mutual benefit. Thus, coercion is being used to create conflicts of interest rather than to resolve them, by using force to enable one person to profit at the expense of another. If each stands to gain by the trade, it will most likely take place of its own accord.

But how do prices fit into this framework of free exchange? The use of a medium of exchange in the economy facilitates trade relationships between men—this is the source of the value of money; it is good for the purpose of trade. However, money is only of worth to an individual consumer in that it can be exchanged for values; *the degree of its value is only meaningful in the full context of the worth of the many commodities it can be traded for*. But what is the relation of prices to the consumer's values and goals? The price of an item is not its value; they are related but not identical. As previously observed, the item acquires value only in relation to the consumer's goals, and money gains its value from the worth to the purchaser of the things he can buy with it. Then the price only affects the relative gain to each party from the exchange.

Choosing Among Alternatives

However, the individual consumer runs into many problems in deciding what specific exchanges to make. One of these is that of *calculating* a value previous to use, i.e., previous to exchanging another value for it. One person may buy a book for 95c which changes his life, gives him a whole new approach and outlook, and ultimately shows him the way to achieve happiness. Another may buy the same book and after reading it decide that he was gypped. The first person profited immeasurably from the exchange, and the second person's action resulted in what he considered a loss. However, at the time of purchase both bought the book because they felt that they would be better off from the exchange. This is a difficulty that many socialist planner-theorists seem to overlook. In a market based on free exchange, at least, a consumer occasions a loss only from his own miscalculations, and may even learn from them and apply that knowledge to future choices, so as to avoid repetition of error.

The chances are, however, that the consumer will gain from exchanges, unless he is completely irrational in his choices, because of the way the market operates on producers' profits. We saw that both parties gain from a voluntary exchange; the price merely determines the relative degree that each profits. But in a competitive economy producers' profit-rates tend toward an average minimum. From this observation it could be argued that the largest profits in the free market are those that accrue to people as consumers!

Thus, it is my contention that the conventional view of profits as only accruing to the businessman's end of the exchange relationship is too narrow; that it gives a false picture of the true nature of voluntary trade. There is no conflict of interests inherent in trade relationships. Mutual profit provides the incentive for people to produce and trade; it is the all-important fuel which keeps the economic engine progressing through human action toward the betterment of everyone.

Satisfy the Customer

In the light of my approach to values and demand, then, what is the source of producers' profits? If the use of coercive measures is not open to him (i.e., if the government acts to protect free exchange between individuals rather than to inhibit it, and does not engage in policies of protectionism, etc.), he has only one means by which he is able to *make money*. He must seek out and identify unsatisfied demand and attempt to fulfill it. This he can do by creating a new product which people will value in that it aids them in achieving their goals (thus making them better off); or he can raise his own efficiency in producing commodities already being produced and undersell the other producers, thus giving the consumer a better deal in the trade than his competitors have; or he can devise a new invention which will raise the efficiency of others' production and lower their costs and thus their prices and thus ultimately helping the consumer in that way.

There are many ways of making profits as a producer in a free-exchange economy, but all of them have one thing in common. *They all ultimately must aim at improving the well-being of the consumer*. Through the legal protection of property and of uncoerced exchange, producers are rewarded by the free market commensurate with their ability to and success in satisfying consumer preferences.

However, I have been very careful about qualifying my conclusions relative to *free* exchange: what happens if these voluntary exchange relationships are inhibited by governmental coercion? What happens in a socialist or even a mixed economy in the light of my conclusions? It would appear that, at least in the consumers' own eyes, they would be not better but worse off than under a free-enterprise system, because if an exchange is to be mutually profitable it must be uncoerced. And goods must be produced to be consumed, so producers' profits are as important economically as consumers' profits.

Who Is to Judge?

But here we run into the moral question: are individual consumers competent to decide what is in their own best interests, i.e., what will improve their conditions of existence? Are they competent to decide their own purposes for their own lives? Or, will the planning of production by someone else more nearly reflect the best interests of "society," i.e., of all individual members?

This question has been argued and will continue to be; it remains one of the more basic issues in the conflict between free enterprise and socialism. But if economics as a science is concerned with setting up conditions under which everyone will be better off, in their own estimations, then we can examine the effects of governmental inhibition of free exchange, whether it take the form of interventionism, fascism, socialism, communism, or any of the many variants of each.

Exactly how is this harm done? For example, what are the effects on business decisions of government price-fixing?

Consequences of Price-Fixing

One consequence is that the price is no longer a direct indicator of the dynamic balance between changing consumer value-preferences and evolving production conditions. The price thus is no longer meaningful in the context of market conditions. Thus, the scope of business decisions is considerably narrowed. Business managers no longer must view the price as an indicator of a great many other changing factors; they need only focus on the price itself, relative to their own production costs. Whereas beforehand they based their decisions ultimately on varying consumers' preferences and attempted to anticipate new wants and fulfill them (thus producing directly *for* the consumer), once prices are planned, the scope of the factors upon which decisions are based is constricted and altered.

As for a mixed economy, the degree of interference will determine the extent of the change. Business decisions weigh heavily on price predictions, which in turn under socialism depend on the vagaries of economic planners with near-arbitrary control. Thus, as a result of this redirection in emphasis, in order to better his position the businessman may aim more at gaining political influence so the price can be adjusted to his advantage (at consumers' expense) rather than aiming solely at improving the lot of the consumer by more efficient production of values. Granted, price controls are a means of directing economic production, but let us not rationalize it by saying that it is "in the best interests of the consumer."

Once again we get back to the same basic question. If values are ultimately referable to individuals' purposes, then they cannot be quantified, calculated, and planned by anyone except that individual, and especially not by any central body. Production of *values* is best done by letting producers aim solely at satisfying consumer demand, in an uninhibited market economy. The final issue remains one of whether a central planner can better decide what is in people's interests than they themselves can; i.e., whether businessmen should act according to the dictates of the consumer or of the planner.

The More Complex the Society,
the More Need for Freedom

If values are ultimately referable to individual purposes, they are not calculable or quantifiable in a developed economy. Possibly in an undeveloped, subsistence-level economy, values are to some degree predictable in that, by the very nature of life, survival requires certain actions of men. But when choices and alternatives become complex, and men are not living a hand-to-mouth existence, men develop longer-range, more diversified purposes. Thus their value-hierarchies become more complicated and varied, and unless one aims at directing the very purposes of people's lives, it is best to leave it all to them. Since we are living in a highly integrated, complex society, we must direct our focus onto the problems of socialist planning in that context, in order to cover two final points. First, since attempts at "planning" do get so complicated, and require so much gathering of information, many man-hours must be dedicated to this task. Would not these planners do more good for consumer well-being if they, too, directed their efforts toward the production of values?

Furthermore, a highly developed and specialized economy is one in which many lives are crucially and intricately dependent upon exchange relationships and their fluidity. Men's professional purposes are so specialized that the fruits of their work may only be of value to a small number of others. The fluidity and sensitivity of a market economy enables these men to seek each other out—thus, men are free (to a certain extent) to specialize and exchange their productive work for other values, always to the mutual benefit of both parties. But it might be quite difficult to convince a "disinterested" planner that this highly specialized work was useful (he might not see things in the same light as the person to whose purposes this man's work had value). In such an instance, who is blocking "progress"? This problem might be intensified all the more in that socialism is partly based on the idea of intrinsic values, which, in the planner's eyes, this work might lack.

The practical problems of socialist planning seem to be without limit in their number and complexity. My purpose in this essay has not been primarily to enumerate those difficulties, however, but rather to present my own claim that much socialist and interventionist theory is ultimately based (a) on an erroneous theory of the nature of *value* and (b) on a subsequent misunderstanding of the nature of *exchange* and *profit*. My analysis of the nature of prices and the value of money merely follows from my other conclusions, as well as my espousal of a free exchange economy as the most efficient creator and protector of "social welfare."

Note

F. B. Jennings was educated at Harvard University and is a free-lance writer. "Values, Exchange, and Profits: The Bedrock of Economic Science" is reprinted with permission from *The Freeman* (September, 1966).

Hans F. Sennholz

25 The Formation and Function of Prices

FOR ALMOST TWO thousand years economic investigation was handicapped by the common notion that economic exchange is fair only as long as each party gets exactly as much as he gives the other. This notion of equality in exchange even permeated the writings of the classical economists.

Back in the 1870's the Englishman Jevons, the Swiss Walras, and the Austrian Menger irrefutably exploded this philosophical foundation. The Austrian School, especially, built a new foundation on the cognition that economic exchange results from a *difference in individual valuations*, not from an equality of costs. According to Menger, "the principle that leads men to exchange is the same principle that guides them in their economic activity as a whole; it is the endeavor to insure the greatest possible satisfaction of their wants." Exchange comes to an end as soon as one party to the exchange should judge both goods of equal value.

In the terminology of the economists, the value of a good is determined by its marginal utility. This means that the value of a good is determined by the importance of the least important want that can be satisfied by the available supply of goods. A simple example first used by Böhm-Bawerk, the eminent Austrian economist, may illustrate this principle.

A pioneer farmer in the jungle of Brazil has just harvested five sacks of grain. They are his only means of subsistence until the next harvest. One sack is absolutely essential as the food supply which is to keep him alive. A second sack is to assure his full strength and complete health until the next harvest. The third sack is to be used for the raising of poultry which provides nutriment in the form of meat. The fourth sack is devoted to the distilling of brandy. And finally, after his modest personal wants are thus provided for, he can think of no better use for his fifth sack than to feed it to a number of parrots whose antics give him some entertainment.

It is obvious that the various uses to which the grain is put do not rank equally in importance to him. His life and health depend on the first two sacks, while the fifth and last sack "at the margin" has the least importance or "utility." If he were to lose this last sack, our frontier farmer would suffer a loss of well-being no greater than the pleasure of parrot entertainment. Or, if he should have an opportunity to trade with another frontiersman who happens to pass his solitary log cabin, he will be willing to exchange one sack for any other good that in his judgment exceeds the pleasure of parrot entertainment.

But now let us assume that our frontier farmer has a total supply of only three sacks. His valuation of any one sack will be the utility provided by the third and last sack, which affords him the meat. Loss of any one of three sacks would be much more serious, its value and price therefore much higher. Our farmer could be induced to exchange this sack only if the usefulness of the good he is offered would exceed the utility derived from the consumption of meat.

And finally, let us assume that he possesses only a single sack of grain. It is obvious that any exchange is out of the question as his life depends on it. He would rather fight than risk loss of this sack.

The Law of Supply and Demand

This discussion of the principles of valuation is not merely academic. In a highly developed exchange economy these principles explain the familiar observation that the value and price of goods vary inversely to their quantity. The larger the supply of goods the lower will be the value of the individual good, and vice versa. This elementary principle is the basis of the price doctrine known as the *law of supply and demand*. Stated in a more detailed manner, the following factors determine market prices: the value of the desired good according to the subjective judgment of the buyer and his subjective value of the medium of exchange; the subjective value of the good for the seller and his subjective value of the medium of exchange.

In a given market there can be only *one* price. Whenever businessmen discover discrepancies in prices of goods at different locations, they will endeavor to buy in the lower-price markets and sell in the higher-price markets. But these operations tend to equalize all prices. Or, if they discover discrepancies between producers' goods prices and the anticipated prices of consumers' goods, they may embark upon production in order to take advantage of the price differences.

Value and price constitute the very foundation of the economics of the market society, for it is through value and price that the people give purpose and aim to the production process. No matter what their ultimate motivation may be, whether material or ideal, noble or base, the people judge goods and services according to their suitability for the attainment of their desired objectives. They ascribe value to consumers' goods and determine their prices. And according to Böhm-Bawerk's irrefutable "imputation theory," they even determine indirectly the prices of all factors of production and the income of every member of the market economy.

The prices of the consumers' goods condition and determine the prices of the factors of production: land, labor and capital. Businessmen appraise the production factors in accordance with the anticipated prices of the products. On the market, the price and remuneration of each factor then emerges from the bids of the competing highest bidders. The businessmen, in order to acquire the necessary production factors, outbid each other by bidding higher prices than their competitors. Their bids are limited by their anticipation of the prices of the products.

The pricing process thus reveals itself as a social process in which all members of society participate. Through buying or abstaining from buying, through cooperation and competition, the millions of consumers ultimately determine the price structure of the market and the allocation of the income of each individual.

Prices Are Production Signals

Market prices direct economic production. They determine the selection of the factors of production, particularly the land and resources that are employed—or left unused. Market prices are the essential signals that provide meaning and direction to the market economy. The entrepreneurs and capitalists are merely the consumers' agents, and must cater to their wishes and preferences. Through their judgments of value and expressions of price, the consumers decide what is to be produced and in what quantity and quality; where it is to be produced and by whom; what method of production is to be employed; what material is to be used; and they make numerous other decisions. Indeed, the baton of price makes every member of the market economy a conductor of the production process.

Prices also direct investments. True, it may appear that the businessman determines the investment of savings and the direction of production. But he does not exercise this control arbitrarily, as his own desires dictate. On the contrary, he is guided by the prices of products. Where lively demand assures or promises profitable prices, he expands his production. Where prices decline, he restricts production. Expansion and contraction of production tend to alternate until an equilibrium has been established between supply and demand. In final analysis, then, it is the consumer—not the businessman—who determines the direction of production through his buying or abstention from buying.

If, for instance, every individual member of the market society were to consume all his income, then the demand for consumers' goods would determine prices in such a way that businessmen would be induced to produce consumers' goods only. The stock of capital goods will stay the same, provided people do not consume more than their income. If they consume more, the stock of capital goods is necessarily diminished.

If, on the other hand, people save part of their incomes and reduce consumption expenditures, the prices of consumption goods decline. Businessmen thus are forced to adjust their production to the changes demanded. Let us assume that people, on the average, save 25 per cent of their incomes. Then, businessmen, through the agency of prices, would assign only 75 per cent of production to immediate consumption and the rest to increasing capital.

Our knowledge of prices also discloses the most crucial shortcoming of socialism and the immense superiority of the market order. Without the yardstick of prices, economic calculation is impossible. Without prices, how is the economic planner to calculate the results of production? He cannot compare the vast number of different materials, kinds of labor, capital goods, land, and methods of production with the yields of production. Without the price yardstick, he cannot ascertain whether certain procedures actually increase the productivity and output of his system. It is true, he may calculate in kind. But such a calculation permits no value comparison between the costs of production and its yield. Other socialist substitutes for the price denominator, such as the calculation of labor time, are equally spurious.

Government Interference with Prices

Economic theory reveals irrefutably that government intervention causes effects that tend to be undesirable, even, from the point of view of those who design that intervention. To interfere with prices, wages, and the rates of interest through government orders and prohibitions is to deprive the people of their central position as sovereigns of the market process. It compels entrepreneurs to obey government orders rather than the value judgments and price signals of consumers. In short, government intervention curtails the economic freedom of the people and enhances the power of politicians and government officials.

The price theory also explains the various other economic problems of socialism and the interventionist state. It explains, for instance, the unemployment suffered in the industrial areas, the agricultural surpluses accumulated in government bins and warehouses; it even explains the gold and dollar shortages suffered by many central banks all over the world.

The market price equates the demand for and the supply of goods and services. It is the very function of price to establish this equilibrium. At the free market price, anyone willing to sell can sell, and anyone willing to buy can buy. Surpluses or shortages are inconceivable where market prices continuously adjust supply and production to the demand exerted by the consumers.

But whenever government by law or decree endeavors to raise a price, a surplus inevitably results. The motivation for such a policy may indeed be laudable: to raise the farmers' income and improve their living conditions. But the artificially high price causes the supply to increase and the demand to decline. A surplus is thus created, which finds some producers unable to sell their goods at the official price. This very effect explains the $8 billion agricultural surplus now held by the U.S. Government.

It also explains the chronic unemployment of some 5 million people in the United States. For political and social reasons and in attempted defiance of the law of supply and demand, the U.S. Government has enacted minimum wage legislation that is pricing millions of workers right out of the market. The minimum wage is set at $1.25 per hour—to which must be added approximately 30c in fringe costs such as social security, vacations and paid holidays, health, and other benefits—so that the minimum employment costs of an American worker exceed $1.55 an hour. But in the world of economic reality, there are millions of unskilled workers, teenagers, and elderly workers whose productivity rates are lower than this minimum. Consequently, no businessman will employ them unless he is able to sustain continuous losses on their employment. In fact, these unfortunate people are unemployable as long as the official minimum wage exceeds their individual productivity in the market. This kind of labor legislation, even when conceived in good intentions, has bred a great variety of problems which give rise and impetus to more radical government intervention.

The price theory also explains most money problems in the world.

For several years after World War II, many underdeveloped countries suffered a chronic gold and dollar shortage. And in recent years, the United States itself has had serious balance-of-payments problems, which are reflected in European countries as a dollar flood.

No matter what the official explanations may be, our knowledge of prices provides us with an understanding of these international money problems. Price theory reveals the operation of "Gresham's Law," according to which an inflated depreciated currency causes gold to leave the country. Gresham's Law merely constitutes the monetary case of the general price theory, which teaches that a shortage inevitably results whenever the government fixes an official price that is below the market price. When the official exchange ratio between gold and paper money understates the value of gold, or overstates the paper, a shortage of gold must inevitably emerge.

And finally, our knowledge of the nature of prices and of the consequences of government interference with prices also explains the "shortages" of goods and services suffered in many countries. Whether the interference is in the form of emergency or wartime controls, international commodity agreements, price stops, wage stops, rent stops, or "usury laws" that artificially limit the yield of capital—and whether they are imposed on the people of America, Africa, Asia, or Europe—government controls over prices control and impoverish the people. And yet, omnipotent governments all over the world are bent on substituting threats and coercion for the laws of the market.

Note

Hans F. Sennholz is professor and Head of the Department of Economics at Grove City College. He has written widely for journals in economics. He translated several works by the noted Austrian economist Eugene Böhm-Bawerk and is also one of the outstanding scholars in the Austrian tradition of free market economics.

"The Formation and Function of Prices" is reprinted with permission from *The Freeman* (February, 1965).

Yale Brozen

26

Automation: The Retreating Catastrophe

AMATEUR SOCIAL SCIENTISTS such as Norbert Wiener (a professional mathematician) predicted, in 1949, that we faced "a decade or more of ruin and despair" from the wholesale unemployment which would occur in the 1950's. Cybernation and automation were going to abolish jobs at an unprecedented rate. The prediction was reaffirmed by a parade of witnesses in the mid-1950's before a Congressional committee investigating automation. Yet, the "decade or more of ruin and despair" from the unemployment that was going to be caused by automation appears to have been postponed by at least 17 years. Nevertheless, we still have doom criers who say that this consequence of automation will be appearing in the near future.

The Ad Hoc Committee on the Triple Revolution has issued a Manifesto (March 1964) which declares that the advent of complex computers and self-regulating machines introduces an historical break in the evolution of social processes. "A new era of production has begun. Its principles of organization are as different from those of the industrial era as those of the industrial era were different from the agricultural." The new machines introduce an era of unlimited productive capacity. The new machines are displacing people in droves from manufacturing and agriculture and will soon displace them from the service industries. Men cannot compete with these machines. Poverty is expanding and it has become impossible to achieve full employment.

Judgement Day is coming. Despite the fact that the predictors of its coming have been constantly disappointed, it will be upon us soon, you sinners, so repent while there is still time.

These predictions of wholesale unemployment seem to be repeated at shorter intervals as more of such predictions fail to materialize. In the late 1700's, machines such as the loom and the spinning jenny were about to bring the end of the world upon us. Edward Baines, the historian, writing in 1834, made the following comment about these predictions:

At the accession of George III (1760), the manufacture of cotton supported hardly more than 40,000 persons; but since machines have been invented by means of which one worker can produce as much yarn as 200 or 300 persons could at that time, and one person can print as much material as could 100 persons at that time, 1,500,000 or 37 times as many as formerly can now earn their bread. . . .

And yet there are still many, even scholars and members of Parliament, who are so ignorant or so blinded by prejudice as to raise a pathetic lament over the increase and spread of the manufacturing system . . . there are persons who regard it as a great disaster when they hear that 150,000 persons in our spinning works now produce as much yarn as could hardly be spun with the little handwheel by 40,000,000.

In the 1870's and 1880's, the spread of mechanization showed that the end was in sight. David Ames Wells, writing on *Recent Economic Changes* in 1889, reported that:

The power to excavate earth, or to excavate and blast rock, is from five to ten times as great as it was when operations for the construction of the Suez Canal were commenced, in 1859–'60. The machinery sent to the Isthmus of Panama, for the excavation of the canal at that point, was computed by engineers as capable of performing the labor of half a million of men.

The displacement of muscular labor in some of the cotton mills of the United States, within the last ten years, by improved machinery, has been from thirty-three to fifty percent, and the average work of one operative, working one year, in the best mills of the United States, will now, according to Mr. Atkinson, supply the annual wants of 1,600 fully clothed Chinese, or 3,000 partially clothed East Indians. In 1840 an operative in the cotton mills of Rhode Island, working thirteen to fourteen hours a day, turned off 9,600 yards of standard sheeting in a year; in 1886 the operative in the same mill made about 30,000 yards, working ten hours a day. In 1840 the wages were $176 a year; in 1886 the wages were $285 a year.

The United States census returns for 1880 report a very large increase in the amount of coal and copper produced during the ten previous years in this country, with a very large comparative diminution in the number of hands employed in these two great mining industries; in anthracite coal the increase in the number of hands employed having been 33.2 percent, as compared with an increase of product of 82.7; while in the case of copper the ratios were 15.8 and 70.8, respectively. For such results, the use of cheaper and more powerful blasting agents (dynamite), and of the steam drill, furnish an explanation. And, in the way of further illustration, it may be stated that a carload of coal, in the principal mining districts of the United States, can now (1889) be mined, hoisted, screened, cleaned, and loaded in one half of the time that it required ten years previously.

The report of the United States Commissioner of Labor for 1886 furnishes the following additional illustrations:

In the manufacture of agricultural implements, six hundred men now do the work that, fifteen or twenty years ago, would have required 2,145 men—a displacement of 1,545.

The manufacture of boots and shoes offers some very wonderful facts in this connection. In one large and long-established manufactory the proprietors testify that it would require five hundred persons, working by hand processes, to make as many womens' boots and shoes as a hundred persons now make with the aid of machinery—a displacement of eighty per cent.

Another firm, engaged in the manufacture of children's shoes, states that the introduction of new machinery within the past thirty years has displaced about six times the amount of hand-labor required, and that the cost of the product has been reduced one half.

On another grade of goods, the facts collected by the agents of the bureau show that one man can now do the work which twenty years ago required ten men.

In the manufacture of flour there has been a displacement of nearly three fourths of the manual labor necessary to produce the same product. In the manufacture of furniture, from one half to three fourths only of the old number of persons is now required. In the manufacture of wallpaper, the best evidence puts the displacement in the proportion of one hundred to one. In the manufacture of metals and metallic goods, long-established firms testify that machinery has decreased manual labor 33⅓ per cent.

In 1845 the boot and shoe makers of Massachusetts made an average production, under the then existing conditions of manufacturing, of 1.52 pairs of boots for each working day. In 1885 each employee in the State made on an average 4.2 pairs daily, while at the present time in Lynn and Haverhill the daily average of each person is seven pairs per day, showing an increase in the power of production in forty years of four hundred per cent.

In the early 1900's electrification meant that the end was at hand. Then in the 1930's, the heavens cracked and the deluge descended because, it was said, there was *too little* technological change, a reversal of the earlier stand. But we are now back at the old stand again. Technology is about to engulf us. Job opportunities are about to be swallowed up, once again, by technological change, which we now call automation and cybernation.

Frankly, I am puzzled by this increasingly repeated belief in a judgement day which is constantly postponed. I am especially puzzled in view of facts which demonstrate that, if ever a judgement day threatened, it is farther in the future than ever. More jobs exist today than ever existed at any time in our history. The number of jobs has grown, not declined or even remained static. More jobs are vacant and more employers are searching for additional help than at any time in our recent history. And this is not because there is a greater gap between the skills required to fill jobs and the skills possessed by those seeking jobs. There are more people at work today filling jobs than at any time in our history. Not only are more people at work than ever, but the proportion of those aged 18 to 64 who are at work has been growing. The population in the 18 to 64 age bracket has increased at a 0.9% per year rate since 1947. Total civilian employment has increased even faster, mounting at a 1.3% per year rate since 1947. The growth rate in number of civilians employed is 40% faster than the growth rate of population in the age brackets that furnishes most of the available tenants for jobs. Yet the Ad Hoc Committee blandly states that the labor force participation rate is declining because people are losing jobs. They tell us that the unemployment figures do not tell the actual unemployment because they do not include those who have withdrawn from the market because they have found the quest for jobs to be hopeless.

Where do we find this spectre of declining job opportunities with which the doom criers are constantly trying to haunt us? The major place where we find it is among Negro teen-agers. After the statutory minimum wage rate was increased to $1.00 an hour in 1956, the unemployment rate among this group leaped to 18% of those who would like to have jobs (from a range of 7 to 13% in the preceding decade). After the statutory minimum wage was raised to $1.15 in 1961, the unemployment rate among this group jumped to 21%. With the further increase in the statutory minimum wage rate to $1.25 in 1963, the unemployment rate in this group rose further to 24%.

Now a proposal is before Congress to increase again the statutory minimum to $1.40 next year and then to $1.60 and to extend further the number of jobs covered by this wage law. We seem to be intent on forcing more and more teenagers into unemployment. We seem to be eager to foreclose the opportunities to learn a skill and become productive enough to be worth employing at wage rates well in excess of the statutory minimum in the later years of life.

A major part of our education is obtained while at work. We are foreclosing educational opportunities by these successive increases in the statutory minimum wage rate. We pushed the statutory minimum wage up by 212% from 1949 to 1963 in a period when the average wage of all employees rose less than 80%. It is no wonder that unskilled, inexperienced workers are finding it difficult to land jobs.

The inability of a major number of teen-agers to find jobs is hardly attributable to automation. The arbitrary price set by law that employers must pay must take the major share of the blame for the lack of employment opportunities for this group.

Mass unemployment, or even a minor amount of unemployment, has not been caused by automation. We are closer to a mass shortage of *employees* in the 20 to 64 year age bracket than we are to a shortage of jobs.

Since 1949, when alarms were sounded about the expected effect of automation, the number of people at work has increased by 14 million and the number of jobs by 16 million. At the same time, the average hourly compensation of factory employees has increased from $1.90 (measured in 1965 dollars) to $2.90. This is a 55% increase in real terms (i.e., measured in dollars of constant purchasing power). If the demand for employees had been depressed by automation, we would have seen a drop in the real wage, not a 55% rise, particularly in view of the rising size of the labor force.

This is not a pronouncement that no person ever lost a job because of automation. I am saying that the number of unemployed persons has not increased because of automation. Automation has created more jobs than it has destroyed. Unemployment has dropped because of it, although there are some people among the unemployed who would not have been there if there had been no automation. But there are a great many more people among those employed because of automation than are among the unemployed because of automation. Although automation has displaced some employees, the total number unemployed is smaller today than it would have been without automation, given the present wage structure.

Most of the unemployment of those 20 years of age and over is the normal unemployment that we will always have with us because of the constant shifting among jobs. People voluntarily quit jobs in very large numbers in order to seek better jobs. Normally, six million or more persons a year do this. During the period in which they are choosing among the jobs available, they are classed as unemployed and seeking work. They are not unemployed because of economic disaster, however. They are unemployed because they are taking time to canvass the

market and choose among alternative openings or because they are
doing some work at home and are not counted among the employed
even though they are employed. If they average two months between the
time they quit one job and the time they start a new one chosen from
among the many openings available, the average unemployment appearing in the statistics from this one source would be over one million.

Automation does result in a redeployment of the work force. This,
however, is an old story in America. A hundred years ago, there was no
automobile industry, no aircraft industry, no electric generating industry, no camera or film industry, no motor boat industry, no radio and
television industry, no telephone industry, etc. Today, these are all very
substantial industries employing large numbers of people. Without a
redeployment of the work force, these industries would not be in
existence. Automation-caused redeployment is simply another facet of
the redeployment of labor which has been a constant fact in American
life.

Why Is Automation Alarming?

In the face of this data, why do some cry that doomsday is
coming? What is it about automation that causes alarm? Why is it that
workers asked about their attitude toward mechanization feel no threat,
yet appear frightened when asked about their feelings toward automation?

The hallmarks of automation, to distinguish it from simple mechanization or automatic methods, are its sensing, feed-back, and self-
adjusting characteristics. Because it senses changing requirements and
adjusts without human intervention, it presumably does away with the
need for human attendants or human labor. This is very fearful indeed
to those who depend upon jobs for their livelihood.

Fear of automation can be traced to four sources. One is based upon
the assumption that there is a fixed amount of goods, which buyers
want. Any new method which enables us to turn out more goods per
man-hour will, it is believed, enable us to turn out the fixed amount of
goods and services with fewer men. If a man helped by an automatic
machine can produce twice as many widgets per hour as he formerly
did, then, presumably, only half as many hours of work will be available
for each man to do. If work weeks are not shortened, only half as many
jobs could, it is asserted, be provided in these circumstances. The
President of the United States used this sort of logic when he said "that
approximately 1.8 million persons holding jobs are replaced every year
by machines."

The second source of fear springs from the idea that automation or cybernation is something more than the latest stage in the long evolution of technology. Automation is said to be so different in degree that it is profoundly different in its effect. Automated machines controlled by computers do not simply augment muscle power as previous machines did. They replace and out-perform human intelligence. In the future, machines will not only run machines; they will repair machines, program production, run governments and even rule men. Union leaders will collect no dues and business will have no customers because, presumably, there will be no production workers required. Human beings will, it is believed, be made as obsolete by these machines as horses were by the tractor and the automobile.

The third source of fear lies in the fact that we are much more aware of the people displaced by automation and concerned about them than we are of the other unemployed. Among the three million unemployed are several thousand persons laid off because their skills are not usable by concerns installing automated processes to replace previously used technology. Presumably, possessing only obsolete skills there are no job opportunities open to them. Others who are laid off or who are among the unemployed because they have voluntarily quit their jobs are less worrisome because their skills are not obsolete and they will have new jobs in a few weeks.

A fourth source of fear is the high incidence of joblessness among the unskilled. It is felt that the unskilled are unemployed because automated production reduces the demand for unskilled workers. Any increases in the demand for labor occurring because of automation are believed to be concentrated on highly skilled workers.

Is The Alarm Justified?

Let us analyze these presumptions which make automation so fearful to some. First, is there a fixed amount of work to be done? Does an improvement in technology which enables us to do a fixed lump of work with fewer men mean there will be fewer jobs?

In terms of a very recent type of automation, the use of electronic data processing equipment, a United States Department of Labor study of large firms which introduced such equipment concluded that: despite the reduction in labor requirements for the tasks performed by the computers, total employment of the offices as a whole rose. Over the four years from December 1953 to December 1957, total office employment at 17 offices studied increased an average of 7 percent. The experience of these offices suggests the possibility of expanding employment in new areas of office activity to handle information which had previously been uneconomical to acquire.[1]

This experience of increasing office employment despite reduced labor requirements per unit of output is a specific instance of what has been going on generally in our economy. From 1919 to 1962, man-hours required per unit of output in the American economy dropped by 67 percent, yet total number of jobs rose from 42 million to 68 million. The tripling of output per man-hour did not reduce the number of jobs by two-thirds as those who believe in a fixed amount of work available would predict.

One group which subscribes to the fixed lump of work philosophy has pointed to the 1960-65 annual rise in output per man-hour of 3.6 percent with alarm. It has said that this exceeds the long term average annual rise of 2.4 percent from 1909 to 1963 and the average annual postwar rise of 3.0 percent. This, it has said, indicates that the pace of technological change is accelerating and will create a great unemployment problem.

The more rapid rise of output per man-hour from 1960 to 1965 was accompanied by an increase in the number of *civilian* jobs from 67 million to 72 million—an increase of 5 million. An even more rapid rate of increase in output per man-hour from 1949 to 1953, amounting to 4.0 percent per year, was accompanied by increase in civilian jobs from 59 million to 62 million. On the other hand, a slowed rate of increase in output per man-hour from 1953 to 1954, when output per man-hour rose by only 1.8 percent, well below the long run average rise of 2.4 percent, was accompanied by a drop in employment from 62 million to 61 million. "It is noteworthy that while many Americans worry about the loss of jobs due to technological change, the much more rapid increase in productivity abroad has been accompanied by a great reduction, not an increase, in unemployment."[2] It would seem that a more rapid rise in output per man-hour should be welcomed as a means of creating jobs more rapidly than they can be destroyed by other factors at work in our economy.[3]

The primary effect of automation and increased output per man-hour is not a reduction in the number of jobs available. Rather, it makes it possible for us to do many things which otherwise could not and would not be done. Automation enables us to earn larger incomes and lead fuller lives. It will, in the future, literally make it possible to travel to the moon. It saves lives through the aid it gives doctors. By controlling traffic signals in response to traffic flows and reducing traffic congestion, it adds hours to the free time of commuters every week. It helps scientists, with the aid of high-speed data processing, to develop new knowledge that otherwise would not be available in our lifetimes. We are increasing the scale of educational activities because mechanization, automation, cybernation, or whatever we choose to call our new technology, makes it possible to do more than we could formerly. With the coming of automation, men are able to do more and have more. Both sublime and mundane activities are being enlarged and the number of jobs has grown as a consequence, not declined.

The second source of fear—the idea that automation is something more than the latest stage in the long evolution of technology—the idea that it is so different in degree that it is profoundly different in effect—is an equally specious hobgoblin. The first thing to be said is that automation is not a new phenomenon.

Although we may grant that automation differs from other kinds of technology, we should not blind ourselves to history to the point of saying it is completely new. Perhaps the earliest automated device was the pressure cooker invented by Denis Papin in 1680. He originated a pressure control which is still one of the most widely used regulators. Despite this automated device, and others such as thermostatic oven controls, cooks are still extensively employed and housewives still find it necessary to devote time to their kitchen work. Although homemakers may spend less time in the kitchen, this has simply freed them to do more of other kinds of work, such as better educating their children and decorating their homes.

During the eighteenth century, several types of automatic regulators were applied to windmills. An automatic, card-programmed loom was devised by Jacquard over 150 years ago. An automatic flour mill was built in 1741. Eighteenth century steam engines were controlled by governors which had sensing, feed-back, and resetting characteristics which are the hallmark of automation. Automation has been increasingly applied over the last two centuries, yet employment has risen continually.

If automation is so remarkably different in degree than previous technological change, it should show in the data on productivity. I have said above that output per man-hour has risen in the last five years at a 3.6% annual rate. If automation is doing such profoundly different things to us, that rate, then, should be a markedly higher rate of increase than ever before experienced. Yet, in contrast, output per man-hour in manufacturing in the post World War I decade rose at a 5.0% per year rate—a rate which has not been matched in any ten year period you want to pick since World War II. If automation is such a profound leap in technology, it has yet to manifest itself as such in economically significant terms.

As to the third source of fear—the fear that our skills will be made obsolete much more rapidly because of automation and we will lose our jobs for that reason and, with obsolete skills, be unable to find any other job—there is simply no evidence that workers are becoming unemployed in greater numbers for this reason and are unable to find other jobs because their skills are obsolete. The only group which has suffered a significant increase in the incidence of unemployment are teen-agers seeking their first job. I have already indicated that this is a consequence of man-made legislation—the stupendous increase in the minimum wage rates set by statutes passed by Congress and state legislatures.

When skill requirements on jobs change, most of the affected employees are retrained by their employers for new jobs. The average production worker in General Motors is retrained six times in ten years. The average airline spends $100,000 per pilot over a pilot's career retraining him for flying new aircraft as old aircraft are phased out and replaced. Industry in general is spending well over $20 billion a year on employee training and retraining.

The U.S. Bureau of Labor Statistics studied the experience of twenty major firms converting to electronic accounting and found that only one employee of the 2,800 employees involved was laid off. In seven companies installing automation equipment which were intensively studied by the Stanford Research Institute, not one employee was laid off. When the South Chicago Works of U.S. Steel was replaced by an automated mill, of the 1,346 employees involved, only one was laid off.

Automation has resulted in the re-deployment of the work force—not in discarding obsolete men for whom there is no further use. I said earlier that this is an old story. The extent of the redeployment which has occurred may startle many readers.

Only a century ago, fifty out of every one hundred workers toiled on farms producing the nation's supply of food and fiber. Only two or three out of every one hundred workers were producing educational, medical, recreational, and other services which contribute to a richer, fuller, healthier life. Today, the number of workers in these life-enriching occupations is relatively five times as great. Those toiling on farms have been reduced to one-seventh their former number. They now direct machines instead of using animal power and their own muscles. The quality of life has been improved and brute toil has been reduced because technology has increased our incomes to the point where we can afford these services and these machines.

Most of this redeployment occurred before we ever heard of automation, much less had any effects produced by it.

The fourth source of fear of automation apparently springs from the high incidence of joblessness among the unskilled. Some of the doom criers tell us the unskilled are unemployed because automation has reduced the demand for unskilled workers even though it may, in some instances they grudgingly admit, increase the demand for skilled workers.

If the unskilled were the victims of automation, we should expect a steadily growing volume of unemployed among the unskilled as the economy becomes increasingly automated. Instead, we find, for example, that the age group 14 to 17 "had particularly severe declines (in employment) from 1950 to 1951, 1955 through 1957, and 1960 to 1961. These declines in employment for this group coincide with Federal increases in minimum wages and the extension of coverage." After the surge in teen-age unemployment coinciding with the last increase in the minimum wage rate in 1963, the unemployment rate has started dropping. If we believe that automation causes unemployment among the unskilled, the unemployment rate in this group should have continued to rise.

There is abundant evidence that the increased unemployment among the unskilled is a result of the rise in the statutory minimum wage rate and extension of the number of jobs covered by the statutory minimum. There is now a large literature which displays the data establishing this fact.

The evidence available concerning the effects of automation leads to these conclusions:

1. If no technological change had occurred in the past decade, the number of civilian jobs available and occupied could have grown as it has from 63 million to 72 million only at the price of restricting increases in wage rates.

2. The technological change of the last decade has increased the average employee's earnings by $400 per year compared to what they would be if there had been no automation.

3. Automation increased the number of jobs available at the 1955 wage level by 20 million. Since only 9 million additional people have joined the work force and become available to fill jobs, there would be a shortage of 11 million workers today if wage rates had not increased. The increase in wage rates has reduced the demand for labor to the point where there are few shortages of most types of labor.

4. The overly large increase in the wage rate for the unskilled as a

result of minimum wage legislation, has destroyed so many jobs for these people that we have a surplus of unskilled teen-agers for filling unskilled jobs in some sections of the country. This surplus is not a result of automation but of over-pricing.

5. Automation and other forces such as the growth in the stock of capital are doing a major job in alleviating poverty. If we define poverty in terms of a $3,000 per year family income measured in 1962 dollars, the incidence of poverty has fallen from 32% of all family units in 1947 to 18% in 1964 and to approximately 15% today. The declarations of the Ad Hoc Committee on the Triple Revolution that there is an increasingly large disadvantaged group in our society, that there is a growing permanently depressed class, and that poverty is worsening simply do not square with the facts.

6. Instead of being alarmed about growing automation, we ought to be cheering it on. The catastrophe that doom criers constantly threaten us with has retreated into such a dim future that we simply cannot take their pronouncements seriously.

Let us have more automation, more mechanical slaves to work for us, and stop wasting our time and dwelling on the threat of hobgoblins which exist only in the imaginations of those who refuse to look about them at what is going on in the economy.

Notes

Professor Yale Brozen is one of the most distinguished members of the Chicago school of economics. His articles have appeared in *The Journal of Law and Economics, The American Economic Review, Econometrica, Land Economics, Ethics, Social Research, Il Politico, Political Science Quarterly, Revista Brasileira de Economia, Saturday Review, Barron's, New Individualist Review, The Intercollegiate Review, The Freeman, Reason,* etc. He is professor of business economics at the Graduate School of Business, The University of Chicago.

"Automation: The Retreating Catastrophe" is reprinted with permission from *Left and Right* (Fall 1966).

1. U.S. Bureau of Labor Statistics, *Adjustment to the Introduction of Office Automation,* Bulletin No. 1276 (Washington: U.S. Government Printing Office, 1960), p.4.

2. R. N. Cooper "International Aspects," *Automation and Technological Change,* edited by J. T. Dunlop (Englewood Cliffs: Prentice-Hall, 1962), p. 148.

3. A study by S. Fabricant for the pre-war period found that

"trends in unit labor requirements have been negatively correlated with trends in man-hour employment in different industries" (that is, decreases in hours of labor per unit of product—increases in output per man-hour—have been correlated with increased employment while increases in hours of labor per unit of product have been correlated with a decline in employment). *Employment in Manufacturing, 1899–1939* (New York: National Bureau of Economic Research, 1942).

27

Yale Brozen

Wage Rates, Minimum Wage Laws, and Unemployment

ALONG WITH THE WEATHER, sex, health, and taxes, one of the most widely discussed topics in America is wage rates. We have had an abundance of guide posts offered for determining the changes which should be made in wage rates. Union strategists have insisted in times past that wage rates should rise when the cost of living goes up, whatever "cost of living" may mean. They do not accept the converse proposition that wage rates should go down when the cost of living goes down, however. In the latter case, they argue that a decline in cost of living means a depression is coming or has arrived and, therefore, wage rates should be raised to increase purchasing power and prevent the depression.

Another guide post offered in times past (and last year by Mr. Reuther) concerns the relationship between wage rates and profits. Still another relates wage rates to an acceptable level of living. Most recently, wage rates and changes in them have been linked to changes in average output per man-hour. The General Motors contract of a decade ago provided for changes in wage rates linked to the change in the consumer price index of middle income urban families, plus an annual improvement factor which happened to be approximately the same as the increase in output per man-hour in the American economy in the preceding several decades.

Four years ago last January, the Council of Economic Advisors entered the discussion of guide posts for wage rate increases. They were moved to do this because, as they said at the time, "... wage decisions affect the progress of the whole economy" and, therefore, "... there is legitimate reason for public interest in their content and consequences."[1] They repeated their suggested guide posts in 1964 because, as they said, "If cost . . . pressures should arise through the exercise of market power . . . we would be forced once more into the dreary calculus of the appropriate trade off between 'acceptable' additional unemployment and 'acceptable' inflation."

The Economic Advisers have advised that, "The general guide for wages is that the percentage increase in total employee compensation per man-hour be equal to the national trend rate of increase in output per man-hour."[2] The Council has provided a measure of recent trends (1952–64) in the annual rates of growth of output per man-hour in the private economy. They suggest that the latest five-year trend in productivity, amounting to 3.2 per cent, should be *the* guide for wage rate increases. They seem to believe that if wage rates plus fringe benefits in each industry rise by 3.2 per cent, then the average cost of labor will rise by 3.2 per cent.

If hourly labor costs increase by 3.2 per cent on the average *in each industry*, however, average compensation per man-hour would rise by 4 per cent. Many wage earners obtain wage increases by leaving low paying jobs (such as those in agriculture) for higher paying jobs— without any change in the rates paid for specific positions. The average wage does rise, then, without any change in wage rates, about 0.6 to 0.8 per cent per year. Subtracting this out of the 3.2 per cent rise in output per man-hour for the total private economy would imply that the Council's suggested guide rate would be achieved with an average annual rate of change of 2.5 per cent per year in money wage rates (including fringe benefits as part of the wage, or employee compensation) in each industry.

The Council does not believe that every wage rate should be increased exactly by the rate of overall productivity increase. Their report says that "specific modifications must be made to adapt (the guide posts) to the circumstances of the particular industry."[3] For instance, they say "Wage rate increases would fall short of the general guide rate in an industry *which could not provide jobs for its entire labor force*."[4] Also, they would fall short where "wage rates are exceptionally high because the bargaining position of workers has been especially strong."[5]

The Council of Economic Advisors should be complimented for its recognition of the fact that wage rates in some industries are too high to permit all those who would like jobs in those industries to obtain them. They should also be complimented for recognizing that money wage rate increases must be smaller in the future if we are to have more rapid economic growth and decreased unemployment without inflation. The Council recognizes that the upward movement of some wage rates and prices is the result of agreements between strong unions and employers, and that "the post-Korean war years were marked by the coincidence of relatively large wage increases with declines in industry employment."[6] The fact that unduly high wage rates decrease the number of jobs available and the number of people working in an industry is obviously understood by the Council and is clearly implied in its report.

Several things are left unsaid, however, which should receive explicit recognition. The Council dwells on the inflation which may be caused by large wage rate increases. They fail to recognize that large wage rate increases for some workers come not only at the expense of causing some to become unemployed, absent inflation, but also at the expense of workers in other sectors of the economy.

I would estimate that 10 per cent of the labor force of the United States receives wage rates about 15 per cent higher than they would in the absence of wage laws and governmental support of trade unions.[7] The result is that 90 per cent of the U.S. labor force receives wage rates about 5 per cent lower than they would otherwise obtain. The *net* result is greater inequality in the division of income and about 3 per cent less total wage income for U.S. wage earners, or about 10 billion dollars less than they would otherwise earn as a group (including those whose wage rate is excessive).

To illustrate this in terms of the experience of one state, let us consider some occurrences in Michigan. Wage rates in transportation equipment manufacturing in Michigan not only rose more than in other manufacturing industries in the state, but also rose, between 1950 and 1957, by 10 per cent more than in the *same* industry in the other four East North Central states (Wisconsin, Ohio, Indiana, and Illinois).[8] Overall employment in the auto industry declined in part as a result of overly large employment cost increases. In Michigan, where the greatest increase in wage rates occurred, the decline in employment was greater than for the industry as a whole. Between 1954 and 1958, there were 85,000 more jobs lost in Michigan than in the other four East North Central states. In 1954, Michigan employed 41,000 *more* workers in transportation equipment manufacturing than the other four states. In 1958 it employed 44,000 *fewer* workers in the industry than the other states. Michigan became a depressed area, in employment terms, largely because employment costs increased so drastically in its major industry.

Not only did employment in Michigan suffer; in addition, workers in other industries in Michigan suffered. Those becoming unemployed in the transportation equipment industry sought jobs in other fields. Many found jobs in other manufacturing industries. The consequence was, however, lower compensation for those in the other industries. More jobs were made available only by restricting the rise in wages which otherwise would have occurred. Hourly earnings in these "other" industries rose 6 per cent less than the rise in these same industries in the other four East North Central states. Although employment in these industries in Michigan increased more than in other states, this represents a less productive use of the labor than its employment in transportation equipment. If wage rates and other employment costs in transportation equipment had not been raised so much in Michigan, hourly earnings would have gone up more in the other manufacturing industries. High hourly earnings for auto workers came at the expense of workers in other industries.

This brings us to the second point which the Council failed to make explicit in its concern over the inflationary impact of unduly large wage rate increases. The power of unions is focused on certain sectors of the economy, such as transportation, auto manufacturing, and coal mining. Their use of power and the consent of employers to agreements which incorporate unduly high costs of employment decreases the number of jobs available in these sectors of the economy. Since these are industries in which output per man-hour is high, declining employment in these industries forces men to take jobs in low productivity sectors of the economy. The net result is a lower average output per man-hour for the economy than otherwise would be attained. Excessive wage hikes in some parts of the economy cause our productivity to rise less rapidly (and average wage income to rise more slowly) than it otherwise would.

The experience of coal miners illustrates this point. Coal mining hourly earnings rose by $1.95 or 163 per cent from 1945 to 1960; bituminous coal mining employment dropped from 385,000 to 168,000. By way of comparison, in the same period, manufacturing production worker hourly earnings rose $1.24 or 122 per cent, and manufacturing employment rose from 15,524,000 to 16,762,000. The differential in hourly earnings in favor of coal miners increased from 18 to 39 per cent. Many of the coal miners who lost their jobs (and men who would have found employment in coal mines) took manufacturing jobs. In these jobs, their productivity and their wage income is lower than in coal mining. If we had more coal miners mining coal and fewer coal miners in other industries today, average output per man-hour in the private sector of the economy would be higher (and the record of the annual rate of increase in output per man-hour would be better), average wage income would be higher, and inequality would be less.

Excessive wage hikes in some industries slow the increase in output per man-hour in the economy as a whole for another reason besides forcing people out of high productivity into low productivity occupations. To make men worth employing in coal mining or auto manufacturing at high wage rates, the amounts of capital per man employed must be increased enough to raise the productivity of the men remaining in the industry to the point where employment costs can be covered. This is the process known as automation. Concentration of large amounts of the available capital on a few men in these industries reduces the capital available per man in the rest of the economy. With less capital per man, output per man-hour in other industries is lower than it otherwise would be. The distortion in the allocation of capital caused by distortions in the wage structure prevents average output per man-hour from reaching otherwise attainable levels. The result is a poorer record of increase in output per man-hour, a poorer record of growth, and lower incomes on the average for all.

The most important point that the Council has overlooked is that their proposed guides will have no influence on the determination of wage rates anyway. They worry about some wage rates being too high, about the unemployment caused in some areas of the economy by the overpricing of labor, about the slowing in the growth rate caused by increasing unemployment; but they suggest no effective means for preventing these unhappy events from occurring. They suggest that "an informed public . . . can help create an atmosphere in which the parties to (wage decisions) will exercise their powers responsibly."[9] This is much like expecting the flood waters rolling toward a threatened town to stop because an informed public recognizes the tremendous damage that will be done.

If an "informed public" does recognize that it and the country are being damaged by excessive wage increases, and that these excessive wage increases are the result of union power and legislative enactments, what should it do? The Council proposed no action! It seems to be sufficient for the Council that the public recognize that the wage increases are excessive and damaging. The President has added that it is his intention to "draw public attention to major actions by either business or labor that flout the public interest in non-inflationary price and wage standards."

It is up to the public, evidently, to figure out what it should do. The

Council is not about to tackle this thorny problem. One thing the public might do is to tell the Council to tell the Secretary of Labor to stop raising the minimum wage rates he sets under the powers vested in him by the Walsh-Healy and Davis-Bacon Acts. In 1964, he raised a great many rates. Most of these he raised by much more than 2.5 per cent— usually by 5 per cent or more. Most of these rates were excessive before he raised them. According to the Council's guide posts, they should not have been raised at all. He raised rates in one case to $6.10 an hour, surely a clear instance in which the advice of the Economic Advisors would have been not to raise such a high minimum wage rate.

Since the Secretary of Labor has surely read the Council's report, however, I would advise the public to forget about asking the Council to speak to the Secretary of Labor. Instead, the public should speak to its Congressmen about repealing the Walsh-Healy and the Davis-Bacon Acts. These are pernicious Acts which, on the one hand, increase costs to the government and increase our taxes, and, on the other hand, prevent people from getting jobs who would like to have them.

Additional steps I would suggest to make the Council's advice effective is to reduce the power of labor unions. The public should insist on enforcement of laws during strikes. Assaulting and threatening people on their way to work is against the law in any jurisdiction about which I know.

Still another step I would suggest is the repeal of the increases which have occurred in the minimum wage rate set by the Fair Labor Standards Act. On September 3, 1965, there was an increase in the minimum wage from $1.15 to $1.25 an hour for a large group of employees, in addition to the group whose minimum wage was raised to $1.25 in September 1963. This will be and was an increase of 8.7 per cent in the wage rate of the very groups now suffering the greatest incidence of unemployment. It comes on top of a 15 per cent increase made two years ago. Not only is this a much greater increase than the 3.2 per cent rate of rise suggested by the Council—it is an increase for a group of people *who cannot now find jobs*. The Council has said "wage rate increases [should] fall short of the general guide rate (in occupations) which cannot provide jobs for their [entire] labor force."[10] The greatest unemployment we have is among the less educated, less skilled, low productivity, low wage groups. Teen-age unemployment amounts to 13 per cent, and Negro unemployment is 9 per cent. The Council's advice points strongly to the inadvisability of any wage rise in this group, much less an 8.7 per cent increase.

Certainly, this is not a time to enact still higher minimum wage rates. Yet, a bill is now before Congress which would increase rates from $1.25

to $1.60 and extend coverage to seven million additional jobs. When this passes we will doubtless find the number of applicants for the Job Corps skyrocketing.

We have seen the damage done by previous increases in the minimum wage rates. Newspapers a few months ago reported 1,800 women discharged in crab meat packing plants in North Carolina because of the increase in the minimum from $1.15 to $1.25 which went into effect last September. When the rate was increased from 75 cents to $1.00 in 1956, unemployment among workers under nineteen and females over forty-five rose, despite an increase in total employment by 1.8 million in 1956 over the levels prevailing in 1955, and a decline in unemployment in all other groups. Normally, increasing employment decreases unemployment in all groups.[11] It failed to do so in 1956 because of the overpricing of less skilled workers.

I remember vividly a dramatic example of the effect of the increase in the 1956 minimum wage. I visited friends in Nashville late in 1956 and remarked on the fact that they had acquired a maid since my previous visit in 1955. They told me that they had hired a Negro girl because the wage rate of maids had dropped, and they had to pay only 50 cents an hour. I expressed my astonishment and asked what had happened. They told me that local textile mills had been hiring girls at 80 cents an hour in 1955. When the minimum wage rate went up to $1.00 an hour in 1956, many of the mills reduced their work force and were no longer hiring Negro girls.[12]

Similar results occurred in 1950 when the minimum wage rate was raised from 40 cents to 75 cents an hour. Professor John Peterson of the University of Arkansas found, from surveys of large southern pine saw mills before and after the imposition of the 75 cent minimum wage in January 1950, that 17 per cent of the workers in mills whose average wage had been below the minimum lost their jobs.[13] Again, when the Fair Labor Standards Act came into operation in October 1938, workers in the seamless hosiery industry in Western Pennsylvania suffered unemployment. The imposition of a minimum wage rate of 25 cents an hour at that time caused layoffs and a drop in employment in Western Pennsylvania at the very time when employment in the United States was rising.

In addition to the actual unemployment caused by increased minimum wage rates, there is also a decrease in the opportunities for youngsters to obtain training which prepares them for productive employment. To put this in terms of a specific example, an automobile parts jobber testified: "We had always had a training program for new employees which in itself is expensive, and when the minimum wage was increased, we had to discontinue this training program and hire only people as we needed them on a productivity basis. In other words, the average number of employees that we now have is about 5 per cent lower than before the minimum wage was increased."

I could go on giving illustrations of the unemployment caused by minimum wage laws and their effects on freedom of choice among occupations, but this should be sufficient to convey the point. Instead, let me turn to another kind of minimum wage imposition and its effect.

We are very concerned in Chicago about the large number of adolescents who drop out of high school and are unable to find jobs. The problem manifests itself in part in high juvenile delinquency rates. These boys would like to engage in some kind of activity, preferably filling a job. Many of them used to be employed as elevator operators at $1.00 to $1.25 an hour. The elevator operators union has succeeded in imposing a minimum wage of $2.50 an hour for operators in downtown Chicago buildings. The result is that owners of buildings have found it economical to spend $30,000 per elevator to automate their lifts and make them self-operating. Since the tax, insurance, depreciation, and interest costs of automating an elevator amount to $8,000 per year, it did not pay to automate when two shifts of operators cost only $5,000 per year. The union has succeeded in driving the two-shift cost of operation to over $10,000 per year. The result is elevator automation, no jobs for elevator operators, and a policing problem of unskilled teen-agers which is getting out of hand. I think this example speaks for itself. Thirteen per cent of the teen-agers who would like to have jobs cannot find them because of the minimum wage rates set by the unions, by the Secretary of Labor, and by law.

Perhaps I should quote the words of a U.S. Senate report at this point, "The conditions of insecurity and hopelessness that characterize the lives of many unemployed young people threaten their acceptance of traditional American ideals. What they need and cannot find is jobs. Given jobs, many of them will make a successful transition into the adult world and a useful contribution to the nation's strength. Without jobs, continuing moral degeneration is inevitable."

The power of unions to prevent people from taking jobs they would like to have is a major factor in causing some people to suffer the circumstances described in this Senate report. Perhaps it is an anticlimax to add that the power concentration in union hands is also a major factor in causing some wage rates to rise much more rapidly than the Council of Economic Advisors' guide lines would allow. Yet the Council has made no suggestion for limiting concentrations of power. It simply offers some meaningless rhetoric about the necessity for having an informed public opinion as a way of enforcing its suggestions.

There is quite a list of actions the Council could have suggested which would make its words meaningful. The fact that its words are not is demonstrated by a series of wage rate increases which have occurred since their guide posts were suggested—wage rate increases exceeding 3.2 or even 4 per cent. The New York electricians' increase is a notorious instance. Typographers on New York newspapers struck for a 26 per cent increase in compensation, surely an amount far in excess of 3.2 per cent. Longshoremen were granted an 8 per cent increase as a result of the pressures exerted by the Federal government during a strike. The Teamsters negotiated a contract providing a 5 per cent annual increase just a year ago. In the first six months of this year, the average wage increase in new settlements amounted to 4 per cent, exclusive of increases in fringe benefits. One-third of the workers covered by new settlements received increases of 5 per cent or more. The agreement negotiated last fall between the Communication Workers and the Michigan Bell Telephone Company provided a 5 per cent increase in wage rates and fringe benefits. The U.A.W. won a 4.9 per cent annual increase for each of three years in 1964. This is 50 per cent higher than the guide line.

The Council's guide lines for wage setting are meaningless in terms of informing the public, providing a guide for employer-union bargaining, or for guiding employers who have no union with which to contend. Certainly, no one has paid much attention to the Council's guide posts, except where unions have used them as an argument for getting a bigger wage increase than they might otherwise be able to justify. However, they are meaningless for very good reasons other than the fact that no one uses them.

First, the increase in average output per man-hour is highly variable year to year. The overall trend of several past years has no necessary relationship to the change in any one year. If one examines productivity changes from year to year, it is clear that average output per man-hour decreased between 1920 and 1921, increased between 1923 and 1924, decreased between 1926 and 1928, decreased again between 1929 and 1933, etc. This is highly variable behavior. Any constant rate of increase even in real wage rates, much less money wage rates, would result in unemployment in some years, shortages of labor in other years, and allocation of much labor to the wrong places every year.

Aside from the fact that past output-per-hour trends do not provide a guide for *real*-wage rate changes in a specific year, they are of no help at all in judging proper changes in *money* wage rates. Money rates fell from 56 cents an hour in 1920 to 52 cents an hour in 1921—a 7 per cent decrease—yet real wage rates went up 4 per cent because of an even greater decline in consumer prices. If money wage rates had been increased 3 per cent between 1920 and 1921, we would have had a 14 per cent rise in real wage rates and 10 million unemployed instead of 5 million in 1921.

The Council pays little attention to the possibility that real wage rates may increase through a declining level of product prices as well as by a rising level of money wage rates. In view of our balance of payments problems at this time, this should be the preferred method of raising real wage rates.

If we are going to engage in the sport of setting guide posts for wage increases, I would like to enter a candidate. I would like to suggest my guide post in the form of an answer to the question, "How can employers recognize the circumstances which dictate a change in the wage level or wage structure?" Of course, any time a company's profits fall or it incurs a loss, it would like to decrease its wage costs. In some cases, this may be the proper action to take; but, in other cases, a decrease in wage rates may increase costs or may cause the company to lose even more.

On the other hand, when profits increase, as they did for General Motors last year, for example, should wage rates be raised? Again this may or may not be the proper action. It depends upon the circumstances. How can we tell what to do, then, if the proper action is not directly related to profitability?

The best single guide to the proper action is the relationship of the quit rate of currently employed persons to the rate of receipt of qualified applications for jobs. If the quit rate in a given company exceeds the qualified-applicant rate, the wage rate may be too low. People do not ordinarily quit jobs in appreciable numbers unless alternative jobs are available which are more attractive than those they are leaving. If the quit rate is high, we would probably find that better paying jobs, or jobs more attractive for some other reason, are available. A low qualified-applicant rate also indicates this sort of situation. Retaining a work force, then, may require an increase in the level of wage rates.

Now, one may notice that my suggested guide line is in the form of advice to employers. I am not interested in getting the public into the act, nor in getting government into the act. The only people in the act should be those who are employing men, and the men who would like to have the jobs. This is true for the determination of overtime rates as well as straight time wage rates. We should not impose penalty rates by law on employers for employing men over forty hours a week. If men desire additional income, wish to work more than forty hours per week, and are willing to do so for rates less than those required by the Fair Labor Standards Act, that should be their privilege as free men.

Further, one may notice that my advice to management is hardly necessary. It simply says, pay as much as you must to obtain the labor force you require; but do not pay any more than you must. Any company not trying to do this is not a business—it is a philanthropic operation. How long it can survive depends only on how long it can go on giving money away, or rather, how long the stockholders are willing to hold stock in a company giving away their money. Also, any company paying higher wage rates than it *must* to attract the work force it wants, and keep turnover rates as low as is profitable, is not serving the public well. It is providing fewer jobs than men would like to have and less product than its customers would like to have. If employers will follow their own interests by raising wage rates only when their quit rates go up (or threaten to do so), they will be serving the economy in general as well as their own interests.

In advising that quit rates should be the primary indicator in determining the appropriateness of a wage change, all I have really said is that wage rates should be set at the levels at which free markets would set wage rates. Perhaps this might be better said by using a quotation from Henry Simons. He pointed out that

The proper wage in any area or occupational category is . . . the wage that will permit the maximum transfer of workers from less attractive, less remunerative, less productive employments. . . . We imply that any wage is excessive if more qualified workers are obtainable at that wage than are employed—provided only that the industry is reasonably competitive as among firms. Reduction of rates (in these circumstances) would permit workers to enter who otherwise would be compelled to accept employment less attractive to them and less productive for the community or to accept involuntary unemployment. . . .

*   The basic principle here is the freedom of entry—freedom of migration, between localities, between industries, between occupational categories. If such freedom is to exist . . . wages must fall to accommodate new workers in any area to which many qualified persons wish to move. Freedom of migration implies freedom of qualified workers, not merely to seek jobs but to get them; free entry implies full employment for all qualified persons who wish to enter. Whether the wage permits an adequate family scale of living, according to social service workers, is simply*

irrelevant ... what really matters is the judgment of workers who would be excluded by an excessive wage as to the relative merits of the employment in question and of employment in less attractive alternatives actually open to them. Other things equal, the wage is too high if higher than the wage in actually alternative employments. Ethically, one cannot go beyond the opinion of qualified workers seeking to transfer. If in large numbers they prefer employment here to the alternatives and cannot get it, the wage is excessive.[14]

I should add that the Council of Economic Advisors itself believes this, although it tries to avoid saying so. The Council does not think much of its own guide posts and prefers the one suggested here, as I will demonstrate shortly.

What is frightening about the Council's discussion of guide lines for the economy is the implication that they know how to make wage decisions and price decisions which are in the public interest. Some idiot is likely to take this seriously and set up a regulatory agency to set wage rates and prices. It is not a long step from setting guide lines for the economy to guiding the economy. Down that road lies tyranny.

That the possibility is real is evidenced by the appointment two years ago of a member of the Council who believes the government should set up an Industry Economics Agency which would set specific prices and wage rates—not just generalized national guide lines—and which would hold corporations over a certain size and unions to "new standards of public accountability." The Council has not yet gone this far, but there is talk about a so-called early warning group to watch for price and wage changes which do not conform to the guide lines.

The Council of four years ago did not even take its own rule for wage setting in terms of change in output per man-hour seriously. After offering its general rule it said, "wage rate increases would exceed the general guide rate in an industry which would otherwise be unable to attract sufficient labor."[15] This, of course, is what any employer does when he finds he cannot obtain as many employees as he wishes. He bids a higher wage to attract more people, frequently bidding substantial premiums above even union-set wage rates when he cannot find enough men. Also, the Council said, "wage rate increases would fall short of the general guide rate in an industry which could not provide jobs for its entire labor force."[16] This, of course, usually occurs in markets where there are large numbers of unemployed men—and no legal minima, or union power to prevent this. What the Council has said in these statements is that supply and demand in free markets should determine wage rates.

I am heartily in favor of those measures and those laws which maximize wage income and minimize inequality. If the labor legislation which I have discussed, and the guide lines proposed for determining changes in wage rates were good for labor as a whole, that would be the end of the matter for me. I question the virtue of these measures because they decrease labor income, limit the opportunity to obtain jobs and to engage in meaningful activity, and increase inequality.

Notes

Professor Yale Brozen is one of the most distinguished members of the Chicago school of economics. His articles have appeared in *The Journal of Law and Economics, The American Economic Review, Econometrica, Land Economics, Ethics, Social Research, Il Politico, Political Science Quarterly, Revista Brasileira de Economia, Saturday Review, Barron's, New Individualist Review, The Intercollegiate Review, The Freeman, Reason,* etc. He is professor of business economics at the Graduate School of Business, The University of Chicago.

"Wage Rates, Minimum Wage Laws, and Unemployment" is reprinted with permission from the *New Individualist Review* (Spring 1966), vol. 4, no. 3.

1. "Annual Report of the Council of Economic Advisors," *Economic Report of the President* (Washington: Government Printing Office, 1962), p. 185.

2. "Annual Report of the Council of Economic Advisors," *Economic Report of the President* (Washington: Government Printing Office, 1965), p. 108. This same advice appeared first in the 1962 report where the Advisors said, "The general guide for non-inflationary wage behavior is that the rate of increase in wage rates (including fringe benefits) in each industry be equal to the trend rate of over-all productivity increase." (p. 189)

3. "Annual Report of the Council of Economic Advisors," *Economic Report of the President* (Washington: Government Printing office, 1962), p. 189.

4. *Ibid.*

5. *Ibid.*

6. *Ibid.*, p. 175.

7. For the data on which this estimate is based, see H.G. Lewis, *Unionism and Relative Wages in the United States* (Chicago: University of Chicago Press, 1963), pp. 8–9, 286–95.

8. S.P. Sobotka, "Michigan's Employment Problem: The Substitution Against Labor," *Journal of Business*, XXXIV (1961), 124. For a fuller

treatment of the subject see S.P. Sobotka, *Profile of Michigan* (New York: Free Press of Glencoe, 1963).

9. "Annual Report of the Council of Economic Advisors," *Economic Report of the President* (Washington: Government Printing Office, 1962), p. 185.

10. *Ibid.,* p. 189.

11. *Ibid.,* p. 232.

12. Y. Brozen, "Minimum Wage Rates and Household Workers," *Journal of Law and Economics*, V (1962), 103–9.

13. J.M. Peterson, "Employment Effects of Minimum Wages, 1938–50," *Journal of Political Economy*, LXV (1957), 419.

14. H.C. Simons, "Some Reflections on Syndicalism," *Economic Policy for a Free Society* (Chicago: University of Chicago Press, 1948), pp. 140–41.

15. "Annual Report of the Council of Economic Advisors," *Economic Report of the President* (Washington: Government Printing Office, 1962), p. 189.

16. *Ibid.*

part six

The
Free Society:
Studies

The studies below focus on some of the issues people today believe to be in some way related to government, law, and public policy. Surely the topics of race, education, advertising, conscription, and ecology are foremost in people's minds—or, at least are foremost on their lips. (The latter, of course, denotes hypocrisy.)

When a culture acquires the statist atmosphere, its individuals begin to believe what the common dogma asserts, namely, that they are impotent to cope with their problems and only the state can. Not quite willing and/or able to recognize that states are people as well, many people accept this belief of impotence. A need, however, to address themselves to the problems verbally seems to be felt by most people. Thus talk shows, panels, commissions, study groups, rap sessions, associations, and rallies abound, all involved in virtually idle talk; the result usually amounts to no more than the resolution to go to government with a problem, never to undertake its solution. Thus, only lip service—that is, the utterance of words and sentences *believed to be appropriate* but certainly not fully understood—is paid to issues. And, as the old saying goes, talk is cheap. It is cheap if we aren't considering where it leads. For such idle talk usually costs a good deal to the taxpayer when he is forced to support not only the attempted political (non)solution of problems, but the *study* of the failure and corruption associated with most of the political problem-solving efforts.

The immense cultural impotence which statism creates cannot be measured comparatively—other societies are in deeper trouble, on the whole, than is the United States. What is necessary is a conceptualization of the possible. This is a rational endeavor, not fit for visionary speculation, science fiction, or religious prophesy. And without it, there is simply no other avenue toward improvement. That the dominant thinking is comparative, at best, and dogmatically statist may be seen by the fact that the idea of statism is never even seriously examined. Must the post office be run by government? Must schools and bus lines be run by the government? And this failure of perception is right in the face of massive flops on all fronts. Medicare, urban renewal, integration, Head Start, Job Corps, VISTA, etc. Despite the occasional challenges from within statist (liberal, ADA democrat) circles as well as from conservative, radical left, and counterculture elements, the established bureaucracy is so well entrenched, the challenges are so unsystematic that serious change is unlikely. One can only hope that by applying intellectual pressure on all fronts a gradual erosion of statism will come about.

The present chapter offers an example of a systematic approach to problems, pointing out areas where government may be of use and showing where people alone, in free associations, can make headway. And clearly, it is better to have unsolved problems than to have problems which are unsolved but appear solved, as is the case with the problems handled by governments acting outside its proper jurisdiction.

Anne Wortham

28 Individualism versus Racism

THE DECLARATION OF INDEPENDENCE of July 4, 1776, laid the foundation for a new society among men on grounds that each individual of right ought to be free to act on his own judgment, for his own goals, by his own choice. Human dignity, in other words, involves self-responsibility for life, liberty, and one's pursuit of happiness.

That essence of the Declaration of Independence is being subordinated and forgotten by today's black and white leaders of the Negro Revolution whose banner is "equality."

Let us recall what Abraham Lincoln said about this: "I protest against that counterfeit logic which concludes that because I do not want a black woman for a *slave*, I must necessarily want her for a *wife*. I need not have her for either; I can just leave her alone. In some respects she certainly is not my equal; but in her natural right to eat the bread she earns with her own hands without asking leave of anyone else, she is my equal, and equal to all others."

There can be no greater condition of equality among men than this. Anything less than this is slavery; and the direction in which the American people today are being led by civil rights leaders, in and out of government, tends toward slavery. A free man is not something emerged from a stew called society. The nature of a man's thoughts and actions, the life he lives, his concept of himself are the qualities of being human—the qualities of individuality, rather than the gray sameness of imposed equality.

The Constitution of the United States was designed to protect the rights of the individual against trespass by other individuals, or by government. But the original code made no provision for the abolition of slavery or recognition of the Negro as an individual. Section 9 of Article I denied to Congress power to prohibit the importation of slaves prior to 1808, and Section 2 of Article IV required the states to comply with the claims of lawful owners for the return of fugitive slaves. Based in part upon these provisions, the United States Supreme Court ruled in 1857 that Dred Scott—a Negro slave—did not acquire the rights of citizenship when taken into a free state.

A Civil War was waged before the Thirteenth Amendment cleared the Constitution of a serious contradiction and established that, if men are to live as men, they must be free to do so. The Reconstruction Era further clarified the extent to which *states' rights* could be practiced without interfering with the individual's *human rights* and without denying his *civil rights*. While these rights had been defined before, they had not been extended to Negroes.

The Constitution, as supplemented by the Bill of Rights and subsequent amendments, makes clear that the powers of the state governments as well as of the Federal government extend no further than needed for protection of the human and civil rights of the individual against encroachment by government and other individuals. Neither mentioned nor recognized are any "rights of society," society having no rights. By 1875, all questions concerning citizenship for Negroes in the United States, and their rights as individuals, were answered in the Constitution.

Solving the Problem Voluntarily

During the last quarter of the nineteenth century, the question before the people—all citizens, with inalienable rights as members of the human race—was this: How are we to live together? "In all things purely social we can be as separate as fingers, yet one as the hand in all things essential to mutual progress," answered Negro leader, Booker T. Washington in 1895. The national concensus at the close of the nineteenth century was that black and white men should live separately; but such concensus did not empower governments to legislate how men should live or where each must sit, eat, dance, learn, and otherwise lead his life.

Nevertheless, the United States Supreme Court's separate-but-equal doctrine of 1896 had stood as law until 1954, when the Court reversed itself to the effect that henceforth men must live, sit, eat, dance, and learn in the same places. But the compulsory integration of the schools was no more required by the Constitution nor necessary for fulfillment of the human rights and civil rights of Negroes than had been the compulsory separation before 1954. Education is no more the business of the Federal government than is eating or dancing or the seating arrangement on a train or bus.

The Negro role in the civil rights movement gained impetus after the Supreme Court decision in 1954, and their main thrust was to the effect that Negroes had been deprived of their rights as a group. Scarcely anyone bothered to ask what rights inhere in groups or to stand in defense of the rights of the individual. It seems safe to say there were few individuals, if any, among the 210,000 marchers on Washington on August 28, 1963; and the net effect was a Congress and a nation made more race conscious than ever before. The resultant Civil Rights Act of 1964 elevated the dubious principles of altruism, collectivism, and racism above life, liberty, and the pursuit of happiness.

A Staggering Sense of Guilt

The brotherhood of selfless love espoused by Martin Luther King, Jr., has not left a situation of mutual respect among Negroes and whites but a nation staggered by a sense of guilt. Irresponsible leadership in the name of civil rights is conning a nation out of its incentives to productivity into sanctioning the undeserved, causing the freest people on earth to sacrifice that freedom for the compulsory equality of slaves.

Civil rights leaders and their followers stress self-sacrifice to the point that self-respect is made to seem a sin. To love and choose without discrimination displaces sound reasons among men to love or choose one person or thing above another. This strained and strange love of racist agitators provokes men to hate them more. They turn simple prejudices into acts of crazed violence—that they might passively endure and resist. They twist man's right to discriminate into an immorality, thrown at a nation as its major guilt. As virtuous victims, they demand freedom, equality, and respect for the pitiable little they have to offer, challenging the nation to redeem itself by redeeming them.

How goes the redemption? Look in the eyes of blacks and whites who are afraid to think, to judge, to discriminate, and you will see an uncertainty embedded in hatred. Negroes, who are told they have gained the respect and gratitude of society but who have no self-esteem, are frightened by a power of redemption which they secretly know they —as individuals—have not earned.

No rational, self-responsible individual relies upon the racism that plagues the nation. He does not beg for patronage, sympathy, and smiles. Instead of asking that others grant him a living, he knows he has been born with an inalienable right to whatever life he is capable of earning, according to his own purpose, his own virtues, which others cannot give to him and cannot take away.

Student Demonstrations

It was inevitable that the youthful students of America would be drawn by their immaturity into the fight for civil rights. From the beginning of the collective movement, climaxed by the March on Washington, the racism of the nation was reflected by the young and selfless black and white youth of America.

White youths, in all sincerity, wanted to share the plight of their Negro counterparts. They had no "cause," so they made his cause their own. They evaded the real issue—that they did not know themselves—and transformed this ignorance into a feeling of guilt for being different from the Negro. In search of virtue, they marched and shouted, "Freedom Now," clenching a Negro's hand, entering restaurants with him where they knew he would not be served, scouting the countryside singing songs of deliverance for him.

Young Negroes joined their white counterparts, believing that any happiness to be achieved on earth must be achieved collectively; they had never been allowed to forget the collective misery of their fore-fathers. Lacking the individuality that can only come through earned self-esteem, they were content with the motives of the group. Personal motives? None.

Among black and white youth alike, their relationship with the group was primary when it should have been secondary. They hid behind the apron of a race, a church, a university, an SNCC, a CORE; and they claimed identities according to the characteristics of such groups. They repeated to themselves what others said of them; their self-regard was the regard they thought others had for them; their self-esteem dependent upon the esteem of others; their achievements what others claimed to be achievements; their failures what others said were failures; their place in the world where others said it was. They had no standards of their own; and so these youths were misled. Their guilt was not in being *black* or *white*, but in being nothing, in seeking virtue in the impossible, encouraging one another simply to suffer and wave flags.

The fact is that within the context of our society, they will always be black or white; and by some persons they will be treated as such, regardless of laws, treaties, and proclamations to the contrary. But a more important truth that escaped those young persons is that they are human beings; that each has a life for which he is responsible; that this is what he holds in common with other human beings; that to live with one another in peace, each must first manage to live with himself.

Such were the "drummer boys" of America who led forth a nation, their elders following, in the revolutionary movement capped by the signing of the Civil Rights Act on July 2, 1962. This new law of the land deals with eleven basic aspects of what the nation's legislators call civil rights: voting, public accommodations, public (governmentally managed) facilities, school desegregation, the Federal Civil Rights Commission, nondiscriminatory use of Federal funds, equal employment opportunity, voting census, a Federal Community Relations Service, civil rights court procedures, and jury trials.

A careful study of the detailed provisions of these 11 titles under the Act may reveal some minor clarifications of points already covered by the Constitution and existing legislation, as in Title 1 on Voting and Title 10 on Court Procedures. But these are hardly what the civil rights revolution was all about. For the most part, the major provisions of the new Act tend to arrogate powers to the Federal government, in the name of Civil Rights, that are none of the government's business because they have to do with regulation and control of what ought to be strictly private business relationships.

The overwhelming tendency of the Act is to deny the civil rights of producers—property owners—in favor of the wishes of those seeking something for nothing, making the Federal government the instrument of compulsion for the implementation of such injustice. Thus, the attempt to appease organized racists has invoked a condition of legislative enslavement on the entire nation—and it will take a police state to enforce this condition.

Note

Anne Wortham is a graduate of Tuskegee Institute who served in the Peace Corps and is now in communications and economic research. Ms. Wortham has written several articles in the field of economics and social studies.

Milton Friedman

29 Is a Free Society Stable?

THERE IS A STRONG tendency for all of us to regard what is as if it were the "natural" or "normal" state of affairs, to lack perspective because of the tyranny of the status quo. It is, therefore, well, from time to time, to make a deliberate effort to look at things in a broader context. In such a context anything approaching a free society is an exceedingly rare event. Only during short intervals in man's recorded history has there been anything approaching what we would call a free society in existence over any appreciable part of the globe. And even during such intervals, as at the moment, the greater part of mankind has lived under regimes that could by no stretch of the imagination be called free.

This casual empirical observation raises the question whether a free society may not be a system in unstable equilibrium. If one were to take a purely historical point of view, one would have to say that the "normal," in the sense of average, state of mankind is a state of tyranny and despotism. Perhaps this is the equilibrium state of society that tends to arise in the relation of man to his fellows. Perhaps highly special circumstances must exist to render a free society possible. And perhaps these special circumstances, the existence of which account for the rare episodes of freedom, are themselves by their nature transitory, so that the kind of society all of us believe in is highly unlikely to be maintained, even if once attained.

This problem has, of course, been extensively discussed in the literature. In his great book, *Lectures on Law and Public Opinion in the Nineteenth Century*, written at the end of the nineteenth century, A. V. Dicey discusses a very similar question. How was it, he asks, that toward the end of the nineteenth century there seemed to be a shift in English public opinion away from the doctrine of liberalism and toward collectivism, even though just prior to the shift, individualism and *laisser-faire* were at something like their high tide, seemed to have captured English public opinion, and seemed to be producing the results that their proponents had promised in the form of an expansion of economic activity, a rise in the standard of life, and the like?

As you may recall, Dicey dates the change in public opinion in Britain away from individualism and toward collectivism at about 1870–90. Dicey answers his question by essentially reversing it, saying that in its original form, it may be a foolish question. Perhaps the relevant question is not why people turned away from individualism toward collectivism, but how they were induced to accept the queer notion of individualism in the first place. The argument for a free society, he goes on to say, is a very subtle and sophisticated argument. At every point, it depends on the indirect rather than the direct effect of the policy followed. If one is concerned to remedy clear evils in a society, as everyone is, the natural reaction is to say, "let's do something about it," and the "us" in this statement will in a large number of cases be translated into the "government," so the natural reaction is to pass a law. The argument that maybe the attempt to correct this particular evil by extending the hand of the government will have indirect effects whose aggregate consequences may be far worse than any direct benefits that flow from the action taken is, after all, a rather sophisticated argument. And yet, this is the kind of argument that underlies a belief in a free or *laisser-faire* society.

If you look at each evil as it arises, in and of itself, there will almost always tend to be strong pressures to do something about it. This will be so because the direct effects are clear and obvious while the indirect effects are remote and devious and because there tends to be a concentrated group of people who have strong interests in favor of a particular measure whereas the opponents, like the indirect effects of the measure, are diffused. One can cite example after example along this line. Indeed, I think it is true that most crude fallacies about economic policies derive from neglecting the indirect effects of the policies followed.

The tariff is one example. The benefits that are alleged to flow from a tariff are clear and obvious. If a tariff is imposed, a specified group of people, whose names can almost be listed, seem to be benefited in the first instance. The harm that is wrought by the tariff is borne by people whose names one does not know and who are unlikely themselves to know that they are or will be harmed. The tariff does most harm to people who have special capacities for producing the exports that would pay for the goods that would be imported in the absence of a tariff. With a tariff in effect, the potential export industry may never exist and no one will ever know that he might have been employed in it or who would have been. The indirect harm to consumers via a more inefficient allocation of resources and higher prices for the resulting products are spread even more thinly through the society. Thus the case for a tariff seems quite clear on first glance. And this is true in case after case.

This natural tendency to engage in state action in specific instances can, it would seem, and this is Dicey's argument, be offset only by a widespread general acceptance of a philosophy of non-interference, by a general presumption against undertaking any one of a large class of actions. And, says Dicey, what is really amazing and surprising is that for so long a period as a few decades, sufficiently widespread public opinion developed in Britain in favor of the general principle of non-intervention and *laisser-faire* as to overcome the natural tendency to pass a law for the particular cases. As soon as this general presumption weakened, it meant the emergence of a climate of opinion in favor of specific government intervention.

Dicey's argument is enormously strengthened by an asymmetry between a shift toward individualism and a shift away from it. In the first place, there is what I have called the tyranny of the status quo. Anyone who wants to see how strong that tyranny is can do no better, I believe, than to read Dicey's book now. On reading it, he will discover how extreme and extensive a collectivist he is, as judged by the kinds of standards for governmental action that seemed obvious and appropriate to Dicey when he wrote his lectures. In discussing issues of this kind, the tendency always is to take *what is* for granted, to assume that it is perfectly all right and reasonable, and that the problem to argue about is the next step. This tends to mean that movements in any one direction are difficult to reverse. A second source of asymmetry is the general dilemma that faces the liberal—tolerance of the intolerant. The belief in individualism includes the belief in tolerating the intolerant. It includes the belief that the society is only worth defending if it is one in which we resort to persuasion rather than to force and in which we defend freedom of discussion on the part of those who would undermine the system itself. If one departs from a free society, the people in power in a collectivist society will not hesitate to use force to keep it from being changed. Under such circumstances, it is more difficult to achieve a revolution that would convert a totalitarian or collectivist society into an individualist society than it is to do the reverse. From the point of view of the forces that may work in the direction of rendering a free society an unstable system, this is certainly one of the most important that strengthens Dicey's general argument.

Perhaps the most famous argument alleging the instability of a free enterprise or capitalist society is the Marxian. Marx argued that there were inherent historical tendencies within a capitalist society that would tend to lead to its destruction. As you know, he predicted that as it developed, capitalism would produce a division of society into sharp classes, the impoverishment of the masses, the despoilment of the middle classes, and a declining rate of profit. He predicted that the combined result would be a class struggle in which the class of the "expropriated" or the proletarian class would assume power.

Marx's analysis is at least in part to be regarded as a scientific analysis attempting to derive hypotheses that could be used to predict consequences that were likely to occur. His predictions have uniformly been wrong; none of the major consequences that he predicted has in fact occurred. Instead of a widening split among classes, there has tended to be a reduction of class barriers. Instead of a despoilment of the middle class, there has tended to be, if anything, an increase in the middle class relative to the extremes. Instead of the impoverishment of the masses, there has been the largest rise in the standard of life of the masses that history has ever seen. We must therefore reject his theory as having been disproved.

The lack of validity of Marx's theory does not mean that it has been unimportant. It had the enormous importance of leading many, if not a majority, of the intellectual and ruling classes to regard tendencies of the kind he predicted as inevitable, thereby leading them to interpret what did go on in different terms than they otherwise would. Perhaps the most striking example has been the extent to which intellectuals, and people in general, have taken it for granted that the development of a capitalist society has meant an increased concentration of industrial power and an increase in the degree of monopoly. Though this view has largely reflected a confusion between changes in absolute size and changes in relative size, in part also, I think, it was produced by the fact that this was something they were told by Marx to look for. I don't mean to attribute this view solely to the Marxian influence. But I think that in this and other instances, the Marxian argument has indirectly affected the patterns of thinking of a great many people including many who would regard themselves as strongly anti-Marxian. Indeed, in many ways, the ideas have been most potent when they have lost their labels. In this way, Marx's ideas had an enormous intellectual importance, even though his scientific analysis and predictions have all been contradicted by experience.

In more recent times, Joseph Schumpeter has offered a more subtle and intellectually more satisfactory defense of essentially the Marxian conclusion. Schumpeter's attitude toward Marx is rather interesting. He demonstrates that Marx was wrong in every separate particular, yet proceeds both to accept the major import of his conclusions and to argue that Marx was a very great man. Whereas Marx's view was that capitalism would destroy itself by its failure, Schumpeter's view was that capitalism would destroy itself by its success. Schumpeter believed that large scale enterprises and monopoly have real advantages in promoting technological progress and growth and that these advantages would give them a competitive edge in the economic struggle. The success of capitalism would therefore, he argued, be associated with a growth of very large enterprises, and with the spread of something like semi-monopoly over the industrial scene. In its turn, he thought that this development would tend to convert businessmen into bureaucrats. Large organizations have much in common whether they are governmental or private. They inevitably, he believed, produced an increasing separation between the ultimate owners of the enterprises and the individuals who were in positions of importance in managing the enterprises. Such individuals are induced to place high values upon technical performance and to become adaptable to a kind of civil-service socialist organization of society. In addition, this process would create the kind of skills in the managerial elite that would be necessary in order to have a collectivist or governmentally controlled society. The development of this bureaucratic elite with its tendency to place greater and greater emphasis on security and stability and to accept centralized control would tend, he believed, to have the effect of establishing a climate of opinion highly favorable to a shift to an explicitly socialized and centralized state.

The view that Schumpeter expressed has much in common with what Burnham labelled a managerial revolution although the two are not by any means the same. There is also much in common between Schumpeter's analysis and the distinction that Veblen drew in his analysis of the price system between the roles of entrepreneurs and engineers, between "business" and "industry." There are also large differences. Veblen saw the engineer as the productive force in the society, the entrepreneur as the destructive force. Schumpeter, if anything, saw matters the other way. He saw the entrepreneur as the creative force in society, and the engineer as simply his handmaiden. But I think there is much in common between the two analyses with respect to the belief that power would tend to shift from the one to the other.

For myself, I must confess that while I find Schumpeter's analysis intriguing and intellectually fascinating, I cannot accept his thesis. It seems to me to reflect in large part a widespread bias that emphasizes the large and few as opposed to the small and numerous, a tendency to see the merits of scale and not to recognize the merits of large numbers of separate people working in diverse activities. In any event, so far as one can judge, there has been no striking tendency in experience toward an increasing concentration of economic activity in large bureaucratic private enterprises. Some enormous enterprises have of course arisen. But there has also been a very rapid growth in small enterprises. What has happened in this country at least is that the large enterprises have tended to be concentrated in communication and manufacturing. These industries have tended to account for a roughly constant proportion of total economic activity. Small enterprises have tended to be concentrated in agriculture and services. Agriculture has declined in importance and in the number of enterprises, while the service industries have grown in both. If one leaves government aside, as Schumpeter's thesis requires one to do, so far as one can judge from the evidence, there seems to have been no particularly consistent tendency for the fraction of economic activity which is carried on in any given percentage of the enterprises to have grown. What has happened is that small enterprises and big enterprises have both grown in scale so what we now call a small enterprise may be large by some earlier standard. However, the thesis that Schumpeter developed is certainly sophisticated and subtle and deserves serious attention.

There is another direction, it seems to me, in which there is a different kind of a tendency for capitalism to undermine itself by its own success. The tendency I have in mind can probably best be brought out by the experience of Great Britain—Great Britain tends to provide the best laboratory for many of these forces. It has to do with the attitude of the public at large toward law and toward law obedience. Britain has a wide and deserved reputation for the extraordinary obedience of its people to the law. It has not always been so. At the turn of the nineteenth century, and earlier, the British had a very different reputation as a nation of people who would obey no law, or almost no law, a nation of smugglers, a nation in which corruption and inefficiency was rife, and in which one could not get very much done through governmental channels.

Indeed, one of the factors that led Bentham and the Utilitarians toward *laisser-faire*, and this is a view that is also expressed by Dicey, was the self-evident truth that if you wanted to get evils corrected, you could not expect to do so through the government of the time. The government was corrupt and inefficient. It was clearly oppressive. It was something that had to be gotten out of the way as a first step to reform. The fundamental philosophy of the Utilitarians, or any philosophy that puts its emphasis on some kind of a sum of utilities, however loose may be the expression, does not lead to *laisser-faire* in principle. It leads to whatever kind of organization of economic activity is thought to produce results which are regarded as good in the sense of adding to the sum total of utilities. I think the major reason why the Utilitarians tended to be in favor of *laisser-faire* was the obvious fact that government was incompetent to perform any of the tasks they wanted to see performed.

Whatever the reason for its appeal, the adoption of *laisser-faire* had some important consequences. Once *laisser-faire* was adopted, the economic incentive for corruption was largely removed. After all, if governmental officials had no favors to grant, there was no need to bribe them. And if there was nothing to be gained from government, it could hardly be a source of corruption. Moreover, the laws that were left were for the most part, and again I am oversimplifying and exaggerating, laws that were widely accepted as proper and desirable; laws against theft, robbery, murder, etc. This is in sharp contrast to a situation in which the legislative structure designates as crimes what people individually do not regard as crimes or makes it illegal for people to do what seems to them the sensible thing. The latter situation tends to reduce respect for the law. One of the unintended and indirect effects of *laisser-faire* was thus to establish a climate in Britain of a much greater degree of obedience and respect for the law than had existed earlier. Probably there were other forces at work in this development but I believe that the establishment of *laisser-faire* laid the groundwork for a reform in the civil service in the latter part of the century—the establishment of a civil service chosen on the basis of examinations and merit and of professional competence. You could get that kind of development because the incentives to seek such places for purposes of exerting "improper" influence were greatly reduced when government had few favors to confer.

In these ways, the development of *laisser-faire* laid the groundwork for a widespread respect for the law, on the one hand, and a relatively **incorrupt, honest, and** efficient civil service on the other, both of which are essential preconditions for the operation of a collectivist society. In order for a collectivist society to operate, the people must obey the laws and there must be a civil service that can and will carry out the laws. The success of capitalism established these preconditions for a movement in the direction of much greater state intervention.

The process I have described obviously runs both ways. A movement in the direction of a collectivist society involves increased governmental intervention into the daily lives of people and the conversion into crimes of actions that are regarded by the ordinary person as entirely proper. These tend in turn to undermine respect for the law and to give incentives to corrupt state officials. There can, I think, be little doubt that this process has begun in Britain and has gone a substantial distance. Although respect for the law may still be greater than it is here, most observers would agree that respect for the law in Britain has gone down decidedly in the course of the last twenty or thirty years, certainly since the war, as a result of the kind of laws people have been asked to obey. On the occasions I have been in England, I have had access to two sources of information that generally yield quite different answers. One is people associated with academic institutions, all of whom are quite shocked at the idea that any British citizen might evade the law—except perhaps for transactions involving exchanging pounds for dollars when exchange control was in effect. It also happens that I had contact with people engaged in small businesses. They tell a rather different story, and one that I suspect comes closer to being valid, about the extent to which regulations were honored in the breach, and taxes and customs regulations evaded—the one thing that is uniform among people or almost uniform is that nobody or almost nobody has any moral repugnance to smuggling, and certainly not when he is smuggling something into some country other than his own.

The erosion of the capital stock of willingness to obey the law reduces the capacity of a society to run a centralized state, to move away from freedom. This effect on law obedience is thus one that is reversible and runs in both directions. It is another major factor that needs to be taken into account in judging the likely stability of a free system in the long run.

I have been emphasizing forces and approaches that are mostly pessimistic in terms of our values in the sense that most of them are reasons why a free society is likely to be unstable and to change into a collectivist system. I should like therefore to turn to some of the tendencies that may operate in the other direction.

What are the sources of strength for a free society that may help to maintain it? One of the major sources of strength is the tendency for extension of economic intervention in a wide range of areas to interfere directly and clearly with political liberty and thus to make people aware of the conflict between the two. This has been the course of events in Great Britain after the war and in many other countries. I need not repeat or dwell on this point.

A second source of strength is one that has already been suggested by my comments on law obedience. In many ways, perhaps the major hope for a free society is precisely that feature in a free society which makes it so efficient and productive in its economic activity; namely, the ingenuity of millions of people, each of whom is trying to further his own interest, in part by finding ways to get around state regulation. If I may refer to my own casual observation of Britain and France a few years after the war, the impression that I formed on the basis of very little evidence but that seemed to me to be supported by further examination was that Britain at the time was being economically strangled by the law obedience of her citizens while France was being saved by the existence of the black market. The price system is a most effective and efficient system for organizing resources. So long as people try to make it operate, it can surmount a lot of problems. There is a famous story about the man who wrote a letter to Adam Smith, saying that some policy or other was going to be the ruin of England. And Adam Smith, as I understand the story, wrote back and said, "Young man, there is a lot of ruin in a nation."

This seems to me an important point. Once government embarks on intervention into and regulation of private activities, this establishes an incentive for large numbers of individuals to use their ingenuity to find ways to get around the government regulations. One result is that there appears to be a lot more regulation than there really is. Another is that the time and energy of government officials is increasingly taken up with the need to plug the holes in the regulations that the citizens are finding, creating, and exploiting. From this point of view, Parkinson's law about the growth of bureaucracy without a corresponding growth of output may be a favorable feature for the maintenance of a free society. An efficient governmental organization and not an inefficient one is almost surely the greater threat to a free society. One of the virtues of a free society is precisely that the market tends to be a more efficient organizing principle than centralized direction. Centralized direction in this way is always having to fight something of a losing battle.

Very closely related to this point and perhaps only another aspect of it is the difference between the "visibility" of monopolistic action whether governmental or private and of actions through the market.

When people are acting through the market, millions of people are engaging in activities in a variety of ways that are highly impersonal, not very well recognized, and almost none of which attracts attention. On the other hand, governmental actions, and this is equally true of actions by private monopolies, whether of labor or industry, tend to be conducted by persons who get into the headlines, to attract notice. I have often conducted the experiment of asking people to list the major industries in the United States. In many ways, the question is a foolish one because there is no clear definition of industry. Yet people have some concept of industry and the interesting thing is that the result is always very similar. People always list those industries in which there is a high degree of concentration. They list the automobile industry, never the garment industry, although the garment industry is far larger by any economic measure than the automobile industry. I have never had anybody list the industry of providing domestic service although it employs many more people than the steel industry. Estimates of importance are always biased in the direction of those industries that are monopolized or concentrated and so are in the hands of few firms. Everybody knows the names of the leading producers of automobiles. Few could list the leading producers of men's and women's clothing, or of furniture, although these are both very large industries. So competition, working through the market, precisely because it is impersonal, anonymous, and works its way in devious channels, tends to be underestimated in importance, and the kinds of personal activities that are associated with government, with monopoly, with trade unions, tend to be exaggerated in importance.

Because this kind of direct personal activity by large organizations, whether it be governmental or private, is visible, it tends to call attention to itself out of all proportion to its economic importance. The result is that the community tends to be awakened to the dangers arising from such activities and such concentration of power before they become so important that it is too late to do anything about them. This phenomenon is very clear for trade unions. Everybody has been reading in the newspapers about the negotiations in steel and knows that there is a labor problem in the steel industry. The negotiations usually terminate in some kind of wage increase that is regarded as attributable to the union's activities. In the post war period, domestic servants have gotten larger wage increases without anyone engaging in large scale negotiations, without anyone's knowing that negotiations were going on and without a single newspaper headline except perhaps to record complaints about the problem of finding domestic servants. I think that trade unions have much monopoly power. But I think the importance of trade unions is widely exaggerated, that they are nothing like so important in the allocation of labor or the determination of wage rates as they are supposed to be. They are not unimportant—perhaps 10 or 15% of the working force have wages now some 10 or 15% higher than they otherwise would be because of trade unions, and the remaining 85% of the working class have wages something like 4% lower than they would otherwise be. This is appreciable and important, but it does not give unions the kind of power over the economy that would make it impossible to check their further rise.

The three major sources of strength I have suggested so far are the corroding effect of the extension of state activities and state intervention on attitudes toward the enforcement of the law and on the character of the civil service; the ingenuity of individuals in avoiding regulation; and the visibility of government action and of monopoly. Implicit in these is a fourth, namely the general inefficiency in the operation of government.

These comments have been rather discursive. I have been attempting simply to list some of the forces at work tending to destroy a free society once established, and tending to resist its destruction. I have left out of consideration the force that in some ways is our most important concern; namely, the force of ideas, of people's attitudes about values and about the kind of social organization that they want. I have omitted this force because I have nothing to say about it that is not self-evident.

No very clear conclusion can be drawn from this examination of the forces adverse and favorable to a free society. The historical record suggests pessimism, but the analysis gives no strong basis for either great optimism or confirmed pessimism about the stability of a free society, if it is given an opportunity to exist. One of the most important tasks for liberal scholars to undertake is to examine this issue more fully in the light of historical evidence in order that we may have a much better idea of what factors tend to promote and what factors to destroy a free society.

Note

Milton Friedman, Professor of Economics at The University of Chicago, is a contributing editor to *Newsweek*, the author of *Capitalism and Freedom* and co-author, with Anna J. Schwartz, of *A Monetary History of the United States, 1867–1960* and *The Great Contraction*.

"Is a Free Society Stable?" is reprinted with permission from *New Individualist Review* (September 1964).

Nathaniel Branden

30

Free Will, Moral Responsibility, and the Law

I. Introduction

In his celebrated criminal defenses Clarence Darrow argued for a position that amounted to the annihilation of the concept of moral responsibility. He maintained, in effect, that the accused were helpless victims of an unfortunate environment and/or a defective heredity, and that if any of the jurors had been victims of a similar environment and heredity, *they* would be standing on trial at that moment. Darrow, in other words, was a staunch advocate of psychological determinism.[1]

The issue of free will versus determinism has profound importance to the profession of law. Indeed, the issue of free will versus determinism is the most crucial question in any study of man. Before one can draw any further conclusions about the activities or states proper to him, it is necessary to know: Does man possess free will, *i.e.*, volitional control over the function of his consciousness and therefore control over his actions—or is man an automaton, a complex robot operated by forces over which he has no control, a robot whose every action and reaction is determined by what reality or experience or environment or inanimate matter or an inherited Id or an inherited chemistry or other people happen to have imprinted on him, a robot who, at any given moment, is pushed by whatever sum such influences may have added up to, and is powerless to resist?

Above all, this question has to be answered before one ventures into any of the "normative" sciences, *i.e.*, sciences which proscribe or recommend certain courses of action for man, sciences such as ethics, education, political philosophy, law.

If man has freedom of choice, one can advise him which actions to take and which to avoid; one can teach him to distinguish between rational pursuits and irrational ones, between good and evil; one can expect him to be able to differentiate between actions which do and do not violate the rights of other men; one can hold him responsible for his actions, one can praise him or blame him accordingly, one can reward him for his virtuous actions or punish him for crimes.

But if man has no freedom of choice, no power of control over his actions, then ethics and law are the first two sciences that have to be abandoned: it would be senseless to expect man to obey any moral code if he has no power to control his actions; it would be senseless to admire or condemn any human action, be it an act of heroism or knavery, if the actors could not help it in any case; it would be sheer brutality to punish any criminal, if he could not have acted differently, if the (apparently) most cold-blooded premeditated killing were, in fact, an involuntary act, determined by a complex mechanism of fate.

It is the purpose of this paper to present and argue for a new concept of free will—and, collaterally, to argue for the reality of moral responsibility.

II.   The Nature of Volition

There are two facts of man's nature which are essential to an understanding of his psychology and behavior. The first is the fact that reason is man's basic means of survival: *i.e.*, his capacity for conceptual thought is the means by which man apprehends the facts of reality[2] and thus is able to guide and direct his behavior. The second is that the exercise of his rational faculty, unlike an animal's use of his senses, is not automatic—conceptual thought is not automatic—the decision to think is not biologically "programmed" in man—*to think is an act of choice*.

It is the novelist-philosopher Ayn Rand who first located man's "free will" specifically in the capacity of his mind to initiate a process of conceptual thought or to abstain from doing so.

"The key ... to 'human nature' ... is the fact that man is a being of volitional consciousness. Reason does not work automatically; thinking is not a mechanical process; the connections of logic are not made by instinct. The functions of your stomach, lungs or heart are automatic; the function of your

mind is not. In any hour and issue of your life, you are free to think or to evade that effort. But you are not free to escape from your nature, from the fact that reason is your means of survival—so that for you, who are a human being, the question 'to be or not to be' is the question 'to think or not to think.'"[3]

In her subsequent writing, Miss Rand does not provide a theoretical elaboration of this statement. Let us proceed to do so here.

A full exposition of this concept of free will requires that we begin by placing the issue in a wider biological context—that we consider certain basic facts about the nature of living organisms.

An organism's life is characterized by and dependent upon a constant process of internally generated *action*. This is evident in the process of growth and maturation, in the process of self-healing—and in the actions of the organism in relation to its environment. The *goal-directedness* of living action is its most striking feature. This is not meant to imply the presence of purpose on the non-conscious levels of life, but rather to stress the significant fact that there exists in living entities a principle of self-regulating action, and that that action moves toward, and normally results in, the continued life of the organism. For example, the complex processes involved in metabolism, or the remarkable self-repairing activities of living structures, or the integrated orchestration of the countless separate activities involved in the normal process of an organism's physical maturation. Organic self-regulation is the indisputable, fascinating and challenging phenomenon at the base of the science of biology.

Life exists on different levels of development and complexity, from the single cell to man. As life advances from simpler to higher levels, one may distinguish three forms or categories of self-regulatory activity, which I shall designate as: the *vegetative* level of self-regulation—the *conscious-behavioral* level—the *self-conscious* level.

The vegetative level is the most primitive. All the physiological-biochemical processes within a plant, by which the plant maintains its own existence, are of this order. This pattern of self-regulatory activity is operative within a single cell and in all higher life-forms. It is operative in the non-conscious physiological-biochemical processes within the bodies of animals and men—as in metabolism, for example.

The conscious-behavioral level of self-regulation appears with the emergence of consciousness in animals. The vegetative level continues to operate within the animal's body—but a new, higher level is required to protect and sustain the animal's life, as the animal moves through its environment. This level is achieved by the animal's power of awareness.

Its senses provide it with the knowledge it needs to hunt, to move around obstacles, to flee from enemies, etc. Its ability to be conscious of the external world enables the animal to regulate and direct its motor activity. Deprived of its senses, an animal could not survive. For all living entities that possess it, consciousness—the regulator of action—is the basic means of survival.

The sensory-perceptual level of an animal's consciousness does not permit it, of course, to be aware of the issue of life and death as such; but given the appropriate physical environment, the animal's sensory-perceptual apparatus and its pleasure-pain mechanism function automatically to protect its life. If its range of awareness cannot cope with the conditions that confront the animal, it perishes. But, within the limit of its powers, its consciousness serves to regulate its behavior in the direction of life. Thus, with the faculty of locomotion *and* the emergence of consciousness in animals, a new form of self-regulatory activity appears in nature, a new expression of this biological principle of life.

In man, both life and consciousness reach their most highly developed form. Man, who shares with animals the sensory-perceptual mode of consciousness, goes beyond it to the conceptual mode—to the level of abstractions, principles, explicit reasoning and *self-consciousness*. Unlike animals, man has the ability to be explicitly aware of his own mental activities, to question their validity, to judge them critically, to alter or correct them. Man is not rational automatically; he is aware of the fact that his mental processes may be appropriate or inappropriate to the task of apprehending reality; his mental processes are not, to him, an unalterable given. In addition to the two previous forms of self-regulating activity, man exhibits a third: *the power to regulate the action of his own consciousness.*

In one crucial respect, however, the nature of this regulatory activity differs radically from the two previous ones.

On the vegetative and conscious-behavioral levels, the self-regulation is "wired in" to the system. A living organism is a complex integrate of hierarchically organized structures and functions. The various components are controlled in part by their own regulators and in part by regulators on higher levels of the hierarchy. For example, the rhythm of the heart is directly under the control of the heart's own "pacemaker" system; the pacemaker system is regulated by the autonomic nervous system and by hormones; these are regulated by the centers in the brain. The ultimate regulative principle, inherent in and controlling the entire system of sub-regulators, from the nervous system to the heart down to the internal action of a single cell, is, clearly, the life of the organism, *i.e.,* the requirements of the organism's survival. The organism's life is the implicit standard or goal that provides the integrating principle of the organism's internal actions. This ultimate regulator is "programmed" into the organism by nature, so to speak, as are all the sub-regulators; the organism has no choice in the matter.

Just as, on the vegetative level, the specific nature of the self-regulation, the controlling and integrating principle, is "wired in" to the system—so, in a different form, this is equally true of the conscious-behavioral level in animals. The ultimate standard and goal, the animal's life, is biologically "programmed"—through the animal's sensory-perceptual apparatus and its pleasure-pain mechanism—to regulate its behavior.

Now consider the *self-conscious* level of self-regulation.

The basic function of consciousness—in animals and in man—is *awareness*, the maintenance of sensory and/or conceptual contact with reality. On the plane of awareness that man shares with animals, the sensory-perceptual plane, the integrative process is automatic, *i.e.*, "wired in" to the nervous system. In the brain of a normal human being, sensations (primary sensory inputs) are automatically integrated into perceptions. On the sensory-perceptual level, *awareness* is the controlling and regulating goal of the integrative process—by nature's "programming."

This is *not* true of the conceptual level of consciousness. Here, the regulation is not automatic, not "wired in" to the system. Conceptual awareness, as the *controlling goal* of man's mental activity, is necessary to man's proper survival, *but it is not implanted by nature*. Man has to provide it. Man has to select that purpose. Man has to direct his mental effort and integrate his mental activity to the goal of conceptual awareness—by choice. The *capacity* of conceptual functioning is innate; but the *exercise* of this capacity is volitional.

To engage in an active process of thinking—to abstract, conceptualize, relate, infer, to *reason*—man must focus his mind: he must *set* it to the task of active integration. The choice to focus, in any given situation, is made in choosing to make *awareness* one's goal—awareness of that which is relevant in the given context.

One activates and directs the thinking process by setting the goal: awareness—and that goal acts as the regulator and integrator of one's mental activity.

The goal of awareness is set by giving oneself, in effect, the order: "Grasp this."

That this goal is not "wired in" to man's brain by nature, as the automatic regulator of mental activity, scarcely needs to be argued. One does not need to design special laboratory experiments in order to demonstrate that thinking is not an automatic process, that man's mind does not automatically "pump" conceptual knowledge, when and as man's life requires it, as his heart pumps blood. The mere fact of being confronted with physical objects and events will not force man to abstract their common properties, to integrate his abstractions, to apply his knowledge to each new particular he encounters. Man's capacity to default on the responsibility of thinking is too easily observable. Man must *choose* to focus his mind; he must *choose* to aim at understanding. On the conceptual level, the responsibility of self-regulation is his.

The act of focusing pertains to the *operation* of a man's consciousness, to its method of functioning—*not* to its content.

A man is in focus when and to the extent that his mind is set to the goal of awareness, clarity, intelligibility, with regard to the object of his concern, *i.e.*, with regard to that which he is considering or dealing with or engaged in doing.

To sustain that focus with regard to a specific issue or problem is to *think*.

To let one's mind drift in will-less passivity, directed only by random impressions, emotions or associations, or to consider an issue without genuinely seeking to understand it, or to engage in an action without a concern to know what one is doing—is to be out of focus.

What is involved here is not an issue of the degree of a man's intelligence or knowledge. Nor is it an issue of the productiveness or success of any particular thinking process. Nor is it an issue of the specific subject-matter with which the mind may be occupied. It is an issue of the basic regulating principle that directs the mind's activity: Is the mind controlled by the goal of awareness—or by something else, by wishes, fears or the pull of lethargic passivity?

To be in focus is to set one's mind to the purpose of *active cognitive integration*. But the alternative confronting man is not simply optimal consciousness or absolute unconsciousness. There are different levels of awareness possible to man's mind, determined by the degree of his focus. This will be manifested in (a) the clarity or vagueness of his mind's contents, (b) the degree to which the mind's activity involves abstractions and principles or is concrete-bound, (c) the degree to which the relevant wider context is present or absent in the process of thinking.

Thus, the choice to focus (or to think) does not consist of moving from a state of literal unconsciousness to a state of consciousness. (This, clearly, would be impossible. When one is asleep, one cannot suddenly choose to start thinking.) To focus is to move from a *lower* level of awareness to a *higher* level—to move from (relative) mental passivity to purposeful mental activity—to initiate a process of directed cognitive integration. In a state of passive (or relatively passive) awareness, a man can apprehend the need to be in full mental focus. His choice is to evade that knowledge or to exert the effort of raising the level of his awareness.

The decision to focus and to think, once made, does not continue to direct a man's mind unceasingly thereafter, with no further effort required. Just as the state of full consciousness must be initiated volitionally, so it must be maintained volitionally. The choice to think must be reaffirmed in the face of every new issue and problem. The decision to be in focus yesterday will not compel a man to be in focus today. The decision to be in focus about one question will not compel a man to be in focus about another. The decision to pursue a certain value does not guarantee that man will exert the mental effort required to achieve it. In any specific thinking process, man must continue to monitor and regulate his own mental activity, to "keep it on the rails," so to speak. In any hour of his life, man is free to suspend the function of his consciousness, to abandon effort, to default on the responsibility of self-regulation and let his mind drift passively. He is free to maintain only a *partial* focus, grasping that which comes easily to his understanding and declining to struggle for that which does not.

Man is free not only to evade the effort of purposeful awareness in general, but to evade specific lines of thought that he finds disconcerting or painful. Perceiving qualities in his friends, his wife or himself that clash with his moral standards, he can surrender his mind to blankness or switch it hastily to some other concern, refusing to identify the meaning or implications of what he has perceived. Dimly apprehending, in the midst of an argument, that he is being ridden by his emotions and is maintaining a position for reasons other than those he is stating, reasons that he knows to be untenable, he can refuse to integrate his knowledge, he can refuse to pause on it, he can push it aside and begin to shout with righteous indignation. Grasping that he is pursuing a course of action that is in blatant defiance of reason, he can cry to himself, in effect: "Who can be sure of anything?"—plunge his mind into fog and continue on his way.

In such cases, a man is doing more than defaulting on the responsibility of making awareness his goal: he is actively seeking *un*awareness as his goal. This is the meaning of evasion.

In the choice to focus or not to focus, to think or not to think, to activate the conceptual level of his consciousness or to suspend it—and in this choice alone—is man psychologically free.

Man's freedom to focus or not to focus, to think or not to think, is a unique kind of choice that must be distinguished from any other category of choice. It must be distinguished from the decision to think about a particular subject: *what* a man thinks about, in any given case, depends on his values, interests, knowledge and context. It must be distinguished from the decision to perform a particular physical action, which again depends on a man's values, interests, knowledge and context. These decisions involve causal antecedents of a kind which the choice to focus does not.

The primary choice to focus, to set one's mind to the purpose of cognitive integration, is causally irreducible: It is the highest regulator in the mental system; it is subject to man's direct, volitional control. In relation to it, all other choices and decisions are *sub*regulators.

The capacity of volitional choice presupposes, of course, a normal brain. A condition of disease can render *any* human faculty inoperative. But this analysis assumes an intact, normally functioning brain and nervous system.

To recognize that man is free to think or not to think is to recognize that, in a given situation, a man is able to think and he is able to refrain from thinking. The choice to think (not the *process* of thinking, but the *choice* to think) and the process of focusing his mind are an indivisible action, of which man is the causal agent.

The choice to focus one's mind is a primary, just as the value sought, *awareness*, is a primary. It is awareness that makes any other values possible, not any other values that antecede and make awareness possible. Awareness is the starting-point and pre-condition of goal-directed (value-directed) human action—not just another goal or value along the way, as it were. The decision to focus one's mind (to value awareness and make it one's goal) or not to focus, is a basic choice that cannot be reduced further.

It must be stressed that volition pertains, specifically, to the conceptual level of awareness. A child encounters the need of cognitive self-regulation when and as he begins to move from the perceptual to the conceptual level, when and as he learns to abstract, to classify, to grasp principles, to reason explicitly. So long as he functions on the sensory-perceptual level, he experiences cognition as an effortless process. But when he begins to conceptualize, he is confronted by the fact that this new form of awareness entails mental *work*, that it requires an effort, that he must choose to generate this effort. He discovers that, on this new level of awareness, he is not infallible; error is possible; cognitive success is not automatically guaranteed to him. (Whereas, on the perceptual level, to look is to see—on the conceptual level, to ask a question is not automatically to know the answer; and to know what question to ask is not automatic, either.) He discovers the continual need to monitor and regulate his mind's activity. A child does not, of course, identify this knowledge verbally or explicitly. But it is implicit in his consciousness, by direct introspective awareness.

Just as a man cannot escape the implicit knowledge that the function of his mind is volitional, so he cannot escape the implicit knowledge that he *should* think, that to be conscious is desirable, that his efficacy as a living entity depends on it. But he is free to act on that knowledge or to evade it. To repeat: Nature has not "programmed" him to think automatically.

(In some cases, the "motive" of non-focusing or non-thinking is anti-effort, *i.e.*, a disinclination to exert the energy and accept the responsibility that thinking requires. In other cases, the "motive" is some wish, desire or feeling which one wants to indulge and which one's reason cannot sanction—and so one "solves" the problem by going out of focus. In other cases, the "motive" is escape from fear, a fear to which one knows one should not surrender, but to which one does surrender, suspending one's consciousness and negating one's knowledge. These "motives" are not causal imperatives; they are feelings which a man may choose to treat as decisive.)

As focusing involves expanding the range of one's awareness, so evasion consists of the reverse process: of *shrinking* the range of one's awareness. Evasion consists of refusing to *raise* the level of one's awareness, when one knows (clearly or dimly) that one should—or of *lowering* the level of one's awareness, when one knows (clearly or dimly) that one shouldn't. To evade a fact is to attempt to make it unreal to oneself, on the implicit subjectivist premise that if one does not perceive the fact, it does not exist (or its existence will not matter and will not entail any consequences).

Consciousness is man's tool for perceiving and identifying the facts of reality. It is an organ of integration. To focus is to set the integrative process in purposeful motion—by setting the appropriate goal: awareness. Non-focus is non-integration. Evasion is willful disintegration, the act of subverting the proper function of consciousness, of setting the cognitive function in reverse and reducing the contents of one's mind to disconnected, unintegrated fragments that are forbidden to confront one another.

Man's life and well-being depend upon his maintaining a proper cognitive contact with reality—and this requires a full mental focus, maintained as a way of life.

The act of focusing, as a primary mental set, must be distinguished from the act of problem-solving. Problem-solving entails the pursuit of the answer to some specific question; as such, it presupposes a state of focus, but is not synonymous with it. For example, a man who goes for a walk on a sunny day, intent only on the enjoyment of his activity, with no immediate concern for any long-range problems, may still be in mental focus—if he knows clearly what he is doing and why, and if he preserves a fundamental alertness, a readiness for purposeful thought, should the need for it arise.

To be in focus does not mean that one must be engaged in the task of problem-solving every moment of one's waking existence. *It means that one must know what one's mind is doing.*

The more consistently and conscientiously a man maintains a policy of being in full mental focus, of thinking, of judging the facts of reality that confront him, of knowing what he is doing and why, the easier and more "natural" the process becomes. The steadily increasing knowledge he acquires as a result of his policy, the growing sense of control over his existence, the growing self-confidence—the conviction of living in a universe that is open to him—all serve to put every emotional incentive on the side of his continuing to think. Further, they reduce the possibility of an incentive that could even tempt him to evade. It is too clear to him that reality is not and can never be his enemy—that he has nothing to gain from self-inflicted blindness, and everything to lose.

No, this does not mean that, for such a man, the policy of rationality becomes automatic; it will always remain volitional; but he has "programmed" himself, as it were, to have every emotional incentive for rationality and none for irrationality. To borrow a term from Aristotle, he has learned to make rationality "second-nature" to him. That is the psychological reward he earns for himself. But—and this must be emphasized—his psychological state must be maintained *volitionally;* he retains the power to betray it. In each new issue he encounters, he still must *choose* to think.

Conversely, the more a man maintains a policy of focusing as little as possible, and of evading any facts he finds painful to consider—the more he sabotages himself psychologically and the more difficult the task of thinking becomes for him. The inevitable consequences of his policy of non-thinking are feelings of helplessness, of inefficacy, of anxiety—the sense of living in an unknowable and inimical universe. These feelings undercut his confidence in his ability to think, in the usefulness of thinking—and he tends to feel overwhelmed by the enormity of the inner mental chaos which he has to untangle. Further, the countless fears to which his policy of evasion inevitably condemns him put the weight of his emotions on the side of additional evasions, of growing self-deception, of an increasingly frantic flight from reality.

No, this does not mean that his evasion and irrationality become automatic; they remain volitional; but he has "programmed" himself to find rationality harder and harder, and the temptation to evasion stronger and stronger. That is the psychological punishment which his nature imposes on him for his default.

But he retains the power to change his course. This side of psychosis, and assuming no interfering structural or chemical disorders, every man retains that power, regardless of his previous mental practices. Volition pertains exclusively to one issue: Is awareness the goal of one's consciousness—or not? What repeated evasion and irrationality can affect is, not the ability to choose to focus, but the efficiency, speed and productiveness of a given thinking process. Since the habitual evader has spent his time, not on improving the efficacy of his mind, but on sabotaging it, he suffers the consequences in terms of mental strain, slowness, internal chaos, when he does decide to think. If he perseveres, he can redeem and raise the efficacy of his thinking. But the mental effort he refused to exert formerly, must now be exerted tenfold.

In a given moment, a man may be so overcome by a violent emotion —particularly fear—that he may find it difficult or impossible to think clearly. But he has the power *to know that he is in this state*—and, unless instant action is required, to defer acting or drawing final conclusions until his mind has cleared. In this manner, he can remain in control even under acute stress. (It is worth mentioning, in passing, that the more a man surrenders to his emotions in *non*acute situations, when he could have easily done otherwise, the more susceptible he is to becoming psychologically incapacitated and helplessly blinded under pressure; he has no firmly established "habit" of rational self-discipline to support him.)

An incentive is not a necessitating cause. The fact that a man has good reason to want to think about some issue, does not guarantee that he will do so; it does not *compel* him to think. And the fact that a man is afraid to think about some issue, does not make it impossible for him to do so; it does not *compel* him to evade.

A man's *behavior, i.e.,* his actions, proceeds from his values and premises, which in turn proceed, in the context of the knowledge available to him, from his thinking or non-thinking. His actions may be said to be free in that they are under the control of a faculty which is free, *i.e.* which functions volitionally. *This is the reason why man is held responsible for his actions.*

III.   Volition and the Social Environment

A man's social environment can provide incentives to think or it can make the task harder—according to the degree of human rationality or irrationality that a man encounters. But the social environment cannot *determine* a man's thinking or nonthinking. It cannot force him to exert the effort and accept the responsibility of cognition and it cannot force him to evade; it cannot force him to subordinate his desires to his reason and it cannot force him to sacrifice his reason to his desires. In this issue, man is inviolately a self-regulator. The social environment can provide man with incentives for good or for evil, but—to repeat—an incentive is not a necessitating cause.

The environment consists only of facts; the meaning of those facts—the conclusions and convictions to be drawn from them—can be identified only by a man's mind. A man's character, the degree of his rationality, independence, honesty, is determined, not by the things he perceives, but by the thinking he does or fails to do about them.

At any step of the way, a man can make honest mistakes of knowledge or judgment; he is not infallible; he may identify incorrectly the meaning or the significance of the events he observes. His power of volition does not guarantee him protection against errors; but it does guarantee that he need not be left helplessly at the mercy of his errors for the rest of his life: he is able to leave his mind open to new evidence that will inform him that his conclusions are wrong and must be revised.

If, for instance, a child is brought up by irrational parents who give him a bewildering, frightening and contradictory impression of reality, he may decide that all human beings by their nature are incomprehensible and dangerous to him; and if he arrests his thinking at this point, if, in later years, he never attempts to question or overcome his chronic feeling of terror and helplessness, he can spend the rest of his life in a state of embittered paralysis. But such does not *have* to be his fate: if he continues to struggle with the problem, or, as he grows older, if he decides to consider the new, wider evidence available to him, he can discover that he has made an unwarranted generalization and he can reject it in favor of a fully reasoned and conscious conviction.

Another child, in the same circumstances, may draw a different conclusion. He may decide that all human beings are unreliable and evil, and that *he* will beat them at their own game: he will act as ruthlessly and dishonestly as possible, to hurt them before they hurt *him*. Again, he can revise this conclusion later in the light of wider evidence, if he chooses to think about it. The facts of reality available to him will give him many opportunities to discover that he is wrong. If he does not choose to think, he will become a scoundrel—not because his parents were irrational, but because he defaulted on the responsibility of forming his convictions consciously and of constantly checking them against the facts of reality.

A third child, in the same circumstances, may decide that his parents are wrong, that they are unjust and unfair, or at least that they do not act intelligibly, and that *he* must not act as they do. He may suffer at home, but keep looking for evidence of better human behavior, among neighbors or in books and movies, refusing to resign himself to the irrational and the incomprehensible as inevitable. Such a child will draw an enormous advantage out of his misfortune, which he will not realize until many years later: he will have laid the foundation of a profound self-confidence.

If an adolescent grows up in a neighborhood where crime flourishes and is cynically accepted as the normal, he can, abdicating the independence of his judgment, allow his character to be shaped in the image of the prevailing values, and become a criminal himself; or, choosing to think, he can perceive the irrationality and humiliating self-degradation of those who accept a criminal's mode of existence, and fight to achieve a better way of life for himself.

If a man is pounded since childhood with the doctrine of Original Sin, if he is taught that he is corrupt by nature and must spend his life in penance, if he is taught that this earth is a place of misery, frustration and calamity, if he is taught that the pursuit of enjoyment is evil—he does not have to believe it. He is free to think, to question and to judge the nature of a moral code that damns man and damns existence and places its standard of the good outside of both.

Of any value offered to him as the right, and any assertion offered to him as the true, a man is free to ask: *Why?* That "Why?" is the threshold that the beliefs of others cannot cross without his consent.

It is conceivable, of course, that a young child could be subjected, from the first months and years of his life, to such extraordinarily vicious irrationality—such bewildering, contradictory and terrifying behavior on the part of his parents—that it would be impossible for him to develop normally, because of the limited evidence available to him; it might be impossible for him to establish any firm base of knowledge on which to build. It is conceivable that a child could be paralyzed psychologically—or severely retarded mentally—in this manner. But this would represent the *destruction*, not the "conditioning," of a child's mind; it is scarcely the pattern of the overwhelming majority of mankind; and this is *not* what is meant by those who claim that man is the product of his background.

Let us consider the case of the individual who *does* appear to be the product of his background, of his social environment. Let us analyze, as an example, the case of the boy who, brought up in a bad neighborhood, becomes a criminal.

In the actions of a boy who thus allows himself to be shaped by his environment, the most obviously apparent motive is the desire "to swim with the current." The root of that desire is the wish to escape the effort and responsibility of initiating his own course of action. In order to choose one's own actions, one has to choose one's own goals, and to do that, one has to choose one's own values, and to do that, one has to think. But thinking is the first and basic responsibility that such a boy rejects.

Having no values or standards of his own, he is led—by his desire for "security"—to accept whatever values are offered to him by the social group in which he finds himself. To swim with the current, one has to accept the ocean or the swamp or the rapids or the cesspool or the abyss, toward which that particular current is rushing. Such a boy will want to swim with the current, he will want to follow any course of action readymade for him by others, he will want to "belong."

And so, if the boys in the neighborhood form a gang at the corner pool-room, he will join; if they start robbing people, he will start robbing people; if they begin to murder, he will murder. What moves him is his *feelings*. His feelings are all he has left, once he has abandoned his mind. He does not join the gang by a conscious, reasoned decision: he *feels* like joining. He does not follow the gang because he honestly thinks they are right: he *feels* like following. If his mother objects and tries to argue with him, to persuade him to quit the hoodlums, he does not weigh her arguments, he does not conclude that she is wrong—he does not *feel* like thinking about it.

If, at some point, he begins to fear that the gang may be going too far, if he recoils from the prospect of becoming a murderer, he realizes that the alternative is to break with his friends and to be left on his own; he does not weigh the advantages or disadvantages of being left on his own; he chooses blindly to stick with the gang—because he *feels* terror at the prospect of independence. He may see, across the river or just a few blocks away, people who lead a totally different kind of life, and boys of his own age who, somehow, did *not* become criminals; he has many means of access to a wider view of the possibilities of life; but this does not raise in his mind the question whether a better kind of life is possible to him, it does not prompt him to inquire or investigate—because he *feels* terror of the unknown. If he asks himself what it is that terrifies him about breaking with his background, he will answer, in effect: "Aw, I don't know nobody out there and nobody knows *me*." In reason, this is not an explanation: there is nothing objectively terrifying in that statement; but it satisfies him—because he feels an overwhelming dread of loneliness, and *feelings* are his only absolute, the absolute not to be questioned.

And if, at the age of twenty, he is dragged to jail to await execution for some monstrously bloody and senselessly wanton crime—he will scream that he could not help it and that he never had a chance. He will not scream it because it is true. He will scream it because he *feels* it.

In a sense opposite to that which he intends, there is one element of truth in his scream: given his basic policy of *antithought*, he could *not* help it and he never had a chance. Neither has any other human being who moves through life on that sort of policy. But it is not true that he or any other human being could not help running from the necessity to think, could not help riding blindly on his feelings.

On every day of this boy's life and at every crucial turning-point, the possibility of thinking about his actions was open to him. The evidence on which to base a change in his policy was available to him. He evaded it. He chose not to think. If, at every turning-point, he had thought carefully and conscientiously, and had simply reached the wrong conclusions, he would be more justified in crying that he could not help it. But it is not helplessly bewildered, conscientious thinkers who fill reform schools and who murder one another on street corners—through an error in logic.

If one wishes to understand what destroyed this boy, the key lies, not in his environment, but in the fact that he let himself be moved, guided and motivated by his feelings, that he tried to substitute his feelings for his mind. There was nothing to prevent him from thinking, except that he did not feel like it.

To the extent that a man defaults on the responsibility of thinking, he *is*, in significant measure, "the product of his environment." But such is not the nature of man. It is an instance of pathology.

The attempt of most psychologists to explain a man's behavior without reference to the degree of his thinking or non-thinking—by attempting to reduce all of a man's behavior to "causes" either in his "conditioning" or in his heredity[4]—is profoundly indicative of the extent to which man is absent from and ignored by most current psychological theories. According to the view prevalent today, man is only a walking recorder into which his parents, teachers and neighbors dictate what they please—such parents, teachers and neighbors themselves being only walking recorders carrying the dictations of other, earlier recorders, and so on. As to the question of where *new* ideas, concepts and values come from, it is left unanswered; the helpless chunk of putty, which allegedly is man, produces them by virtue of some chance concatenation of unknown forces. It is interesting to consider the personal confession contained in the social determinist's dismay, incredulity *and indignation* at the suggestion that original, self-generated thinking plays any significant role in a man's life.

IV. The Contradiction of Determinism

"Free-will"—in the widest meaning of the term—is the doctrine that man is capable of performing actions which are not determined by forces outside his control; that man is capable of making choices which are not necessitated by antecedent factors. As one writer formulates it: "In the case of an action that is free, it must be such that it is caused by the agent who performs it, but such that no antecedent conditions were sufficient for his performing just that action."[5]

The nature of these free choices, to what human faculty they pertain, how they operate and what are their limits—are questions on which various theories of free will differ. Predominantly, theories of free will have attempted to argue that certain desires or physical actions are "free," *i.e.*, causally irreducible—a position that is flagrantly insupportable.[6]

Man's free will consists of a single action, a single basic choice: to think or not to think. It is a freedom entailed by his unique power of self-consciousness. This basic choice—given the context of his knowledge and of the existential possibilities confronting him—controls all of man's other choices, and directs the course of his actions.

The concept of man as a being of volitional consciousness stands in sharp opposition to the view that dominates our culture in general and the social sciences in particular: the doctrine of psychological determinism.

Psychological determinism denies the existence of any element of freedom or volition in man's consciousness. It holds that, in relation to his actions, decisions, values and conclusions, man is ultimately and essentially *passive*; that man is merely a *reactor* to internal and external pressures; that those pressures determine the course of man's actions and the content of his convictions, just as physical forces determine the course of every particle of dust in the universe. It holds that, in any given situation or moment, only one "choice" is psychologically possible to man, the inevitable result of all the antecedent determining forces impinging on him, just as only one action is possible to the speck of dust; that man has no *actual* power of choice, no *actual* freedom or self-responsibility. Man, according to this view, has no more volition than a stone: he is merely confronted with more complex alternatives and is manipulated by more complex forces.

Although they usually do not care to have it formulated so explicitly, nor to accept its full implications, this is the view of man's nature that most contemporary psychologists accept. They accept it, many of them candidly admit, as "an article of faith." That is, the majority do not claim that this view has been proven, has been logically demonstrated. They profess a belief in psychological determinism because they regard it as "scientific." This is the single most prevalent and destructive myth in the field of psychology today.

The doctrine of determinism contains a central and insuperable contradiction—an *epistemological* contradiction—a contradiction implicit in any variety of determinism, whether the alleged determining forces be physical, psychological, environmental or divine.

The determinist view of mind maintains that whether a man thinks or not, whether he takes cognizance of the facts of reality or not, whether he places facts above feelings or feelings above facts—all are determined by forces outside his control; in any given moment or situation, his method of mental functioning is the inevitable product of an endless chain of antecedent factors; *he* has no choice in the matter.

That which a man does, declare the advocates of determinism, he *had* to do—that which he believes, he *had* to believe—if he focuses his mind, he *had* to—if he evades the effort of focusing, he *had* to—if he is guided solely by reason, he *had* to be—if he is ruled instead by feeling or whim, he *had* to be—*he couldn't help it.*

But if this were true, no knowledge—no *conceptual* knowledge—

would be possible to man. No theory could claim greater plausibility than any other—including the theory of psychological determinism.

Man is neither omniscient nor infallible. This means: (a) that he must work to *achieve* his knowledge, and (b) that the mere presence of an idea inside his mind, does not prove that the idea is true; many ideas may enter a man's mind which are false. But if man believes what he has to believe, if he is not free to test his beliefs against reality and to validate or reject them—*if the actions and content of his mind are determined by factors that may or may not have anything to do with reason, logic and reality*—then he can never know if his conclusions are true or false.

Knowledge consists of the correct identification of the facts of reality; and in order for man to know that the contents of his mind *do* constitute knowledge, in order for him to know that he has identified the facts of reality correctly, he requires a means of testing his conclusions. The means is the process of *reasoning*—of testing his conclusions against reality and checking for contradictions. It is thus that he validates his conclusions. But this validation is possible only if his *capacity* to judge is free—*i.e.*, non-conditional (given a normal brain). If his capacity to judge is *not* free, there is no way for a man to discriminate between his beliefs and those of a raving lunatic.

But then how did the advocates of determinism acquire *their* knowledge? What is its validation? Determinists are conspicuously silent on this point.

If the advocates of determinism insist that their choice to think and their acceptance of reason is *conditional*, dependent on factors outside their control—which means: that they are *not* free to test their beliefs against the facts of reality—then they cannot claim to *know* that their theory is true; they can only report that they feel helpless to believe otherwise. Nor can they claim that their theory is highly probable; they can only acknowledge the inner compulsion that forbids them to doubt that it is highly probable.

Some advocates of determinism,[7] evidently sensing that epistemological dilemma, have sought to escape it by asserting that, although they are determined to believe what they believe, the factor determining them is *logic*. But by what means do they know this? Their beliefs are no more subject to their control than those of a lunatic. They and the lunatic are equally the pawn of deterministic forces. Both are incapable of judging their judgments.

One of the defining characteristics of psychosis is *loss* of volitional control over the power of rational judgment—but, according to determinism, that is man's normal, metaphysical state. There *is* no escape from determinism's epistemological dilemma.

A mind that is not free to test and validate its conclusions—a mind whose judgment is not free—can have no way to tell the logical from the illogical, *no way to ascertain that which compels and motivates it,* no right *to* claim knowledge of any kind; such a mind is disqualified for such appraisals by its very nature. The very *concept* of logic is possible only to a volitional consciousness; an automatic consciousness could have no need of it and could not conceive of it.

The concepts of logic, thought and knowledge are not applicable to machines. A machine does not reason; it performs the actions its builder sets it to perform, and those actions alone. If it is set to register that two plus two equal four, it does so; if it is set to register that two plus two equal five, it does so; it has no power to correct the orders and information given it. If "self-correctors" are built into it, it performs the prescribed acts of "self-correction," and no others; if the "self-correctors" are set incorrectly, it cannot correct itself; it cannot make any independent, self-generated contribution to its own performance. If man, who is not "set" invariably to be right, were merely a super-complex machine, engineered by his heredity and operated by his environment, pushed, pulled, shaped and molded by his genes, his toilet training, his parental upbringing and his cultural history, then no idea reached by him could claim objectivity or truth—including the idea that man is a machine.

Those who propound determinism must either assert that they arrived at their theory by mystical revelation, and thus exclude themselves from the realm of reason—or they must assert that *they* are an exception to the theory they propound, and thus exclude their theory from the realm of truth.

That knowledge is possible to man, cannot be contested without self-contradiction. It is a truth that must be accepted even in the act of seeking to dispute it. Any theory that necessitates the conclusion that man can know nothing, is self-invalidating and self-refuting by that very fact. Yet such is the conclusion to which the theory of determinism inescapably leads.

In appraising any theory of the nature of man's mind and its operations, it is necessary to consider that, since the theory is itself a product of man's mind, its claim to truth must be compatible with its own existence and content. For example, if a man were to declare, as an alleged fact of reality: "Man is incapable of knowing any facts"—the logical absurdity of his statement would be obvious. The epistemological contradiction of determinism is—in a subtler and more complex way— of the identical order.

Determinism is a theory whose claim to truth is incompatible with its own content. It exhibits what may be termed *the fallacy of self-exclusion*.

A number of thinkers,[8] attacking the theory of classical association-ism, point out that the associationist theory of mind does not allow the possibility of ever establishing associationism as true; that the theory does not allow the possibility of *any* knowledge. But associationism is merely one version of psychological determinism. What has not been recognized is that the same objection applies to—and invalidates—*any* version of determinism.

It does not matter whether man's mind is alleged to be passively under the sway of the "laws of association"—or of conditional reflexes— or of environmental pressures—or of Original Sin. *Any* theory of mind that denies man's volitional control over his faculty of judgment, collapses under the weight of the same inescapable and insuperable contradiction.

Only because man *is* a being of volitional consciousness, only because he *is* free to initiate and sustain a reasoning process, is conceptual knowledge—in contradistinction to irresistible, unchosen beliefs—possible to him.

V.   Volition and the Law of Causality

Two notions—both mistaken—are especially influential in propagating the mystique of psychological determinism. The first is the claim that psychological determinism is logically entailed by the law of causality, that volition contradicts causality. The second is the claim that, without determinism, no science of psychology would be possible, there could be no psychological laws and no way to predict human behavior.

What is involved, in the first of these claims, is a gross misapprehen-sion of the nature of the law of causality. Let us begin, therefore, by considering the exact meaning of this law.

As Ayn Rand writes:

The law of causality is the law of identity applied to action. All actions are caused by entities. The nature of an action is caused and determined by the nature of the entities that act, a thing cannot act in contradiction to its nature.[9]

This is the first point that must be stressed: all actions are actions *of entities*. (The concept of "action" logically requires and presupposes *that which* acts, and would not be possible without it. The universe consists of entities that act, move and change—not of disembodied actions, motions and changes.)

The actions possible to an entity are determined by its nature: what a thing can *do*, depends on what it *is*. It is not "chance," it is not the whim of a supernatural being, it is in the inexorable nature of the entities involved that a seed can grow into a flower, but a stone cannot—that a bird can fly, but a building cannot—that electricity can run a motor, but tears and prayers cannot—that actions *consistent* with their natures are possible to entities, but *contradictions* are not.

Just as what a thing can do, depends upon what it is—so, in any specific situation, what a thing *will* do, depends on what it is. If iron is exposed to a certain temperature, it expands; if water is exposed to the same temperature, it boils; if wood is exposed to the same temperature, it burns. The differences in their actions are caused by differences in their properties. If an automobile collides with a bicycle, it is not "chance" that the bicycle is hurled into the air, rather than the automobile: if an automobile collides with a train, it is not "chance" that the automobile is hurled into the air, rather than the train. Causality proceeds from identity.

Causality pertains to a relationship between *entities and their actions*.

The law of causality is a very wide abstraction; per se, it does not specify the *kind* of causal processes that are operative in any particular entity, and it does not imply that the *same* kind of causal processes are operative in *all* entities. Any such assumption would be gratuitous and unwarranted.

The actions of a stone, for example, are only *re*actions to other objects or forces; a stone, which moves by a mechanistic type of causation, cannot *initiate* actions. It cannot start rolling down a hillside, unless it is pushed by a man's hand or by the wind or by some other force *outside* itself. It can generate neither action nor goals. But an animal possesses the power of locomotion, it can initiate movement, *goal-directed* movement, it can start walking or running: the source of its motion is *within* itself. That the animal may start running in response to the perception of some stimulus-object is irrelevant in this context. What is relevant is that the animal has the capacity to respond in a manner impossible to a stone: by originating, within its own body, the motion of running—and moving toward a goal. Different causal processes, different principles of action, are involved in these two cases.

The nature of a *living* entity gives it the capacity for a kind of action impossible to inanimate matter: self-generated, goal-directed action (in the sense defined above). Man's greatest distinction from all other living species is the capacity to originate an action of his consciousness—the capacity to originate a process of abstract thought.

Man's unique responsibility lies in the fact that this process of thought, which is man's basic means of survival, must be originated volitionally. In man, there exists the power of *choice*, choice in the primary sense, choice as a psychologically irreducible natural fact.

This freedom of choice is not a negation of causality, but a category of it, a category that pertains to man. A process of thought is not causeless, it is caused by a man. The actions possible to an entity are determined by the entity that acts—and the nature of man (and of man's mind) is such that it necessitates the choice between focusing and non-focusing, between thinking and non-thinking. Man's nature does not allow him to escape this choice, it is his alone to make: it is not made for him by the gods, the stars, the chemistry of his body, the structure of his "family constellation" or the economic organization of his society.

If one is to be bound by a genuine "empiricism"—*i.e.*, a respect for observable facts, without arbitrary commitments to which reality must be "adjusted"—one cannot ignore this distinctive attribute of man's nature. And if one understands the law of causality as a relationship between entities and their actions, then the problem of "reconciling" volition and causality is seen to be illusory.

But it is not thus that the law of causality is regarded today. That is the source of the confusion.

The historical turning-point came at the Renaissance. Windelband, in his *A History of Philosophy*, describes it as follows:

> The idea of cause had acquired a completely new significance through Galileo. According to the [earlier] conception . . . causes were substances or things, while effects, on the other hand, were either their activities or were other substances and things which were held to come about only by such activities: this was the Platonic-Aristotelian conception . . . Galileo, on the contrary, went back to the idea of the older Greek thinkers, who applied the causal relation only to the state— that meant now to the motions of substances—not to the Being of the substances themselves. Causes are motions, and effects are motions.[10]

This was the view that dominated post-Renaissance science and philosophy: causality was seen as a relationship between *actions* and *actions*—not between entities and actions. The "model" of causality was mechanics: the essence of the causal relationship was identified with the relationship of impact and counter-impact, of action and reaction.

Long after the time when the mechanical "model" was recognized by physicists as inapplicable to many aspects of the physical world, *i.e.*, inapplicable even to many inanimate, deterministic systems within the universe (electromagnetic phenomena, for example), a disastrous legacy remained: the insidiously persistent notion that every action, including every action of man, is only a *re*action to some antecedent action or motion or force.

The view of causality as a relationship between motions is entirely spurious. It is worth noting that, if one accepts this view, there is no way to prove or validate the law of causality. If all that is involved is motion succeeding motion, there is no way to establish *necessary* relationships between succeeding events; one observes that B follows A, but one has no way to establish that B is the *effect* or *consequence* of A. (This, incidentally, is one of the reasons why most philosophers, who accept this notion of causality, have been unable to answer Hume's argument that one cannot *prove* the law of causality. One can't—unless one grasps its relationship to the law of identity. But this entails rejecting the motion-to-motion view of causality.)

Furthermore, the motion-to-motion view obscures the explanatory nature of the law of causality. If one wishes to understand *why* entities act as they do, in a given context, one must seek the answer through an understanding of the properties of the entities involved. And, in fact, any explanation via references to antecedent actions always implies and presupposes this understanding. For example, if one states that the *action* of a wastebasket catching fire was *caused* by the *action* of a lighted match being thrown into it, this constitutes a satisfactory causal explanation only if one understands the *nature* of paper and of lighted matches; a description of the action sequence, in the absence of such knowledge, would explain nothing.

The premise that every action is only a reaction to an antecedent action, rules out, arbitrarily and against the evidence, the existence of self-generated, goal-directed action. The way in which this premise has impeded progress in the science of biology is outside the scope of this discussion. What is directly pertinent here is the disastrous consequences of this premise for psychology; it is this premise that forbids men to grasp the possibility of a volitional consciousness.

On this premise, thinking or non-thinking is merely a necessitated reaction to an antecedent necessitated reaction to an antecedent necessitated reaction, etc. Such a view makes man wholly passive. It is entirely incompatible with the fact of man as a cognitive self-regulator. But it is not the fact of cognitive self-regulation that must be questioned and rejected; it is the mistaken notion of causality.

(It is an error to demand: "What *made* one man choose to focus and another man choose to evade?" This question almost invariably reflects the mistaken notion of causality discussed above. The question implies one's failure to grasp the meaning of *choice* in the primary sense involved in the act of focusing or thinking. The questioner is asking: "To what is the action of focusing or thinking a reaction?")

As applied to physical nature, determinism may be regarded, and commonly is regarded, as synonymous with universal causality. But as applied to man, *i.e.*, in a psychological context, the term has a narrower meaning, as defined above, which is *not* entailed by the law of causality and which is demonstrably at variance with the facts.

Now, let us consider the issue of psychological law and prediction.

Man's consciousness or mind has a specific nature; it has a specific structure, it has specific attributes, it has specific powers. Its manner of functioning exhibits specific principles or laws which it is the task of psychology to discover and identify. None of this is contradicted by the fact that the exercise of man's reason is volitional.

His mind is an organ over which man has a specific, delimited, regulatory control. Just as the driver of an automobile can steer the car in a chosen direction, but cannot alter or infringe the mechanical laws by which the car functions—so man can choose to focus, to aim his cognitive faculty in a given direction, but cannot alter or infringe the psychological laws by which his mind functions. If a man does not steer his car properly, he has no choice about the fact that he will end in a smash-up; neither has the man who does not steer his mind properly.

For example, a man is free to think or not to think, but he is not free to escape the fact that if he fails to think, if he characteristically evades facing any facts or issues which he finds unpleasant, he will set in motion a complex chain of destructive psychological consequences, one of which will be profound loss of self-esteem. This is a matter of demonstrable psychological law.[11]

Or again, if a man forms certain values—as a result of his thinking or non-thinking—these values will lead him to experience certain emotions in certain situations. He will not be able to command these emotions out of existence by "will." If he recognizes that a specific emotion is inappropriate, he can alter it by re-thinking the value(s) that evokes it—but he can do so only in a specific, "lawful" manner, *not* by arbitrary whim.[12]

"Free will" does *not* mean arbitrary, omnipotent power—*unlimited* power—over the workings of one's own mind.

Thus, to the extent that one understands the principles by which man's mind operates, one can predict the psychological consequences of given ideas, values, conclusions, attitudes and thinking policies. One can predict, for example, that a man of authentic self-esteem will find intellectual stagnation intolerable; that a man who regards sex, life and himself as evil will not be attracted to a woman of intelligence, independence and guiltless self-confidence, will not feel at ease and "at home" with her romantically; that a man whose guiding policy is "Don't antagonize anyone," will not be the first to stand up for and champion a radical new idea or theory.

One cannot predict with certainty that these men will not change their thinking. Therefore, one's predictions must take the form of "all other things being equal," or "assuming no new factors enter the situation." But this is true of prediction in the physical sciences also.

If one is to understand man psychologically, a cardinal requirement is that one identify the fact of volition. A genuinely scientific psychology must repudiate the mystique of determinism and the spurious theory of causality on which it rests.

VI. Conclusion

Such, then, is the nature of man's "free will," and as such, it justifies the concept of moral responsibility.

To recognize that man is a being of volitional consciousness is not to deny that under certain circumstances—as in insanity—a man's volitional capacity may be rendered inoperative. Thus, it is reasonable for the law to inquire, for instance, "was the accused a free agent in forming the purpose to kill and in carrying out that purpose?"—in contexts where there are objective grounds to question the normalcy of the accused's mental condition.

In other words, nothing that has been said here should be construed as a denial of the fact that there *are* times when a man may not be responsible for his acts (whatever the difficulties may be in making such determinations). Rather, it has been my purpose to establish that such a state of affairs is the *exception*, the *abnormal*—*not* the universal condition of all men, as deterministic theories would lead us to conclude.

Observe the sophistry by which some advocates of psychological determinism strive to reconcile such advocacy with their belief in the validity of legal punishment. I quote Judge Herbert Silverman:

A person can be held responsible for his behavior, whether he is determined or not. It can be held that he and no one else is the author of his behavior and that society would not be possible without the premise that we are all responsible for what we do. It may be that this is a necessary illusion . . . or a convenient fiction held for the individual's well being and for the well being of the social group of which he is a part. Nevertheless, it is a useful and pragmatic fiction.[13]

Thus does a guardian of justice "justify" the incarceration of a man in prison for many years, or even his execution, *for an action he had no power to avoid taking*.

The issue can be evaded, but the simple truth of the matter cannot be wiped out of existence: psychological determinism amounts to the annihilation of the foundations of morality and law. One cannot have one's cake and eat it, too.

Notes

Dr. Nathaniel Branden is a psychologist and practicing psychotherapist in Los Angeles, California. He is the author of three books—*The Psychology of Self-Esteem, Breaking Free,* and *The Disowned Self* —and a number of articles on topics ranging from psychology to the philosophy of science.

"Free Will, Moral Responsibility, and the Law" is reprinted with permission from the *Southern California Law Review* (1969) vol. 42:264. The article is based on a chapter from Dr. Branden's *The Psychology of Self-Esteem.*

1. See Edwards, "Hard and Soft Determinism," in *Determinism and Freedom* 117–25, Sidney Hook (ed.) (1958).

2. The term "facts of reality" means simply: that which exists.

3. A. Rand, *Atlas Shrugged* 1012 (1957).

4. See, *e.g.*, B. Skinner, *The Behavior of Organisms* (1938); C. Hull, *Essentials of Behavior* (1951); and other works by these authors.

5. R. Taylor, *Metaphysics* 50 (1963).

6. Branden, "Emotions and Values," *The Objectivist*, May 1966, at 1.

7. See *e.g.*, Blanshard, "The Case for Determinism," in *Determinism and Freedom* 19–30 (1958).

8. See *e.g.*, 2 B. Blanshard, *The Nature of Thought* 98–129 (1939).

9. A. Rand, *Atlas Shrugged* 1037 (1957).

10. 2 W. Windelband, A History of Philosophy 410 (1938).

11. Branden, "Self-Esteem," *The Objectivist*, March at 1, April at 5, May at 8, June at 1, September at 8, 1967.

12. Branden, "Emotions and Values," *The Objectivist*, May 1966, at 1.

13. Silverman, "Determinism, Choice, Responsibility and the Psychologist's Role as Expert Witness," 24 *American Psychologist* 5, 6 (1969).

Thomas S. Szasz

31 Involuntary Mental Hospitalization: A Crime against Humanity

FOR SOME TIME I have maintained that commitment—that is, the detention of persons in mental institutions against their will—is a form of imprisonment; that such deprivation of liberty is contrary to the moral principles embodied in the Declaration of Independence and the Constitution of the United States; and that it is a crass violation of contemporary concepts of fundamental human rights. The practice of "sane" men incarcerating their "insane" fellowmen in "mental hospitals" can be compared to that of white men enslaving black men. In short, I consider commitment a crime against humanity.

Existing social institutions and practices, especially if honored by prolonged usage, are generally experienced and accepted as good and valuable. For thousands of years slavery was considered a "natural" social arrangement for the securing of human labor; it was sanctioned by public opinion, religious dogma, church, and state; it was abolished a mere one hundred years ago in the United States, and is still practiced in some parts of the world, notably Africa. Commitment of the insane has enjoyed equally widespread support since its origin, approximately three centuries ago. Physicians, lawyers, and the laity have asserted, as if with a single voice, the therapeutic desirability and social necessity of institutional psychiatry.

My claim that commitment is a crime against humanity may thus be countered—as indeed it has been—by maintaining, first, that the practice is beneficial for the mentally ill, and second, that it is necessary for the protection of the mentally healthy members of society. This conventional explanation is but a culturally accepted justification for certain quasimedical but extralegal forms of social control exercised against both individuals and groups whose behavior does not violate criminal laws but threatens established social values.

Mental illness is a metaphor. If by *disease* we mean a disorder of the physicochemical machinery of the body, then we can assert that what we call functional mental diseases are not diseases at all. Persons said to be suffering from such disorders are socially deviant or inept, or in conflict with individuals, groups, or institutions. Since they do not suffer from disease, it is impossible to "treat" them for any sickness.

Although the term *mentally ill* is customarily applied to persons who have no disease, it is sometimes also applied to persons who do. However, when patients with demonstrable diseases of the brain are involuntarily hospitalized, the primary purpose is to exercise social control over their behavior; treatment of the disease is, at best, a secondary consideration. Frequently, therapy is nonexistent, and custodial care is dubbed "treatment."

Even if, as a result of future research, certain conditions now believed to be "functional" mental illness were shown to be "organic," my argument against involuntary mental hospitalization would remain unaffected.

In free societies, the relationship between physician and patient is predicated on the legal presumption that a person "owns" his body and his personality. The physician can examine and treat a patient only with his consent; the latter is free to reject treatment (for example, an operation for cancer). After death, "ownership" of the person's body is transferred to his heirs; the physician must obtain permission from them for a postmortem examination. John Stuart Mill explicitly affirmed that "each person is the proper guardian of his own health, whether bodily, or mental and spiritual." Commitment is incompatible with this moral principle.

Commitment practices flourished long before there were any mental or psychiatric "treatments" of "mental diseases." Indeed, madness or mental illness was not always a necessary condition for commitment.[1]

The claim that commitment of the "mentally ill" is necessary for the protection of the "mentally healthy" is more difficult to refute, not because it is valid, but because the danger that "mental patients" supposedly pose is of such an extremely vague nature.

However, in the absence of disease there is no medical justification for isolating patients with mental illness as there is for isolating patients with leprosy or tuberculosis.

If the so-called mental patient threatens others by virtue of his beliefs or actions, he could be dealt with by methods other than "medical": if his conduct is ethically offensive, moral sanctions might be appropriate; if forbidden by law, legal sanctions might be appropriate. In my opinion, both informal sanctions such as social ostracism or divorce and formal judicial sanctions such as fines and imprisonment are more dignified and less injurious to the human spirit than involuntary hospitalization.

To be sure, confinement does protect the community from certain problems. However, the question we ought to ask is not *whether* commitment protects the community from "dangerous mental patients," but rather, from precisely *what danger* it protects and by *what means*?

Slavery, too, protected the community: it freed the owners from manual labor. Commitment likewise shields the nonhospitalized members of society: first, from having to accommodate themselves to the annoying or idiosyncratic demands of persons who have not violated any criminal statutes; and, second, from having to apprehend and prosecute community members who have broken the law but who either cannot be convicted in court, or, if convicted, might not be restrained as effectively or as long in prison as in a mental hospital.

I have stated that commitment constitutes a social arrangement whereby one part of society secures certain advantages for itself at the expense of another part. To do so, the oppressors must possess an ideology to justify their actions; and they must be able to use the police power of the state. It may be argued that such use of state power is legitimate when law-abiding citizens punish lawbreakers. What is the difference between this use of state power and its use in enforcing slavery or involuntary commitment?

"Criminals" are subject to such controls because they have violated laws applicable equally to all; "psychotics" and "slaves" are subjected to the coercive controls of the state because they are members of a special class of inferior beings.

The principal purpose of imprisoning criminals is to protect the liberties of law-abiding members of society. Since the individual subject to commitment is not considered a threat to these liberties in the same way as the accused criminal is (if he were, he would be prosecuted), his removal from society cannot be justified on the same grounds. Justification for commitment must thus rest on its therapeutic promise and potential: it will help restore the "patient" to "mental health." But if this can be accomplished only at the cost of robbing him of liberty, this goal is no more compatible with the moral principles of a free society than is the drafting (in the absence of a national emergency) of young men to serve as doctors or farmers; or of women, as nurses or maids.

Critical examination of the practice of involuntary mental hospitalization compels one to confront the basic moral dilemma of contemporary psychiatry: in a conflict between the values of liberty and mental health (no matter how defined) which should rank higher? The architects of the open society chose liberty; I want to reecho their choice. The architects of the therapeutic society chose mental health; the present-day supporters of commitment procedures reecho their choice.

The fundamental parallel between master and slave on the one hand, and institutional psychiatrist and involuntarily hospitalized patient on the other, lies in this: in each instance, the former member of the pair *defines* the social role of the latter, and *casts* him in that role by force.

Wherever there is slavery, there must be criteria for who may and who may not be enslaved. In ancient times, any people could be enslaved; bondage was the usual consequence of military defeat. After the advent of Christianity, although the people of Europe continued to make war on each other, they ceased enslaving prisoners who were Christians. By the time of the colonization of America, the peoples of the Western world considered only black men appropriate subjects for slave trade.

The criteria for distinguishing between those who may be incarcerated in mental hospitals and those who may not be are similar: poor and socially unimportant persons may be, and Very Important Persons may not be. This rule is manifested in two ways: first, through our mental hospital statistics, which show that the majority of institutionalized patients belong in the lowest socio-economic classes; second, through the rarity and difficulty with which VIPs are committed. Yet even the sophisticated social scientists often misunderstand or misinterpret these correlations by attributing the low incidence of committed upper-class persons to a denial of the "medical fact" that "mental illness" can "strike" anyone. To be sure, powerful people may feel anxious or depressed, or behave in an excited or paranoid manner; but that, of course, is not the point at all.

Let us suppose that a person wishes to study slavery. How would he go about doing so? First, he might study slaves. He would then find that such persons are, in general, brutish, poor, and uneducated, and he might accordingly conclude that slavery is their "natural" or appropriate social state. Such, indeed, have been the methods and conclusions of innumerable men throughout the ages. Even the great Aristotle held that slaves were "naturally" inferior and hence justly subdued. "From the hour of their birth," he asserted, "some are marked for subjection, others for rule." This view is similar to the modern concept of schizophrenia as a genetically caused disease.

Another student, "biased" by contempt for the institution of slavery, might proceed differently. He would maintain that there can be no slave without a master holding him in bondage; and he would accordingly consider slavery a type of human relationship and, more generally, a social institution supported by custom, law, religion, and force. From this point of view, the study of masters is at least as relevant to the study of slavery as is the study of slaves.

The latter point of view is generally accepted today with regard to slavery, but not with regard to institutional psychiatry. "Mental illness" of the type found in psychiatric hospitals has been investigated for centuries, and continues to be investigated today, in much the same way as slaves were studied in the antebellum South and before. The "existence" of slaves was taken for granted; their biological and social characteristics were noted and classified. Similarly, the "existence" of "mental patients" is now taken for granted; indeed, it is widely believed that their number is steadily increasing. The psychiatrist's task is to observe and classify their biological, psychological, and social characteristics.

This perspective is a manifestation, in part, of what I have called "the myth of mental illness"—that is, of the notion that mental illnesses are similar to diseases of the body; and in part, of the psychiatrist's intense need to deny the fundamental complementarity of his relationship to the involuntary mental patient. The same complementarity obtains in all situations where one person or party assumes a superior or dominant role and ascribes an inferior or submissive role to another; for example, master and slave, accuser and accused, inquisitor and witch. (Sometimes people willingly assume a submissive role and cast their partners in a dominant role. I am not concerned with this aspect of the problem here.)

A basic assumption of American slavery was that the Negro slave was racially inferior. "There is no malice toward the Negro in Ulrich Phillips' work," wrote S. M. Elkins about that author's book, *American Negro Slavery*,[2] a work sympathetic to the Southern position. "Phillips was deeply fond of the Negroes as a people; it was just that he could not take them seriously as men and women; they were children."

Similarly, the basic assumption of institutional psychiatry is that the "mentally ill" person is psychologically and socially inferior. He is like a child: he does not know what is in his best interests and therefore needs others to control and protect him. Psychiatrists often care deeply for their involuntary patients, whom they consider—in contrast with the merely "neurotic" persons—"psychotic," which is to say, "very sick." Hence, such patients must be cared for as the "irresponsible children" they are considered to be.

The perspective of paternalism has played an exceedingly important role in justifying both slavery and involuntary mental hospitalization. Aristotle defined slavery as "an essentially domestic relationship"; in so doing, wrote D. B. Davis, in *The Problem of Slavery in Western Culture*,[3] he "endowed it with the sanction of paternal authority, and helped to establish a precedent that would govern discussions of political philosophers as late as the eighteenth century." The relationship between psychiatrists and mental patients has been and continues to be viewed in the same way. The fact that, as in the case of slavery, the physician needs the police power of the state to maintain his relationship with his so-called patient does not alter this self-serving image of the oppressive institution.

Paternalism is the crucial explanation for the stubborn conflict about whether the practices employed by slaveholders and institutional psychiatrists are "therapeutic" or "noxious." Masters and psychiatrists profess their benevolence; their slaves and involuntary patients protest against their malevolence. As S. L. Halleck, a defender of contemporary mental health practices, put it in *Psychiatry and the Dilemmas of Crime*,[4] ". . . the psychiatrist experiences himself as a helping person, but his patient may see him as a jailer. Both views are partially correct." Not so. Both views are completely correct. Each is a proposition about a different subject: the former, about the psychiatrist's self-image; the latter, about the involuntary mental patient's image of his captor. In *Ward 7*,[5] Valeriy Tarsis presents the following dialogue between his protagonist-patient and the mental hospital physician: "This is the position. I don't regard you as a doctor. You call this a hospital, I call it a prison. . . . So now, let's get everything straight. I am your prisoner, you are my jailer, and there isn't going to be any nonsense about my health . . . or treatment."

This is the characteristic dialogue of oppression and liberation. The ruler looks in the mirror and sees a liberator; the ruled looks at the ruler and sees a tyrant. If the physician has the power to incarcerate the patient and uses it, the relationship between the two will inevitably fit into this mold. If one cannot ask the subject whether he likes being enslaved or committed, whipped or electroshocked—because he is not a fit judge of his own "best interests"—then one is left with the contending opinions of the practitioners and their critics.

The defenders of slavery claimed that the Negro was happier as a slave than he could have been as a free man because of the "peculiarities of his character." The defenders of involuntary mental hospitalization claim that the mental patient is healthier—the twentieth-century synonym for *happier*—as a psychiatric prisoner than he would be as a free citizen because of the nature of his illness. It requires no great feat of imagination to see how comforting—indeed, how absolutely necessary—these views are, even when contradicted by fact.

For example, although it was held that the Negro slave was happy, there was an ever-lurking fear of Negro violence and revolt. As S. M. Elkins put it: "The failure of any free workers to present themselves for enslavement can serve as one test of how much the analysis of the 'happy slave' may have added to Americans' understanding of themselves."[6]

The same views and the same inconsistencies apply to involuntary psychiatric hospitalization. Defenders of the system maintain that the committed patient is better off in the hospital; at the same time, the patients are feared for their potential violence, their escapes from captivity occasion intense manhunts, and their crimes are prominently featured in the newspapers. Moreover, as with slavery, the failure of free citizens to present themselves for involuntary psychiatric hospitalization can serve as a test of how much the currently popular analysis of mental health problems may have added to Americans' understanding of themselves.

The social necessity, and hence the basic value, of involuntary mental hospitalization, at least for some people, is not seriously questioned today. It is thus possible to debate *who* should be hospitalized, or *how*, or for *how long*—but not whether *anyone* should be. I submit, however, that just as it is improper to enslave anyone—black or white, Moslem or Christian—so it is improper to hospitalize anyone without his consent, whether· he is depressed or paranoid, hysterical or schizophrenic.

Our unwillingness to look at this problem searchingly may be compared to the unwillingness of the South to look at slavery. ". . . a democratic people," writes Elkins, "no longer 'reasons' with itself when it is all of the same mind. Men will then only warn and exhort each other, that their solidarity may be yet more perfect. The South's intellectuals, after the 1830s, did really little more than this. And when the enemy's reality disappears, when his concreteness recedes, then intellect itself, with nothing more to resist it and give it resonance, merges with the mass and stultifies, and shadows become monsters."

Our growing preoccupation with the menace of mental illness may be a manifestation of just such a process. A democratic nation, as we have been warned by Tocqueville, is especially vulnerable to the hazards of a surfeit of agreement: "The authority of a king is physical, and controls the actions of men without subduing their will. But the majority possesses a power that is physical and moral at the same time, which acts upon the will as much as upon the actions, and represses not only all contests, but all controversy."

There are essential similarities in relationship between masters and subjects—no matter whether owners and slaves or psychiatrists and confined patients.

To maintain a relationship of personal or class superiority, it is necessary, as a rule, that the oppressor keep the oppressed uninformed, especially about matters pertinent to their relationship. In America the history of the systematic efforts by the whites to keep the Negro ignorant is well known. A dramatic example is the law, passed in 1824 by the Virginia Assembly, that provided a fifty-dollar fine and two months' imprisonment for teaching *free* Negroes to read and write. Nor was the situation very different in the North. In January 1833, Prudence Crandall admitted to her private school, in Canterbury, Connecticut, a young lady of seventeen, the daughter of a highly respected Negro family. Miss Crandall was thereupon ostracized and persecuted by her neighbors. She was formally tried for breaking a law that forbade the harboring, boarding, or instruction in any manner of any person of color and was convicted. Finally, her school was set on fire.

A similar effort to educationally degrade and psychologically impoverish their charges characterizes the acts of the managers of madhouses. In most prisons in the United States, it is possible for a convict to obtain a high-school diploma, to learn a trade, to become an amateur lawyer, or to write a book. None of these is possible in a mental hospital. Moreover, the principal requirement for an inmate of such an institution is that he accept the psychiatric ideology about his "illness," and the things he must do to "recover" from it. The committed patient must thus accept the view that he is "sick," and that his captors are "well"; that his own view of himself is false, and that of his captors, true; and that to effect any change in his social situation he must relinquish his "sick" views and adopt the "healthy" views of those who have power over him. By accepting himself as "sick," and his institutional environment and the various manipulations imposed on him by the staff as "treatment," the mental patient is compelled to authenticate the psychiatrist's role as that of a benevolent physician curing mental illness. The mental patient who maintains the forbidden image of reality, i.e., that the institutional psychiatrist is a jailer, is considered paranoid. Moreover, since most patients—as do oppressed people generally—sooner or later accept the ideas imposed on them by their superiors, hospital psychiatrists are constantly immersed in an environment in which their identity as "doctors" is affirmed. The moral superiority of white men over black was similarly authenticated and affirmed.

In both situations, the oppressor first subjugates his adversary, and then cites his status as proof of his inferiority. Once this process is set in motion, it develops its own momentum and psychological logic.

Looking at the relationship, the oppressor will see his superiority and hence his well-deserved dominance; the oppressed will see his inferiority and hence his well-deserved submission. In race relations in the United States, we continue to reap the bitter results of this philosophy, and in psychiatry, we are even now sowing seeds of this poisonous fruit, whose eventual harvest may be equally bitter and long.

Convicts are entitled to fight for their "legal rights"; but not involuntary mental patients. Like slaves, such patients have no rights except those granted them by their medical masters. According to Benjamin Apfelberg, clinical professor of psychiatry and medical director of the Law-Psychiatry Project at New York University: "Our students come to realize that by fighting for a patient's *legal* rights they may actually be doing him a great disservice. They learn that there is such a thing as a person's *medical* rights, the right to get treatment, to become well."[7]

The "medical right" to which Apfelberg refers is a euphemism for the *obligation* to remain confined in a mental institution, not the *opportunity* to choose between hospitalization and no hospitalization. But calling involuntary mental hospitalization a "medical right" is like calling involuntary servitude in antebellum Georgia a "right to work."

Oppression and degradation are unpleasant to behold and are, therefore, frequently disguised or concealed. One method for doing so is to segregate—in special areas, such as camps or "hospitals"—the degraded human beings. Another is to conceal the social realities behind the fictional facade of what we call, after Wittgenstein, "language games." While psychiatric language games may seem fanciful, the psychiatric idiom is actually only a dialect of the common language of oppressors. Thus slaveholders called the slaves *livestock*, mothers *breeders*, their children *increase*, and gave the term *drivers* to the men set over them at work. The defenders of psychiatric imprisonment call their institutions *hospitals*, the inmates *patients*, and the keepers *doctors*; they refer to the sentence as *treatment*, and to the deprivation of liberty as *protection of the patient's best interests*.

In both cases, the semantic devices are supplemented by appeals to tradition, morality, and social necessity. The proslavery factions in America argued that the abolitionists were wrong because they were seeking to overthrow an ancient institution recognized by the Scriptures and the Constitution.

The contemporary reader may find it difficult to believe how unquestioningly slavery was accepted as a natural and beneficial social arrangement. Even as great a liberal thinker as John Locke did not advocate its abolition. Moreover, protests against the slave trade would have provoked the hostility of powerful religious and economic groups.

Similar considerations apply to challenging the institution of involuntary mental hospitalization.

In Western nations and the Soviet bloc alike, there are two views on commitment. According to the one, involuntary mental hospitalization is an indispensable method of medical healing and a humane type of social control; according to the other, it is a contemptible abuse of the medical relationship and a type of imprisonment without trial. We adopt the former view and consider commitment "proper" if we use it on victims of our choosing whom we despise; we adopt the latter view and consider commitment "improper" if our enemies use it on victims of their choosing whom we esteem.

The change in perspective—from seeing slavery occasioned by the "inferiority" of the Negro and commitment by the "insanity" of the patient, to seeing each occasioned by the interplay of, and especially the power relation between, the participants—has far-reaching practical implications. In the case of slavery, it meant not only that the slaves had an obligation to revolt and emancipate themselves, but also that the masters had an even greater obligation to renounce their roles as slaveholders. Naturally, a slaveholder with such ideas felt compelled to set his slaves free, at whatever cost to himself. This is precisely what some slaveowners did.

Their action had profound consequences in a social system based on slavery. For the act led almost invariably to the former master's expulsion from the community—through economic pressure or personal harassment or both. Such persons usually emigrated to the North. For the nation as a whole, these acts and the abolitionist sentiments behind them symbolized a fundamental moral rift between those who regarded the Negroes as objects or slaves, and those who regarded them as persons or citizens. The former could persist in regarding the slave as existing in nature; whereas the latter could not deny his own moral responsibility for creating man in the image, not of God, but of the slave-animal.

The implications of this perspective for institutional psychiatry are equally clear. A psychiatrist who accepts as his "client" a person who does not wish to be his client, defines him as a "mentally ill" person, then incarcerates him in an institution, bars his escape from the institution and from the role of mental patient, and proceeds to "treat" him against his will—such a psychiatrist, I maintain, creates "mental illness" and "mental patients." He does so in exactly the same way as the white man who sailed for Africa, captured the black man, brought him to America in shackles, and then sold him as if he were an animal, created slavery and slaves. To be sure, in both cases, the process is carried out in accordance with the law of the land. The assertion that only the "insane" are committed to mental hospitals is, in this view, comparable to the claim that only the black man is enslaved. It is the most damaging evidence, for it signifies that the oppressor recognizes the "special" condition of his adversary.

The parallel may be carried one step farther. The renouncing of slave holding by some slaveowners led to certain social problems, such as Negro unemployment and a gradual splitting of the country into pro- and anti-slavery factions. The renouncing by some psychiatrists of relationships with involuntary mental patients has led to certain professional problems in the past, and is likely to do so in the future. Psychiatrists restricting their work to psychoanalysis and psychotherapy have been accused of not being "real doctors"—as if depriving a person of his liberty required medical skills; of "shirking their responsibilities" to their colleagues and to society by accepting only the "easier cases" and refusing to treat the "seriously mentally ill" patient—as if practicing self-control and eschewing violence were newly discovered forms of immorality.

The psychiatric profession has, of course, a huge stake, both existential and economic, in being socially authorized to rule over mental patients, just as the slaveowning classes did in ruling over slaves. In contemporary psychiatry, indeed, the expert gains superiority not only over members of a specific class of victims, but over nearly the whole of the population, whom he may "psychiatrically evaluate."

The economic similarities between chattel slavery and institutional psychiatry are equally evident. The economic strength of the slaveowner was determined by the number of slaves he owned. The economic strength of the institutional psychiatrist lies, similarly, in his involuntary mental patients, who are not free to move about, work, marry, divorce, or make contracts, but are, instead, under the control of the hospital director. The income and power of the psychiatric bureaucrat rises with the size of the institution he controls and the number of patients he commands. Moreover, just as the slaveholder could use the police power of the state to help him recruit and maintain his slave labor force, so can the institutional psychiatrist rely on the state to help him recruit and maintain a population of hospital inmates.

Finally, since the various governments have vast economic stakes in the operation of psychiatric hospitals and clinics, the interests of the state and of institutional psychiatry tend to be the same. Formerly the state and federal governments had a vast economic stake in the operation of plantations worked by slaves, and hence the interests of the state and of the slaveowning classes tended to be the same. The wholly predictable consequence of such an arrangement is that the oppressive institution is invincible; its defects, no matter how glaring, cannot be much improved. On the other hand, once such an institution loses the support of the state, it rapidly disintegrates; there can be no oppression without power.

If this argument is valid, pressing the view that psychiatrists now create mentally sick clients just as slaveholders used to create slaves is likely to lead to a cleavage in the psychiatric profession, and perhaps in society generally, between those who condone and advocate the relationship between psychiatrist and involuntary mental patient and those who condemn and oppose it.

It is not clear whether, or on what terms, these two psychiatric factions could coexist. The practices of coercive psychiatry and of paternalistic psychiatrists do not, in themselves, threaten the practices of noncoercive psychiatry and of contracting psychiatrists. Economic relations based on slavery coexisted over long periods with relations based on contract. But the moral conflict poses a more difficult problem. For just as the abolitionists tended to undermine the social justifications of slavery and the psychological bonds of the slave, so the abolitionists of psychiatric slavery tend to undermine the justifications of commitment and the psychological bonds of the committed patient.

Ultimately, the forces of society will probably be enlisted on one side or the other. If so, we may, on the one hand, be ushering in the abolition of involuntary mental hospitalization and treatment; on the other, we may be witnessing the fruitless struggles of an individualism bereft of popular support against a collectivism proffered as medical treatment.

We know that man's domination over his fellowman is as old as history; and we may safely assume that it is traceable to prehistoric times and to prehuman ancestors. Perennially, men have oppressed women; white men, colored men; Christians, Jews. However, traditional reasons and justifications for discrimination have lost much of their plausibility. What justification is there for man's age-old desire for domination of his fellowman? Modern liberalism (in reality, a type of statism), allied with scientism, has met the need for a fresh defense of oppression and has supplied a new battle cry: Health!

In this therapeutic-meliorist view of society, the ill form a special class of "victims" who must, both for their own good and for the interests of the community, be "helped"—coercively and against their will, if necessary—by the healthy; and among the healthy, especially by physicians, who are "scientifically" qualified to be their masters. This perspective developed first and has advanced farthest in psychiatry, where the oppression of "insane patients" by "sane physicians" is by now a social custom hallowed by medical and legal tradition. At present, the medical profession as a whole seems to be emulating this model. In the therapeutic state toward which we appear to be moving, the principal requisite for the role of big brother may be an M.D. degree.

Notes

Dr. Thomas Szasz is Professor of Psychiatry in the college of medicine at the State University of New York in Syracuse. Dr. Szasz received his degree in medicine from the University of Cincinnati.

"Involuntary Mental Hospitalization: A Crime Against Humanity," is reprinted with permission from *Medical Opinion & Review* (May 1968).

1. See Szasz, "Medical Ethics: A Historical Perspective," *Medical Opinion & Review*, February, 1968.

2. Phillips, *American Negro Slavery* (New York: D. Appleton & Co., 1918).

3. Davis, *The Problem of Slavery in Western Culture* (Ithaca, New York: Cornell, 1966).

4. Halleck, *Psychiatry and the Dilemmas of Crime* (New York: Harper & Row, 1967).

5. Tarsis, *Ward 7* (New York: E. P. Dutton & Co., Inc., 1965).

6. Elkins, *Slavery: A Problem in American Institutional and Intellectual Life* (Chicago: University of Chicago Press, 1959).

7. *SK&F Psychiatric Reporter* (Smith, Kline & French Laboratories), July–August, 1965.

Ruth S. Maynard

32 Who Conserves Our Resources?

"WHO SHOULD CONSERVE our resources?" If a poll were taken, a large majority probably would answer: "Our federal and state governments." And if one were to ask why this view is so widely held, he would find among other "reasons" the following:

(1) that the free market is chaotic, gives profits to the few, and is unmindful of the great "waste" of our diminishing resources;

(2) that "people's rights" are above "private or special interests" and only the government can properly serve the public interest;

(3) that government has access to more funds;

(4) that government has the power and facilities to obtain all the necessary data and to do the research needed for the best "scientific" decisions on resource conservation;

(5) that the price system does not operate in the interests of conservation because of the "unrestrained pursuit of self-interest";

(6) that the concentration of power in some corporations further threatens our dwindling resources and must be regulated by government.

These "reasons," of course, do not indicate how a government agency would go about attempting a solution to the conservation problem—this is always just assumed—but consider them briefly:

(1a) The free market is anything but chaotic. Competing natural market forces reflect in prices the wishes of both buyers and sellers—millions of individuals, separately accountable and responsible for their own actions in their own field of economic activity. All persons seek their own advantage when allowed a choice, but in the free market a producer cannot profit unless he pleases consumers better than his competitor does. Since he must think of efficiency and lowered costs in order to survive, it is false to assume that he alone profits from the use of natural resources from which are made the products wanted by consumers. All gain who use the resulting products.

(2a) Can there be "people's rights" superior to the rights of individuals? All individuals have special and private interests and rights. Therefore, the "people" cannot have rights except individually; and the right to life carries with it the right to maintain it by private and special means.

(3a) The government has no funds that have not been taken from the people by force, whereas many a large private undertaking has come forth from voluntarily contributed funds. In fact, the entire industrial development in this country has been a continuous example of this voluntary way of creating the facilities for production by giving the consumer what he wants at the price he is willing to pay in competition.

(4a) Offhand it would seem that a government might have access to more data about scarce resources than would a private enterpriser. But government cannot bring forth the detailed information so vital to sound decision. The kind of detailed knowledge needed simply isn't "given to anyone in its totality," as Hayek has pointed out.[1] "Knowledge of the circumstances of which we must make use never exists in concentrated or integrated form," he states, "but solely as dispersed bits of incomplete and frequently contradictory knowledge which all the separate individuals possess." Yet, producers need such information before they can decide how to act. The chief communicator of this knowledge is free price movements. If the price of a given resource continues upward, this tells producers all they need to know about its increasing scarcity and signals them to conserve it, to use it sparingly and for the most valuable products. Advocates of government planning never seem to grasp how this works, for they are constantly tampering with market forces, distorting the delicate price signals that could otherwise guide them. Thus, government planners must rely on using *general* data obtained by crude polling methods which are unreliable for action in specific economic areas and are out of date before they can be collected, analyzed, and summarized. Moreover, such studies cannot tell the government controller as much as free price movements tell individuals acting in a particular market as buyers or sellers.

(5a) The role that prices play in the free economy is so little understood that many people believe government must set prices lest they reflect only the "selfish interest" of the producers. The price system not only tells producers and consumers when scarcity of a product exists (prices rise) or when it has become more plentiful (prices drop); it also supplies the incentive to act in the interests of conservation by seeking a substitute for the high-priced scarce material. Competitive prices allocate scarce resources to those who will *pay* more (not those who *have* more, as is alleged) for the right to try to serve consumers efficiently as well as profitably.

(6a) If concentration of power in corporations is too great to be permitted, what about the ultimate concentration of power in a government institution beyond the regulation of market forces? Government is unaccountable in the sense that it is not obliged to please consumers in order to stay in business. If it does not show a profit, its losses can be covered by tax money. Big corporations can behave in monopolistic fashion only if they enjoy government privileges of some kind. Potential competition, substitution, and elasticity of demand force them to keep prices close to the competitive level.[2]

When Government Controls

The foregoing arguments, however, do not touch upon the basic problem involved in the conservation of resources. Let us assume that Congress passes a conservation law setting up "The Federal Bureau of Conservation." Tax money must then be appropriated for this Bureau. The director, a political appointee, must find a building and hire a staff large enough to justify his salary. To investigate and collect data on what is being done is a time- and tax-consuming job.

Turning the conservation problems over to an agency with police power does not mean solution, however. It only means that the director has been given the authority to find a solution and to force it on those individuals who are in the market for natural resources. This does not assure the public that the director has any special grant of wisdom concerning the problems involved, or that he will even know what they are. This appointment would lead him to assume that individual enterprisers were not doing their jobs well. He would undoubtedly define his task as one of finding what individual enterprisers are doing wrong and stopping it. Such interference could only prevent private individuals from utilizing their creativity and energy in seeking a solution to both immediate and long-run conservation problems. Having stopped this flow of creative endeavor, he would need to find a "positive" solution—such as stockpiling by force certain quantities of those materials deemed most scarce.

But for whom would the director be stockpiling? Would he sacrifice the present generation to future ones? And, if so, which ones? The next generation, the one after that, those living a hundred years from now, or whom? And how could he possibly know what those generations would want or need? Moreover, he would have the problem of what quantities to stockpile and what grades (best or worst) to save. Would some items have alternative uses? Would he plan for possible added or new uses in the future? These questions never seem to be asked by the authors of books and articles on conservation, whose specialty is to condemn private enterprise.

Stockpiling only aggravates the very scarcity given as the reason for stockpiling. The more scarce a stockpiled item, the higher the price, and the more complaints to be heard from the users. Whereupon, the director probably would seek power to fix prices lower than market levels. This, of course, could only lead to increased demand and pressure on prices, leading to black markets or government rationing, or both. Allocation by rationing would present the problem of whom to favor and whom to slight. His authority to discriminate would subject the director to strong political pressures. If not by political favoritism, the director could select by personal preference, or first come, first favored. Any system is discriminatory. The system of government planning implies arbitrary discrimination by one man with police power who decides who shall get what. Without personal favoritism, the free market "discriminates" *against* those who would waste scarce materials— it lets their businesses fail—and "discriminates" *for* those who would most efficiently use the resource to serve consumers—their profit depends on their capacity to conserve the scarce resource.

The government system is based on arbitrary decisions of man over man, with strong probability of political influence; the free market system is influenced by nonpolitical and nonpersonal forces. There is no other alternative. The first system leads to static conditions which cannot meet the changing needs and desires of consumers, the "people" most involved and presumably those whom a conservation agency ought to protect. The business way encourages search for substitutes when price rises indicate growing scarcity. This not only aids conservation but also affords the consuming public more reasonably priced alternatives in times of scarcity. When prices are fixed below market levels by the government director, this discourages conservation and gives a false signal as to the degree of scarcity all the way from the natural resource level to the final consumer.

Is It Not Worth Saving?

Until someone discovers that a resource has a specific use, it has no value for which it should be conserved. Alexander the Great had no use for the reservoir of oil beneath his domain. The underdeveloped countries do not lack resources. But they have not yet found the key (personal saving and competitive private enterprise) by which to utilize the resources to meet the people's needs. Private enterprisers are constantly trying to find new materials and new uses for known resources, always looking ahead to see which ones will be available and how efficiently they can be utilized. Pick up any trade journal and note the articles on how to cut costs, utilize waste materials, be more efficient. Because the government told them to? No. The hope of profits acts as a powerful compulsion to be efficient, to improve, to conserve. The following examples show how private enterprisers eliminate waste and utilize natural resources to meet the needs of the consuming public.

Until natural gas was known to be useful as a fuel, petroleum producers burned it to get rid of it. Until ways were found of storing and transporting gas with safety, it had only local use. Competition forced the search for further uses and wider markets, and profits rewarded those who best served consumers. As ways were found to handle gas beyond local markets, consumers elsewhere gained a wider choice of fuel, and other fuels were thereby conserved.

Reliance on Hindsight

Accusations of waste in private industry are always based on hindsight. Any statistics of inadequate use of natural resources are history. When a new method or new use is discovered, it is easy to point out past waste and misuse. The assumption is that industrialists are wasteful if they haven't seen in advance all possible uses for all materials.

The meat-packing industry over the last century has used all but the squeal of the pig. But this did not come all at once. Nor did or could it have come from government decrees. It came slowly through individual efforts to cut costs and increase profits in competition with others.

In the lumber and pulp-paper industries, uses have been found for virtually all of a tree, including the bark, branches, and sawdust which were formerly "wasted." The "waste" lignin, after removal of the carbohydrates, has been the concern of many a pulp company as well as scientists at The Institute of Paper Chemistry, who have yet to find a use that will meet adequately the competitive market test of consumer choice.

With the increasing scarcity of pure water, the pulp and paper industry has used less and less of it per ton of product. When wood became scarce in Wisconsin, the "Trees-for-Tomorrow" program was instigated, encouraging farmers to grow trees as an added cash crop. As salt cake from Saskatchewan grew scarce, the Southern kraft-pulp mills learned how to reclaim it and cut the amount needed per ton of pulp by two-thirds or more. Could such a conservation measure have been forced by government decree? It is most doubtful.

In the agricultural field are many illustrations of continuous improvement: of tools (the history of the plow alone would make an impressive volume); of methods of utilizing land, fertilizers, insecticides, and seeds; of knowledge of genetics, hydroponics, and radioactive materials. All of these have played a vital part in getting better farm products to the people with fewer manhours and at less cost. These all conserve time.

Time also is a resource. Conserving time can save lives from starvation, give relief from backbreaking jobs, enable individuals to further achieve their respective purposes. Improved tools have won time for more leisure, for increasing recreational, cultural, educational, and religious activities.

Individual Improvement

Improvement of the well-being of individuals, rather than conservation, is the chief goal in the utilization of resources. Absolute conservation could lead to the absurdity of not utilizing our resources at all, and thus conserving to no purpose—no freedom and no improvement of our lives. J. S. Mill has expressed it thus: "The only unfailing and permanent source of improvement is liberty, since by it there are as many possible independent centers of improvement as there are individuals." The energy of the police force of a government agency must by its very nature be negative. Enterprisers are positive, constantly trying to solve specific problems. It is impossible to force the release of the creative energy of millions of individuals who, if free, are each highly motivated to release it in trying to improve their status. Thus, force only inhibits the real sources of improvement.

Because individuals have been free to find the best use of land resources, the American farmer today feeds himself and at least 25 others. In our early history food production was the principal occupation, and in some countries today as high as 90 per cent of the population still spends long hours of backbreaking work farming for a bare subsistence.

Who Is Responsible for Waste?

The real waste in resources comes from government policies. It is seen especially in wartime, but more and more in peacetime programs. The government farm program has encouraged waste of land, seeds, fertilizers, labor, and capital by subsidizing the production of surpluses to be stored in bins that dot the countryside. The foreign aid program has wasted various resources, sending them to countries where little if any use has been or could be made of them. Waste occurs in such projects as the TVA that floods permanently many fertile acres which formerly provided millions of dollars worth of food products and which the Army Engineers have estimated would not be flooded by the natural forces of the Tennessee River in 500 years.

Rising taxes also promote waste. The corporate income tax of 52 per cent of earnings, for example, encourages industrialists to engage in questionable and wasteful projects which appear justified only when purchased with a 48-cent dollar. This is not in the interests of conservation.

However, the errors individuals make and their waste of resources are small and inconsequential compared with those made by government agents in controlling a major supply of a scarce resource. Those in civil service positions are rarely dismissed or otherwise held accountable for their errors. A private individual stands to lose personally if he wastes resources in his field of economic activity, and has a built-in motivation for attempting to correct his mistakes as soon as they are reflected in rising costs or decreasing demand. A government agent, however, risks no personal loss when he misuses resources, he cannot recognize mistakes by rising costs when prices are fixed arbitrarily, nor is he motivated to correct his mistakes even when recognized.

Natural resources are best utilized and conserved where they meet specific economic requirements in the most efficient way as determined by competition in the free market. Government control of natural resources reduces the freedom of choice of producers in using these materials and this affects adversely the freedom of choice of consumers who buy the final products made from them. There is no effective method of determining the economic requirements of the people when the free market is not allowed to reflect them, nor can force solve the problem of conservation. It is a false panacea that is centuries old, advocated by those who desire power over others whom they neither trust nor respect. Conservation will take place in the best sense where individuals are allowed to seek solutions to their own personal problems as they arise. Necessity is the mother not only of invention but of conservation as well.

Notes

Ruth S. Maynard is a retired teacher of economics. She last taught at Lake Erie College.

"Who Conserves Our Resources?" is reprinted with permission from *Essays on Liberty*.

1. F. A. Hayek, "The Use of Knowledge in Society," *The American Economic Review*, Vol. XXXV, No. 4, September, 1945.

2. Hans Sennholz, "The Phantom Called Monopoly," *Essays on Liberty*, Vol. 7, p. 295.

David J. Dawson

33 John Locke, the Draft, and the Divine Right of Kings

THERE ARE TWO ways to form an army: by compulsion—the draft; and by voluntarism—a volunteer armed force. Ever since the founding of the republic, both these methods have been used in the United States. A government founded on the revolutionary principle that governments should operate ultimately through the consent of the governed has never been able to make up its mind whether to compel men to defend it, or to leave that to free choice.

Recruitment by free choice predominated until World War II. Though it is true that most of the colonies had draft laws on their books (Pennsylvania included a draft in its 1776 constitution), the draft was not of much consequence in the Revolutionary War. Nor was it in the Civil War—not militarily—though use of conscription created political division and even violence both in North and South. Our participation in World War I was brief: the draft came and went in two years. It was not around long enough to imbed itself in American life—but it set the precedent that would be followed in the next war.

World War II saw the beginning of something new. From then to now, except for a period of little over a year in the late forties, there has been a draft. As L. Mendel Rivers, Chairman of the House Armed Services Committee, pointed out in the Committee's 1966 hearings on the draft, "we have literally raised a generation of Americans under the Selective Service System."

For the first time in history, forced military service has now been institutionalized in the United States. It is thought of less and less as a temporary necessary evil that can *only* be put up with because it is temporary. More and more, legislators and administration spokesmen view the draft as a permanent institution. Until World War II, Americans thought of peacetime conscription as a European institution. It was particularly associated with France, Prussia and Czarist (and later Soviet) Russia. One of the prime reasons for the flood of immigrants to the United States during the late nineteenth and early twentieth centuries was to escape this dreaded institution.

We cannot postpone making up our minds about conscription forever. If we do, history will decide for us, and we will have a conscript state by default. We must decide just how basic individual rights will be in the United States of the future. On this issue, we are not standing still; we cannot have rights *and* conscription. We either move further toward compulsion, or we move toward recognizing the right of choice.

Today, in large measure because of the draft, we are moving toward an entire society based on compulsion. Today, when we violate the individual rights of young men through the draft, we are laying the foundations for a future in which every man's rights (and every woman's) will be violated as a matter of course, by custom and by law. A volunteer armed force is not a dangerous luxury; it would not, as L. Mendel Rivers put it in 1966, jeopardize "our national security and in turn, our precious heritage of freedom." On the contrary, the existence of such a force is a necessity if we are to be a free society. That is, a society which recognizes individual rights.

We all have a commonsense notion of what rights are. Rights involve being allowed to do what you want, when you want, provided you don't attack other people or other people's property. Under a government based on rights, the individual citizen is left alone to make a living, or to express ideas, or to invent, or to found a business, or as a prime document of the United States puts it, to engage in the "pursuit of happiness."

But "rights" is a political term, and the commonsense usage is only a reflection of complex ideas, ideas which were very consciously in the minds of the founders of the country. If any one man is philosophically the father of the United States, that man is the seventeenth-century English philosopher John Locke. Locke's influence is most strikingly seen, perhaps, in the Declaration of Independence (its author, Thomas Jefferson, was a student of Locke's political philosophy), but virtually all of the delegates to the constitutional convention were so well acquainted with Locke's ideas that they were provided with a common philosophical base which enabled them to agree on a basic and complex document in the short space of one summer. There was virtual unanimity on the meaning of rights and on their necessity to man, and therefore on the principle that the purpose of government was to protect rights. This was the animating principle behind the main articles and sections of the Constitution; this was the explicit reason that James Madison gave for insisting that if there was to be a Bill of Rights there must also be a provision stating that the people retained rights which were not enumerated in it—the Ninth Amendment in the Bill of Rights. The United States was not to be a tyranny. All forms of governmental violation of the rights of man were to be left behind in Europe.

Locke's view of the nature of rights represented a complete reversal of the view of the proper relationship of the state to its citizens which had prevailed until his time. For Locke, the rights of man precede government rather than being derived from it. Locke's major political work was *Two Treatises of Government*, considered for some time by scholars as having been written to justify Great Britain's "Glorious Revolution" of 1688. Recent scholarship, as well as the discovery of Locke's own annotated copy of the work in the Cambridge University library, now indicates that the work was begun as early as 1679, thus making it a cause of the Revolution in England, not an *ex post facto* justification of it. It is also now held by the British scholar, Peter Laslett, that the second treatise, the famous *Of Civil Government*, was in fact written first, and that the whole work was primarily intended as a refutation of the work of Sir Robert Filmer. Filmer had justified patriarchal kingship by quoting from the Bible, and had specifically denied the growing intellectual assumption that men were free and equal. Laslett considers that Locke formulated his theory of property in response to this. "It may well be," he writes in his long Introduction to the Cambridge University Press edition of *Two Treatises of Government*, "that some of Locke's arguments would never have been developed at all if it had not been for Filmer. We have seen that he showed no sign of an interest in the theory of property before he sat down to his polemic and found himself faced with an argument in favor of primitive communism which was very difficult to refute unless a new justification of ownership was devised." The result was, says Laslett, a book that "was at once a response to a particular political situation and a statement of universal principle, made as such and still read as such."

Filmer advocated "primitive communism" combined with the so-called Divine Right of Kings—he advocated a patriarchal state in which the monarch was all-powerful and controlled his people absolutely, while he doled out benefits to all. If one substitutes for the single monarch of Filmer the modern semi-anonymous bureaucracy, one can see points in common between this theory and the implicit view of many who support the draft—that the state is the great benefactor, whose motives and powers are therefore not to be questioned.

In chapter two of Locke's *Of Civil Government*, he declares that the "State all Men are naturally in ... is a *State of perfect Freedom* to order their Actions, and dispose of their Possessions, and Persons as they think fit, within the bounds of the Law of Nature, without asking leave, or depending upon the Will of any other Man." Further in the same chapter he says, "The *State of Nature* has a Law of Nature to govern it, which obliges everyone: And Reason, which is that Law, teaches all Mankind, who will but consult it, that being all equal and independent, no one ought to harm another in his Life, Health, Liberty, or Possessions."

He is undeviating in this view that man, each individual man, has an unequivocal right to himself. In chapter five he states, "... every Man has a *Property* in his own *Person*. Thus no Body has any Right to but himself. The *Labour* of his Body, and the *Work* of his Hands, we may say, are properly his."

Thus he sets up the essence of man's relationship to man. It is natural for man to own himself, to possess, to be free. This is his state in nature but, as he says, "In the state of nature there are many things found wanting." Each man must be his own government, must judge and punish. Too easily this leads to one man harming another.

Hence, he reasons, there is a proper role for government. In chapter nine he declares that in this state of nature man "is very unsafe, very insecure. This makes him willing to quit a Condition, which however free, is full of fears and continual dangers ... he seeks out, and is willing to joyn in Society with others ... for the mutual *Preservation* of their Lives, Liberties and Estates. . ."

But not just any society will do. Locke calls for government established by the consent of the governed, which is ruled by the majority in order to preserve these rights. He rejects the absolute state, as not being based on the consent of the governed. Men do not willingly choose "to be devoured by *Lions*."

This rule by the majority, which is to be based in an elective process, has limits, very definite limits. "Government has no other end but the preservation of property." By "property" he means not only possessions but life and liberty as well. Quite clearly, for Locke this means that majorities may not act like "*Lions*"; they may not act to devour those whom they govern. On the contrary, the purpose of civil government is to create a society that is secure and safe, where "Men ... joyn and unite into a Community, for their comfortable, safe, and peaceful living one amongst another, in a secure Enjoyment of their Properties. . ."

The key term in the Lockean notion of the state is that its purpose is the "preservation" of rights naturally belonging to man. This is the meaning behind the phrase in the preamble to the Constitution that one of the purposes of that constitution was to "secure the Blessings of Liberty to ourselves and our Posterity." There is a total denial here, and in all of the Lockean approach, of the idea that governments are the source of rights and may therefore at will change the nature of rights. Rights are prior to governments, the safeguarding of rights is the purpose of proper government, not the granting of privileges.

Thus did John Locke brilliantly overturn the notion that man was the servant and property of the state. Man has a nature and it is that nature that government must serve. That nature requires freedom: the right to life, liberty and property. "No man in Civil Society can be exempted from the Laws of it," says John Locke, and that includes officials of the government. There can be no such thing as a "right" by government to violate rights.

Yet in effect that is what the government is trying to do when it sets up compulsory military service. For a man to live at all he must have a right to his life. Yet now the government can seize him against his will and risk that life at its will. For a man to live in accord with his nature as a thinking being, he must have the liberty to think and act freely on the basis of that thought as long as he respects the rights of others. Yet the draft allows no liberty of action, it takes men when the government wills and they do what it wills. For a man to live for any length of time, he must own his own labor and keep the products of it. Yet through the draft, the government seizes that labor and claims that it cannot afford to pay what its citizens would for comparable work.

Whatever else the government is doing when it drafts, it is not acting for the "preservation of . . . Lives, Liberties, and Estates." What the draft represents is a reversion to the old view that man is owned by the state and governed by the state's will. This can only be justified by the philosophy of government that Locke was at such pains to refute.

Whether one reasons from John Locke's position, or simply from common sense, the draft violates the rights of man. In a nation set up to embody those very same rights, the first nation in history to do so, this is a grave charge. The fact that both John Locke and the Founding Fathers violated their own basic principles by countenancing the continued existence of slavery in the American colonies is no reason that other violations of rights should be sanctioned. Slavery has long since been repudiated by principled men who insisted that it was the grossest injustice to be born subject to involuntary servitude. The Negro need no longer be a slave just because he was born a Negro. Must a man still be a soldier, just because he was born a man?

The answer given to that question is really no answer at all. It is, in essence, "the draft isn't un-American, because the Department of Defense says we need an army." L. Mendel Rivers in the 1966 House Hearings said that, "for a nation whose traditions and philosophy are predicated on the concept of individual freedom and liberty, a law conscripting manpower must necessarily always be unpalatable." He then proceeded to say that it was necessary. Here he simultaneously recognizes and ignores the contradiction [behind] the draft, the contradiction that men must enslave one another in order to be free.

Statement after statement both in the 1966 and the 1967 Hearings of the House Armed Services Committee on Selective Service reflected this same contradiction. It was repeatedly [stated], in effect, that the draft violated individual rights, but was necessary in order to preserve those same rights.

However, the law itself attempts to invoke the contradiction even more blatantly. The law admits the prior rights of man in its ... provisions while setting up the institutionalization of the violation of those very rights.

This admission lies in the concept, codified in law, of conscientious objection. Pause and consider this anomaly, that in a law asserting the universal military obligation of all, some are exempted by reason of the opinions they hold as to the nature of the universe, the existence of deity, and the supposed dictates of this belief with respect to the waging of war.

As the law now reads it does not "require any person to be subject to combatant training and service in the Armed Forces of the United States who, by reason of religious training and belief, is conscientiously opposed to participation in war in any form, but no person so exempted shall be exempted from service in the Armed Forces in any capacity that the President shall declare to be noncombatant. Any person found ... to be conscientiously opposed to both combatant and non-combatant training and service may immediately upon induction into the Armed Forces, be furloughed ... to perform twenty-four months of civilian service contributing to the maintenance of the national health, safety or interest. . ."

On the basis of what political principle can one grant that a person's deep convictions determine his availability for compulsory military service? Only on the basis of the primacy of man's rights, specifically his right to think and to act on his convictions.

On what basis can a government require that a man surrender life, liberty and property at the government's will, to serve the government's purposes? On the basis of the political principle that government should be a patriarch which cares for those whom it coerces.

Both of these principles are invoked by the same act of legislation. There is no reason in principle why conscientious objectors may be excluded from combatant training and service while other young men of equally deep nonreligious conviction must accept such training and its ultimate danger to life and health.

Once a person grants the rightness of conscientious objection, there is no argument which that person can muster to justify the draft in principle.

So the present dialogue between the proponents of compulsion and the proponents of voluntarism is embodied in the draft law itself.

Unfortunately, the draft is not some small unpleasant political sickness that can be isolated from the rest of the body politic, an illness to be admitted and deplored but having little effect on the body as a whole. Once you violate rights in one place it becomes epidemic. Once the individuals of one group have their liberties systematically violated by the law of the land, there is precedent by which to seek the violation of every man's liberty. Notice that sign of the totalitarian state, the card of identity, which has been planted as a seemingly minor accompaniment to the draft in the requirement that each draft registrant must carry his draft card. What's more, he must notify his board of changes of address, changes in status, and even, if the law is read strictly (according to some lawyers), must carry the card after he is classified 5A as "too old to serve." The whole idea of having to carry identification papers of any sort is contrary to American tradition and principles. But so is the draft, and one thing leads to another.

Something else new is being added to political discourse in America, something as new, and as foreign, as the idea that men must carry cards of identity.

It is not done openly. Politicians do not name the spread of tyranny for what it is. Often they do not fully recognize it themselves—they merely have no articulate arguments against it. They respond to a symbol which conceals the true nature of their acts, both from themselves and from the public, some ideal which covers the act by justifying it.

In the case of the *military* draft the ideal is national security. This is at least somewhat definable. Separated from the draft, it is a proper purpose of government—a purpose, by the way, which can be readily achieved with a fully volunteer armed force, as I have attempted to show in other articles.

But there is another ideal, not so definable, and not defined, which is called upon to justify the draft; and further, to justify other kinds of forced service, service encompassing whole fields outside of the military such as charity, hospital work, overseas service, education, land improvement, reforestation, and domestic police work.

This ideal comes up again and again, an incantation of supposed necessity. It is the ideal of a "democratic" society. Let us start with the testimony of General Lewis B. Hershey, Director of the Selective Service System for more than a generation. For him, the draft has far more than military possibilities. In his hands it is a tool for shaping the lives of the nation's young men. In his own words, "the selective service system has been what we call a channeler." Through the application of the threat of being drafted "we have channeled people into training for professions and occupations . . . necessary for national life." At the 1966 House Hearings he proudly cited figures which he said bore out the wisdom of this purpose of the draft. He talked of thousands of physicians, doctors of philosophy, teachers, and engineers which "the nation produced." Presumably these multitudes of individuals would not on their own have chosen these professions had not the fear of the draft, of government power, urged them to their choices.

But why? What is the ideal in General Hershey's mind that requires the massive use of fear as official government policy? General Hershey is not a theoretician. But no man can sit for hours, as he did at the 1966–67 House Hearings on the draft, and not show at least a hint of political theory. It can be no surprise to anyone that General Hershey believes in the draft. In fact it should not be a surprise to learn that he advocates the spread of military training as universally as possible. He would hardly have held the job he has for all these years if he didn't have such belief . . . but why does he believe?

A particular term came up in his testimony a few times. Each time, it formed the core of his justification of the draft. Advocating not only the present draft but its extension to include as many men as possible, he said, "You are not going to have a *democracy* when not more than 20 or 30 per cent of the individuals can carry the responsibilities." [Italics mine] Thus he called for the armed forces to be used to "uplift the citizenry." With respect to those individuals who are rejected for educational, moral, and relatively minor physical reasons, he stated in the 1966–67 Hearings that the incentives for them not to improve themselves to the point where they would be acceptable by the military were too great. They must be *made* to improve themselves. If they don't, "it means avoidance of a duty that a person in a *democratic* society owes." [Italics mine]

From his own words one can get a dim idea of what he means by "democracy" or "democratic." He means a society in which everyone has a potential obligation to do the things the duly elected representatives of all the people think ought to be done for the good of all the people. It is obvious that all the people must be defended. So, in his words at the hearings, "We got to make men better so they can defend us."

Why can't we depend upon a free labor market for these men? It wouldn't be evenly enough spread, it wouldn't involve everyone. He doesn't want the economic principle of the division of labor to apply. "We must never get ourselves to the place where only the few serve the many," he stated, and did not go on to say why. Only a "few" physicians serve the "many," only a "few" teachers, policemen, engineers, industrialists, business executives, serve the "many." A free society's economy depends upon minorities of productive specialists. That is one of the reasons for its seemingly unlimited productivity. All of this General Hershey ignores.

It is my guess that General Hershey believes that the division of labor not only should not but in fact cannot apply to the military profession. This is an ironic twist from a man whose entire adult life has been in the military. He doesn't seem to believe that free men would choose the military as a career. "If you give everybody their individual rights you won't send anybody into the Armed Forces."

Let us go to the opposite extreme, to a professional academician who, like Hershey, embraces compulsion as politically good.

That man is Morris Janowitz. Professor of sociology at the University of Chicago, he has written several works on the military. In an article, "American Military Service," in the March 1967 *Trans-Action*, he proposed an alternative to the selective service system which he believed "to be more compatible with the needs and goals of political democracy."

In his opinion the present draft results in the "lower classes" having "higher casualties." On the other hand, a volunteer system would mean that the more disadvantaged would tend to join the military to improve themselves and this would result in a social inequity also, particularly with respect to Negroes, who he asserts might well entirely fill the ranks of a volunteer army.

For him, a very important value in a society is homogeneity. Everyone must do everything. And so he calls for national service for men and women, a mixed system of forced and voluntary service. Under government compulsion and/or urging all youths would go into the military, the police cadet corps, the national teacher corps, the national health corps, VISTA, and the Peace Corps. He would have a 400,000-man National Job Training corps which would be a substitute for military service.

In the second session of the 89th Congress, Senator Jacob K. Javits (R.,N.Y.), offered a resolution calling for a program of universal national service very much like that of Professor Janowitz's except that he calls unequivocally for every young male to be compelled to serve either "militarily or non-militarily." At the 1966–67 Hearings he stated that as of now "the law falls far short of universality." Like Hershey and Janowitz, the Senator is disturbed by the present inequity in which only some are forced to serve. So the answer, the way to make it democratic, is to use force against all.

The Senator, like Hershey and Janowitz, claims that only force can adequately shape the citizenry. In the Hearings, General Hershey repeatedly called for the use of forced military service to "raise the quality of our citizenry educationally, physically and particularly morally." Janowitz shows a fear of individuals being left on their own. Force must be used to counter this. National service should be "designed to develop intense and close group solidarity, based on collective rather than individualistic goals."

Senator Javits holds that his proposed universal forced service is a means to "equip our youth of today for the challenge of tomorrow."

All three agree on the same general principle: it is both proper and necessary for the state to shape citizens by forcing them to do things for the good of the community that they otherwise would not choose to do.

If one reads the remarks of these men (and the many others both in and out of government who have come out with variants on these proposals) one can notice an interesting tone. It is that of a father about his children. Equip our youth, give them goals, shape up the ignorant and unruly. These are all fatherly worries, and yet these gentlemen make them governmental.

Can it be that after almost three centuries we are back again with the Divine Right of Kings? General Hershey has said: "What I'm proposing isn't like Hitler. If this country decided to do this kind of thing, it would be the people who decided to do it, and not some dictator." But isn't he saying that, collectively, the people *are* the King, and have therefore not only the power (like Hitler) but the justification to do anything at all to each other—as long as it's supposed to be beneficial to the country?

If ever there should be a dead issue in America, this is it, and yet here it stands. Of course, here there is no king. But substitute the word "government" for "king" and substitute the word "democratic" for "divine" and you have the idea in modern American dress, the Democratic Right of Governments in which the endowment of power is not from God but from the "people." As they say, *Vox populi, Vox Dei.*

How does this really differ from Sir Robert Filmer's formulation justifying the absolute power of the king? On the basis of a tortuous theological citation and interpretation he "proved" that since those who bore children gave them life from God and for this reason owned those children, in the same manner a king (ultimately descended from Adam) owned his "children," the people in his kingdom. This meant that the king had a responsibility to God, to take care of his children for their good, and that here on earth he, the king, was judge of this; the "children" could not know what was good for them and so should bow to royal power. As James II of England said, "The king is from God, and law is from the king." Thus "rights" were really privileges granted by the king. That meant that for Filmer government antecedes rights.

But we have come full circle, for, as we have already seen, it was this position that John Locke challenged in his *Two Treatises of Government.*

The original actors may be long since dead, but the dialogue has not ended. The terms have been changed, but this "new" argument which declares that the state must use force against its own citizens to benefit those same citizens is but divine right, thinly disguised.

Are we going to abandon our tradition of individual rights? To understand the immediate implications of such suggestions, each individual might ask himself the following questions:

Have I chosen the things I most value, or was it necessary for some government official to come to me and force me to have the values I now have?

Do I believe that I would not have become human unless the government had made me so?

Do I want someone to come to me and force me to take certain training in order for me to be equipped to live tomorrow?

Many more such questions could be asked. I ask these to bring out one fact. When these generals, professors and senators, and the too many others like them, talk about the necessity of forcing citizens to serve, they are talking about the individual, either actually or potentially. They are telling him that he will not defend himself, will not equip himself for tomorrow, will chose values inimical to others. And they have to hold this view, because they have to have an intellectual position that justifies the draft. According to the theory of the Democratic Right of Governments, the people delegate, not the protection of their rights, but unlimited, absolute power to their representatives to do anything that needs to be done. Congress can pass, and the Executive can carry out, anything that the people will put up with. They can shape citizens so that they have the proper values, they can force them to do good things that would not otherwise be done. The citizen learns, serves—and is drafted.

And it is only right that it should be so—once you grant the propriety of any form of conscription.

If, on the other hand, one is against universal compulsory service, one cannot consistently be for a military draft in any form, in any degree, under any circumstances.

Why is anyone for it? For a variety of reasons: indifference to philosophical issues, fear of communism, desire for power—the reasons can be relatively innocent or deeply suspect. But the fact remains that men *do* have rights, and effective performance is reduced to the extent that they cannot exercise their rights. A free society is, as John Locke maintained, the only moral form of government—it is also the most practical form of government.

This means that if this is ever to be a free society fully based on individual rights, then that society must defend itself by means of a fully voluntary armed force.

After all, there is only one alternative to freedom.

Note

David J. Dawson was the president of the libertarian Metropolitan Young Republican Club of New York from 1964-1967. He was the publisher of the libertarian magazine *Persuasion* from its incorporation in 1965 to its closing in 1968. During this same period, Mr. Dawson gave courses on educational theory and argumentation for capitalism in his studio in New York City, and as chairman of MYRC's Committee for the Abolition of the Draft spoke on college campuses throughout the Northeast and appeared on many radio and television programs. In 1970, he and his wife, Joan Kennedy Taylor, moved to Stockbridge, Mass., where he now has his design studio, and where he has been the managing director of the Playwright's Workshop of the Berkshire Theatre Festival.

"John Locke, the Draft, and the Divine Right of Kings" is reprinted with permission from *Persuasion* (May 1968).

Israel M. Kirzner

34

Advertising

ADVERTISING HAS BEEN badly treated by many scholars who should know better. Not only Marxists and liberals, but even conservatives have given advertising a bad press. Let us examine some of the criticisms.

First, many advertising messages are said to be offensive—by esthetic or ethical and moral standards. Unfettered, unhampered, laissez-faire capitalism, it is contended, would propagate such messages in a way that could very well demoralize and offend the tastes and morals of members of society.

Second, advertising, it is argued, is deceitful, fraudulent, full of lies. Misinformation is spread by advertising, in print, on the airwaves, and this does harm to the members of society; for that reason advertising should be controlled, limited, taxed away.

Third, it is argued that where advertising is not deceitful, it is at best persuasive. That is, it attempts to change people's tastes. It attempts not to fulfill the desires of man but to change his desires to fit that which has been produced. The claim of the market economist has always been that the free market generates the flow of production along the lines that satisfy consumer tastes; their tastes determine what shall be produced— briefly, consumer sovereignty. On the contrary, the critics of advertising argue, capitalism has developed into a system where producers produce and then mold men's minds to buy that which has been produced. Rather than production being governed by consumer sovereignty, quite the reverse: the consumer is governed by producer sovereignty.

A fourth criticism has been that advertising propagates monopoly and is antithetical to competition. In a competitive economy, it is pointed out, there would be no advertising; each seller would sell as much as he would like to sell without having to convince consumers to buy that which they would not otherwise have bought. So, advertising is made possible by imperfections in the market. More seriously, it is contended, advertising leads toward monopoly by building up a wall of good will, a protective wall of loyalty among consumers which renders a particular product immune to outside competition. Competing products, which do not share in the fruits of the advertising campaign, find themselves on the outside. This barrier to entry may gradually lead a particular producer to control a share of the market which is rendered invulnerable to the winds of outside competition.

Finally—and this in a way sums up all of these criticisms—advertising is condemned as wasteful. The consumer pays a price for a product which covers a very large sum of money spent on advertising. Advertising does not change the commodity that has been purchased; it could have been produced and sold at a much lower price without the advertising. In other words, resources are being used and paid for by the consumer without his receiving anything that he could not have received in their absence.

These are serious criticisms. We have learned to expect them to be emphasized by contemporary liberal economists. To Marxist thinkers, again, advertising is essential for capitalism; it is seen as a socially useless device necessary in order to get excess production sold. They see no positive elements in advertising at all. But even conservative thinkers and economists have pointed out some apparent limitations, weaknesses, criticisms of advertising.

The Free Economy and How It Functions

It is not my purpose here to defend each and every advertising message. I would rather discuss a free economy, a laissez-faire economy, pure capitalism. I would like to show that in such a world, advertising would emerge with a positive role to play; that it would add to the efficiency with which consumer wants are satisfied; and that, while the real world is far from perfect, a large volume of the criticism would fade away were it understood what role advertising, in fact, has to play in a pure market economy.

Let me imagine a world, a free market, in which there are no deceitful men at all. All the messages beamed to consumers and prospective consumers would be, as far as the advertisers themselves believe, the strict truth. We will consider later the implications of the fact that men are imperfect and that men succumb to the temptation in selling something to say a little bit less, a little bit more, than the exact truth. In the meantime, let us talk about a world of honest men, men who do not try to deceive.

Further, let us imagine a pure market economy with government intervention kept to the absolute minimum—the night watchman role. The government stands to the sidelines and ensures the protection of private property rights, the enforcement of contracts freely entered into. Everyone then proceeds to play the game of the free market economy with producers producing that which they believe can be sold to the consumers at the highest possible money price. Entrepreneur producers, who detect where resources are currently being used in less than optimum fashion, take these resources and transfer them to other uses in the economy where they will serve consumer wants which the entrepreneurs believe are more urgently desired, as measured by the amounts of money consumers are willing to pay for various products.

We will assume that there is freedom of entry into all industries. No entrepreneur has sole control over any resource that is uniquely necessary for the production of a given product. No government licenses are required in order to enter into the practice of a given profession or to introduce a particular product. All entrepreneurs are free to produce what they believe to be profitable. All resource owners are free to sell their resources, whether labor, natural resources, capital goods. They are free to sell or rent these resources to the highest bidder. In this way the agitation of the market gradually shuffles resources around until they begin to be used to produce those products which consumers value most highly. Consumers arrange their spending to buy the commodities they believe to be most urgently needed by themselves. And the market flows on in the way that we understand it.

Open Competition

We say this is a free market, a laissez-faire, competitive system. But we do not mean a *perfectly* competitive market, as this notion has been developed by the neo-classical economists. In a perfectly competitive market, each seller faces a demand curve which is perfectly horizontal. That is to say, each seller believes that he can sell as much as he would like to sell without having to lower the price. Each buyer faces a perfectly horizontal supply curve and each buyer believes that he can buy as much as he would like to buy of anything without having to offer a higher price. In such a world of "perfect competition," we have what we call an "equilibrium" situation, that is a situation where all things have already been fully adjusted to one another. All activities, all decisions have been fully coordinated by the market so that there are no disappointments. No participant in the economy discovers that he could have done something better. No participant in the economy discovers that he has made plans to do something which it turns out he cannot do.

In this model of the perfectly competitive economy, there would in fact be *no* competition in the sense in which the layman, or the businessman, understands the term. The term "competition" to the businessman, the layman, means an activity designed to outstrip one's competitors, a rivalrous activity designed to get ahead of one's colleagues, or those with whom one is competing. In a world of equilibrium, a world of "perfect competition," there would be no room for further rivalry. There would be no reason to attempt to do something better than is currently being done. There would, in fact, be no competition in the everyday sense of the term.

When we describe the laissez-faire economy as competitive, we mean something quite different. We mean an economy in which there is complete freedom of entry: if anyone believes that he can produce something that can serve consumers' wants more faithfully, he can try to do it. If anyone believes that the current producers are producing at a price which is too high, then he is free to try to produce and sell at a lower price. This is what competition means. It does not mean that the market has already attained the "equilibrium" situation, which goes under the very embarrassing technical name of "perfectly competitive economy."

Non-Price Competition

Now, economists and others understand generally that competition means price competition: offering to sell at a lower price than your competitors are asking, or offering to buy at a higher price than your competitors are bidding. Entrepreneurs will offer higher prices than others are offering for scarce labor. They will offer to sell a product at lower prices than the competing store is asking. This is what price competition means. This is the most obvious form in which competition manifests itself.

However, we must remember that there is another kind of competition, sometimes called "nonprice competition," sometimes called "quality competition." Competition takes the form not only of producing the identical product which your competitors are producing and selling it at a lower price, not only in buying the identical resource which your competitors are buying and offering a higher price. Competition means sometimes offering a better product, or perhaps an inferior product, a product which is more in line with what the entrepreneur believes consumers are in fact desirous of purchasing. It means producing a different model of a product, a different quality, putting it in a different package, selling it in a store with a different kind of lighting, selling it along with an offer of free parking, selling through salesmen who smile more genuinely, more sincerely. It means competing in many, many ways besides the pure price which is asked of the consumer in monetary terms.

With freedom of entry, every entrepreneur is free to choose the exact package, the exact opportunity which he will lay before the public. Each opportunity, each package has many dimensions. He can choose the specifications for his package by changing many, many of these variables. The precise opportunity that he will lay before the public will be that which, in his opinion, is more urgently desired by the consumer as compared with that which happens to be produced by others. So long as there's freedom of entry, the fact that my product is different from his does not mean that I am a monopolist.

A Disservice to Economics

The late Professor Edward H. Chamberlin of Harvard did economics a great disservice in arguing that because a producer is producing a unique product, slightly different from what the fellow across the street is producing, in some sense he is a monopolist. So long as there's freedom of entry, so long as the man across the road *can* do exactly what I'm doing, the fact that he is *not* doing exactly what I'm doing is simply the result of his different entrepreneurial judgment. He believes that he can do better with *his* model. I believe I can do better with *mine*. I believe that free parking is more important to consumers than fancy lighting in the store. He gives a different package than I do. Not because he couldn't do what I'm doing, not because I couldn't do what he's doing, but because each believes that he knows better what the consumer is most anxious to acquire. This is what we mean by competition in the broadest sense, not merely price competition, but quality competition in its manifold possible manifestations.

Professor Chamberlin popularized a distinction which was not original with him but which owes its present widely circulated popularity primarily to his work. That is a distinction between "production costs" and "selling costs." In his book of almost forty years ago, *The Theory of Monopolistic Competition*, Chamberlin argued that there are two kinds of costs which manufacturers, producers, sellers, suppliers incur. First, they incur the fabrication costs, the costs of producing what it is they want to sell. Second, they incur additional expenditures that do not produce the product or change it or improve it, but merely get it sold. Advertising, of course, is the most obvious example which Chamberlin cited. But "selling costs" of all kinds were considered by him to be sharply different from "production costs." In his original formulation, Chamberlin argued that "production costs" are costs incurred to produce the product for a given Demand Curve while "selling costs" simply shift the Demand Curve over to the right. That is to say, the same product is now purchased in greater quantities at a given price but the product is the same.

A False Distinction

The fallacy in the distinction between production costs and selling costs is fairly easy to notice. In fact, it is impossible for the outside observer—except as he resorts to arbitrary judgments of value—to distinguish between expenditures which do, and expenditures which do not, alter the product. We know as economists that a product is not an objective quantity of steel or paper. A product is that which is perceived, understood, desired by a consumer. If there are two products otherwise similar to the outside eye which happen to be considered to be different products by the consumer, then to the economist these *are* different products.

Ludwig von Mises gives the example, which cannot be improved upon, of eating in a restaurant. A man has a choice of two restaurants, serving identical meals, identical food. But in one restaurant they haven't swept the floor for six weeks. The meals are the same. The food is the same. How shall we describe the money spent by the other restaurant in sweeping the floor? "Production costs" or "selling costs?" Does sweeping change the food? No. Surely, then, it could be argued that this is strictly a "selling cost." It is like advertising. The food remains the same; but, because you have a man sweeping out the floor, more people come to this restaurant than to that. But this is nonsense. What you buy when you enter a restaurant is not the food alone. What you buy is a meal, served in certain surroundings. If the surroundings are more desirable, it's a different meal, it's a different package. That which has been spent to change the package is as much production cost as the salary paid to the cook; no difference.

Another example that I recall was the case of the coal being run out of Newcastle and traveling along the railroad toward London. Every mile that coal travels nearer the London drawing room, the Demand Curve shifts over to the right. How shall we describe that transportation cost? "Production cost" or "selling cost?" Of course, it's "production cost." In fact, it's "selling cost" too. All "production costs" are "selling costs." All costs of production are incurred in order to produce something which will be more desirable than the raw materials.

You take raw meat and turn it into cooked steak. The act of changing the raw meat into cooked steak is to make the consumer desire it more eagerly. Does this simply shift the Demand Curve over to the right? Of course, it does that. It does it by changing the product.

Another example supposes there are two identical pieces of steel, except that one piece has been blessed, while the other piece is subject to a spiritual taint, which to the scientist is not there but which is very vivid and vital to the consumer. How shall we describe the expenditure on the commodities? Shall we describe the difference between them as non-existent? Or should we not recognize that, if something is spiritually tainted to the consumer—in his view, not necessarily in mine or yours or the economist's or other than in the mind of the consumer—then he will not buy the tainted item, even though to the objective laboratory scientist there's no difference between the items? The economist has recognized these as two different commodities. There'll be two Demand Curves. The fact that the scientist doesn't see any difference—they look the same, they smell the same, if you touch them they feel the same—is irrelevant. We know, as economists, that what we find in a commodity is not the objective matter that is inside it, but how it is received by the consumer.

Clearly then, the distinction between a so-called "selling cost" and "production cost" is quite arbitrary. It depends entirely on the value judgments of the outside observer. The outside observer can say that this particular selling effort does not change the product, but in that situation he is arrogating to himself the prerogative of pronouncing what is and what is not a product. That is something which violates our fundamental notions of individual consumer freedom: that a consumer's needs are defined by no one else other than himself. This may seem quite a detour from advertising and yet it is all relevant to the question of what role advertising has to play.

The Provision of Information

Let us consider how some of these notions apply to the matter of information. One of the standard defenses for advertising is that it provides a service which consumers value: the provision of knowledge, the provision of information. People buy books. People go to college. People enroll in all kinds of courses. Advertising is simply another way of providing information. To be sure, it would seem that the information provided by suppliers comes from a tainted source, but don't forget that we are imagining for the meantime a world without deceitful people.

We can even relax that assumption for a moment. It may be cheaper for the consumer to get his information from the supplier or the producer than from an outside source. In other words, if you, a consumer, have the choice of acquiring information about a particular product—either more cheaply from the producer or more expensively from an outside, "objective" source—you may decide that, on balance, you're likely to get a better deal, penny-for-penny, information-wise, by reading the information of the producer, scanning it perhaps with some skepticism, but nonetheless relying on that rather than buying it from an outside source. Technically, this involves what is known as the problem of transactions costs. It may be more economical for the information to be packaged together with the product, or at least to be produced jointly with the product, than to have the information produced and communicated by an outside source. This is a possibility not to be ignored.

Advertising provides information, and this goes a long way to explain the role which advertising and other kinds of selling efforts must play. Does this not seem to contradict the point just made, that there is no distinction between "production costs" and "selling costs"? Surely, information about a product is distinct from the product. Surely the costs incurred to provide information are a different kind of costs than the costs incurred to produce the product. The answer is clearly, no. Information is produced; it is desired; it is a product; it is purchased jointly with the product itself; it is a part of the package; and it is something which consumers value. Its provision is not something performed on the outside that makes people consume something which they would not have consumed before. It is something for which people are willing to pay; it is a service.

You can distinguish different parts of a service. You can distinguish between four wheels and a car. But the four wheels are complementary commodities. That is to say, the usefulness of the one is virtually nil without the availability of the other. The car and gasoline are two separate products, to be sure, and yet they are purchased jointly, perhaps from different producers, different suppliers, but they are nonetheless parts of a total package, a total product. If it happens that the information is produced and sold jointly with the product itself, then we have no reason to question the characteristics of the costs of providing information as true "production costs," not producing necessarily the physical commodity about which information is produced, but producing information which is independently desired by consumers, independently but jointly demanded, complementarily used together with the "product" itself. In other words, the service of providing information is the service of providing something which is needed just as importantly as the "product" itself.

Why the Shouting?

There is another aspect of advertising which is often overlooked. Information is exceedingly important. But, surely, it is argued, information can be provided without the characteristics of advertising that we know, without the color, without the emotion, without the offensive aspects of advertising. Surely information can be provided in simple straight-forward terms. The address of this and this store is this and this place. These and these qualities of commodities are available at these and these prices. Why do illustrated advertising messages have to be projected? Why do all kinds of obviously uninformative matter have to be introduced into advertising messages? This is what renders the information aspects of advertising so suspect. The Marxists simply laugh it away. They say it is ridiculous to contend that advertising provides any kind of genuine information. If one rests the defense of advertising on its informative role, then one has a lot of explaining to do. One has to explain why information that could be provided in clear cut straightforward terms is provided in such garish and loud forms, in the way that we know it.

The answer, I think, is that advertising does much more than provide information which the consumer wishes to have. This is something which is often overlooked, even by economists. Supposing I set up a gas station. I buy gasoline and I have it poured into my cellar, my tanks. I have a pump carefully hidden behind some bushes, and cars that come down the road can buy gas if they know that I'm here. But I don't go to the effort to let them know I'm here. I don't put out a sign. Well, gas without information is like a car without gas. Information is a service required complementarily with the gas.

Customers Want to Know Where to Find the Product

Supposing, then, I take a piece of paper, type very neatly in capital letters, "GAS," and stick it on my door. Cars speed down the road in need of gas, but they don't stop to read my sign. What is missing here? Information is missing. Don't people want information? Yes. They would like to know where the gas station is, but it's a well kept secret. Now, people *are* looking for that information. It's my task as an entrepreneur not only to have gas available but to have it in a form which is known to consumers. It is my task to supply gas-which-is-known-about, not to provide gas *and* information.

I have not only to produce opportunities which are available to consumers; I have to make consumers aware of these opportunities. This is a point which is often overlooked. An opportunity which is not known, an opportunity to which a consumer is not fully awakened, is simply not an opportunity. I am not fulfilling my entrepreneurial task unless I project to the consumer the awareness of the opportunity. How do I do that? I do that, not with a little sign on my door, but with a big neon sign, saying GAS; and better than that I chalk up the price; and better than that I make sure that the price is lower than the price at nearby stations; and I do all the other things that are necessary to *make* the consumer *fully* aware of the opportunity that I am in fact prepared to put before him. In other words, the final package consists not only of abstract academic information but in having the final product placed in front of the consumer in such a form that he cannot miss it.

Free $10 Bills!

The strange thing about the world in which we live is that it is a world in which $10 bills are floating around, free $10 bills! The problem is that very few of us notice these $10 bills. It is the role of the entrepreneur to notice the existence of $10 bills. An entrepreneur buys resources for $10 and he sells the product for $20. He is aware that resources available for $10 are currently being used in less than optimum fashion, that commodities for which consumers are willing to pay $20 are not being produced, and he puts these things together. He sees the $10 bill and makes the combination which other people do not see. Anybody might do it—freedom of entry. The entrepreneur notices

the $10 bill, gets it for himself by placing in front of the consumer
something which he had not noticed. If the consumer knew where he
could buy resources for $10 and get the product that is worth $20, he
wouldn't buy from the entrepreneur. He would do it himself. Since he
doesn't know, I, as entrepreneur, have to create this opportunity and
make the consumer aware.

It is not enough to buy gas and put it in the ground. The
entrepreneur puts it in the ground in a form that the consumer
recognizes. To do this requires much more than fabrication. It requires
communication. It requires more than simple information. It requires
more than writing a book, publishing it, and having it on a library shelf.
It requires more than putting something in a newspaper in a classified
ad and expecting the consumer to see it. You have to put it in front of
the consumer in a form that he *will* see. Otherwise, you're not performing your entrepreneurial task.

The Growth of Advertising

Advertising has grown. Compare the volume of advertising today with the volume of 100 years ago and it has grown
tremendously. More! Consider the price of a commodity that you buy in
a drug store or in a supermarket. Find out what portion of that price can
be attributed to advertising costs and it turns out that a much larger
percentage of the final cost to the consumer can be attributed to
advertising today than could have been attributed 50 years ago, 70 years
ago, 100 years ago. Why is this? Why has advertising expenditure grown
in proportion to total value of output? Why has advertising expenditure
grown in proportion to the price of a finished commodity? Why has
advertising apparently grown more offensive, more loud, more shrill?
It's fairly easy to understand.

I give, as example, the lobby walls of a college building that I know
very well. At one time this was a handsome lobby with walls of thick
marble; you could walk from one end of the building to the other and
the walls would be clear. Some years ago an enterprising entrepreneur
decided to use some free advertising space. He pasted up a sign. It was
the only sign on the wall; everybody looked at it, saw the message. I don't
remember what the message was or whether it was torn down, but I do
remember that soon afterward those walls were full of signs. As you
walked down the passage, you could read all kinds of messages, all kinds
of student activities, non-student activities. It was fairly easy to learn
about what was going on simply by reading the signs.

At first, the signs did not have to be big. But as advertisers saw the opportunity, the free space gradually filled up. The Ricardian rent theory came into play; all the free land was in use. And as the free land or space was taken, of course, it became more and more important to get up early to paste up your sign. That was the "rent," the high price, getting up early. But more than that, it became necessary now to arouse all kinds of interest in me in order to get me to read these signs. In other words, the variety and multiplicity of messages make it harder and harder to get a hearing.

The Price of Affluence

We live in a world which is often described as an "affluent society." An affluent society is one in which there are many, many opportunities placed before consumers. The consumer enters a super-market and if he is to make a sensible, intelligent decision he is going to have to spend several hours calculating very carefully, reading, re-reading everything that's on the packages and doing a complete research job before feeding all the information into the computer and waiting for the optimum package to be read off. It's a tough job to be a consumer. And the multiplicity of opportunities makes it necessary for advertisers, for producers, to project more and more provocative messages if they want to be heard. This is a cost of affluence. It is a cost, certainly; something that we'd much rather do without, if we could; but we can't.

The number of commodities that have been produced is so great that in order for any one particular product to be brought to the attention of the consumer a large volume of advertising is necessary. And we can expect to get more and more. Is it part of production costs? Very definitely, yes. It is completely arbitrary for anyone to argue that, whether or not the consumer knows it, the commodity is there anyway, so that when he pays the price which includes the advertising communi-cation he is paying *more* than is necessary for the opportunity made available. For an opportunity to be made available, it must be in a form which it is impossible to miss. And this is what advertising is all about.

One more word about the offensiveness of advertising. Ultimately in a free market, consumers tend to get what they want. The kinds of products produced will reflect the desires of the consumer. A society which wants moral objects will get moral objects. A society which wants immoral objects will tend to get immoral objects. Advertised communi-cation is part of the total package produced and made available to consumers. The kind of advertising we get, sad to say, is what we deserve. The kind of advertising we get reflects the kind of people that we are. No doubt, a different kind of advertising would be better, more moral, more ethical in many respects; but I'm afraid we have no one to blame but ourselves, as in all cases where one deplores that which is produced by a market society.

A final word about deceit. Of course, deceitful advertising is to be condemned on both moral and economic grounds. But we have to put it in perspective. Let me read from one very eminent economist who writes as follows:

The formation of wants is a complex process. No doubt wants are modified by Madison Avenue. They are modified by Washington, by the university faculties and by churches. And it is not at all clear that Madison Avenue has the advantage when it comes to false claims and exaggerations.[1]

Take with a Grain of Salt

In other words, we live in a world where you have to be careful what you read, to whom you listen, whom to believe. And it's true of everything, every aspect of life. If one were to believe everything projected at him, he would be in a sorry state.

It is very easy to pick out the wrong messages to believe. Now, this doesn't in any way condone or justify deceitful messages of any kind. We have to recognize, however, while particular producers may have a short-run interest in projecting a message to consumers of doubtful veracity, that so long as there's freedom of competition the consumer has his choice not only of which product to buy but who to believe. And notice what is the alternative in this world of imperfect human beings. The alternative, of course, is government control—still by imperfect human beings. So there is no way to render oneself invulnerable to the possibility of false, fraudulent, deceitful messages.

It would be nice to live in a world where no deceitful men were present. It would be cheaper. You could believe any message received. You wouldn't have to check out the credentials of every advertiser. But that is not the world in which we live. You check out the credit standing of individuals, the character of people with whom you deal; and this is an unavoidable, necessary cost. To blame advertising for the imperfections and weaknesses of mankind is unfair. Advertising would exist under any type of free market system. Advertising would be less deceitful if men were less deceitful. It would be more ethical, less offensive, if men were less offensive and more ethical. But advertising itself is an integral, inescapable aspect of the market economy.

Note

Israel Kirzner is Professor of Economics at New York University. He has written for many scholarly journals. His books include *The Economic Point of View, Market Theory and Price System*, etc. Dr. Kirzner has written for the *Journal of Political Economy*, the *Southern Economic Journal* and other scholarly publications.

"Advertising" is reprinted with permission from *The Freeman* (September 1972).

1. H. Demsetz, "The Technostructure, Forty-Six Years Later." (*Yale Law Journal*, 1968), p. 810.

part seven

Prospects and Obstacles to Freedom

In my preface, I remark briefly upon the response of conscientious libertarians to the present cultural and political situation. More needs to be said about this, however. In historical terms, in the light of what we know about social change, what is likely to happen? It is clear that if people pay attention to the libertarian argument, consider the alternative, and undertake to act, the prospects for a free society are very good; *that* follows simply from the fact that such a society is indeed good for people, and possible as well. But the "if" is very important. No guarantees exist. People *cannot* be *forced* to think about anything. So even if it were in some sense desirable to have them conned into making the right moves, doing so is simply impossible.

Yet it is also true that most people are more positive in their attitude toward life than they are given credit for by social analysts, psychiatrists, and other commentators. A positive attitude toward life is evident from the fact that life is, looked at in a historical perspective, getting better *and* is lasting longer for most people in the Western world. There is a real sense in which it is possible to *count* on people's basic willingness, in the main, to improve on their own lives. After all, to fail to do so *must* lead to suicide. And if there is anything to the notion of the eventual survival of the fittest in the realm of concepts and theories—a notion that seems to be valid, more or less, within most sciences, and the arts—it is not unreasonable to look toward the future with some optimism. The following essays discuss just these issues in considerable detail.

Tibor Machan

35

On Reclaiming America's Unique Political Tradition

THE AUTHORS APPEARING in this book and I want to reclaim or reinstate America's unique political tradition. By political tradition I mean the political viewpoint which best characterizes *and* distinguishes the American historical tradition. Of course, there is no consensus on any one political philosophy as *the* American view. The historical record is being set straight constantly and just what can be subsumed under the "American political tradition" is an open issue. I am interested in what can be consistently identified as the *unique* features of the American political tradition, the features that constitute America's ideological tradition as well as its actual history.

In this paper I will present what I believe to be the American political tradition and will offer an argument in support of what it would take to reclaim it.

Two features of any political viewpoint concern the political philosopher: first, the statements which constitute the substance of the political theory (its view of man, morality, optimal human social and political conditions, etc.), and second, the specifications for implementing the theory (administrative procedures such as checks and balances, separation of powers, and jurisdictional provisions). A political theory and its instituting procedures are not separable, in the sense that the elements of the former will imply something about those of the latter. For instance, if free expression of one's views is regarded as a right within a political society, the institutional provisions for sustaining such a society cannot reasonably require the suppression of free expression. That is, of course, provided internal consistency is a virtue which a political theorist accepts. (I do not believe it to be outrageous to *assume* this virtue and to omit discussion of possible political theories which renounce it—what would it be to renounce rationality within the realm of political theory?)

It seems appropriate to claim that the central and unique feature of American political theory is a concern for the moral priority of the individual human being *within the social context*. Of course, there have been many instances where this feature was not implemented within political and legal practice. Some philosophers might wish to argue that cases that appear to indicate contradictory practices in fact do not (e.g., there is a view of slavery which has it that insofar as the American Negro was not viewed as a human being, slavery did not contradict the concern with the moral priority of individual men). But most of these arguments rest on conventionalism—the view that since the prevailing conventions accepted the "contradictions" as consistent, it is illegitimate to view them otherwise. This line of reasoning makes shambles of criticism on virtually all fronts—most people who make mistakes, or fail morally, do not, *at the time*, admit that theirs is a mistake or failure. According to the Soviets, while the Stalinist era was in effect, it was fully consistent with the Marxist designs of Soviet society—only in retrospect were discrepancies admissible. Still, we know better. (Obviously, the problem to be resolved in these cases is objectivity about one's present thinking and action.)

Suffice it to say that in America the bulk of political activities, principles, institutions, and teachings, as well as the substance of political philosophy,* emphasized the primacy of the moral autonomy of individuals. In short, in the American political tradition political theory influenced political practice so much that the scale was tipped from the state toward the individual.

The American political tradition contained as its central, distinctive (and extraordinary) feature the individual as the value focus. Therefore, one would expect a legal–political system within which the governing, basic principle was a statement identifying individual human rights. The Bill of Rights, despite some flaws in the midst of considerable integrity, appears to testify to the above expectation, if only in intention.

It is true that the political philosophy of the American states had concern for the many traditional political virtues, including stability, order, authority, justice, duty, power, and sovereignty. Yet clearly these are not the virtues that stand out, they are not what set off the American tradition conceptually and historically. (No one can miss this point who has ever listened to the view of America presented by the bulk of Europe's citizenry. Their romantic vision of the United States still overshadows all the antiAmerican rhetoric of the sophisticated—and properly left wing or royalist—European intelligentsia.)

I must emphasize that this distinctive American political tradition is properly *political*—it comprises the intended political practices as well as a political philosophy. There is no clear cultural, ethical, or psychological pattern in American history comparable to this political one. Even though America was influenced by the "Protestant ethic," the frontiersman mentality, and Yankee ingenuity, there simply is no widespread, cohesive philosophical tradition that touches any realm so persistently as individualism touches the political. The *political* realm served, after all, as the unifying factor; it provided the one feature of the culture that could claim virtual universal (tacit or explicit) adherence from a citizenry as varied as there ever has been in human history. The personal, religious, cultural, ethnic, and other elements of people's lives did not unify the whole populace. In most national–geographical units that we call countries there seems to occur ethical, cultural, and even psychological uniformity to the point that it is meaningful to talk of the Irish, Italian, or Spanish mentality. Specific mores and patterns of culture discernible in these countries were not embraced by America as a whole; even today attempts to fix upon *the* American culture, manners, or mentality usually end in absurdity.

With this in mind, I should like to mention yet another point: the distinctively American political *tradition* no longer distinguishes the American political reality of *our age*. Not because the rest of the world has adopted the tradition, but because America no longer exhibits it except in its documents and occasional rhetoric. Within the purview of politics the last fifty years there has been a clearly identifiable decline of expressed preference for actions (legislative, judical, educational, scholarly, diplomatic, etc.), favoring the individualist approach. Perhaps the only areas where this decline appears to be countered are within certain provisions of criminal law, civil liberties, and considerations for personal privacy. Yet even in these areas the arguments are no longer grounded on the individualist political tradition. For example, many of the considerations accused persons receive have to do with psychological theories pertaining to social versus personal responsibility (a sort of reflexive sympathy for criminals and those accused of crimes—as if it were *a priori* impossible that there should be *any* criminals. Civil liberties emerged in response not to general notions about human rights but special concerns with collective units such as blacks, women, chicanos, and Indians; the atmosphere surrounding the language of civil liberties reeks of power politics even if some of the results do justice to individualistic goals. And considerations about privacy emerge all too frequently in response to official attempts to identify individuals who are suspected of some form of criminal, including treasonous, activity, as well as in cases where the "horrors of technology" have been employed by government and business.

The thinking of those persons countering the decline of the individualist approach is rarely that the sphere of individual authority ought to be unimpeded, in line with general principles of individualism (that would commit those involved in this issue to altogether too much for their ideological comfort), but that the American establishment must be opposed on all counts—on principle. (The curious thing is that as the American state apparatus grows, many who supported its growth in the first place, or their brethren, now find that their principle of anti-Americanism makes it impossible for them to stick by their original commitments. I can't begin to consider all the reasons why so many of the intellectuals find it psychologically imperative to demean anything even remotely American. I believe that Dr. Ludwig von Mises' *The Anti-Capitalist Mentality* and Dr. Helmut Schoek's *Envy* offer the best hints toward understanding this phenomenon. If there are dominant intellectual trends these days, rarely do they express any of the tenets of the American political tradition *as such*. Though at times it is just those tenets that have become fashionable—perhaps under the guise of being early Marx or neo-Freud—individualism and capitalism still must be dutifully, if perversely, renounced.

What needs to be done in order to reintroduce one of the healthiest trends in political theory and practice here and/or anywhere on earth? How do we reinstate individualism as the guiding political theory within our society? Or, how do we reclaim the American political tradition?

At this point I want to make a brief case for the view that individualism as a political philosophy and tradition is indeed healthy, that it is indeed the right approach to organizing a human society—especially once the division of labor is accomplished.

The argument for individualism has its difficulties. Because my argument leads to a statement about what sort of political arrangement ought to be adopted by people, it is thought to be a normative thesis reducible to mere preference and incapable of rational support. Yet, these days it is no longer respectable to assume without question the "is–ought" gap—too many philosophers have pointed out the fallacies in

Hume, G. E. Moore, Charles Stevenson and others who accept their view, that statements about what *ought* to occur, how people *ought* to act in various circumstances cannot be supported or given a sound defense.

My argument here goes some way toward indicating the answer to the question about reclaiming individualism. If some of the connections I identify are indeed acceptable, then it would appear that the individualist political philosophy must in part be *grounded* on them.

Before one can argue for what is politically right, correct, good, or just, some view of what is generally right must be introduced. Not just in politics, but in all areas of our lives we require standards of judgment. Can we produce anything like a *general* standard of right conduct from which we can get a clue to what constitutes the *politically* good?

We must start by answering the question "What kind of thing is a man and what renders someone a *good* one?" For in determining the excellence of anything, we must know what is crucial about it—a good apple cannot taste like an orange, an excellent dish of chicken paprika won't be one if it conforms to the recipe of chicken chow mein. Good football players aren't ones because they hit home runs. In short, the excellence of anything is identifiable first of all by reference to what *sort* of thing it is.

But to present a definition of the nature of man leads to complaints that producing definitions leads to a closed world view and, consequently, to both dogmatism and skepticism. However, I believe that those who complain have a limited and wrongheaded view of what can count as defining something. *To our best current understanding,* what renders people the distinguishable things they are is their capacity to choose to be conceptually aware of things (including themselves). (The view of free will I rely on here is that it is up to man to make use of his distinctive capacity—conceptual knowledge. Denying this view leads to very serious troubles in attempting to *make sense* of things to ourselves so we need to accept it.)

The nature of human beings is that they are rational and free to choose some of their actions. Since their lives require some of these actions, the excellence of the actions and the agents consists in *choosing* to perform them. Of those actions their lives require judging and acting on judgment seem most crucial. These are what lead some people to moral excellence and others to moral failure. The man unawake to the world around him (taking into consideration his own abilities and circumstances) defaults on his humanity.

For a quick outline of the basic issues of a moral philosophy the above will have to do. It seems to omit none of the basic considerations of most traditional moral positions and it implies the answers to the objections of moral skeptics.

In the light of the above, individualism does appear to be the political theory most suited to human beings. Indeed, if it is man's rationality and freedom that make his moral excellence (and failure) possible—and each man must be considered individually, for only he can be held responsible or given credit for making *his* choices—then the fostering of the moral life in a social context requires the discouragement of the mutual *imposition* of our wills and judgments upon each other. No genuine moral development can come from running another person's life—it simply is impossible that moral worth should accrue to anyone from paternalism, from dictating his actions (once maturation has been reached).

What a sound political system requires, then, is the individualist principle that free action in matters not impinging on one's fellows *must* be respected and protected above all else. Such a system is good for people. Its correctly applied implementation *must* benefit everyone as a human, moral being—a necessary condition.

I have put forth only a sketchy defense of individualism and have **not** shown how we might go about reinstating it, reviving it, reclaiming it for ourselves and our offspring. The above outlined argument gives the hint.

The American political tradition requires an ethical base. The morality that justifies individualism as *the* sound political system for human beings must itself become a part of the world view of those who see the political value in individualism. Political ideas and ideals are intimately connected with ethical ideas and ideals. The acceptance of political ideals into the conceptual framework of individuals and into the culture (arts, literature, film, television, poetry, etc.) is conditional upon the acceptance of certain ethical notions. I am speaking very generally, of course. I do not mean to argue for perfect consistency throughout a culture between the moral and political principles people find acceptable. I do mean to suggest that there needs to be a greater degree of consistency between people's politics and ethics than America has ever enjoyed. (Recall my earlier mention of the uniquely unifying function of America's political ideology in its cultural history.) A greater consistency between politics and ethics is precisely what is required for the maintenance of a political–legal system which invests the life of an individual man with so much political value.

The drastic difference between statements that capture our political tradition ("a man has the right to life, liberty, and the pursuit of happiness") and those of the dominant ethics ("our primary obligation is toward the furtherance of our fellows' welfare and happiness") cannot but contribute to undermining the more remote part of our value system, politics. The contradiction must be eradicated between the American's political ideals (of the past!) and the ideals that are espoused by those who give voice to and teach the personal codes by which Americans attempt to guide their conduct. Or the goal of reclaiming the American political tradition must be abandoned. There does not seem to be any alternatives left.

I believe that the goal of reverting from a serious backsliding in our and in humanity's political evolution must be undertaken. We must make the difficult, strenuous, patient, and *personal* effort to explain to people that *they* indeed have the right to *their* lives, liberty, and pursuit of happiness—and that no other person has the right to theirs, nor do they have the right to anyone else's. As the prime moral duty, service to society is plainly incompatible with this program. The valuing of oneself is a prerequisite to upholding a political system which values each individual equally in the eyes of the law.

I have no doubt about the *possibility* of accomplishing the reinstatement of the individualism which at one time achieved a temporary breakthrough in political theory. This individualism led to the eradication of political elitism—the reign of privilege that subjected countless numbers who were guilty of nothing but were deprived of their dignity as members of mankind although they were no better or worse, intrinsically, than their "noble" brothers. But possibilities are one thing, success another.

My considered opinion is pessimistic—that implies that, on the one hand, the effort of regenerating the individualist political tradition will take time, and that failure may well kill off permanently the American tradition of libertarian politics. Yet my opinion is optimistic, as well, considering the above mentioned point about the possibilities open to us. In fact, what we need is plain realism: the choice as to what will happen lies with people, including—importantly—with ourselves.

Note

*Some argue that the correct ascription of philosophical influence goes not to the radical individualist Locke, but to the gradualist-cautionary Burke. In terms of what renders the tradition *distinctive* Burke is, so to speak, nothing new for political philosophy; Machiavelli focused attention on matters which were Burke's primary concern.

R. A. Childs, Jr.

36

Liberty and the Paradigm of Statism

Introduction

IN HIS CONTINUING STRUGGLE to live and prosper on this planet, man is faced with many difficult and complex problems which he must solve. Two of the most fundamental problems are that to live man must act and choose between alternatives, and that he can make mistakes. And the consequences of mistaken notions and actions can come home to roost days, years, or even decades after the initial choice was made. These possible consequences, plus the necessity for man's planning out courses of action across a span of time, make it all the more important not only that man's ideas and actions be basically life-serving and correct, but that they be based on principles, since it is principles alone that enable man to project integrated courses of action over long spans of time.

Like all other life forms, man must engage in certain processes in order to remain alive. And like most other life forms, his continued existence does not depend upon his own efforts and exertions alone; if he is to raise himself above subsistence level, man requires the cooperation of other members of his own species. Thus man is a "social animal"; that much abused phrase signifies only that he must associate with other men in order to survive and prosper. But man is different from other social animals in that he possesses no inborn pattern of association; unlike bees and other insects, he possesses no inborn impulse to associate in a *specific* way. Thus is man, in the Aristotelian sense, a *political* animal, that is, he must determine the forms and means of associating with other men by *choice*.

Not only is life itself a problem for man to solve by means of thought and effort, but the proper forms of human association must be so determined as well. Man possesses a specific nature with specific needs; if this were not true, then it would make no difference what kinds of associations, if any, he formed. If man did not possess specific needs which required specific means for fulfilling them, if the problems which confront man were equally solvable under any and all systems, if the choices and actions of other human beings were not capable of affecting him adversely as well as beneficially, then there would be no need for man to concern himself with politics in the broad Aristotelian sense.

Unfortunately, his nature is such that it *does* make a difference, and the nature of political systems is such that a mistake in this extraordinarily complex realm can cause untold harm—everything from starvation to mass murder.

The fact that most of mankind throughout history has suffered considerable harm would seem to suggest that the political forms which man has chosen have not been adequate for his needs. My main consideration in this essay is indeed the particular form of association which men have chosen, or have had forced upon them: the state (as it has historically existed). My contention is that the state is causally connected to most of the problems that men have historically faced.

My thesis is that statism, as a political doctrine, as a reality, and as a systematic paradigmatic attempt to solve problems faced by man, is a failure, and that this failure is a result of certain inner contradictions in statism itself. According to my analysis, not only does the statism paradigm, or model solution, fail to solve the fundamental problems of man, but in the very attempt to solve problems, it generates new problems of even greater complexity. I hope to show how and why human responses to these problems tend to be an actual *extension* of the paradigm of statism, and why this extension is self-defeating. Finally, I will, after briefly developing this thesis, apply it to American history as a case study, attempting to predict, in broad terms, what the prospects for the future are. I also will consider and examine the prospects of an alternative paradigm: the paradigm of libertarianism.

Before proceeding further, let us consider the nature and function of paradigms themselves.

The Structure of Paradigms

Perhaps the greatest breakthrough recently in the historiography of science has been Thomas Kuhn's pioneering work, *The Structure of Scientific Revolutions*.[1] Putting aside its implications for epistemology, Kuhn's thesis is a brilliant sociological insight into the origin, acceptance, and rejection of scientific theories. More than any other work, this book has popularized the notion of paradigms.

At root, Kuhn's thesis constitutes a radical overhauling of what Murray N. Rothbard has called "the whig theory of science,"[2] namely, that scientific progress consists of a gradual, accumulative, step-by-step growth in man's knowledge. Kuhn states that in recent years, more and more scientists have been finding this notion of scientific progress difficult to defend and have begun considering alternative explanations.

Kuhn's book constitutes perhaps the most interesting reinterpretation to appear yet. Essentially, Kuhn sees progress as occurring through "scientific revolutions," rather than cumulatively.

In any context of science, Kuhn sees the existing structure of scientific knowledge as being organized into a dominant paradigm, which he takes to be a theory which is almost universally recognized as a model solution to problems that are seen as fundamental to a science. Paradigms do not always exist in a science, but in many ways we cannot say that a coherent science exists before a paradigm becomes widely accepted. Without a paradigm, all of the facts that pertain to a certain science are likely to be seen as equally relevant. Experiment and research tends to appear random. Furthermore, in these preparadigm periods, we find scientists engaging in frequent and deep debates over legitimate methods, problems, and criteria.

After a time, some individual manages to discover or construct an integrated model which solves most of the crucial or fundamental problems in a given field, and a paradigm is born. The paradigm initially serves to define the legitimate problems and methods of a research field for fellow scientists. But how is it able to do this? Kuhn gives us two answers: (a) the model, the scientific achievement, was sufficiently new to attract a relatively permanent group of adherents away from competing modes of scientific activity, and (b) while the achievement managed to solve some of the major problems, it was "sufficiently open-ended to leave all sorts of problems for the redefined group of practitioners to resolve."[3] Those who come to work within this framework begin practicing "normal science" and spend much of their time in what Kuhn calls "mopping up operations"—filling in the gaps and implications of the basic paradigm.

Why does one theory become accepted as a paradigm? As a problem-solving device, "a theory must seem better than its competitors, but it need not, and in fact never does, explain all the facts with which it can be confronted." The younger scientists tend to accept the new paradigm, and the older schools are either converted or else die out. Indeed, "the new paradigm implies a new and more rigid definition of the field."

The new paradigm is usually very limited in scope and precision—it is adopted because it is more successful than its competitors in solving "a few problems that the group of practitioners has come to recognize as acute."

But as the outlines of the paradigm become increasingly sketched out and filled in, problems often develop. Anomalies pile up—Kuhn calls them "violations of expectations." This means that puzzles continue to develop which the paradigm appears to be incapable of solving. At first, the result is intensified research and experimentation in the precise area where the anomalies develop. The basic paradigm may be modified slightly in an attempt to explain the problems and solve the puzzles. But if the puzzles are increasingly basic and fundamental and pile up more and more quickly, then we have what Kuhn calls a "crisis period," where the paradigm itself may be called into question.

A paradigm is never rejected outright. If it cannot solve some important problems, then ad hoc explanations and solutions may ensue, or else the problems may be ignored. Facts alone never unseat a paradigm; a rival and more successful paradigm is needed to replace it. Discussing case histories, Kuhn states, "In each case a novel theory emerged only after a pronounced failure in the normal problem-solving activity . . . The novel theory seemed a direct response to crisis."

Why is a paradigm never rejected outright? Kuhn does not explicitly discuss this, but I can offer a few important reasons as hypotheses which have not been conclusively verified.

We already know that paradigms give man the sense of having an integrated set of readily applicable solutions to important problems. My hypothesis is that, as such, paradigms may serve the function of increasing man's *sense of control* over some aspect of reality, or some aspect of his own life. If this is so, then we would expect that a straightforward abandonment of a paradigm would threaten that sense of control. This hypothesis is indeed nothing more than an extension of psychologist Nathaniel Branden's insight into the nature of neurotic symptoms. Branden's theory, itself only sketchily developed at this point,[4] is that virtually every kind of neurotic symptom which is psychologically caused represents a given individual's solution to the problem of dealing with some experienced threat to his sense of efficacy or control. Branden points out that in different contexts throughout his life an individual will find himself up against various such threats and that "neurotic symptoms in effect represent the organism's solutions to problems posed by some kind of threat to the organism's effective functioning." One important difference between a sense of control and actual effective control is that the latter is in fact reality-based, whereas the former might not be. A reality-based control would not only be consistent with the facts of reality, but consistent with the basic needs of man's nature. A "sense of control" in this context might easily be applied to the case of paradigm acceptance or rejection.

Indeed, this is part of the thesis that I shall develop: the reason the paradigm of *statism* has been accepted and extended in response to problems is that it serves the function of maintaining, or increasing, people's sense of control, particularly for members of significant groups.

Relating this thesis to Kuhn's discussion, paradigms tend to be held onto after they have been shown to be wanting because they represent an apparent solution to a whole nest of problems, a solution which must have been, in some sense and in some context, partially effective. Outright rejection of the paradigm would therefore only serve to undermine the sense of control already existing, no matter how unstable it has become. Indeed, as Kuhn shows, even when anomalies are piling up and paradigms more and more appear incapable of resolving important puzzles, the practitioners of science often react as though they themselves were under attack. As Kuhn also states: "once it has achieved the status of a paradigm, a scientific theory is declared invalid only if an alternate candidate is available to take its place." This means that "the act of judgement that leads scientists to reject a previously accepted theory is always based upon more than a comparison of that theory with the world. The decision to reject one paradigm is always simultaneously the decision to accept another, and the judgement leading to that decision involves the comparison of both paradigms with nature *and* with each other." And if the problems or puzzles are particularly perplexing? "Very often scientists are willing to wait. . . ."[5]

Now I shall pinpoint the preconditions for a scientific revolution, in anticipation of my later analysis of the prospects for libertarianism—the doctrine of liberty.

I have noted already that one major precondition is the piling up of puzzles, anomalies, which cannot be solved in the conventional paradigmatic framework. When crisis proportions are reached—determined by the fundamentality rather than the *number* of problems—there occurs a "blurring of the paradigm and the consequent loosening of the rules for normal research."[6] This situation is much like the preparadigm period, except that the freedom is narrower in scope.

A crisis is followed by an intensification of research in the problem areas, and it is "particularly in periods of acknowledged crisis that scientists have turned to philosophical analysis as a device for unlocking the riddles of their field." The scientists begin to take a different view of the existing paradigms, and "the proliferation of competing articulations, the willingness to try anything, the expression of explicit discontent, the recourse to philosophy and to debate over fundamentals, all these are symptoms of a transition from normal to extraordinary research."[7]

Thus we reach the scientific revolution itself, which consists of "those non-cumulative developmental episodes in which an older paradigm is replaced in whole or in part by an incompatible new one."[8] A crucially important aspect of the revolution is the growing sense among the community that the paradigm is malfunctioning.

The process by which a new candidate for paradigm replaces its predecessors is as one would suspect: the new interpretation emerges in the mind of one or a few individuals, who begin to develop the theory. Paradigm testing, or application, then takes place. Verification proceeds, as the best among the actual alternatives is selected. In this critical process, "probably the single most prevalent claim advanced by the proponents of a new paradigm is that they can solve the problems that have led the old ones to a crisis. When it can legitimately be made, this claim is often the most effective one possible."[9]

This, then, is the basic means of scientific progress. But is Kuhn's thesis only applicable to science, or does it also apply to other realms of thought, and political reality as well?

The Paradigm of Statism vs. the Paradigm of Liberty

Many people today hold that there are *no* paradigms operative today in the realms of the social sciences and politics. But this belief is not self-evident. What seems to be true instead is that different communities of thought and institutional reality *operate* according to specific paradigms, but they either have not brought facets of their paradigms into clear focus, or else they simply do not recognize the paradigms that they operate by. This would not be at all unusual, since a great many principles of thought and action often operate at a preverbal, subconscious stage.

I maintain that in the sphere of politics and the social sciences there is a clear and basic paradigm operative.

In fact, in the entire history of Western civilization, perhaps no single paradigm has been so unshakeable, despite its ability to solve practically *no* problem whatever, as the paradigm of statism, which is fundamental to nearly every ideology and political program.

This paradigm has two interrelated aspects: (a) that the use of aggression, of physical force or the threat of it, is a legitimate or functional means of solving social problems or attaining ends, and (b) that a monopoly of such aggression should be rested with the state apparatus, this being man's basic political tool for solving such social and political problems. Within this paradigm there are many subvariants, but all uphold the validity of the basic premise and the efficacy of statism.

By now, my thesis can be restated with new meaning: I hold that the fundamental political paradigm is statism as a doctrine and as a reality; that as a systematic attempt to solve problems, the state is a failure; and that this failure is a result of certain inner contradictions in statism itself. Furthermore, not only does statism fail to solve any fundamental problem of man, but in man's very attempt to solve problems by means of it, anomalies are generated and puzzles and problems are increasingly the result. Although this paradigm is not always explicit, reliance on it is nearly universal. A state's recourse to this paradigm in most instances of domestic and foreign interventionism is prevalent today, and has been throughout history, because it *increases the sense of control which significant groups feel that they have.* In other words, instances of statism, of governmental interventionism, serve to increase various groups' sense of control. Finally, statism as a paradigm is life-negating, and actually, in the long run, destroys people's actual control of their own lives.

Domestic and foreign policy may be explained in terms of the response of various individuals and groups to problems created by the state apparatus. Solutions are always adopted to increase the sense of stability and control within the context of the paradigm of statism, and the result is increasing problems of greater complexity.

Paradigms of all kinds are model solutions to problems, and problems exist in a hierarchy. Because of a different perspective and purpose, what is a problem in one context may not be in another. Furthermore, a particular solution to one problem might in fact generate new puzzles which would not be puzzles had an alternative approach been used instead. Thus in the case of statism we might find a whole nest of problems and puzzles which are only problems in the context of statism and which a free society, a society of liberty, could not give rise to. This also means that if my thesis is correct, then statism might have, by now, generated a whole nest of problems which would not arise otherwise—a nest which itself exists hierarchically. Some problems generated by statism might not be solvable in the context of statism, but as statism is rolled back, contexts will arise which will allow for these problems to *become* open to solution.

One minor point should be covered at this juncture. What justifies using Kuhn's analysis for an area and field that he did not intend it? All thought and action involves problem-solving, and Kuhn's thesis is therefore applicable in principle to *any* context where integrated theories and institutions exist in order to solve problems. Anomalies can result in any area that involves model solutions to problems and attendant expectations of the sort with which Kuhn deals in physics. The concept of a paradigm applies to the realm of both the physical sciences and politics simply because a paradigm is an ordered set of model solutions.

At this point I will elaborate that aspect of my theory which holds that the paradigm of statism creates new problems for man necessarily, in the very act and process of applying it.

A 'problem' in this context shall be taken to be any obstacle in the path of achieving a goal. This leaves us with the task of specifying what goal will serve as a standard against which to evaluate the efficacy of the means under consideration—the paradigm. This is necessary because if we specified that our goal was in fact to destroy man, then statism might *not* present problems, but might be a highly efficient means to achieve that end. Thus, the necessity for an objective, nonarbitrary, end or purpose.

This ultimate end, or value, can be determined by an analysis of the context and nature of all values, of that which gives rise to them. Quoting Ayn Rand:

> *'Value'* is that which one acts to gain and/or keep. The concept *'value'* is not a primary; it presupposes an answer to the question: of value to whom and for what? It presupposes an entity capable of acting to achieve a goal in the face of an alternative. Where no alternative exists, no goals and no values are possible . . . *'There is only one fundamental alternative in the universe: existence or nonexistence, and it pertains to a single class of entities: to living organisms. The existence of inanimate matter is unconditional, the existence of life is not: it depends on a specific course of action. Matter is indestructible, it changes forms, but it cannot cease to exist.* It is only a living organism that faces a constant alternative: the issue of life or death. Life is a process of self-sustaining and self-generated action. If an organism fails in that action, it dies; its chemical elements remain, but its life goes out of existence. It is only the concept of 'Life' that makes the concept of 'Value' possible. It is only to a living entity that things can be good or evil. . . .

Without an ultimate goal, or end, there can be no lesser goals or means: a series of means going off into an infinite progression toward a nonexistent end is a metaphysical and epistemological impossibility. It is only an ultimate goal, an end in itself, that makes the existence of values possible. Metaphysically, life is the only phenomenon that is an end in itself . . . Epistemologically, the concept of 'value' is genetically dependent upon and derived from the antecedent concept of 'life.' To speak of 'value' as apart from 'life' is worse than a contradiction in terms. It is only the concept of 'Life' that makes the concept of 'Value' possible.[10]

Thus, our ultimate end must logically be the preservation and further-ance of the life of the organism with which we are concerned: man. Our standard will be: that which is required for man's survival *qua* man. "Since everything man needs has to be discovered by his own mind and produced by his own effort, the two elements of the method of survival proper to a rational being are: thinking and productive work."[11]

Statism as a paradigm can be considered self-defeating and life-negating if it is opposed, in principle and practice, to the requirements of either thinking or productive work. Man needs to think about the things which his life requires and to translate his thought into action by means of a process of production. In a social context, he needs to have the liberty to produce, and to exchange the results of his production with others, on mutually agreeable terms. He must be free to think, to act, to produce, and to keep the results. The state attacks all of these.

Statism subjects men in society to the arbitrary control and power of a group of men who have become the most powerful institution in a given geographical area, and who proceed to rule that area by means of physical force, with or without the consent of the territory's inhabitants. The most fundamental way in which the state attacks the requirements of man's proper survival is by taxation, which is the coercive extracting of a portion of a person's property from him without his explicit consent. It then proceeds to regulate an individual's autonomous actions, compels exchanges and gifts between its subjects and itself, and either compels or prohibits actions, including exchanges, between a pair of subjects. All of these are examples of hegemonic relationships, in contradistinction to the voluntary, contractual relations developing in the society of liberty.[12]

A free market society is one based on voluntary relationships. A free market, as such, is a system of units; the units are acts of exchange. Exchanges, of course, are exchanges of property titles. What distin-guishes a free market from a nonfree market is that people are free to trade property titles which they have justly acquired with each other on any terms that are mutually agreeable. A free market is a society where acts of aggression are absent, where no man or group resorts to aggression. Libertarianism as a political philosophy is the doctrine which holds that no man or group of men may legitimately seek to gain values by the use or threat of aggression. As a positive doctrine, libertarianism holds that anyone may do anything that he pleases, so long as he does not aggress against the person or just property of another.

Thus in *fundamental* terms, we can see that libertarianism is consistent with the criteria we have set down, and statism is not. This means that statism necessarily acts to place obstacles in the path of attaining human well-being and happiness, of promoting human life. Statism institutionalizes aggression; libertarianism does not.

As a corollary, we can see that statism sets up a society where there are *necessarily* fundamental conflicts of interest among men, while libertarianism does not. Indeed, the doctrine that there *are fundamental conflicts of interest among men* has been a handmaiden of statism for centuries. The doctrine as stated by Ludwig von Mises is: *"the gain of one man is the damage of another; no man profits but by the loss of others.* The dogma was already advanced by certain ancient authors. Among modern writers Montaigne was the first to restate it; we may call it the *Montaigne dogma.* It was the quintessence of the doctrines of Mercantilism, old and new. It is at the bottom of all modern doctrines teaching that there prevails, within the frame of the market economy, an irreconcilable conflict among the interests of various social classes within a nation and furthermore between the interests of any nation and those of all other nations."[13]

Libertarianism, on the contrary, holds that there are fundamentally *no* conflicts of true interests among men, that all men possess in common the interests in increasing production and exchange.

To see how statism causes specific problems, and to pinpoint the libertarian solution, let us take a few problems which are popularly held to be fundamental in importance today.

1. Unemployment.

On the free market there is no problem of unemployment per se. There is only the "problem" of how to help sustain the lives of those who are physically incapable of producing for themselves. On a market, labor, like everything else, is sold at a price. When the pricing system is left alone, in any given context the supply and demand for labor will match each other, otherwise there is a gradual bidding up or down of prices, that is, of wages. Unemployment results when the state undertakes to raise some wages above the free market price by means of force, regardless of the productive context and capacities, thus throwing off a natural adjustment mechanism which tends to bring wages and work into an equilibrium appropriate for a specific context. Statism causes the problem by preventing wages from being bid downward slightly, thus causing a surplus. Often, a price for labor even 3 percent higher than the market price will cause an unemployment problem of 5 percent, since labor tends to be "elastic"; that is, a slight change in the price of labor can cause more drastic changes in the supply or demand. Statism is the cause; the solution is to let the pricing mechanism adjust wages to economic reality.[14] Unions too, backed by state power, restrict the supply of labor, at the expense of the unemployed, to raise the wages of union members slightly.

2. Monopoly.

There is no problem of "monopoly prices" or of growing centralization of industry on the free market. Economically, there is no way of determining what is, and what is not, a "monopoly price" on the free market,[15] thus the concept does not apply. Furthermore, since economies of scale are limited, there is no reason to postulate an inherent market tendency toward centralization. Finally, historical research has shown that in the case of the nineteenth century, which is generally focused upon, the trend was actually toward growing competition and decentralization.[16] What, then, is the root of the problem? State intervention and grants, direct and indirect, of special monopoly privileges to favored industries and individuals. "Redistribution of wealth" is usually taken to mean a distribution from the rich to the poor; in practice, the reverse is often the case, as the power of the state is used to attain and maintain a monopoly-elite status for a select group of power-lusters. The libertarian solution to the problem of monopoly is to abolish the privileges and allow the working of the market forces to press on with decentralization.

3. Depressions.

Depressions are not something which have existed, or could exist, on a free market. Depressions are large-scale liquidations of massive malinvestments in an economic system—malinvestments which result from state action in credit manipulation–expansion. Such state actions separate economic activity from the economic context of reality. In a free market, every commodity that is sold (such as the commodity of money) is simultaneously buying something else; thus, there can be no problem

of *general* overproduction. Malinvestment occurs when the state distorts
the signals of economic reality, throwing off the economic equilibrium of
a free market.

4. Imperialism.

Imperialism is one of the greatest of modern problems. Every state
system is a system of exploitation and aggression, a system of benefitting
some at the expense of others. Imperialism is a system of "double
exploitation," a system of special restrictionist privileges imposed by one
state on top of the exploitations already imposed by another state
system. Thus, imperialism is a hierarchical system of privileges involving
at least two state systems. Fundamentally, imperialism is the result of two
interrelated restrictions: domestic interventionism (which is the cause of
the primary system of exploitation) and the denial, on an international
level, of free trade (which is the cause of the secondary imposition of
restrictions and exploitation). Imperialism is a logical outcome of the
older pre-laissez-faire mercantilism, supported by conservative defenders of the old order of caste and privilege. In modern times,
imperialism has had two champions: the conservatives and the socialists,
particularly the British Fabians and their fellow travelers.

5. Inflation.

Inflation is normally taken to be a rise in the general price level. As such,
it means that the prices of goods have risen relative to that of money,
that is, the exchange ratios have changed so that money is worth less vis-
à-vis other commodities. What can cause this? Only two things: a general
decline in the quantity of other exchangeable commodities, which can
only be caused, barring a natural disaster, by state destruction of goods,
or else a drastic increase in the money supply. This last has been for
centuries a monopoly of the state, and accordingly it is responsible for
"inflation." The free market libertarian solution is simply to take money
out of the hands of the state, and to rest the money supply on a
commodity base, such as gold or silver.

In all of these cases we find that the state causes the problems which
later on it allegedly is attempting to solve. I purposefully have left out of
consideration here the motives of the state for taking these actions;
sometimes the motive is explicitly to benefit certain groups, sometimes to
"solve" another problem. I shall specify these motives more later, in
considering a historical case study.

The basic pattern of state aggression is as follows. We begin with the
large-scale acceptance of the paradigm of statism itself, with the belief

that the state is a proper and effective means of solving certain perceived problems. The paradigm is applied as an ad hoc solution; for example, the state causes a depression, which makes many businesses discover that they cannot sell their products at profitable prices; then there is a general cry for the state to increase purchasing power and to find and guarantee foreign markets. The first it does by means of inflating the money supply; the second it does by means of adopting an expansionistic, imperialistic policy. In both cases the consequences are worse than if the state had simply done nothing and allowed businesses to adjust to economic reality. The consequences of the initial action begin to show up, causing more and more problems. Generally, people begin to feel their sense of control threatened, and resort to an ad hoc extension of the paradigm to solve these further problems, and to increase their sense of control. In the case I mentioned, the foreign policy adopted to gain new markets in other nations might involve later a growth in militarism, the adoption of conscription, and resorting to war.

These alleged solutions, too, only alleviate the problems temporarily, and, as more and more problems pile up, statism becomes more and more an integrated hierarchy of erroneous solutions to perceived problems.

Thus, the basic conflict between the paradigm of statism and the paradigm of liberty. I shall presently consider how the paradigm of statism has, in fact, functioned in the United States and how it is responsible for the present context of America. There is no similar empirical test for the paradigm of liberty, for unlike the literally dozens of variants on the theme of statism, liberty—the doctrine of libertarianism—stands untried and untested. But in today's context, when we are dealing with such political ideas and ideologies as have existed, perhaps that is a mark in its favor.

The Paradigm in Action: American History, 1860–1972

Any attempt at "panoramic history" must necessarily stay on the level of essentials; thus, I will consider only the areas where the paradigm is admittedly relevant: domestic and foreign situations, beginning with the Civil War.

Why the Civil War? The Civil War was a turning point in American history. As Arthur Ekirch states in his book *The Decline of American Liberalism:* "Among the ironies of the struggle to maintain the American Union was the fact that nothing seemed to effect so great a transformation in the fundamental character of that Union as did the Civil War."[17] Both ideologically and in terms of the politico–economic system, the effects of the Civil War are major and fundamental.

In economic matters the war . . . occasioned a tremendous expansion of the role of the Federal government. Along with the obvious part played by official Washington in contracting for the purchase of army supplies there was the important financial legislation passed by the new Republican administration. In place of the low duties current in the era from Jackson to Lincoln, the Republican Congress returned to the Whig theory of a protective tariff for American manufacturers. At the same time the business and agricultural interests were rewarded for their support of the party by the passage of the homestead law, and by the granting of Federal lands and funds for railroad building. . . . Finally the position of the Federal government as against the individual or the separate states was strengthened by such wartime legislation as the National Bank Act, an unprecedented income tax, and a variety of excise taxes which were the equivalent almost of a universal sales tax.[18]

As Ekirch also states: "Later, in the postwar period, it would be forgotten that many of the national problems associated with the rise of big business and monopoly had had their origins in this earlier era of expansion and consolidation during the Civil War."[19]

Ideologically, too, there were changes. "In place of John Locke and other philosophers of the natural rights and compact theories of government, American political theorists glorified the role of the state."[20] And "the enlarged scope of the powers of the Federal government was reflected in the political theory of the generation after the Civil War. The remnants of the older natural rights and state rights philosophies of government were now replaced by the new teachings of nationalism."[21]

The Civil War did more to initiate and sustain a system of privileges *as a system* than did anything else up to that time. For the Civil War effectively eliminated the opposition of the South to the growth in statism benefitting northern industrialists. As economist and historian Walter Grinder has stated,

One of the most important and long lasting developments of this period which was to set the course of America's future was the reenforcement and further development of the ties between the United States government and the emerging industrial class. The dislocations in the structure of the economy produced by this business–industrial elite by way of selective tariffs, subsidies, war contracts, wartime inflation, charters, favors and more subsidies led to a centralized capital accumulation in the hands of selected Yankee businessmen which altered the whole course of American history.[22]

Yet the results were predictable. The government helped to promote drastic malinvestments and misallocations of resources (considered from the perspective of the objective needs of the economy as reflected in the free market), and produced something inherently unstable. For unless such support continues, the forces of the market will work themselves out and show these investments for what they would have been without state aid: inherently uneconomic and unprofitable. Yet during this period of American history, the support of the industrialists by the federal government tended to be unstable and shifting. Thus, once the initial favors were granted to the railroads, the railroads found themselves in economic trouble, unable to maintain their level of functioning without government aid, which was not always forthcoming. The result, inevitably, was a depression, beginning in the 1870s.

Depression was therefore a problem which the politicians and key industrialists faced during the post–Civil War era. The result was the extention of the paradigm of statism in order to increase their sense of control. The theory of depressions prevalent at the time held that they were caused by overproduction and by too few markets for goods. Thus, what arose simultaneously on the part of the industrialists, financiers, intellectuals, and politicians was a twofold push for domestic regulation of smaller competitors which threatened the giants and for an interventionistic foreign policy designed to secure new markets for American goods. The Progressive Movement, indeed, was the fountainhead of both of these policies, and it was bankrolled and supported by the major business and financial leaders. Domestically, regulation took the form of the antitrust laws; foreign policy promoted the new imperialist movement.

Ideologically, imperialism was an offshoot of two trends that met and worked together in opposing laissez-faire and in promoting statism: the conservative and the socialist.[23] Economically, imperialism was a regression to mercantilism.

Again, both of these policies—domestic and foreign interventionism —were advocated as solutions to problems which key groups faced, and the statist paradigm appeared to be appropriate.

The entire history of the twentieth century is largely an extension and elaboration on the theme of interventionism, not just in America, but in all the countries in the world. The pattern is that state interventionism creates crises, and solutions are sought in both domestic and foreign interventionism. The rush for foreign colonies, spearheaded by the statist doctrines of nationalism and protectionism, resulted in the conflicts that led to World War I.

America's entry into the war was no accident; it was determined by the ideas and interests of the elite of financial, industrial, and political leaders. Economically, J. P. Morgan and other financiers were heavily involved with loans and investments to Britain; when defeat appeared to be a possibility, they stood to lose hundreds of millions of dollars. Many other financiers and industrialists feared a German victory for this reason and also because they feared German competition in world markets. Ideologically, the war was portrayed as a crusade to make the world safe for democracy.

Very important consequences resulted from American intervention, which determined the fate of the 1920s. Besides the triumph of a new nationalism, militarism, conscription, and censorship, there were even more far-reaching results of America's entry into the war. As Murray N. Rothbard has written:

More than any other single period, World War I was the critical watershed for the American business system. It was a 'war collectivism,' a totally planned economy run largely by big business interests through the instrumentality of the central government, which served as the model, the precedent, and the inspiration for state corporate capitalism for the remainder of the twentieth century.[24]

The entire history of the 1920s can be traced in terms of the policies resulting from the problems generated by the First World War. The American farmer, who had drastically expanded production for the war effort, found himself faced with falling markets, a rising European protectionism, and falling prices. High tariffs, put through to protect American industry from foreign competition, merely made it even more impossible for Europeans to buy American goods. Britain was faced with an increasingly shaky monetary system, which the U.S. Federal Reserve System attempted to help maintain and prop up by massive credit expansion during the 1920s.[25] The result of this was the Great Depression, which was the liquidation of the malinvestments carried on during the postwar boom generated by credit expansion engineered by the Federal Reserve System.

The case of the depression is the best single instance of the failure of the statist paradigm. For not only did the state *cause* the depression, it deepened it and maintained it until the Second World War, by using state controls to fight the depression itself. Since a depression is the process of liquidation of malinvestments, any attempt to prop up failing industries is self-defeating, *if* one's purpose is economic recovery. For it is precisely the adjustment to reality that is so vitally needed. Yet under both Hoover and FDR, the American government systematically attempted to *prevent* adjustment, by supporting uneconomic businesses. It also attempted to hold up wages (purchasing power) at a time when all other prices were falling, resulting in massive unemployment.

It is at this point that foreign policy becomes more relevant. The treaty ending World War I had imposed on the world an unstable statist status quo, which exploded when Germany attempted to retake the Danzig corridor (which had been seized from it at the conclusion of the war), and Britain and France declared war. The actual causes of the war were more complex; they involved statist rivalry during the 1930s and a desperate attempt for all three countries to find a permanent recovery from the depression.

American interest in foreign affairs was heightened during this period because the New Deal had failed to cure the depression. The old theory of foreign markets was dug up, and once the war had begun, American political and economic leaders began to watch with envy the colonial systems of Britain and France. Entry into the war (achieved in the face of massive public opposition by means of provoking Japan into attacking the American colony of Hawaii) was seen as a partial cure for the depression (whose effects had persisted until 1939) and as a means of gaining a bargaining position within the British and French colonial–imperialistic systems.

With the end of the war, both Britain and France were too economically destitute to actively sustain their colonial systems, and it was within this framework that the United States first became involved, on a large scale, with imperialism.

In the broadest terms, American foreign policy since World War II has been based on imperialism. American businessmen and financiers have sought foreign markets and access to raw materials and have depended on force and the military might of the U.S. government. The U.S. government has paved the way for investments through diplomacy and actual military interventions, and through such "international" agencies as the World Bank and International Monetary Fund. Although foreign markets and investments are thereby established, the dynamics of the situation do not stop at that point. As foreign markets and investments are established (not by means of free trade, but through protectionist, restrictionist grants of monopoly privileges), it is a natural tendency for those doing the investing to seek to stabilize the domestic situations of other countries—to freeze the *status quo*—and they use the military might of the U.S. government to attain that end. The foreign governments thus manipulated and sustained in power have nothing to do, of course, with the nonexistent "free world."

Feudalism, an inherently unstable system which all the military force in the world cannot sustain, is the structure of most of the foreign countries with which the corporations and financial institutions are so intricately involved. Thus, when the local populations rise up in revolutions against the increasing dominance of their lives by their own and foreign governments and business interests, American corporations and financial institutions seek to increase their sense of control by promoting American military intervention, by financially supporting the local ruling castes, or by attempting to establish control over the revolution itself. It is this process that has led to the Vietnam War and other, similar, events.[26]

The result, of course, is continued problems in areas such as Latin America, Africa, and Asia, which are tackled with the paradigm of statism. Needless to add, the revolutionary movements themselves also are incapable of solving their problems, since they accept the same ideology of statism as their oppressors.

Domestically, the U.S. has been suffering many effects of statism. In an attempt to take over Britain's preeminence as a world monetary center, the U.S. has engaged in constant monetary and financial manipulations. These manipulations have led to increased inflation and to a balance of payments problem, a problem caused by pairing two contradictory policies: a coercive fixing of the price of gold vis-à-vis the U.S. dollar, and a constant expansion of the currency. This situation has led to economic problems at home which the government has responded to with unworkable wage and price controls, as well as other regulations.

Anomalies and Revolution

What, then, of the future? In foreign policy, the U.S. is becoming increasingly interventionistic, involved in more and more countries. Whereas it had troops in no foreign countries in 1939, today it has troops in over 116 countries. The military budget has grown so rapidly in the last thirty years that a large segment of the American economy has become dependent on government contracts. When any attempt is made to end the contracts, and the war contractors are forced to liquidate malinvestments, political pressures are put on the government to take actions to prevent the liquidations, as in the case of Lockheed. Moreover, the American coercive union system has made it impossible for workers thrown out of jobs by the ending of war contracts to compete elsewhere for jobs. Thus, effective liquidation is prevented. Thus, too, there has come to be a host of economic groups that have a vested interest in maintaining the American defense budget and its consequent expansionistic military policies; e.g., the businesses involved, their workers, the military, and the bureaucracy whose interests have become so intertwined with the current establishment.

Furthermore, American investments and loans are becoming increasingly threatened in the so-called third world, and the pressure is greater than ever for interference in many other nations.

Domestically, malinvestments and misallocations of resources are greater than ever; a large number of American economic interests have a vested interest in evading economic reality. There is no "politically popular" means of decontrolling, for the largest businesses and financial institutions are precisely the ones that would be harmed the most by such deregulation. The situation is becoming increasingly worse.

And anomalies pile up increasingly.

Let us now look at the prospects for liberty, that is, the prospects for a revolution, for a *fundamental* change—a change in paradigms. At first glance, the future does not look too promising.

There are two things that can be done at this point. One is to test the theory I am proposing here empirically, that is, to continue extending the paradigm of statism as an attempted solution to social and political problems, and to see if, in fact, the problems are solved, or, on the contrary, if new problems are generated by this very process. The alternative is to use abstract reasoning, such as I have been doing (in an admittedly sketchy manner), to predict the consequences of the extension or maintenance of the paradigm and to show, by means of such reasoning, that these consequences will or will not occur, as the theory would lead us to anticipate. Since human action is qualitative and not quantitative, no specifically quantitative predictions can result from this second alternative. But if the theory is valid, it should enable us to predict *what* will happen, even if we cannot pin down the "when" or the "to what extent" by means of statistics.

The social sciences and humanities today, having decided to ape the methodology of the physical sciences, are decidedly "empirical," in the narrow sense of that term, in their approach to prediction and verification of theories. This leads us to expect that most social scientists will take the first rather than the second option at this point. They will wait for the theory proposed to be empirically confirmed.

Yet, there are at least three substantive objections to this procedure. First, it is enormously costly and time consuming. Secondly, since we are dealing with qualitative and not quantitative matters, there is no objective cutoff point, after which it is possible to say conclusively that the theory has been completely verified—because the variables cannot be controlled. Thirdly, if the theory is correct, as the paradigm is extended it will tend to produce more problems. Therefore, even if the intellectuals and political leaders decide that the paradigm is invalid and should be abandoned, it will become more and more difficult to abandon it because an integrated system of statism will have been created.

Of the three objections to empirical verification, the first, cost, is clearly the most important. The cost is in terms of untold human misery and destruction. If the paradigm continues unabated, the result will be continued bloodshed and poverty, continued repression and war. It increasingly is becoming apparent that most human beings in the world can ill afford the experiment with statism to continue. Regretfully, it looks as though more than ninety-nine percent of the modern intellectuals are willing to risk such an awesome cost. So much for the alleged humanitarianism of modern conservatives and liberals alike.

Is there a final solution to the problem? Are the preconditions for a true radical revolution operative? At this point I shall return briefly to Thomas Kuhn to see the relevance of his theory for our own future. I shall do so by answering a number of questions implicit or explicit in Kuhn's analysis.

Are we in a crisis period, in the strict sense of that term? Yes. The paradigm of statism has proved incapable of solving problems, and a growing number of intellectuals are beginning to realize it. Various aspects of the paradigm have been under assault for years now, such as the structure of imperialism, the welfare state, public education, the monetary system, and foreign aid. Crucial aspects of the paradigm itself are therefore being called into question. The large-scale desertion of the radical left from the ranks of the establishment is one indication that a crisis is operative.

Notice also that crisis periods are always followed by an intensification of research in the problem areas. Is this research happening now? Yes, especially with respect to education, monetary matters, and imperialism and foreign policy.

Certainly anomalies and puzzles have been piling up consistently, and at a growing pace. And again, a growing number of intellectuals believe the paradigm to be *incapable* of solving the problems.

Are there "violations of expectations"? Again, yes. Inflation, war, imperialism, depressions, monetary crises, underdeveloped countries— in all cases the events that are occurring are not what were anticipated by liberals.

Is there explicit dissent on fundamental issues? Yes.

Is there an increase in interest in philosophical analysis today? Yes, more so than at any time for the last several decades, and, as Kuhn suggests, "it is ... particularly in periods of acknowledged crisis that scientists have turned to philosophical analysis as a device for unlocking the riddles of their field."

We can, I think, conclude that the "objective conditions" for a revolution in paradigms exist. What about the "subjective conditions," by which is meant the existence of an alternate paradigm or attempted solution to problems?

This, too, is being developed—the ideology of libertarianism. As Kuhn suggests, "often a new paradigm emerges, at least in embryo, before a crisis has developed far or has been explicitly recognized." This paradigm does indeed claim to have better solutions to fundamental problems than statism, and both the broad theory and the "mopping up operations" are presently going on side by side. But does libertarianism qualify as a paradigm, as a potentially widespread doctrine? Yes, for while libertarianism is what Kuhn calls "sufficiently new," and has at least theoretically solved some of the major problems which men face, politically speaking, it is also "sufficiently open-ended to leave all sorts of problems for the redefined group of practitioners to solve."

In addition, it is precisely the younger "problem solvers" who are retreating from statism and looking for new alternatives, and an increasing number of them are attracted to libertarianism.

We may now turn to Kuhn's own analysis of the analogies between political and scientific revolutions. "Political revolutions are inaugurated by a growing sense, often restricted to a segment of the political community, that existing institutions have ceased adequately to meet the problems posed by an environment that they have in part created. . . . In both political and scientific development the sense of malfunction that can lead to crisis is prerequisite to revolution."[27]

Political revolutions aim to change political institutions in ways that those institutions themselves prohibit. Their success therefore necessitates the partial relinquishment of one set of institutions in favor of another, and in the interim, society is not fully governed by institutions at all. . . . In increasing numbers individuals become increasingly estranged from political life and behave more and more eccentrically within it. Then, as the crisis deepens, many of these individuals commit themselves to some concrete proposals for the reconstruction of society in a new institutional framework. At that point the society is divided into competing camps or parties, one seeking to defend the old institutional constellation, the others seeking to institute some new one. And once that polarization has occurred, political recourse fails.[28]

This, of course, is precisely the state of a large part of the world, and is increasingly the state of society in the United States. The interesting fact, however, is that there is no widely accepted alternative; statism is accepted in principle even by many of the disenchanted.

The time is ripe for a real revolution, and a new paradigm. Will that paradigm be libertarianism? No one can be sure. Unlike the physical sciences, today's political institutions can abolish and prevent effective change by means of physical force and destruction of opposition. But libertarianism alone is a fundamental challenge to the paradigm of statism.

Except in broad terms, then, no prediction is possible. We know that as long as statism is resorted to, conflicts and problems will be the inevitable result.

We also know that there might be a viable alternative: liberty. Whether or not liberty will succeed depends upon factors so complex that no one can determine the results with precision. If statism is resorted to because of people's need for a sense of control, and if it continues to erode that sense of control, perhaps enough people may come to loosen their own mental guidelines to enable them to rethink their premises and ideas. For a true sense of control must be in harmony with the facts of reality. And the facts of reality are on the side of liberty, not statism.

Notes

R. A. Childs, Jr., is one of the most active intellectual theoreticians in this country. His articles have appeared in the *Individualist, Libertarian Forum, Outlook, Reason, Rampart Journal* and elsewhere. He taught at Rampart College, edits Books for Libertarians, and has participated in numerous workshops dealing with political philosophy, ethics, and economics.

1. Thomas Kuhn, *The Structure of Scientific Revolutions,* 2nd ed. (Chicago: University of Chicago Press, 1970).

2. Murray N. Rothbard, "Ludwig von Mises and the Paradigm for Our Age," *Modern Age,* Spring 1971. I have incorporated a great many of Rothbard's insights into this essay.

3. Kuhn, *op. cit.,* p. 10. All further quotations in this section are from this work, unless otherwise noted.

4. *Seminar,* no. 30, a monthly recorded discussion of psychology and related issues. See also the discussion by Nathaniel Branden in an interview in *Reason* magazine, May 1973.

5. Kuhn, *op. cit.,* p. 77.

6. Ibid., p. 84.

7. Ibid., p. 91.

8. Ibid., p. 92.

9. Ibid., p. 153.

10. Ayn Rand, "The Objectivist Ethics," *The Virtue of Selfishness* (New York: New American Library, 1964), pp. 15–17.

11. Ibid., p. 23.

12. For a detailed analysis of the workings of a free market economic system, and that of statism, see Murray N. Rothbard, *Man, Economy and State* (Los Angeles: Nash Publishing Co., 1971) and *Power and Market* (Menlo Park, Calif.: Institute for Humane Studies, 1970).

13. Ludwig von Mises, *Human Action* (New Haven: Yale University Press, 1949), p. 660.

14. Rothbard, *Power and Market*, p. 42.

15. Rothbard, *Man, Economy and State*, pp. 604–614.

16. See Gabriel Kolko, *The Triumph of Conservatism* (Glencoe, Ill.: The Free Press, 1965).

17. Arthur Ekirch, *The Decline of American Liberalism* (New York: Atheneum, 1969), p. 119.

18. Ibid., pp. 128–129.

19. Ibid., p. 129.

20. Ibid., p. 137.

21. Ibid., p. 135.

22. In an unpublished essay.

23. See Bernard Semmel, *Imperialism and Social Reform* (New York: Doubleday, 1960) and George Lichtenheim, *Imperialism* (New York: Praeger Publishing Co., 1971).

24. Murray N. Rothbard and Ronald Radosh, eds., *A New History of Leviathan* (New York: E. P. Dutton & Co., 1972), p. 66.

25. M. N. Rothbard, *America's Great Depression* (Los Angeles: Nash Publishing Co., 1972).

26. See Gabriel Kolko, *The Politics of War* (New York: Random House, 1968) and Joyce and Gabriel Kolko, *The Limits of Power* (New York: Harper & Row, 1972).

27. Kuhn, *op. cit.*, p. 92.

28. Ibid., p. 93.

Murray N. Rothbard

37

Left and Right: The Prospects for Liberty

THE CONSERVATIVE HAS LONG been marked, whether he knows it or not, by long-run pessimism: by the belief that the long-run trend, and therefore Time itself, is against him, and hence the inevitable trend runs toward left-wing statism at home and Communism abroad. It is this long-run despair that accounts for the Conservative's rather bizarre short-run optimism; for since the long-run is given up as hopeless, the Conservative feels that his only hope of success rests in the current moment. In foreign affairs, this point of view leads the Conservative to call for desperate showdowns with Communism, for he feels that the longer he waits the worse things will ineluctably become; at home, it leads him to total concentration on the very next election, where he is always hoping for victory and never achieving it. The quintessence of the Practical Man, and beset by long-run despair, the Conservative refuses to think or plan beyond the election of the day.

Pessimism, however, both short-run *and* long-run, is precisely what the prognosis of Conservatism deserves; for Conservatism is a dying remnant of the *ancien regime* of the pre-industrial era, and, as such, it *has* no future. In its contemporary American form, the recent Conservative Revival embodied the death throes of an ineluctably moribund, Fundamentalist, rural, small-town, white Anglo-Saxon America. What, however, of the prospects for *liberty*? For too many libertarians mistakenly link the prognosis for liberty with that of the seemingly stronger and supposedly allied Conservative movement; this linkage makes the characteristic long-run pessimism of the modern libertarian easy to understand. But this paper contends that, while the short-run prospects for liberty at home and abroad may seem dim, the proper attitude for the libertarian to take is that of unquenchable long-run optimism.

The case for this assertion rests on a certain view of history: which holds, first, that before the 18th century in Western Europe there existed (and still continues to exist outside the West) an identifiable Old Order. Whether the Old Order took the form of feudalism or Oriental despotism, it was marked by tyranny, exploitation, stagnation, fixed caste, and hopelessness and starvation for the bulk of the population. In sum, life was "nasty, brutish, and short"; here was Maine's "society of status" and Spencer's "military society." The ruling classes, or castes, governed by conquest and by getting the masses to believe in the alleged divine *imprimatur* to their rule.

The Old Order was, and still remains, the great and mighty enemy of liberty; and it was particularly mighty in the past because there was then no inevitability about *its* overthrow. When we consider that basically the Old Order had existed since the dawn of history, in all civilizations, we can appreciate even more the glory and the magnitude of the triumph of the liberal revolution of and around the eighteenth century.

Part of the dimensions of this struggle has been obscured by a great myth of the history of Western Europe implanted by antiliberal German historians of the late 19th century. The myth held that the growth of absolute monarchies and of mercantilism in the early modern era was necessary for the development of capitalism, since these served to liberate the merchants and the people from local feudal restrictions. In actuality, this was not at all the case; the King and his nation-State served rather as a super-feudal overlord re-imposing and reinforcing feudalism just as it was being dissolved by the peaceful growth of the market economy. The King superimposed his own restrictions and monopoly privileges onto those of the feudal regime. The absolute monarchs were the Old Order writ large and made even more despotic than before. Capitalism, indeed, flourished earliest and most actively precisely in those areas where the central State was weak or non-existent: the Italian cities, the Hanseatic League, the confederation of seventeenth century Holland. Finally, the Old Order was overthrown or severely shaken in its grip in two ways. One was by industry and the market expanding through the interstices of the feudal order (*e.g.*, industry in England developing in the countryside beyond the grip of feudal, State, and guild restrictions). More important was a series of cataclysmic revolutions that blasted loose the Old Order and the old ruling classes: the English Revolutions of the seventeenth century, the American Revolution, and the French Revolution, all of which were necessary to the ushering in of the Industrial Revolution and of at least partial victories for individual liberty, *laissez-faire*, separation of church-and-state, and international peace. The society of status gave way, at least partially, to the "society of contract"; the military society gave way partially to the "industrial society." The mass of the population now achieved a mobility of labor and place, and accelerating expansion of their living standards, for which they had scarcely dared to hope. Liberalism had indeed brought to the Western world not only liberty, the prospect of peace, and the rising living standards of an industrial society, but above all perhaps, it brought hope, a hope in ever-greater progress that lifted the mass of mankind out of its age-old sink of stagnation and despair.

Soon there developed in Western Europe two great political ideologies, centered around this new revolutionary phenomenon: the one was Liberalism, the party of hope, of radicalism, of liberty, of the Industrial Revolution, of progress, of humanity; the other was Conservatism, the party of reaction, the party that longed to restore the hierarchy, statism, theocracy, serfdom, and class exploitation of the Old Order. Since liberalism admittedly had reason on its side, the Conservatives darkened the ideological atmosphere with obscurantist calls for romanticism, tradition, theocracy, and irrationalism. Political ideologies were polarized, with Liberalism on the extreme "Left," and Conservatism on the extreme "Right," of the ideological spectrum. That genuine Liberalism was essentially radical and revolutionary was brilliantly perceived, in the twilight of its impact, by the great Lord Acton (one of the few figures in the history of thought who, charmingly, grew *more* radical as he grew older). Acton wrote that "Liberalism wishes for what ought to be, irrespective of what is." In working out this view, incidentally, it was Acton, not Trotsky, who first arrived at the concept of the "permanent revolution." As Gertrude Himmelfarb wrote, in her excellent study of Acton:

> *his philosophy develop(ed) to the point where the future was seen as the avowed enemy of the past, and where the past was allowed no authority except as it happened to conform to morality. To take seriously this Liberal theory of history, to give precedence to "what ought to be" over "what is," was, he admitted, virtually to install a "revolution in permanence."*
>
> *The "revolution in permanence," as Acton hinted in the inaugural lecture and admitted frankly in his notes, was the culmination of his philosophy of history and theory of politics ... This idea of conscience, that men carry about with them the*

knowledge of good and evil, is the very root of revolution, for it destroys the
sanctity of the past . . . "*Liberalism is essentially revolutionary,*" *Acton observed.*
"*Facts must yield to ideas. Peaceably and patiently if possible. Violently if not.*"[1]

The Liberal, wrote Acton, far surpassed the Whig:

The Whig governed by compromise. The Liberal begins the reign of ideas . . . *One*
is practical, gradual, ready for compromise. The other works out a principle
philosophically. One is a policy aiming at a philosophy. The other is a philosophy
seeking a policy.[2]

What happened to Liberalism? Why then did it decline during the
nineteenth century? This question has been pondered many times, but
perhaps the basic reason was an inner rot within the vitals of Liberalism
itself. For, with the partial success of the Liberal Revolution in the West,
the Liberals increasingly abandoned their radical fervor, and therefore
their liberal goals, to rest content with a mere defense of the uninspiring
and defective status quo. Two philosophical roots of this decay may be
discerned: First, the abandonment of natural rights and "higher law"
theory for utilitarianism. For only forms of natural or higher law theory
can provide a radical base outside the existing system from which to
challenge the *status quo*; and only such theory furnishes a sense of
necessary immediacy to the libertarian struggle, by focussing on the
necessity of bringing existing criminal rulers to the bar of justice.
Utilitarians, on the other hand, in abandoning justice for expediency,
also abandon immediacy for quiet stagnation and inevitably end up as
objective apologists for the existing order.

The second great philosophical influence on the decline of Liberalism was evolutionism, or Social Darwinism, which put the finishing
touches to Liberalism as a radical force in society. For the Social
Darwinist erroneously saw history and society through the peaceful,
rose-colored glasses of infinitely slow, infinitely gradual social evolution.
Ignoring the prime fact that no ruling caste in history has ever
voluntarily surrendered its power, and that therefore Liberalism had to
break through by means of a series of revolutions, the Social Darwinists
looked forward peacefully and cheerfully to thousands of years of
infinitely gradual evolution to the next supposedly inevitable stage of
individualism.

An interesting illustration of a thinker who embodies within himself
the decline of Liberalism in the nineteenth century is Herbert Spencer.
Spencer began as a magnificently radical liberal, indeed virtually a pure
libertarian. But, as the virus of sociology and Social Darwinism took over

in his soul, Spencer abandoned libertarianism as a dynamic historical movement, although at first without abandoning it in pure theory. In short, while looking forward to an eventual ideal of pure liberty, Spencer began to see its victory as inevitable, but only after millenia of gradual evolution, and thus, in actual fact, Spencer abandoned Liberalism as a fighting, radical creed; and confined his Liberalism in practice to a weary, rear-guard action against the growing collectivism of the late nineteenth century. Interestingly enough, Spencer's tired shift "rightward" in strategy soon became a shift rightward in theory as well; so that Spencer abandoned pure liberty even in theory *e.g.*, in repudiating his famous chapter in *Social Statics*, "The Right to Ignore the State."

In England, the classical liberals began their shift from radicalism to quasi-conservatism in the early nineteenth century; a touchstone of this shift was the general British liberal attitude toward the national liberation struggle in Ireland. This struggle was twofold: against British political imperialism, and against feudal landlordism which had been imposed by that imperialism. By their Tory blindness toward the Irish drive for national independence, and especially for peasant property against feudal oppression, the British liberals (including Spencer) symbolized their effective abandonment of genuine Liberalism, which had been virtually born in a struggle against the feudal land system. Only in the United States, the great home of radical liberalism (where feudalism had never been able to take root outside the South), did natural rights and higher law theory, and consequent radical liberal movements, continue in prominence until the mid-nineteenth century. In their different ways, the Jacksonian and Abolitionist movements were the last powerful radical libertarian movements in American life.[3]

Thus, with Liberalism abandoned from within, there was no longer a Party of Hope in the Western world, no longer a "Left" movement to lead a struggle against the State and against the unbreached remainder of the Old Order. Into this gap, into this void created by the drying up of radical liberalism, there stepped a new movement: Socialism. Libertarians of the present day are accustomed to think of socialism as the polar opposite of the libertarian creed. But this is a grave mistake, responsible for a severe ideological disorientation of libertarians in the present world. As we have seen, Conservatism was the polar opposite of liberty; and socialism, while to the "left" of conservatism, was essentially a confused, middle-of-the-road movement. It was, and still is, middle-of-the road because it tries to achieve Liberal *ends* by the use of Conservative *means*.

In short, Russell Kirk, who claims that Socialism was the heir of classical liberalism, and Ronald Hamowy, who sees Socialism as the heir of Conservatism, are *both* right; for the question is on what aspect of this confused centrist movement we happen to be focussing. Socialism, like Liberalism and against Conservatism, accepted the industrial system and the liberal *goals* of freedom, reason, mobility, progress, higher living standards for the masses, and an end to theocracy and war; but it tried to achieve these ends by the use of incompatible, Conservative means: statism, central planning, communitarianism, etc. Or rather, to be more precise, there were from the beginning two different strands within Socialism: one was the Right-wing, authoritarian strand, from Saint-Simon down, which glorified statism, hierarchy, and collectivism and which was thus a projection of Conservatism trying to accept and dominate the new industrial civilization. The other was the Left-wing, relatively libertarian strand, exemplified in their different ways by Marx and Bakunin, revolutionary and far more interested in achieving the libertarian goals of liberalism and socialism: but especially the smashing of the State apparatus to achieve the "withering away of the State" and the "end of the exploitation of man by man." Interestingly enough, the very Marxian phrase, the "replacement of the government of *men* by the administration of *things*," can be traced, by a circuitous route, from the great French radical *laissez-faire* liberals of the early nineteenth century, Charles Comte (no relation to Auguste Comte) and Charles Dunoyer. And so, too, may the concept of the "class struggle"; except that for Dunoyer and Comte the inherently antithetical classes were not businessmen vs. workers, but the producers in society (including free businessmen, workers, peasants, etc.) *versus* the exploiting classes constituting, and privileged by, the State apparatus.[4] Saint-Simon, at one time in his confused and chaotic life, was close to Comte and Dunoyer and picked up his class analysis from them, in the process characteristically getting the whole thing balled up and converting businessmen on the market, *as well as* feudal landlords and others of the State privileged, into "exploiters." Marx and Bakunin picked this up from the Saint-Simonians, and the result gravely misled the whole Left Socialist movement; for, then, *in addition* to smashing the repressive State, it became supposedly necessary to smash private capitalist ownership of the means of production. Rejecting private property, especially of capital, the Left Socialists were then trapped in a crucial inner contradiction: if the State is to disappear after the Revolution (immediately for Bakunin, gradually "withering" for Marx), then how is the "collective" to run its property without becoming an enormous State itself in fact even if not in name?

This was a contradiction which neither the Marxists nor the Bakuninists were ever able to resolve.

Having replaced radical liberalism as the party of the "Left," Socialism, by the turn of the twentieth century, fell prey to this inner contradiction. Most Socialists (Fabians, Lassalleans, even Marxists) turned sharply rightward, completely abandoned the old libertarian goals and ideals of revolution and the withering away of the State, and became cozy Conservatives permanently reconciled to the State, the *status quo*, and the whole apparatus of neo-mercantilism, State monopoly capitalism, imperialism and war that was rapidly being established and riveted on European society at the turn of the twentieth century. For Conservatism, too, had re-formed and regrouped to try to cope with a modern industrial system, and had become a refurbished mercantilism, a regime of statism marked by State monopoly privilege, in direct and indirect forms, to favored capitalists and to quasi-feudal landlords. The affinity between Right Socialism and the new Conservatism became very close, the former advocating similar policies but with a demagogic populist veneer: thus, the other side of the coin of imperialism was "social imperialism," which Joseph Schumpeter trenchantly defined as "an imperialism in which the entrepreneurs and other elements woo the workers by means of social welfare concessions which appear to depend on the success of export monopolism . . ."[5]

Historians have long recognized the affinity, and the welding together, of Right-wing socialism with Conservatism in Italy and Germany, where the fusion was embodied first in Bismarckism and then in Fascism and National Socialism: the latter fulfilling the Conservative program of nationalism, imperialism, militarism, theocracy, and a right-wing collectivism that retained and even cemented the rule of the old privileged classes. But only recently have historians begun to realize that a similar pattern occurred in England and the United States. Thus, Bernard Semmel, in his brilliant history of the social-imperialist movement in England at the turn of the twentieth century, shows how the Fabian Society welcomed the rise of the Imperialists in England.[6] When, in the mid-1890's, the Liberal Party in England split into the Radicals on the left and the Liberal-Imperialists on the right, Beatrice Webb, co-leader of the Fabians, denounced the Radicals as "*laisser-faire* and anti-imperialist", while hailing the latter as "collectivists and imperialists." An official Fabian manifesto, *Fabianism and the Empire* (1900), drawn up by George Bernard Shaw (who was later, with perfect consistency, to praise the domestic policies of Stalin *and* Mussolini *and* Sir Oswald Mosley), lauded imperialism and attacked the Radicals, who "still cling to the fixed-frontier ideals of individualist republicanism (and) non-interference." In contrast, "a Great Power ... must govern (a world empire) in the interests of civilization as a whole." After this, the Fabians collaborated closely with Tories and Liberal-Imperialists. Indeed, in late 1902, Sidney and Beatrice Webb established a small, secret group of brain-trusters called The Coefficients; as one of the leading members of this club, the Tory imperialist, Leopold S. Amery, revealingly wrote: "Sidney and Beatrice Webb were much more concerned with getting their ideas of the welfare state put into practice by any one who might be prepared to help, even on the most modest scale, than with the early triumph of an avowedly Socialist Party ... There was, after all, nothing so very unnatural, as (Joseph) Chamberlain's own career had shown, in a combination of Imperialism in external affairs with municipal socialism or semi-socialism at home."[7] Other members of the Coefficients, who, as Amery wrote, were to function as a "Brains Trust or General Staff" for the movement, were: the Liberal-Imperialist Richard B. Haldane; the geo-politician Halford J. Mackinder; the imperialist and Germanophobe Leopold Maxse, publisher of the *National Review*; the Tory socialist and imperialist Viscount Milner; the naval imperialist Carlyon Bellairs; the famous journalist J. L. Garvin; Bernard Shaw; Sir Clinton Dawkins, partner of the Morgan bank; and Sir Edward Grey, who, at a meeting of the club first adumbrated the policy of Entente with France and Russia that was to eventuate in the First World War.[8]

The famous betrayal, during World War I, of the old ideals of revolutionary pacifism by the European Socialists, and even by the Marxists, should have come as no surprise; that each Socialist Party supported its "own" national government in the war (with the honorable exception of Eugene Victor Debs' Socialist Party in the United States) was the final embodiment of the collapse of the classic Socialist Left. From then on, socialists and quasi-socialists joined Conservatives in a basic amalgam, accepting the State and the Mixed Economy (=neo-Mercantilism=the Welfare State=Interventionism=State Monopoly Capitalism, merely synonyms for the same essential reality). It was in reaction to this collapse that Lenin broke out of the Second International, to re-establish classic revolutionary Marxism in a revival of Left Socialism.

In fact, Lenin, almost without knowing it, accomplished *more* than this. It is common knowledge that "purifying" movements, eager to return to a classic purity shorn of recent corruptions, generally purify further than what had held true among the original classic sources. There were, indeed, marked "conservative" strains in the writings of Marx and Engels themselves which often justified the State, Western imperialism and aggressive nationalism, and it was these *motifs*, in the ambivalent views of the Masters on this subject, that provided the fodder for the later shift of the majority Marxists into the "social imperialist" camp.[9] Lenin's camp turned more "left" than had Marx and Engels themselves. Lenin had a decidedly more revolutionary stance toward the State, and consistently defended and supported movements of national liberation against imperialism. The Leninist shift was more "leftist" in other important senses as well. For while Marx had centered his attack on market capitalism *per se*, the major focus of Lenin's concerns was on what he conceived to be the highest stages of capitalism: imperialism and monopoly. Hence Lenin's focus, centering as it did *in practice* on State monopoly and imperialism rather than on *laissez-faire* capitalism, was in that way far more congenial to the libertarian than that of Karl Marx. In recent years, the splits in the Leninist world have brought to the fore a still more left-wing tendency: that of the Chinese. In their almost exclusive stress on revolution in the undeveloped countries, the Chinese have, in addition to scorning Right-wing Marxist compromises with the State, unerringly centered their hostility on feudal and quasi-feudal landholdings, on monopoly concessions which have enmeshed capital with quasi-feudal land, and on Western imperialism. In this virtual abandonment of the classical Marxist emphasis on the working class, the Maoists have concentrated Leninist efforts more closely on the over-throw of the major bulwarks of the Old Order in the modern world.[10]

Fascism and Nazism were the logical culmination in domestic affairs of the modern drift toward right-wing collectivism. It has become customary among libertarians, as indeed among the Establishment of the West, to regard fascism and Communism as fundamentally identical. But while both systems were indubitably collectivist, they differed greatly in their socio-economic content. For Communism was a genuine revolutionary movement that ruthlessly displaced and overthrew the old ruling élites; while Fascism, on the contrary, cemented into power the old ruling classes. Hence, fascism was a counter-revolutionary move-ment that froze a set of monopoly privileges upon society; in short, fascism was the apotheosis of modern State monopoly capitalism.[11] Here was the reason that fascism proved so attractive (which Communism, of course, never did) to big business interests in the West—openly and unabashedly so in the 1920's and early 1930's.[12]

We are now in a position to apply our analysis to the American scene. Here we encounter a contrasting myth about recent American history which has been propagated by current conservatives and adopted by most American libertarians. The myth goes approximately as follows: America was, more or less, a haven of *laissez-faire* until the New Deal; then Roosevelt, influenced by Felix Frankfurter, the Intercollegiate Socialist Society, and other "Fabian" and Communist "conspirators," engineered a revolution which set America on the path to Socialism, and, further on, beyond the horizon, to Communism. The present-day libertarian who adopts this or a similar view of the American experience, tends to think of himself as an "extreme right-winger"; slightly to the left of him, then, lies the Conservative, to the left of that the middle-of-the road, and then leftward to Socialism and Communism. Hence, the enormous temptation for some libertarians to red-bait; for, since they see America as drifting inexorably leftward to Socialism and therefore to Communism, the great temptation is for them to overlook the intermediary stages and tar all of their opposition with the hated Red brush.

One would think that the "right-wing libertarian" would quickly be able to see some drastic flaws in this conception. For one thing, the income tax amendment, which he deplores as the beginning of socialism in America, was put through Congress in 1909 by an overwhelming majority of both parties. To look at this event as a sharp leftward move toward socialism would require treating President William Howard Taft, who put through the Sixteenth Amendment, as a Leftist, and surely few would have the temerity to do that. Indeed, the New Deal was not a *revolution* in any sense; its entire collectivist program was anticipated: proximately by Herbert Hoover during the depression, and, beyond that, by the war-collectivism and central planning that governed America during the First World War. Every element in the New Deal program: central planning, creation of a network of compulsory cartels for industry and agriculture, inflation and credit expansion, artificial raising of wage rates and promotion of unions within the overall monopoly structure, government regulation and ownership, all this had been anticipated and adumbrated during the previous two decades.[13] And this program, with its privileging of various big business interests at the top of the collectivist heap, was in no sense reminiscent of socialism or leftism; there was nothing smacking of the egalitarian or the proletarian here. No, the kinship of this burgeoning collectivism was not at all with Socialism-Communism but with Fascism, or Socialism-of-the-Right, a kinship which many big businessmen of the 'twenties expressed openly in their yearning for abandonment of a quasi-*laissez-faire* system for a collectivism which they could control. And, surely, William Howard Taft, Woodrow Wilson, and Herbert Clark Hoover make far more recognizable figures as protofascists than they do as crypto-Communists.

The essence of the New Deal was seen, far more clearly than in the conservative mythology, by the Leninist movement in the early 1930's—that is, until the mid-thirties, when the exigencies of Soviet foreign relations caused a sharp shift of the world Communist line to "Popular Front" approval of the New Deal. Thus, in 1934, the British Leninist theoretician R. Palme Dutt published a brief but scathing analysis of the New Deal as "social fascism"—as the reality of fascism cloaked with a thin veneer of populist demagogy. No conservative opponent has ever delivered a more vigorous or trenchant denunciation of the New Deal. The Roosevelt policy, wrote Dutt, was to "move to a form of dictatorship of a war-type"; the essential policies were to impose a State monopoly capitalism through the NRA, to subsidize business, banking, and agriculture through inflation and the partial expropriation of the mass of the people through lower real wage rates, and to the regulation and exploitation of labor by means of government-fixed wages and compulsory arbitration. When the New Deal, wrote Dutt, is stripped of its "social-reformist 'progressive' camouflage," "the reality of the new Fascist type of system of concentrated state capitalism and industrial servitude remains," including an implicit "advance to war." Dutt effectively concluded with a quote from an editor of the highly respected *Current History Magazine*: "The new America (the editor had written in mid-1933) will not be capitalist in the old sense, nor will it be Socialist. If at the moment the trend is towards Fascism, it will be an American Fascism, embodying the experience, the traditions and the hopes of a great middle-class nation."[14]

Thus, the New Deal was not a qualitative break from the American past; on the contrary, it was merely a quantitative extension of the web of State privilege that had been proposed and acted upon before: in Hoover's Administration, in the war collectivism of World War I, and in the Progressive Era. The most thorough exposition of the origins of State monopoly capitalism, or what he calls "political capitalism," in the U.S. is found in the brilliant work of Dr. Gabriel Kolko. In his *Triumph of Conservatism*, Kolko traces the origins of political capitalism in the "reforms" of the Progressive Era. Orthodox historians have always treated the Progressive period (roughly 1900–1916) as a time when free-market capitalism was becoming increasingly "monopolistic"; in reaction to this reign of monopoly and big business, so the story runs, altruistic intellectuals and far-seeing politicians turned to intervention by the government to reform and regulate these evils. Kolko's great work demonstrates that the reality was almost precisely the opposite of this myth. *Despite* the wave of mergers and trusts formed around the turn of the century, Kolko reveals, the forces of competition on the free market rapidly vitiated and dissolved these attempts at stabilizing and perpetuating the economic power of big business interests. It was precisely in reaction to their impending *defeat* at the hands of the competitive storms of the market that big business turned, increasingly after the 1900's, to the federal government for aid and protection. In short, the intervention by the federal government was designed, not to curb big business monopoly for the sake of the public weal, but to *create* monopolies that big business (as well as trade associations of smaller business) had not been able to establish amidst the competitive gales of the free market. Both Left and Right have been persistently misled by the notion that intervention by the government is *ipso facto* leftish and anti-business. Hence the mythology of the New-Fair Deal-as-Red that is endemic on the Right. Both the big businessmen, led by the Morgan interests, and Professor Kolko almost uniquely in the academic world, have realized that monopoly privilege can only be created by the State and not as a result of free market operations.

Thus, Kolko shows that, beginning with Theodore Roosevelt's New Nationalism and culminating in Wilson's New Freedom, in industry after industry, e.g., insurance, banking, meat, exports, and business generally, regulations that present-day Rightists think of as "socialistic" were not only uniformly hailed, but conceived and brought about by big businessmen. This was a conscious effort to fasten upon the economy a cement of subsidy, stabilization, and monopoly privilege. A typical view was that of Andrew Carnegie; deeply concerned about competition in the steel industry, which neither the formation of U.S. Steel nor the famous "Gary Dinners" sponsored by that Morgan company could dampen, Carnegie declared in 1908 that "it always comes back to me that Government control, and that alone, will properly solve the problem." There is nothing alarming about government regulation *per se*, announced Carnegie, "capital is perfectly safe in the gas company, although it is under court control. So will all capital be, although under Government control . . ."[15]

The Progressive Party, Kolko shows, was basically a Morgan-created party to re-elect Roosevelt and punish President Taft, who had been over-zealous in prosecuting Morgan enterprises; the leftish social workers often unwittingly provided a demagogic veneer for a conservative-statist movement. Wilson's New Freedom, culminating in the creation of the Federal Trade Commission, far from being considered dangerously socialistic by big business, was welcomed enthusiastically as putting their long-cherished program of support, privilege, and regulation of competition into effect (and Wilson's war collectivism was welcomed even more exuberantly.) Edward N. Hurley, Chairman of the Federal Trade Commission and formerly President of the Illinois Manufacturers Association, happily announced, in late 1915, that the Federal Trade Commission was designed "to do for general business" what the ICC had been eagerly doing for the railroads and shippers, what the Federal Reserve was doing for the nation's bankers, and what the Department of Agriculture was accomplishing for the farmers.[16] As would happen more dramatically in European fascism, each economic interest group was being cartellized and monopolized and fitted into its privileged niche in a hierarchically-ordered socio-economic structure. Particularly influential were the views of Arthur Jerome Eddy, an eminent corporation lawyer who specialized in forming trade associations and who helped to father the Federal Trade Commission. In his *magnum opus* fiercely denouncing competition in business and calling for governmentally-controlled and protected industrial "cooperation," Eddy trumpeted that "Competition is War, and 'War is Hell.'"[17]

What of the intellectuals of the Progressive period, damned by the present-day Right as "socialistic"? Socialistic in a sense they were, but what *kind* of "socialism"? The conservative State Socialism of Bismarck's Germany, the prototype for so much of modern European—and American—political forms, and under which the bulk of American intellectuals of the late nineteenth century received their higher education. As Kolko puts it:

The conservatism of the contemporary intellectuals, . . . the idealization of the state by Lester Ward, Richard T. Ely, or Simon N. Patten . . . was also the result of the peculiar training of many of the American academics of this period. At the end of the nineteenth century the primary influence in American academic social and economic theory was exerted by the universities. The Bismarckian idealization of the state, with its centralized welfare functions . . . was suitably revised by the thousands of key academics who studied in German universities in the 1880's and 1890's . . .[18]

The ideal of the leading ultra-conservative German professors, moreover, who were also called "socialists of the chair," was consciously to form themselves into the "intellectual bodyguard of the House of Hohenzollern"—and that they surely were.

As an exemplar of the Progressive intellectual, Kolko aptly cites Herbert Croly, editor of the Morgan-financed *New Republic*. Systematizing Theodore Roosevelt's New Nationalism, Croly hailed this new Hamiltonianism as a system for collectivist federal control and integration of society into a hierarchical structure. Looking forward from the Progressive Era, Gabriel Kolko concludes that

a synthesis of business and politics on the federal level was created during the war, in various administrative and emergency agencies, that continued throughout the following decade. Indeed, the war period represents the triumph of business in the most emphatic manner possible ... big business gained total support from the various regulatory agencies and the Executive. It was during the war that effective, working oligopoly and price and market agreements became operational in the dominant sectors of the American economy. The rapid diffusion of power in the economy and relatively easy entry virtually ceased. Despite the cessation of important new legislative enactments, the unity of business and the federal government continued throughout the 1920's and thereafter, using the foundations laid in the Progressive Era to stabilize and consolidate conditions within various industries ... The principle of utilizing the federal government to stabilize the economy, established in the context of modern industrialism during the Progressive Era, became the basis of political capitalism in its many later ramifications.

In this sense progressivism did not die in the 1920's, but became a part of the basic fabric of American society.[19]

Thus, the New Deal. After a bit of leftish wavering in the middle and late 'thirties, the Roosevelt Administration re-cemented its alliance with big business in the national defense and war contract economy that began in 1940. This was an economy and a polity that has been ruling America ever since, embodied in the permanent war economy, the full-fledged State monopoly capitalism and neo-mercantilism, the military-industrial complex of the present era. The essential features of American society have not changed since it was thoroughly militarized and politicized in World War II—except that the trends intensify, and even in everyday life men have been increasingly moulded into conforming Organization Men serving the State and its military-industrial complex. William H. Whyte, Jr., in his justly famous book, *The Organization Man*, made clear that this moulding took place amidst the adoption by business of the collectivist views of "enlightened" sociologists and other social engineers. It is also clear that this harmony of views is not simply the result of naiveté by big businessmen—not when such "naiveté" coincides with the requirements of compressing the worker and manager into the mould of willing servitor in the great bureaucracy of the military-industrial machine. And, under the guise of "democracy," education has become mere mass drilling in the techniques of adjustment to the task of becoming a cog in the vast bureaucratic machine.

Meanwhile, the Republicans and Democrats remain as bipartisan in forming and supporting this Establishment as they were in the first two decades of the twentieth century. "Me-tooism"—bipartisan support of the *status quo* that underlies the superficial differences between the parties—did not begin in 1940.

How did the corporal's guard of remaining libertarians react to these shifts of the ideological spectrum in America? An instructive answer may be found by looking at the career of one of the great libertarians of twentieth-century America: Albert Jay Nock. In the 1920's, when Nock had formulated his radical libertarian philosophy, he was universally regarded as a member of the extreme left, and he so regarded himself as well. It is always the tendency, in ideological and political life, to center one's attentions on the main enemy of the day, and the main enemy of that day was the conservative statism of the Coolidge-Hoover Administration; it was natural, therefore, for Nock, his friend and fellow-libertarian Mencken, and other radicals to join quasi-socialists in battle against the common foe. When the New Deal succeeded Hoover, on the other hand, the milk-and-water socialists and vaguely leftish interventionists hopped on the New Deal bandwagon; on the Left, only the libertarians such as Nock and Mencken, and the Leninists (before the Popular Front period) realized that Roosevelt was only a continuation of Hoover in other rhetoric. It was perfectly natural for the radicals to form a united front against FDR with the older Hoover and Al Smith conservatives who either believed Roosevelt had gone too far or disliked his flamboyant populistic rhetoric. But the problem was that Nock and his fellow radicals, at first properly scornful of their new-found allies, soon began to accept them and even don cheerfully the formerly despised label of "conservative." With the rank-and-file radicals, this shift took place, as have so many transformations of ideology in history, unwittingly and in default of proper ideological leadership; for Nock, and to some extent for Mencken, on the other hand, the problem cut far deeper.

For there had always been one grave flaw in the brilliant and finely-

honed libertarian doctrine hammered out in their very different ways by
Nock and Mencken; both had long adopted the great error of pessimism. Both saw no hope for the human race ever adopting the system of
liberty; despairing of the radical doctrine of liberty ever being applied in
practice, each in his own personal way retreated from the responsibility
of ideological leadership, Mencken joyously and hedonically, Nock
haughtily and secretively. Despite the massive contribution of both men
to the cause of liberty, therefore, neither could ever become the
conscious leader of a libertarian movement: for neither could ever
envision the party of liberty as the party of hope, the party of revolution,
or *a fortiori*, the party of secular messianism. The error of pessimism is
the first step down the slippery slope that leads to Conservatism; and
hence it was all too easy for the pessimistic radical Nock, even though
still basically a libertarian, to accept the conservative label and even come
to croak the old platitude that there is an *a priori* presumption against
any social change.

It is fascinating that Albert Jay Nock thus followed the ideological
path of his beloved spiritual ancestor Herbert Spencer; both began as
pure radical libertarians, both quickly abandoned radical or revolutionary tactics as embodied in the will to put their theories into practice
through mass action, and both eventually glided from Tory tactics to at
least a partial Toryism of content.

And so the libertarians, especially in their sense of where they stood
in the ideological spectrum, fused with the older conservatives who were
forced to adopt libertarian phraseology (but with no real libertarian
content) in opposing a Roosevelt Administration that had become too
collectivistic for them, either in content or in rhetoric. World War II
reinforced and cemented this alliance; for, in contrast to all the previous
American wars of the century, the pro-peace and "isolationist" forces
were all identified, by their enemies and subsequently by themselves, as
men of the "Right." By the end of World War II, it was second nature
for libertarians to consider themselves at an "extreme right-wing" pole
with the conservatives immediately to the left of them; and hence the
great error of the spectrum that persists to this day. In particular, the
modern libertarians forgot or never realized that opposition to war and
militarism had always been a "left-wing" tradition which had included
libertarians; and hence when the historical aberration of the New Deal
period corrected itself and the "Right-wing" was once again the great
partisan of total war, the libertarians were unprepared to understand
what was happening and tailed along in the wake of their supposed

conservative "allies." The liberals had completely lost their old ideological markings and guidelines.

Given a proper reorientation of the ideological spectrum, what *then* would be the prospects for liberty? It is no wonder that the contemporary libertarian, seeing the world going socialist and Communist, and believing himself virtually isolated and cut off from any prospect of united mass action, tends to be steeped in long-run pessimism. But the scene immediately brightens when we realize that that indispensable requisite of modern civilization: the overthrow of the Old Order, was accomplished by mass libertarian action erupting in such great revolutions of the West as the French and American Revolutions, and bringing about the glories of the Industrial Revolution and the advances of liberty, mobility, and rising living standards that we still retain today. Despite the reactionary swings backward to statism, the modern world stands towering above the world of the past. When we consider also that, in one form or another, the Old Order of despotism, feudalism, theocracy and militarism dominated every human civilization until the West of the 18th century, optimism over what man has and can achieve must mount still higher.

It might be retorted, however, that this bleak historical record of despotism and stagnation only reinforces one's pessimism, for it shows the persistence and durability of the Old Order and the seeming frailty and evanescence of the New—especially in view of the retrogression of the past century. But such superficial analysis neglects the great change that occurred with the Revolution of the New Order, a change that is clearly irreversible. For the Old Order was able to persist in its slave system for centuries precisely because it awoke no expectations and no hopes in the minds of the submerged masses; their lot was to live and eke out their brutish subsistence in slavery while obeying unquestioningly the commands of their divinely appointed rulers. But the liberal Revolution implanted indelibly in the minds of the masses—not only in the West but in the still feudally-dominated undeveloped world—the burning desire for liberty, for land to the peasantry, for peace between the nations, and, perhaps above all, for the mobility and rising standards of living that can only be brought to them by an industrial civilization. The masses will never again accept the mindless serfdom of the Old Order; and *given* these demands that have been awakened by liberalism and the Industrial Revolution, long-run victory for liberty is inevitable.

For only liberty, only a free market, can organize and maintain an industrial system, and the more that population expands and explodes, the more necessary is the unfettered working of such an industrial economy. *Laissez-faire* and the free market become more and more evidently necessary as an industrial system develops; radical deviations cause breakdowns and economic crises. This crisis of statism becomes particularly dramatic and acute in a fully socialist society; and hence the inevitable breakdown of statism has first become strikingly apparent in the countries of the socialist (*i.e.*, Communist) camp. For socialism confronts its inner contradiction most starkly. Desperately, it tries to fulfill its proclaimed goals of industrial growth, higher standards of living for the masses, and eventual withering away of the State, and is increasingly unable to do so with its collectivist means. Hence the inevitable breakdown of socialism. This progressive breakdown of socialist planning was at first partially obscured. For, in every instance the Leninists took power not in a developed capitalist country as Marx had wrongly predicted, but in a country suffering from the oppression of feudalism. Secondly, the Communists did not attempt to impose socialism upon the economy for many years after taking power; in Soviet Russia until Stalin's forced collectivization of the early 1930's reversed the wisdom of Lenin's New Economic Policy, which Lenin's favorite theoretician Bukharin would have extended onward towards a free market. Even the supposedly rabid Communist leaders of China did not impose a socialist economy on that country until the late 1950's. In every case, growing industrialization has imposed a series of economic breakdowns so severe that the Communist countries, against their ideological principles, have had to retreat step by step from central planning and return to various degrees and forms of a free market. The Liberman Plan for the Soviet Union has gained a great deal of publicity; but the inevitable process of de-socialization has proceeded much further in Poland, Hungary, and Czechoslovakia. Most advanced of all is Yugoslavia, which, freed from Stalinist rigidity earlier than its fellows, in only a dozen years has desocialized so fast and so far that its economy is now hardly more socialistic than that of France. The fact that people calling themselves "Communists" are still governing the country is irrelevant to the basic social and economic facts. Central planning in Yugoslavia has virtually disappeared; the private sector not only predominates in agriculture but is even strong in industry, and the public sector itself has been so radically decentralized and placed under free pricing, profit-and-loss tests, and a cooperative worker ownership of each plant that true socialism hardly exists any longer. Only the final step of converting workers' syndical control to individual shares of ownership remains on the path toward outright capitalism. Communist China and the able Marxist theoreticians of *Monthly Review* have clearly discerned the situation and have raised the alarm that Yugoslavia is no longer a socialist country.

One would think that free-market economists would hail the confirmation and increasing relevance of the notable insight of Professor Ludwig von Mises a half-century ago: that socialist States, being necessarily devoid of a genuine price system could not calculate economically and therefore could not plan their economy with any success. Indeed, one follower of Mises in effect predicted this process of de-socialization in a novel some years ago. Yet neither this author nor other free-market economists have given the slightest indication of even recognizing, let alone saluting this process in the Communist countries— perhaps because their almost hysterical view of the alleged threat of Communism prevents them from acknowledging any dissolution in the supposed monolith of menace.[20]

Communist countries, therefore, are increasingly and ineradicably forced to de-socialize, and will therefore eventually reach the free market. The state of the undeveloped countries is also cause for sustained libertarian optimism. For all over the world, the peoples of the undeveloped nations are engaged in revolution to throw off *their* feudal Old Order. It is true that the United States is doing its mightiest to suppress the very revolutionary process that once brought it and Western Europe out of the shackles of the Old Order; but it is increasingly clear that even overwhelming armed might cannot suppress the desire of the masses to break through into the modern world.

We are left with the United States and the countries of Western Europe. Here, the case for optimism is less clear, for the quasi-collectivist system does not present as stark a crisis of self-contradiction as does socialism. And yet, here too economic crisis looms in the future and gnaws away at the complacency of the Keynesian economic managers: creeping inflation, reflected in the aggravating balance-of-payments breakdown of the once almighty dollar; creeping secular unemployment brought about by minimum wage scales; and the deeper and long-run accumulation of the uneconomic distortions of the permanent war economy. Moreover, potential crises in the United States are not merely economic; there is a burgeoning and inspiring moral ferment among the youth of America against the fetters of centralized bureaucracy, of mass education in uniformity, and of brutality and oppression exercised by the minions of the State.

Furthermore, the maintenance of a substantial degree of free speech and democratic forms facilitates, at least in the short-run, the possible growth of a libertarian movement. The United States is also fortunate in possessing, even if half-forgotten beneath the statist and tyrannical overlay of the last half-century, a great tradition of libertarian thought and action. The very fact that much of this heritage is still reflected in popular rhetoric, even though stripped of its significance in practice, provides a substantial ideological groundwork for a future party of liberty.

What the Marxists would call the "objective conditions" for the triumph of liberty exist, then, everywhere in the world, and more so than in any past age; for everywhere the masses have opted for higher living standards and the promise of freedom and everywhere the various regimes of statism and collectivism cannot fulfill these goals. What is needed, then, is simply the "subjective conditions" for victory, *i.e.*, a growing body of informed libertarians who will spread the message to the peoples of the world that liberty and the purely free market provide the way out of their problems and crises. Liberty cannot be fully achieved unless libertarians exist in number to guide the peoples to the proper path. But perhaps the greatest stumbling-block to the creation of such a movement is the despair and pessimism typical of the libertarian in today's world. Much of that pessimism is due to his misreading of history and his thinking of himself and his handful of confrères as irredeemably isolated from the masses and therefore from the winds of history. Hence he becomes a lone critic of historical events rather than a person who considers himself as part of a potential movement which can and will *make* history. The modern libertarian has forgotten that the liberal of the seventeenth and eighteenth centuries faced odds much more overwhelming than faces the liberal of today; for in that era before the Industrial Revolution, the victory of liberalism was *far* from inevitable. And yet the liberalism of that day was not content to remain a gloomy little sect; instead, it unified theory and action. Liberalism grew and developed as an ideology and, leading and guiding the masses, made the Revolution which changed the fate of the world; by its monumental breakthrough, this Revolution of the eighteenth century transformed history from a chronicle of stagnation and despotism to an ongoing movement advancing toward a veritable secular Utopia of liberty and rationality and abundance. The Old Order is dead or moribund; and the reactionary attempts to run a modern society and economy by various throwbacks to the Old Order are doomed to total failure. The liberals of the past have left to modern libertarians a glorious heritage, not only of ideology but of victories against far more devastating odds. The liberals of the past have also left a heritage of the proper strategy and tactics for libertarians to follow: Not only by leading rather than remaining aloof from the masses; but also by not falling prey to *short-run* optimism. For short-run optimism, being unrealistic, leads straightway to disillusion and then to long-run pessimism; just as, on the other side of the coin, long-run pessimism leads to exclusive and self-defeating concentration on immediate and short-run issues. Short-run optimism stems, for one thing, from a naive and simplistic view of strategy: that liberty will win *merely* by educating more intellectuals, who in turn will educate opinion-moulders, who in turn will convince the masses, after which the State will somehow fold its tent and silently steal away. Matters are not that easy; for libertarians face not only a problem of education but also a problem of power; and it is a law of history that a ruling caste has never voluntarily given up its power.

But the problem of power is, certainly in the United States, far in the future. For the libertarian, the main task of the present epoch is to cast off his needless and debilitating pessimism, to set his sights on long-run victory and to set about the road to its attainment. To do this, he must, perhaps first of all, drastically realign his mistaken view of the ideological spectrum; he must discover who his friends and natural allies are, and above all perhaps, who his enemies are. Armed with this knowledge, let him proceed in the spirit of radical long-run optimism that one of the great figures in the history of libertarian thought, Randolph Bourne, correctly identified as the spirit of youth. Let Bourne's stirring words serve also as the guidepost for the spirit of liberty:

youth is the incarnation of reason pitted against the rigidity of tradition. Youth puts the remorseless questions to everything that is old and established—Why? What is this thing good for?

And when it gets the mumbled, evasive answers of the defenders it applies its own fresh, clean spirit of reason to institutions, customs, and ideas, and finding them stupid, inane, or poisonous, turns instinctively to overthrow them and build in their place the things with which its visions teem . . .

Youth is the leaven that keeps all these questioning, testing attitudes fermenting in the world. If it were not for this troublesome activity of youth, with its hatred of sophisms and glosses, its insistence on things as they are, society would die from sheer decay. It is the policy of the older generation as it gets adjusted to the world to hide away the unpleasant things where it can, or preserve a conspiracy of silence and an elaborate pretense that they do not exist. But meanwhile the sores go on festering just the same. Youth is the drastic antiseptic ... It drags skeletons from closets and insists that they be explained. No wonder the older generation fears and distrusts the younger. Youth is the avenging Nemesis on its trail ...

Our elders are always optimistic in their views of the present, pessimistic in their views of the future; youth is pessimistic toward the present and gloriously hopeful for the future. And it is this hope which is the lever of progress—one might say, the only lever of progress ...

The secret of life is then that this fine youthful spirit shall never be lost. Out of the turbulence of youth should come this fine precipitate—a sane, strong, aggressive spirit of daring and doing. It must be a flexible, growing spirit, with a hospitality to new ideas, and a keen insight into experience. To keep one's reactions warm and true is to have found the secret of perpetual youth, and perpetual youth is salvation.[21]

Notes

Professor Murray N. Rothbard is the most prolific and eloquent representative of the Austrian school of economics actively working in his field as well as making numerous contributions to political theory and general social studies (history, political science, etc.). He teaches economics at the Polytechnic Institute of Brooklyn. His monumental *Man, Economy and State* is now a classic. His other books include *America's Great Depression, The Panic of 1819* and *Power and Market*. He is editor of *Libertarian Forum*.

"Left and Right: The Prospects for Liberty" is from *Left and Right*, vol. 1, no. 1 (Spring 1965).

1. Gertrude Himmelfarb, *Lord Acton* (Chicago: University of Chicago Press, 1962), pp. 204–205.

2. *Ibid.*, p. 209.

3. Cf. Carl Becker, *The Declaration of Independence* (New York: Vintage Books ed., 1958), Chapter VI.

4. The information about Comte and Dunoyer, as well indeed as the entire analysis of the ideological spectrum, I owe to Mr. Leonard P. Liggio. For an emphasis on the positive and dynamic aspect of the Utopian drive, much traduced in our time, see Alan Milchman, "The Social and Political Philosophy of Jean-Jacques Rousseau: Utopia and Ideology," *The November Review* (November, 1964), pp. 3–10. Also cf. Jurgen Ruhle, "The Philosopher of Hope: Ernst Bloch," in Leopold Labedz, ed., *Revisionism* (New York: Praeger, 1962), pp. 166–178.

5. Joseph A. Schumpeter, *Imperialism and Social Classes* (New York: Meridian Books, 1955), p. 175. Schumpeter, incidentally, realized that, far from being an inherent stage of capitalism, modern imperialism was a throwback to the pre-capitalist imperialism of earlier ages, but with a minority of privileged capitalists now joined to the feudal and military castes in promoting imperialist aggression.

6. Bernard Semmel, *Imperialism and Social Reform: English Social-Imperial Thought, 1895–1914* (Cambridge: Harvard University Press, 1960).

7. Leopold S. Amery, *My Political Life* (London, 1953), quoted in Semmel, *op. cit.*, pp. 74–75.

8. The point, of course, is *not* that these men were products of some "Fabian conspiracy"; but, on the contrary, that Fabianism, by the turn of the century, was Socialism so conservatized as to be closely aligned with the other dominant neo-Conservative trends in British political life.

9. Thus, see Horace B. Davis, "Nations, Colonies, and Social Classes: The Position of Marx and Engels," *Science and Society* (Winter, 1965), pp. 26–43.

10. The schismatic wing of the Trotskyist movement embodied in the International Committee for the Fourth International is now the only sect within Marxism-Leninism that continues to stress exclusively the industrial working-class.

11. See the penetrating article by Alexander J. Groth, "The 'Isms' in Totalitarianism," *American Political Science Review* (December, 1964), pp. 888–901. Groth writes: "The Communists . . . have generally undertaken measures directly and indirectly uprooting existing socio-economic elites:

the landed nobility, business, large sections of the middle class and the peasantry, as well as the bureaucratic elites, the military, the civil service, the judiciary and the diplomatic corps . . . Second, in every instance of Communist seizure of power there has been a significant ideological-propagandistic commitment toward a proletarian or workers' state . . . (which) has been accompanied by opportunities for upward social mobility for the economically lowest classes, in terms of education and employment, which invariably have considerably exceeded the opportunities available under previous regimes. Finally, in every case the Communists have attempted to change basically the character of the economic systems which fell under their sway, typically from an agrarian to an industrial economy . . .
Fascism (both in the German and Italian versions) . . . was socio-economically a

counter-revolutionary movement . . . *It certainly did not dispossess or annihilate existent socio-economic elites* . . . *Quite the contrary. Fascism did not arrest the trend toward monopolistic private concentrations in business but instead augmented this tendency* . . .

Undoubtedly, the Fascist economic system was not a free market economy, and hence not 'capitalist' if one wishes to restrict the use of this term to a laissez-faire system. But did it not operate . . . *to preserve in being, and maintain the material rewards of, the existing socio-economic elites?"*

Ibid., pp. 890–891.

12. For examples of the attractions of fascist and right-wing collectivist ideas and plans for American big businessmen in this era, see Murray N. Rothbard, *America's Great Depression* (Princeton: Van Nostrand, 1963). Also cf. Gaetano Salvemini and George LaPiana, *What To Do With Italy* (New York: Duell, Sloan, and Pearce, 1943), pp. 65ff.

   Of the fascist economy, Salvemini perceptively wrote: "In actual fact, it is the State, i.e., the taxpayer who has become responsible to private enterprise. In Fascist Italy the State pays for the blunders of private enterprise . . . Profit is private and individual. Loss is public and social." Gaetano Salvemini, *Under the Axe of Fascism* (London: Victor Gollancz, 1936), p. 416.

13. Thus, see Rothbard, *passim.*

14. R. Palme Dutt, *Fascism and Social Revolution* (New York: International Publishers, 1934), pp. 247–251.

15. See Gabriel Kolko, *The Triumph of Conservatism: A Reinterpretation of American History, 1900-1916* (Glencoe, Ill.: The Free Press, 1963), pp. 173 and *passim.* For an example of the way in which Kolko has already begun to influence American historiography, see David T. Gilchrist and W. David Lewis, eds., *Economic Change in the Civil War Era* (Greenville, Del.: Eleutherian Mills-Hagley Foundation, 1965), p. 115. Kolko's complementary and confirmatory work on railroads, *Railroads and Regulation, 1877–1916* (Princeton: Princeton University Press, 1965) comes too late to be considered here. A brief treatment of the monopolizing role of the ICC for the railroad industry may be found in Christopher D. Stone, "ICC: Some Reminiscences on the Future of American Transportation," *New Individualist Review* (Spring, 1963), pp. 3–15.

16. Kolko, *Triumph of Conservatism*, p. 274.

17. Arthur Jerome Eddy, *The New Competition: An Examination of the Conditions Underlying the Radical Change That Is Taking Place In the*

Commercial and Industrial World—The Change from A COMPETITIVE TO A COOPERATIVE BASIS (7th Ed., Chicago: A. C. McClurg and Co., 1920).

18. Kolko, *Triumph of Conservatism*, p. 214.

19. *Ibid.*, pp. 286–287.

20. One happy exception is William D. Grampp, "New Directions in the Communist Economies," *Business Horizons* (Fall, 1963), pp. 29–36. Grampp writes: "Hayek said that centralized planning will lead to serfdom. It follows that a decrease in the economic authority of the State should lead away from serfdom. The Communist countries may show that to be true. It would be a withering away of the state the Marxists have not counted on nor has it been anticipated by those who agree with Hayek." *Ibid.*, p. 35. The novel in question is Henry Hazlitt, *The Great Idea* (New York: Appleton-Century-Crofts, 1951).

21. Randolph Bourne, "Youth," *The Atlantic Monthly* (April, 1912); reprinted in Lillian Schlissel, ed., *The World of Randolph Bourne* (New York: E. P. Dutton and Co., 1965), pp. 9–11, 15.

Bibliography

ALCHIAN, ARMEN A. and Allen, William R. *University Economics*. Belmont, California: Wadsworth Publishing Co., 1964.

Anderson, Benjamin M. *Economics and the Public Welfare*. Princeton, N.J.: D. Van Nostrand Co., Inc., 1949.

Anderson, Martin. *The Federal Bulldozer: A Critical Analysis of Urban Renewal, 1949–1962*. Cambridge, Massachusetts: The MIT Press, 1964.

Bailey, Martin. *National Income and the Price Level*. New York: McGraw-Hill, 1962.

Bakewell, Paul, Jr. *Curious Errors About Money*. Caldwell, Idaho: Caxton Press, 1962.

Ballvé, Faustino. *Essentials of Economics*. Irvington-on-Hudson, N.Y.: Foundation for Economic Education, Inc., 1969.

Bastiat, Frederic. *Economic Sophisms and Economic Harmonies*. Princeton, N.J.: D. Van Nostrand Co., 1964.

_____. *Selected Essays on Political Economy*, Princeton, N.J.: D. Van Nostrand Co., 1964.

_____. *The Law*. Irvington-on-Hudson, N.Y.: Foundation for Economic Education, 1962.

Baudin, Louis. *A Socialist Empire: The Incas of Peru*. Princeton, N.J.: D. Van Nostrand, 1961.

Bauer, P. T. *Indian Economic Policy and Development*. New York: Praeger, 1961.

Bauer, P. T. and Yamey, B. S. *The Economics of Underdeveloped Countries*.

Böhm-Bawerk, Eugen von. *Capital and Interest.* South Holland, Ill.: Libertarian Press, 1959.

————. *Shorter Classics of Böhm-Bawerk.* South Holland, Ill.: Libertarian Press, 1962.

————. *The Exploitation Theory and Value and Price.* South Holland, Ill.: Libertarian Press, 1960.

Buchanan, James M. and Tullock, Gordon. *The Calculus of Consent.* Ann Arbor, Michigan: University of Michigan Press, 1962.

Campaigne, Jameson G. *Check-Off: Labor Bosses and Working Men.* Chicago: Henry Regnery, 1961.

Chodorov, Frank. *Out of Step.* New York: Devin-Adair, 1962.

Davenport, John; DeGraff, Herrell; Hayek, F. A. and Morley, Felix. *The Spiritual and Moral Significance of Free Enterprise, A Symposium.* (pamphlet available from the National Association of Manufacturers, 2 E. 48th St., New York 17, New York)

Friedman, Milton. *Capitalism and Freedom.* Chicago: University of Chicago Press.

Friedman, Milton and Schwartz, Anna J. *A Monetary History of the United States, 1867–1960.* Princeton, N.J.: Princeton University Press for the National Bureau of Economic Research, 1963.

————. *The Great Contraction.* Princeton, N.J.: Princeton University Press, 1965.

Groseclose, Elgin. *Money and Man.* New York: Frederich Ungar.

Hart, H. L. A. *Law, Liberty and Morality.* Stanford: Stanford University Press, 1963.

Hayek, Friedrich von. *The Constitution of Liberty.* Chicago: University of Chicago Press, 1962.

Hazlitt, Henry. *Economics in One Lesson.* New York: Harper & Row, Publishers, 1946.

————. *Man Versus the Welfare State.* New Rochelle, N.Y.: Arlington House, Inc., 1969.

————. *The Conquest of Poverty.* New Rochelle, N.Y.: Arlington House, Inc., 1971.

————. *Time Will Run Back.* New Rochelle, N.Y.: Arlington House, Inc., 1970.

Hempstone, Smith. *Rebels, Mercenaries and Dividends: The Katanga Story.* New York: Praeger, 1962.

Hunold, Albert, ed. *Freedom and Serfdom.* Reidel, Dordrecht, Holland, 1961.

Huszar, George B. de, ed. *Fundamentals of Voluntary Health Care.* Caldwell, Idaho: Caxton Press.

Jacobs, Jane. *The Death and Life of Great American Cities*. New York: Harpers, 1961.

Kintner, William R. and Kornfeder, Joseph Z. *The New Frontier of War*. Chicago: Henry Regnery, 1962.

Kuznets, Simon. *Capital in the American Economy*. Princeton University, Princeton, 1961.

Leoni, Bruno. *Freedom and the Law*. Princeton, N.J.: D. Van Nostrand, 1961. (Los Angeles: Nash Publ. Co., 1971).

Lively, John. *The Social and Political Thought of Alexis de Tocqueville*. Oxford: Oxford University Press.

Lukacs, John. *A History of the Cold War*. New York: Doubleday, 1961.

Lutz, Vera. *French Planning*. Washington, D.C.: American Enterprise Institute, 1965.

Martin, James J. *American Liberalism and World Politics, 1931–1941*. New York: Devin-Adair, 1963.

McCormick, John and MacInnes, Mairi. *Versions of Censorship*. Chicago: Aldine Press, 1962.

Mises, Ludwig von. *Bureaucracy*. New Haven, Connecticut: Yale University Press, 1945.

———. *Human Action*. New Haven, Connecticut: Yale University Press, 1951. Revised edition, Chicago: Henry Regnery Co., 1963.

———. *Omnipotent Government: the Rise of the Total State and Total War*. New Haven, Connecticut: Yale University Press, 1944.

———. *Planning for Freedom*. South Holland, Ill.: Libertarian Press, 1952.

———. *Socialism*. New Haven, Connecticut: Yale University Press, 1951.

———. *The Anti-Capitalistic Mentality*. Princeton, N.J.: D. Van Nostrand Co., Inc., 1956.

———. *The Free and Prosperous Commonwealth*. Princeton, N.J.: D. Van Nostrand.

———. *Theory and History*. New Haven, Connecticut: Yale University Press, 1957. Reprinted, New Rochelle, N.Y.: Arlington House, Inc., 1969.

———. *Theory of Money and Credit*. Irvington-on-Hudson, N.Y.: Foundation for Economic Education, 1971.

Nutter, G. Warren. *The Growth of Industrial Production in the Soviet Union*. Princeton, N.J.: Princeton University Press, 1962.

Paterson, Isabel. *The God of the Machine*. New York: G. P. Putnam's Sons, 1943. Reprinted, Caldwell, Idaho: Caxton Printers, Ltd., 1964.

Perlman, Richard. *Wage Determination: Market or Power Forces*. Boston: D. C. Heath and Co., 1965.

Petro, Sylvester. *The Labor Policy of the Free Society*. New York: Ronald Press, 1957.

Rand, Ayn. *Atlas Shrugged*. New York: Random House, Inc., 1957.

————. *Capitalism: the Unknown Ideal*. New York: New American Library, Inc., 1967.

————. *The Virtue of Selfishness*. New York: New American Library, Inc., Signet Books, 1964.

Read, Leonard E. *Elements of Libertarian Leadership*. New York: Foundation for Economic Education, 1962.

Robinson, Claude. *Understanding Profits*. Princeton: Van Nostrand, 1962.

Rothbard, Murray. *Man, Economy, and the State*. Princeton, N.J.: D. Van Nostrand Co., 1962. (Reissued, Los Angeles: Nash Publ. Co., 1971).

————. *Power and Market*. Menlo Park, California: Institute for Humane Studies, 1970.

————. *The Panic of 1819*. New York: Columbia University Press, 1962.

Schoeck, Helmut and Wiggins, James W. *Relativism and the Study of Man*. Princeton: D. Van Nostrand, 1961.

Schuyler, Phillippa. *Who Killed the Congo?* New York: Devin-Adair, 1962.

Sennholz, Hans F. *The Truth about the GREAT DEPRESSION*. Lansing, Michigan: Constitutional Alliance, Inc., 1969.

Smith, Adam. *The Wealth of Nations*. 1776.

Spencer, Herbert. *Social Statics*. New York: Robert Schalkenbach Foundation, 1970.

————. *The Man Versus the State*. Caldwell, Idaho: Caxton Printers, Ltd., 1940.

Stigler, George J. *The Intellectual and the Market Place and Other Essays*. New York: The Free Press of Glencoe, 1963.

Taylor, A. J. P. *Origins of the Second World War*. London: Hamish Hamilton, 1961.

Tuccille. *Radical Libertarianism*. Indianapolis, Ind.: Bobbs-Merrill Co., 1970.

Woodcock, Dover. *Anarchism*. New York: Meridian, 1962.

Appendix

Acton, H. B. *The Morals of Markets*. New York: Humanities Press, 1972.

Anderson, Martin. *Conscription*. Stanford, Cal.: Hoover Press, 1976.

Armentano, D. T. *The Myths of Antitrust*. New Rochelle, N.Y.: Arlington House.

Block, Walter. *Defending the Undefendable*. New York: Fleet Press, 1976.

Blumenfeld, Samuel L., ed. *Property in a Humane Economy*. La Salle, Ill.: Open Court, 1975.

Buchanan, James. *The Limits of Liberty*. Chicago: University of Chicago Press, 1975.

Cranston, Maurice, ed. *Human Rights Today*. London.

Hayek, F. A. *Law, Legislation, and Liberty*, 2 volumes. Chicago: University of Chicago Press, 1974, 1976.

Hellman, Arthur D. *Laws Against Marijuana: The Price We Pay*. Urbana, Ill.: University of Illinois Press, 1975.

Hessen, Robert. *Steel Titan*. New York: Oxford University Press, 1976.

Hospers, John. *Libertarianism*. Los Angeles: Nash, 1971 (paper Santa Barbara, Cal.: Reason Press, 1972).

Hutt, W. H. *The Theory of Idle Resources*. Indianapolis: Liberty Classics, 1977.

Kirzner, Israel. *Competition and Entrepreneurship*. Chicago: University of Chicago Press, 1973.

MacBride, Roger L. *A New Dawn for American: The Libertarian Challenge*. Ottawa, Ill.: Green Hill, 1976.

Machan, Tibor R. *Human Rights and Human Liberties*. Chicago: Nelson-Hall, 1975.

_____. *The Pseudo-Science of B. F. Skinner*. New Rochelle, N.Y.: Arlington House, 1974.

Martin, James J. *Men against the State: The Expositors of Individualist Anarchism in America, 1827-1908*. DeKalb, Ill.: Adrian Allen, 1953.

Norton, David L. *Personal Destinies: A Philosophy of Ethical Individualism*. Princeton: Princeton University Press, 1976.

Nozick, Robert. *Anarchy, State, and Utopia*. New York: Basic Books, 1974.

Oppenheimer, Franz. *The State*. New York: Vanguard Press, 1926.

Rothbard, Murray N. *Conceived in Liberty*, 3 volumes. New Rochelle, N.Y.: Arlington House, 1974, 1975, 1976.

_____. *For a New Liberty*. New York: Macmillan, 1973.

Siegan, Bernard H. *Land Use without Zoning*. Lexington, Mass.: Lexington Books, 1972.

_____. *Other People's Property*. Lexington, Mass.: Lexington Books, 1976.

Sowell, Thomas. *Race and Economics*. New York: David McKay, 1975.

Spooner, Lysander. *Natural Law*. Boston: Williams, 1882.

_____. *No Treason: The Constitution of No Authority*. Larkspur, Col.: Pine Tree Press, 1966.

Stigler, George. *The Citizen and the State*. Chicago: University of Chicago

Press, 1976.

Szasz, Thomas S. *Law, Liberty, and Psychiatry*. New York: Macmillan, 1963.

————. *Psychiatric Slavery*. New York: Free Press, 1977.

Twight, Charlotte. *America's Emerging Fascist Economy*. New Rochelle, N.Y.: Arlington House, 1976.

Tucker, Benjamin. *Individual Liberty*. New York: Vanguard Press, 1926.

————. *Instead of a Book*. New York, 1893.

Wallis, W. Allen. *An Overgoverned Society*. New York: Free Press, 1976.

West, E. G. *Education and the State*. London: Institute of Economic Affairs, 1965.

Wilson, James Q. *Thinking about Crime*. New York: Basic Books, 1975.

About the editor

Tibor R. Machan is an associate professor of philosophy at SUNY at Fredonia. Previous to this assignment he was instructor in political theory at Santa Barbara City College, Santa Barbara, California and assistant professor of philosophy at California State College, Bakersfield.

Born in Budapest, Hungary, from which he escaped in 1953, he lived for three years in Munich, Germany, before emigrating to the United States in 1956. He lived in Cleveland and Philadelphia before entering the U.S. Air Force in which he served for four years.

He received his undergraduate degree from Claremont Men's College in 1965. He did his graduate work at New York University (M.A., 1966) the University of California at Santa Barbara (Ph.D., 1971).

His published articles have appeared in scholarly journals including *Educational Theory, The Personalist, Journal of Aesthetics and Art Criticism,* and *Journal of Human Relations*, as well as in the general periodicals *Barron's, Freeman, Individualist, New Guard, Indian Libertarian*, and *Reason*.

Machan is working on manuscripts dealing with government regulation, the foundations of labor legislation, and a new theory of natural law. He lives in Fredonia with his wife, Marty Zupan, a free lance writer and professional editor.